A Prima Donna's Progress

A Prima Donna's Progress

The Autobiography of
JOAN SUTHERLAND

Weidenfeld & Nicolson
LONDON

First published in Great Britain in 1997 by
Weidenfeld & Nicolson

A catalogue reference is available
from the British Library

ISBN 0 297 81321 8

Typeset by Selwood Systems, Midsomer Norton
Printed in Great Britain by Butler & Tanner Ltd, Frome and London

Weidenfeld & Nicolson

The Orion Publishing Group Ltd
Orion House
5 Upper Saint Martin's Lane
London, WC2H 9EA

CONTENTS

ILLUSTRATIONS

SECTION TWO (*between pages 342 and 343*)

As Giorgetta in *Il Tabarro*, 1952

As Clotilde in *Norma*, 1952 (*Roger Wood*)

As the Countess in *The Marriage of Figaro*, 1953 (*Angus McBean*)

As Frasquita in *Carmen*, 1953/4 (*Helga Sharland*)

Richard playing the harpsichord continuo (*Foto Film*)

With Dino Dondi in Bellini's *Beatrice de Tenda*, 1961 (*Foto Piccagliani*)

La Fille du Régiment, 1966 (*Donald Southern*)

Singing with Marilyn Horne in *Norma*, 1967 (*Donald Southern*)

Rodelinda, 1973 (*Maria Austria*)

Singing the Czardas at Orlofsky's Party, *Fledermaus*, 1973 (*Carolyn Mason Jones*)

Violetta in *La Traviata*, 1975 (*Stuart Robinson*)

The Australian Opera *Lakmé*, 1976

As Esclarmonde, 1976 (*J Heffernan/Metropolitan Opera*)

As Donna Anna in *Don Giovanni*, 1978 (*Beth Bergman*)

The *Lucia* Mad Scene, 1982 (*J Heffernan/Metropolitan Opera*)

Australian Opera's *Alcina*, 1983 (*Branco Gaica*)

With Margreta Elkins after a performance of 'Mira, o Norma', 1983 (*Mirror Australian Telegraph Publications*)

Semiramide, 1983 (*Branco Gaica*)

The 1983 Met production of *La Fille du Régiment* (*J Heffernan/Metropolitan Opera*)

Adriana's denunciation in *Adriana Lecouvreur*, 1984 (*Branco Gaica*)

The 1984 Canadian Opera production of *Anna Bolena* (*Robert Ragsdale*)

As Olympia with Graeme Ewer in 1984 production of *The Tales of Hoffman* (*Paul Richardson*)

Curtain calls with Ric after *The Merry Widow*, 1988 (*Branco Gaica*)

On Our Selection cast at Kate's wedding (*Robert McFarlane*)

The magnificent Australian Opera farewell

The Covent Garden farewell, New Year's Eve 1990 (*Clive Barda/PAL*)

FOREWORD

It has been one of the great joys of my life that, as well as writing about artists I admire, I have been able to know them as friends. When you first meet performing artists, it is striking how much that you know from their music-making seems reflected in their personalities. So it was when, soon after her spectacular leap to international stardom at Covent Garden in February 1959, I first met Joan Sutherland, the most unspoilt prima donna you could ever imagine, a great giving character to whom one instantly warms.

From that moment, it has been a joy to follow her in one glory after another, a career that has few if any parallels in history, both for the scale of achievement and its extraordinary span. If anyone has claims to be the Singer of the Century, it is surely Joan. And yet here is an artist who, from first to last, has kept her sense of wonder, of gratitude, taking nothing for granted, the last person to give herself the sort of airs assumed by far too many leading singers. Joan has remained the great Joan to whom I instantly responded, both as a person and as an artist.

I shall never forget the matinée performance at Covent Garden of Mozart's *The Magic Flute*, when, with Joan singing Pamina, I first registered the emergence of an unforgettable voice, magnetic both in sound and expression. I was initially disappointed that in the very early recordings she made, the engineers seemed unable to convey the full individuality of the Sutherland timbre. But then, after the triumph of February 1959, the Decca engineers quickly found the answer, giving us over the years an astonishing library of great singing, even if one has always had to hear Joan in the flesh to appreciate fully the weight and volume of the glorious voice, as well as its unique combination of richness, brilliance and flexibility. No wonder that her early advisers, before Richard Bonynge became her guide, thought she was destined to be a Wagnerian.

My happy memories include many from recording sessions, starting with those for her first double-album recital, *The Art of the Prima Donna*, when she made light of all problems in her dazzling account of the Queen's aria from Meyerbeer's *Les Huguenots*. The sparkling recording she made of Donizetti's *La Fille du Régiment* – one of her first opposite

Pavarotti – was another great landmark, and so in a different way were the sessions for Puccini's *Turandot* with Zubin Mehta conducting, and the generosity with which she ceded first place to Montserrat Cabballé as Liu in their single Act 3 confrontation. Generosity is a quality that has always marked her work, partly because she is the opposite of self-obsessed, seeing herself very clearly, and as I say, keeping a sense of wonder.

Make no mistake, Joan Sutherland is a great heroine, but it is no secret that she never expected to be one, and has always been firmly determined to see things in proportion. I remember meeting her unexpectedly once in the Grand'rue in Montreux, near her Swiss home, shopping-bag in hand, wearing an ordinary raincoat. When I asked her what her plans were, she replied in a jolly, matter-of-fact way, 'Just a few *Sonnambulas* at the Met,' adding that she felt she was 'getting a bit long-in-the-tooth' for that girlish role. To my delight, she then did an imitation of herself tripping on as Amina, holding her shopping-bag in front of her like a posy. I cannot imagine any other soprano in the world, let alone one of Sutherland's stature, sending herself up in that way. So far from diminishing her, it confirmed her greatness, both as a person and as an artist.

And though over the years no one has filled the role of diva more magnificently than Sutherland as she received ovations at the end of a performance, what dominated even then was her natural jollity and exuberance. The cheerful grin, as well as reflecting genuine pleasure, seemed also to be telling us that this was all a bit of a lark. No great diva has let us, as mere mortals, share her joy quite so completely. It could not be more welcome now that in this book she has set down her feelings and memories.

Edward Greenfield

PART ONE

Life in Australia and London
1926–1961

No great diva has let us, mere
mortals, share her joy of singing and
living so completely.

Ilgvaram dzimšanas dienā

Čučuš

27.04.2006

✧ 1 ✧

FOR THE RECORD I was born in Sydney on November 7, 1926.

That anyone at the age of sixty and more can clearly recall the days of their childhood and youth has been a mystery to me all my life. Now, when confronted with the task of writing about my own, I can only conjure up disjointed 'flashes' of those early days.

I see the sparkling waters of Sydney Harbour and those unreal blue skies – I never see clouds and rain. I picture the garden at what was then 6 Wolseley Road, Point Piper, terraced from the house to the beach below with one hundred and eleven steps (counted by all who had to climb them). There was always a blaze of flowers, nurtured daily by my father – delphiniums, larkspur, ranunculus, zinnias, lupins, stock, cinnerarias, phlox, low hedges of plumbago and lantana, a passionfruit vine and a riot of sub-tropical shrubs including various oleanders. There was a mango tree right at the bottom of the garden, jacarandas, a mulberry tree (we fed silkworms on the leaves) and lemon trees. There was an old gardener who came to mow. I loved to 'help' him and my father, and my love of flowers and trees probably began then.

I remember the long summer days when my half-sisters were at work and my half-brother and sister at school. (My father's first wife died in the influenza epidemic after the First World War, leaving three daughters and a son.) I would go 'walkabout' and cause my mother not a little anxiety by my disappearance. There was a longish beach to walk before reaching the rocks on the point and many times I would forget about the tide coming in, making it difficult to get back the way I had come. Sometimes I climbed up through the garden of a neighbour and found my way back by the road. And sometimes I got 'lost' and was brought home by the baker or milkman – a great treat, for they both had a horse and cart.

I also spent long hours with my mother and our ample laundress, Mrs Fisher, watching the various housekeeping chores and being delighted to be permitted to help hang out the handkerchiefs and table napkins to dry and then, even more so, to be allowed to iron them. Of course, the laundry process in those days was very different – a fuel copper which boiled the white linens, which had to be lifted, soaking

3

wet, into the tub for rinsing and then lifted again to go through the blue (Reckitt's, of course) then put through the wringer (turned by hand) and into the clothes basket to be hung on the line in the backyard to dry. Many things had to be starched after the blueing process and damped when dry before they could be ironed properly – no washing machines, driers or steam irons in every household then.

The greatest joy of all was to sit with my mother when she did her daily vocal exercises. Although her teacher (Mr Burns-Walker, a pupil of Mathilde Marchesi, Melba's teacher) had wanted my grandfather to send her to Europe for further study, Mother declined, saying she was too nervous to embark on a singing career, preferring to enjoy it as a hobby. I fear it was a great loss to the opera-goers of her day, for it was a glorious sound – rich, true and even from bottom to top of her considerable range. I compare her to Ebe Stignani. But their loss was to be my gain, for I was able from the age of three to imitate her scales and exercises and, as she was a mezzo-soprano, I worked very much in the middle area of my voice, learning the scales and arpeggios and even the dreaded trill without thinking about it. The birds could trill, so why not I? I even picked up her songs and arias and sang them by ear, later singing duets with her – Manrico to her Azucena. I always had a voice.

I remember when I was about five years old we spent a summer holiday in a rented house at Newport – about twenty kilometres from the centre of Sydney. It was prior to the opening of the Harbour Bridge and we travelled to Manly across the harbour by ferry, then by bus or horse cab to Newport. Today it is a thriving seaside resort – then it was a general store-cum-post office with a number of weatherboard weekenders. The surf, of course, hasn't changed but nowadays the parking lot is full of cars and trailers bearing surfboards and teenagers in wetsuits, summer and winter, with take-out food stores and some excellent clothing shops, also a large second-hand bookshop, much frequented by Richard – and even myself.

There was a boy, Norman, living next door at Point Piper, with whom I had a typical childhood relationship – I liked him if we agreed and disliked him if we didn't. He had a fabulous electric train which he set up in the ballroom of Danmark, his home. His father, W. J. Smith, used to take me and my sister Barbara, who was four years my senior, to his factory which later became incorporated in the larger company of Australian Consolidated Industries. Norman, Barbara and I loved to watch the bottles being made – and the returns being sterilised and recreated. We also saw what I believe were the first Australian glass bricks being made. We were fascinated by it all.

My father had been born in Port Skerra, a fishing village in the north of Scotland, and he loved to visit either Watsons Bay or the Fish Markets at weekends and bring home fish for dinner – garfish, flathead, bream, snapper, whiting, and sometimes prawns or lobsters. Occasionally, the family used to go prawning or collecting rock oysters from our own bay of the harbour. To a Sydney-sider, there is nothing better than a Sydney rock oyster.

My father was also a great believer in a good walk and if we went to visit my grandfather and aunt and uncle in Woollahra, we had plenty of opportunity. We would catch the bus or tram from the bottom of Wolseley Road to Edgecliff and walk up Ocean Street to my grandfather's house on Queen Street – quite a stiff climb. The best thing about it was that the return trip was downhill. If we were really lucky it might rain, in which case we would take a horse cab one way at least – hopefully *up* the hill.

I remember the dilapidated shops and Post Office on the corner of Ocean Street and New South Head Road, opposite the grounds of Ascham Girls School – one of the most expensive private schools in Sydney to this day. There was a terrible fuss when plans were made to develop that corner and incorporate the Eastern Suburbs Railway station within the complex. It was held up for years by quibblers and now that it has finally been completed it looks splendid – much more attractive than it ever did. At least it is one good mark for the 'developers'.

On one of those visits to Grandpa I apparently heard him say, 'They'll never conquer droughts and floods until they harness the waters of the Snowy River.' He was also a great advocate of the Eastern Suburbs Railway, anticipating the growth of the city of Sydney. These two projects were bandied about by politicians and finally managed to emerge during the Sixties and Seventies to great acclaim and ultimate success. Unfortunately, though, the Eastern Suburbs Railway was terminated before it reached the ever-growing Sydney Airport – a foolish economy on the part of the Government as every other big city in the world had or has since built a railway connection to its main airport.

My grandfather was a master builder and stone mason. He died in 1930 so never saw his 'dream' come true. However, he left his mark on Sydney in some of the old Victorian stone buildings such as the old Medical School of Sydney University; portions of the Sydney Hospital and the Victoria Barracks; the conversion of the Darlinghurst Gaol to the Sydney Technical College and the Gladesville Lunatic Asylum (not so called today).

Back to those childhood memories – of the early morning swims, of weekends spent almost exclusively at the bottom of the garden with a portable gramophone churning out the latest jazz hits or an aria from

Caruso, Tibbett or Galli-Curci. My half-sisters would entertain their 'beaux', and picnics would be the order of the day.

My eldest half-sister, Heather, was a young and promising architect and used to put up with me watching her work on her huge board set up in the 'breakfast room', which would be called a rumpus or family room today. We all used it for our own particular needs – homework, games, sewing, pasting up our scrap-books, drawing, painting and trying to listen to the wireless: a crystal set with earphones. The telephone was also in that room, attached to the wall, with a handle you cranked to raise the exchange and ask for your number.

I remember the excitement aroused by the daring flights of Charles Kingsford Smith and Amy Johnson and the beginnings of national and international air travel, never dreaming of anything like the huge modern jet aircraft, or that I would be one of their millions of regular travellers. I also remember the 'scandal' of Captain de Groote cutting the ribbon to open the Sydney Harbour Bridge anticipating the Labour Premier, Jack Lang. How everyone laughed over the event and admired de Groote for his rather Hollywood-style act, riding up on horseback and slashing the ribbon with a sword.

My father was a master tailor and I loved any opportunity to visit his workroom and see the bolts of beautiful suitings and tweeds – indeed tartans, for he was a Highlander and not only wore the kilt with style but also made it, and the accompanying intricate jackets and waistcoats. I used to play with the buttons and chalks, and was intrigued by all the different tacking systems, interfacings and trimmings. Daddy, or 'Pop' as we usually called him, was also a pillar of the Presbyterian Church in Sydney, being an Elder at St Stephens which was then in Phillip Street. Every Sunday the family trooped off with Pop in the lead. I was mostly left at home as I was considered too young and fidgety, but I do remember the old Phillip Street church and my mother trying to stop my father singing the hymns at the top of his voice – he was tone deaf, but he believed he was making a joyful noise and was not about to hush up.

Barbara and I adored our half-brother Jim – he was so patient and kindly and has never changed. He must have longed for male company other than that of his father, with six women in the family. Heather, Ailsa and Nancye were a good deal older and, between their work and various social pursuits, we didn't see that much of them.

I was a very happy child and enjoyed my days immensely. There was very little radio to listen to and no television at all, so I spent hours out of doors on fine days or if the weather was bad I would look at the many books in the house or pester Mother to sing and play the piano with me – or I would pick out tunes for myself; and I had a scrap-book in which I stuck postcards, fashion pictures, animals, flowers and anything else that caught my eye.

There was a spiteful child called Marie Gray living next door in an apartment house called The Anchorage. We used to play together because our mothers thought we were company for each other but there was no love lost between us. She seemed to delight in pointing out imaginary things of interest – a sailing boat, a liner or a bird – then either punching or hitting me and running away when I was fool enough to turn my head to look. One day she hit me with a heavy garden stake, whereupon my mother no longer insisted on our 'friendship'. I was always big for my age and maybe Marie thought her cunning ruse would prevent my flattening her. I certainly felt like it often enough, especially when she indulged her irritating habit of singing out raucously, 'I'll put you down the lavatory' over and over again.

I remember being in the garden one day, singing for myself, when our next-door neighbour, Dame Mary Barlow, called to me from her window, 'Joan! Joan! Go and tell your mother that our wonderful songbird is dead!' Dame Mary had heard the sad news of Melba's death on the radio just minutes before.

Death was something I very soon had to cope with on a much more personal basis, for on my sixth birthday my father died on returning from his morning swim. He had not been feeling too well when I opened my presents (one of which was a green-and-white bathing suit) and Mother had told him not to go down to the beach and face the stiff climb back, but I was eager to try out my new bathers so he decided to go. Mother, at an upstairs window, saw him falter when almost back to the top of the garden and called to him to stay where he was, hurrying down herself, but he insisted on climbing the rest of the way and died in her arms. Although I was so young I remember the heart-break still.

Both Barbara and I missed him terribly and Mother was distraught but trying all the time not to break down in front of us. He had been quite a strict head of the family but a loving bear of a person and very fair, if stern at times. He had been a member of the Highland Society of New South Wales and a Freemason, having many good friends in these organisations who were of the greatest help to my mother and family.

Things moved rapidly. Mother found that not only did Pop die intestate but there were two mortgages on the house at Point Piper about which she knew nothing and his business was in very bad shape, due to the general Depression. Pop had not wanted to refuse his clients, although many had large outstanding accounts – everyone was feeling the pinch. But Mother never understood why he hadn't told her how bad things were. Her father had already died by this time and only Auntie 'Blos' and Uncle Tom, together with great-uncle Arthur, lived in their old house in Queen Street, Woollahra, which, while not the greatest, had a big garden and rooms enough. The result was that Mother, Barbara and I moved to the Woollahra house and the three older girls moved into an apartment together, Jim finding digs with a pleasant family at Bellevue Hill. He was a splendid student and should have gone to university, but it was essential for him to earn a living and a friend of Pop kindly took Jim into his firm, Macdonald Hamilton, the P & O Company agents in Sydney, and arranged for him to study accountancy at night. He passed with flying colours, becoming in due course, after war service and prisoner-of-war camp in the Malayan zone, Chief Accountant and finally Secretary of the firm. His six children still reap the benefit of his patience and good judgement.

'Whatever happens, life goes on' was a lesson I learned very early. At 115 Queen Street there was no sea, no swim every morning before breakfast – Bondi was a half-hour away by tram. But our aunt and uncle tried hard to make us welcome. Auntie Blos had always been a favourite and continued to enchant us. Her names were the very Victorian Annie Ethel, but Uncle Tom had dubbed her 'Blossom' when she went to spend considerable time with cousins Bill and Minnie Boucher on their farm at Hagley in Tasmania, the nickname being that of their favourite cow. She was Blos to everyone thereafter – except to Uncle Tom who gave her the name, then persisted in calling her Ethel – or, much to her chagrin, 'Etty pet'. She helped me to read, spell, write, do my mathematical problems in a trice – not the way the school taught but always producing the correct answer, which I could seldom get with the method we used at school. She was tall and angular, and as straight as an arrow. She also made our dresses and let us watch and help with hand sewing once we were able.

Uncle Tom had something of a dual personality. I think he was frustrated in a way. He had a good education at Camden Grammar School, a very old boys' school outside Sydney and looked after my grandfather's properties, collecting rents, seeing to repairs, doing the banking and coping with the tenants' complaints. He never worked at a steady job until, during the Second World War, a friend engaged in the non-essential industry of picture-framing was short of staff and Uncle Tom went to 'help him out' at well over retiring age. He had never enjoyed himself so much and stayed on as long as he could manage the hours. He, too, was a great gardener, specialising in outsize dahlias. I always found them very stiff flowers and much preferred his sweet peas, climbing roses, iceland poppies, cinnerarias, phlox, carnations, watsonias and the rock lilies which 'jus' growed'. He was

Secretary of the Eastern Suburbs Rugby Union Football Club (to which Richard's father Carl Bonynge also belonged) and of the local Presbyterian church choir. He had a reasonable baritone voice and knew an inexhaustible number of hilarious – and sometimes rather risqué – music-hall and vaudeville songs, along with operetta, comic opera and grand opera favourites. I only wish I could remember more of those old songs now – my mother or aunt used to say, 'Tom! That's not fit for the child! Sing her something decent!' Of course the songs were quite innocent but Mother appeared to be shocked by the least impropriety. One of his favourites was:

> My old woman's an awful boozer
> In the pub, well, I tried to lose 'er.
> Ginger ale and gingerette
> Used to make 'er ****, you bet!
> Then one day she signed the pledge –
> Signed it on our window-ledge.
> That very night I bought the old dear
> A nine-gallon keg of ginger beer.
> In less than an hour it was out of sight
> And when we was lyin' in bed that night
> She went
> Pop! Pop! Poppety-pop!
> Poppety-poppety-pop!
> I shouted Murder! Police! 'elp! Fire!
> Me ole' girl 'as busted 'er pneumatic tyre
> I got under the bed, yer know,
> Doin' a flippety flop
> For every time she moved she went
> Poppety-poppety-pop!

My garden was now flat instead of terraced and I watched, instead of the sailing boats, ferries and liners on the harbour, the trams, buses and cars passing by in Queen Street, also the people, who intrigued me.

Soon after our move it was time for me to go to school. Mother and Auntie had a friend who owned and ran the 'Fairy Godmother' Kindergarten. I was very nervous the first day but from then on I *loved* school. I think I was happy to be with people my own age and younger instead of being the baby of the family. Because I was a rather large 'baby' I was never allowed to be the fairy or the beautiful princess in our school games. Sometimes I got to be the handsome prince (if we were short of boys) but mostly I was the villain – giant, evil stepfather, or wicked witch. However, I was noticed in the singing games and asked to go on the Fairy Godmother's radio show. I was all of six and a half or seven and Mother was not in favour of it – but I did appear on it once, during my year at this school, singing 'The Bonnie Banks o' Loch Lomond'.

About this time began long-standing relationships with my dentist and the ear, nose and throat specialist. In my childhood the water in and around Sydney was beautifully soft, with no added fluorides. The result was a generation of people with fairly poor teeth, not helped by the fact that most mothers were good cooks, and cakes, biscuits and sweet desserts were the norm. All the tooth brushing in the world didn't do much good. I had, too, a tendency to catarrh and ailments of the ears and throat which are common enough in Australia and possibly caused by all that swimming and surfing. My first trip to the ENT specialist was because Mother thought I should have my tonsils removed to prevent my innumerable colds and sore throats – it was all the rage. Dr Mansfield was adamant that the tonsils stay put and extracted a promise from Mother and myself that I would only ever go to the best ENT specialist available, wherever I might be. He said that my vocal cords were so responsive that no doctor worth his salt would presume to operate in their vicinity unless there was considerable infection. Mother told him that I sang quite nicely, which he rather expected, and as he was getting towards retiring age advised her to take me to a much younger specialist in Sydney, Dr George Halliday, should I have further problems. I think he knew I would, but didn't want to frighten Mother or myself. However, his choice was a blessing, for there never was a more gentle and knowledgeable surgeon. He looked after my chronic sinusitis for about fourteen years, until I left Sydney for London and, at the time of writing, Sir George is still a consultant in Macquarie Street, Sydney. He, too, refused to operate because of the vocal cords. He found there was a 'kink' in my rather narrow eustachian tubes which helped create a blockage from time to time, causing the intense inflammation and pain to sinus and ears. The treatment was not pleasant, but he at least made it bearable.

After the kindergarten followed days at St Catherine's Church of England Grammar School for Girls. It is the oldest girls' school in Australia and was originally called the Clergy Daughters' School, founded for the education of daughters of the clergy. They were happy days and I stayed with the same group of classmates until I left to do a secretarial course at the age of sixteen. Our granddaughter, Natasha Bonynge, is already a pupil at the same school. When I first attended there were about seventy pupils altogether. It grew while I was there and has further expanded until now there are about three hundred pupils, with fantastic facilities for a wider education than we had, providing an orchestra, choir and ballet classes. My only musical pursuit there was a weekly 'Musical Appreciation' class when we listened to records and sometimes were lucky enough to attend one of the Children's Concerts in the Sydney Town Hall, with Bernard Heinze conducting the Sydney Symphony Orchestra. I did study the piano for about two years with the daughter of Augustus Juncker – he composed an operetta (*Ma Mie Rosette*) which included the charming 'I Was Dreaming', a great favourite with the darling of the Australian operetta scene, Gladys Moncreiff. I later recorded it. My piano practice was only of interest until I could just manage to accompany myself in simple songs and arias, then my set work was forgotten. Mother had to struggle to pay for the lessons so I was told there'd be no more if I didn't do what Miss Juncker required. Foolish child that I was, I continued to play what I wanted and have regretted it ever since as Mother kept her word and the piano lessons stopped.

But I still had Mother singing every day, Uncle Tom in a different vein, and all the music belonging to them and Uncle Arthur to browse through – *Chu Chin Chow*, *The Country Girl*, *The Maid of the Mountains*, *Land of Smiles* and a host of collections of songs and operatic arias, including all the Highland airs. We also had a small, box-like wireless, so we could listen to the various musical programmes and the fine plays that were broadcast from time to time. Everyone in the household sang to a greater or lesser degree and Mother and Auntie Blos played well enough, so we used to have musical evenings about once a month. Sometimes friends of Mother, who also played, would join us – 'Auntie Thalia' on the violin (very out of tune) and our cousin John Ritchie and his wife, both of whom sang. We all found it great fun and my interest in performing grew. I didn't like to say too much about it, but I thought it would be wonderful to sing at Covent Garden some day. Meanwhile I'd settle for the Sydney Town Hall.

Various events came to mind from those school years. Every Easter there was a big show put on by the Royal Agricultural Society in their showground, a mini-world fair with agricultural and pastoral exhibits predominating, but with household goods and manufactured foodstuffs on display and bags of samples for sale by all the various biscuit and chocolate makers, canning companies, etc. with side shows, shooting galleries, wood-chopping competitions and, every day, the Grand Parade of prize-winning Merino sheep, cattle, horses or Hereford bulls – a marvellous sight. There were rodeo events and sheepdog trials – all taking place on the fringe of the city and within walking distance of Queen Street. We loved it all, especially the sample bags. They had been free in my aunt's young days but have steadily increased in price over the years.

There was also the Jubilee of King George V and Queen Mary, followed by the scandal of the abdication of Edward VIII and his marriage to Wallis Simpson, the coronation of King George VI and

Queen Elizabeth and the hundred and fiftieth anniversary of the founding of the Australian Colony at Farm Cove – the last two celebrated by splendid firework displays. The rise of Hitler and Mussolini and the outbreak of yet another 'war to end wars' seemed, at first, very distant from Australian shores. But soon our young men, including Jim and his friends, were joining up and being sent to the various war zones. Jim was in an Ambulance Unit in Kuala Lumpur and was taken prisoner when Malaya fell. We had no news of him for ages but always hoped for his return and rejoiced when he came back.

School days came to an end and I knew that I had to earn my living, so a singing career was out of the question – unless I could manage to work during the day and study singing and a bit of Italian and German in my spare time. I went to the Metropolitan Secretarial College for a year, during which time I did night classes of tailoring and dressmaking. I was never *very* good at the latter, particularly drafting patterns, but the training has come in very handy.

❖ 2 ❖

MY FIRST SECRETARIAL job was with the Council for Scientific and Industrial Research Radiophysics Laboratory. It was situated in the grounds of Sydney University, not far from the Medical School built by my grandfather. It was a very interesting job and one had the pleasant lawns of the University for lunch-time recreation. But, quite apart from the fact that I was losing my shorthand speed, as I was typing from manuscript reports about radar all the time, I was too far out of town to permit of any singing lessons at lunch-time or to participate in any of the vocal competitions taking place during the City of Sydney Eisteddfod. I therefore managed to find a position with a firm of country suppliers back in the centre of the city within easy distance of the Sydney Conservatorium and Palings Studios, where most of the teaching was focused.

Whilst reading the advertisements in the *Sydney Morning Herald*, my eyes had fallen on one announcing a scholarship for two years' free vocal tuition to the successful candidate. My mother was a little wary of my entering, as she knew nothing of the teacher, Aida Summers; however, she felt she would still be at hand to guide me if she disapproved too much of the method of teaching and I had a fair grounding from her in the rudiments of voice production. Money was short and maybe I had a chance of winning.

I won and, after a few weeks' work with Aida, was shocked by her telling me I was definitely *not* a mezzo-soprano but a dramatic soprano. This caused much apprehension on the part of my mother and was a challenge for me. Somehow I had to convince Mother that no harm was being done by taking the voice into a somewhat higher register – especially as it did not always respond easily and smoothly. I had grown to like Aida and felt she was quite justified in her effort to extend the range of the voice upwards, particularly when we began to have results. I had long admired Kirsten Flagstad's voice and began to visualise myself as Brünnhilde or Sieglinde – even Isolde! So I set about trying to make secure the few tentative extra notes I had gained. With hindsight I see the danger of studying heavy repertoire too early, but I made progress and won some prizes in the Sydney Eisteddfod. This annual competition was a starting point for many young artists in

13

Australia and was not limited to vocal entrants, there being instrumental sections as well. Many past and current members of the Australian Opera were competitors and were known to me as far back as those mid-forties years. One of the staunchest of friends and colleagues has been Elizabeth Allen, who retired only in 1989 from the Australian Opera, and who often went along with me to some of the weeding-out sessions in the various sections. She was a contralto, so we seldom had to compete against each other and, if we did, were hugely pleased when either of us won a place.

There were regular Youth Concerts given by the Sydney Symphony Orchestra and I believe it was at one of these that Richard and I were first introduced by a mutual friend. From then on we met frequently as we were both members of a group of young musicians who entertained each other in their homes and who sometimes performed at Music Club concerts both in Sydney and the country districts of New South Wales. Richard was a full-time student at the NSW Conservatorium of Music and studied piano with Lindley Evans who had been Nellie Melba's last accompanist. The result was that he was encouraged to accompany singers and instrumentalists (not too difficult to manage as he had a cousin, Denise Thompson, who was a coloratura soprano) and was asked by the Director of the Conservatorium, Eugène Goossens, to play for the student opera rehearsals. From that day forward he was passionately keen to acquaint himself with the vast operatic repertoire. There was no sudden romance between us. I think we were each intent on pursuing our own career and although there was a certain admiration of each other's talent we were also critical.

What with my full-time job, my singing lessons, Italian and German sessions, the concerts and a little family life, I always seemed to be hurrying from one place to the next. My employers were fairly strict and we had to sign on each morning and after our lunch break. If we were ten minutes late in one week we had to forfeit our one free Saturday morning per month. This became too restricting, so I sought a position with another firm of country suppliers of everything from rabbit traps to combine harvesters, pre-fab sheds and fine wines. Here, the checking-in times were much more easygoing and I had an adorable boss, 'Pop' Clyde, who was most interested in my vocal goals.

For some time there had been a group of people working to found a permanent opera company in Sydney, headed by Mrs Clarice Lorenz, the wife of the well-known optician, C. T. Lorenz. Another organisation was formed called 'Singers of Australia', with which they were also involved. The President and Founder was Mr Oliver King (who had been a founder of the Federated Music Clubs of Australia) and a large percentage of the singing teachers of Sydney were on the Council. The Musical Director was Henry Krips, younger brother of Josef. I joined their Bach Choral Society and the Ladies Choir and was happy to sing in the seventy-member group, our first appearance being a performance of the *Christmas Oratorio* on December 12, 1946. Two of the soloists, Rosina Raisbeck and Raymond Nilsson, both became colleagues of mine later at Covent Garden and Rosina was a stalwart performer with the Australian Opera until she retired in 1988. Charles Mackerras was engaged to play the solo oboe part.

One of my co-members of the Choir suggested to Henry Krips that I should be doing solo work with the organisation and after he and Mr King heard me sing again, Henry was sufficiently impressed to engage me for a Wagnerian Operatic Concert in the Sydney Town Hall on March 22, 1947, with four other soloists including Ronald Dowd (soon to travel to London to further his career) and the Ladies Choir. Henry Krips accompanied us on the piano. The programme included the Spinning Chorus and Senta's Ballad from *The Flying Dutchman*; the Bridal Chorus and the bridal chamber scene from *Lohengrin*; and the monologue, duet and Prize Song and quintette from *The Mastersingers* – all in English. My fee was £10 and the critic of the *Sun* newspaper wrote:

> The Sutherland voice, powerful and warmly resonant, responded to pressure without stridency. But her head tones of much beauty can be made more secure.

The *Australian Musical News*:

> The Sutherland voice is a dramatic soprano of warm quality and evenly tempered throughout the scale, yet to gain some further weight of metal in the head range.

There were reservations, not the least of which were my own – but I had been given a chance and had a sufficient success with the Singers of Australia to be asked to sing with them Handel's *Acis and Galatea* on June 20 and July 19 of the same year and *Dido and Aeneas* of Purcell on Saturday, August 30.

A tour of the Riverina Music Clubs followed in September. We performed in Leeton on Monday, Narrandera on Tuesday, Wagga Wagga on Wednesday, Cootamundra on Thursday and Griffith on Friday. My travelling days had begun.

I was still working full time as a secretary at D'Arcy Shelley Pty Ltd and managed to get time to do the tours and various broadcasting dates by taking portions of my annual leave. Fortunately many of the Music Club concerts were in the suburbs of Sydney so I could manage to fit those in – after work, or with just one day off. It was becoming evident that sooner or later I would have to choose between the security of a full-time job and the possibility of a career in singing.

Meanwhile, I continued to enter the local competitions, the Eisteddfod, and the Concerto and Vocal Competition (sponsored by the Australian Broadcasting Commission), and in 1948 I reached the final concert with the Sydney Symphony Orchestra conducted by Eugène Goossens. The pianist, Laurence Davis, won on that occasion and there were remarks in the press that there should be separate prizes for singers and instrumentalists. I don't think I was too worried about that – there was still the Sun Aria Competition (which had about three hundred entrants each year) and the Vacuum Oil Company launched their 'Mobil Quest' in 1949. This carried an ultimate prize of £1000 (approximately Australian $25,000 today). Each heat and semi-final was broadcast by 3DB and a network of some forty radio stations nationwide, using the Australian Symphony Orchestra and its musical director, Hector Crawford. All the preliminaries were held in Melbourne and our expenses handsomely paid by the sponsors who also endeavoured to put us at our ease.

It was during this period that my brother Jim married a charming girl, Frances Hammett, and of course I sang at the wedding. She was the daughter of the well-known jazz musician, Al Hammett and much loved by us all.

Also at that time, my sister Barbara had developed many health problems and become very frustrated at not being able to sustain a full-time position. She felt she was schizophrenic and took herself to a psychiatrist. She also was friendly with an older man who appeared interested in marriage. We all tried to help her, although she seemed not to want to talk about her problems and fears to the family. Then Mother telephoned me at the office one day and told me that Barbara had taken her life by throwing herself off the cliff at South Head, an area known as the Gap. The terrible fact for all of us to face was that we had no idea she was so disturbed. If only she had talked more with us instead of struggling on, giving the impression that all was well. To my mother, particularly, it was a terrible shock; she had a big guilt complex, feeling she had failed as a mother to Barbara.

I finally had to relinquish my position with D'Arcy Shelley. Dear old 'Pop' Clyde assured me that if I hadn't resigned he would have 'kicked me out' so that I would be forced to try my luck in the musical world. My co-workers were very sweet and sent flowers to my concert appearances.

The Grand Final of the 1949 Mobil Quest was held in Melbourne Town Hall on September 15, and Ronal Jackson was the proud winner of the £1000 first prize, with Trudy Daunt second, William Smith third and myself fourth. It was a very exciting evening and the Vacuum Oil Company followed up the competition with a 'Stars of Mobil Quest' tour to Hobart, Adelaide, Brisbane, Newcastle and Sydney, by which time I had entered and won, at the fourth attempt, the Sun Aria Competition, a prize of £300 and a great deal of prestige in Australia. Indeed, the two competitions having had such widespread publicity, I received many requests to perform – with the ABC Military Band under Stephen Yorke; various 'Returned Soldiers' concerts; a performance of *Elijah*; 'Carols by Candlelight' in Hyde Park, Sydney; the annual 'Scottish Concert' of the Highland Society of NSW and a spate of Music Club recitals – one of them in Lithgow on November 28, 1949 with Richard as joint artist. He did not play my accompaniments on that occasion but was busy enough with Beethoven, Chopin, Weber and Albeniz, whilst I sang two Massenet arias, some lieder and some art songs. Around this time I heard him play the Beethoven Fourth Concerto, the Liszt Eb in Sydney Town Hall conducted by Goossens and the Mozart A Major K 449 at the Conservatorium with the orchestra conducted by Henry Krips. We performed at Killara Music Club on April 11, 1950 in a different programme and, on June 17, I appeared in 'A Farewell Concert to Richard Bonynge, pianist, who is leaving shortly for overseas to continue his studies'.

The 1950 Mobil Quest was already in progress and I was again participating. I also gave a concert for the Young Musicians' Group at the Lyceum Club, with Richard and Elizabeth Allen taking part, and a performance of Handel's *Samson* with the Royal Philharmonic Society of Sydney on July 15. Of this last, the critic (Lindsay Brown) of the *Sydney Morning Herald* wrote scathingly of most of the soloists, concluding with 'and Joan Sutherland whose fine voice might have been singing hey-nonny-nonny, so inadequately did it realise the dramatic shape of the text'. Another concert with Richard was held at the Conservatorium in aid of the Rachel Forster Hospital on July 21 and this was the last time we performed together prior to his departure for London to take up his scholarship at the Royal College of Music. He had graduated from the Sydney Conservatorium with both performer's and teacher's diplomas – the highest accolade. A group of us bade him farewell on one of the old P & O vessels, the *Mooltan*, and we all hoped to follow soon.

Early September brought the Grand Final of the Mobil Quest and this time I was the lucky winner! Cousin John had said if I won he would double the prize – so I had £2000 to go into my savings account for that long-awaited trip abroad. This was further augmented by fees for our 1950 Mobil Quest Tour going to Brisbane, Canberra, Sydney, Newcastle, Kalgoorlie, Perth, Adelaide, Launceston and Hobart.

Again the engagements kept coming, all of them great experience, and I notice from the funny old photographs that I had begun to pay a little more attention to my appearance. There was a *Messiah* with the Sydney Symphony Orchestra; more Music Club concerts and, on

April 20, 1951, a Testimonial Farewell Concert in Sydney Town Hall, with several of my colleagues singing gratis for my benefit. I had decided the time had come to see if my voice would be good enough to gain me some kind of career in England. I had one ambition in those days and that was to sing at Covent Garden. Mother and I were booked on the P & O ship *Maloja*, due to sail from Sydney on July 17 of that year.

At the time it didn't occur to me that, although I had done a fair number of joint recitals and a few oratorios, I was completely inexperienced for the opera stage. I had sung arias, but never sustained a complete role – indeed, had never learned a complete role, except for Purcell's Dido and Handel's Galatea which I sang with the score. And I had the audacity to think I might land a contract to appear at Covent Garden if they heard me do an audition! How naïve I must have been.

Before I left, during June, Eugène Goossens gave me the opportunity to appear on stage in six performances as the heroine of his opera *Judith*. He conducted this Australian première and was most kind and helpful. I wanted desperately to do well as he had such faith in my ability. The press was neither ecstatic nor unkind. The *Sunday Sun* said:

> Joan Sutherland sang the title role broadly and boldly, but was histrionically defeated by a part that would take the resources of a Sybil Thorndike to present plausibly.

The *Daily Sun*:

> Joan Sutherland sang Judith's part fluently and with great power, but moved and acted too stiffly, as though in slow motion, for a temptress who could lure a general from a large band of camp followers.

The stage direction *did* leave much to chance and I relied a lot on my colleagues for help. There were a few mishaps – one when Holofernes (James Wilson) slipped off his bed with a terrible thump and a loud curse just as I was walking offstage with 'his' gruesome papier-mâché head, in a blood-soaked bag, rather killing the dramatic effect. Another night, Ronald Dowd (as the Chief Eunuch) must have been feeling the winter cold and forgot to take off his brilliant red and black socks before making his entrance.

Lina Belle, who was my handmaid in *Judith*, was also booked on the *Maloja* and after a few more concerts and many farewell parties we found ourselves on board the friendly old ship and fêted in each Australian port we visited (Melbourne, Adelaide and Fremantle-Perth) by local representatives of the Vacuum Oil Company. They also met

Mother and me at Tilbury when we finally reached England on August 27 – six weeks after leaving Sydney, having called at Colombo, Aden, Suez, Port Said and Algiers.

✧ 3 ✧

THE THRILL OF being in London cannot be described. Here we were with no conception of the size of the city, only knowing a few Australians like ourselves and booked into a private hotel in Pembridge Square, Notting Hill Gate, for a stay of a week or so while we hunted for 'digs'. Once again, the Vacuum Oil Company representatives were helpful, not only meeting us at Tilbury but seeing us safely ensconced in our modest accommodation, then arranging to take me to the theatre two nights later. Mother assumed that my rendezvous at 6 p.m. would mean dinner before the show and I would be brought home immediately after. Not at all – I was taken to meet the rest of our party and have drinks, then to the theatre and on to a late after-theatre meal and dancing in one of the Mayfair night-clubs. I felt embarrassed and uncomfortable – not only because of my unstylish clothes but knowing that Mother would be anxious. I was not mistaken on this last point for, to my horror and dismay, when the car and my charming escort, Jack Vecsey, finally did arrive back at the hotel, there was Mother in her night attire at the reception desk just about to send out a police call, I was sure. I said my thanks and good-nights very hastily and hoped my kind host hadn't noticed Mother through the glass doors.

The day after, Richard met me – we had been writing to each other as friends – and he couldn't wait to show me all his favourite galleries – the Wallace Collection, the Tate, the National Portrait Gallery – and our round of theatre-going, as well as ballet and opera, began. We also started talking about doing some work together and I began to get in touch with various people whose names had been given me by friends and colleagues in Australia, among whom were the Baroness Ravensdale, a great benefactress to promising artists; Clive Carey, who was head of the Opera School at the Royal College of Music; and Wilfred van Wyck, an agent of prominence. Although I was not performing, there was a flurry of activity trying to make the most of the September days to visit Kew Gardens, Hampton Court and the like, before I was involved in study and the winter weather began.

Irene Ravensdale was very friendly and invited me to a memorable performance of *Dido and Aeneas* at the old Mermaid Theatre, with

Kirsten Flagstad and Maggie Teyte. It was one of the only two times I heard my idol in person and although I was enchanted I felt she was holding back the volume of sound for that very small house – I would have given a great deal to have heard her final performances at Covent Garden as Richard had the year previously. Irene kindly introduced me to many of her friends and at one of her musicales (in July 1952) I was a soloist with Ivor Newton as my accompanist. I had never liked singing in a room once I'd felt the thrill of a concert hall, so chose some lieder and art songs rather than operatic arias as being more suitable for the drawing-room. Ivor Newton was, I'm sure, trying to be helpful when he went through the items and said that Elisabeth Schumann sang a piece like so and someone else did something else, but it made me feel very inadequate and doubly nervous. I remember thanking him for his advice and adding that as the soirée was imminent there wasn't much I could do about it and would he please try and do the best he could for me nevertheless. The room was packed when the evening came and I was horribly nervous – I wished I'd sung better. But there were a few genuine compliments and once I'd sat down again I was delighted to be entertained by Joyce Grenfell who was a regular at those evenings.

I had made contact with Clive Carey and went to see him on September 20. Having read my various introductions and references, he heard me sing and said I should come and work at the Opera School for a year and study voice production with him. I had wanted to work with him (he had studied with the de Reszkes and been teaching in Australia for a number of years just prior to and during the Second World War) but couldn't believe that I would be accepted into the RCM Opera School with no formal musical study behind me; Clive just laughed and said he thought that could be managed – so my London training had begun.

The Opera School was an eye-opener to 'the girl from Australia'. There were some very friendly and amusing girls among the group, all much more knowing than I, and they unwittingly taught me a great deal. The male complement was an even more mature group, many of them doing repat training after their time in the Services. Among them were several with whom I sang later, including the two Scots, Kenneth McKellar and David Ward. The language could be fairly ripe at times and I know they used every opportunity to shock in my presence as I blushed so easily. The movement and dancing classes with Margaret ('Peggy') Rubel were hilarious for all of us but more so for people like David, Judith Pierce and myself who were rather larger than the rest of the group. The only consolation was that everyone felt a fool, especially when we had to pretend to be butterflies or mice. The amazing thing was that we heavier ones were quite light-footed.

There were speech-training and diction classes and, as well as preparing scenes from *Hansel and Gretel* and *The Magic Flute*, we did excerpts from *Iphigenia* (the play). For the operatic excerpts we were coached by the conducting students; two of these were Alexander Gibson and William Reid, both of whom went on to have excellent careers in Britain and abroad. Bill Reid was for a number of years Director of the Elizabethan Trust Orchestra in Sydney, which played for both the Australian Opera and the Australian Ballet.

I met Isobel Baillie, that charming English soprano, and we spent a pleasant hour or so. We heard her sing a *Messiah* exquisitely. She remained in touch and we had lunch with her a few years ago, a very endearing old lady.

In early October I auditioned for the BBC and made contact with Wilfred van Wyck. He seemed to think the thing to do was continue at the Opera School and do a Wigmore Hall recital to launch my career in London at some later date – in a year perhaps. I wasn't sure I wanted to wait that long (impatient, like all young singers).

Meetings with Richard were becoming more frequent as we were working together as often as possible. He was not happy at the Royal College as he had not been permitted to take lessons with the teacher he preferred, nor to study conducting. As he had graduated from the Conservatorium in Sydney with marks which won him the RCM Scholarship, he found the restrictions of the College unreasonable and the repetition of work he had done already in Sydney futile. He left and studied with Herbert Fryer, a darling old man and a pupil of Busoni. Ric was passionately interested in the operatic works of the early nineteenth century and infused me with the same enthusiasms. Recordings of Callas were thrilling the listeners and already I had been persuaded by Ric to study the Mad Scene from *I Puritani*, although the upper register of the voice was not controlled – in fact I doubted it could ever be improved and Mother was very sceptical. ('He's ruining my daughter's voice,' she said.) Besides working with me to solidify my technique, he also played for various singing teachers, one of the regulars being Professor E. Herbert Caesari whose vocal method gave him quite a few ideas, also Elena Gerhardt. He came with me to my lessons with Clive Carey and we spent most of our time at the opera, a concert or ballet, or straight theatre. We frequently sat in the 'gods' or stood to see everything and everyone – Ljuba Welitsch, Margherita Grandi, Schumann, Flagstad, Schipa, Gigli and others. There were always discussions during intermissions and afterwards about the performers. There were some things I couldn't (and still can't) bear and they were forced, over-enlarged voices and off-pitch singing – the latter usually the result of the former. Tucked into a busy day at the College on October 16, I notice I had an audition at 2.45 p.m. at the

Wigmore Hall. Was this my first audition for Covent Garden? Be that as it may, the very eventful year of 1951 was drawing to a close and Mother and I had, by this time, found a mini-apartment in the attic of a house in Pembridge Crescent. Early in January a small, rather beat-up piano was hoisted into our attic and now Richard and I really worked. He was slowly convincing me that I had a much wider range both of voice and music at my command.

With the New Year, rehearsals proceeded at the Opera School with excerpts from *Richard III* (!), *Don Giovanni*, *Così fan tutte*, *Tannhäuser* and an operetta, *All at Sea*, this last causing much hilarity.

During February I met Eugène Goossens and he was again encouraging. When he returned to Sydney he said it was 'high time Australia took steps to keep her talent at home. If we had a fine national opera house with performances the year round and adequate financial rewards for our singers, they would think twice before leaving the country.' He never let up on his dream of an opera house for Sydney and although the realisation of that dream leaves much to be desired *vis-à-vis* practicality as a workable theatre, without him and those around him of like mind, the Sydney Opera House would not exist – nor would the Australian Opera (now Opera Australia).

There were many Australians in Britain at that time and an Australian Musical Association group was formed. This aimed at helping young Australian musicians by providing a small showcase for them in the form of a recital or shared recital at Australia House. Richard and I were both early members and performers and the Association continues to do very good work.

In July I was to sing Giorgetta in Puccini's *Il Tabarro* at the Opera School. The BBC hired me to understudy Irma Kolassi in *Oedipus Rex* (a mezzo-soprano part) and I did small recitals on the Home Service. On May 22 there was another audition – for Covent Garden – and rehearsals for the final productions of the year at the College were intensive and exciting. There was much friendly rivalry but we found time to organise an outing on the Thames. The 'boys' were very gallant handlers of the punts but the weather was unkind and we finally abandoned the river and sought shelter in a handy pub where Bill Reid accompanied all and sundry in an impromptu operatic concert – to start with and then just anything any of us could remember or felt like singing.

On July 10 there is an entry in my diary which says: '5.30–5.45 p.m.: Covent Garden.' Was it the third audition for the Opera House? That same afternoon I'd had a Stage and Orchestra for *Il Tabarro* at the College, and Irene Ravensdale's soirée, in which I was to sing, was the same evening. It's the sort of schedule I have shunned for years. My performances of *Il Tabarro* were on July 16 and 18 at 5.30 p.m., and according to my diary I sang on the Third Programme at 10.30 on the morning of the sixteenth. I suppose I thought I'd not be asked again if I had said I had another important engagement later that day.

Of the *Il Tabarro* performance, Arthur Jacobs wrote in the September issue of *Opera*:

> ... the most arresting portrayal came from Joan Sutherland's Giorgetta: here is a dramatic soprano of high quality and well-controlled power. Doubtless Clive Carey, Director of Opera at the College, has assisted Miss Sutherland to develop her considerable stage presence; and one may confidently look forward to hearing more of her.

Clive Carey in his Report on Individual Studies for the year said:

> SINGING: A voice of great power, quality and remarkable range and flexibility – in fact, the very rare type of dramatic soprano that is capable of brilliant coloratura work also, such as is demanded by Bellini and Donizetti. With her musicality she will, I am sure, at once find a high place. If she realised fully the importance of complete relaxation (in which she has already made some progress) she would without doubt find her way to the very top, for there is nothing that she cannot do.
>
> OPERA: She has had a considerable stiffness of body to contend with, and has already gone far in the way of release and movement in the short time with us, but needs continually to give her mind to improvement here, and might do so much towards it on her own if she but knew how. She has a good stage sense which is developing and she has gained much in ability to express her emotions and these qualities, with her splendid voice, should take her far.

Joyce Wodeman on DRAMA:

> Has made very remarkable progress in this short time. She has shown a feeling for the stage and has a fine stage presence. She is beginning to realise how to use her own assets – humour and warmth and capacity for emotion and to bring them into her work. She must work always for greater fluidity and gesture and get rid of the tendency to stiffen when she is nervous. She is very co-operative and I wish her great success.

Representatives from Covent Garden came to the Royal College end-of-year performances and I think it was seeing and hearing me in the Parry Theatre that prompted the fourth summons to the Royal Opera House on July 22. On the morning of the twenty-fourth, Sir Steuart Wilson (Deputy General Administrator) told me I was accepted into the Company, rehearsals to begin on September 10.

Apparently on the strength of my promised contract with the Royal Opera House (£10 per week), Mother and I went to Scotland for ten days, making Edinburgh our headquarters and tripping out from there, also meeting up with a cousin from Thurso. Back in London we worked. Richard was as nervous as I about my imminent launching and wanted to have me prepared for my first role – the First Lady in *The Magic Flute*.

✧ 4 ✧

THE GREAT DAY of initiation arrived and five days later I had my first production call in the foyer with Christopher West and the young conductor, John Pritchard. This was the beginning of a long association with John, and I think Christopher (who was Resident Producer with the Company) immediately wanted to help me as much as his busy schedule permitted. I found all the other members of the Company very helpful and there was always a good deal of fun at rehearsals, as well as the serious business of the day. I cannot say that I have ever worked with a spiteful or unkind colleague in all my forty-odd years, except for one or two conductors. One had always read of jealousies and rivalries and I expected to find this at 'the Garden'. But the friendly acceptance of myself and the encouragement I was given by them all, throughout the House, was very heart-warming and a great lesson for me in the future when I began to meet the younger generation of singers who seemed to hold me in such awe.

The policy of the House was to present works in English, and as most of the principals were imported – at least for the opening performances of a new production – there was, frequently, some very amusing pronunciation. Even the British contingent could not seem to disguise their local dialect, particularly in spoken dialogue. Some of the translations left much to be desired too, although I have always found the Dent translations of Mozart charming.

As the Opera House was only finding its feet after having been a dance-hall during the war years, the majority of singers were relatively young and eager, and I discovered some pleasant comrades among those in my first opera. The lovely Adèle Leigh was singing Pamina and Monica Sinclair was the Third Boy, whilst my Second and Third Lady companions were Janet Howe and Jean Watson. How helpful they all were, showing me around the labyrinth of the back-stage area, much more congested than it is now, and locating all the rehearsal rooms, some right up in the gallery or amphitheatre bars. When you had a call there, you made sure you were ahead of time so you could catch your breath. The Retiring Room of the Bedford Box, with its quaint Victorian blue-flowered lavatory bowl complete with antique plunger, was also pointed out.

I was sometimes surprised and even shocked by the levity of my colleagues – for me it was such a serious step and a wonderful opportunity to learn about the inside workings of the theatre I had visited in the audience so many times during the previous year. But gradually I relaxed and we had some wonderful times together, later working with Barbara Howitt who was so witty and vivacious. All 'the girls' helped me with hints on make-up – no make-up artist except for special character roles – and then you had to learn how to manage it yourself after the dress rehearsals and first night. They even tried to advise me with my street clothing, although not very successfully as I was always rather too large for anything off the rack and had most dresses made – or made them myself which was usually disastrous.

There were fittings to attend and I shall never forget the excitement of putting on the charming costume designed by Oliver Messel for the First Lady. He also had designed *The Marriage of Figaro*, and the Countess's gowns were a dream, particularly the midnight-blue velvet appliquéd in silver. It was thought I could wear Sylvia Fisher's skirt for *Figaro* and perhaps have a new bodice made. I didn't care about it being new or not – just to wear it made one feel fabulous. The Wardrobe Mistress, Olivia Cranmer, was apparently quite a tartar to her staff – and they certainly turned out beautifully constructed costumes. Barbara Matera of New York and William Paterson, head of the Australian Opera Wardrobe, have been making costumes in the same way ever since their early days at Covent Garden. The bodices were all stiffly boned, then laced at the back to allow either for a singer having put on or lost weight, or so that in the event of a cast change the new singer could be laced in tighter or looser. In those days there were sometimes two sets of costumes for the leading lady – one smaller than the other 'just in case'.

As well as the main Wardrobe where the large gowns and tutus were made (a block or so away from the Opera House in Wellington Street) there was the Current Season Wardrobe within the theatre where Gertie Stelzel organised repairs and adaptations, as well as overseeing pressing before every performance and cleaning where necessary. Gertie was also in charge of the dressers and helped with Principal Ladies – especially when they were German-speaking and/or 'difficult'. The dressers at that time were mostly cockney ladies of middle age and more, very outspoken and not what some of our visiting German sopranos had been used to. We had some wonderful laughs with them all backstage.

At the time I joined the Royal Opera House, the surrounding area was still occupied by the fruit, vegetable and flower market and conjured up visions of Eliza Doolittle. The market porters were darting to and fro and many were the humorous (not to say fresh) epithets tossed our way. Although one left sufficient time to get to the Garden from home, there was always the possibility of the cranky old elevator at Covent Garden station being out of action and of having to climb the stairs, or perhaps there was a delay on the Underground. Then one would emerge from the station flustered and make a dash for the Stage Door, eliciting remarks like: 'Runnin' late, are we darlin'?' ... ''ullo luv – not 'ear the alarm this morning?' ... 'Too many late nights, Joanie girl?' It was amazing how they got to know our names and sometimes exactly what we were doing in the theatre. Our dear Stage Door man, Joe Kettley, sometimes came out of his cubby-hole to get some air and maybe spoke with one or two. Much gossip was also heard at the Nag's Head pub opposite the Stage Door where we went for a counter lunch – no canteen at that time.

The old market area is all very 'boutiquy' and smart now, but I miss the scent of rotting cabbage and carnation, and banana peels underfoot. It was amazing how the hustle and bustle of the pre-ten-thirty rehearsal time vanished by the time we had our lunch break and the congestion of the big produce-bearing trucks and vans disappeared, to be replaced later by the stream of vehicles dropping elegantly dressed patrons of the opera, only to change again by the time the curtain came down – so that certain aroma never really went away.

At last the great night of October 28 came and my début in *The Magic Flute*. I was petrified, to say the least. Another Australian, John Lanigan, was Tamino, Welsh Geraint Evans was the Speaker, Scottish William McAlpine the First Priest, the New Zealander Inia Te Wiata was Sarastro and Australian Arnold Matters the Papageno. I have little recollection of the evening. All I know is that Ric and Mother were pleased.

Performances of *The Magic Flute* continued but even before it opened I had begun studying Clotilde in *Norma*, the High Priestess in *Aida*, the Countess in *Figaro* and Amelia in *Masked Ball*, for which I was the official cover and had to sit in at all rehearsals when I was not otherwise engaged. This was wonderful experience as I was able to watch all Amelia's scenes take shape from scratch, with Gunther Rennert producing in his very dynamic fashion.

There was no Green Room or canteen in the theatre in which to relax, so I used to go into the auditorium and look at whatever was being rehearsed, be it ballet or opera. I learned so much from watching and listening. I was fascinated by the ballet and saw some wonderful dancers: Danilova, Toumanova, Chauviré, Eglevsky, Markova, Dolin, Fonteyn, Beryl Grey.

I continued to do BBC recitals and had committed myself to a solo recital in the Wigmore Hall, with Gerald Moore accompanying me, to take place on my birthday, November 7.

Before that, there was the thrill of working in the rehearsals for the début performance at Covent Garden of Maria Meneghini Callas in *Norma*, with that grand old mezzo-soprano, Ebe Stignani, as Adalgisa. The impact of hearing Callas in the flesh was something one cannot forget, and when the voices of Norma and Adalgisa blended in their fantastic duets and trio, I doubted if I would ever experience such a thrill again. Stignani was very much 'old school' and Maria young and ambitious, but they were both a great example to a young soprano. I didn't dare approach either of them outside of my minimal role but they were both very kindly – Maria having quite a few joking asides with me in her Brooklyn vernacular. But what a professional she was and, although she knew the role inside out she was content to rehearse until things were right. Her eyesight was appalling and contact lenses not yet the norm, so she would pace out her movements with her thick glasses on, counting the number of steps she could take from point to point, and only removing them when we reached the final Dress Rehearsals. I doubt if she could see the conductor (Vittorio Gui) but they had worked together a great deal and all went well. Richard and I were also fortunate to hear Maria sing performances of *Aida* and *Il Trovatore* the following season and later in 1957 or 1958, her Violetta was unforgettable, but by this time she had lost considerable weight and the voice, although coloured incredibly to project her emotions, was showing signs of strain.

As if I hadn't enough to think about, I was suddenly requested to sing for Sir Thomas Beecham at his home in St John's Wood. It was suggested I sing some Handel – so I rushed to Ric at Willesden and we got together on 'Let the Bright Seraphim' and 'Rejoice Greatly'. In fear and trembling, I presented myself. When I entered the room Sir Thomas was seated in a huge wing chair and asked what I was going to sing. When I told him, he exploded with 'Oh! Not more Handel! Sing "Voi che sapete"!' I tried to say that I'd been asked to sing Handel and that I was a soprano and not a mezzo, but he countered with 'If you can sing "Voi che sapete" you can sing anything'. So, as I had sung the aria as an exercise with my mother when I was about twelve, I sang it. I left, knowing he was not interested.

In later years, as a guest artist in each opera house I usually only had just one work to perform at a time, but as a Company Member, and a new one with no repertory, I was rehearsing and performing all the time. Some of the roles were small. The High Priestess in *Aida* was off-stage and very short, so I was able to arrive a half-hour before I sang and leave immediately after. But I had to be there and fitting everything in was hectic.

On Friday, October 31, I had a 10 a.m. stage call for *Norma*, which went on until 1 p.m.; at 1.30 p.m. a costume fitting; and at 2.30 p.m., musical calls on *The Marriage of Figaro* and *Aida*. The second night of *The Magic Flute* was on Saturday, November 1, with a 10 a.m. General Rehearsal of *Aida*; Sunday the second a morning musical call of *Norma*; Monday the third the opening night of *Aida*, with dear Sir John Barbirolli conducting; Tuesday the fourth a 10.30 *Norma* rehearsal in costume, no make-up; Wednesday the fifth the same (and a *Figaro* call that was mercifully cancelled); Thursday the sixth *Norma* at 10.30 a.m., again on-stage, in costume without make-up, and an *Aida* performance at night. On Friday, November 7, my birthday, I had the Dress Rehearsal of *Norma* at 10.00 a.m. and my Recital at Wigmore Hall at 7.30 p.m., followed the next day by the opening night of *Norma*. It's the sort of schedule I advise young singers to avoid – but it was do or die, and I survived.

I can't say the critics went wild about the recital, but they did give encouragement, if not always in the right direction, *The Times* saying:

> This young Australian has the voice and physique to make her a dramatic soprano capable of tackling either heavy Italian or Wagnerian roles.

The *Daily Telegraph* critic said:

> Here was a rare voice, here the possibilities of a truly eminent singer. At present, Miss Sutherland is no accomplished technician. Her legato still wants an even line; control is spasmodic. But the tone is generously rich, and if things go well she should in a couple of years' time be a splendid heroine in, for instance, *Trovatore*.

Encouragement indeed – but I did not sing Verdi's wonderful heroine until September 1975.

In *Norma*, the following night, the excitement in the theatre was tremendous, backstage as well as in the front of House. The audience went wild, the majority only having heard *Norma* on record before, as it had not been performed in England since 1930. If I wasn't on-stage in view of the audience, I was peering through a very convenient hole in the scenery, as I couldn't bear to miss a note of the opera. This was what I'd wanted all my life and I almost had to pinch myself to make sure it was not a dream.

I was thrilled to receive wonderful flowers from David Webster, the General Administrator, after the performance. For him to include me in the recipients of floral tributes from the House for such a small role on a grand occasion meant a great deal to me. I was somewhat in awe of him at that stage but came to admire him immensely for his sympathetic ear and canny foresight – he would listen and advise me with a good sense of humour and understanding. I felt he was a father figure to us all, whether in the opera or the ballet.

The critic for *The Times* on November 10 used abusive terms like 'a tedious opera ... insipid ... musical vapidity ... rum-tum wind chords ... historical curiosity ... so bald a score ... a byword for absurdity'. How taste has changed.

I had difficulty coming down to earth after those nights and wondered what it would be like to have sung the role of Norma myself and received such an ovation.

During the run of the *Flute* London experienced a terrible 'killer' fog, possibly the last of its kind because of the resultant insistence on smokeless fuel. It was incredible how the sulphuric fumes seeped into the theatre. The performance at Sadler's Wells was cancelled. At the Garden the show went on but the beautifully lit gloom of many scenes became much deeper and two candelabra on the false proscenium failed to work. The conductor, John Pritchard, disappeared from time to time in the all-enveloping haze, reappearing like some gesticulating spirit only to vanish again. It was hard to remain serious. Then, in our quaint Dent translation, Tamino says: 'What a terrible night! Why are we always left in darkness? Papageno, are you there?' Of course, the whole cast, orchestra and public laughed uproariously and the performance was a triumph.

I was asked to take a score of *Der Rosenkavalier* from the library and look at the role of the Marschallin. Richard went into a tail-spin over this! 'Quite apart from three big roles to learn [by this time, I was covering Aida as well as the Countess in *Figaro* and Amelia in *A Masked Ball*] you have your current parts to sing and anyway, you're much too young and immature to play the Marschallin. You want to have a long, steady career. Tell them you don't think it's right for you yet – if ever!' I was feeling a bit bogged down with the amount of work I was having to do to learn everything, but I was afraid to complain about the Marschallin. I thought, better let it go for a while and see what happens – I only had an occasional call on it and I rather liked the musical challenge.

My mother's cousin kindly sent us a brace of pheasants for part of our Christmas cheer. Either they had hung too little or too long, or just didn't agree with me, but I was violently ill after Christmas and was still feeling very unwell on December 29 when the Company Manager telephoned me. He explained that the soprano for that evening's performance of *A Masked Ball* (Helene Werth) had cabled to say that she was ill and would I please sing the role of Amelia for them? I said I felt I didn't really know the part well enough:

'Oh, but Mr Pritchard was very pleased when you sang a portion of the Sitzprobe due to the late arrival of Miss Werth, because of fog over the channel.'

'I had the score in front of me,' I said, 'and I've only watched the production rehearsals and not actually moved about the stage at all.'

'We will have plenty of stage-managers and people to remind you where to go and would appreciate your coming in for a costume fitting at noon. We don't ever like to change the opera or cancel a performance and will not penalise you if you don't have a success. We understand your reservations but want you to do this for us.'

What was I to do? I knew I couldn't get through the opera without a few errors even with the score at hand. If I sang I could perhaps be kicked out – if I didn't, likewise.

'Very well, then, I'll be in for the fitting.'
'Good girl! Thank you very much.'

What had I done! Mother wondered if I'd been hasty saying I'd do it but I felt strongly that if I didn't it would not be to my advantage – better to take the chance and know that I'd tried.

There was a flurry of activity, rushing in for the fitting and back again to look at my score, trying to have a rest but anxious to get to the theatre to have plenty of time to make up and dress. Finally at the theatre I barely registered that I was actually in the Star dressing-room. I got through Amelia's first entrance to Mlle Arvidson's (Ulrica's) and during the intermission was asked to go to the Conductor's Room as Mr Pritchard wanted to see me. I went and he, probably with the best intentions, asked me to sing through the big gallows scene. I started to and then said:

'I'm sorry Mr Pritchard, but I feel I need every ounce of energy for "out there". I'll do the best I can but I can't sing it now and again immediately after – please let me go back to my dressing-room and try to compose myself!'

He probably thought I was crazy, but he let me go and by the time I got back to my room with a few more tweaks of the costume and wig I was 'on'.

All sorts of emotions were experienced that night and I was so grateful to Edward Downes who was in the prompt box. I was not used to the prompting technique at all but Ted was so clear that I vow he saved the performance. John Pritchard, too, was helping all he could and my co-singers, Edgar Evans, Frederick Dalberg, Mike Langdon and Jess Walters, all were wonderful to me. After the performance Ted Downes was one of the first to greet me – all smiles – saying 'You did it!' Later he confessed that prior to that evening, at one of the regular weekly staff meetings, he had suggested I not be re-engaged the following season as he felt I was such a slow learner. That performance changed his mind.

During the run of *A Masked Ball*, the early performances of Amelia were sung by two German sopranos. I believe it was Helena Werth singing on the night Eugenia Zareska was heard to remark in a very loud whisper from her seat in the House: 'Zat voman hass no English! She says "Modders prayer" alvays. Doesn't she know it should be "Muzzahs"?' She was covering the part of the Fortune-teller, Mlle Arvidson/Ulrica, and sang performances later in the season – also Cherubino and, then, Carmen – in English, of course.

The eventful year came to an end and with the beginning of 1953 the musical calls on *Rosenkavalier* were resumed, much to Richard's chagrin. They continued until the opening night of the opera in the House with Sylvia Fisher as the Marschallin, which Richard and I attended. He pointed out sections of the role that were less than suitable for my voice and convinced me to speak out at my calls regarding our reservations over it.

Rehearsals for the Countess and Amelia intensified as I had been told I would have a chance to do both these operas during the spring tour which was to open in Cardiff on February 16. Ric was working on the roles with me, two or three times a week, and now that I was a member of the opera company we were able to attend performances even more frequently. I could get standing passes and the jolly Commissionaire, Sergeant Martin, checked the House at first intermission and told us where the vacant seats were.

We both went to Clive Carey once or twice a week, depending on my schedule, still working to relax and polish the upper register of the voice. Clive had been bowled over when we took him *I Puritani* for the first time.

On February 4, 1953 I sang the role of Aida in an English concert version of the opera with the Plymouth Choral Society. The *Western Morning News* critique for February 5 said:

Dominating the cast was the Australian soprano from Covent Garden, Joan Sutherland. Miss Sutherland has the remarkably wide range required for the part of Aida, and her voice is just as much at ease in the top register as when it drops into the realms of the mezzo-soprano. She sang this exacting role with startling brilliance, combining a powerful sense of the theatre with purity of tone.

The diary for February 3 and 6 denotes *Orpheus* at the Opera House, the moving Kathleen Ferrier performances, which Ric and I saw, not realising that she was so close to death. In fact, there were buckets in the wings for her to use when leaving or returning to the stage. My ear, nose and throat doctor, dear Ivor Griffiths, who was House Doctor at the Garden, told me that when the performances with Kathleen were mooted her doctors were asked their opinion as to whether she would be well enough to fulfil her engagement. They agreed that she would certainly be in pretty bad shape by then but she wanted so desperately to do the performances, and they knew how strong-willed and stoic she was that, if Covent Garden was prepared to take the chance, she should go ahead and complete the contract. What courage she had.

Rehearsals continued up to and during the tour which visited Cardiff, Edinburgh, Glasgow, Liverpool, Manchester and Birmingham – a total of nine weeks. My salary in London had been £10 per week and as I had to 'live away from home' it was raised to £15 for the tour. There were lists of theatrical 'digs' on the notice board and I was advised for and against by experienced fellow artists. Finding the shillings for the gas meter in the bedroom was a problem as a rule, and coping with some of the landladies' chatter used to drive us out in spite of the cold and drizzly early-spring weather. I can remember it was so cold one night in Cardiff that Barbara Howitt, Ann Finley, Ted Downes and myself all got into Ted's double bed, fully clothed, to keep warm between our evening meal and bedtime. It was much too cold to sit in a chair and read a book or chat. How we envied those who could afford to stay at the Angel Hotel.

During the tour I sang my first Countess in *Figaro*, at the Empire Theatre in Edinburgh (February 24). More performances of the opera followed on the tour and I also did more Amelias in *A Masked Ball* than those for which I was scheduled, as Elfriede Wasserthal was indisposed. The performances were conducted by Vilem Tausky with whom I had the pleasure to work again, several times, when I sang Mimi and Butterfly with the BBC Midland Light Orchestra. I apparently managed to 'sing [Amelia] with poise and great vocal assurance' according to the *Birmingham Gazette* and warranted a headline in the *Edinburgh Evening News* (February 28): 'Newcomer Shines in Verdi Opera'. The writer went on to give a short biography and to say: '... it could be said she rose magnificently above the strain of a very challenging role.'

Whilst in Manchester, the Hallé Orchestra had a Wagnerian concert scheduled and, at the last minute, had to change the programme, requiring the presence of Brangäne in the *Tristan and Isolde* excerpt from Act 2 of the opera. Sir John Barbirolli asked for me to do it and Ted Downes hammered it into me all weekend. The London *Daily Express* made much of my small contribution, saying:

Her voice, round and confident, rose above the strength of a full symphony orchestra to the utmost reaches of the hall. It was heart-warming. Then she closed her score – she sang in German – and went back to her small hotel.

The tour ended in Birmingham on April 18 and it was back to London and rehearsals for *Elektra* conducted by Erich Kleiber and produced by Rudolf Hartmann of the Munich Opera. I was singing my unfavourite role of the Overseer but I got to work with Kleiber and Hartmann and the Elektra – Erna Schlüter – was most impressive. Richard and I were much more interested in seeing performances of Markova in *Giselle* and, in early June, Maria Callas sang Aida with Giulietta Simionato as Amneris and Kurt Baum as Radames.

Two days before that, on June 2, was the Coronation of Queen Elizabeth II, and Mother and I had wonderful seats in the stand outside Westminster Abbey. The pageantry was magnificent with all the dignitaries in their finest robes riding in coaches or open landaus – notably Queen Salote of Tonga. When Noël Coward was asked who was the little man sitting opposite her, he replied very swiftly 'Her lunch'. I believe it was the Sultan of Zanzibar. The young Queen and all the Royal Family looked radiant and after the long day in the stand, Mother and I walked to the Palace and stood with the crowd to watch them appear on the balcony. It was an emotional scene.

The following Monday there was a gala performance at the Opera House 'On the Occasion of the Coronation of Her Majesty Queen Elizabeth II'. Mother and I had seats in the balcony stalls on the curve, so could look down into the Royal Box area in the centre of the grand tier. The flowers festooning the theatre were magnificent (designed by Oliver Messel, as was the souvenir programme) and the jewels worn by the audience seemed fabulous – until the Royal party arrived in flashing tiaras and necklaces and all their Orders. The public went wild and I'm sure the performance was late starting – unheard of, then, at the Garden.

The opera was the first performance of Benjamin Britten's *Gloriana*, with Peter Pears as the Earl of Essex and Joan Cross as Queen Elizabeth I and an all-British supporting cast. Jennifer Vyvyan sang the role of Penelope Rich (Essex's sister) and I think maybe the only reason I was able to get such good seats in the House was because I was covering this part, and was to do performances later in the year in Bulawayo. It was a very spectacular show with Svetlana Beriosova dancing beautifully during the Masque. I also remember a quaint touch during the last-act London street scene when Edith Coates, the grand English mezzo-soprano, emptied the contents of a chamber pot over one of the Essex supporters, crying out: 'I'll damp your courage – take that, you wastrel!' There was criticism that it was not quite right to show the ageing Elizabeth I, bereft of wig and looking haggard surrounded by fawning and intriguing courtiers, as a homage to our new Queen. But the opera was historical in content, written by the best-known British composer of the day and cast mostly from singers in the resident Company.

Four more performances of *Norma* were presented with Maria Callas and the same cast as previously, except for the Adalgisa, sung on these occasions by Giulietta Simionato, probably the greatest mezzo of her time. She was very elegant and I sang with her again on a somewhat more equal footing some eight years later with great pleasure.

On July 10 my mother sailed to Sydney, her return due to the breaking up of the Queen Street home. Uncle Tom and Auntie Blos were growing too old to manage the big house and Mother went back to attend to the sale of what was left of my grandfather's estate in Paddington and Surry Hills, and to dispose of the predominantly Victorian furnishings of the old home. Before she left, we had moved from our attic to a first-floor studio apartment nearer the Notting Hill Gate tube station: much more convenient for me and certainly less of a strain for mother climbing the stairs. On arrival in Sydney she set about clearing out cupboards, apparently burning all our old photographs and any old music they couldn't give away – Ric and I were stunned and not a little cross. But they were leaving the house, my aunt coming ultimately to London to live with Mother in an apartment, and my uncle going to stay with friends and then to my brother Jim and his wife and young family.

The organising of the trip by the Company to Bulawayo was a formidable task, as the big jet aircraft were not yet in service. We travelled in what I think were converted bombers or troop carriers. We stopped at Malta, Khartoum (where the heat was unbelievable and Adèle Leigh had a 'fit of the vapours'), Entebbe, where we stayed overnight on Lake Victoria, then on to Livingstone. Our welcome by the press and the residents was somewhat overwhelming but we all thoroughly enjoyed being fêted at Government House receptions and private dinner parties and outings. The big exhibition ground was of great interest with much local colour, an 'African village', tribal dancing and wild animals. Many of my colleagues went to one or other of the game reserves but I seemed to be either performing or 'covering' roles which didn't leave sufficient days free to go and be back in time.

There was a very carefree attitude with all the Company members and I can remember they used to sunbathe on the roof of our hotel – to the amazement of the staff who tended, like me, to keep out of the sun. Some did daily exercises and I remember Hilde Zadek, Frances Yeend and Hella Toros having a competition as to who could stand on their head the longest. It was like a grand holiday and work seemed incidental. We managed to see fascinating cave paintings and visit the magnificent Victoria Falls, travelling in a boat on the Zambesi, seeing hippos, crocodiles, elephants and myriads of monkeys, even landing on a small island to have our packed lunches, the remains of which the monkeys were eager to devour. The Stage Director (Elizabeth Latham) and the Stage Managers (Ande Anderson and Stella Chitty – the latter the stalwart Director of the Stage at the Garden until 1993) and all the backstage staff did a fabulous job in getting the productions together and running smoothly, but still managed to join in our outings.

The tour ended on August 29 after presenting thirty-one performances – eight of *Aida*; seven *Marriage of Figaro*; nine *La Bohème* and seven *Gloriana*. Some of the company went home via Cairo but for me the wonders of Egypt had to wait another thirty-six years. At the end of this very full and eye-opening season, I had done sixty performances:

First Lady	6
Priestess (*Aida*)	25
Clotilde	9
Amelia	7
Countess	3
Overseer (*Elektra*)	4
Penelope Rich	6

There were only three other members of the soprano/mezzo roster who did more, and I was in my first season. What was in store?

✧ **5** ✧

AS I WAS now living alone, I frequently went out to dinner with friends or colleagues or to the theatre and dinner after. Ric and I worked constantly and although hitherto we had been merely friends a warmer relationship developed.

In the second week of September 1953, the Munich Opera played for two weeks at the Opera House – a Strauss season of *Arabella*, *Capriccio* and *Die Liebe der Danae*. We were captivated by these beautiful productions, particularly *Die Liebe der Danae* and the voluptuous voice and performance of Leonie Rysanek.

Back to rehearsal at the Garden on September 28 with Helmwige in *Walküre*, Frasquita in the new production of *Carmen* and the Woodbird in *Siegfried*. The *Carmen* was a very lovely-looking production designed by Georges Wakhevitch and produced for the most part by Anthony ('Puffin') Asquith, the English screen director. He was a charming person to work with, having fanciful ideas like wishing Micaela to make her entrance on a donkey with panniers. But he was used to the screen technique of many re-takes, and to hurry things along so that all would be ready on opening night, Tyrone Guthrie together with Joan Cross were brought in. Ultimately the production worked very well but again there was a conglomeration of accents in the spoken dialogue. We had two Americans as Carmen and Micaela (Nell Rankin and Frances Yeend), James Johnston the Irish tenor as Don José, the Czech Marko Rothmüller as Escamillo, two Welshmen, a couple of English in Barbara Howitt (Mercédès) and Michael Langdon (Zuniga), and myself – the dialogues were hilarious. *Walküre* was also a source of much fun among the warrior maidens – Blanche Turner, Edith Coates, Jean Watson, Monica Sinclair, Constance Shacklock, Barbara Howitt and Emily Hooke. We still had a very old production, complete with helmets and ultra-long spears. I remember singing my first 'Ho-Yo-To-Ho' from the prompt side of the stage on a high rostrum and then having to run around the back of the cyclorama and pick up my spear before making an entrance. Some of us couldn't control our spears and tended to trip ourselves – or others – up. Worse, a sudden turn from a colleague and you might be swiped across the shins or have to duck to save your head, although the helmets did give

38

protection. When all of us were cowering beneath the wrath of Wotan (Karl Kammann who had a surfeit of saliva) on one occasion, Edie was heard to mutter, 'I say, darlings, he's dribbling a bib full.' We could barely sing for laughing. The conductor was Fritz Stiedry from the Metropolitan Opera and Brünnhilde that imposing American, Margaret Harshaw. Stiedry seemed to like me and Margaret Harshaw, who was very nervous over her début at Covent Garden, wrote me a charming and encouraging 'Thank-you' note for a few flowers I sent her.

My very sincere thanks to you for your warm wishes and lovely flowers. It was a joy to work with you and you certainly gave me support on an important occasion in my life.

For you, I have great hopes and I am sure you will have a most wonderful future – your voice is very beautiful. You have my sincere best wishes for a successful year and God bless you.

signed Margaret Harshaw
London, October 24, 1953

Earlier in October, *Luisa Miller* was performed at Sadler's Wells with David Ward singing splendidly as Count Walter, also Oreste Kirkop, who later had a rather short-lived movie career as 'Oreste'. Richard and I still remember the thrill of that evening. David's future was assured. We also had the good fortune to hear Maria Callas sing *Il Trovatore* during the season at the Garden and again we were mesmerised by her presence.

Before the year was out I had a few more BBC engagements and a memorable concert in the Orpington Civic Hall with Alfred Deller and Heddle Nash. Memorable because it was the first time Richard or I had heard a countertenor singing solos. (We really were innocents abroad.) Ric was in the audience and was overcome with mirth at the rather stocky, moustachioed and macho-looking Alfred Deller singing alto arias from *Messiah* and the *Christmas Oratorio*.

About this time I signed a contract with Ingpen & Williams – virtually a one-woman agency directed by Joan Ingpen who found all manner of engagements for me outside of the Opera House.

Richard was pursuing his piano studies privately with Herbert Fryer and continuing to play for vocal students at their lessons with various teachers. We went to the performances at Covent Garden together whenever possible and frequently to Sadler's Wells. We had made several friends among the theatre-goers and two of our favourites were Roy Hobdell and Phillip Harris. Roy was an artist with Unilever but we loved his Arcimboldesque paintings and the wonderful decorated furniture in his apartment. He also designed sets for several operas for his own pleasure and later did a fantasy painting of myself as Alcina and another as Lucia.

On February 4, my compatriot Joan Hammond was scheduled to sing *Aida*, but was ill and I was on, with Leonne Mills singing my usual High Priestess role. Mercifully, I had studied Aida a little longer and better than Amelia and had plenty of opportunity to see and hear several casts. When I was being 'touched up' by Gertie Stelzel and Albert Sargood to go on in the final scene my dresser Beattie blurted out, 'Ooh, Miss Sutherland, you've only got one more scene to do and you'll be through – but that's the one where they all sing flat!'

The Opera House had mounted a new production of Weber's *Der Freischütz* this season conducted by Edward Downes with Sylvia Fisher singing the leading soprano role of Agathe, Adèle Leigh as Aennchen, James Johnston as Max, Otakar Kraus as Caspar, Michael Langdon as the Hermit, Jess Walters as Ottokar and Geraint Evans as Cuno in the Edward Dent translation – another League of Nations, and dialogue, of course. There were some embarrassing lines to put over, one of Agathe's worst being: 'Don't shoot Max! I am the dove!' This said while running down a ramp on to the stage. No matter how hard one tried to tread lightly, the rostrum was hollow and sounded like a drum being beaten with every step. Neither Sylvia nor I (who sang the role for the first time on the spring tour) was petite and we both hated that point in the opera. The audience thought it a great joke.

At this time it was decided to send me to work with Norman Ayrton, who was then Assistant Principal of the London Academy of Music and Dramatic Art (LAMDA). My first session with Norman was on February 12, 1954 and neither of us could have foreseen that a friendship and collaboration of over forty years' duration would result. He helped tremendously to loosen me up and progress was made by the time I had to do performances of Agathe.

When I sang the role in May at the Royal Opera House, the critics were very impressed, *The Times* saying:

Miss Sutherland has been heard in smaller roles, and has taken larger ones, too, in time of need. This, it is believed, is the first major role that has been deliberately allotted to her. Her appearance and behaviour are, to the life, those of the demure, gentle country maiden. She managed the two scenes with Aennchen with fine dramatic effect. Her firm, well-focused appealing voice brought out the freshness of Weber's music, 'Leise, leise' did not go more than promisingly, but she moulded the long lines of 'Und ob die Wolke' with rare purity and warm artistry: the first of the two phrases culminating in an A flat above the stave was eloquent, exquisitely controlled.

Cecil Smith, in the *Daily Express*, said:

Take a note – it's a voice to watch.

In *Opera* magazine, the same critic wrote:

> Up to now the Covent Garden management has kept the talents of the Australian soprano Joan Sutherland pretty much hidden under a bushel. Once, about a year and a half ago, she was slipped into the part of Amelia in *A Masked Ball* at the last moment, but the press was kept in ignorance of this move until after the fact; and I gather she also sang an Aida. On tour she has had a number of opportunities in leading roles, to be sure. In London, however, her appearance as Agathe was her first advertised demonstration of her powers in an assignment more extensive than Clotilde or the Overseer.
>
> With a competence as impressive as it was modest, she established herself as one of the whitest hopes of the soprano department. Her voice is a true operatic lyric soprano. It is large enough to carry across the orchestra all the time in all registers. It is round and rich, yet pure and clear. Her A flats in 'Und ob die Wolke' were as enchanting in texture as any tones we have heard all year.

Richard was extremely excited by the reaction both of the press and the audience but he was not about to let me rest on my laurels. Work went on to improve the role and also a myriad of other things. Two cycles of the complete *Ring* were coming on at the end of May through to the end of June, and I had something to do in each of the four operas. I had been spending some time learning 'A Song of Welcome' by Sir Arthur Bliss (Master of the Queen's Music) written to welcome back to Britain Her Majesty The Queen and the Duke of Edinburgh after their long tour. Sir Malcolm Sargent was the conductor. I also was studying the part of the Marchesa Lucinda in *La Buona Figliuola* which was recorded and transmitted by the BBC conducted by Charles Mackerras.

I remember a very hectic day when I was late for a *Götterdämmerung* rehearsal because I'd a fitting for my Rhinemaiden 'costume' – tights and leotard, sparsely covered in a very realistic-looking silver, blue and green rubber seaweed. Although I had lost about five inches around my middle and hips since joining the Company – not dieting, just a metabolic change because I was doing what I wanted, perhaps – I was still no sylph and, while gazing in the mirror in the fitting-room, was begging for more of the seaweed to cover thighs and knees. It took time to drape it realistically and I was already late for Fritz Stiedry, our conductor – and still had to dress and run from Wellington Street to the theatre and upstairs to Room A where the conductor held his piano rehearsals. I fell into the room in time to hear Stiedry saying, 'I'll wait ten minutes for anyone, but no more – not even for a Sutherland!' I fear he had to wait for what seemed like another ten minutes before I regained my breath.

The press for Stiedry was not the best for the cycle and yet the singers enjoyed working with him, and Richard and I thought his handling of that mammoth work most expressive and lyrical. The other Rhinemaidens were Rosina Raisbeck and Marjorie Thomas; Rosina also sang Gerhilde in *Die Walküre* where we again had many laughs backstage.

Another Australian, Eleanor Houston, had joined the Covent Garden Company doing performances of the Countess in *Figaro* during the Bulawayo tour and other roles including Freia in the *Ring*. Elsie Morison, who had come from Australia to study at the RCM and then done a couple of seasons at Sadler's Wells, joined the Company, and a little later Una Hale from South Australia swelled the soprano ranks along with English Amy Shuard, who had also been singing at the Wells.

During the Diamond Jubilee Prom Season that year I sang Lisa's aria from *The Queen of Spades* in a Tchaikovsky–Dvořák concert, and throughout the summer looked forward to the start of rehearsals for the 1954–5 season, when I was to sing more performances of Agathe and then Antonia in *The Tales of Hoffman*, later singing the Doll (Olympia) and Giulietta in a new production by Gunther Rennert, conducted first by Inglebrecht and ultimately by Edward Downes who had a great deal to do with the version's preparation. Ric wanted me to sing all the roles on the one night but this was not to be for some years.

As well as these tried and true operas, I was to create the role of Jenifer in Michael Tippett's opera *The Midsummer Marriage*, to be given its world première on January 27, 1955.

With all these tempting roles to look forward to and the knowledge that I was obviously in London to stay, I made up my mind to hunt for better accommodation. Mother was due to come back in October or November and my aunt was following later, so I decided to rent an apartment big enough to house the three of us, complete with piano. Richard joined me on the hunt and it was not long before we both were attracted by a charming mews house in Aubrey Walk, Kensington, with two bedrooms, a very large studio looking on to its own small garden, and a large dining-room-kitchen opening to the garden – luxury after living in cramped quarters for three years. I did some very quick arithmetic and worked out I could afford it as my salary had been steadily increased to the sum of about £40 per week during the season.

In September we had the opportunity of seeing the visiting Vienna State Opera. *Le Nozze di Figaro* with Lisa della Casa, Rita Streich, Sena Jurinac, Erich Kunz and Paul Schoeffler; *Don Giovanni* with George London, Elisabeth Grümmer, Sena Jurinac, Leopold Simoneau and

Erich Kunz; also *Così fan tutte* with Seefried and Jurinac.

During this year I had been encouraged to 'do something' about my hair by Ric, so one day took myself to Raymond's salon in Dover Street, just off Berkeley Square. I was duly designated to a Miss Pamela who conferred with Mr Gordon, the manager of the salon, and I came out with a much more youthful style – and blonde streaks in my mousy brown hair. I wasn't sure what Ric would think but it pleased him immensely. I continued to go to the salon for some years after, going to Mr Gerald and then, when he left, to Mr Gordon who had opened a salon of his own in Connaught Street, much nearer home and on the way to everywhere. Kenneth Dryland from New Zealand worked with Mr Gordon, then went out to Australia, and I still go to his charming salon in a quiet suburb of Sydney when I am there. Mr Gerald went to America, to a large salon in one of the big stores in San Francisco, and I continued to go to him whenever I was in that city. They knew exactly how I like my hair and I always could rely on them fitting me in, however busy they might be.

One evening early in the 1954–5 season I was ironing after Ric had come for dinner and he proposed we be married – preferably before Mother reached London again to raise any objections. She had already left Sydney by ship. I thought it was a splendid idea and may have said something like 'I thought you'd never ask!' and we were married quietly in Kensington Methodist Church on October 16 – one week after we had decided. Clive Carey gave me away and Elizabeth Allen and a London friend, Vicky Fox, were witnesses, along with a very old friend of Richard's mother. There was no time or need for bridal finery. I managed to find something to fit me in Bond Street – a red fine-corduroy dress which I wore with a grey hat and gloves – and just before I went to the church a beautiful bouquet of red carnations arrived from David Webster, whom I had told out of courtesy. So the bride wore red. We sent a cable to Mother on the ship at Colombo so she would have some time to get over the shock. She was worried that possibly having a family might bring the career that was moving along so well to an abrupt end – a career she had been very dubious about at the outset.

There was a party at David Webster's house the night after and Muriel Kerr (David's secretary) acted the part of a major-domo when we arrived and announced: 'Ladies and Gentlemen – Mr and Mrs Richard Bonynge.' That caused a stir and we had a wonderful evening.

There was no time for a honeymoon – that had to wait until the summer of 1955 – as there was so much work for me to learn and now Ric was able to be with me full time so we worked whenever I was free of official rehearsal at the Garden. When I was at the Opera House, Ric was practising for a solo recital he was to give at the

Wigmore Hall on October 28 and continuing to work with several singers and singing teachers, as well as taking his lessons with Herbert Fryer.

Mother arrived back and life was much easier for me knowing I had not to cope with running the house entirely on my own, nor to cook our meals. There was much more time for working and Richard was forever wanting more legato, more expression, rounder tone, clearer diction, greater intensity, until I reached the end of my patience and would say 'I can't'. This was rather like a red rag to a bull with either Ric or Norman Ayrton, when I worked with one or other of them, and I would be bullied (I thought) to try again. Sometimes it would work and others not. I remember collapsing on the floor in hopeless laughter frequently at Norman's classes and sometimes he would join in, but Richard used to get impatient and angry at any waste of time. We always worked for an hour or so, then had a break for tea or coffee and resumed work until we agreed on another break. However, the time between the pauses was for serious work. I fear I would lose my concentration and be thinking of the host of other things I needed to attend to besides learning my roles and perfecting my technique. Mother would frequently worry that I was doing too much and possibly taxing my voice, but there were obvious improvements in range and timbre and so work continued. Ultimately, by taking advantage of my 'relative' as opposed to 'perfect' pitch, Richard tricked me into singing up to a high E in scales, having started them on a higher note than was usual during our vocalises.

My début as Antonia in *The Tales of Hoffman* was brought forward due to Elsie Morison straining her back. Andrew Porter in the *Daily Express* wrote:

ONE VOICE SAVES AN OPERA

'It's a voice to watch,' wrote Cecil Smith when Australian ex-secretary, Joan Sutherland was given her first big role at Covent Garden last year.

I wish he had been back in this country to hear her at Covent Garden last night, when she saved a performance of *The Tales of Hoffman* from hitting rock-bottom.

The home team was batting in this opera for the first time, after the foreign guest-artists had left. Only Miss Sutherland, the consumptive heroine of the second act who sings herself to death, reached enjoyment level.

Tall, with pre-Raphaelite looks as sweetly attractive as her voice, she acted convincingly and sang with artistry and beautiful tone.

So here was more encouragement and a feeling that all the work we had done was beginning to be evident in performance – not that it meant we could relax our efforts.

✧ 6 ✧

AROUND THIS TIME, Richard and Mother came up for a performance of *Messiah* in Liverpool, conducted by John Pritchard. I had been accustomed to have a simple meal at about 4.30 in the afternoon if I was singing at night. Being away from home we wandered into a likely café and all I fancied was fish and chips. Mother and Ric were worried I'd swallow a bone but all was well – until I got up to sing 'I know that my Redeemer liveth'. I got as far as 'I know –' and burped loudly through the second half of that note. There was no way I could stop it – I've never eaten so late on the day of a performance since.

On December 22, I was in the revival of *Der Freischütz* which apparently was in trouble that night. Cecil Smith wrote in the *Daily Express*:

> Weber's melodrama of magic bullets and compacts with the Devil was often a comedy of errors last night.
>
> People forgot their lines, or stumbled over them, or said the same thing twice. (Frederick Dalberg predicted that Agathe, the heroine, would 'dry of grief'). Rhydderch Davies tried to sing in spite of a cold, and made about as much noise as a kitten.
>
> But the performance was worthwhile whenever the Australian soprano, Joan Sutherland was on the stage, caressing the music with her radiant, floating tone.

The performance was broadcast by the Home Service of the BBC on December 24.

With the beginning of 1955 there were further performances of Agathe in *Der Freischütz* and the première of Michael Tippett's brainchild *The Midsummer Marriage*. The plot was unfathomable – at least to this singer. One knew it was to do with sexual love and a binding of spirits after trials similar to those of Pamina and Tamino along with vague mythological points, but nothing seemed to come together and one went through the motions and sang the music hoping the audience might comprehend what was going on. I'm afraid when asked about the opera at rehearsal Michael Tippett (whom we all respected and liked immensely) answered: 'I don't know, darlings. It was something inside me that had to come out! You just sing it beautifully, and it will all be clear and right.' The sets and costumes were by the British sculptress Barbara Hepworth. I was not terribly impressed by my costumes and was intrigued to find them in somewhat modified form in the Christmas number of *Vogue* magazine when I was at the hairdresser's one day in January.

Well, we all did what we could, although we had the old problem of British regional and colonial accents, along with Otakar Kraus, who had a long and incomprehensible monologue as Kingfisher, after which Edie Coates as the She Ancient sang the memorable line, 'What's he saying now?' It generally raised a laugh as Otakar's English was never that clear and the convoluted text he had to utter was a further impediment.

Very lengthy reports greeted the première, the majority praising the soloists and chorus and, like them, wondering what on earth it was about. There were a few more performances of the opera at the Garden and then we were off on tour, visiting Glasgow, Edinburgh, Leeds, Manchester and Coventry. In Glasgow, I sang Giulietta in *Tales of Hoffmann* for the first time, singing Aida the night after and four nights later both Giulietta and Antonia, which I did together again in Manchester. On the tour I sang altogether eight Giuliettas, three Aidas and four Antonias. Of the *Aida* performance in Glasgow, *The Scotsman* critic wrote:

> The principals were familiar to us in their roles, with one exception – Joan Sutherland in the title role. Miss Sutherland is a comparative newcomer to the part, and we have seen many fine Aidas in Glasgow, but last night's characterisation could stand comparison with any of them. This young singer has a warmth of voice; a keen dramatic sense; she can portray the emotion admirably, and she moves naturally about the stage. Her singing with Johnston and Walters in the Nile Scene was sensitive and compellingly beautiful.

Back in London I had three performances of the Beethoven *Missa Solemnis* with Rudolf Schwarz conducting and Peter Pears, Elsa Cavelti and Richard Standen completing the quartet. Two cycles of the *Ring*, conducted by Rudolf Kempe followed in May–June at Covent Garden. In these performances my co-Rhinemaidens were Una Hale and Glenice Halliday. Una, like myself, had been worried about covering hips and thighs with sufficient seaweed. Unfortunately, during our time on the stage making seductive swimming motions, half hidden by a huge 'rock', one of Una's legs became trapped behind the other by a loop of the seaweed and instead of smoothly disappearing she was forced to bunny-hop into the wings as both legs were firmly held together.

During these performances I made my début as Olympia in *The Tales of Hoffmann* which I repeated four more times, plus three or four High

Priestesses. These last *Aidas* were criticised for having greatly increased prices for an 'Italian' performance and singers of mediocre quality – except for Tito Gobbi as Amonasro and: 'The most frankly praiseworthy piece of singing came from an invisible Joan Sutherland as the Priestess.'

The Covent Garden season closed in July and I had one more concert before going on holiday. This was the Dvořák *Te Deum* at the Proms with the London Symphony Orchestra and Basil Cameron conducting. The *Te Deum* was in the second half of the programme and while I was waiting in the dressing-room the cap on one of my front teeth just fell into my mouth. There I was with an ugly gap right in the middle of my upper teeth and I had to go and face a full Albert Hall audience in minutes. The St John Ambulance attendants had nothing that might help, not even any chewing gum which might have worked. So, in spite of having been told by Richard to acknowledge any applause by pleasantly smiling I had to be very prim and not smile broadly. The singing was another problem, as certain consonants created a current of air through the gap causing a faint whistle. I doubt if I've ever been so preoccupied – but I got through and at the end again bowed very seriously, trying not to show the gap. When Ric came round to pick me up I said 'I'm sorry I didn't smile but don't you think it's just as well?' and flashed a huge smile at him. We had a good laugh. A quick trip to the dentist, then off to Lake Garda for a month's holiday and delayed honeymoon.

We stayed in a charming family hotel at Fasano and enjoyed days of lazing about by the lake, swimming and visiting towns nearby like Salo and Gardone. It was my first visit to Italy and I was enchanted. I loved the narrow streets and all the stalls selling not only fruit and vegetables that we'd not seen much since leaving Australia but the colourful ceramics and clothing – and, of course those wonderful Italian meals, taken on the terrace.

By this time I was pregnant and we were busy choosing names. We both hoped it would be a boy as the Bonynge line was dwindling and who knew whether we'd manage another infant with my career steadily taking over our lives. I was rudely healthy and only once felt slightly exhausted. We had seats in the Verona arena for *Carmen* with Giulietta Simionato and Mario del Monaco and the performance was stupendous, in spite of the fact that a thunderstorm forced it to be suspended for about an hour. We reached Fasano again about 4.30 the following morning, agreeing that the long day had been very worthwhile.

One humorous incident during our stay was a remark from a small English boy who was also staying at the hotel and was forever asking questions. One day Ric, who could take the sun much more than I could, had gone ahead to the lake shore to sun himself. The said child was playing on the shore and plying Ric with the usual barrage of questions. Finally he said 'Where is she?' prompting Ric to say 'Who is she?' The child replied, 'You know – Mrs Bonnet – your mother!' Of course, I was 'Mrs Bonnet, Ric's mother' for quite a while after that.

Our artist friend Roy Hobdell introduced us to John Vickers, the London photographer, and his wife Jean who produced some very smart clothing. I became a fairly frequent client of hers and one outfit lasted me through my pregnancy – a green velvet hip-length smock with black frogging worn with a black skirt. I think all my colleagues, as well as myself, never wanted to see that again. She also made a Greco-Roman white crêpe gown for me to wear at my second London recital.

By this time the blonde streaks in my hair had taken over and I was more blonde than anything else. Now it became the habit at Covent Garden to use my own hair as a basis and attach pieces instead of providing a full wig.

Prior to the recital and the Covent Garden season in September, Fritz Stiedry asked me to sing the role of Euryanthe in Weber's opera of the same name which he was conducting for the BBC Third Programme. Other roles were sung by Kurt Böhme, Franz Vroons, Otakar Kraus and Marianne Schech. It was a pleasure to be working with Stiedry again and the role was one with a great deal of scope for me, although the plot of the opera was rather far-fetched.

The recital with Richard at the piano was on October 7 in the Wigmore Hall, and a fairly full programme was presented of Handel, Arne, Mozart, Schubert, Rossini and Verdi. *The Times* said:

> ... She showed extraordinary skill in singing Arne and Schubert with a light touch and Mozart with acquired flexibility. Her Mozart singing, however, has a little way still to go – the tone needs to be smoother and the delivery easier. But the top part of her voice is glorious and she uses it well. To music for which she has not the natural aptitude she brings intelligence and her lieder singing had the essential quality of presenting in a short space the concentrated essence of each song.

When I had told David Webster of my pregnancy he had wanted to know how I felt about continuing at the Garden as long as possible up to the birth. I said I was feeling fine and it was suggested I sing the role of Micaela in *Carmen* which was being revived in the 1955–6 season. The role was one Ric wanted me to sing and the costume was rather elaborate and hung from below the bustline to the floor over a large hooped underskirt, totally concealing any sign of my condition. David said that I would be listed to sing until the end of the year but if either I or the Company felt my performance was not satisfactory I could relinquish the part at any time. I was very grateful, as I felt I needed the steady income, especially with the baby due in February, and hoped I would be able to fulfil my obligation.

The *Carmen* opened on October 20 and the conductor, Edward Downes, bore the brunt of the critics' displeasure. However, there was a fair amount of success for myself so I settled into the run of ten performances which I enjoyed immensely. The Don José was James Johnston, the Irish tenor, and one night he said in his dialogue, 'Ah, Mi-coy-elah, what're yer doin' in Brazil?' The line was, of course, 'Ah, Micaela – what are you doing in Seville?' I nearly dropped my basket of goodies and could hardly respond for laughing.

I was very fond of James Johnston with whom I had worked in *Aida*, *Der Freischütz* and *Carmen* previously. He was yet another helpful colleague and I remember he was nearby when I opened my first Income Tax account at the Stage Door. I asked him what I was supposed to do about it and he very kindly suggested that I should see a good tax accountant as it would save me a lot of headaches and, probably, money. He gave me the address of the firm he was with and although the name has changed several times because of retiring partners and so on, Richard and I have happily remained with the Group and their legal advisers in Britain and Switzerland ever since.

There was one more London concert that year – my first in the Royal Festival Hall on November 9. It was the British première of Frank Martin's *Golgotha* with Marjorie Thomas, Walter Midgley, Gwyn Griffiths and Trevor Anthony, the BBC Symphony and Sir Malcolm Sargent conducting. I was not terribly happy singing that piece and I never enjoyed singing in the Festival Hall. The platform seemed much too low and the audience much too close for comfort.

Now we waited rather impatiently for the happy day when 'the baby' would arrive. I made the customary visits for check-ups and was still rudely healthy and not very obviously in 'a certain condition'. Ric and I still went to ballet and opera performances and visited friends. The lessons with Norman and Clive Carey continued.

I had accepted the part of Vitellia in two performances of Mozart's *La Clemenza di Tito* for the BBC on March 11 and 12 with John Pritchard conducting. The rehearsals were to begin on March 1 and I was told by my doctor to expect the baby about February 17. I said I thought it should come a week earlier than that and certainly hoped so.

Ric and I often went to a Sunday matinée movie, the only day I was free to relax. On February 12 we walked from the house in Aubrey Walk to the Kensington Odeon to see Humphrey Bogart in *The Desperate Hours*. During intermission we saw Jess Walters and his wife Emma, who said to me, 'Do you think you should be seeing this movie? It's a very dramatic story and aren't you just about due?' I told her, somewhat in jest, it was one of the reasons I'd come, as I needed to have the baby within the next couple of days. We all laughed and after the film (which was exciting) Jess insisted on driving us home. We'd had a large midday dinner and I began to feel decidedly uncomfortable when I went to bed but thought it was due to the supper of beans on toast; Mother, however, had other ideas and called Queen Charlotte's Hospital where I was booked. I was protesting that she was only going to embarrass me at the hospital and that I'd be sent back, when an ambulance arrived – quite unnecessary in my view. The result was that our son, Adam, was born very early on Monday, February 13.

The matron of Queen Charlotte's was a splendid person and, whereas most maternity patients were sent home after a very short period I was able to stay for nine days, during which time I was well initiated into the habits of young Adam. He was a good sleeper and enjoyed his meals – this hasn't changed much, except that he tries to work off the latter with cycling, jogging, tennis, golf and swimming. A young nanny was completing her hospital training and she and Matron agreed that it would be good for her to come to 'live in' for a time. So I was very fortunate to have someone to take Adam on his walks who was kind and capable, and able to combine my shopping needs with her duties for him – and even cook a little. Mother, together with Auntie Blos who had arrived from Australia, moved into a flat in Ladbroke Grove which my half-sister Ailsa had vacated after a few years' stay in London. So I had plenty of help with Adam and even Ric managed to cope with his needs now and then.

I was going off to rehearse for the *Clemenza di Tito* performances about the second of March when a neighbour asked Ric when the baby was due, only to be told that he was already two and a half weeks old. I evidently didn't look much different. However, I had somewhat underestimated the drain on one's stamina after childbirth and found the role of Vitellia much more taxing than when I'd been rehearsing the music while very pregnant. The performance went well enough and I was intrigued by Richard Lewis in rehearsal who appeared to be sight-reading a rather difficult role. He had just arrived back from a trip to the United States and I expect had not had much chance to study.

A week or so later I was in Coventry singing the Verdi *Requiem* with the Midland Symphony Orchestra and on Good Friday I sang *Messiah* in Cardiff. I also rushed to Liverpool and Manchester to be on hand to sing Micaela if need be on the tour and do some rehearsing with the Company. Back to Covent Garden in April with more *Hoffmann* performances (Antonia), First Lady in *The Magic Flute*, First Rhine-maiden in *Das Rheingold* and *Götterdämmerung*, also Helmwige in *Die Walküre*.

In May I did a performance of the Pergolesi *Stabat Mater* and various sacred solo items together with Norma Procter in Brecon Cathedral. What a lovely voice that was and a kindred spirit. We were to perform together frequently and enjoy each other's company. In fact, I appeared with her in the first performance in England of Mahler's *Das Klagende Lied* with the London Symphony Orchestra just one week later, on May 13 in the Festival Hall with Walter Goehr conducting. It must have been my 'Mahler Period' as I had sung in his Symphony No. 4 with the Royal Philharmonic Orchestra and Rudolf Kempe conducting earlier the same month. The *Telegraph*'s J. W. said of the Fourth:

> Joan Sutherland's bright pure tone was well suited to the finale's Cockayne-like vision of heaven, and she followed charmingly Mahler's instructions to sing 'with clear, childlike expression'.

During the last week of May I started taking the train to Lewes for rehearsals at Glyndebourne, where I was to sing eight performances of the First Lady in *The Magic Flute* and six of the Countess Almaviva in *The Marriage of Figaro* and four more with the Company in Liverpool in September. These were to be my first Mozart operas in the original language. Our 'calls' there were always something of a riot, as the cast of singers were very genial and cosmopolitan: Sesto Bruscantini (Italian) as Figaro; Elena Rizzieri (Italian) as Susanna; Michel Roux (French) as the Count; Ian Wallace (Scottish) as Dr Bartolo; Monica Sinclair (English) as Marcellina; Cora Canne Meijer (Dutch) as Cherubino; Hugues Cuénod (Swiss) as Don Basilio.

Musical rehearsals were very precise, with the outrageous coach Jani Strasser telling everyone how to sing by illustrating with his terrible voice. He was teased a lot by both the *Figaro* and *Magic Flute* casts – and was forever trying to find his glasses. There seemed to be three pairs of them on strings around his neck but they were never the right ones. He also spent a great deal of time trying to make the Three Ladies (Cora Canne Meijer, Monica Sinclair and myself) sing impossibly piano phrases. But the end results in both operas were splendid and I was thrilled to be working there with such casts and a producer and conductor like Carl Ebert and Vittorio Gui. The way Ebert moved when portraying the Countess was incredible – so refined and elegant – and I tried very hard to imitate his deportment and gestures. The designer of both operas was Oliver Messel and our costumes were glorious, although I thought his gown for the Countess's third and fourth acts was even more stunning at Covent Garden.

This was the Mozart Bicentenary Festival season and I felt honoured to be given such roles in so important a venue. *The Times* critic said: 'She finally vindicated her claim to be a true Countess Almaviva in the beauty of the phrase in the last act with which she brought reconciliation to end the intrigue.'

Although the setting was so different and the piece sung in Italian, the experience of having sustained a role like the Countess in English for the Covent Garden performances was of great value and my Glyndebourne colleagues were so helpful. Michel Roux had a beautifully produced baritone voice and a very aristocratic manner but was humorous and sometimes quite naughty on stage. I remember we did, as well as the performances in costume, a special one on July 30 for the Home Service of the BBC – live from the stage at Glyndebourne with an audience, but with the singers in lounge suits and cocktail dresses. It was so hard to go through all the production movements using props and sets, but in ordinary dress and knowing that there was a huge unseen audience out there as well as that in the theatre visualising an eighteenth-century scene. Very early on the bats (for which that theatre was notorious) started swooping about our heads and twittering. Finally one of them landed on the stage, fluttering and dazzled. Michel Roux had his prop box of tools handy to break down the door into 'Milady's chamber' so proceeded to kill the bat with his hammer – all of us continuing to sing without missing a beat but hopelessly out of character and either nauseated or laughing. I wonder how it sounded to those listening in?

Another time for hilarity was the long dinner interval when the artists tended to gather in the Green Room in various stages of dress and undress, particularly in *The Magic Flute*. At this time I heard some of the most outrageous and risqué stories and limericks, each member of the cast seeming to vie with the others, endeavouring to cap the last tale. Tom Hemsley and Hugues Cuénod had us laughing so much I ultimately decided to stay in my dressing-room as all that laughter didn't help me sing well after the interval.

The *Flute* cast was quite splendid, with the lovely Pilar Lorengar as Pamina. Pilar continued to have an international career and we frequently sang together (or during the same part of a season) at the Met or some other House. I remember being worried about how much luggage I had taken to New York one season – until I saw Pilar and her mother shepherding porters with twice as many bags as Richard and I had.

❖ 7 ❖

DURING THE SEASON at Glyndebourne we had become quite friendly with Jani Strasser's wife Irene and had talked about having a holiday somewhere – maybe going to Vienna and Salzburg as it was the Mozart Bicentenary year. We had no car as yet and Irene had the brilliant idea that if we paid for the gasoline and her board she would drive us to Vienna and back in hers. We organised for Mother and Auntie Blos to stand guard, along with Nanny Pat, over our Adam and on the sixteenth off we went on a fabulous trip through Belgium and Germany via Nuremberg to the Salzkammergut, staying on the Mondsee for four nights and travelling all over the area to Bad Ischl, St Wolfgang and, of course, Salzburg. We saw a performance of *The Marriage of Figaro* with Elisabeth Schwarzkopf, Irmgard Seefried and Dietrich Fischer-Dieskau. I was rather upset as I couldn't hear very well and even when I changed places with Irene found the work very under-sung and 'precious'.

We reached Vienna via the fantastic abbeys of St Florian and Melk, and delighted in visiting Schönbrunn, the Belvedere Gardens, the Prater, the museums and had some time for shopping over the four and a half days there. Then back via Munich (with rebuilding and renovating going on everywhere to repair the dreadful bomb damage), Strasbourg, Soissons, Montreuil, Boulogne and back in London by the night of September 1. It had been a wonderful trip and gave us a great perspective of the culture and background of that area of Europe.

The following day I had a rehearsal for the Prom in the Albert Hall on September 3, singing 'Martern aller Arten' in the Mozart half of a Mozart–Elgar programme. Sir Adrian Boult was conducting the London Philharmonic Orchestra and Noël Goodwin wrote a rather humorous crit in the *Daily Express* next day.

COBWEBBY? THEN KEEP IT THAT WAY

Joan Sutherland – fast-rising star among Covent Garden's group of Australian sopranos – made her reputation shine even brighter at last night's Prom in the Albert Hall.

'I felt a bit cobwebby,' she told me – she is just back from a fortnight's holiday in Germany and Austria with pianist husband Richard Bonynge – 'and I'm sure I wore the wrong dress.'

On the contrary. Her Grecian-draped gown of white silk and three-inch pearl drop-earrings suited her tall, blonde and slightly aggressive dignity. It gave a commanding air to the testing scene she sang from Mozart's opera *Il Seraglio*, wherein the heroine determinedly resists the attentions of a Turkish pasha.

Every note in its huge range was squarely pitched, glowing in tone at the top, and impassioned.

During this very important year for both of us we had decided that although the house in Aubrey Walk was charming we were paying (for those days) a fairly large rent. It was eleven pounds a week. We felt that now we were very proud parents we should own our home, so decided to buy a ground-floor flat in one of the large houses in Cornwall Gardens, off Gloucester Road. There was a beautiful communal garden where we could sit with Adam (who was growing apace and would soon be terrorising old ladies and their lap-dogs in the selfsame garden) and the shops and public transport were much closer. It was a wrench to leave our little house and rather cramped by comparison but we managed to survive the move and Ric became more of a collector than ever, covering every wall with framed Victorian song covers or prints of singers and actors of the past, and adding to his collection of Staffordshire figures. We already had a few nice pieces of furniture, one of them a beautiful Regency desk which I treasure and use to this day. We saw it on one of our excursions to Portobello Market, sitting in a shop window in Westbourne Grove asking to be bought. I remember I was almost sick with anxiety signing the cheque and thinking it cost more than I was paid for a week – and we had a new baby and had to pay the nanny and the rent. Richard's maxim was always, 'It'll only cost more next year!' How right he was.

It had been a great experience and privilege to work with the Glyndebourne group: indeed, I was apparently the first British artist to sing the Countess with the Company and the 'showcase' with them had far-reaching effects. I was henceforth frequently engaged to sing eighteenth-century music and the coloratura attributes of the voice became more controlled and confident, consolidating the whole vocal range.

Rehearsals began on September 4 at Covent Garden and at this time I was working on the Mozart *Mass in C Minor* which I sang twice during October, once in Llanelli and once in Coventry with the Philharmonic Society there and the Boyd Neel Orchestra.

There had not been a Musical Director at the Royal Opera House since Karl Rankl had relinquished the post, and his death in early

1956 was mourned by all those who had worked with him there. Rafael Kubelik had joined the Company as Musical Director in October 1955. Kubelik brought many new works into the Company's repertoire and we all enjoyed working with him. I sang both Pamina in *Magic Flute* and Eva in *Mastersingers* with him.

The critic of *The Times* was obviously not enamoured of the *Flute* production – and I must say I preferred the old Oliver Messel one – but mentioned

> Miss Sutherland, whose voice and artistry have matured rapidly in her four years' service with the company. Her Pamina is acted with dignity and restraint, yet warmly, and it is sung with a vocal beauty and musical understanding that give constant pleasure and seem liable to develop to one knows not what heights. Mr Piper's costume, which became Miss Elsie Morison, is utterly unsuited to Miss Sutherland's more classic physique; he should quickly design an alternative.

The last remark of the critic was very much to the point and attention to costume details is something that has always been a major concern of both Richard and myself. When one was a company member and went into a role as third or fourth cast there wasn't much to be done about adapting a design. But once you were fortunate enough to be cast for the opening of a new production there was sometimes a difference of opinion between the designer and the singer as to what the character was to wear. If the said designer knew enough about the cutting and fitting of clothes, he was usually amenable to a compromise to enhance the appearance of the wearer. For instance, I have never been slim but have always had a waist. Two things I have always abhorred in costume design are cartridge-pleated skirts to provide fullness (especially in heavy velvets and grosgrains) and short waists. The former filled in the ellipse of the waistline and the latter did nothing to help my proportions – merely made me look deformed. I also hated costumes with several different patterned materials used in combination unless managed very artfully by the designer and costumier together.

Another problem could be the Empire line with the 'waist' immediately under the bosom. Although the last-mentioned portion of my anatomy has never been very large – indeed Zeffirelli insisted on padding my bust – my rib-cage is, so I always felt like a large column walking about the stage in a costume cut that way. The length from the Empire line to the floor was too great and, again, clever cheating had to be accomplished by the costumier. I was very fortunate from the Sixties on to have someone like Barbara Matera make so many of my costumes and also William Paterson who now makes for the Australian Opera. Bonn and Mackenzie of London were also excellent and all those who made for me latterly were adept at arriving at those long, pointed bodices in which I felt so comfortable. There is nothing more daunting than to appear on stage in a costume that is uncomfortable or you feel is unflattering. In latter years I've been most fortunate in having splendid designers like José Varona, Michael Stennett and Kristian Fredrikson do many of my most beautiful gowns. Needless to say, I did *not* have a new costume designed for Pamina, nor was it the last of my unflattering ones.

The year drew to its close with more performances of Pamina, rehearsals for *Mastersingers* and several BBC appearances – one a Haydn and Mozart programme conducted by Charles Mackerras – and the usual party going over Christmas and New Year – our first Christmas as parents.

The opening night of *The Mastersingers* was on January 28 in a production designed by Georges Wakhevitch. The settings and costumes were very traditional medieval and the cast predominantly English-speaking, working well together. I enjoyed my scene with Sachs (James Pease) and the Quintet very much, however the critics didn't seem to think the whole thing had quite 'jelled' but would probably settle down in due course. Geraint Evans singing his first Beckmesser was very well received. There were five performances all told until the end of February. On Sunday, February 17, the whole cast assembled on stage at 9.30 a.m. in costume and make-up to film the final scene of the opera. This was for an English movie (*Davy*) starring Harry Secombe as a would-be opera singer with Adèle Leigh playing the part of his girl-friend. I think we were there all day and Harry Secombe was keeping us amused being more like his *Goon Show* characters than Walther von Stolzing. Yes, in the film he made it to Covent Garden! One learned how little is used of the feet of film shot when the movie was released – but the pay wasn't bad for one day of sitting about waiting; and you can recognise me by my yellow gown.

Also during this period I sat for an Australian artist, Phyllis Cram, in one of my Eva costumes and the portrait was entered by her for the Archibald Prize – the annual Australian Portrait Competition held at the New South Wales Art Gallery. It was the first of many portrait sessions.

Performances of *Midsummer Marriage* and then Pamina on tour in Cardiff, Manchester and Southampton followed. Tucked in there, during early March, I did a programme for the BBC on the eminent eighteenth-century soprano Mrs Elizabeth Billington and two momentous performances of *Alcina* for the Handel Opera Society at St Pancras Town Hall.

I say 'momentous' as it was probably my singing of the role of the sorceress which finally convinced the Garden that my future lay away from the dramatic works of Strauss, Wagner and later Verdi, and most definitely in the grand and varied bel canto repertoire. The performances were done on a shoe-string and the costumes borrowed from old Sadler's Wells stock. I had jewellery made from chandelier drops wired together and a beautiful Brazilian topaz and pearl ring given me by Richard, which he found in Portobello Market. I prize it to this day.

As Ruggiero we had, instead of a mezzo-soprano, a 'male soprano' in John Carvalho but the technique to cope with the beautiful flow and legato of Ruggiero's music was lacking. Monica Sinclair, on the other hand, was in her element as Bradamante, being encored for her great vengeance aria. Andrew Porter in the *Financial Times* wrote:

> ... in the title role we can enjoy singing of altogether exceptional accomplishment and art. This comes from Joan Sutherland, the Covent Garden soprano. ... Now that in Miss Sutherland we have a first-rate Handelian soprano, who phrases, flourishes, trills and embellishes with lovely tone and exquisite art, we must have Handel added to the national repertory ... This was the first British performance of *Alcina* since 1737!

Needless to say, Richard wrote all my variants then and ever after. He studied countless eighteenth- and nineteenth-century tomes but insists it is only instinct.

There had been so much to learn and a very tight rehearsal schedule – the Dress Rehearsal was on Monday night (following an afternoon and evening rehearsal on the Sunday) and the two performances on Tuesday and Wednesday. Prior to this I had been back and forth between Cardiff and London, doing my Pamina performances in Cardiff and the early *Alcina* rehearsals in London.

I had also been having more sinus and dental problems and long sessions in the dentist's chair – not very helpful when you have to sing afterwards. Our nanny had left and Mother and Auntie Blos had helped me cope with looking after Adam but it was obvious that we must have younger full-time help. We engaged a lovely young Swiss girl, Ruthli, who forty years later is still with us.

I was rehearsing the part of Gilda in *Rigoletto* for performances at the Garden in May and also the Verdi *Requiem* which I sang in Brangwyn Hall, Swansea. Richard had worked a great deal on the role of Gilda with me. He adored Galli-Curci's singing of 'Caro nome' and we listened over and over again to her recordings. I'm afraid I began to thin the timbre of my voice in an effort to sound more youthful – and like Galli-Curci. This was a most dangerous and foolish thing to do. I have *never* had a voice vaguely like hers and it was the style and phrasing that we admired, also her sincerity. But the voice acquired a certain overlay of that charming singer's quality which I had to work very hard to eradicate. Richard and I agree it is very wrong for young singers to adopt a vocal timbre because they hear another singer on record using it – they must sing with their *own* voice and develop their *own* technique and vocal attributes.

The *Rigoletto* production was quite old but had been rather beautiful, designed by James Bailey. Andrew Porter in the *Financial Times* said:

> Joan Sutherland's 'Caro nome' was beautifully vocalised, with high accomplishment, and called forth rapturous applause. . . . The quality of the Gilda we may confidently expect was perhaps more noticeable elsewhere – particularly in the sensitive, beautifully moulded short phrases which open Act 3, the soprano line of the Quartet, and a silvery, floating 'Lassù in cielo' – for these were not only exquisite, but expressive within the dramatic context.

Noël Goodwin in the *Daily Express*:

ROOM AT THE TOP – FOR JOAN

Australian soprano Joan Sutherland stepped to a place among the greatest at Covent Garden last night.

The tall, 29-year-old blonde sang Gilda, the hunchback jester's daughter, in Verdi's *Rigoletto* for the first time – and scored a triumph.

As the innocent girl who sacrifices her life to save a worthless philanderer, her voice cascaded in a jewelled stream of radiant tone.

Everybody seemed pleased over the success, especially Ric – he was *sure* now that there would be no further suggestions of unsuitable roles, although we knew I was scheduled to sing Desdemona in a revival of Verdi's *Otello* at the end of the year.

The dental problems continued and I now had to be careful at what angles I was photographed, as I had several discoloured teeth which tended to be very evident when I smiled. My dentist thought I should go to a specialist in 'cosmetic dentistry', whereupon I asked what *that* might cost. I was told it would depend what he did, but that considerable bridge work and capping should be done without delay if I wanted to save what was left of my teeth. I approached David Webster who was most sympathetic and arranged for a consultation with Henry Pitt Roche (whom I found a rather fascinating character) and was told that for about £1000 he could reconstruct my mouth, at the same time elongating my back molars to open the bite and, consequently, take the point of the chin a little further away from the point of the nose, improving the profile. Fabulous – but £1000 (today it would be £20,000 or more). When advised of the estimate David said that I would be singing for them next season and, if I wanted, the season after and my salary should increase with the nature of the roles I was to be given. How about the opera company paying the dentist and deducting an amount from my salary every week until we were square?

So it was arranged, work to commence in September, probably taking about a year.

Between the fifth and sixth performances of *Rigoletto*, at the end of May, our au pair girl arrived. Ric went to meet her at Victoria station but was a little late, so the poor girl, already anxious, was near to panic. Then, in the taxi home, Ric, speaking to her in French although she was actually German-speaking from Basel, asked how well she cooked. That was another shock for her, as she had only expected to help with the baby and a bit in the house – cooking hadn't been mentioned by her agency, in spite of Richard having requested help in that area. Then she arrived at the flat to find my mother and aunt sitting on the big couch in our studio giving her 'the once-over' and me, rather incoherent and gabbling away in English, trying to make her feel welcome. The only one really to get across to her was Adam, who held out his arms to her, flashed his most winning smile and just asked to be cuddled and petted. Maybe that did the trick for, through all manner of ups and downs over the past forty years, Ruthli (Ruth Brendle as she was then, now Ruth Ingold with a lovely daughter Rachel who is past her twenty-fourth birthday) has managed our household in the most wonderful way – and what a fantastic cook she has become.

But I leap ahead. There was a good deal of adjusting to do – the cramped quarters didn't help, but at least it was summer time and Kensington Gardens weren't far away. It was incredible how quickly 'Udi' (Adam couldn't say 'Ruthli' and she is known by this name to all our friends) began to pick up English and she now speaks the language very well. It was soon obvious we had a gem, and many are the laughs we've all had together over those early days. I wasn't much use at all, going back and forth to Glyndebourne throughout June for rehearsals of *Der Schauspieldirektor* in which I sang Madame Herz. There were eight performances of the opera between July 5 and 23 and there were four performances of Pamina at the Garden before the middle of July, so much time was spent on trains.

We did manage to entertain a few friends to dinner at our apartment, with the help of our Swiss treasure. She, incidentally, had found out through the 'au pair grapevine' in Kensington that there was a public telephone box just around the corner from us, off Gloucester Road, where you could call anywhere in Europe for the price of a local call – for as long as you liked. She therefore had a 'hotline' to her mother and used it regularly for gleaning a wealth of great Swiss cuisine from that capable lady.

One of our early dinners was for Lord and Lady Harewood who had entertained us at their lovely house in Orme Square and who appeared most interested in my progress. Lord Harewood had, of course, founded with Harold Rosenthal *Opera* magazine and was involved in so many of the musical activities around Great Britain, not the least of which was the Royal Opera House. Ruthli was practically paralytic with anxiety and when the doorbell rang went to it to take the coats, in true Swiss fashion extending her hand and saying 'Good evening' first. George took the hand and responded with a smile and Marion did neither. After seeing the Harewoods into the studio I went to tell Udi what they would like to drink – and see how dinner was progressing. She was livid: 'Who duss she sink she iss? Ven she goes to de bassroom she makes de same ass me!'

I think my profession puzzled Udi at first because she was a big pop music fan and adored Ella Fitzgerald, Frank Sinatra, Shirley Bassey and the like. But slowly she became interested and intrigued, more so when she got to know some of our operatic friends, most of whom she got along with splendidly – and they with her, especially when she fed them.

More work for the BBC during early August, including the role of Laodice in Scarlatti's opera *Il Mitridate Eupatore* with my old friend Monica Sinclair.

Immediately after this Richard and I went to Lake Garda again and had a most enjoyable time with our friends Philip and Roy who were there for part of our stay. I remember Ric and I were very cross with a party of women staying at the hotel who invariably smoked small cigars during their meals, breakfast being no exception. All of us, especially Ric, made derogatory remarks in English as they spoke some Nordic language all the time. After a particularly smoky breakfast (and many rude comments from Ric) they arose and went to the reception desk together, asking the owner in perfect English for their accounts. We learned never to be quite so outspoken again in *any* language.

There was a broadcast of *Emilia di Liverpool* conducted by John Pritchard and narrated by Bernard Miles in early September – a Donizetti piece of which there are a few pirate tapes about. Then back to rehearse at Covent Garden – and the beginning of my many trips to Henry Pitt Roche with long hours (seven or eight at a stretch) in the chair while he carefully took impressions, filed down my teeth to a minimum to use as a post – or inserted platinum or gold posts where necessary – all prior to possessing the 'supersonic' drill. There were a few extractions, too. He was an amateur sculptor – he did a very good head of Adam but mine looked like Beethoven. He played classical records all through the dental sessions and I had to beg him not to play certain composers' music after he had almost ruined Tchaikovsky for me during a particularly gruelling session. I used to present myself to him at 9 a.m. most Monday mornings (and at other times if need be, rehearsals permitting) and very often stagger into rehearsal at the

Garden during the afternoon, although I was mostly able to plead off the rest of the day on Monday. If he had not been so considerate and gentle I think I'd never have gone back after the first appointment.

There were further performances for me of *Rheingold* and *Götterdämmerung* during September–October with Kempe conducting, and more Antonias and Micaelas to take me up to mid-December. The *Carmen* performances during this period were conducted by Kubelik who had not rehearsed with me, due to my dental problems and because the Company *répétiteurs* were aware that I had sung the part so frequently. I arrived at the Sitzprobe to find that he launched straight into my aria without the lovely accompanied recitative, so I asked him why we weren't rehearsing it. He told me that it was dialogue and never had been recitative in this particular production at which I begged to differ and fortunately some members of the orchestra agreed that we had always done Micaela's recitative. When Kubelik was adamant I felt embarrassed but said if there was no recitative I would prefer to relinquish the part. It didn't come to that, and I was able to continue to create the atmosphere leading to that most expressive outpouring of Micaela's fears and courage.

The Carmen in these performances was the American Regina Resnik who was most impressive in the part and with whom I later recorded the opera for Decca. Both Richard and I have worked with her frequently and we have become very friendly. She has a great dramatic sense and also marvellous humour which she put to good use in those operas that we later did together or that she produced.

Rehearsals for Desdemona began in early October and I enjoyed the role. I'd watched many rehearsals of the opera with Gré Brouwenstijn and looked forward to wearing the very beautiful costumes, as well as singing that haunting love duet. Then, in November, the rehearsals for Poulenc's *Dialogues of the Carmelites* began. This is a fascinating, most dramatic and moving work. The short play by Georges Bernanos (after a novel by Gertrude von Le Fort) was read by all of us in the cast and it was wonderful to work with Poulenc himself during the final production calls. He even made a couple of musical changes for me. I sang the role of Madame Lidoine, the New Prioress, and was chosen to act as a 'model' for the correct Carmelite habit, a photograph being sent to the Carmelite Monastery in North London to check that the wardrobe had interpreted the various garments and veils correctly. A letter came back to John Sullivan (our Technical Director) that everything was exactly right and went on:

> What interests us still more is Miss Sutherland's face. It is an ideal face for the part of a Carmelite – a definitely Carmelite face. Contrary to the popular idea of an enclosed contemplative a Carmelite – a genuine one

in the full sense of the word – generally has a face full of character – neither pretty-pretty nor pious! I do congratulate you. In the small picture especially, she could be taken for a real Carmelite.

But first there were the *Otello* performances which were rehearsed by Peter Potter until we went on-stage. There, unfortunately – or fortunately, I'm not sure – Peter was absent as he succumbed to a particularly virulent influenza virus and was very ill. So Ramon Vinay himself steered me through the stage rehearsal, seeming very sexy in our intimate scenes and making me all a flutter. But whatever he did, the performances were a success and I loved the part. It was my first major role in Italian at the Garden, and I only sang three performances of it that December 1957, then two in Vienna in December 1959. It was January 1981 – just over twenty-one years later – before I sang the role again, doing sixteen performances with the Australian Opera – ten in Sydney and six in Melbourne with Carlo Felice Cillario conducting.

Of the performance at Covent Garden Percy Cater in the *Daily Mail* wrote:

Joan Sutherland, 29-year-old blonde Australian soprano [I was thirty-one] had a distinguished success at Covent Garden last night in her new role of Desdemona.

Musically and dramatically the part was made so poignant that we all sorrowed with the cruelly wronged and fatally slandered wife.

This voice, the clearness and sweetness of which form its special charm, seemed to have strengthened itself for the requirements of Verdi's tempestuous tragedy.

The singing throughout had a beautiful line, splendid truthfulness of intonation, and a fine emotional sensitiveness.

Andrew Porter in the *Financial Times*:

The development of the young Australian soprano, Joan Sutherland is highly gratifying. We, and she, may rejoice that she was not born an Italian – that she is not singing her lovely voice away in a matter of years through a rackety international career. Instead, she is moving from role to role in an artistic progress based on pure tone, sound technique, and the musical way of going about things.

Desdemona, in Verdi's *Otello*, is perhaps the most important of her assignments so far; it is also her greatest success. Miss Sutherland could quite easily make her assumption more patently effective in the short run – by sacrificing purity to power, by forcing the note of despair, by lurching on to chesty tones. But this is not her way; and five years on we shall bless her for not endeavouring now to be 'exciting' but, instead, lyrical and beautiful. This is not to say that the note of passion was missing, only that it was never forced.

We note too that she has accepted her height for the virtue it is, and moves gracefully, with dignity, without awkwardness. Also that, especially in conversational exchanges, a new timbre has come into her voice – one that recalls, surprisingly, Toti dal Monte's, in seeming to fall right from the lips, warm and ripe.

So we came to our second Christmas as parents, with Adam much more aware of what was going on, and we were glad to have a few quiet days to ourselves.

✧ 8 ✧

THE NEW YEAR of 1958 had me off and running with the continuing dental visits and rehearsals with Margherita Wallmann, the producer of *The Carmelites*. These were very intensive and all of us became very involved in the work. I think we all felt that the characters we were playing were such real people as opposed to some of the more glossy and showy roles in the repertoire.

I did seven performances of the opera between January 16 and March 24, two of them being in Oxford and Manchester on tour with the Company. Once more, it was a role I was not to sing until twenty-six years later. I repeated performances of Madame Lidoine nine times with the Australian Opera in Sydney in September 1984 in Elijah Moshinsky's riveting production, again cast mostly with Company members.

There were some further appearances for the BBC in January and February, and a concert with Harry Blech and the London Mozart Players – the Mozart concert aria 'Vorrei spiegarvi, oh Dio' and Beethoven's 'Primo amore'. Also in February I had six performances of Gilda in *Rigoletto* (still in English) at the Garden and a further four on tour in Oxford and Manchester, with more scheduled back in London in April and May.

At this time I must have been fairly exhausted and was dashing back and forth between concerts and opera performances, learning pieces for the BBC, the *Resurrection* Symphony (the Second) of Mahler for the Hallé, the *St Matthew Passion* for performance in Liverpool Cathedral, the Haydn Cantata *Applausus* and still the fairly harrowing visits to the dentist.

In Manchester I developed a sinus cold and was given several penicillin injections which may or may not have helped cure the sinus infection, but I then developed two very swollen and painful knees. I managed to do Beethoven's Ninth Symphony for the BBC (recorded from their Maida Vale Studio), the *Passion* in Liverpool and, half seated on a high stool, record for Decca at Broadhurst Gardens two arias from *Alcina* – 'Tornami a vagheggiar' and 'Ombre pallide'. But the pain in the knees increased and they were like two huge pumpkins so I sought medical advice, ending up in West London Hospital. There I remained for two weeks having 'tests' and physiotherapy with not much progress being made, except that the swelling seemed to be somewhat less, likewise the pain. There had been a performance of *Rigoletto* at the Garden on April 5 with the Maltese tenor Oreste Kirkop who had such a success at Sadler's Wells, went to Hollywood and then returned to the opera stage. Unfortunately, I had to cancel the next two performances from the hospital. Then I said I couldn't stay there for ever while they tried various experiments and was told they thought that maybe my teeth were the cause of the trouble and I should have them all extracted.

That was it! I said after all I had been through to get them to their present state I was *not* going to have them removed, and besides, I hadn't even finished paying for them. I decided to leave the hospital – against their advice – and signed a waiver of any responsibility on their part should I become worse or permanently disabled. Anyway, I had to get myself in shape to sing with the Hallé Orchestra and dear Sir John Barbirolli on May 14 and 15 – and it was already the sixth. Fortunately nothing too disastrous happened and the knees gradually went back to almost normal, although they have always had a tendency to swell after long hours of standing for staging rehearsals and kneeling has increasingly become a problem. However, I did my concert with the Hallé and less than a week later, after various rehearsals, the Haydn Cantata *Applausus* for the BBC Third Programme in London.

On June 10 there was to be a gala performance at Covent Garden and I was to sing 'I Dreamt I Dwelt in Marble Halls' and the lovely duet from *The Bohemian Girl* with John Lanigan, another Australian stalwart in the Company. There was a great deal of excitement over this Centennial Gala and, as is so often the case, too many items on the programme. The result was last-minute cutting and I remember Ric and I being rather 'miffed', to put it mildly, that the duet was drastically cut, including a long cadenza, whilst Maria Callas sang the whole of a very slow Mad Scene from *I Puritani*. It seemed unfair at the time, as one had worked hard and the last-minute changes were awkward to memorise. However, nothing could really damp our spirits as we had heard from David Webster that a new production of *Lucia di Lammermoor* was to be mounted at the Royal Opera House and I was to be the Lucia, with that grand old man of Italian opera, Tullio Serafin, conducting and the young designer who had been Visconti's assistant, Franco Zeffirelli, doing the sets and costumes and producing the opera. Richard was ecstatic, as he had been working on the role with me and had often talked about the part being ideal for my voice, let alone my Scottish background.

Meanwhile, I was having further sinus problems and Ivor Griffiths was becoming convinced that there would have to be an operation and cleansing of the whole sinus area if there was ever to be any real cure. He was worried that the lungs would become infected and did not want me to go through another winter without having the operation. I replied that it was just not possible, as I was to have a fantastic chance with the *Lucia* and who knew what would happen if the operation wasn't successful? He would just have to get me through until after the performances were over.

About this time I became disenchanted with my blonde hair – it seemed too light a colour for my skin and the hair itself was very dry and tended to break. I talked with Gerald at Raymond's and it was decided that a nice deep auburn would be very good for the hair and also make a good contrast for the stage. So that day I returned home a redhead, wondering what Ric might have to say. He loved it, and the colour, with variations according to what country or hairdresser I visited, remained for many a long year.

I had been invited to sing the role of Donna Anna in *Don Giovanni* for the First Vancouver International Festival and with my dental work complete, flew off on July 8 feeling a little lonely (we could not afford for Richard to accompany me) and unsure of myself as the cast was very famous. George London was the Don, Léopold Simoneau and his wife Pierrette Alarie were Don Ottavio and Zerlina, Jan Rubes the Czech-Canadian was Leporello and Milla Andrew was Donna Elvira. The opera was designed by Ita Maximovna and produced by Gunther Rennert. I knew some of the cast by repute but had only previously met Rennert fleetingly, at Covent Garden where I had admired his drive and energy when I'd watched him rehearsing during my first season there.

Nicholas Goldschmidt (the Artistic and Managing Director of the Festival) had seen and heard me at Glyndebourne and had engaged me as Donna Anna. The members of the cast were charming and I treasure my opening night programme of July 26, 1958 dedicated and signed by them all. The rehearsals were arduous but never boring and Rennert was very decisive about what he wanted. I was grateful that Ric had worked with me so much to have the role word perfect and vocally secure – though I missed his usual criticism and comment on what was happening in the production.

During that visit I made many friends in Vancouver and met some of the other artists like Marcel Marceau (who frequently appeared either before or after me in cities all over the globe) also Jan Rubes who has remained a friend and colleague, together with his wife Susan Douglas and their family. The press was enough to turn one's head! Eric McLean in the *Montreal Star*:

> ... of Miss Sutherland I can say without the slightest hesitation that she is the greatest Donna Anna I have heard. It is not difficult to understand

why the Royal Opera, Covent Garden rates her so highly. A voice of thrilling power and extraordinary control, an imaginative and tasteful appreciation of the music, and a winning stage presence qualify her for a wide range of soprano roles, but particularly for Donna Anna.

and John Kraglund in the *Globe and Mail*:

Outstanding among several first-class vocal performers was Joan Sutherland ... It is difficult to call to mind any other soprano who combined so admirably a sense of Mozart style with vocal purity, ease of production in the most florid passages and interpretive insight. In addition, she moved with the grace and dignity appropriate to the role of Donna Anna.

Gunther Rennert's production was very straightforward, with no gimmicks and a simplicity and sincerity that helped the singers project the drama. Ita Maximovna's costumes were very elegant and comfortable.

George London was most helpful and arranged for me to go to New York from Vancouver and sing what turned out to be an ill-advised audition at the old Metropolitan Opera House. His intentions were the best but I was tired after the whirlwind run and the trip to New York alone (still no jets) and performed very much below my capabilities, even being misguided enough to sing 'Caro nome' in English in a house that did everything in the original language. I also had the impression I was being a nuisance to whoever was listening – it was August and the House was officially closed.

I finally arrived back in London exhausted and was supposed to join Ric in Italy, where he had preceded me, for a short holiday. But instead I sent him a telegram to Positano saying all were well at home but it was impossible to join him, sent my love and asked him to come home. He did so and we had some time with young Adam and Udi before rehearsals began again at the Garden in the second week of September for *The Ring*.

Two cycles of *The Ring* were interspersed with rehearsals for Handel's *Samson* which was being prepared for performance at the Leeds Centenary Music Festival. Designed by Oliver Messel, produced by Herbert Graf and conducted by Raymond Leppard, there were five performances in Leeds on consecutive days in October. We later did it at Covent Garden.

Again the critics were very complimentary, with headings like: 'The Best Soprano in 12 Years' ... 'No Equal' ... 'Joan Sutherland Triumphs in Handel Opera' – and I had only one aria to sing, right at the end of the opera.

Ric and I had done a recital together for the Sevenoaks Music Club's Silver Jubilee in early October and I sang in Horsham later that month.

At the recital with Ric I tried my wings on 'Regnava nel silenzio', the big opening aria for Lucia and in Horsham I sang the 'hit tune' from *Samson*, 'Let the Bright Seraphim'. We have always enjoyed trial runs of key pieces.

Some time during the autumn I went into the theatre to find the stage being hung with the very old *Louise* sets – pre-First World War. I was told that *Lucia* was probably being cancelled and replaced by performances of *Louise*. I didn't want to believe it and thought maybe it was someone's idea of a joke, knowing how keen I was to do the Donizetti piece. So up I marched to David Webster's office. He saw me immediately, sat me down and laughed. 'My dear,' he said, 'I've told them the scenery's impossible to repair – the rats have been at it! It's being hung to prove my point and you'll get your *Lucia*, no matter who thinks you're not ready for it.' It appears that Walter Legge and possibly some others on the Board were against having a Company member given such a chance in what promised to be a spectacular new production. Or was there a fear on that gentleman's part that EMI's prize recording star, Maria Callas, might have a rival if the plans went ahead? Whatever the reasons or objections, it made Ric and me all the more determined that David's faith in my capability would not be in vain and we worked harder than ever.

The *Samson* performances at the Garden began on November 15, where *Lucia* musical rehearsals had already started, and on the nineteenth there was a concert in Leeds of Honegger's *King David* with the Royal Liverpool Philharmonic Orchestra and Sir Malcolm Sargent conducting, narrated by Richard Attenborough. The next day I was in Dublin where I was to do four performances of *Don Giovanni* for the Dublin Grand Opera Society at the Gaiety Theatre.

More *Samson* performances, three *Messiahs* in Liverpool on three successive weekends (each time a different version) and then I was free, from January 3 until the projected opening night of *Lucia* on February 17. Eight performances had been planned for February–March but Ivor Griffiths was adamant that the sinus operation should be done without further delay and it was agreed that I do five, have the operation and recuperate, ready to do more *Lucias* in July. Ensemble rehearsals for the opera continued at the Garden and I was delighted to have as my Alisa my compatriot Margreta Elkins who had joined the Company – she was a shade taller than I, for which I was grateful.

David Webster had agreed with Maestro Serafin to send me, together with Ric, to Venice to work with the Maestro who was conducting *Falstaff* at the Fenice Theatre there. We spent ten wonderful days, working with the charming old man, who wore his hat indoors constantly. He was most complimentary to Ric, telling him he had taught me the role very stylishly and he was very pleased with the big cadenza in the Mad Scene and all the variants, saying there was nothing more, really, he could teach me. Oh, he had many suggestions and asked me to pay great attention to pronunciation of the Italian. Indeed, I still have in my score at the beginning of 'Regnava nel silenzio' in his handwriting: 'g / *ginger* and dolor, no dollor'. He was kind and humorous and we loved to work with him. We also went to *Falstaff* and saw Stabile in the title role, on his seventieth birthday, with Anna Moffo singing the most delightful Nanetta. We fortunately had time to visit many of the treasures of Venice and just walk about enjoying that beautiful, unique city without the usual milling tourists, as it was between seasons and very romantic in the January fog.

Back to London in time for the final ensemble rehearsals before the beginning of the production rehearsals with Franco Zeffirelli. What a revelation *they* were. Here was this young and vigorous man who had designed magical sets and costumes – much of both he painted himself between attending to the production – proceeding to bring alive in the most romantic way every facet of each character in the opera. His attention to detail was extraordinary and he seemed to be everywhere at once. He was charming in the extreme and spoke excellent colloquial English with a steady flow of witticisms. The cast – the whole theatre, I think – adored him.

My first fitting with him in the Opera Wardrobe was a riot. I was very embarrassed as it was the first time I'd had to strip quite so far for a male designer. His eye for proportion was incredible and first off he wanted to accentuate my natural waistline and compensate for my lack of bosom. Much feeling, pushing and pummelling went on until he achieved the effect he desired and I had become his most adoring fan.

The experience of everything gradually coming together and the genius of both Zeffirelli and Serafin was incredible. The dear old Maestro was horrified when he saw Lucia's Mad Scene costume spattered liberally with 'blood' and was told my hands were likewise to be covered. He was used to the pristine négligé, whereas Franco had read his Walter Scott and wanted Lucia to appear really to have struggled with her unwanted husband, stabbing him many times, as in the novel. How could she not have blood on her hands and shift? He won, and the costume was a triumph, with a flimsy veil which might have been part of the bedding used to great effect.

I was still seeing Ivor Griffiths through the final stage rehearsals and was trying to conserve as much energy as possible by cutting completely any social activities. The rehearsals were very exciting, with wonderful atmosphere created by the combination of Zefirelli and Serafin, but at the end of the day I was only interested in getting home to relax and be ready for the next day's work.

The Dress Rehearsal finally arrived and I was not made any more at ease by learning that among those present in the House were Maria Callas, Elisabeth Schwarzkopf and her husband Walter Legge. I would have preferred not to have been told until afterwards, but there they were and I just had to go out and do my very best. They were most complimentary afterwards in my dressing-room and a number of good-humoured photographs appeared.

✦ 9 ✦

AT LAST, THE next night, that of February 17, 1959 and the long-awaited first performance of *Lucia di Lammermoor* in the House since 1925, when it had not been a success and was, in fact, withdrawn. We were all very excited and I became anxious when Franco, who had promised to help with my make-up but, with so much to attend to on the stage and checking everyone else's costumes, was very much later than he'd anticipated getting to my room. We also had a last-minute change of tenor – Joao Gibin with whom we had rehearsed was ill and the Australian, Kenneth Neate, bravely stepped in at a few hours' notice. With all the good wishes of friends and colleagues, members of the chorus and the Administration, Ivor Griffiths, telegrams and cards, gifts and flowers I was in a daze and was very grateful for that opening scene with Enrico (played by Geraint Evans and later by John Shaw), Raimondo (Michael Langdon – later Joseph Rouleau) and Normanno (Raymond Nilsson) and the chorus to gain a few moments to myself before being seated beside 'the fountain' in Lucia's elegant blue satin gown with its trailing tartan plaid.

The long fountain-like harp solo began, the curtain still down, and I was glad to have the sweet posy of flowers to hold (a Zeffirelli touch) as my hands were shaking and my pulse racing. But, as the curtain went slowly up, we had been so well rehearsed that anxiety and nerves gradually disappeared and at the close of the entrance aria and cabaletta ('Regnava nel silenzio' and 'Quando rapito in estasi') I knew that the public was thoroughly enjoying what they could see and hear – we just had to sustain the interest and excitement with the sincerity that Franco had asked of us.

All the sets were very romantic and dramatic and the costumes exquisite, the whole effect being that of a beautifully tinted lithograph. As scene followed scene the absorption of the audience deepened and the Sextet received tumultuous applause. Thankfully, Serafin was opposed to encores – and I still had my big Mad Scene in the following Act.

The gaiety of the wedding feast, interrupted by Raimondo's tragic news of Arturo's death by the hand of his unhinged wife who was gibbering over his blood-soaked body, led up to the astonishing entrance

71

of Lucia, who flitted like some spectre to splay herself against the wall at the head of a flight of some eighteen to twenty curving stairs. Franco's inspiration evoked gasps not only from the assembled wedding guests as rehearsed, but from the audience as well. Those stairs were formidable in a way, but at least they were all the same height and had good wide treads – not like some with which I had to cope in later productions. They also helped in physically interpreting the early part of the scene and both Franco and I found ways of using them.

He had so many graphic touches: the vision to Lucia of the phantom ... the scent of roses ... the recognition of the priest ... the enactment of the wedding scene. Then, with the flute cadenza, the first time we rehearsed the scene I had automatically snapped my head sharply up, listening, and risen from the kneeling position to follow it. 'Keep it! Keep it!' Franco said excitedly, then asked me how much I could move while singing. I said quite a bit, as long as it didn't make my voice wobble when I ran. And so Lucia's 'flights' during the flute cadenza evolved. The response of the audience that first night – and ever after – was unbelievable and I wondered if I would ever be able to continue with the cabaletta.

The curtain finally descended on the scene and many, many calls were taken during the set change to the graveyard for the wonderful tenor aria. I was elated, exhausted, longing to remove my costume and change into some dry clothes – but had to wait until the end of the opera and appear on stage with Serafin and Zeffirelli and the rest of the cast, never anticipating the roar of applause and 'Bravos', nor the number of times my weary body would bow – and the flowers! It was all overwhelming and I couldn't believe the number of callers to my dressing-room and the crowd waiting at the Stage Door for autographs. It was difficult to have a few moments alone with Richard and Mother who were both jubilant, although Ric and I knew I could do better.

What pleased us most was the obvious satisfaction that the performance had given Zeffirelli and Serafin. Indeed, the Maestro (who had given me sixpence for my top E flat during a rehearsal) was most complimentary in an interview he granted Noël Goodwin of the *Daily Express*. He said:

I cannot tell you how delighted, how moved I am to find a British singer who not only has a lovely voice but can interpret her part so fully.

When I started, audiences were only interested in voices. And singers were only interested in applause. Now we expect singers to put the music above all. But it is not enough to sing. They must create life as well.

That is what your Miss Sutherland did. She followed me perfectly and made her part a living character. You cannot be born a Callas, you know, nor become one overnight. I am sure Joan Sutherland has just as big a future if she goes about it the right way.

Andrew Porter, in the *Financial Times*, said:

Briefly: Franco Zeffirelli's production of *Lucia di Lammermoor* for Covent Garden takes its place beside the great Scala revivals of ottocento opera which have been so striking a feature of post-war musical life: and with her performance of the title role the young Australian soprano Joan Sutherland becomes one of the world's leading prima donnas.

... Anyone who has heard Joan Sutherland sing could have deduced that she would vocalise Lucia's music with high accomplishment. The surprise of the evening was the new dramatic power she brought to her impersonation. The traces of self-consciousness, of awkwardness on the stage, had disappeared; and at the same time she sang more freely, more powerfully, more intensely – also more bewitchingly – than ever before.

The great soprano that her admirers have always felt she would be was now conclusively revealed (and since the war only Mme Callas has won an ovation at Covent Garden to equal last night's after the Mad Scene). A new beauty shone in her face; her gestures, her bearing, were unfailingly expressive. Zeffirelli, who produced her, and Tullio Serafin (under whose baton both Ponselle and Callas rose to greatness) must have helped her to achieve this triumph – the climax to which Miss Sutherland's Pamina, Gilda and Desdemona had been pointing.

Early on in *The Bride of Lammermoor*, when he first describes his heroine, Scott tells us that those people were mistaken who failed to discern beneath Lucy's apparent sweet mildness a stronger current of feeling. Those sopranos who merely drop sweet notes into place are also mistaken in their interpretation of the role.

From the start, in the recitative to the Fountain aria, Miss Sutherland showed that Lucia was made of stronger mettle than, say, Ophelia: she had the stuff of violent tragedy in her. Her singing was exquisite: particularly notable were the sustained notes, followed by an octave drop. Her decorations were tastefully and justly conceived, and beautifully executed. Arpeggios were delicate and lovely, trills were confident. But beyond this, there was a *meaning* in everything she did. A singer who can make florid decorative bursts in thirds with the flute heart-rending in effect has understood the secret of Donizetti's music.

Philip Hope-Wallace in the *Manchester Guardian*:

JOAN SUTHERLAND'S TOUR DE FORCE AS LUCIA

... Her voice, intrinsically beautiful, was under the strictest control, the ornaments evenly delivered, nothing shirked, and the entire shaping of the scene put to the most dramatic effect. The producer Zeffirelli deserves his place in the catalogue of excellence and the veteran Maestro Serafin likewise, but the audience was in no two minds about where the final credit lay: namely with this lyrical coloratura soprano who, on this crucial occasion, surprised her most ardent admirers. The pathos of her 'Alfin son tua' seized the whole house. This was exceptional operatic singing, radiant, pure and vivid, and it won an ovation of the kind usually reserved for the favourite ballerina.

Desmond Shawe-Taylor, in the *Sunday Times*, said:

The current Covent Garden revival is a triumph for Joan Sutherland, the soprano – and also for a previously unknown creature, Joan Sutherland, the tragic actress: it is a triumph for Tullio Serafin and the forces he so admirably controls – and also for Franco Zeffirelli, who produced and designed.

... In previous performances Miss Sutherland had often given grounds for high hope, but had never quite shaken off a certain angularity of vocal and dramatic deportment. Now all is changed. The voice, always pure, has gained richness and colour, and a remarkable fullness in the upper register: the vocalisation is brilliant, but never merely decorative; both style and accent are convincingly Italian; the singer's appearance is appropriate and touchingly beautiful, while her acting underlines at every point the pathos of this ill-used, but by no means insipid, heroine of the North. When, after the murder of her husband, preceded by horrified attendants, she appears in a cold, grey light on the steps of a spiral staircase, we know that Ravenswood Castle will shortly have a second and more terrifying ghost. Her performance was all of a piece, musically exquisite, dramatically veracious and intense.

On February 24 there was a note in *The Times* to the effect that:

Because of the tremendous success achieved by Australian soprano Miss Joan Sutherland in the present production of Donizetti's *Lucia di Lammermoor* at Covent Garden, the BBC Third Programme have decided to take the exceptional steps of changing all their advertised programmes for Thursday evening in order to broadcast the opera in full from 7.30 p.m.

Then, on February 27, commenting on the broadcast performance, Andrew Porter, in the *Financial Times*, wrote:

... No soprano of our century has recorded the great scenes from *Lucia* with so rare and precious a combination of marvellously accomplished singing and dramatic interpretation of the music.

TEARS AND FIRE

On the first night Miss Sutherland was spell-binding; yet in last night's performance she was even finer. Tears and fire were commingled in her tone; there was more passion in her duologues with Enrico and with the Chaplain, even more tenderness in the lyrical passages of the Mad Scene. There were phrases which burnt themselves on the memory – phrases that look plain in the score (such as 'E il giuramento?' in the study scene) but which became great moments. The most famous Donizetti singers, from Pasta to Maria Callas, have been remembered for these sudden flashes of dramatic characterisation: and this amazing performance by Miss Joan Sutherland places her, I truly believe, in their company.

Of course the critics were correct in assuming that Zeffirelli and Serafin had an enormous amount to do with the extraordinary success of the performances, but they were also the fruition of all the hard work put in by Richard and his faith in the bel canto repertoire being the right road for me to follow. I would not have felt as secure in my success without those very important formative years at Covent Garden. Although it certainly thrust me into the international field it was not really an 'overnight success' and I have always been grateful for this.

The routine that Richard and I had evolved over the years stood us both in very good stead. It was to become more difficult to study new roles satisfactorily as we were to be constantly on the move, away from home for long periods and with an exhausting travel and performance schedule, not to mention obligatory social engagements, especially in the United States. However, we had a fairly disciplined mode of life and continued to keep to it as much as possible, wherever we were.

The Italian papers were full of the success of the production and Zeffirelli and Serafin were keen to do performances of other bel canto operas with me. There was such a demand for interviews and a great number of offers to perform in Europe and the United States were received. The recording company of L'Oiseau Lyre, owned by an Australian (Mrs Louise Hanson-Dyer) for whom I had already recorded the *Alcina* arias, planned for me to record eighteenth-century arias and songs in May. The recordings were made and pressed under an agreement with the Decca Record Company, using their technical staff. Decca also planned to record the two big *Lucia* scenas with other arias and asked me to sing in their recording of the Beethoven Ninth Symphony, both in April.

It was all very thrilling, but within three days of the last *Lucia* performance I entered the London Clinic and finally underwent the long-postponed sinus operation, with Ivor Griffiths most attentive, visiting me each evening from his home across the road. I had grown so accustomed to the painful attacks and regular 'washings' of the passages that the discomfort afterwards was not so hard to bear. When

Ivor was asked what medication I should have for the pain I think the sister was shocked when he replied: 'Give her a couple of Veganin every four hours – every three hours if she needs it.' But it really was sufficient and eight days later I was home, then off to the South of France.

Funds being limited, Richard and I went by train to a charming apartment at Cap d'Ail for ten days. We had splendid weather and walked a lot, even to Monte Carlo, and enjoyed the markets in Monaco and Nice, buying those wonderful carnations by the armful. We also visited the Opera House and Casino – but no winnings.

It was very warm in our sleeper at the beginning of our trip back to London and I cast off all but the lightest covering. Whether from the air-conditioning or the cooler air once we were away from the coast I don't know, but I developed a heavy cold and raw throat, just what Ivor Griffiths wanted to avoid. I tried to sing after a few days and felt no resonance at all – the sound was dry and hard and unlike any sensation I had felt previously. We were terrified. So off to Ivor, who had a good look at nose, throat and ears and pronounced that everything was in tip-top shape and there appeared to be no reason why I shouldn't make the same sounds as before – or better. He suggested that I go home and, no matter how foreign I felt the sensations and sounds were, gently keep singing with the same technical approach as always and see what happened by Monday evening, when he would see me again. It was Friday evening, so I had three days.

Slowly the old feelings returned and by the Monday visit we were able to report that all was well. Ivor was so relieved that he invited Richard and me for a glass of sherry in his home upstairs. He then confessed he hadn't known for sure if his 'prescription' would work, but felt I had been so used to the passages being clogged and inflamed that naturally, now that they were completely free, I would have different sensations to which I must adapt. He also told me just how anxious he had been over the operation – not the actual surgery, but the administering of the anaesthetic. He had not told me (and I'd not thought about it) that this was given by a tube down the throat and, if removed carelessly, could have nicked the vocal cords, doing irreparable damage. He said it was bad enough to feel the operation was finally a necessity, but after I'd had such a success with the *Lucia* he was doubly apprehensive. All we could do was thank him for not enlightening us beforehand.

So, with all that drama over we got back to work. During the last week of April I went to Geneva and recorded the Ninth Symphony with Ansermet in the Victoria Hall. I remember the asparagus was in season and all of us made the most of it at practically every meal.

After two and a half days there, I was off to Paris, where Ric joined me and I recorded the *Lucia* arias, also the 'Bolero' from *I Vespri Siciliani*, 'Ernani Involami' from *Ernani* and 'O luce di quest'anima' from *Linda di Chamounix*. The conductor was Nello Santi, with whom we had some very pleasant evenings, together with his wife. Ric found literally hundreds of scores, many autographed (particularly works of Massenet, Offenbach and Meyerbeer) in the old bookshops.

By the afternoon of May 2 we were back in London and I was again recording for the BBC 'Commonwealth Concert' and on the fifth went to Manchester to do performances of the Beethoven Ninth with the Hallé Orchestra and Sir John Barbirolli conducting.

There was a panic call from Köln as the Westdeutscher Rundfunk had planned a concert performance of Handel's *Alcina* and their protagonist had become unavailable. Norma Procter was singing the role of Bradamante and had mentioned my name as being the only person she knew who had sung the part of Alcina. That I had only done the opera in English and their performance was in Italian didn't seem to matter. In no time at all we were on a plane and rehearsing in Köln, with me trying to fit the different language to the music. The ill-fated Fritz Wunderlich was the Ruggiero and Nicola Monti the Oronte, but I can't remember much about the event as I was so anxious over my own words and it is a rather long and involved part. I do recall that Norma Procter told me much later that Monti and Wunderlich both came to rehearsal having learned the same role (Oronte) and Wunderlich undertook to sight-read the part of Ruggiero and sing it in the performance only days later – quite a feat.

Back to London and into rehearsal of another Handel opera, *Rodelinda*, also the recording sessions in Watford Town Hall of the eighteenth-century pieces, then *Acis and Galatea* with Sir Adrian Boult and Peter Pears. As well as all this Handel there were rehearsals for a revival of *Samson* at Covent Garden – to inaugurate the 'official' Purcell–Handel Festival of 1959. However, before the *Rodelinda* performances (at Sadler's Wells) Richard and I gave a recital on 18 June for the Australian Musical Association at Australia House in the presence of Her Royal Highness Princess Alexandra of Kent. Evan Senior wrote of it in *Music and Musicians*:

Joan Sutherland sang one of the most arduous programmes of any recent song recital at a concert for the Australian Musical Association at Australia House on June 18.

It ranged from the grand vocal histrionics of *I Puritani* – the Mad Scene – and *Ernani* – 'Ernani, involami' – through the formalities of Handel arias from *Atalanta*, *Rodelinda* and *Alcina*, to the simplicity of English and French songs.

In a large theatre it is possible to throw something of a veil over imperfections of vocal technique, however good a voice is to start with. In a comparatively small hall, and at close range, a voice must be perfectly used as well as fine in texture to pass muster. This was an astonishing performance on all counts, for loveliness of tone and texture, for perfection of use of both. This was a recital that should have been heard by a wider audience. A world audience would have acclaimed it as the work of a singer who is not only a great technician but a great artist as well.

The *Rodelinda* performances were on June 24 and 26, with a *Samson* at Covent Garden on the twenty-fifth – it was only one aria but it meant one had to be on top form three nights running. *The Times* said of *Rodelinda*

Miss Sutherland's performance is paramount, momentous in beauty and dignity, pathos and electric vigour; and because she has recently made startling progress as a singing actress, she uplifts the title part into a thrilling experience.

In the *Financial Times* Andrew Porter wrote:

... A highly distinguished cast has been assembled for this performance. Miss Sutherland's Rodelinda is on a level with her Lucia di Lammermoor – confirmation that we have in our midst one of the great sopranos of the world. The brilliance and beauty of her coloratura are matchless. But no less notable is the exquisitely drawn phrasing of the slow melodies, and of the recitative, the subtle and intricate line and play of tone-colours by which she gives to Handel's music such meaning and eloquence. With one aria in particular last night, in prison when she believes her husband has been slain, she ravished the ear and melted the heart: but it is unfair to single out just one passage when the role, a magnificently rewarding one, offered so many treasures. Miss Sutherland's acting was also marked by the tenderness and the fire which distinguished her Lucia: expression, gesture and bearing were always such as to enhance the music.

Margreta Elkins as my deposed husband Bertarido gave an eminent performance and we had a delightful duet. It was the first of many Handel opera performances together spanning nearly thirty years. The opera was broadcast on the Third Programme.

Two weeks after the last *Rodelinda* there were four further performances of *Lucia* at the Garden, bringing us to the end of the Royal Opera House season. Happily, the tenor was not taken ill and it was the first time I had the great pleasure of singing with Alfredo Kraus who was to be the tenor on so many future occasions (again over a thirty-year period) throughout Europe and America – in *La Sonnambula, La Traviata, I Puritani, Lucrezia Borgia, La Fille du Régiment,* and many more performances of *Lucia di Lammermoor*. My great regret is that we never recorded together – the only recordings which are available are on pirate tapes or CDs.

✧ 10 ✧

IT HAD BEEN an action-packed year and now we had our customary month (more if possible) without singing a note. This year we had arranged through our London Anglo-Italian friends to take an apartment in Sorrento and we were hoping to improve our Italian, as well as provide a holiday for ourselves, Adam and Udi. Ric's mother was coming from Australia and was also arriving in Naples on July 22 to join us also. The apartment was rather strange, with all the furniture in the salon in white dust sheets which we were told not to remove. As we were out of doors most of the time we were not too put out, but our Italian friend was very cross and tried to have the rent reduced because of it.

We had gone to Naples and on to Sorrento a few days ahead of Adam and Ruthli, who were to be met by Ric on their arrival in Naples. Unfortunately, neither party knew there were two stations and Ric was waiting at the wrong one. Once again poor Ruthli was in a panic, with a very tired little boy, as well as being exhausted herself after the long trip and a mix-up over their reservation – they'd had no seat from Rome on. But they soon revived and we had a great time, walking to the beach every day and enjoying the marvellous outdoor restaurants, especially the pizzas and the abundance of fruits we knew in Australia. We also made our first visit to Capri and were as captivated as any other tourist. As usual, Ric and Ruthli were very soon suntanned whilst I kept covering myself up, wearing a big hat and sitting in the shade whenever possible.

After a month, Adam and Ruthli went back to London and Ric, his mother and I spent some time in Rome, staying just off the Piazza di Spagna at a charming pensione, the terrace of which looked across to Franco Zeffirelli's apartment. As a result of all this Richard's Italian was greatly improved. Mine was still fairly non-existent, but my ear was better attuned and I could understand very much more. As with French, it was the grammar that defeated me.

There was no contract with the Royal Opera House for the forthcoming season, just one for performances of *La Traviata* in January–February, 1960. I had concerts booked in London and Manchester and was to do two performances each of *Don Giovanni* and *Otello* at the

Vienna State Opera in December. There were to be many performances in 1960 – many new opera house audiences to conquer, especially in Italy – and three big new roles to learn!

Both Richard and I had signed a contract with the American agency of Colbert La Berge and were booked to do a spring tour in the United States in February and March 1961. Having had such a well-reported success, we now had to make sure the standard was maintained and had a lot of hard work ahead of us.

First on the agenda was a recording of *Don Giovanni* for EMI. Other than the Bach Cantata No. 147 this was the only recording I made with that company. The other soloists in the opera were Eberhard Waechter, Giuseppe Taddei, Elisabeth Schwarzkopf, Graziella Sciutti and Luigi Alva. Giulini conducted the Philharmonic Choir and Orchestra for the discs but we did two concert performances with the same cast in the Festival Hall at the end of the recording sessions on October 18 and 20 which were conducted by Colin Davis.

There were two other concerts in October, one for Robert Meyer and the other for the Victoria League. This last was attended by Princess Alice The Countess of Athlone, deputising for Queen Elizabeth The Queen Mother, who was ill. The Australian pianist Eileen Joyce was the other soloist, with Sir Adrian Boult conducting the Royal Philharmonic Orchestra. I sang two Handel arias and the Mad Scene from *I Puritani*.

At this time Richard was doing a great deal of accompanying, both for singers and instrumental soloists, and on November 3 we did a recital together in Manchester with the violinist John Bacon playing the obbligato to the Mozart aria 'L'Amero, saro costante'. Then back to London for a charity concert at the New Theatre and two performances of the Beethoven Ninth Symphony with Otto Klemperer conducting in the Festival Hall. The other soloists were Jon Vickers, Ursula Böse and Gottlob Frick.

As well as the performances, I was still catching up on many of the requested interviews with journalists and radio talk shows, and appeared on that old favourite radio show *Desert Island Discs*. There were also fittings for concert gowns and suitable street clothes, plus work with Ric and Norman Ayrton learning *La Traviata* – and we even did a mini-concert for the prisoners at Wormwood Scrubs.

The second presentation of the Ninth Symphony was on November 30 and on December 1 we went to Vienna for the performances of *Don Giovanni*. There was what was laughingly called a rehearsal with Eberhard Waechter, Walter Berry, Gerda Scheyrer, Anton Dermota and Hilde Güden. Gerda Scheyrer (Elvira) and I were the newcomers to the cast, the rest of whom were either talking or reading the newspaper most of the time. They were, of course, thoroughly inside their roles, but for the two of us it was scant preparation for a début the following day. I was most touched that Eberhard Waechter took me aside and said that he would come to my dressing-room before curtain-up to show me the set, as the staircase down which we were to make our struggling entrance was rather awkward. He was as good as his word and I have never forgotten his kindness. Although there was so little rehearsal, the performances on the third and fifth were well received, especially by the audiences. One reviewer stated I was the best Donna Anna since Lilli Lehmann.

Back to London for *La Traviata*. The production of this opera at Covent Garden was charming but quite old and, as new costumes had to be made for me, Franco (Zeffirelli) had agreed to design them and see to their making while he was in London.

I also had a little time with Adam. We had been fortunate in his being accepted by the Lycée Français at South Kensington, within walking distance of our apartment. I felt the lack of fluency in at least one other European language myself and we were delighted at the prospect of Adam being trilingual, picking up German from Udi as well.

Back to Vienna on December 13 and the same sort of rehearsal for *Otello*, although we managed a little more stage work as the Otello (Carlos Guichandut) made himself available. We laughed at our respective heights and were somewhat glad there was a big rake to the stage so I tended to keep well forward, while he opted for the few extra inches a more up-stage position gave him. In spite of the dismal weather I managed to do some shopping, finding interesting goodies for Christmas.

Back in London I was working day and night to get the role of Violetta learned and had probably been travelling about too much, with the events of the year catching up with me; when the opening night came I felt terrible, with a tight, raw throat and a high temperature. I thought it was a super attack of nerves but soon found out that I had no middle and bottom voice – only the high head tones were there.

Thankfully, Ivor Griffiths was in the house with his little bag and in the first interval he came to my dressing-room, took a look at my throat and diagnosed severe tracheitis. There was nobody else on hand to continue the performance so he gave me an injection to relax my nervous tension and, somehow, I got to the end of the opera. Whatever the injection was, it made me completely unperturbed when no sound was emitted as a result of my efforts, so I just went on doing the best I could and sometimes the voice came normally. It was a very awkward situation – and the next two weeks' performances were sung by Virginia Zeani, as I was completely out of action.

One thing I remember about that terrible experience was the gorgeous floral tribute from Hardy Amies, an avid opera buff and needlepointer, as well as a great couturier. As camellias were not in season he had the florist carefully wire gardenias to camellia branches and I had a beautiful, scented tree while the blossoms lasted. I was overjoyed by his thought, having become one of his many happy clients about that time. The first travelling outfit he made me consisted of a purple and green tweed suit with blouse, overcoat and matching hat – and thirty years later the overcoat was still worn for shopping trips by Ailsa. I love his simple creations which are easy to pack and wear – and are so well fitted that a few pounds more or less don't mean that you have to rush to have the outfit altered or discard it. On the contrary, the clothes last for ever and somehow remain fashionable. Hardy (now Sir Hardy, I'm pleased to say) was such fun to be with – so energetic and lively, and his needlepoint exquisite. I feel my efforts are very poor beside his.

On reading the critics' reports of that opening performance and those of Virginia Zeani I notice that all of them remark on the 'lugubrious tempi', the 'undistinguished', 'heavy', 'plodding', 'slack', 'non-adventurous' conducting of Nello Santi who was making his Covent Garden début. Of the Zeani performance Edward Greenfield remarked that 'Madame Zeani, like Sutherland on Friday last, had to suffer from the efforts of Nello Santi as conductor'.

There had been a great deal of expectation and publicity about these first Violettas and I felt very depressed over the outcome. But it had been a great lesson to us both – we vowed never to accept a new role unless we were sure of sufficient time not only to learn the part but to sing it well 'into the voice' and have all the vocal hazards under control as much as possible well in advance. This was easier said than done, as my future bookings were beginning to be two and three years ahead. How could one gauge the amount of time to apply to the learning and 'digesting' of each projected opera? One thing was certain: we would endeavour to have a breathing space at home between each block of performances and not accept everything that was offered without analysing what amount of time we would need to work on a piece satisfactorily.

The two weeks' rest with no singing and time to think about the part unflurried worked wonders, and by January 22 I was again able to return to the Garden for three more performances, with the Australians Marie Collier (as Flora again) and John Lanigan as Alfredo. Of the final performance on January 30 Andrew Porter wrote:

JOAN SUTHERLAND'S TRIUMPH

After the first performance of *La Traviata* this season, I wrote harshly of Miss Sutherland. Though making it plain that she was quite obviously in vocal distress, so that detailed criticism would be irrelevant, I suggested that the Covent Garden direction had been foolish to allow her to undertake Violetta without providing a strong producer and a strong conductor.

I was wrong about Miss Sutherland's dependence. Laryngitis compelled her to retire from the next performances. I went again to the last one she gave – and heard, and saw, a new Violetta. And in so far as this entirely successful performance was achieved without those Svengalis, Serafin and Zeffirelli, being at hand, it can be reckoned an even more brilliant achievement than her *Lucia di Lammermoor*. Last year there was only one soprano equipped to sing every part of this most taxing role: now there are two.

Sparkling First Act

Gone was the monotony of a single tearladen timbre, and of a dynamic that never rose to forte. Gone the wilting gentleness which had marked the first night Violetta from the opening scenes. Gone that too persistent pathos which had led some critics to deem this Violetta an extension of Lucia. The very costumes took on a new expressive quality. Miss Sutherland sparkled as the hostess of the first-act party: she was vivacious and brilliant; the contrast of 'Ah! fors'è lui' made its full effect.

In Act 2 she was loving with Alfredo, dignified with Germont, in phrase and gesture realising the creature of Verdi's imagination. The dramatic intensity of her acting in the next scene was remarkable. The little shudder of dismay as she realised Alfredo was there too, her agony as he forced her to avow love for Duphol, the gesture by which she tried to silence his outburst – all these were beautifully handled. And in the final act she found not only the pathos of resignation, but also moments of fierce defiance, of will to live followed by the bitter realisation that it was, indeed, too late.

Miss Sutherland had regained all the necessary colours and the necessary techniques for the music; and now the delicate portamentos, the subtle and supple phrasing, and the long-sustained trill at the close of 'Ah! fors'è lui' took on dramatic significance. There was a glitter, not merely vocal, which made one believe in a Violetta who had all Paris at her feet. And there was a consistent dramatic progression. The warmth of feeling, the passionate outbursts, were vividly projected.

It is good news that we are, in all likelihood, to have more *Traviatas* later in the year. Miss Sutherland has transformed what was nearly a failure into a triumph, acclaimed by an excited audience.

In fact, the role of Violetta became one of my favourites. She was, for me, all woman, whereas many of the characters I interpreted were somewhat artificial. The realities of the drama and her noble sacrifice are so powerfully and sympathetically expressed by Verdi, along with the brilliance and gaiety of the two party scenes. Zeffirelli's costumes were a great success and I wore them at the Metropolitan Opera and many other houses in America.

There were four performances of *Lucia* in early February at the Garden with André Turp as Edgardo and John Shaw as Enrico. During these *Lucias* I had the first of many attacks of back discomfort, brought about by a broken vertebra at the base of the spine and the consequent pinching of nerves by the maladjustment. Perhaps it was the result of my rather substantial body perfecting falls – but I continued to do them up to my last *Lucias* and *Borgias*.

Ric and I were then off to Venice to rehearse *Alcina* in a superb spectacle designed and produced by Franco Zeffirelli and conducted by Nicola Rescigno, with costumes by Anna Anni. Compared to the St Pancras effort this was a dream realised, with the appearance of the beautiful Teatro La Fenice carried through on to the stage and rich Court furnishings (from the ante-rooms of the theatre) used for the assembled 'Chorus of Courtiers'.

Monica Sinclair again sang the role of Ruggiero, Cecilia Fusco that of Morgana, Oralia Dominguez was Bradamante, Nicola Monti again sang Oronte and Plinio Clabassi was Melisso. The action took place mostly on a huge rock-like structure on a central turntable which had three sections to provide different areas of Alcina's magic island. The basic colourings of the principals' costumes were pearly pinks, blues and greys to silver, and the skilful lighting gave the impression of glistening water. Zeffirelli was adamant that the harpsichord continuo player should wear costume and make-up and be on stage which the musician engaged to play refused to do. As Richard knew the work so well he was pressed into service and made his Italian début with me, wearing an outrageous wig with his stylish costume.

Although the Italian audiences were unused to the Handelian style in opera they appeared to enjoy the experience and I even sang an encore of 'Let the Bright Seraphim' with an Italian text at the apparent request of the 'Duke' who had organised the Court extravaganza. The performances won me the title of 'La Stupenda' – and a bevy of faithful Italian fans. I was quite thrilled by my new title.

Apart from the performances, Ric and I had a great time revisiting museums, churches and restaurants in Venice. There were various receptions given by the theatre Direction and the British Consul and we had tea with Toti dal Monte who was adorable.

The association with Zeffirelli and Serafin continued immediately after the Italian début with performances in March and April of *Lucia di Lammermoor* in the Teatro Massimo in Palermo, and the same production went to Genoa and Paris during that period. In Palermo and Genoa my Edgardo was Gianni Raimondi, with whom I sang many later performances and, together with his wife Gianna, Richard and I enjoyed happy and relaxed moments sightseeing and dining by the sea.

The press in Palermo and Genoa were again ecstatic, remarking on the size of the voice and its agility in the coloratura passages and cadenzas, 'with an exceptional beauty of colour and purity of tone'.

The Teatro Carlo Felice in Genoa was a lovely old theatre, but very much in need of renovation and repair after the war. There seemed to be only one toilet, used by stagehands and soloists alike, male and female, which was very basic and somehow tucked into the wings so everybody on the stage knew when someone used it. There was a skylight-cum-window which opened on to the main piazza so one seemed to be visible to everyone in the square, too. If you didn't have the window open you were overcome by the smell – once the performance started it was unwise to flush the bowl as the noise penetrated to the stage.

These early performances in Italy brought us many new friends, with some of whom we have remained in touch to this day. Their kindness to us over the years and their assistance with the Italian language (to myself, especially Dr Tito Gallacci when learning the text of *Norma*) has been invaluable and will always be remembered. We also are grateful for their help in finding much of the beautiful furniture in our home, having accompanied Ric on many excursions to the antique shops.

It was becoming more obvious that we needed a larger residence – but where? Both Richard and I loved the English countryside, particularly the Lake District, but were also enamoured of Italy. The climate was better for two antipodeans and perhaps, if we lived there, it would help our Italian language. I also had a great number of future engagements there. But was it really stable financially and politically? Then the great idea of the Ticino in southern Switzerland took a hold and we went on an exploratory excursion to the Locarno area on Lake Maggiore. Ascona had been growing as a resort and there were a great number of expensive modern residences, but we – especially Ric – fancied something a little more romantic. With his house-hunting luck he found the most beautiful villa perched high above the Bellinzona end of the lake, near Minusio, set in a huge park and with open terraces on three sides, all looking out on spectacular views. The owner was a charming man, Signor Baccillieri, who had been the engineer on the building of the Simplon Tunnel and he agreed to us having a five-year lease, also to let us make first offer if ever he wished to sell 'Rocca Bella' as the villa was called.

Ivor Griffiths was delighted that I would be living in a more equable climate and our accountant and lawyer were also pleased as they were worried about our projected earnings, especially the record royalties, making our taxes over-burdensome in Britain. But I think Udi was most pleased because, as she had elected to stay on with us, it meant she would be closer to her family in Basel and they could even come and stay – there was plenty of room. The prospect of all that space to move about indoors, plus the garden and the beautiful views with a certain solitude because of its position, and its proximity to Milan had us very excited and eager to be there.

We'd had no car but that, too, was becoming a necessity, so Ric was learning to drive. Meanwhile, we had two very good friends who helped us out. One was Maggie Sorley who lived in the apartment above us in Cornwall Gardens and was taking Ric on practice runs in the car, and the other Fiona Ede who had become a part-time secretary–chauffeuse and kept our 'scrap-books' up to date. We relied very much on the services of the Regency-Taylor car hire firm to transport us to and from performances in the London area and the airport and still do. However, it was obvious that we would need a car to negotiate the trip from Rocca Bella to Locarno for supplies, let alone the trips back and forth to Milan – and even London. So there was great excitement when we purchased our very own Sunbeam which served us extremely well and made life much easier.

The Paris performances followed immediately after and were another enormous success. The comparisons by the press to Callas which had begun in a small way in London and been enlarged upon by the Italian journalists now became much more positive. *France Soir* said: 'The equal of Callas and Renata Tebaldi'. *Le Figaro*: '*Tragédienne autant que chanteuse.*' And Marc Pincherle remarked: 'Never, since Maria Barientos ... a trill like this!'

As if the splendid setting of the Palais Garnier were not enough I had the added thrill of being given the dressing-room of Madame Fanny Heldy. Although she had long-retired – her heyday was during the 1920s – Madame still had the right to designate who might or might not use the room. It was decorated in a charming fashion and very comfortable, and I felt highly honoured.

Ric had dreamed up a Giselle-like apparition of Lucia during Edgardo's final scene for these Paris performances and so Franco draped me in veils, carrying a bouquet of lilies and I rose from behind the tombstones in an unearthly, shimmering light – the nearest I got to being a ballerina.

Paris loved the performances and Ric and I were fêted – a late dinner with that famed society organiser Elsa Maxwell and her retinue; an invitation from the restaurant Lasserre to partake of a specially prepared dish in my honour 'L'Aile de Bresse Sutherland' and a dinner at Maxim's with that seemingly ageless performer Maurice Chevalier. It also became more difficult to pursue our private sightseeing trips, as the spring tourists were already afoot and I became a target for those who had visited the Opéra – or had read the considerable press coverage.

In the Paris cast were Alain Vanzo as Edgardo, Robert Massard as Enrico, my dear colleague from Covent Garden Joseph Rouleau as Raimondo and Guy Chauvet as Arturo. The performances were conducted by Pierre Dervaux.

The last *Lucia* in Paris was squeezed in between two performances of *La Traviata* at Covent Garden and rehearsals for *I Puritani* at Glyndebourne, and I became very overtired and consequently somewhat unwell. It was a shock to find that news of my slight indisposition travelled immediately to Palermo (where I was to sing again early in 1961) and to receive a query from them as to whether I would be honouring my contract to perform in *I Puritani* the following January or having a baby.

I had a deal of preparation ahead and constant performances, notably over three months at Glyndebourne doing not only ten Elviras in *I Puritani* but also twelve Donna Annas in *Don Giovanni*, as well as preparing and recording *The Art of the Prima Donna* for Decca. I had signed an exclusive contract with that excellent recording company and remained with them for over thirty years. The projected album consisted of sixteen very diverse coloratura arias, each dedicated to a famous singer from the past, and I had previously sung only half of them – not always in the original language. The autumn and winter were crowded with engagements, not the least of which was my début in yet another Bellini opera, *La Sonnambula*, at the Royal Opera House in October.

It was obvious from our forward bookings that there would be no time for a holiday that year so we rented a house within twenty minutes of Glyndebourne and installed ourselves for the whole period, hoping to rest quietly between rehearsals and performances, preparing together for future appearances. Adam would join us for weekends with Ruthli until they could stay full time during the school vacation, also my mother, and from time to time friends like Norman Ayrton and the extremely talented couturier Heinz Weber Riva. Heinz had worked in Paris with Balenciaga, and the cut and line of his designs were, naturally enough, very akin to those of that magnificent artist. He also had a wonderful eye for perspective and, before I went to the United States early in 1961 for my first big tour there, he created two stunning concert gowns for me which those American audiences remember to this day. One of them (in emerald-green satin) was featured on the cover of one of the many reissues of *The Art of the Prima Donna*. The original cover was a *trompe-l'oeil* composite painting of Sutherland–Bonynge memorabilia by that other dear friend Roy Hobdell.

The rehearsal period was, as always at Glyndebourne, a very friendly and happy time with pleasant wanders through the park trying to avoid the obnoxious Sock – John Christie's snuffly pug dog. The conductor was Vittorio Gui and the producer Gianfranco Enriquez with whom I later worked in Italy. Nicola Filacuridi (who later emigrated to Australia) sang the role of Arturo and Ernest Blanc was Riccardo. The part of my uncle (Giorgio) was sung by Giuseppe Modesti and my old friends Monica Sinclair and David Ward were Queen Henrietta and Lord Walton. The opera was designed by Desmond Heeley whose treatment of the broken-down wedding attire in the Mad Scene was captured to perfection by the photographer Guy Gravett in 'soft focus'. Many praised the Glyndebourne administration for bringing I Puritani back into the professional repertory. It had not been performed in England since 1887!

The soprano role is difficult enough and requires sustained long stretches on stage, whereas the tenor role has become well-nigh impossible to cast, as the Arturo has to attain high C sharp, D and, possibly, F. With the shift upwards of today's pitch compared to Bellini's day this understandably puts the tenor in a panic. The opera has remained a great favourite with both Richard and me, also the general opera-going public, retaining its place in the repertory.

Not all the days at Glyndebourne were balmy that season and I remember one particularly grey and drizzly weekend. I had unloaded our weekend grocery order and placed the empty containers on the back porch until the rain stopped. Adam was amusing himself with an enamel bowl and large spoon making 'pudding' with a plentiful supply of mud whilst I helped Ruthli prepare dinner. Soon we heard Adam talking continuously on the other side of the half-open door. We crept up to see what prompted the monologue and realised what he was saying. Over and over again, like a broken record he quoted a well-known TV advertisement: 'So *don't* give your dog ornery meat – Give him P A L – P A L – Prolongs actig life! PAL meat for dogs!' One of the boxes carrying the groceries bore the PAL brand and our four-year-old was already an avid children's TV watcher. He had picked up the exact inflexion and emphasis.

During this period (June 12) I sang the Verdi Requiem at the Royal Festival Hall in London. Carlo Maria Giulini conducted the Philharmonia Orchestra and Chorus and the other soloists were Fiorenza Cossotto, Luigi Ottolini and Ivo Vinco. This concert was repeated with the same artists in the Usher Hall, Edinburgh, on August 21 during the Edinburgh Festival run of Glyndebourne's I Puritani. In his Edinburgh Festival Notebook Rex Bawden wrote:

Last night, appropriately enough at the opening concert of the Fourteenth International Festival, the audience at the Usher Hall was privileged to witness the setting of the seal of fame upon Joan Sutherland, the Australian soprano, whose performance in Verdi's *Requiem* was little short of phenomenal.

The progress of this tall, auburn-haired girl has been quite remarkable. Less than a decade ago, she was unknown outside her native land, and for several years she did nothing spectacular at Covent Garden.

But the seeds of greatness were always there. Only recently have they come to full bloom, moving one eminent critic to compare her recent recordings with those of Tetrazzini – or, indeed, any other soprano of any age.

This is high praise, but last night's audience would endorse it. For here is a voice which not only sounds beautiful, but has that indefinable quality which can raise a lump in the throats of the strongest men, and tears of gratitude that any human endeavour can rise to a quality so ethereal.

In sheer power, too, Miss Sutherland is utterly thrilling. Against choir and orchestra, brass, drums and all, going full blast, she rings out loud and clear.

Before going to Edinburgh I took part in a concert performance of Handel's *Samson* at All Souls Church given by artists of the Royal Opera House in memory of the Australian baritone David Allen. He had died after being involved in a road accident, aged only thirty-five, at the beginning of a very promising career.

The *I Puritani* performances at Glyndebourne finished on June 24 and *Don Giovanni* (which had already been in rehearsal for some weeks) opened on July 1 with John Pritchard conducting. The production was again by Gunther Rennert who had helped me so much in Vancouver and Ita Maximovna again designed the sets and costumes. Mirella Freni and Ilva Ligabue were my colleagues and they were both a joy to work with. Now Mirella and I exchange notes on our grandchildren when we meet!

The *New York Saturday Review* said: '... such fluent, effortless and beautiful singing, which allowed one to sit back and savor many passages normally fraught with anxiety.' *The Times* called attention to the ensembles, particularly the maskers' trio, the 'Al desio' duet and the final sextet, stating the overall production may well have been the 'finest of all' those of *Don Giovanni* given at Glyndebourne to that date.

I Puritani opened in Edinburgh at the King's Theatre on August 24 and the headlines were again voiced in superlatives:

A TRIUMPH FOR JOAN SUTHERLAND – ONE WOMAN OPERA IN EDINBURGH.

A THRILL LIKE CALLAS – ELECTRIFYING.

BRAVO JOAN — THE QUEEN OF SONG.

'GOLDEN VOICE' OF THE FESTIVAL IN BELLINI OPERA.

And so on.

It was during the performances with the Glyndebourne Company that announcements were made that I would be singing at La Scala, Milan the following season and also making my United States début in Dallas in November of 1960 singing the role of Alcina in Zeffirelli's glorious Venice production, together with Donna Anna in his *Don Giovanni*.

Before this, Richard and I gave a recital at St James's Palace. We were privileged to sit down to supper at a small table for four with Her Majesty The Queen Mother, looking resplendent in one of her sparkling gowns with complementing jewels and tiara. The Queen Mother was wonderful at putting people at ease. I tentatively took a brown-bread sandwich, whereupon the Queen Mother, discovering the brown bread ones were all smoked salmon, pulled a wry face and said she didn't like smoked salmon, turned to me and asked, 'Do you, Miss Sutherland?' 'Not really,' I said. 'Take another you *do* like,' she said, laughing, and passed the sandwiches to me. My taste has since changed and I am very fond of smoked salmon.

During this same busy year of 1960 I had, as I have said, worked with Richard preparing a two-disc album of sixteen operatic arias, bearing the title of *The Art of the Prima Donna*, each scena dedicated to an opera singer of the past. Richard had chosen a stunning array of varied and difficult pieces ranging from 'The Soldier Tir'd' from Arne's *Artaxerxes* (a favourite aria of the eighteenth-century soprano Elizabeth Billington) through arias of Mozart, Rossini, Bellini, Meyerbeer, Gounod, Thomas, Delibes and Verdi which had been sung by the likes of Giulia Grisi, Jenny Lind, Adelina Patti, Luisa Tetrazzini and Galli-Curci. Richard also provided some fiendish variants as a foretaste of those to come in later years. The original album was accompanied by a charming collection of biographies of singers, together with a likeness of each taken from miniatures, lithographs and photographs in the collection of either Richard and myself or that of Terry McEwen who was still a member of the Decca Recording Company, although by this time in New York.

It was a huge undertaking, given the time available. It was recorded in the splendid old Kingsway Hall, right in the heart of London, with the Orchestra and Chorus of the Royal Opera House, Covent Garden, conducted by Francesco Molinari-Pradelli. He was also well acquainted with most of the arias but only too happy to confer with Richard over those he had not encountered before. The recording sessions went very well and the album has remained a great – possibly the *greatest* – favourite with the record collectors.

Along with the news that I had been asked to sing at La Scala during April and May of 1961 came reports in the Italian newspapers quoting the magazine *Le Ore* as saying that I had 'surpassed Maria Callas as the world's leading soprano' and that Callas had threatened to walk out on her contract for the opening of the season at La Scala with Donizetti's *Poliuto* in December because they had engaged me. These reports were immediately taken up by the English and Australian press, together with, I'm happy to say, a denial by Maria. This was published in the *Rome Daily American* of November 8, with Madame Callas calling the story 'the most ridiculous and silliest stunt I ever saw in my life,' blaming the magazine for starting the rumour.

> I have expressed a highly favorable opinion of that young Australian soprano [she said] and several newspapers printed my remarks about her.
> It is only regrettable, to put it mildly, that someone literally invented a story and published it [she said of the jealousy rumour].

The rehearsals for *La Sonnambula* at the Garden began in September and the opening performance on October 19 – and that of the 1960–1 season – was a gala in honour of the King and Queen of Nepal (who were on a three-day State Visit) in the company of the Queen, the Duke of Edinburgh and most of the other members of the Royal Family. The Court Circular of the *Telegraph* dated October 20 reads like the attendance at the Royalest of weddings.

The opera house had been decorated by Carl Toms who had been assistant to that wizard of theatrical design Oliver Messel. The results of his several years' training with Messel were evident in the dazzling eighteenth-century oriental splendour with which Carl Toms converted the theatre, particularly the centre of the Grand Tier. This was transformed into a pavilion of yellow and white silk, fringed with silver and gold in festoons and garlands, topped off by Nepalese emblems and ostrich plumes. There were even palm trees flanking this temporary and extremely large Royal Box. The remainder of the house was hung with garlands of yellow and white chrysanthemums.

During an interval members of the cast were presented to the Royal party in the Crush Bar – and what a crush it was! Excitement was running high and the sight of the Royal regalia and jewels was breathtaking. It was a cold and rainy night but the glamorous regal line-up belied the wintry weather. I progressed along the protocol-appointed way and came to Princess Margaret who had been a fairly regular visitor to the opera at that time and whom I had met previously. After I had taken her extended hand and done my somewhat restricted 'bob' curtsey the Princess said, 'My dear Miss Sutherland, you know my ...'

I thought she was going to say 'husband' and extended my hand to Mr Antony Armstrong Jones. But the Princess continued, '. . . Aunt, the Duchess of Gloucester.'

Being completely confused I crossed my left hand over and gave it to the Duchess of Gloucester, doing my 'bob' and set them all laughing by saying: 'Oh! There are too many of you!' At that Princess Margaret rejoined, 'We know!'

This was fairly near the end of the line and I was able to escape to change into my next costume, embarrassed and asking Sir David Webster if I had been too gauche and rude. He laughed in turn and said they were probably delighted – they hadn't laughed for three days, apparently.

La Sonnambula had not been performed in London for fifty years, the last protagoniste being the great Luisa Tetrazzini, and there was a deal of interest in it, the most charming of Bellini's works. The normal first night (October 21) followed the gala and I developed a very heavy cold between the two, possibly resulting from my visiting Royalty in my night attire. There was also a downpour as the audience was leaving the opera house after the gala, causing havoc with the excessive traffic of limousines. Once all the Royal party had gone there was utter chaos and Richard and I waited in the cold at the Stage Door for an hour before our car could get to us and take us on to a very late supper party. I managed to get through that regular performance with, according to the press, flying colours, but I know I should not have had to sing.

Having Tullio Serafin in charge in the pit helped me, as he knew and loved every bar of the score. In this production, instead of sleep-walking on the rotting bridge over the mill-stream, Amina (the heroine) appeared on top of the roof and came safely down steps at the side of the mill. Another variant was to have Amina's first sleep-walking scene take place on a loggia outside Count Rodolfo's bedroom rather than in the room, somewhat weakening the impact of her discovery there. I loved singing the role and the rest of the cast was extremely good, particularly Joseph Rouleau as the Count. This was a part he repeated whilst on the Sutherland–Williamson tour to Australia in 1965. There was a total of seven performances up to and including November 7 which happened to be my birthday. From the staunch gallery-going fans on that last night I received a greater ovation than usual – if that were possible – and many good wishes for my successful début in the United States, which was to take place nine days later in Dallas.

✧ 11 ✧

THE SCRAMBLE TO pack and be off on Richard's and my first trip to the United States together was only one of many such crises. We had to change planes upon arrival at Idlewild Airport in New York after going through the immigration process and our agents Ann and Henry Colbert greeted us with a thermos of Martinis, which they proceeded to pour for us in the VIP Lounge. It was election day, and there was a total ban on the sale of liquor whilst the populace decided whether Nixon or Kennedy would be the next President. Ann and Henry were so kind and welcoming, having eased the whole business of entry into the United States – and quite unaware that my only tipple was a glass of wine or beer, never any spirits.

They saw us on to the plane for Dallas and when we arrived there (still only on November 9) we were met by representatives of the Dallas Civic Opera and I was presented with a Scroll of Greeting from the Mayor, declaring that I had been made an honorary citizen of Dallas, Texas and 'under this Charter shall hold and enjoy a place of high esteem in the minds and hearts of the people of this City'.

After theatres like Covent Garden and the Paris Opéra it was something of a shock to see the State Fair Music Hall where we were to perform – it resembled a made-over aeroplane hangar. However, we were made so welcome by the ladies of the Opera Guild and our particular hostesses, Mary Ann Clark and Juanita Miller, plus being plunged into adapting the Venice *Alcina* to its new surroundings and with an almost totally different cast, that we settled down to a routine there very quickly. The biggest problem was that rehearsals started (and finished) so late, and the jet-lag didn't help. Another lesson was learned for future planning – try to leave a space between one set of engagements and the next, however persuasive the agent or manager and no matter how tempting the prospective dates may be.

The other members of the cast were Blanche Thebom as Ruggiero, Monica Sinclair as Bradamante, Luigi Alva as Oronte, Nicola Zaccaria as Melisso and Joan Marie Moynagh as Morgana, together with the Joffrey Ballet and Nathalie Krassovska as prima ballerina. Nicola Rescigno conducted. We were a happy group and as the performances were as soon as November 16 and 18, with the *Don Giovanni* on 20 and 23, I was exceedingly glad that I knew both roles very well and had done them quite recently.

As well as the rehearsals – most of which were held in the evening, due to the semi-professional chorus who held other jobs during the day or were housewives – there was a round of social functions and interviews with members of the press, our first exposure to the American publicity machine. There was even a complete Texas-designed wardrobe presented to me.

Although *Alcina* had been composed some 225 years previously, the Dallas performances were the first in the United States. The 'Double Début' met with huge coverage in the local press and also in the likes of the *Christian Science Monitor* and the *New York Times*. In this last newspaper Harold C. Schonberg wrote:

> ... One waits until Sunday's *Don Giovanni* for a more accurate estimate. *Alcina* is, after all, an unknown opera. But it was clear that Miss Sutherland has a voice far beyond the average. And when she ended the opera with a fortissimo, secure, effortless high D, the audience went wild, in the full realization that a great voice had come to America.
>
> It is a warm-coloured voice, of very large size, and of unusual fluency. One might almost call Miss Sutherland a dramatic coloratura. What with a soaring lyric line, a superb technique, a trill that really is a trill and not a wobble, an enormous range, rapid scales and even registers, she seems equipped to handle almost any soprano role in the repertory.

The *New York Herald Tribune* wrote:

> ... Miss Sutherland enthroned herself as a most remarkable prima donna assoluta, blessed with an incredibly flawless technique and vocal expressivity that is the finest of our time, certainly, and possibly as great as any in musical history.
>
> Her trills alone are not to be believed in an age of flagrant technical cheating. Miss Sutherland is a mistress of bel canto whose impact is stupendous.

There was a memorable supper at the Sheraton Hotel where hundreds of flowers were imported from France – fragrant lilac, gardenias, wisteria and a host of others transforming the banquet hall into a Mediterranean garden. The food and wines were splendid and all the Dallas opera-goers appeared to be present, along with the members of the cast. It was a breath-taking and wonderful party – and I was later told the host and hostess who had been very richly garbed that night skipped town without paying a cent.

The interest generated by the glowing press for the dazzling Zeffirelli production of *Alcina* and its splendid musical presentation brought many more opera buffs from all parts of the United States to the second performance and curtain calls became somewhat of a riot. All this was most exciting, but we had to get on with such minimal rehearsal as there was for *Don Giovanni*, opening with the matinée performance on Sunday, November 20.

Franco had designed quite massive costumes and there was no time at all to accustom oneself to their whims – they had a habit of getting under one's feet, or someone else's. I was understandably tired and tried hard to sleep late in the morning, something that has always been difficult for me. However, the long evening rehearsals rather forced the issue. They were another fact of operatic life that I could never adapt to comfortably. In fact, as one of the *Don Giovanni* rehearsals went on and on I complained that it was far too late and we were not accomplishing anything – just standing about waiting for scene changes. Larry Kelly (the General Manager of the Dallas Opera) did not endear himself to me when he countered, 'Maria would work until two or three in the morning to get things right!' I quickly snapped, 'And look what's happened to her!'

Both Richard and I firmly believe that three hours at any one time of intensive rehearsal is about the limit of any artist's true con-centration. A break of an hour and a further three hours' work – and that is plenty for one day. Longer than six full working hours not only tire the body and voice but tend to become unproductive due to the lack of proper attention to the work in hand by the cast.

Because all the artists were well acquainted with their roles and the action scenes of the opera were very obvious, we had another huge success. The Don was again Eberhard Waechter, Elvira was Elisabeth Schwarzkopf, Leporello was Giuseppe Taddei and Don Ottavio was Luigi Alva. The Commendatore was Nicola Zaccaria, Masetto John Reardon and Zerlina Eugenia Ratti. Franco had dressed Eugenia out-rageously in a flurry of what appeared to be pink tulle – the prototype for Miss Piggy's outfit when dancing with Nureyev in the *Muppet Show*.

Luigi and I enjoyed singing together very much and I was intrigued by Elisabeth's know-how on the stage. I remember her making an entrance from the balcony of her inn room, commencing the recitative 'In quali eccessi, o numi', hissing 'Lights!' into the wings as her follow spot had not appeared and continuing with the recit calmly and in tempo. I also remember that Richard was fascinated by her antics with a large handkerchief scarf during Alva's singing of 'Il mio tesoro'. He vows all eyes were on Elisabeth, *not* Luigi.

In my dressing-room for the opening matinée performance I found a huge vase of four dozen red roses from Elsa Maxwell. At the party after the opera I thanked her for her lovely thought, at which she roared laughing. 'Oh,' she said, 'enjoy them. I arrived today and found them in my hotel room. I thought I'm only here tonight and Joan has her first night of *Don Giovanni*. It's Sunday and I don't know where to get flowers so I had them delivered to you at the theatre!' Her honesty gained my respect and I *did* enjoy the beautiful roses.

We were nearly killed by Texan hospitality and we have experienced it many times since with friends made on that first momentous trip.

During the end of the year there were further reports of rivalry with Callas in the Italian papers, all unfounded. There were three more performances of *La Sonnambula* and four of *Lucia di Lammermoor* at Covent Garden before Christmas. At the end of the Mad Scene on the last night of *Lucia* a great number of the audience remained in the auditorium applauding and roaring 'Brava' through the whole of the intermission, only stopping as the final bells rang and those who had gone to the bars returned for the final scene. It was noted in the press next day that the previous record set by Margot Fonteyn (fifteen curtain calls in twelve and a half minutes' applause) had been broken. I had managed to take seventeen calls in the twenty-minute interval, the then post-war record.

Christmas 1960 was a very happy occasion, with Mother and Auntie Blos joining us, although we were preparing to leave the next day – Richard, Ruthli, Adam and myself – for Barcelona where I was to make yet another début at the Gran Teatro del Liceo, with three performances of *I Puritani*.

On Boxing Day off we went to the airport, only to find that Richard and I (with Australian passports) should have procured visas to enter Spain. Adam had a British passport, Ruthli her Swiss one, so they were quite legal. We had to talk very hard at the check-in counter to make it clear I was expected for rehearsals in Barcelona. Finally Richard and I were allowed to board the plane with Adam and Ruthli, after signing an agreement not to hold British Airways (or BEA as it was then) responsible for any problems encountered upon our arrival. Fortunately we were able to phone our British agents and they contacted the Liceo and the Consulate in Barcelona so that we were met there and assisted through immigration, much to our relief. The experience made me very conscious of the need to be sure of all travel documents being in order well ahead of time – something of a joke within our family, especially with Richard!

The Barcelona stay was extremely pleasant, the first of many such sojourns in that most beautiful and interesting city, let alone the joy of working in the theatre. We had been in the city barely one night when two Australians presented themselves at our hotel and asked if they could be of any assistance to us with sightseeing, shopping or just interpreting. This last was of foremost importance and Mrs Jess Burgess and her son Tom, the latter very fluent in the Spanish languages, were both a great boon, remaining friends over the years.

There were very few rehearsals for *I Puritani* and the conductor, Luciano Rosada, was most charming and helpful. Richard had insisted on my asking Glyndebourne to lend me the costumes Desmond Heeley had designed for me in their production and I was very grateful to have them and know they worked so well. The first night was on December 30, 1960 and the public went wild with their applause. The rest of the cast were mostly Spanish with Manuel Ausensi as Riccardo.

During that period it was impossible to transfer money out of the country. As we were paid in cash during each performance it was burning a hole in our pockets. Richard had the brilliant idea of buying some splendid antique furniture and having it shipped to the villa we had leased on Lake Maggiore. That was quite permissible and the furniture has been shipped again and again to grace our home wherever it happened to be. One great buy was a set of six Isabella II gilt salon chairs and a huge matching sofa. I ultimately worked needlepoint pieces to cover all the chairs, with Udi helping, but the sofa was too daunting.

On January 6, 1961 the third and last *I Puritani* performance was held as a

> *Homenaje y despedida de la eximia soprano*
> *Joan Sutherland*
> *y despedida de los grandes artistas*
> *Gianni Iaia y Manuel Ausensi*

The programme went on to say that at the end of the performance of the opera I would sing an encore for the public of an aria from *La Sonnambula* – 'Ah, non giunge'. Not only was I presented with a gold medal of esteem by the Liceo, but a flight of turtle-doves was released in the theatre. They even called me the 'New Malibran'. I don't know what time we went to bed, as it appeared that half the public wanted autographs outside the theatre and then escorted us up the Ramblas to our hotel.

That same morning we all left for Palermo via Nice, with Adam looking very pale and sickly, having caught measles during his stay. But the doctor had said he could travel and he managed very well until, just half an hour before landing in Palermo, we ran into a frightful electrical storm. Udi was terrified and trying not to show it, Adam was violently ill – and Richard and I were not far from it.

There were only four days to work on the production of *I Puritani* there as the opening night at the Teatro Massimo was on Thursday, January 12. Franco Zeffirelli was again the producer and Tullio Serafin the conductor, with the costumes designed by Peter John Hall who had been in the wardrobe department at Covent Garden. So we felt very much at home and managed to fit in a reasonable amount of sightseeing around the city of Palermo, notably a visit to Monreale where Richard took some delightful photographs of Adam. The first night – which was the opening night of the season – was a very grand affair, with Princess Paola and Alberto of Belgium present and a tumultuous reception from the audience. Gianni Raimondi sang Arturo and Mario Zanasi Riccardo. There were twenty curtain calls at the end of the opera and a rain of flowers, many torn from the beautiful garlands decorating the theatre.

The press reports, too, were ecstatic, praising the great interpretation by Serafin of I Puritani and his loving attention to the Bellini style and to the singers. They spoke of the quality of 'the Sutherland voice', sparkling 'like diamonds in the sun', extolling its flexibility, the 'silvery trill' and the range, particularly at the top. Several articles were headed 'The Voice of the Year in Italy', another reported the gift of the sixpence. They did not report that he had been furious with Zeffirelli one day when he learned that Franco had taken me at great speed in his open sports car around the coast to a restaurant for lunch and back prior to a rehearsal. 'All that sea air blowing in your face could be fatal – very bad for the voice, and we have the performances to think of!' Serafin raged, more at Franco than me.

Adam appeared to have a wonderful time and recovered well from his attack of measles. The big excitement for him was when he attended a dress rehearsal and was fitted out backstage with sword, cape and hat belonging to Mario Zanasi, making a very happy boy and another cute photograph.

Although the time in Palermo was relatively short we had grown to love the city and Sicily generally, fortunately going back several times over the years. One of the great evenings was spent at the beautiful Villa Tasca, home of the Conte and Contessa Tasca and their family. The house was fabulous, with marble floors, painted ceilings and sweeping staircases to the romantic garden and its ornamental lake, all used some years later in the film of The Leopard for the grand party scene. Indeed, we experienced just such a grand party in reality there, with the guests lavishly dressed, sparkling with jewels and a wonderful table laid for what seemed like upwards of sixty people with the most delicate porcelain and crystal, a white-gloved footman behind each chair. The Tascas were charming and warm-hearted and the wines from their vineyards are still some of the smoothest in Sicily.

The third and last performance was on January 17 and we took an early flight to Venice, via Rome, where I had three performances of Lucia di Lammermoor on January 24, 26 and 29. We stayed at the Regina-Europa hotel and there was a large group of American senior citizens doing the Grand Tour of Europe. They made a great fuss of

Adam and he reacted by expecting such attention all the time, and getting it, too, even in the theatre. I had thought to keep him out of school and travel with him more as I felt I was missing the greater part of his growing up. But after the exposure of this trip both Richard and I, as well as Ruthli, realised it was impossible and Adam would be much better with the steady routine of daily school. Already his sweet temperament and personality were showing signs of becoming more boisterous, rude and somewhat unmanageable. He was probably missing his young friends and we decided that after Easter he should go back to the Lycée in London, which served him very well until he went to boarding-school in Switzerland at the age of twelve.

The *Lucia* production was again Zeffirelli's from Palermo with that delightful young tenor Renato Cioni as Edgardo.

Although it seems all too taxing now, we must have flown home to London on January 30, with Adam and Ruthli going by train to Basel where they were to spend the next few months with Ruthli's parents. It was here that Adam perfected his 'Basel Deutsch' as the Brendles spoke no English. It has been of great use to him in his profession as an hotelier, and some of his colleagues were quite surprised to learn that he was not Swiss but British by birth.

Richard and I left again on the thirty-first for New York, leaving my mother and Auntie Blos to live in the Kensington apartment. As we were departing for the airport Mother threw her arms about us both and tearfully wished us good luck for our first United States concert tour and my New York début, saying she feared she wouldn't see us again. We tried to cheer her up, with Richard saying we were all moving to the lovely Villa Rocca Bella on Lake Maggiore when we came back and there was so much to look forward to, including my début at La Scala. Mother pulled herself together in true Alston–Sutherland style, admonished by Auntie Blos for putting a damper on our farewell, and we left, smiling but somewhat uneasy.

✧ 12 ✧

THERE WAS NO time to become accustomed to New York, as the day after our arrival we flew from Newark to Charlotte, North Carolina and were taken by car to Rock Hill, South Carolina where we were to give the first recital at Winthrop College (now Winthrop University) Auditorium on Thursday, February 2. This was one of the many American colleges with a very fine concert series and the Colberts had a strong belief that by their artists performing in these venues they built up a young audience for the future. We were quite shocked to learn that there was such segregation in the South and there were no black pupils at this all-female college. Also that a singer of the calibre of Leontyne Price would not be invited to perform there. How rapidly all this changed over the next few years.

The programme consisted of three Handel arias, a group of Italian and English eighteenth-century arias, 'Regnava nel silenzio' from the first act of *Lucia di Lammermoor*, a group of Victorian songs and arias, two songs from Rossini's *Soirées Musicales* and two French pieces, ending with the Mad Scene from Thomas's *Hamlet*. This remained the basic recital for the whole tour with a few changes from time to time.

The *Rock Hill Evening Herald* of the next day wrote:

SUTHERLAND CAPTIVATES ROCK HILL AUDIENCE IN US DEBUT
After receiving rave notices abroad, last night's performance marked Miss Sutherland's American recital début.

Miss Sutherland's tones could only be described as golden, as her voice seemed to fill every corner of the spacious hall. She thoroughly captivated her audience, holding each individual in breathless awe, as she put on a tremendous display of pitch, range, feeling for her music – and even a sense of humour.

Overnight there was a severe snowstorm and our flight back to Newark was cancelled. Mrs Colbert organised our taking the train and she came to the station to pick us up. We couldn't believe the scene on the Manhattan streets, with the parked cars all covered and making snowy walls about five or six feet high on either side. Such cars as were moving were slipping and sliding about. It was our first experience of many in such conditions.

The recital was repeated on Sunday, February 5 in Danbury, Connecticut, with an orchestral concert almost completely of Handel works on the seventh at Dumbarton Oaks, Washington. Paul Callaway conducted.

In Washington we were invited to stay at the Australian Embassy. Our ambassador to the United States at that time was Sir Howard Beale and he and his charming wife were delightful hosts. The residence was in a magnificent position with perfect reception rooms and garden and a pleasant, thoughtful staff whom we got to know quite well over ensuing years and other visits.

On February 8 TWW released in Britain the thirty-minute television show that had been recorded in Bristol with Geraint Evans at the end of 1960. The programme included the duet with Enrico from *Lucia di Lammermoor* and 'Ah fors'è lui' from *La Traviata*. It was a trial sortie into classical music presentation by Independent Television and transmitted quite late – 10.35 at night – so as not to interrupt viewing of the regular evening shows. The result was a spate of letters from viewers begging for more and the press congratulating the TV company for having the courage to present the programme.

Other recitals followed on the eleventh in Pittsburgh, Pennsylvania and on the thirteenth in Oklahoma City, with another orchestral concert in Dallas, Texas on the fifteenth with the Dallas Symphony conducted by Franz Allers. Here I sang the Sleep-walking Scene from *La Sonnambula* and the Mad Scene from *Lucia di Lammermoor* with 'Son vergin vezzosa' from *I Puritani* as an encore.

We then had five days in New York during which we met Marilyn Horne for the first time and rehearsed for the American Opera Society's performance of *Beatrice di Tenda*. The Director of the Society was Allen Sven Oxenburg and he presented concert performances of many operas in Carnegie Hall long before they were seen in full productions in the United States during the present generation, also numerous new international singers.

There was an instant rapport between Marilyn, Richard and myself, and a lasting friendship and collaboration resulted. Both Marilyn and I were making our New York début and we've had several other big 'firsts' together over the years.

Something that thrilled Richard and me was meeting so many well-known performers, past and present, who came to the concerts. Terry McEwen had introduced us to Geraldine Souvaine who organised the Intermission fare for the Texaco Metropolitan Opera Broadcasts and she, in turn, was the means whereby we met many stars – not only in the musical world but some of our favourite movie personalities as well. One evening during this period we went to dinner with Clytie Mundy who had sung at Covent Garden as Clytie Hine during the era of the British National Opera, directed by Sir Thomas Beecham. Ric had a great time quizzing her about her colleagues.

The big début night was February 21, 1961 and on that Tuesday morning Richard had to break the news to me that Mother had died the day before in London. The question arose of my going back for the funeral but there seemed no way I could just walk out on the concert, and when I spoke with Auntie Blos by telephone she was adamant that Mother would have wanted me to stay and fulfil my obligation. As the performance of *Beatrice di Tenda* had sold out by subscription, a second performance had been added at Carnegie Hall on March 1. This also sold out and, as was printed at the back of the original programme

By Overwhelming Demand
Extra and Final Performance
Carnegie Hall Saturday Evening, March 11 at 8.30

So, feeling rather shaky, I managed to get through the evening – possibly with less nervousness than otherwise, as I felt it was my tribute to Mother, rather than yet another first night. Richard says it was one of the most moving performances I ever sang. I hardly knew I was on stage. The audience was well sprinkled with singers, including Leontyne Price, Bidu Sayao and Franco Corelli, also representatives of many of the US musical organisations.

Again the glowing reviews, particularly by Harold Schonberg in the *New York Times*:

The much-anticipated local début of Joan Sutherland took place last night in Town Hall ... She may well be the unique singer of her genre in the world today – a singer who can handle coloratura with complete ease, and yet whose voice is big enough to take on roles like Donna Anna and Norma.

It is a beautifully colored voice, one that ascends effortlessly to the E in alt and, most likely, beyond. Where most sopranos have trouble with B flats and Cs, Miss Sutherland is at her most secure above the staff. And withal she preserves warmth, color and style. In concerted numbers her voice soars over the ensemble, without ever becoming hard or jagged. She is a supreme technician.

... She has numerous ways of changing the color of her voice, in accordance with the stylistic or dramatic needs of the moment, and she does not hesitate to do so.

Like all great singers, she plays to strength. In somewhat altering some of the coloratura writing, she follows precedent. Singers in Bellini's day were expected to embellish the vocal line. Thus when Miss Sutherland interpolated a high E or E flat here and there, she was on secure traditional ground.

In short, she is a great singer. Indeed, as the species goes these days, she is a supreme singer. One only hopes that she will preserve her sense of proportion; that she will retain the present high degree of vocal finish, musicianship and tonal warmth that so mark her work. For a singer of her unusual gifts can easily be turned into a circus performer, coming on stage for the sole purpose of demonstrating her trill (and what a trill she has!) and her high notes instead of making music.

The *Christian Science Monitor*'s 'M. K.':

Not in years has the début of a singer excited New York as that of the Australian soprano Joan Sutherland...

When her clearly focused tones soared immediately and she sang a perfect trill in the process, she revealed a technical mastery of exceptional caliber. Those crystalline tones so beautifully controlled heralded an almost unique performer ... That Miss Sutherland sustained remarkable coloratura and amazing clarity of note throughout the performance made the event memorable.

Yet there were such matters as distinctive phrasing, musicianly controlled dynamics, and subtle interpretative touches to enhance the performance. Truly, all this was phenomenal.

Winthrop Sargeant in the *New Yorker*:

BRAVA! BRAVA! BRAVA!

The New York début of the Australian soprano Joan Sutherland, in the American Opera Society's concert performance of Bellini's *Beatrice di Tenda* on Tuesday night of last week, was one of those rare occasions that cause a music critic to examine his pitifully meagre and worn supply of superlatives and then to discard them, on the ground that he is confronted with an altogether unique phenomenon. To get a clear idea of the magnitude of the phenomenon, it is necessary to point out that in recent years the only soprano to conquer with any degree of success the territory that Miss Sutherland is a complete mistress of has been Maria Callas, and that Miss Callas's conquest of it – remarkable as it was – always seemed to be the result of a strenuous effort of the will, and to involve, now and then, a certain amount of screaming in the higher registers of the voice. Miss Sutherland does not have to scream. On the contrary, her upper notes, which extend to high E, are produced with incredible ease and sensuous beauty, and her command of the trills, ornamentations, and cascading scales of the florid Bellini style is such that she can bring off with complete relaxation and grace technical feats that seem to strain most coloratura voices to the breaking point. Her voice, moreover, is not a cold, flutelike one but a sort of hybrid that combines the agility of the true coloratura with the warm expressiveness of a spinto soprano. In addition to all this, she is an artist. Her sense of musical values is immaculate; she phrases beautifully, and she is capable of restraint and refinement as well as stunning fireworks. I have heard that Miss Sutherland, who is very tall, rather imposing, red-haired and somewhat angular in physical appearance, is also a gifted actress, and even within the formal limitations of the concert performance offered by the American Opera Society this was often hinted at – in telling dramatic inflections, in the emotional sincerity she brought to the role, and in the impressive dignity with which she comported herself. During the evening, I searched my memory for comparisons, only to conclude that in all my not inconsiderable experience in opera houses and concert halls I had never heard a soprano quite like her. Presumably, she is the type of singer for whom Bellini originally wrote his lovely and peculiarly taxing female roles – a type that one reads about in histories of music but almost never finds on today's operatic stage.

Marilyn Horne, who made her New York début in this same performance, had a great success with both public and critics.

For all these concerts and recitals I alternated the two beautiful gowns Heinz Riva had designed and made for me. The favourite was the green satin with a huge stole of the same material lined with white satin and the other a deep lilac satin with a matching cloak-like coat lined and faced in silver grey. With the green dress I wore a lovely antique necklace of emeralds that Richard had bought me when shopping in Barcelona. Both gowns made a lasting impression on members of the audience – and set a high standard of concert garb for me to live up to.

If we had thought the autograph hunters were numerous in Europe, those in the United States were overwhelming. It was unbelievable how so many familiar faces came to performance after performance and always required yet another signed programme, ticket, score – even cheque-book. Indeed, we came to expect certain fans to appear and wondered if they were ill if we didn't see them. But they were a faithful following and very generous with little gifts and remembrances which we appreciated. Birthdays and Christmas still bring stacks of cards.

There had been so much coverage by the press generating public interest that Richard and I found we had an extra recital on February 23 at Englewood, New Jersey which had not been on the original schedule. It was held in a High School gymnasium and, due to its proximity to New York City, was packed with concert- and opera-goers from there. Some were trying to hear me sing ahead of my projected Metropolitan Opera début but had not managed to get tickets for the American Opera Society's concerts – and others because they *had* and wanted to hear more. That concert was certainly a highlight of our career and has remained an outstanding musical event in the memories of so many who attended.

Among those present were several singers who were legendary to us – Jennie Tourel, Anna Case Mackay and Gladys Swarthout of Metropolitan Opera and film fame. Also in the audience was Anya Dorfman, that petite Russian pianist whom Richard had admired since his teens. She was most complimentary of his accompaniments and remained a friend until her death. Later during our extended New York visits she found a suitable apartment for us to rent in the same building as hers on East 94th Street and Madison Avenue.

The tour continued – Richmond, Virginia, on the twenty-fifth, Charlottesville, Virginia, on the twenty-seventh – and also a quick visit to Monticello. Then back to New York where Ric had meetings with RCA Victor and also representatives of the *Bell Telephone Hour*, together with our TV and publicity agent Herbert Breslin. These last were proposing a show for March 17 called at that stage *Shakespeare on Broadway* and wanted me to appear on it in costume singing the Mad Scene from *Hamlet* and the 'Salce' from *Otello*. Staged portions of *West Side Story*, *Kiss Me, Kate* and *The Boys from Syracuse* were included in the plan, together with John Gielgud narrating and reading excerpts from the Bard's plays. Although this show meant delaying by four days our return to London we agreed to do it.

On March 1 the second performance of *Beatrice di Tenda* was held in Carnegie Hall, that beautiful and historic old venue. It was another huge success, the audience response making it difficult for us to leave the hall in time to catch the 11.55 p.m. flight from Idlewild to Chicago, arriving there at 1.15 a.m. for the next appearance on March 3, an orchestral concert of baroque arias with the Little Symphony of Chicago, conducted by Russell Stanger in the Studebaker Theater. It was a similar programme to that I had sung at Dumbarton Oaks, including five long Handel arias and an aria each of Paisiello and Bianchi.

Two of the Chicago critics were falling over themselves with praise. After much preamble, Don Herakan of the *Daily News* went on:

What does this woman have?

A clear wobble-free voice, smoothly and evenly produced throughout more than two octaves. Breath control that is not to be believed – it was as if she had drawn a breath before the concert and then let it out slowly and evenly during seven long, florid arias.

The only practical explanation I could see was that behind her sumptuous satin train lurked a man with a bellows, pumping, pumping, pumping.

HER TRILLS, mordants, turns and other ornaments were not merely the gross vibrato of lesser singers.

They actually varied the pitch so precisely that the notes seemed to be etched in the air.

From Handel's 'Care selve' to his 'Let the Bright Seraphim', her first and last arias, there was not a false or forced note from the serenely handsome singer.

Roger Dettmer wrote:

SUTHERLAND DEBUT HERE TRIUMPHANT

Indisputably, the right place to be seen last evening was in the Studebaker Theater where Joan Sutherland, the statuesque soprano wonder from Down Under, made her local début with the Little Symphony of Chicago, Russell Stanger conducting. Miss Sutherland is a superlative singing mechanism with an even musical temperament, a gracious and untheatrical manner, and a tonal production unfailingly pure, steady and beautiful.

... Plainly and unequivocally, she is the best singer in a generation at least.

The social whirl was quite exhausting, but Board members of the various societies and their donors held supper parties after the concerts and expected to be able to meet and speak with the artists, and Chicago was no exception. Mrs Herrschner (who claimed relationship through a Sutherland ancestor) gave a lovely reception and, as usual, I arrived longing for a drink – preferably of water. I found the central heating and the long concerts very drying. There was a howl of protest, with people pressing me to accept champagne or something stronger, and I finally managed to get by ordering a beer. We met several members of the Chicago Opera there, including Carol Fox, the General Manager.

Ann Colbert had organised the next concert for Monday, the sixth at Wells College, Aurora, in upstate New York, leaving us the weekend free. As we were 'so close' Ann had booked us on a flight to Buffalo so we could spend the two days at Niagara Falls. We were most impressed by the size of the Falls and all the snow and ice made it doubly remarkable – but when the rainbow lights played on this great natural beauty we suffered alternate horror and amusement. Buffalo itself was best forgotten, but the quiet pause away from all the press and adulation was a godsend. My diary reminds me that Richard even had time to write to La Scala and Maestro Gui regarding the version of *Beatrice di Tenda* projected for the Milan début. Maestro Gui had prepared it and cut the final brilliant cabaletta of Beatrice, completely weakening her character and, of course, robbing me of a great vehicle. Richard explained that the concerts in New York had been a huge success and some members of the audience were planning to attend the opera at La Scala. I couldn't possibly cut this dramatic exit aria as

I felt people would think that I had tired and deleted it myself. Ultimately I made my début in Milan singing *Lucia*, with *Beatrice* following about a month later, Maestro Gui having withdrawn from the performance.

It was now obvious that we needed a secretary on hand all the time and Richard's aunt, Anne Roughley (some nine years his senior), was preparing to join us during the La Scala season to live and travel with us. So our quiet weekend was very valuable to us for sorting out some of our pressing problems.

On Monday, March 7 after a three-and-a-half-hour train trip to Syracuse, and a forty-five-minute drive to Aurora where we arrived about 4.15 p.m., we gave our recital at 8 p.m. and the next day it was on to Montreal, where we had afternoon tea with that grand old singer and teacher Pauline Donalda. The Montreal concert was for the 'Ladies' Morning Musical Club' at 2.30 in the afternoon on March 9. The President and Spokeswoman for the Club was Dr Schopflocher and she had protested that our programme was not the sort of music 'her ladies' were accustomed to hearing and requested that it be changed. We had refused, and at the end of the recital there was an uproar of approval from the audience, with Dr Schopflocher twittering, 'My ladies *never* behaved like this before!'

We were able to fly back to New York in the early evening, having dinner there with Terry and Regina Resnik with whom I had sung in the *Carmen* performances at Covent Garden just prior to Adam's birth. Over the years we have kept in touch with Regina, often working in the same Company if not in the same opera, and Richard did performances of *The Queen of Spades* both in Vancouver and Sydney in which she not only sang the old Countess but produced the opera as well, her husband Arbit Blatas designing the scenery and costumes.

The next day we had lunch at the Colony Restaurant with Elsa Maxwell and the Duchess of Windsor. We found the Duchess quite charming and Elsa kept the conversation spinning in her inimitable style. She confessed to Ric and me that she felt responsible for Callas's vocal decline, having introduced her into the whirl of the social jet-setters. This increased our admiration for her apparent candour and directness. We also admired the Duchess's jewellery.

The final *Beatrice di Tenda* was held in Carnegie Hall the following night (Saturday, March 11) and was again a resounding success. A party was given afterwards at her apartment by Geraldine Souvaine, where we met Alexandra Danilova, John Brownlee, Fredric March and his wife Florence Eldridge, Giovanni Martinelli, Dolores del Rio and Jean Dixon and her husband (Mr and Mrs Ted Ely).

Then off to Toronto for a recital and back to New York for the *Bell Telephone Hour*. A lot of time was spent in my dressing-room waiting, but it was exciting to see and speak with Sir John, Violette Verdy,

Jacques d'Amboise, Alfred Drake and Patrice Munsell who were also on the show.

In spite of the heavy work schedule we managed to go to the Chateau Madrid with Elsa Maxwell to see Carmen Amaya.

On March 15 we had dinner at Jennie Tourel's apartment and we met Leonard Bernstein. The following night it was dinner with Mrs Lucy Rosen who was a great benefactress of music and art. She was quite a character and had given recitals on that most odd instrument the theramin when it was in vogue. Photographs showed her caressing it, her hair standing out somewhat like Elsa Lanchester's in *The Bride of Frankenstein*.

The next day the *Telephone Hour* had final rehearsals and was broadcast at 9 p.m. After such a hectic week – as well as what had gone before – I was relieved when the show was over and everyone was congratulating everyone else. I was also most impressed by the precision of timing and efficiency displayed by the whole crew who had only those few minutes of station identification and advertisement to change whole sets and move people off. There was, I believe, one pre-recorded segment due to these pressures, but it was a great feat to accomplish the event so successfully.

PART TWO

The Move to Switzerland
and Débuts at La Scala, San Francisco and the Met
1961–1965

✧ 1 ✧

THE OVERALL SCHEDULE of that first American tour had been exhausting and with the extra performances I was running very late for my next commitment in Italy. There had been the news of Mother's death in London and a constant worry as to how Auntie Blos would be managing. We knew Adam was well and happy with Ruthli and her parents in Basel and were looking forward to seeing them again when we all moved into the Villa Rocca Bella.

So we flew to London on March 18 (after a delay of some three hours before take-off) and had a very brief time with Auntie Blos, trying to convince her to join us at the villa in Switzerland. She was adamant and insisted on staying in London, saying she was too old to move again. We had to leave it at that, thinking we could be more persuasive when we had more time during our next trip back to England.

We arrived in Genoa on March 19 and had a 'brush-up' rehearsal on the twentieth, the Dress Rehearsal on the twenty-first and opened on the twenty-second with the Palermo production of *I Puritani*.

During our stay in Genoa we continued our friendship with two young medical students, Tito Gallacci and Romolo Gazzani who were fervent opera lovers and attended all the performances that were within reach, travelling very long distances by car. As well as taking us to some excellent restaurants and showing us around their city, they took us to the antique shops where some of our favourite pieces of furniture were bought, including a great painted four-poster bed and some lovely chandeliers. We went to Portofino for fabulous seafood.

The last *I Puritani* was on Wednesday, March 29 and as Easter weekend was free we took the opportunity to drive up to the Villa Rocca Bella. Ruthli and Adam were already installed. How spectacular it was, with an uninterrupted view down Lake Maggiore from the terraces and upstairs windows, the house being set well back from and above the road on a mini-plateau. There were all manner of interesting plants and trees in the rambling garden and the climate seemed perfect, although just early April. We could only stay until the end of the holidays, but our anticipation of returning when possible from Milan and staying there for most of the summer was boundless.

So back to the Hotel Duomo in Milan and my first rehearsal at La Scala – at 4 p.m. on April 4 – for *Lucia* with Maestro Antonino Votto and my friendly colleagues Gianni Raimondi and Giuseppe Modesti, together with that splendid baritone Ettore Bastianini who was singing the role of Enrico. Nervous I must have been but Maestro Votto was charming, playing much of the musical rehearsal himself and being most helpful so that I soon relaxed and enjoyed the thrill of working with such a splendid cast. The next day, my first on the huge La Scala stage, was quite an experience and I was delighted to meet the designer Nicola Benois with whom I worked later on in the theatre, together with the producer Mario Frigerio.

Rehearsals were numerous, although they were never very early in the day so we had time to explore Milan, enjoy the gallerias, window shop and even buy a few household articles needed for Rocca Bella. We met the Italian representatives of Decca and they organised some publicity photographs with Renato Cioni at the flower market, by the Duomo, in front of the theatre, etc.

The opening night finally arrived and was another resounding success, with the audience again tearing roses and carnations from the floral decorations in the house and showering them on to the stage during the curtain calls after the Mad Scene. The press had a field day, with titles like

JOAN SUTHERLAND: AT LA SCALA A STAR IS BORN

AT LA SCALA *LUCIA DI LAMMERMOOR* HAS TRULY SPROUTED WINGS

THE PRIMA DONNA OF THE DAY – 28, BORN IN AUSTRALIA

30 CALLS AT LA SCALA AT THE END OF *LUCIA*

SUTHERLAND A VOICE OF PAGANINI – A TRIUMPHAL DÉBUT

Several articles again made comparisons to the voice and personality of Callas, and spoke of her and Renata Tebaldi as having been the reigning Queens of La Scala who would now have to be content with being Queen Mothers.

My grasp of the Italian language was minimal at this stage and I couldn't read all the ecstatic reviews in their entirety. Richard did and, fortunately for my own equilibrium, only confirmed that the critics had agreed with the audience reaction and been generous with their acclamation. The success, of course, prompted the journalists to ask for interviews and there were so many to accommodate. We were very grateful to have our Decca friends to help with translations and it was all very gratifying, if somewhat tiring.

There were four more performances of *Lucia*, the last being on May

3. On this day Anne ('Weenie') Roughley arrived from Australia to begin a six-month trial period of travelling with us as secretary, chauffeuse and general dogsbody. Although jet-lagged and unable quite to believe where she was, she insisted on coming to that last *Lucia* and it has remained her favourite opera. As for the 'trial', she stayed with us for eight and a half years – until December 1969 – and continued to look after the numerous press cutting and pertinent memorabilia books until my retirement.

During the time in Milan we managed to spend each weekend at Rocca Bella, sometimes making the two-hour journey late at night to have the benefit of the whole of the following day there. Although our visits to the villa were brief it was a joy to get away from all the pressures of the city, where there was a constant round of social engagements, rehearsals for *Beatrice di Tenda*, fittings for costumes and also for some smart Italian dresses for me, the press interviews, dinner with the Amici della Scala and even a performance of Britten's *Midsummer Night's Dream* lavishly staged at La Scala in Italian.

I'm afraid we got the giggles when Oberon, a comely mezzo-soprano, sang 'Benvenuto, Pook', and we left after the first act, preferring to have dinner with Sir Geoffrey and Lady Meade who were the British Consul and his wife in Milan at that time. They were very hospitable and remained friends until their death.

Another thrill during our stay in Milan was a special performance of the sextet from *Lucia di Lammermoor* presented on the stage to honour Her Majesty Queen Elizabeth who was on the last day of an Italian tour with the Duke of Edinburgh. At first the Queen was only going to be shown the theatre and stage but the management decided that was not good enough. As *Lucia* had just been in the repertoire and both Gianni Raimondi and I were still in Milan, they arranged for us all to be in costume and make-up and appear to be rehearsing the sextet – in their *I Puritani* set, as the *Lucia* one was deemed too old and decrepit.

Among the staunch supporters of La Scala was Toscanini's daughter, Signora Wally Toscanini. Wally befriended us and we had several enjoyable and entertaining meals together, Richard and I fascinated by her reminiscences. We also met her sister Wanda, the wife of Vladimir Horowitz, discovering they were great friends of Anya Dorfman and lived close by her in New York.

Between all the social engagements rehearsals for *Beatrice di Tenda* progressed, with Antonino Votto conducting in place of Vittorio Gui. The sets and costumes were designed by Attilio Colonnello (who had a passion for the use of red, black, white and gold) and the producer was Franco Enriquez, with whom I had done the Glyndebourne *I Puritani*.

Beatrice was the penultimate opera of Bellini, first presented at the Fenice in Venice in 1833, and had not been seen at La Scala since

1841. The story somewhat resembles *Anna Bolena*, with similar situations. Beatrice, the widow of Facino Cane, has remarried Filippo Visconti, bringing him a huge dowry which helped found his power as Duke of Milan. Filippo is bored with his ageing wife and loves her lady-in-waiting Agnese – who in turn loves Orombello (the tenor) who loves only Beatrice who is faithful to her marriage vows. Agnese's jealousy of Orombello's love for her mistress gets the better of her and she denounces both Orombello and Beatrice to Filippo. Beatrice is tried for adultery and conspiracy, Orombello is forced to make a false confession under torture and, although he later recants, he and Beatrice are put to death. Maybe the very involved plot was responsible for its long years on the shelf, but the music is incredibly beautiful and was a joy to sing.

Dino Dondi sang the role of Filippo, Giuseppe Campora was Orombello and Raina Kabaivanska (a young Bulgarian in Milan for further study) made her début as Agnese. She was very sweet and nervous but with a lovely voice and obvious potential. It has always been delightful to meet up with her again, whether in Italy, Covent Garden or America, and I shall never forget a thoughtful armful of flowers brought by her to my dressing-room, nor some of her spectacular television performances.

The critics were divided as to the merits of the opera, some saying it was a rediscovered treasure, others that it was better left sleeping. But all were of the opinion that the musical and dramatic content of the role of Beatrice showed different facets of the quality and range of my still developing voice. There were five performances of the opera between May 10 and 21, with Ric and me taking the two-hour trip to Rocca Bella and back whenever we could to see Adam and Ruthli.

The morning after the last *Beatrice* I was up early as I had to leave for Venice where performances of *La Sonnambula* were planned, with Sandro Sequi producing and Nello Santi conducting. I was rather exhausted, probably only half awake, and slipped in the bath, hitting my cheekbone on one of the large taps. I was lucky not to have broken the skin, but a heavy bruise began to form under my eye. Unfortunate, but I had to have fittings in Milan, then take the train to Venice where we were supposed to open at the Fenice two days later. The theatre had accepted my very late arrival, knowing I was well prepared in the role and Sandro had talked through the production with me. I had also worked with Nello Santi before. There was not much time to rehearse, only a pre-dress rehearsal and the Dress Rehearsal. Santi's tempi were even more slow and rigid than in the *Traviatas* and the long phrases in the beautiful quintet became impossible. I asked him politely could he take the piece a trifle faster, whereupon he laughed, made a remark to the orchestra and we tried again – no difference, although I tried to force his hand. We stopped again and he said, for all to hear, that I had only come for the money.

The theatre called a 'Pausa' and the management, Santi, Richard, Sandro and myself went into conference. We all wanted the performance to go ahead, but Santi was adamant – *he* was the conductor and that was his tempo. We tried again, to no avail. I left the stage – and Venice as soon as possible.

What a scandal it caused, especially in the Italian press. They even implied my black eye was the result of a family squabble. There were rumours that I was to be sued by the theatre for 'doing a Callas'. On the contrary, they presented me with a dressing case complete with beautiful cut-glass perfume bottles and jars with silver lids. It is one of my treasures. The incident was unpleasant, farcical and should never have happened. I was very ill advised to accept the engagement in the first place, knowing how tight the timing was, but I wanted to do it for Sandro and the Fenice administrators were persuasive, so Ric and I agreed, thinking it could be an enjoyable conclusion to our Italian engagements for the season. We had learned another lesson – the hard way.

The British newspapers were full of the story, of course, and I was loath to be seen in London with my dark glasses and discoloured cheek and eye. However, Margreta Elkins was singing the role of the Princess Marina in *Boris Godunov* at Covent Garden, with Boris Christoff in the title part, and Ric and I went to the performance – slipping into our seats in a box just as the lights went down. I stayed in the box during the intervals, keeping well back, but someone obviously noticed me and towards the end of the second interval applause began, then the whole House stood and turned to the box applauding for some minutes – a spontaneous tribute and an expression of love and appreciation which gave me goose-pimples and a very warm feeling. I blew them a kiss, and Mr Christoff was upset that someone in the audience was stealing his applause and he delayed the curtain for a considerable time.

There were two performances of *Lucia* on June 6 and 9 with Alain Vanzo as Edgardo. Apart from a few rehearsals together I had some free time to catch my breath after all the excitement. During this period in London arrangements were made over a luncheon at the Ritz with Mark Bonham Carter and Russell Braddon for Russ to write my biography over a two-year period, starting immediately. He was going to follow us on our journeys and write as we went along, beginning in Paris in June, then spending time with us at Rocca Bella during our summer holidays and travelling down to Rome where we were to record *Rigoletto* and *Lucia* for Decca.

During this breathing space in London it was announced in the

Queen's Birthday Honours list that I had been awarded the CBE (Commander of the Order of the British Empire). Richard and I had been elated by the letter from Buckingham Palace some time previously asking if I would accept the award, but it was nothing to the excitement once the award was made public.

I was also sitting for one of many subsequent portraits, this one by the artist Etta Pollini. It is dated now because of the 'beehive' hairstyle, the whole painting resembling the original American cover of the *Art of the Prima Donna* recording. Richard has always liked it and it still hangs in the music room of our home.

The two *Lucia* performances during the last weeks of the opera season at Covent Garden were more or less a rehearsal for John Pritchard who was to conduct the recording of the work in Rome. The majority of the critics agreed that his handling of the work was perfunctory and lacking in a love of the music – as though he didn't rate it very highly. The audience gave me a great welcome back after the 'Venice Scandal'.

The following week we returned to Paris for three more *Lucias* on June 16, 19 and 23. These were the last appearances of our 1960–1 season and it was with great relief that we all set off for Rocca Bella and the magical atmosphere of Lake Maggiore.

We had a wonderful holiday for about three weeks, enjoying the nearby town of Locarno and continuing to decorate the house to our liking. We had a steady flow of guests and Weenie would drive us to Ascona and beyond so that we could visit the island of Brissago with its lovely gardens, or the Villa Taranto or, something that Adam loved, take the funicular from Madonna del Sasso up the mountain to our favourite picnic spot. Heinz Riva, Russ Braddon and Greta Elkins were with us and apart from swimming in the lake there was no need to go anywhere. One could happily laze on any of the terraces all day.

Weenie and Ruthli had rooms in a corner of the house where they vowed there were strange noises in the night – and at other quiet times – giving rise to rumours of a friendly ghost. We had theories about the 'ghost', believing it could be squirrels, birds, mice (we could never find anything) or – which we felt was rather more likely – devilment on the part of the caretaker-farmer's boys trying to scare us. They used to play with Adam in the huge park-like garden and got up to some fairly dangerous pranks.

During the second week of July we closed up Rocca Bella and left for Castiglioncello where Franco Zeffirelli had a summer villa by the sea. He had invited us all to come and stay on our way to Rome, where Franco had said we could use his apartment during our recording sessions. Ruthli and Adam went ahead by train and Weenie, Russ, Greta, Ric and I piled into the car with our luggage and arrived very hot and dusty, having meandered a bit to satisfy Ric's curiosity over every antique shop he saw – or town he thought might have one.

Franco had said there was plenty of room for everyone and to this day I'm not quite sure where 'everyone' managed to sleep, as there already appeared to be a houseful when we arrived, with more to come. Among those already resident was Sir John Gielgud who was working with Franco on the forthcoming *Othello* to be presented at Stratford in September, although how they managed to find a quiet place to work I'll never know. Beds were at a premium, so that Greta, Richard and I shared a normal double bed – with me in the middle! None of us could be termed small and sleep was very fitful and elusive due to the cramped conditions and the hot summer weather. Water was also scarce, with the pressure seeming to disappear completely at peak periods. There is a photograph of Greta and me cleaning our teeth at a pump in the garden, and I remember looking forward to being in Rome to take a decent bath.

Even with all the inconvenience it was a memorable holiday. Adam was not the greatest swimmer at that time but showed no fear of the waves breaking on the rocks below the villa. He had asked Sir John his name and been told to call him 'John', which he did and they got along famously. We remember one day when the waves were big and crashing forcibly on the rocks. None of us was inclined to venture in but Adam was there on the edge, playing with a plastic boat and, seeing John sitting far back on the rocks, called to him: 'Come on, John. Aren't you coming in? It's great!'

Whereupon John's splendid voice replied quietly but firmly: 'I don't *think* so, Adam, not today!'

Our doctor friends from Genoa visited and Peter John Hall was there – people were always appearing whom one hadn't noticed before. Franco's Auntie Lidia with her minions in the kitchen managed to provide food for the horde, and a few times we went to the local market and shops and bought trays of the luscious summer fruits, also pastries.

Our party of Greta, Weenie, Ric and myself pressed on to Rome, where Russ was staying in the pensione opposite Zeffirelli's top-floor apartment which housed the rest of us. We arrived at the weekend to be told by the maid that the telephone and electric light had been cut off as Franco had forgotten to pay the bills, so our longed-for baths had to be postponed. We settled the accounts and then spent a fabulous three weeks savouring the sights and atmosphere of Rome, as well as recording *Rigoletto* and *Lucia*.

The recordings were made with the Accademia di Santa Cecilia Orchestra and Chorus and we used to walk from the apartment across the Piazza di Spagna and on to the hall. I was very much slimmer in those days, and the sight of Margreta and me – one tall blonde and one tall redhead – striding through the crowds in the piazza elicited quite a few whistles and comments. We grew to expect these, but were somewhat shocked when approached by two men and asked to accompany them to see 'Maestro Fellini'. We looked at each other and then reluctantly went down a street off the square, with our 'escorts' explaining that Fellini had seen us walking through the square each day and wanted to offer me a film contract. I tried to explain that I was not an actress but an opera singer and in the middle of recording, so couldn't stand about talking to Fellini (who was ensconced in a huge limousine, wearing dark glasses and looking like some Mafioso Boss) or I'd be late for my session. I agreed to think about it, took the card thrust at me by one of his scouts and made off to the hall post haste.

How we laughed over the episode and toyed with the idea of accepting the offer. But Franco wisely told us not to touch it. He knew that Fellini was making *La Dolce Vita*, and although it might mean a good sum of money right away, the opera managers in Italy – and elsewhere – who were eager to engage me would not take me seriously, especially if I flopped when the film was shown. We accepted his advice, but have always wondered just which of Fellini's women I was to be – Anita Ekberg, perhaps?

Rigoletto was sung by Cornell MacNeil. Renato Cioni sang the Duke, Cesare Siepi Sparafucile, Sanzogno conducting. About half-way through the opera I developed a very sore throat and was amazed to find that the Italian doctor's 'cure-all' remedy of suppositories made it possible for me to complete the role of Gilda.

Cornell MacNeil had some slightly different cuts in his score and complained that the conductor had not brought him in on time to which Sanzogno replied with a laugh, 'I will send you a telegram next time.' This response was not appreciated by Mr MacNeil and he walked off the stage. Time cannot be wasted during recording sessions, so it was decided to proceed with a tenor section, whereupon Cioni missed his cue. He grinned and apologised, adding, 'You forgot to send me a telegram' which restored everyone's good humour, including Cornell MacNeil's.

Lucia di Lammermoor followed on immediately with John Pritchard conducting, Renato Cioni as Edgardo, Robert Merrill as Enrico, Cesare Siepi as Raimondo.

These two recordings gave me the opportunity to work with three of the Metropolitan Opera's top stars and I was delighted to find them so friendly and helpful. We have received the Merrills' Christmas card every year since. We all had some wonderful meals together after the day's work with Christopher Raeburn (the Producer), Kenneth Wilkinson ('Wilkie') the Chief Recording Engineer and the other Decca technicians providing some hilarious stories to match those of the singers.

Weenie had spoken from time to time of hearing noises on the roof of the apartment and one night she came from her room vowing she'd seen a face at her window. We were all laughing about her preoccupation with nocturnal noises, both at the villa and there in Rome, when suddenly Russ called out from his terrace across the very narrow street: 'There's a man on your roof!' This resulted in much scuffling both on the roof and inside the apartment, with us all trying to see what was going on, until Russ said that whoever it was had disappeared. Someone had called the police, who searched and went away, doubtless thinking we were crazy. Then we had to hunt right through every room before we felt secure, opening all doors and cupboards. Unfortunately, when we did this in Franco's studio-workroom we all took fright at the draped dressmaker's dummy, lit by moonlight, and when Ric quickly opened a cupboard door there, out fell a heavy old wooden wash-board – right on Weenie's big toe, leaving her with a very nasty and most uncomfortable injury. We never found anybody, but Franco was convinced he knew who it had been.

✧ 2 ✧

RELUCTANTLY WE LEFT Rome and went back to London, where I was to begin recording Handel's *Messiah* in Kingsway Hall. Sir Adrian Boult was conducting the London Symphony Orchestra and the other soloists were Grace Bumbry, Kenneth McKellar and David Ward – these last two old friends from the Royal College of Music Opera School days. There were discussions about appoggiature and variants and whether or not to use them. I believe I was the only noticeable executant. Wilkie opined: 'I like Handel as Handel wrote it!'

Although I had managed to finish both recordings in Rome, there seemed to be some infection remaining in my throat and chest so, as well as the *Messiah* sessions, there were visits to Ivor Griffiths, hairdressers, interviews, long sittings for publicity photographs for Decca and the occasional quiet meal with friends. A hectic ten days – and then off to Edinburgh in the car over the weekend for performances of *Lucia di Lammermoor* at the Festival with the Covent Garden Company. We had two or three days of short rehearsals and opened on August 25.

Lord Harewood was the Director of the Edinburgh Festival during this period and there were some splendid social functions and outings arranged. I was feeling quite tired but managed, at least, to visit Kirkliston Parish Church and the vault where Janet Dalrymple Dunbar's remains are buried. It is said that the legend surrounding her death inspired Sir Walter Scott's *The Bride of Lammermoor*.

As well as the five projected *Lucia* performances I did a short recital for the BBC with Richard and a concert with the English Chamber Orchestra in the Usher Hall.

Between the third and fourth performances of the opera I was persuaded to attend the spectacular Edinburgh Tattoo against my better judgement. This is held out of doors at the Castle. It was a very raw, humid night for the end of the summer and I was still fighting the bug or virus I'd picked up in Rome, as well as feeling tired. Although it had been considered as a pleasant night off with great entertainment, it had disastrous effects. Presumably the infection was given a new lease of life, and by the night before the fourth *Lucia* I knew I couldn't possibly sing it – and probably not the last one either.

I had developed an abscess in both ears and was in a great deal of pain. There was nothing to be done but stay in bed and wait for the inflammation to subside. Richard had the unenviable task of advising Sir David Webster that he would need a substitute Lucia for the last two shows.

In fact, the immediate performance was cancelled and a performance of *Il Barbiere di Siviglia* substituted.

More chaos was to follow, as when I finally travelled to London and saw Ivor Griffiths he forbade me to go on to San Francisco, where I was due to open their opera season on September 15 – again with *Lucia*. Fortunately there were eight days between the first and second performances there, by which time I was able to cope with the long flight to the West Coast and begin not only our long-term association with the San Francisco Opera and its General Director, Kurt Herbert Adler, but our fondness for and enjoyment of California. Kurt had been able to engage Anna Moffo for his opening but, to the day he died, he claimed I owed him one San Francisco Opera Season Opening Night.

I only sang one performance on September 23 before going on a recital tour with Richard. Further performances with the Company were scheduled for the end of October and early November.

On the twenty-fourth we flew to Lawrence, Kansas, for a recital on the twenty-fifth at the University of Kansas, followed on the twenty-eighth by one in the Joslyn Art Museum in Omaha, Nebraska. This was for the Tuesday Musical Club concert series – although it was given on a Thursday. On we travelled to Atlanta, Georgia, then to Syracuse to open their seventy-second season of 'Civic Morning Musicals' in Lincoln Auditorium of Central High School – at 8.20 on Monday evening, October 2. On the fourth we gave the final recital of that particular tour at the University of Connecticut at Stoors. Here, as on some of the other occasions, Richard and I decided to substitute the *Lucia* Mad Scene for 'Lo, here the gentle lark', feeling the audience rather expected an operatic piece – and they loved it.

On this tour we had met many devoted concert- and opera-goers, some of whom became ardent fans and some lasting friends whom we looked forward to seeing whenever we revisited their home towns. Their kindness and hospitality meant a great deal to both of us when we had such a gruelling schedule.

As well as Richard accompanying all the recitals he was fast becoming recognised as my 'manager', if not in the sense of an agent certainly as the person to consult over immediate details and problems on tour. Without him to liaise between our European and American agents, to suggest and agree on repertoire and fees with the various opera house and concert directors, our affairs would have been in a sorry state. With him there I never had to enter into the discussions over future plans alone – if at all – and it left me free to concentrate on the work in hand. He was certainly never at a loss to propose a work if nothing interesting had been put forward. Mrs Colbert was frequently disconcerted by his combined shrewdness and readiness to revive a long-neglected opera. On one occasion a little later Maurice Rosengarten (with whom Ric was discussing our Decca contracts) asked: 'Where did you get your business sense, Mr Bonynge? You're a musician, and you're *not* Jewish!'

From Connecticut we went to New York, staying at the old Navarro Hotel on Central Park South for the few days it took to perform with Musica Aeterna, conducted by Frederic Waldman at the Metropolitan Museum of Art on October 7. I sang three arias from *Alcina* – giving them (according to the *New York Times* critic) 'electrifying immediacy'.

We travelled to Chicago and attended a cocktail party with Carol Fox, the General Manager of the Lyric Opera of Chicago, held in the apartment of Mr and Mrs Nathan Cummings and were stunned by their collection of Impressionist paintings, learning there were bigger and better in their home out of town. We had met Nate Cummings in Paris, introduced by Alicia Markova.

There was not much time for rehearsal and the Lyric Opera's production, including the sets and costumes, was Zeffirelli's from Palermo. There were to be three performances and for the first two my Edgardo was Richard Tucker (soon to be my first Edgardo at the Metropolitan Opera), with Carlo Bergonzi singing the third. Both of these splendid tenors were to become regular partners. I knew the Met was scheduled for the end of November and was embarrassed when Dick Pearlman (Zeffirelli's assistant) went through the moves of our first scene together saying to Richard Tucker 'Miss Sutherland moves here', then 'Miss Sutherland sits there' and 'Miss Sutherland moves quickly over here'. I thought it was a bit much telling the top tenor at the Met what I was doing all the time and finally said to Dick Pearlman: 'Yes, I do as you say, but it's Mr Zeffirelli who *wants* me to be wherever you've said.' I felt Richard Tucker's attitude towards me change immediately.

The mother and sister of President Kennedy were present at the opening performance on October 14, and the big annual fund-raising Opera Ball was held in the Grand Ballroom of the Conrad Hilton Hotel after its conclusion. I was loaned a sapphire to wear that had belonged to Catherine the Great. The reviews were somewhat condescending, implying they expected more, and were critical of the public for their evident enjoyment of the piece.

Back in Manhattan there were various meetings – with a costume designer, lunch with *Life* magazine, a luncheon with the *Bell Telephone Hour* direction – all nobly attended by Richard to try and give me a rest from speaking. I found the incessant talking, especially in crowded restaurants, very taxing and let Richard answer as many of the questions as possible. He was much more articulate about musical matters anyway.

On the evening of October 22 we must have travelled to Worcester, Massachusetts where I rehearsed and sang in a concert the following day with the Detroit Symphony Orchestra, conducted by the venerable Frenchman Paul Paray. This was the opening concert of the hundred and second Worcester Music Festival and there was something of a mix-up over the parts provided for the orchestra, only those for the cabaletta to the Sleep-walking Scene of *La Sonnambula* having arrived. I had planned to sing the whole of this scene with its moving slow section 'Ah, non credea mirarti' as my appearance in the first half of the concert, or the Mad Scene from *Lucia*. Somehow both big scenes were printed on the programme, with 'Ah, fors'è lui' and its cabaletta correctly placed in the second half. As the Mad Scene parts were complete it was decided I sing that in the first half, the *Traviata* as printed and the cabaletta of the Sleep-walking Scene as an encore, if need be.

Unfortunately, the orchestral players' music had been arranged on their stands strictly according to the printed programme, so when Maestro Paray conducted the opening of the *Lucia* there was consternation, confusion and cacophony from the musicians who had *La Sonnambula* in front of them. It was very quickly corrected and the concert was claimed by the press to have thrilled the Festival audience, delighted by the inclusion of the 'encore'.

From Worcester it was back to San Francisco, where there was one performance of *Lucia* on October 25 as a 'brush-up' before going to Los Angeles and San Diego with the Company. Maestro Molinari-Pradelli was making very heavy weather of the opera for everyone and we were relieved to discover he was not conducting my Met début as originally planned. Because of the uncertainty of there being a season at the Metropolitan that year due to Union problems, Molinari-Pradelli had been released from his contract and accepted other engagements.

It was at this stage that Silvio Varviso (who was also conducting with the San Francisco Opera, both *Le Nozze di Figaro* and *Rigoletto*) was suggested and engaged for the Met performances, which delighted all of us. We had met and enjoyed each other's company, and looked forward to being in New York together. Albert Goldberg in the *Los Angeles Times* rounded off his eulogy on the Sutherland voice with a cute line: '... Any other singer who attempts *Lucia* in Miss Sutherland's day is in for a bad time: this is it.'

Although the Shrine Auditorium in Los Angeles where the San Francisco Opera played was a huge and somewhat decrepit theatre, in a not too chic part of the city, I loved singing there. The acoustics reminded me of the Albert Hall – there was that 'ring' to the sound, which you felt was suspended on the air after you had moved on to the next phrase. It was here that I was delighted to receive a huge bouquet of red and white roses and a lovely note from Miliza Korjus whom Ric and I had adored in the film *The Great Waltz*. There was also a telegram from Galli-Curci wishing us continued success. Miliza became a fan and a regular correspondent, sending me jars of her special 'rejuvenating face-cream'. It did not do too much for me!

We went back to San Francisco, where we did a recital in the Opera House on my birthday, November 7.

During these first trips to California we made some good friends who have been particularly hospitable to us over the ensuing thirty-odd years. It has made our return visits such a pleasure and given us the opportunity to enjoy a more relaxed atmosphere, staying in their homes and visiting many of the West Coast beauty spots with them on our free days.

More *Lucia* performances followed in Dallas on November 16 and 18, with Renato Cioni again as Edgardo; Enrico was sung by Ettore Bastianini, Raimondo by Nicola Zaccaria. The role of Arturo was sung by Placido Domingo, 'a splendid young Mexican'. The audience of over 4000 went wild with delight each night. Chairs had to be placed at the rear of the first floor to accommodate the overflow – some sixty-five over the capacity of the hall.

Much as we had enjoyed our third stay in Dallas in a year we were anxious to get back to New York, as Adam was arriving there with Weenie from London. We were to be in and around the city for some five weeks and so, not having seen him since the summer, were happy to be able to spend a little time together, even if involved in rehearsals and performances. Adam was so excited to be flying on such a large plane that Weenie vows he talked almost all the way.

The day after his arrival, Richard and I had a recital at Rutgers University in New Jersey so we travelled there by limousine in the early evening and back after the concert. Rehearsals for the Metropolitan Opera début had already begun and Adam was thrilled to attend the Dress Rehearsal on November 24. During the introduction to the aria of Raimondo preceding the Mad Scene he remarked in a very audible stage whisper, with great relish: 'Now she's cutting him up!' He may have been only five years old, but he knew what was going on in that opera.

The great night of Sunday, November 26, 1961 finally arrived. The performance was a non-subscription benefit for the Metropolitan Opera Guild. The sets were very old and worn, likewise the costumes, having been designed in 1942 and done considerable service. I had, however, brought my own costumes from Covent Garden so felt very comfortable and at home in them, in spite of the great emotional thrill of walking in the footsteps of so many operatic 'greats' on the stage of the old Met.

When I appeared at the beginning of the second scene of the opera I was apparently cheered for a full three minutes before I had sung a note. Each item was greeted with an extended ovation, with a five-minute break in the middle of the Mad Scene and such continued applause at the end of it that there was a great delay in commencing the last scene. I understand the lights were raised and lowered several times, likewise the baton of Silvio Varviso. The ovation went on for twenty minutes, with the audience having risen to its feet *en masse*, cheering and stamping. I had experienced a few good audience reactions but this one beat them all. It was like the fans of a favoured team at a football match and somewhat frightening. It was also quite something to live up to.

I already had a self-appointed 'bodyguard' in Martin Waldron and I needed him that night. Martin was an actor and possessed a very commanding and carrying voice which brooked no argument from over-zealous fans and autograph hunters. He was well known backstage at the Met as a regular opera-goer and also for his handling of the dressing-room traffic after the performances of that splendid star Zinka Milanov, whom he greatly admired. My dresser, Jenny, had assured me that Martin was 'a real gentleman'. He had previously asked if he might be of any help and volunteered to regulate the flow of visitors to my room – doing so for the next twenty-five years or more. He has been a true, much-loved friend to all of us.

When we finally managed to leave the theatre, we went to Geri Souvaine's apartment on Central Park West, where she had another of her splendid parties. There were so many gatecrashers that night that Geri was standing by the maid and butler in the hall asking: 'Who are *you*? I didn't invite you – I don't *know* you!' In spite of there being a few 'ring-ins' the party was wonderful. Birgit Nilsson, Regina Resnik, John Brownlee, Robert Merrill, Fredric March, Jennie Tourel, Giovanni Martinelli, Anya Dorfman, other members of the evening's cast and Met administration, including that mine of operatic information Francis Robinson, were all there.

Also present was Silvio Varviso who, in spite of his success that evening, was moaning that his waistcoat button had flown off during the performance and every time he raised his arms the stiff waistcoat popped apart, giving him the problem of holding it down and conducting at the same time. 'Would this happen to me in a provincial town? No. It had to be at the Met – my début, too!' he wailed.

The reviews were legion, with glowing headlines, each one more rapturous than the last:

DIVA'S DÉBUT TAKES MET BY STORM

JOAN CONQUERS MET — AND NY

SUTHERLAND STOPS THE SHOW

JOAN SUTHERLAND'S MET DÉBUT TEASES MEMORY: MAYBE NOTHING EVER LIKE IT

GREATEST OVATION IN 77 YEARS — NY WILD OVER JOAN SUTHERLAND

In the *New York Times* of November 27 Harold C. Schonberg wrote:

... Old timers in the press room of the Metropolitan Opera could not remember an equivalent reception. The audience refused to let the final scene continue, and carried on with yells and cheers.

Well it might. It would take a long memory to recall a similarly finished, virtuosic piece of singing in *Lucia* and Miss Sutherland's work last night, on the occasion of her Metropolitan Opera début, upheld her reputation as the greatest singing technician before the public.

... Her well-articulated trills, the precision of her scales, the security in her upper range and in addition, the good size of her voice were a throwback to a style of singing that is supposed to be extinct.

The quality of her voice is one of extreme beauty. Some have called it cool, and it is true that it is produced with very little vibrato. This listener does not find it cool at all. It is silvery, delicately colored and capable of extraordinary nuance. In addition, the voice has body. In coloratura it does not thin out but is produced in a full-throated manner. That, too, is something she has in common with singers of a preceding generation, singers who would sing Lucia one night, Donna Anna a few nights later, perhaps Leonora or Elsa after that.

... One thing might be added: the taste with which Miss Sutherland sings. She is not a stunt singer, and she does not throw in high notes on no provocation. She phrases quite elegantly, and with all her heart she tries to use her voice to bring out the musical meaning. In short, at last we have a great coloratura soprano.

Elsa Maxwell wrote a two-and-a-half-column eulogy about the night in her 'Mid-Week Memo' and was hostess at a dinner party at which myself and my 'handsome husband Ricky' shared the honours with Mayor Wagner.

At the second performance of *Lucia* there were several cast changes. Jan Peerce sang Edgardo, Frank Guarrera (who had sung in *L'Elisir d'Amore* the same afternoon and *Turandot* the previous night!) replaced Lorenzo Testi as Enrico, and Bonaldo Giaiotti sang Raimondo. It was thrilling to sing with both Jan and Richard during my first appearances at the Met, having heard them so much on recordings.

With this and all the other grand reviews the monthly magazines, radio, TV – every journalist in town wanted a personal interview, not forgetting the *Ed Sullivan Show* and *Bell Telephone Hour* both wanting appearances. But we managed to take Adam for a trip with us to F. A. O. Schwarz, the Zoo or skating in Central Park and to see the wonderful Christmas window displays.

We couldn't have imagined the hectic schedule of the month between the Met début and Christmas. As well as the remaining performances of *Lucia* between December 2 and 21 there were recitals at Princeton University, New Jersey, on November 28, Constitution Hall in Washington DC on December 11 and Great Neck, New York, on December 13. Added to those dates were the rehearsals for *La Sonnambula* with the American Opera Society, performances being given in Carnegie Hall on December 5 and at the Academy of Music in Philadelphia on the seventeenth.

The critics again remarked on the quality of the voice – 'the smooth, effortless modulated tone that is as beautiful as anything that is to be heard today,' said Harold Schonberg in the *New York Times*. He also spoke of the 'trills, turns and a dizzy variety of flawlessly performed pyrotechnics. The audience, of course, went wild,' he said.

For all the out-of-town dates except Washington we travelled by limousine, going back to New York after the concert to be ready for the following day's appointments – and there were plenty. Fittings for new concert gowns, for costumes for the *Bell Telephone Hour*, photographic sessions for both Richard and myself for Decca, the agents and the Met, rehearsals for the two TV shows, more interviews, trips to my hairdresser Adolfo, a record signing organised by Decca (London Records) at Schirmer's big store – the first of many such efforts – and the various luncheons and dinners with friends and colleagues like Jennie Tourel, Regina Resnik, Dudley Toller Bond from London Records and his wife Nancy, Bert Shevelove, who was directing the *Bell Telephone Hour*, and as much time as possible spent with Adam. The diary for those weeks resembles a maze.

We took the train to Washington and again stayed with the Australian Ambassador and his wife, Sir Howard and Lady Beale. Our recital was given to a packed house of 3800 and elicited tumultuous applause and further rave reviews. Many top members of the Presidential staff and Commonwealth Diplomatic Corps were present and also attended a large supper party given afterwards at the residence. The last guests left about 1 a.m. and an hour later we were on a train back to New York. It was while helping to regulate the flow of autograph hunters at the record-signing session over the lunch-hour of the following day that Weenie became incensed at the young fans greeting me like an old friend and calling me by my christian name. She felt this was impertinent and started to refer to me as 'the PD' (prima donna) instead of calling me Joan. Her ploy worked (although I never liked the nickname) and some of those then teenagers use the term to this day! I actually retaliated by calling Weenie my PD – Pet Dragon – as she tried to keep all and sundry at bay and chased me to sign letters and photographs.

With all the varied work-load Ric and Weenie were a tower of strength. He was able to attend meetings on my behalf with Mrs Colbert concerning future engagements in the United States, fitting them in to the forthcoming European dates. He appeared on the intermission show, such an important feature of the Metropolitan Opera's Saturday matinée broadcasts, organised by Geri Souvaine. He provided the various conductors with copies of my variants and cadenzas, even 'talking through' my arias with the musical directors of the big TV shows. These and many other responsibilities were handled perfectly by him, whilst Weenie did her best to keep the diary straight and not to double-book appointments. She also accompanied me if I had time to go shopping to help ward off the autograph hunters. It was amazing how many people on the busy New York streets, heightened by the frenzied Christmas rush, approached me. There had been so much in the newspapers and on television that heads turned as I passed, very often being heard to say 'That's Joan Sutherland!' or they'd stop and say, 'Aren't you Joan Sutherland?'

Weenie also came with me to the long rehearsal sessions for the *Bell Telephone Hour* and the *Ed Sullivan Show*. I performed one of each live and taped one of each for viewing early in 1962. During one of the *Ed Sullivan Shows* we got into the elevator to go down to the studio from my dressing-room, I in all my concert finery, to be greeted by a very friendly chimpanzee, also part of the show. He promptly picked up my hand and kissed it – and my arm to the elbow – his owner looking on with approval.

There were to have been three performances of *Beatrice di Tenda* at the San Carlo Opera House in Naples on December 26, 28 and 30. Fortuitously, these were postponed until the following May so, after the final *Lucia* in New York, Richard and I went back to London to spend a quiet Christmas with Auntie Blos. Adam and Weenie stayed on in Westchester for a few days, returning between Christmas and New Year, so we all celebrated the beginning of 1962 together.

✧ 3 ✧

THE SCHEDULE DEMANDS of those years of 1960 and 1961, together with that of 1962, became the basis of our lives for the next thirty years. The engagements were different, the cities and countries varied but the day-to-day planning revolved around the current rehearsals and performances and those in the immediate future – with bookings completely covering a period of three years in advance. We had to admit that taking Adam with us, even if he was on school holidays, was not the best for him or us. A steady routine of school with his friends at the Lycée and Ruthli to look after him was what pleased him most. But the apartment was too small for all of us.

While out walking that January in Cornwall Gardens with Adam riding his tricycle we noticed one of the old houses for sale – number 36. It had been neglected and used as a rooming house we were told by the estate agents when enquiring the following day, although it was very sound structurally. When we visited it Richard was in raptures and tried to keep his enthusiasm from the agent, making hasty asides to me regarding all its possibilities, including the fact that the huge first-floor salon was intact, except for an easily removable partition. That would be the music room. I was certainly interested, but just having made the move to a still half-decorated villa on Lake Maggiore and with all the forthcoming engagements, I found the prospect of coping with the restoration and decoration of a large mid-Victorian six-storey house daunting, to say the least. 'Don't you worry about it, dear,' said Ric. 'I'll organise everything, and you'll only have to give your approval. We'll get a good decorator who knows a trusty firm of builders and Ruthli can keep an eye on them all when we're away.'

I wasn't really convinced, but we needed the space and, with Auntie Blos, Weenie, Adam and ourselves to look after, Ruthli would have to have someone else to help. So the purchase was made and the work (which took much longer than expected) begun. We also engaged another au pair girl, this time Gudrun Helm from Germany, the Wagnerian name being part of the attraction. We were again lucky, 'Gudi' fitting in with our rather chaotic life, as well as being another good cook and very adept with decorative effects.

We all agreed that the big house with just two young women, a boy and an eighty-four-year-old rattling around in it if we were on tour was too much of a responsibility for Gudi and Udi. Margreta and Ike Elkins were finding their current apartment a bit small and it was decided that they would move into the basement of number 36 as soon as it was possible, decorating as they wanted. Traumas with the decorators there might be, but at least Greta and Ike would be there to help the two German-speaking girls when the problems arose.

While all this was being organised I had been rehearsing the Queen of the Night in Mozart's *Die Zauberflöte* at Covent Garden, performances being on January 4, 6 and 8 with Otto Klemperer conducting. He was ill and his beat was very slow and irregular – so much so that the orchestra leader, Charles Taylor, said to me: 'Don't watch him, Joan dear! You just go and we'll be with you!' Comforting up to a point, but I was very far upstage and it wasn't always easy to hear the orchestra once I started singing. There was little or no amplification used on stage in those days.

The afternoon of the opening night arrived and I was resting on my bed, alone in the apartment with Auntie Blos. Ruthli was picking Adam up from school and Richard was going over the house we were buying further up the square with the builders. Suddenly Auntie Blos burst into my room saying her bed was on fire. She had been putting her clothes in order to go to the performance and couldn't find her shoes. She thought they might have been kicked under the bed and, not finding a torch, she lit a candle to help her see, the hessian covering the under part of the divan base immediately catching fire. I raced out to her room and tried to remove the mattress, turn the base over and beat out the small blaze with a wet towel. But my aunt grabbed me with such a strong grip I couldn't move. She was afraid my flimsy long dressing-gown would catch alight. I was amazed how strong she was and I must have been twice her size.

At this point Adam and Udi came back and I asked Udi to bring me a bucket of water and to phone the fire brigade. This she did and, unfortunately as it turned out, I threw the water under the bed to dowse the flames, following it with another bucketful. The smoke from the still smouldering fibres was choking, and my eyes were stinging. I threw open the window, letting in the damp and freezing January air, at that moment hearing the fire engines. Seven men, all in muddy Wellington boots and dripping wet rain capes, trooped into the apartment over my newly laid gold Wilton carpet. That was the last straw. I retreated to the front room but the smoke had permeated everything. After the very kindly firemen left and I had surveyed the damage and wrecked carpeting I accepted the invitation of our new overhead neighbour to escape the smoke and have a bath and a cup of tea upstairs. Auntie Blos, nothing daunted, rescued her sodden shoes. She wasn't going to miss the opera.

Quite apart from the effect of the drama of the afternoon on my own performance, the production of *Die Zauberflöte* was not greeted with much enthusiasm. The critics, particularly Arthur Jacobs, complained that Klemperer had been allowed too much say in its presentation. Not only did he conduct the opera but produced it as well, in scenery and costumes by Georg Eisler, who was chosen by him. Because of the 'unimaginativeness of some heavily painted settings' and 'bleak', 'prosaic', 'drab' costumes, along with Klemperer's slow tempi, and raised seat prices (£3.17s.6d maximum) 'the audience reacted with distinctly modified raptures'. I apparently 'did well without scintillating'. It was, however, reported in the *Daily Mirror* that the three-guinea seats for the opera were selling at twenty-five guineas on the black market.

At the completion of the three performances at the Garden, Weenie and I went to Palermo, where I was to sing three performances of *Lucia*, leaving Ric in London to cope with the renovation of Number 36 as the house became known. He was also working with several singers, including the Australians Jon Weaving, Margaret Nisbett and Elizabeth Fretwell whom he coached as Violetta and Leonora (*Trovatore*).

After the first rehearsal at the Massimo in Palermo the chorus and stage hands went on strike, demanding a longer working year. The result was that Weenie and I had a short holiday break in a sunny climate, enjoying little trips about the city and surrounding countryside with Peter John Hall, also unable to work because of the strike. Ultimately I did do one *Lucia*, having been fortunate enough to hear the superb Mario del Monaco singing at the Massimo one of his last performances of the role of Otello.

Weenie and I then flew to Rome, where we met Richard. He was to make his début as a conductor on January 25, 1962. A concert had been arranged by the Accademia Filarmonica Romana under the artistic direction of Massimo Bogianckino, and the organisers had suggested that, as Richard knew the repertoire I was to sing so well, he conduct the Rome Radio Orchestra. It was a magnificent opportunity for him and he grasped it, having a very good success with several pieces the Roman orchestra was not at all accustomed to playing. They comprised a large Handel group with the *Water Music* suite as an opener, together with the *Alcina* suite of dances, 'Ah, Ruggiero, crudel' and 'Ombre pallide', followed by 'Tornami a vagheggiar'. We also did the Mad Scenes from *I Puritani* and *Hamlet*. There was such prolonged applause that Richard accompanied me at the piano in three encore numbers. He must have been incredibly nervous but he finally was doing as he had always wished, made a very favourable impression and has gone on conducting from that day with increasing success.

From Rome we flew to Barcelona where there were three more *Lucia* performances with the very young Jaime Aragall making his début as Arturo.

It was in Barcelona that I was given a small replica of the Madonna of Montserrat by my dresser and told to give her a flower before each performance to ensure my success on that occasion. I was feeling the strain of the constant journeys and exposure to the press and public and she assured me that placing a rose by the tiny effigy would make all the difference. Whether she was right or not I'll never know but Weenie, and after she had left us one or other of the fans, always provided 'a rose for the Madonna', brought or sent to my dressing-room before each performance. I must say, I didn't have to cancel often and the Madonna was an essential part of my 'theatre bag' packing thereafter.

On February 4 we flew to Milan where, after minimal rehearsals, I sang five performances of *La Sonnambula* at La Scala in the beautiful sets and costumes of Piero Tosi. It had been produced initially by Luchino Visconti in 1955 for Maria Callas with Bernstein conducting. Antonino Votto conducted and Alfredo Kraus sang Elvino.

Richard returned to London after the second performance. It was Adam's birthday that week, as well as there being planned meetings with Decca and some agents. Weenie and I enjoyed, among other things, a dinner with Renato Cioni and his family from Elba, partaking of their home-made wine – heady, to say the least – and I sang the remaining *Sonnambulas*.

On February 21 Weenie and I left Milan for Brussels, where we were greeted by members of the police organisation (for whom I was doing a concert) with a motor-cycle escort to Antwerp, the concert to take place in the Queen Elisabeth Hall of the Zoological Gardens there two days later. On the way we visited Rubens's house and were entertained by several police Commissars and their wives in a hotchpotch of French, Flemish and very basic English, made more difficult by the fact that both of us had been trying to cope with Italian and, before that, Spanish, neither of us being great linguists.

Alberto Erede was conducting the Belgian Radio Orchestra. Unfortunately, as I walked on to the platform at the concert my foot slipped on the highly polished floor and, to stop myself measuring my length there, I used my rear foot as a brake, jarring my spine very badly and causing severe pain to my lower back. I managed to sing the programme, *Lucia* and *Hamlet* Mad Scenes and 'Ah, fors'è lui', but the supporting of the breath, particularly when singing in the high register of the voice, created problems of excruciating spasmodic pain. I found I had to hold myself in a particularly stiff way and sitting down was almost unbearable.

Somehow I got through the usual aftermath of curtain calls and congratulations, then entertainment to supper, although I was very preoccupied as to what could be done to ease my pain. I had a train journey to Amsterdam the following morning and a concert there the day after. The packing was a particular problem for me as I have always done it myself so that no one else was to blame for leaving anything behind, also ensuring that my gowns and dresses were folded a certain way to avoid undue creasing.

The journey was a nightmare and I stood most of the way – fortunately not that far. When we arrived at the hotel in Amsterdam the two Dutch agents were very concerned – for me, rather than the concert they'd arranged. They brought a doctor from Utrecht who administered an injection, but when I took a deep breath at the rehearsal I nearly screamed a top G sharp! A charming orthopaedic doctor was brought to the hotel but the verdict was I would need a thorough examination with X-rays. This would take time – but I had a concert that night and didn't want to disappoint. So I sang, firmly wrapped in a maternity binder. This helped, but the pain was still excruciating.

It was my first appearance in the Concertgebouw and Erede again conducted. He was very sympathetic and helped me as much as possible to get through a very exacting programme. I sang 'Ombre pallide' from *Alcina*, 'Son vergin vezzosa' from *I Puritani*, 'Ah, fors'è lui' from *La Traviata* and the Mad Scene from *Lucia*. In spite of my problem the audience went wild and I was asked when would I sing in an opera in Holland by a bevy of new fans.

Weenie got me back to London, my having stood in the plane most of the way. I was longing to collapse into bed – I hadn't slept for four nights, was in constant pain and feared any sudden movement or jerk. Sitting and lying down were worse than standing but I had to get some sleep, as I was faced with a hideously full rehearsal and performance schedule over the next six weeks.

Fortunately, Ivor Griffiths sent me immediately to Mr Tucker, a great orthopaedic surgeon, who gently manipulated my back into a more normal position and had me measured for a corset which we ultimately called my 'armour'. He continued to see me every second day between rehearsals and the massage and the steel-boned surgical corset helped. But I was assured by him that the problem was a broken disc near the base of the spine which caused the spinal column to tilt like the leaning tower of Pisa, pinching the spinal cord as a result. He warned me he could ease the pain with manipulation but that I would have to live with the problem and wear the corset for a couple of years, when the back might stabilise to a certain extent. He could operate and fuse the spine but he said he didn't want to do it unless I couldn't put up with learning to live with it, rounding off his diagnosis with the fact that the operation wasn't always a success.

So, with his sound advice of 'no jerky movements and no falls' I continued rehearsals at Covent Garden for *Alcina* each morning and *La Traviata* every afternoon. The production of *Alcina* was Zeffirelli's, brought from Venice via Dallas, and couldn't have been a better vehicle to try out my restricting support, movement consisting mainly of flowing gestures and the long arias demanding vocal agility rather than great visual histrionics. It was staged very much as an eighteenth-century masque and once I had managed to rise from my throne I could safely stand and walk. The main problem was still the breath support, but I really was learning to live with it.

The *Traviata* rehearsals were a bit more testing. Norman Ayrton was re-directing the old Fedorovitch production – for its last appearances, I believe – and Violetta couldn't be quite so unbending and aloof as the enchantress Alcina. However, we progressed with both characters and I hope managed to make them come alive.

The critics were somewhat severe about Zeffirelli's production of *Alcina*, claiming that it was wrong to present it as a masque as it limited the visual drama too much. They seemed to want to forget he had devised it as an entertainment presented by members of the household of a wealthy nobleman for his family and friends in the grand hall of his palace, and that it was made for the stage – and audience – of La Fenice in Venice. It was a 'first' with the Italian public and Franco's conception and realisation of the piece in that setting had a great deal to do with its success in Italy and the continuing revival of similar works today. Many of the critics harked back to the St Pancras Town Hall production of the Handel Opera Society in 1957, a comparison which I found ludicrous. Half the problem was that the shock of the wonderful musical content of the opera had been removed by that earlier production, being the first time the wiseacres had heard it.

There were also the critics who applauded the spectacle and said it was the perfect way to present the opera. One way or the other, they agreed that there was some fine, virtuoso singing from Monica Sinclair and Margreta Elkins, as well as that 'expected' from Joan Sutherland. I was happy to have managed to sustain the performance and that fact gave me the confidence to continue to cope with the terrifying schedule.

On March 12, between the second and third Covent Garden performances of *Alcina*, we began recording the opera for Decca with Richard conducting. He was so used to attending the sessions with me that he knew the routine and felt at ease with all the technicians. He also knew the work, having prepared it with me for every presentation of it we had done, as well as accompanying the arias in recitals many times. He had chosen to start with my big scena comprising the recitative 'Ah! Ruggiero, crudel' and the aria 'Ombre pallide', followed by some orchestral interludes, and he managed famously. We had begun yet another phase of our working together and a new and far-reaching outlet for Richard's outstanding musical talents.

Because of my own heavy schedule, and availability of the other artists and orchestra involved, the recording sessions were spread over a four-week period. I didn't record again for a week, being totally occupied with final rehearsals for La Traviata and the last two performances of Alcina at Covent Garden. When we reached the final trio on the last night of the latter I was either so tired or so relieved that the run was completed that I relaxed my concentration, made a wrong entry – and threw Margreta and Monica into confusion. I brazened out the situation, evidently making it appear that *they* had made an error. They were cross.

That was on March 17. On the nineteenth the Dress Rehearsal of La Traviata was held at the Garden and we had a relaxing dinner with Russell Braddon who was writing the final pages of his book Joan Sutherland. The next morning Richard, Adam and I went to Buckingham Palace where I received the regalia of Commander of the British Empire from Her Majesty The Queen. What a thrill it was for us. We were just sorry that Mother hadn't lived to be there too. Adam was taken by an equerry to watch the band playing and I wonder if he realised how privileged he was to attend the ceremony.

The opening night of La Traviata was on March 21 – and Richard was not present for the first time in years. He was busy recording Alcina at Walthamstow, where sessions had resumed for him the night before. Norman Ayrton had rehearsed us tirelessly within the old Fedorovitch sets and, with Alberto Erede conducting, the performance went very well indeed.

Neatly slotted in between the Traviatas were the Alcina recording sessions it was essential for me to attend. Fortunately there was only the one trio involving Ruggiero and Bradamante, and the recitatives without full orchestral accompaniment were done at separate sessions. It was a wonderful cast and we had quite a few laughs between takes. Teresa Berganza was Ruggiero, Monica Sinclair sang Bradamante, Graziella Sciutti was Morgana, Luigi Alva sang the role of Oronte, Ezio Flagello was Melisso and Mirella Freni sang the part of the boy Oberto.

We had been booked to do a concert tour to Australia from June 1 until August 18 for the ABC some years previously. With my back in its unstable condition it was impossible to undertake the long trip by air and then the many flights between the state capitals, rehearsing and performing all the time. Mr Tucker insisted that I remain within reasonable range of his treatment and so, very reluctantly, we cancelled the tour. I remember being driven back into London from one of the recording sessions (on March 27) and reading on the news placards:

JOAN SUTHERLAND CRIPPLED

The news of the cancellation had been published in Australia and picked up by the London press. I had such trouble trying to explain that the problem would be controlled and at the moment, with the continuing treatment, the doctor was very hopeful. He did not want me to stop singing. On the contrary, he wanted me to be as mobile as possible but that long trip of nearly thirty hours on a plane was, in his opinion, out of the question. It was most upsetting feeling that people, particularly in Australia, couldn't understand why I could go on singing in Europe but not go out and sing for them.

But go on I did – with a concert presented by Victor Hochhauser in the Royal Albert Hall on April 1. The audience of close on 7000 applauded and shouted 'Brava', as relieved as I was to hear proof that I intended to sing on in spite of the back problem. The press voiced their surprise and pleasure that the concert had been such a success, with headlines such as

JOAN IN RADIANT VOICE

MISS SUTHERLAND'S NIGHT OF TRIUMPH

THE ONE WORD FOR IT — PERFECTION

THUNDEROUS OVATION FOR SINGER

HOMAGE TO LA STUPENDA

These were followed by glowing accounts of the singing and good wishes and hopes for a long-continued career. We had tried to tone down the exaggerated reports of retirement and this concert was proof that nothing was further from my mind.

Sympathetic mail poured in, some offering advice and 'cures'. There was even one from an American music student suggesting I was using my voice incorrectly and should do this and that to rectify my errors or I would certainly lose it within the year. Somehow Weenie and I managed to answer them all – eventually.

❖ 4 ❖

NUMBER 36 CORNWALL Gardens was slowly being refurbished but we had to leave for Milan on April 10 to do four more *La Sonnambula* performances at La Scala. Adam was able to come to the matinée on the fifteenth as he was on Easter holidays from the Lycée and he went with Richard, Fiona and Ruthli to see the opera. We all went back to Rocca Bella in the car afterwards and I was trying to persuade Adam to have a sleep on the way, saying I was tired and so must he be. Quick as a flash he responded: 'You shouldn't be tired. You've been sleeping all evening!' This caused such laughter that coming out of Lugano we suddenly found ourselves on the railway tracks of the goods yard instead of on the road.

We shuttled back and forth between the villa and Milan, spending the Easter weekend and a few days after the last *Sonnambula* in the house, enjoying the spring weather and making the place more lived in.

Richard and I went to Naples, where I sketchily rehearsed and did two performances of Bellini's *Beatrice di Tenda* at the San Carlo on May 4 and 6 to close their season. The conductor was Nicola Rescigno, with whom I had sung the opera making my New York début, as well as so many other opera performances. Margreta Elkins sang Agnese, Renato Cioni Orombello and Mario Zanasi Filippo. It was at one of these performances that, during the curtain calls, the tapes of my white cotton underskirt snapped and I was hobbled by it around my ankles. Unable to walk off thus, I stepped out of it and Renato gallantly picked it up, waved it at the audience and carried it off for me.

The public and critics enjoyed the presentation of the opera immensely, Alfredo Parente of *Il Mattino* remarking that one of the most surprising things was the way in which this singer 'who was not European, not Latin, not Italian understood and executed the role of Beatrice so naturally in the true Bellini style'. He also said, 'The warmth of the middle of the voice, the limpidity and stupendous colour of the high register, intact, without a sign of breathiness or force in the "sopracuti" emitted with the naturalness of a flowing fountain – these are the natural attributes which make the voice of la Sutherland of all

139

sopranos, the organ probably the most complete of our time.' Such a thrill to sing in that beautiful theatre.

We returned to Milan after the Naples run for rehearsals for *Gli Ugonotti* (*Les Huguenots*). It was a pleasantly relaxed period as my part as Queen Marguerite was quite short and concentrated mostly in Act 1, Scene II, with an entrance in Act 2 – on horseback! The opera was done in four acts at La Scala, omitting the fifth. We had luncheon dates with our friends from Genoa, Wally Toscanini, Gladys Swarthout and her husband (the Chapmans) and Amy Shuard, that stalwart English soprano. I also had fittings for costumes and for some personal clothes from the couturier Selia.

There were some difficult ensemble scenes to organise in the opera, so sometimes the rehearsal schedule would be delayed. I didn't mind a bit and would sit in the theatre enthralled and excited by the singing of the splendid male cast. The producer was Franco Enriquez with whom I had worked before and Ricky and I had a friendly relationship with him. The conductor was Gianandrea Gavazzeni and the designer Nicola Benois. The cast was fabulous – never to be repeated: Giorgio Tozzi, Giulietta Simionato, Wladimiro Ganzarolli, Franco Corelli, Nicolai Ghiaurov and Fiorenza Cossotto.

The production of *Gli Ugonotti* was a much-anticipated and exciting event. The opera had not been seen in Milan since 1899 and has always had the reputation of requiring 'seven stars' for the main roles. A considerable amount of the lengthy score was cut and at one point during rehearsals it seemed I would lose the beautiful duet between Raoul and Queen Marguerite – not because of its length, but because Corelli was finding the role difficult to learn in the time he'd allowed himself. Cutting the duet would reduce his anxiety. But Richard was adamant that it should stay in – and rightly so as, not only is it an interesting and lovely piece, but it would take away a good half of my role. Gavazzeni agreed that the music should be heard and I sang most of it as a solo, with Corelli standing by and making the occasional interjection.

The opera opened to great acclaim by the press and public on May 28, with five further performances, the last on June 12. Much was made of my riding a 'temperamental' horse on stage in view of my cancellation of the Australian tour. The only temperament that poor old Giorgio showed was an unwillingness to go on, needing a slap on the rump from his groom to get him going. I mounted with the aid of a block and the groom, riding side-saddle as befitted the Queen. It was rather strange singing in that elevated position and I always wondered if Giorgio would misbehave. One night I could feel great rumblings in his huge body and thought the moment had come. However, he merely broke wind – right in the face of Fiorenza Cossotto who happened to be walking behind him to take up her position in the group. I am told her face was a picture, rather green-looking.

It was a great experience to work in a cast of that calibre and Gavazzeni made the piece come alive. In spite of the many cuts it still lasted four and a half hours and it was obvious that a rearrangement of the scenes into fewer acts and intervals would be necessary if the opera was to be presented again under modern conditions in the theatre. The work from a musical point of view was a revelation, being a crucial orchestral and harmonic milestone for composers during the latter part of the nineteenth century. It influenced the works of Wagner, Verdi, Bizet, Gounod and others, and it was intriguing to discover so clearly the source of some of their inspiration.

Medea was on at La Scala between the *Ugonotti* performances and Ric and Weenie went to see Maria Callas in the opera. Weenie (who always vows she only likes mezzos and contraltos) couldn't understand the 'Callas Mania' and loathed what she heard. It has been impossible to this day to convince her that Maria had done some magical performances, so upset was she by the state of Callas's voice on that occasion.

Trips back and forth to the villa continued, with Ric going to Zurich to talk with Mr Rosengarten of Decca about our future contracts with that company. Weenie went off to Australia for a two-month break to see her ageing mother and two sisters. She had decided already she would stay with us as she found the life varied and interesting, and we looked forward to her return. At last we could snatch two full weeks at Rocca Bella and they were very relaxed. One interesting outing at that time was to Lugano, where we were entertained to lunch by the authoress Marcia Davenport.

By the last week of June we were back in London for four days for dental and medical check-ups, Adam's prize-giving ceremony and some theatre-going, including *Giselle* with Fonteyn and Nureyev. Ric also had a meeting with Sir David Webster regarding the 1963 season at the Garden.

We flew back to Milan on July 2 for fittings of my new gowns, had lunch and drove up to Rocca Bella. Margreta Elkins had come with us expecting to have a long holiday with Udi, Adam and whoever else appeared. Instead she received an urgent request to return to London and audition for the role of Octavian in *Der Rosenkavalier* for Solti. As I had further fittings in Milan on July 6 Greta came with us and flew to London from there, where she was successful in her audition. Ric and I returned to the villa for the weekend and on Tuesday, July 10 went to Milan again early to pick up my new gowns for America, go to the hairdresser and travel on to Genoa, from where we sailed to New York on the *Cristoforo Colombo* the following day.

The voyage was calm and we had a wonderful rest, keeping very much to ourselves and managing to avoid being drawn into the shipboard activities. Ric was studying the orchestral scores for his first concerts as a conductor in the United States, one with the celebrated pianist Byron Janis and the other with myself as soloist, both in the Hollywood Bowl. I was happy to relax, read a book, play the occasional game of cards or Scrabble with Ric and take our couple of walks around the deck daily.

Arrived in New York I sang my first big outdoor concert in the United States – at Lewisohn Stadium, to an audience of 20,000. It was quite an experience to be greeted by the roar of a crowd that size before having sung a note, but it was nothing to the clamour after 'Sempre libera' from *La Traviata* in the first half of the concert and the Mad Scene from *Lucia* in the second. It was very difficult to leave the platform after numerous bows, as no encores had been prepared, but finally, after the Stadium lights were turned up and the orchestra left, the appreciative audience did likewise. The conductor was Joseph Rosenstock.

Sir Eugène Goossens was to have conducted – his first Stadium concert since 1940 – but sadly he died a few weeks prior to the event. Goossens had battled on in spite of the scandal unleashed by the discovery of a large number of 'pornographic' photos in his luggage on his return to Australia from a European trip in March 1956. He was obliged to resign from both the Directorship of the NSW Conservatorium of Music and the Sydney Symphony Orchestra and was ostracised in Australia by a majority of his 'friends' and society generally. With his health and spirit shattered, he returned to England in July of 1956 and endeavoured to re-enter the European musical scene, being slowly accepted.

His work at the Eastman School of Music in forming the Symphony Orchestra in Rochester, NY, his many years with the Cincinnati Symphony and the comparatively short time spent revitalising the musical life and prospects of Sydney and Australia generally, should never be forgotten. At least there is now a bust of him in the Sydney Opera House, presented to the trust in November 1982, and the ABC dedicated to him in 1991 their new rehearsal studio, the Goossens Hall.

The next day we flew to Chicago, where I rehearsed and performed with the Chicago Symphony, conducted by André Cluytens. Once more I sang the Mad Scene from *Lucia di Lammermoor* to an audience of close on 8000.

On we went to Los Angeles to make our débuts in the popular 'Symphonies under the Stars' series with the Los Angeles Philharmonic Orchestra in the Hollywood Bowl. Richard's concert was on July 31 with Byron Janis playing the Rachmaninoff Concerto No. 2 in C Minor. The critics were impressed by Richard's appearance, complimenting him on his rapport with Byron Janis in the Rachmaninoff – not surprising, as it had been one of Ric's concert works as a pianist. Herbert Donaldson, in the *Citizen News*, wrote:

> Bonynge's gifts are considerable. He is a young man and his approach to music is, quite naturally, often exuberant. He fairly danced through some of the ballet music from Gounod's *Faust* as he conducted it. He was totally relaxed and ideally relaxing in his interpretive approach to the Ibert 'Divertissement'. Here is tongue-in-cheek music to be projected laughingly and whole-heartedly.
>
> Bonynge's best contribution to the program was the highly sensitive, sympathetic support given Janis in the piano concerto. Both artists obviously had something to say as regards the concerto's message. They said the same things; they said them together, and they said them with eloquence.

The concert given by the two of us on Thursday, August 2 was a complete sell-out with an attendance of over 20,000. Before the opening number Thomas Cassidy announced that I had agreed to stay on and give another concert the following Wednesday, due to the huge demand for tickets.

The first concert was an all operatic night consisting of the overture to Verdi's *La Forza del Destino*, 'Ah, fors'è lui' and 'Sempre libera' from his *La Traviata*, the ballet music from Rossini's *William Tell*, the Mad Scene from Bellini's *I Puritani*, Queen Marguerite's aria 'O lieto suol' from Meyerbeer's *Gli Ugonotti*, the overture to Rossini's *La Gazza Ladra* and the Mad Scene from Thomas's *Hamlet*. It was again a thrilling sensation to be on the receiving end of the applause and acclamation of such a huge and generous audience. Many Hollywood movie stars were there, but our greatest pleasure was to be greeted afterwards by Jeanette MacDonald whom we had admired as young teenagers in her films. She was just as charming in real life.

Albert Goldberg of the *Los Angeles Times* wrote:

> ... Perfection is a dangerous word but it is one that can safely be applied to Miss Sutherland. She has both a phenomenal voice and a phenomenal technique, but one never thinks of them in separate terms. No matter how startling her feats of agility may be the voice always retains the same luster, the bell-like resonance, the power, the freedom and the musical quality it has in straight melodic singing. It is as uncanny as it is wonderful.
>
> When she sings 'Ah, fors'è lui' from *La Traviata* she sounds like a lyric soprano, with a velvety and beautifully nuanced control of long-spun

phrases. Then she switches into the succeeding 'Sempre libera' and dashes off the glittering passages with just as much ease and with a tone as unerringly poised and phrased with the same amount of subtlety.

She did the same thing in the Mad Scene from Bellini's *I Puritani*. The melting quality of the voice was exquisite in the opening section, the coloratura as flawless in the cabaletta.

He went on to extol the Meyerbeer and Thomas arias, citing 'cascades of scales, staccati, trills – and a more perfect one you will never hear – and stratospheric top tones, all executed faultlessly and with a musical taste that avoided any hint of exhibitionism'.

Rachel Morton wrote that the voice,

in addition to being an amazing coloratura, has an almost Wagnerian middle and lower register, so that the whole range is weighty and warm and velvety ... The agility of the runs and the long spun trills left one breathless in utter amazement. Hers is without doubt the greatest voice in the world today.

Hedda Hopper even had a good word or two to say in her column in the *Los Angeles Times*:

High C: Not since the great Kirsten Flagstad have I heard such purity of tone or power as when I listened to Joan Sutherland sing in the Hollywood Bowl. She doesn't usually give encores, but had to sing two. After her mad song from *Hamlet*, Jeanette MacDonald said 'The only thing she can do now is "The Last Rose of Summer".' And, by gosh, she did. Her conductor-husband, however, distracted me. His gyrations were sort of a cross between St Vitus dance and the Twist. But he's a good-looker and could take over some of Tony Curtis's roles.

Between the two concerts we spent many hours with Marilyn Horne and her husband Henry Lewis. At that time Henry was a member of the Los Angeles Philharmonic Orchestra and beginning his career as a conductor. He helped Ric enormously to improve his control of the orchestra and clarify his directions. The four of us talked incessantly about the fund of music in the bel canto repertoire that had lain in libraries all over the world just waiting for the voices to come along that would warrant the revival of such works with sympathetic conductors. Ultimately, between us all, we didn't score too badly.

The second concert was another huge success, with Amina's first scene from Bellini's *La Sonnambula*, the Mad Scene from *Lucia*, a repeat performance of 'O lieto suol' from *Gli Ugonotti* and, as encore numbers, the cabaletta of the *I Puritani* Mad Scene and 'Sempre libera' from *La Traviata*.

✧ 5 ✧

AT LAST WE were free to return to Europe, check on the progress at number 36 and join Adam and Ruthli at Rocca Bella for a splendid holiday, with friends like Heinz Riva and Norman Ayrton staying from time to time. The area around Locarno was so beautiful and unspoiled compared with today. Now the town seems to extend all the way to the motorway tunnel to Bellinzona, with Villa Rocca Bella almost inaccessible because of it. Thirty years ago we could cross the road, walk under the railway bridge and around the lake to a favourite little cove to swim. That whole area is now covered with apartment houses and hotels.

Feeling thoroughly refreshed we left on September 6 for Florence, where we were to record *La Sonnambula* in the Teatro della Pergola with the orchestra of the Maggio Musicale Fiorentino, Richard conducting. Something like twelve days had been allowed for this, but I believe we managed to complete the opera in less time, it being a relatively short piece. We had a wonderful time between sessions, enjoying the historic city, its monuments and galleries, not forgetting its restaurants. Adam was with us for some of the time, joining Ruthli and her sister on the east coast before we all returned to London.

On October 13 we travelled to Bristol, installed ourselves at the Grand Hotel and spent the entire following day in the TWW Studio recording the hour-long *Joan Sutherland Show* made for Australia and also bought by companies in the United States, Britain and France. It was a huge undertaking to do the complete recording in one day, with orchestral rehearsals, costume changes and the possibility of filming and sound problems. Fortunately videotape was used commercially by then which made it somewhat easier, although the cameras were large and cumbersome and the performers had to 'favour' a specified one at given points, without the freedom of movement possible today with the more compact and manoeuvrable apparatus. It is now available on video-pirate probably.

Michael Denison was the compère and the programme consisted of the overture to *La Belle Hélène*, Queen Marguerite's aria from *Les Huguenots*, the duet 'Mira, o Norma' with Margreta Elkins, 'The Gypsy and the Bird' (Sir Julius Benedict), 'Addio del passato' from *La Traviata*, the duet 'Al bel destin' from *Linda di Chamounix* (Donizetti) and the Mad Scene from *Lucia di Lammermoor*.

At the end of fifteen hours of 'shooting' everyone seemed satisfied and, after being presented with an armful of Australian wildflowers that had been specially flown in for me, we all drove back to London. The show was presented in Australia one month later (on November 18, 1962) and hailed as 'one of the most ambitious and exciting one-hour specials ever screened on television anywhere in the world'.

The pace in London was hectic as usual – working on the pieces for the forthcoming Decca recording *Command Performance*, sitting for a portrait by Michael Garady, business talks with our lawyer (Sir William van Straubenzee) and our agent Joan Ingpen and a very long weekend in Vienna to record the Woodbird in *Siegfried* for the famous Georg Solti–Culshaw *Ring Cycle*.

At the time of writing it is thirty years to the day that Sir Georg bumped into me in the hotel after a recording session and asked me to join him for dinner – he was feeling very depressed as it was his fiftieth birthday. This week he has been fêted by all, celebrating his eightieth birthday – dining with the Prime Minister and his wife at 10 Downing Street and conducting gala performances of *Otello* at Covent Garden with as much energy as ever.

Back again to London from Vienna for the final preparation and beginning of the *Command Performance* recording sessions. The programme for this two-disc set was made up of the type of songs and arias that Queen Victoria might have requested to be performed at one of the many concerts or recitals held at Buckingham Palace or Windsor, and we lent various lithographs and paintings of artists and composers to be reproduced and included in the handsome libretto which accompanied the discs.

The London Symphony Orchestra conducted by Richard, together with the Ambrosian Singers, accompanied me in this wide-ranging collection comprising:

Oberon (WEBER) 'Ocean! thou mighty monster'
Le Cid (MASSENET) 'Pleurez mes yeux'
Dinorah (MEYERBEER) 'Ombre légère' ('Shadow Song')
I Pagliacci (LEONCAVALLO) *Recit and Ballatella*: 'Stridono lassù'
I Masnadieri (VERDI) *Recit and aria*: 'Tu del mio Carlo' *tenor*: John Dobson
Luisa Miller (VERDI) *Aria*: 'Tu puniscimi, o Signore'
La Cambiale di matrimonio (ROSSINI) *Recit and aria*: 'Vorrei spiegarvi'
Beatrice di Tenda (BELLINI) 'Deh! se un'urna' *chorus*: The Ambrosian Singers
'The Gipsy and the Bird' (BENEDICT) *solo flute*: Alexander Murray
'Parla!' (ARDITI)

Crispino e la comare (RICCI) 'Io non sono più l'Annetta'
'Ideale' (TOSTI) *piano*: Richard Bonynge
'Il Bacio' (ARDITI)
'La Serenata' (TOSTI) *piano*: Richard Bonynge
'Mattinata' (LEONCAVALLO)
'Lo, Here the Gentle Lark' (BISHOP) *solo flute*: Alexander Murray
Martha (FLOTOW) 'The last rose of summer'
Maritana (WALLACE) 'Scenes that are brightest'
Bohemian Girl (BALFE) 'I dreamt I dwelt'
Clari (BISHOP) 'Home sweet home' *harp*: Tina Bonifacio

On November 2 we celebrated my birthday nearly a week early so that Auntie Blos and Adam could be with us. Young Adam was very pleased with himself as he had trotted round to the local chemist and bought a large packet of Kleenex for my present with his (not very liberal) pocket money. Most thoughtful, I felt, as I used so many tissues in the theatre and it was the season for colds, too. By the time the seventh came around I was already recording *La Traviata* in Florence with Carlo Bergonzi and Robert Merrill.

Richard and I again had a wonderful time enjoying Florence and staying at the splendid Villa San Michele in Fiesole. Being Italy, there was no recording done until after lunch – usually not before 3 or even 4 p.m. – so we had plenty of opportunity to relax. When the recording was released some eight or nine months later it received almost unanimous acclaim from the critics, saying it was 'undoubtedly Sutherland's finest recorded performance to date'.

Richard had been busy preparing his first big ballet recording, *The Art of the Prima Ballerina*, and when we returned to London we had several pleasant meetings with that fabled ballerina Dame Alicia Markova. We had always admired her magical interpretations and, once we got to know her, the idea evolved of producing a recording of great Romantic ballet excerpts, not only as a homage to her but with her advice as to tempo and style. She and Richard worked together, choosing and discarding from the wealth of repertoire. The result was another two-disc set with a most charming accompanying album of photographs and reproductions not only of Markova herself but of Pavlova, Fokine, Taglioni, Grahn, Grisi, Karsavina, Danilova, Spessivtseva and so on. Although recorded thirty years ago it is still a great favourite and has been used by many of the international ice skaters for their competition displays. The London Symphony Orchestra played superbly and the items were:

SIDE 1

La Bayadère (MINKUS) Grand pas de deux
Les Millions d'Arlequin (DRIGO) Pas de trois
William Tell (ROSSINI) La Tyrolienne Act 3

SIDE 2

Giselle (ADAM) Danse des Vignerons; Pas seul; Peasant pas de deux Act 1
Giselle (ADAM) Grand adage and variations Act 2
La Sylphide (LOVENSKJOLD) Scène de la Sylphide Act 2

SIDE 3

Swan Lake (TCHAIKOVSKY) Grand pas de deux Act 3 (The Black Swan)
La Favorita (DONIZETTI) Ballet Music Act 3
Don Quixote (MINKUS) Grand pas de deux
Bolero 1830 (*Arranged* JAMES O'TURNER) Traditional

SIDE 4

Pas de Quatre (PUGNI)
The Sleeping Beauty (TCHAIKOVSKY) Blue Bird pas de deux Act 3
The Nutcracker (TCHAIKOVSKY) Grand pas de deux Act 2

During this period we were still organising the renovation of number 36, slowly managing to get what we wanted from builders and painters. Auntie Blos had been declining in health although she was as determined as ever to keep going, looking forward to the move as much as we were. We had allotted a large bedroom and small bathroom to her on the ground floor of the house so she would not always have to climb the stairs unless she felt she could manage them. Her doctor advised a week or so in hospital for some tests as she had been having a series of small black-outs. After one night there she had a massive stroke and never regained consciousness, although she lived a further four days in spite of the doctor's firm belief she would be dead by the following evening. We missed her quick wit and sharp comments and were very sorry she had not lived to enjoy the lovely house after being so interested in all that was happening there.

I was now somewhat late for rehearsals of *Semiramide* at La Scala and was upset, thinking I had disrupted them. I needn't have worried as Giulietta Simionato was also late and rehearsals had gone ahead with those who were available.

The conductor was the seventy-seven-year-old Gabriele Santini who, although wonderfully musical, was extremely intolerant and had many outbursts of shouting, screaming, stamping his foot and even jumping up and down on the podium prior to throwing down his baton – if he still had one – and walking off, fuming. He had precious little time for the production of Margherita Wallmann, who tried to liven up the stolid chorus of La Scala by an over-abundance of ballet dancers flitting about between them and the principals, invariably blocking the view of Santini's beat and causing general havoc. At one stage rehearsal he screamed that all he could see was a *culo inglese* (English behind), whereupon I spun about to inform him that it was a *culo australiano* – *that* much Italian I had mastered.

Giulietta Simionato arrived late as she had suffered a nasty tooth extraction and neither of us was word perfect, relying a great deal on Maestro Naldini (the prompt). With all the interruptions we at least had the chance to repeat large sections and gradually the lavish production sorted itself out. Simionato had a good sense of humour and we laughed a lot, particularly over the fact that I was her mother in the opera. When we had costume changes she would pass by my dressing-room and ask 'Ready, Mum?'

We worked hard towards the advertised opening night on Saturday, December 15 but Santini was adamant that nobody was ready and the première was postponed until Monday the seventeenth. At least we had no rehearsals on the Sunday and felt rested for the first performance of *Semiramide* at La Scala for eighty years. The evening was a huge success with the public and certainly for myself. The title role was written for Rossini's Spanish wife Isabella Colbran who was noted for her vocal agility and fioriture. In the *Sunday Times* Desmond Shawe-Taylor wrote of my performance:

> ... As a sheer feat of vocalisation Joan Sutherland's Queen of Babylon was prodigious: it ranks among her very finest achievements. Nothing daunted her, and nothing caused her enraptured listeners the smallest apprehension. Roulades, scales, arpeggios were thrown off with accuracy and ease, while over two and a half octaves her tone remained consistently round; pure and lustrous.
>
> The sheer physical pleasure afforded by such singing at a time when it has grown increasingly rare can hardly be exaggerated. In addition Miss Sutherland phrased neatly, looked handsome and comported herself with regal dignity.

There was criticism of Santini's slow tempi (they *were* rather exhausting) and of the majority of the cast being ill-equipped to cope with Rossini's very florid music. However Giulietta Simionato and I were highly praised for our singing of the wonderful duets together and although there were reservations among the critics as to the wisdom of reviving *Semiramide* at all, surely the fact that performances of the opera have continued regularly over the past thirty years is justification enough.

During those thirty years there have been many revivals of other Rossini works and a spate of performances to commemorate the bicentenary of his birth. Ridiculous as the plot of *Semiramide* may be, that of *Sigismondo*, revived in the autumn of 1992 in Rovigo, Treviso and Savona with Richard conducting, is more so. However, the music warranted its performance, and the fact that young singers were cast with a vocal facility to cope with the Rossinian style admirably.

We squeezed in a lovely Christmas at Rocca Bella with Ann Colbert and our friends Francis Coulson and Brian Sack from Sharrow Bay, Ullswater. Francis, one of Britain's foremost country-house hoteliers, spoiled us by helping Ruthli and Gudi cook the Christmas dinner.

There were festivities at the New Year performances of *Semiramide*, with Simionato bringing glasses of champagne to the dressing-room. This I would appear to sip delightedly, passing the glass to Weenie as soon as Giulietta had departed. I've never really enjoyed anything but the thought of champagne, finding it very drying to the throat and rather indigestible. I certainly would never touch it before or during a performance. Weenie, who sat in my dressing-room through most of them, was very happy to polish off the bubbly for me.

After a few days back in London, Weenie and I boarded the *Queen Mary*, bound for New York. Ric stayed on in London for a few more days to help complete the move to number 36, which was only partially ready.

To our great delight Noël Coward and his secretary Cole Lesley were also making the trip to New York and many were the laughs we had together. Weenie and I were amazed at the 'Master's' quick summing up and witty judgement of fellow passengers. Although I had met Noël previously this was the first opportunity to spend much time together and the basis of a friendship between our two households lasting even after his death to this day.

Arrived in New York, we stayed at the Hampshire House briefly before moving into a pleasant apartment on East 94th Street and Madison Avenue, in the same building as our friend Anya Dorfman. At that time she was still performing and looking forward to her years of teaching at the Juilliard School.

Ric and I went to Washington again – this time for President Kennedy's Inaugural Anniversary Salute at the Armory. All the artists were invited to the home of Vice-President Lyndon Johnson after the concert for supper and to meet the President and Mrs Kennedy. We had a wonderful time with some of our colleagues from the concert – Carol Channing, George Burns, Shirley Bassey, Gene Kelly, Yves Montand, Diahann Carroll, Carol Burnett and stars of the New York City Ballet. We found Lady Bird Johnson very warm and friendly and stayed rather longer than anticipated.

We were supposed to be catching an early plane back to New York next morning, but this was cancelled as there was very heavy fog, and although we went to the airport and waited for some time, we had to return to the city and take the train. This travelled very slowly and made us late for the taping of a Metropolitan Opera Intermission interview with Birgit Nilsson. The plan had been to go to dinner at Birgit's apartment after the taping, but I was very tired – and had to rehearse and tape the *Dinah Shore Show* the next day – so declined to attend dinner. Birgit was very annoyed as she had gone to a lot of trouble making Swedish meat balls and other goodies. Indeed, she didn't speak to me for some years. However, I really felt exhausted and made a large effort to get through the Met Intermission taping, then go home to bed.

The much-loved *Dinah Shore Show* was recorded with Dinah and Ella Fitzgerald. I was very nervous working with such giants of the entertainment world, but I need not have worried. They were great fun, and confessed they were feeling the same about me. The show was a huge success when presented on March 17 and has been replayed (or parts of it) many times. Probably the high points were our trios: 'Three little maids from school' and 'Lover come back to me'. We each sang 'a song about unrequited love' and mine was 'Vissi d'arte' from *Tosca*.

On January 24 it was my great privilege to be the guest of honour at a Lotos Club State Dinner. This old-established New York Club holds dinners to which they invite a guest who is prominent in their field, be it music, art, medicine or whatever. A great deal of research had been done to provide the (at that time) all male members and their guests with a biography noting my recent 'triumphs' and a beautiful sketch had been made of me as Queen Marguerite de Valois in the La Scala production of *Les Huguenots* which was printed on the programme-menu for the event, the original of which was presented to me. Richard and I spent a most enjoyable evening and I have remained an honorary member of the Club. I understand that Mary Garden was the first woman to be honoured in this way in 1922 – and she was the first woman ever allowed in the clubhouse, which was founded in 1870.

On January 26 I appeared in the Academy of Music's 106th anniversary concert with the Philadelphia Orchestra, Leopold Stokowski conducting. I sang the Mad Scene from *Lucia di Lammermoor*. All went well until the end of the cadenza, when I sang my last trill and turn, and hopped on to my high E flat. But instead of a nice solid supporting chord from the orchestra there was nothing. I was left high and dry – then suddenly the concert master brought the players in as I held the note for dear life, hoping my breath would not run out. Stokowski must have been on another planet just then.

On January 31 rehearsals began for *La Sonnambula* at the Met and on the following day rehearsals for the taping of a *Bell Telephone Hour* in Brooklyn. There were also fittings for costumes for both shows, frequent hairdressing by Adolfo and one or two visits per week from my hearty Scandinavian masseuse, Jenny Delerud. We even managed to fit in a few social engagements as well.

During this season in New York our friendships with many New Yorkers and other East Coast dwellers grew and flourished. These included Buddy and Geri Kaufman from South Orange, New Jersey, with whom we spent several relaxed and happy weekends over the years. They were great art and music lovers and Buddy had a seemingly endless fund of stories which kept us laughing.

The *Bell Telephone Hour* was broadcast on February 4 – live. It was quite a mixed bag, with Mindy Carson and Pat Boone (the latter doubling as host), concert pianist John Browning playing the third movement of Brahms's Piano Concerto No. 1, Erik Bruhn and Sonia Arova dancing the Black Swan *pas de deux* from *Swan Lake*, and I concluded the programme with the Sleep-walking Scene from *La Sonnambula*.

Before beginning at the Met Ric and I had orchestral concerts at White Plains (New York) and Englewood (New Jersey).

✧ **6** ✧

THE MET REHEARSALS – and the performances – became rather nightmarish as the set consisted of a large fibre-glass hill covered in what appeared to be green velour. Over this chorus villagers, ballet and soloists were meant to come tripping on. Unfortunately, that's exactly what most of us *did*, it was so slippery. The ballet girls and boys were terrified and ultimately we all had fine non-slip rubber soles stuck to our shoes. This was a help – until the rubber started curling back at the edges, providing a further hazard and necessitating regular inspection and resticking by the dressers.

The whole production was designed by Rolf Gérard and the costumes, too, were a disaster after the glorious Piero Tosi ones at La Scala, in spite of them being executed by that remarkable costumier Karinska in her inimitable balletic style. Unfortunately I had anything *but* a ballet dancer's shape and the layers of pale-pink, green and lavender chiffon, cut on the cross into circular skirts, one over the other, merely clung over my stomach, bottom and hips and fell in an uneven mess at the hemline. The wardrobe was constantly being asked to adjust the length. I felt very uncomfortable and fat in them, but my objections to wearing them were pooh-poohed by the management. I thought the producer, Henry Butler, agreed with me – but this was a brand new production and wear them I did. My ire was somewhat mollified when I was confronted by Niki Gedda as Elvino looking like Little Boy Blue in very tight pale-blue tights and velvet jacket, his behind being quite a feature when he turned upstage. At least we had some laughs. Alicia Markova was in town and helped me immensely with balletic movement.

The opening night of *La Sonnambula* was on February 21, with Silvio Varviso conducting. Immediate reviews of the opera were rather sparse, it being the seventy-seventh day of the New York newspaper blackout, but the vocal aspects of the work were appreciated, if not the dramatic content – or (to some) lack of it. Harold Schonberg wrote in the *New York Times* a fair assessment of the opera itself and the 'economy-sized production', together with references to the authenticity of style and command of the vocal writing by the Sutherland voice, rounding off his article with:

153

... and by the time the last act came around she was stupendous.

This act has the two great arias 'Ah non credea' and 'Ah, non giunge'. The first is a long, unembellished melody that cannot be sung without a flawless technique. The second is one of the all-time coloratura showpieces. In both Miss Sutherland was as perfect as one could desire. She followed the practice of Bellini's time by interpolating cadenzas and other coloratura work into the second stanza of 'Ah, non giunge'.

The aria closes the opera, and when she finished an explosive roar went up from the audience. It was fully deserved. For this was not merely coloratura singing, it was singing in the grand line, and it was the stuff of which legends are made.

The bridge over which Amina did her sleep-walking in the last act looked very perilous from the audience. In fact it was its height (about fourteen feet above the stage) that added to the illusion and I always felt secure there, not suffering a problem with vertigo. However, Rudolf Bing tested it before every performance by walking over it himself. He said he did not expect any of his singers to do anything he wouldn't.

On about the third night of the opera a stage lamp exploded with a mighty bang during some of my pyrotechnics. Whether it was the high pitch of my voice or the state of the lamp I'll never know, but it shocked the audience and me. Weenie thought it might have been an unfriendly soprano out there, but I assured her that as I didn't feel dead I just kept on singing.

The day after the *La Sonnambula* opening Ric and I travelled to Boston, where we did a début concert on February 23 at Symphony Hall.

Richard had been gaining valuable experience conducting so many of the concerts with me and now came the opportunity to make his début preparing and conducting Gounod's *Faust* on stage for the Vancouver Opera. It was strange that I should have made my North American début in the same theatre as Richard made his as an operatic conductor – and fortunate for the two of us.

Irving Guttman was the Artistic Director of the Vancouver Opera Association at that time, as well as Stage Director of the *Faust* production. We had known him for some years, he being an old friend of Terry McEwen from their schooldays in Montreal. Irving had assembled a fine cast of young North American singers, with whom we were to work again frequently, particularly on the tour we did to Australia in 1965.

John Alexander, from the Metropolitan Opera, was Faust, Richard Cross sang Mephistopheles, Doris Yarick was Marguerite and Victor Braun sang the role of Valentin. The costumes were designed by Suzanne Mess.

While Richard was away in Vancouver performances at the Met of
La Sonnambula continued. I also did two concerts with Silvio Varviso
conducting – one at the old Mosque Theater in Newark, New Jersey
on Sunday, March 12 and the other at Brooklyn College on the
sixteenth. Silvio was good company, as well as a fine, sensitive conductor, and the concerts were a pleasure and very well received.

Richard arrived back in New York very happy with the way the
Faust had come together in Vancouver and looking forward to his next
operatic dates. We went, together with Terry McEwen and Alicia
Markova, to a preview of the ill-fated Zeffirelli stage production of *La
Dame aux Camélias*. The sets and costumes were exquisite, in true
Zeffirelli style, and the actors were all very handsome – but the dialogue
was in the most atrocious modern colloquial English, even using slang
terms, with some very tasteless and unnecessary scenes. In spite of all
its visual beauty the presentation was a decided flop, losing $1,000,000,
and was taken off after a week.

Arnold Scaasi was designing gowns for me both for concert and day
wear so there were lengthy fittings with him, continuing visits from
my trusty masseuse, the everlasting trips to the hairdresser and several
dinner parties with Alicia Markova, Ann Colbert and Georg Solti, Anya
Dorfman, the Kaufmans and various other friends, also a business
luncheon with Rudolf Bing. These pleasant occasions were neatly
fitted in between the Met performances and rehearsals with Leonard
Bernstein for my first concert at the relatively new Philharmonic Hall,
Lincoln Center. This was to be a Gala Pension Fund Benefit Concert
and it was exciting to work with Bernstein and the splendid New York
Philharmonic Orchestra in that very glamorous hall. I was quite happy
with the acoustic, but a large number of the regular concert-goers said
it was disgraceful – terrible – and the whole hall must be reassessed
and altered to give a better overall sound.

For this concert, however, we all managed very well, with not only
some of my customary vocal fireworks, but Lenny Bernstein dancing
and almost flying off the podium during the overture to *Mignon*. I was
wearing one of the Scaasi creations – a bright-green and apricot floral
with a voluminous cloak of apricot silk – and Adolfo had gone berserk
with my hair-do, eliciting comments from the critics. It was on this
occasion that Birgit Nilsson, when asked was Miss Sutherland's hair
real, was reported (in Leonard Lyon's column) to have replied: 'I don't
know – I haven't pulled it yet!'

I was very pleased by Harriet Johnson's comments in the *New York
Post* the next day:

> ... Her voice – a true, dramatic coloratura – and her effortless use of it
> are phenomenal. In my experience, I have heard only one singer to

compare with her in vocal greatness, the late Norwegian soprano Kirsten Flagstad, whose voice in a completely different genre – a real dramatic soprano – was also miraculously beautiful and effortless. Today, Miss Sutherland has no peer.

To be thought of as comparable to Kirsten Flagstad was for me – and still is – the height of praise.

The matinée of *La Sonnambula* at the Met on March 30 will never be forgotten by us. Silvio, Terry McEwen, Ric and myself were invited by Francis Robinson to a splendid dinner after the show at Toscanini's favourite restaurant, then back to his apartment to hear some of his recordings of previous great singers and a nightcap. Much champagne was consumed by all during the wonderful evening of music, laughter and anecdotes from Francis's seemingly inexhaustible store, and when we finally went down to the car we were all very merry. Silvio seemed all arms and legs when we left him at his hotel (the 'Myflovver' as he called the Mayflower) and when we reached the door of our apartment Ric said, 'Last one into the bedroom's a rotten egg!' We both made a dive for the room, ending up in a giggling heap on the floor.

The day after the ninth (and second-last) *Sonnambula* at the Met we travelled to Los Angeles where, in the Shrine Auditorium, we performed a Special Benefit Concert with the Los Angeles Philharmonic Orchestra. Miliza Korjus requested tickets in the front row and appeared in all her splendour, *Merry Widow* hat and all, with a present of her 'magic anti-wrinkle cream'.

From Los Angeles we went to San Francisco where we were presented by Sol Hurok in the San Francisco Opera House on April 7. The audience went wild, cheering and stamping for ten minutes and I sang 'Son vergin vezzosa' from *I Puritani* as an encore with the orchestra, also 'When Daisies Pied' with Ric at the harpsichord. The critics extolled the 'soaring top tones', the 'vocal agility', the 'rococo floridity'(!), stating that it was 'the most phenomenal coloratura singing this city has heard within living memory'.

On April 8 we flew back to New York for the last *Sonnambula* at the Met on the twelfth, rehearsals for the American Opera Society's *I Puritani* and fittings for the *Firestone Hour* TV Show which was to be recorded and presented live between 10.30 a.m. and 10.30 p.m. on Sunday, April 21.

On Tuesday, April 16 we performed Bellini's *I Puritani* in Carnegie Hall with Richard making his New York conducting début, earning praise for his contribution to the stylishness of the evening and his 'spirited pacing, precision and expert orchestral accompaniment'. Again the audience went wild and the critics were ecstatic over the work as a whole and the interpretive ability of the artists, with great praise for the 'floods of tone', 'cascades of scale and arpeggio passages' and the show-stopping duet in the third act with Niki Gedda and myself. Ernest Blanc and Justino Diaz were also splendid.

As was so often the case, there was a supper party after the concert. Whilst chatting with Betty Allen who had sung the Queen, a distinguished-looking gentleman told her how much he had enjoyed her performance.

She, with her customary wit, replied, 'Oh, it's just one of my stagnant royalty parts.'

'I suppose you might say I come into that category,' he responded. He was Prince Vladimir Alexeivitch Romanoff.

On Thursday, April 18 *I Puritani* was presented with the same cast in the Academy of Music, Philadelphia. Ric and I travelled back after the concert, and the next morning there was a four-hour rehearsal of the *Firestone Hour*. More rehearsing the next day and the show recorded and presented live as planned on Sunday, April 21.

The theme song of the show had been composed by the sponsor's wife and every soloist appearing sang it in the finale. I lost my way at one point so let the chorus get on with it until I felt the end was approaching, threw in a high note and made a typical Sutherland grimace – which the camera caught in detail.

It has been extremely interesting to see this and many other shows re-recorded on video and released for public sale almost thirty years later. The clarity of the film and even the sound (which was usually less than good on TV for various technical reasons) are amazing. All the shows are living documents of the history of show business and music on television and it is wonderful that they have been preserved. What with Union restrictions and the costs having soared, I doubt if such programmes could be made on a regular basis today.

After a second *Puritani* in Carnegie Hall we made another trip to Washington to perform at Constitution Hall a Benefit Concert for the Congressional Circle for Friendship House, under the patronage of Mrs John F. Kennedy and the Australian Ambassador and Lady Beale. The concert was one of our stock ones for the season with a baroque first half and a nineteenth-century operatic second half. To open this second half I sang 'Io non sono più l'Annetta' by the brothers Ricci which was considered rubbish by the critic Paul Hume. A letter written two days later from Arlington, Virginia was sent on to me in London. It read:

Dear Madame Sutherland,

Nuts to Paul Hume! We like what we like. We (Ruth and I) loved 'Io non sono più l'Annetta'. Please do it as often as you like. Really, it allows you to reveal a lively, free sensuousness that appeals to all who feel. Thank you for it, and may you be blessed.

Sincerely,

signed Hal Crowley

I was very touched that someone would take the trouble to write in this way and I certainly did sing it as often as I chose, finding that the Crowleys were not the only ones who enjoyed it.

Back in London immediately after the Washington concert we finally had possession of number 36 and although 'the girls' (Udi and Gudi) had done a splendid job of coping with the painters and decorators there were still a lot of things to be sorted out. We needed time to catch our breath and study Handel's *Julius Caesar*, and the part of Micaela in *Carmen* in French (I was to record the role in a few weeks' time and had only sung it in English on stage) and also learn the repertoire for the next recording of arias – *The Age of Bel Canto* with Marilyn Horne and Richard Conrad, which was to take place in early June.

The massage for the back problem continued, but I had managed to find a much lighter and very satisfactory surgical corset in New York which restricted my movement a great deal less and was altogether more comfortable to wear. Four of the same model remained the most important part of my luggage henceforth – three in the suitcase and one on my person. The only problem was that the heavy metal bones set off the alarm when security checking became essential and I had to explain and be frisked at every check-point. Finally, well into the Seventies, I was able to wear a very natty French boneless corselet and only don the surgical monster on performance nights – or if my back showed signs of strain from carrying heavy hand-luggage or too much gardening.

Watching the lovely old house gradually absorb all the furnishings and drapes, not to mention some splendid wallpapers, mantels and chandeliers, was very exciting and gratifying. Richard had done a great job on his various sorties to auctions and out-of-town antique dealers and the house became a much-loved home very soon. We all appreciated the space after having been so cramped in the apartment, especially Adam who had plenty of room for his fleet of toy cars, trains and all the other paraphernalia boys love. He could also invite a friend for the weekend from time to time.

But we couldn't remain idle for ever. At the end of May we went to Geneva for the *Carmen* recording, Thomas Schippers conducting L'Orchestre Suisse-Romande with Regina Resnik as Carmen, Mario del Monaco as Don José, Tom Krause as Escamillo and Yvonne Minton as Mercedes. The *New York Times* said of my performance:

Miss Sutherland's glinting tone graces Micaela's music in a manner that delights the ear. Furthermore, she creates a charmingly naive character through her singing. She shows how capable she is of contributing more than just beautiful vocalism to a role.

On June 4 we returned to London and on the fifth rehearsals for *Julius Caesar* at Sadler's Wells began in earnest, with the first session of *The Age of Bel Canto* being recorded on the night of the seventh.

Richard's father Carl had recently retired and come to stay with us for a few months, intending to return to Australia with Weenie when she went back on her next holiday. As we were so busy, Weenie had taken him to Scotland via the Lake District for a spring tour, during which it rained most of the time. They returned rather earlier than expected, as Weenie said, 'to warm up and dry off'. Also staying in the house was Richard Conrad, who was participating on *The Age of Bel Canto*. By this time Margreta and Ike Elkins were installed in the basement apartment of number 36, so we were quite a jolly household. There was also Jedda, Greta's golden labrador, who frequently managed to find her way up to our dining-room to sleep under the table where it was quiet, except at mealtimes, when she would drowsily appear in the hope of titbits (breaking wind in the process), Greta often having fed her leftover cabbage.

As well as preparing the *Caesar* production and making the recording, we also found time to do a charity recital at Fairfield Hall, Croydon on June 10 in aid of the British Home and Hospital for Incurables. Margreta and I sang a fairly popular programme, with Richard accompanying.

It would appear that some of the residents of Cornwall Gardens were having more than enough music during the pleasant June days. What with Neville Marriner living diagonally opposite and rehearsing at times, and Richard busy with Greta, myself, Marilyn Horne and Richard Conrad, it must have been a bit tiresome. One day there was a strangled noise from outside, where a neighbour was standing on his balcony furiously imitating the vocal sounds – making more noise than all of us together. From the garden below another neighbour had been enjoying what she called 'the afternoon performance' – we *never* worked in the evening at home. The man on the balcony leaned over and shouted at the passers by: 'Just listen to that! Did you ever hear anything like it?'

All this was reported in a couple of the daily papers. But other than someone next door playing back my *Lucia* Mad Scene very loudly at 1.45 a.m. – after I'd just sung a theatre performance and was trying to get some sleep before a heavy study day – we had no further problems of that nature.

The sessions of *The Age of Bel Canto* progressed with a flamboyant mixture of eighteenth- and nineteenth-century vocal gems, including some duets and trios. Marilyn, Richard Conrad and I all enjoyed a good joke and we had a lot of fun as well as hard work making the recording. When it was issued (a two-disc set) it was accompanied by a charming and informative libretto with many reproductions of prints of the original performers and the composers, Ric having been responsible for providing most of the material from his collection.

Two orchestras were used – the London Symphony Orchestra and the New Symphony Orchestra of London – and the set was acclaimed for its interesting repertoire, the spectacular vocal ability of the artists and particularly the overall standard of performance from Richard and the orchestras. It was reissued on CDs in 1996.

JOAN SUTHERLAND • MARILYN HORNE • RICHARD CONRAD
THE LONDON SYMPHONY ORCHESTRA
THE NEW SYMPHONY ORCHESTRA OF LONDON
RICHARD BONYNGE CONDUCTOR

1. 'Furia di donna' *La Buona Figliuola* PICCINNI Joan Sutherland
2. 'Care selve' *Atalanta* HANDEL Richard Conrad *Cello obbligato* Ambrose Gauntlett
3. 'Superbo di me stesso' *Meraspe* LAMPUGNANI Marilyn Horne
4. 'With plaintive note' *Samson* HANDEL Joan Sutherland
5. 'Iris hence away' *Semele* HANDEL Marilyn Horne
6. 'Mio caro ben' *Astarto* BONONCINI Joan Sutherland and Richard Conrad
7. 'O too lovely' *Artaxerxes* ARNE Marilyn Horne *Cello obbligato* Douglas Cameron
8. 'Light as thistledown' *Rosina* SHIELD Joan Sutherland
9. 'When William at eve' *Rosina* SHIELD Joan Sutherland
10. 'Voi che fausti' *Il re pastore* MOZART Richard Conrad
11. 'O zittre nicht' *Die Zauberflöte* MOZART Joan Sutherland
12. 'Ich baue ganz' *Die Entführung aus dem Serail* MOZART Richard Conrad
13. 'Ma Fanchette est charmante' *Angéla* MME GAIL & BOIELDIEU Joan Sutherland, Marilyn Horne and Richard Conrad
14. 'Serbami ognor' *Semiramide* ROSSINI Joan Sutherland and Marilyn Horne
15. 'Ferme tes yeux' *La Muette de Portici* AUBER Richard Conrad
16. 'Und ob die Wolke' *Der Freischütz* WEBER Joan Sutherland *Cello obbligato* Nelson Cooke
17. 'Angiol di pace' *Beatrice di Tenda* BELLINI Joan Sutherland, Marilyn Horne and Richard Conrad
18. 'Tornami a dir' *Don Pasquale* DONIZETTI Joan Sutherland and Richard Conrad

19. 'Il segreto' *Lucrezia Borgia* DONIZETTI Marilyn Horne
20. 'Santo di patria ... allor che i forti corrono' *Attila* VERDI Joan Sutherland
21. 'Un ritratto? – Veggiam' *La Straniera* BELLINI Joan Sutherland and Richard Conrad
22. 'Ecco ridente' *Il Barbiere di Siviglia* ROSSINI Richard Conrad *Guitar accompaniment* Sydney Del Monte
23. 'Bolero' ARDITI Marilyn Horne
Harpsichord continuo on first record only, Hubert Dawkes

All the recording sessions had been neatly juggled to fit in with the rehearsals of Handel's *Julius Caesar*, Marilyn and Richard Conrad recording when I was needed for rehearsals by Norman Ayrton and Charles Farncombe, who was conducting the opera. Margreta Elkins was singing the role of Caesar and was to make her entrance standing on the prow of a 'ship', wearing a magnificent feathered helmet. The ship was not about to co-operate during rehearsal, making a very jerky approach, and Greta detested wearing hats and headgear so begged to carry the helmet. There was a heated and lengthy discussion between Norman and Greta while the ship-handlers endeavoured to make their charge glide on satisfactorily. Greta finally flatly refused to wear the helmet – a great shame, as it looked most imposing and added to the grandeur of the scene – and the ship worked admirably.

Apart from a few more minor hiccups *Julius Caesar* opened at Sadler's Wells on June 20, with further performances on June 22 and 26, this last being a gala in aid of the Sunshine Homes and Schools for Blind Children. It was in the presence of Princess Margaret, Countess of Snowdon and the Earl of Snowdon and was broadcast on the BBC Third Programme.

The production received mixed reviews but there was general agreement that the work was hampered by dreary settings and the 'plodding and unexciting' conducting. The public appeared to enjoy the opera and it was hoped there would be further opportunities to see and hear it.

On July 2 we had a 'Housewarming' dinner at number 36 to which we invited several dear friends including Alicia Markova, Hilary Watson, Mr Norman Barrett and his wife Elizabeth and Mrs 'Cee Bee' Pilling. The latter caused quite a ripple of laughter when, during a pause in the general conversation, she was heard to announce very decisively to Elizabeth Barrett: 'I always say there are those who read Proust and those who don't!'

The next day (and for the three succeeding ones) we recorded excerpts from *Julius Caesar* with Margreta Elkins as Giulio Cesare, Marilyn Horne as Cornelia, Monica Sinclair as Tolomeo and Richard

Conrad as Sesto. The New Symphony Orchestra of London was conducted by Ric, and the disc, when issued, was greeted with enthusiasm by critics and public alike, many lamenting that the whole opera had not been recorded.

$$\diamond \; 7 \; \diamond$$

THIS CONCLUDED OUR work for the 1962–3 season in London and the household set off for Villa Rocca Bella by various routes and detours Ric and I to Florence to record Bellini's *I Puritani*. We again stayed at the Villa San Michele in Fiesole, enjoying the slightly countryfied atmosphere there. Weenie and Carl drove down from Rocca Bella and between the recording sessions we had some pleasant times together.

Franco Corelli, as a long-standing Decca artist, had been requested to sing the very taxing role of Arturo in the opera with its famed high Ds and possible F. However, very close to the recording period he had sent a message (accompanied by X-rays) to say his throat was inflamed and he was unable to appear. He was replaced by the young Canadian tenor Pierre Duval who, in view of the short notice and hurried trip, managed manfully. Riccardo was to have been sung by Wladimiro Ganzarolli who had, we were told, 'the same complaint as last year' so was replaced by Renato Capecchi. The rest of the cast consisted of myself as Elvira, Ezio Flagello as Giorgio, Margreta Elkins as Queen Enrichetta and the trusty Piero de Palma as Bruno. Richard conducted the Chorus and Orchestra of Il Maggio Musicale Fiorentino.

The recording was made between July 15 and 26 and was considered an outstanding achievement by the critics. Comparisons were made between it and the decade-old Angel album with Maria Callas, conducted by Tullio Serafin. The Decca set was deemed 'more effective, with livelier tempi and greater musical propulsion secured by Richard Bonynge, who appears to be developing his considerable promise as a conductor'.

Anxious to get back to Villa Rocca Bella to rest, spend time with Adam and study *Norma*, Weenie and I drove off, leaving Ric to hear a few play-backs of the recording and show his father some of the Tuscan beauty spots. They arrived at the villa looking very sun-tanned some days later and we had a wonderful August swimming in the lake, picnicking in the hills behind Locarno with Adam and lazing about on the terrace or in the garden of the house. We had difficulty making time to study but managed to spend a part of most days working on Bellini's wonderful opera. I was finally going to sing the role that had replaced my Wagnerian aspirations, that of the Druid High Priestess

Norma. We were to give performances of *Norma* in Vancouver, commencing on October 17, and Ric and I wanted to make them successful. Memorising the words was, as usual with me, the longest process so I would wander about muttering them to myself, becoming exasperated at my persistent errors and lapses and appearing to be ready for the insane asylum.

The household returned to London briefly, Carl and Weenie flying off to Australia, Ric and I to New York on 1 September, and Adam returning with Udi and Gudi and going back to school at the Lycée. It was good to know that Margreta and Ike were living in the downstairs flat and on hand if needed.

Our stays in New York were very brief, Ric travelling on to San Francisco the next day as he was to begin rehearsals there for *La Sonnambula*, which was to be his conducting début with the San Francisco Opera. The General Director of the company, Kurt Herbert Adler, had great faith in Ric's ability and musical integrity and continued to champion him throughout his reign over the company. He even agreed to mount the splendid production of Massenet's *Esclarmonde* several years later (1974) fired by Ric's enthusiasm for the work, as I doubt Kurt had even been aware of its existence.

I followed two days later, after a few appointments in Manhattan, and was pleased to meet Lotfi Mansouri who was producing the opera. Somehow I knew immediately that we would get along well and that it would be a no-nonsense, straightforward presentation. I was also impressed to find that Lotfi was practically word-perfect and could actually sing all the music – not always the case with opera producers. It was the first of many enjoyable collaborations with him over the next thirty years.

It was a very friendly company, consisting of singers that we either had worked with previously or would do many times in the future – Dorothy Cole, Renato Cioni and Richard Cross. I had brought my own costumes from the La Scala production and felt comfortable in them after my Met experience. Our rehearsals progressed well, Lotfi being very helpful and attentive to everyone, and we finally transferred from the regular rehearsal hall to the stage of the opera house. Here Mr Adler, from his vantage point in the theatre, started criticising what Lotfi was doing with us on stage in front of the whole assembled Company, and when he complained about my interpretation I couldn't control my anger and asked him across the footlights was *he* producing the opera or Mr Mansouri. We weathered the little storm and all went on to have a good success, with Richard's conducting of the work being 'strong and compelling'.

There were three performances, on September 14 and 17 and the Sunday matinée on the twenty-second. As they were so nicely spaced there was time to enjoy the splendid weather with picnics and visits to the Napa Valley and Chinatown. Jack Shelton was host on several occasions and invited us to stay in his house above Sausalito on our way to Los Angeles from Vancouver later on, in November that year. We had numerous interviews and a record-signing session over the lunch-hour at Sherman Clay's big store. With all the social functions I was pleased that my faithful hairdresser, Gerald Smith from Raymond of London, had settled in San Francisco and was always happy to fit me in.

After the last *Sonnambula* we returned to New York for ten days for meetings with various producers and opera directors, including Sarah Caldwell and Rudolf Bing, and set off for Vancouver on October 3, plunging into rehearsals for *Norma* and interviews the next day.

The opera consisted of solo, duo and trio scenes so we were able to progress well with the production during the periods when no chorus was available. The cast was one of dear colleagues and friends – Marilyn Horne, John Alexander, Richard Cross and I were all singing our roles for the first time, with costumes designed by Suzanne Mess, the sets by Gail McCance, Irving Guttman producing and Richard conducting.

Weenie had returned from Australia to join us and was delighted by the various mishaps as well as the glorious music when she attended rehearsals – the gong in the last act flying off its stand at the third mighty stroke, Marilyn and I having difficulties with our trailing robes (in spite of years of experience) and dear John Alexander in the piano-dress rehearsal appearing with a half-finished attempt with putty at a more Roman nose, his tunic far too long (more like a nightshirt), one laced-to-the-knee sandal and his wig on back to front. We laughed so much we needed a repair job on our make-up. Francean Campbell in *Opera News* wrote:

Joan Sutherland's first *Norma* was the subject of much celebration here. She sang five performances of Bellini's opera with the Vancouver Opera Association, and to report that her interpretation was a success would be to understate the case. With her husband, Richard Bonynge, conducting, with a carefully assembled cast of fellow-principals, and with a leisurely, unhurried period of rehearsal, an only slightly nervous Sutherland won nothing short of triumph on her opening night. Succeeding performances, two or three days apart, lent an increased confidence, a deepened intensity, and a flowering of the distinctively personal voice itself: the clarion upper range (to D in the first act, E flat in the second), the melting lower one, the fabulous trill, and the nearly faultless articulation of the swiftest passages.

Richard Bonynge has without question arrived as a talented, intelligent and serious conductor. The insight that he brought to the music of *Norma* lent strength and confidence to orchestra and singers. His sensitivity to music of this genre, and to the niceties of its balance and ensemble, set him far ahead of his years of experience.

What with the length and stature of the role of Norma, it having been a goal for ten years, the close proximity of the performances (five between October 17 and 26) with, on the twenty-ninth, a gala concert for the Vancouver Opera Endowment Fund and the very late suppers given by various members of the Board, I was exhausted. Although I resisted many invitations on the days between perform- ances and rested quietly in my hotel I developed stomach cramps and severe nausea, both of which disappeared once I was on stage, returning with a vengeance after the performance. The year had been a very busy one and there were still more obligations to fulfil.

Both Ric and I felt the improvements in vocal stamina and interpre- tation with each successive performance. The costumes became man- ageable and indeed, the brilliant orange-red velvet cloak I wore in the last act was a great feature and eye-catcher, photographed by Barry Glass and used as the cover of the original *Norma* recording for Decca. We knew the role was a perfect one for me, but realised that I could not continue to sing such a mammoth part with only one day free between performances. After this experience, somewhat to our agents' displeasure, we established the system of only two performances per week of such large roles, giving me two whole days free, plus the day of the second performance. It took a while before we could enforce it because of commitments already made, but it was a system that we adhered to and which probably helped account for the longevity of my career. I also was very strict about refusing invitations for the night before a performance, preferring to spend it quietly at home (or in my hotel) than to have to raise my voice to be heard above the babble of sound in a smoke-filled room or restaurant. Any function I may have missed along the way was nothing to compare with the feeling of freshness and relaxation that was mine each night I had to 'deliver the goods'.

The day after the concert we flew to San Francisco, to stay with our friends Jack Shelton and Jack Juhasz in their home in Sausalito, before going on to Los Angeles for two performances of *La Sonnambula* with the San Francisco Opera at the Shrine Auditorium. While at Sausalito, Jack arranged for me to receive medical advice from a very charming doctor. He agreed with me that my discomfort and nausea could be 'nervous exhaustion' but advised me to check with my doctor when finally I returned to London that there was not a gall bladder problem. Meanwhile I should rest quietly as much as possible. Fortunately, the unpleasant condition gradually subsided and there were no further similar symptoms.

Sonnambula earned rave reviews from the critics and 'almost frenzied demonstrations' from the audiences. Among the latter we were again favoured by the presence of Miliza Korjus. This time she was not in the front row, but sitting with our friends 'the Jacks'. After the performance Jack Shelton related gleefully that, as the applause waned after many curtain calls, the people in the row in front of Miliza rose to leave. Up jumped Miliza, towering over them with her more than six feet, placed her hands on the shoulders of the nearest of them, forcing him back into his seat and saying, 'Sit down and applaud!' The whole group was so astonished that they did.

Rachel Morton in the *Independent* of November 4 credited me as having 'THE GREATEST voice in the world today', while Albert Goldberg in the *Los Angeles Times* waxed eloquent about 'what singing it was!'

Everything in the whole arsenal of bel canto was there: sustained cantilena of exquisite purity and artfully molded inflection, trills of an evenness to make a nightingale blush with envy, scales like perfectly matched pearls, cascading roulades and cadenzas, rippling arpeggios, stratospheric tones never pinched or shrill, and every note squarely on pitch...

For the seriousness and the style that pervaded the production one is willing to credit Richard Bonynge, for it was obviously his understanding that shaped the stylistic excellence of all the singers, Miss Sutherland included.

After Los Angeles it was back to New York, still feeling most unwell, for a single performance of *La Traviata* in the Academy of Music for the Philadelphia Lyric Opera Company on November 12. The General Manager at that time was Aurelio Fabiani who became a very dear friend. He had a great fund of stories gleaned from a career not only in musical pursuits but as a promoter of wrestling and boxing events. He had led the orchestra during the early days of the Chicago Lyric Opera and we loved to hear his comments on the performances then. He apparently helped support the Philadelphia Lyric Opera with his gains from the wrestling–boxing promotion. He told us a story about the great beauty Lina Cavalieri. The poster outside the opera stated: LINA CAVALIERI – MANON. Some wag (or rival) had written after the Manon '*Si sente!*' – that is '*ma non si sente*' – but you can't hear her!

Somewhere, either in New York or more likely while rehearsing in Philadelphia, I had my thirty-seventh birthday – but I've no recollection of it whatsoever.

In the cast of *La Traviata* was that dearly loved mezzo-soprano Thelma Votipka as Flora, John Alexander as Alfredo and Gabriel

Bacquier (with whom Richard and I worked many times thereafter, greatly admiring him) as Giorgio Germont. Richard conducted and the opera was produced by Irving Guttman.

Back to New York for rehearsals and taping of yet another *Bell Telephone Hour* (part of which was live) shown on November 19. The following day we flew to Toronto and gave a concert on the twenty-second in Massey Hall, Richard conducting the Toronto Symphony Orchestra in our usual programme of an eighteenth-century first half followed by nineteenth-century numbers, including the *Lucia* Mad Scene. This last prompted the audience to show their appreciation with not one, but two standing ovations – half-way through and at the end of the scene. We had been shocked at the lunch-hour that day to witness on television the assassination of President Kennedy and thought the concert would be cancelled. However, the promoters decided against that move and were probably right. So many members of the audience remarked as we were leaving the hall that they needed such a concert after the horror of the day.

On November 27 and 28 a TV show was recorded by the CBC for their hour-long *Festival* series. This consisted of comments by me on some of the great sopranos of the past – Melba, Albani, Patti – with photographs of them in various roles, selections of which I then proceeded to sing. The show was produced jointly by Franz Kramer and Irving Guttman and now appears in pirate video thirty years later.

To New York again for brush-up rehearsals of *La Sonnambula* and *La Traviata* at the Met. There were just two performances of *Sonnambula*, in my own costumes this time.

Me to Mr Bing: 'I refuse to wear those horrible costumes. They are cheap and nasty.'

Mr Bing to me: 'Nasty perhaps, my dear Miss Sutherland, but certainly *not* cheap!'

The *Traviata* costumes were again by Rolf Gérard, but I had brought my own, designed by Franco Zeffirelli for my début in the role at Covent Garden. For the second act Barbara Matera had made a simple green organza gown, worn with a large straw hat with trailing green ribbons – copied from Greta Garbo's gown when she appeared in the film *Camille*.

The criticisms were quite contradictory, some, like Winthrop Sargeant of the *New Yorker*, who said:

Miss Sutherland is one of the wonders of the world precisely because she is a coloratura soprano of exceptional warmth as well as unusual power. Her Violetta on Saturday evening, December 14th, brought her into direct competition with the great sopranos who sing the so-called standard repertoire, and she won hands down. It also offered her a role that was not only believable but extremely touching. I should say that her Violetta is the most beautifully sung and one of the best acted that our generation has encountered. Her 'Sempre libera' was of extraordinary brilliance, and the emotional scene leading up to it was projected with rare conviction. The letter reading in the last act was done as only a consummate actress could do it. Altogether, hers was a performance to remember.

Another, abhorring the fact that I had been engaged for the role by the management, was surprised that I managed not only to sing it but provided a more than reasonably well-acted interpretation of Violetta. Whatever they thought about the singers – and they were not too glowing over the rest of the cast other than Justino Diaz – they agreed that the conducting of George Schick left much to be desired. He was accused of conducting 'with a somewhat heavy hand', also 'in a rather bandmasterish fashion' and other remarks in the same vein.

I ultimately sang seven performances that season at the Met with at least five different tenors. I can remember after Sándor Kónya it was Flaviano Labo who was about half my height but very clever at hiding the fact, and with a most beautiful and powerful voice. Next was Niki Gedda, then Richard Tucker and after that Barry Morell. Weenie would arrive with me at the theatre and I'd send her to find a programme and tell me who was singing Alfredo on that particular night.

We had plenty of social engagements with the approach of Christmas and I had some beautiful photos taken by the great fashion photographer Hiro. Adam and Ruthli arrived to spend Christmas and we had some good times – going to *The Nutcracker* at City Center, to the circus at the Coliseum, skating in the Park, to town shopping and, of course, to the Met *Traviata*. Adam apparently had a bit of a sniffle and weep over his mum being so ill in the last act, but cheered up at the thought of dinner. He was also taken on a sightseeing trip with Udi and Martin Waldron and entertained by some friends of Jan and Susan Rubes. Ruthli enjoyed herself immensely, going to Harlem with Ric and Martin Scheepers to listen to the jazz.

On Sunday, January 5, the Met presented me in a Gala Evening in which I performed Act 1 of *La Traviata*, the Mad Scene from *Lucia* and the last act of *La Sonnambula*. It was a great honour to have been given such a gala so early in my career at the Met, these evenings usually being given as an anniversary homage after many years with the Company.

On January 12 Ric and I flew to Cleveland for a concert of eighteenth- and nineteenth-century works.

Back to New York again, not only for the last two Met *Traviata* performances on January 21 and 24, but to have fittings with Barbara Matera for costumes for *I Puritani* which was being produced in Boston by Sarah Caldwell the following month. I had been bowled over by Barbara's expertise and requested that she make my costumes on every possible occasion. She also took over making my concert gowns in due course, continuing to do so until I retired.

On January 25 I flew to Los Angeles for two concert performances of *Semiramide* with Marilyn Horne singing Arsace. On February 1 we flew back to New York and were off again on the fifth to Boston where, after five days' rehearsal, we presented *I Puritani* in a splendid production designed by Lloyd Burlingame, with costumes designed by Fred Voelpel and staged by Sarah Caldwell – for one performance only. Many old friends – Richard Cross, Spiro Malas, Charles Craig and Dorothy Cole – were in the cast. Richard 'gave lustrous shape to the Bellini score as he welded the singing forces with the orchestra, made up largely of Boston Symphony players'.

Harold Schonberg in the *New York Times* of February 14 rounded off his glowing review with:

> ... It was an exciting evening, and it is no disservice to the other participants to give Miss Sutherland most of the credit. For, where most of them were good, she was spectacular. And it must be said that when she sings, it is an event and realised as such by the audience. Something of the glamour and electricity of a vanished age of prima donnas stalks the house when she is in action.

To New York for two performances of *Semiramide* with the American Opera Society (February 18 and 20), then to Hartford, Connecticut on the twenty-first for a concert. Richard conducted all these appearances.

We had a farewell dinner with Terry McEwen on February 23, doubtless to celebrate the conclusion of a very successful North American tour of five and a half months, together with the release of several Decca London recordings, including *I Puritani*, *La Traviata* and *Command Performance*.

✧ 8 ✧

THE PACE IN London was no easier than in the United States. Talks had already begun regarding the proposed tour to Australia in 1965 under the auspices of the old theatrical firm there of J. C. Williamson. Sir Frank Tait, Director of 'The Firm', had been involved with the three Melba–Williamson Companies when they toured the country in 1911, 1924 and 1928, and his dearest wish was to sponsor a tour by the Sutherland–Williamson International Grand Opera Company before he died. Being advanced in years (already in his eighties) he wanted this to be accomplished as soon as possible. Norman Ayrton was to be Resident Producer and undertake the scheduling of all rehearsals, as well as producing five of the seven operas to be presented. Martin Scheepers was to produce the other two. There were many consultations during this period regarding casting, music staff, designs, juxtaposition of operas and a host of details all to be sorted out – mostly with Richard who was Artistic Director of the Company.

Rehearsals began immediately at Covent Garden for I Puritani, designed and produced by Franco Zeffirelli in Palermo with costumes by Peter John Hall.

I was asked to join Carlo Maria Giulini and Frederick Ashton judging the costumes at the Opera Ball on March 5, which had a Shakespearean theme that year. I wore a Scaasi creation in black lace which Weenie called my 'Diamond Lil' gown and had a good time with the adjudicators and Lord and Lady Harewood. Each of the judges had a course of the dinner dedicated to them, together with what was considered a fitting quotation from Shakespeare. The menu read:

Shallow Fried Trout Giulini
  'Provision give thee sweet conduct' (King Lear)
Rare Sutherland Turkey
  '... and so sweet a breath to sing' (Twelfth Night)
Ashton Cream Puffs
  '... dances and delight' (A Midsummer Night's Dream)

The opening night of I Puritani was on March 20 and we held a supper party at number 36 for the cast members and some of our friends. There were about thirty people, including Zeffirelli, Nureyev and Franco's guests the Maharanee of Baroda and her son. The display of jewels on both of them had to be seen to be believed – and they had a couple of tough-looking security guards in tow to see that they weren't robbed. I think everyone was relieved when they finally left and we could be more relaxed.

Richard was making his début as a conductor at Covent Garden, 'proving himself equally adept at accompanying tricky vocal ornamentation and in shaping the big set-piece choruses with a firm, eloquent hand'. There were reservations about the massive Zeffirelli sets, but the public loved the opera and voiced their appreciation in no uncertain terms. I adored the sets.

There were six further performances. The days between these were always packed with appointments and dinner dates with old friends like Hardy Amies, Bert Shevelove, Sir Frank Tait and his lovely wife Viola, Howard Hartog who took over the Ingpen & Williams agency, John Copley, David Webster and a host of others.

To New York again, this time for the Met tour. Ric remained in London, where he was recording *Pas de Deux* – a collection of ballet music – auditioning singers for the Australian tour and sorting out various contractual details and casting. Weenie and I spent a few days in Manhattan, during which time I rehearsed with Eugene Ormandy in Carnegie Hall for a concert I was to do at the end of the month at Ann Arbor, Michigan. We then went to Boston for a matinée performance of *Lucia* on Sunday, April 19 at the Music Hall. Silvio Varviso conducted and Anselmo Colzani and Barry Morell were the male protagonists.

We returned to New York immediately after the matinée and were able to attend a performance of the Noël Coward musical *High Spirits* from his delightful play *Blithe Spirit*. Tammy Grimes and Beatrice Lillie were both hilarious, although the latter had a little trouble sticking strictly to the text and Noël, whose guests we were, was not amused.

Next stop on the tour was Cleveland, Ohio, with another *Lucia*, then an exciting performance back at the Met of Verdi's *Falstaff* conducted by Leonard Bernstein and designed by Zeffirelli was a really great night in the opera house. It was the year of the New York World Fair and the Metropolitan Opera presented a special Gala Season.

On the twenty-ninth we went to Ann Arbor, Michigan, for the concert with Eugene Ormandy conducting the Philadelphia Orchestra. I sang 'Ah fors'è lui' and 'Sempre libera' from *La Traviata* and the Mad Scene from *Lucia*, receiving a thunderous standing ovation from audience and orchestra combined. Back to New York – and a small rehearsal for *La Sonnambula* which was presented as part of the Gala Season at the Met on Sunday, May 3 and Saturday, May 9. In between, there was a grand supper party at Sherry's to launch this special season, and Leontyne Price, Renata Tebaldi, Anna Moffo and I were each seated at a separate table as a 'Guest of Honour'.

In between performances I managed to do some interviews, attend the World Fair twice with the Jacks from Sausalito, the ballet with Tony Blum and Martin Scheepers and the musical *Funny Girl*.

There were further *Lucias* in Atlanta on May 15, Minneapolis on May 22 and Detroit on the twenty-sixth.

Back to Europe – and on June 1 Richard and I flew to Berne where we performed a concert in aid of the Pestalozzi Children's Home on the fourth. This was widely broadcast in Europe and, I believe, televised. Five more *Lucias* (a new production designed by Alessandro Benois) in Milan at La Scala followed, conducted by Nino Sanzogno with Piero Cappuccilli (making his first appearance at La Scala) and Gianni Raimondi.

This production was being taken to Moscow in August–September and I was excited at the prospect. However, during my summer break at Rocca Bella I was told by Maestro Sicilliani that there were many Italian-born singers complaining about the large number of foreigners engaged for leading roles on the tour, and to avoid a possible strike and cancellation of the whole project, the Scala administration reluctantly asked me to withdraw. It meant that I could have a much longer holiday and, as I had not defaulted and possessed a perfectly watertight contract, the Scala paid me. Renata Scotto sang *Lucia* on the Russian tour.

But back to June 1964, and prior to the opening night in Milan Noël Coward and Coley, his secretary, had arrived there and we dined together. The conversation was very lively and we spoke of slipping up to the villa in Ticino after the opening for the weekend. Noël was surprised that we were so happy with that area and said it was inaccessible. This was true at that time. When our lease expired (which was the following year) he said we should come and live in the canton of Vaud, near Montreux and his home in Les Avants. An autoroute was being constructed that would make a trip to Geneva airport only an hour – door to door – and one should start looking for a property now.

I was not too pleased at the thought of moving again; however, arrangements were made that Weenie and Ric (who were driving back to London the following week) would call in at the Coward residence *en route*, stay a few nights and go house-hunting during the day. This they did, and after some disappointing excursions (somewhat hair-raising, as Noël drove very fast in his own open car) with no property either appealing or being within our means, Ric said over dinner that the only place he was really interested in was the chalet he could see through the trees, next door to Chalet Coward. The owner agreed to sell and we bought Chalet Monnet – from which name we deleted one 'n', having more affinity with the artist than the family who built the house originally. The property enjoyed fabulous views on all sides and although the chalet was enlarged by us at the back, towards the forest, the other three façades remain very much as they were when we bought it. The windows have been enlarged to capture the vistas and more light.

A welcome addition to our household at this time was Paul Garner who was Canadian and had worked with Decca in London, where we met him. With Richard performing more, and very often works for which the orchestral material was in a sorry state, requiring much editing and cleaning up, it was necessary to have more assistance with the secretarial work. There was also organising to be done for the Australian tour the following year and Paul was a great help in many ways. He stayed with us for several years, finally leaving to work for Placido Domingo in the same capacity.

We were saddened to learn at this time that Fiona Ede was dying of leukaemia. She had organised all our books of press cuttings, attended to the early fan mail and kept us supplied with tapes of radio performances that we missed due to our travels. We had appreciated her cheerful common sense and ever-ready assistance, especially when we were without a car, and we still remember her with great affection.

On June 26 we commenced recording *Norma* for the RCA label, a reciprocal arrangement with that Company and Decca, using the latter's technicians. As Adalgisa we had Marilyn Horne, John Alexander was Pollione, Richard Cross was Oroveso and we had Yvonne Minton as Clotilde, with Joseph Ward as Flavio. Richard conducted the London Symphony Orchestra and Chorus, and the reviews were highly complimentary to all, especially in view of the comparisons with the Callas, Ponselle and Cigna interpretations. The majority of critics were struck by the youthfulness of all the protagonists and praised the insight Richard had into the work.

Many of the singers who were to accompany us to Australia started working on their respective roles with Richard in between the recording sessions and there were all manner of meetings and appointments. The recording sessions finished on the evening of July 15 and Richard flew to Toronto the next day, where he was to conduct nine performances of *The Marriage of Figaro* for the Stratford (Ontario) Festival between August 4 and 22.

His cast was predominantly a young one – with a couple of well-seasoned singers in the roles of Figaro (Jan Rubes, with whom I had sung in the Vancouver *Don Giovanni* in 1958) and Doctor Bartolo (sung by Howell Glynne, a stalwart of my Covent Garden days). Susanna was sung by Laurel Hurley, Cherubino by Huguette Tourangeau (who had won the Met Auditions that year), Count Almaviva was sung by Cornelis Opthof, Don Basilio by John Bonhomme (who joined the Sadler's Wells Company later that year) and the Countess by Ilona Kombrink. Several of the singers received excellent reviews, also Richard who '... gave brio and wit to the sparkling overture, and was unremitting in his consideration of the singers' privileges. He received prolonged acclaim at the end of the opera.'

I left London at the same time as Ric, Adam being on school holidays, travelling to Villa Rocca Bella by car with Weenie and Gudrun. I spent some time studying *Faust* for the forthcoming season in the United States, and much more enjoying the summer weather and being with Adam. I paid a short visit to Noël Coward to check the Chalet Monet and met Charlie Chaplin and his wife Oona.

Having returned to London, Richard and I flew to New York on September 18, where he had arranged for us to stay in a charming duplex flat with a minute garden on West 9th Street in Greenwich Village. The Village area was such fun for shopping and just walking about at that time.

After a long and rather fraught rehearsal period at the Met, due to a deadlock of labour negotiations with the orchestra, the season there opened on October 12 with more performances of *Lucia di Lammermoor*. The production was new and made with the move to the larger stage of the Lincoln Center Met in mind. This was the second-last season at the old theatre and there was a tendency to overstate the scenery and costumes. There was so much greenery framing the Fountain Scene that I called the opera 'Lucia of the Rain Forest' and the costumes by Attilio Colonello were far too rich for an impoverished girl, forced to marry for money and gain by her brother. All the costumes appeared to be black, red and white, and would have been perfect for *Maria Stuarda*. But the public was excited by the vocal performances and gave us a splendid and prolonged ovation of some fourteen curtain calls. There were nine or ten performances of the opera at intervals until Christmas Eve, with Flaviano Labo and John Alexander singing the role of Edgardo at times.

As usual there were plenty of social functions in New York. Bob Merrill (who was beginning his twentieth season in the house and singing Enrico) gave a party after the Met opening, and Geri Souvaine a magnificent dinner party. Barbara Matera had undertaken to make all my costumes for the Australian tour. These were designed by Tonina Doráti, the daughter of the Hungarian conductor Antal Doráti. Indeed, she had been asked to design all the costumes and sets for the complete season of seven operas – a mammoth task. Tonina came to New York and discussed with Barbara the possible materials and trimmings for my costumes, leaving most of the decisions to Barbara. In all there were about twenty wonderful creations, the *Faust* and

Semiramide being aired in Philadelphia and Boston respectively prior to Australia.

It was during this period that the photograph of Renata Tebaldi, Elisabeth Schwarzkopf, Lisa della Casa and myself was taken – rather a feat to bring us all together! It was a publicity shot for the Met Gala to be held at the end of November.

At this time Richard made a quick trip to Melbourne to audition singers for the chorus of our touring company – one hundred and fifty applicants for a chorus of only thirty-six. It was difficult for him to choose, as the voices were so good, and the ultimate group made a glorious sound and were very handsome. Many of those chorus members became soloists with the Australian Opera or remained choristers with them, only retiring three or four years ago. They were one of the greatest assets of the tour.

Richard arrived in San Francisco ahead of me to rehearse *La Traviata* and I travelled out ten days later, after taping an *Ed Sullivan Show*. Other artists on the show were Van Johnson, the group called The Animals and Topo Gigio, that adorable mouse. There were three performances of *La Traviata* in San Francisco – on November 1, 3 and 5 – and two with the Company in Los Angeles on the eighth (a matinée) and the tenth. Lotfi Mansouri was the Stage Director.

Alfred Frankenstein wrote in the *San Francisco Chronicle* of November 2:

> The size of her voice, its three-dimensional quality, its endlessly surprising glints and sparkles of color, and the polished correctness of her vocalism all fall together to produce one of the true musical marvels of our time.

Rachel Morton wrote a splendid review in the *Independent* after the matinée at the Shrine Auditorium in Los Angeles, asking how long must they wait to hear me sing *Norma* and saying that Richard had 'conducted with sensitivity and authority'.

Ric left for Vancouver after Los Angeles as he had rehearsals and five performances there of *The Marriage of Figaro* between November 19 and 28.

I returned to New York immediately for two more *Lucias* and the Met gala on the twenty-ninth. This last consisted of the first acts of *Der Rosenkavalier*, *La Bohème* and *La Traviata* and was a Benefit in aid of the Welfare and Pension Fund. I shared the evening with Elisabeth Schwarzkopf, Lisa della Casa, Otto Edelman, Renata Tebaldi, Carlo Bergonzi and Cesare Siepi.

There was an unscheduled performance that night. The dog fondled by the Marschallin didn't show up and as Renata Tebaldi's poodle New had accompanied her to the theatre, he went on, acquitting himself very well. At the end of his scene he trotted back to his mistress with a ten-dollar bill in his collar – the standard fee for a performing dog at the Met.

There was a *Lucia* matinée on December 5 and we flew to Montreal the next day for a concert. The second half commenced with my singing of the Glière Concerto (Opus 82) for Coloratura and Orchestra. It was the first time the orchestra had played the piece – and I believe it was the first time I sang that haunting vocal work in public. I had originally heard it sung in Australia by Erna Berger and was enchanted by it then.

There were two performances with the Houston Symphony, on December 17 and 19. The Glière Concerto was again a hit with the critics and audience, who were amazed that they had not known of the piece, although it was written some twenty-two years previously.

We were back in New York as soon as possible, as Adam and Gudrun were arriving on the afternoon of the twenty-first to spend Christmas with us. We had dinner with Frances Yeend, with whom I had sung at Covent Garden in *Carmen* – Frances as Micaela and me singing Frasquita back in the Fifties. We had also been in Bulawayo together, and it was great to talk and laugh over those times.

There was a *Lucia* on Christmas Eve at the Met – the last there for some time – and we spent a quiet Christmas Day together. Adam was fortunate that Jan and Susan Rubes were in town with their family of boys, so he was able to have some fun with them.

Before the New Year we were already rehearsing for the American Opera Society performances of Handel's *Alcina*. These were held in Carnegie Hall on January 3 and 5, 1965, with Margreta Elkins as Ruggiero, Monica Sinclair as Bradamante, André Montal as Oronte, Laurel Hurley as Morgana and Spiro Malas as Melisso. Richard conducted 'with a feeling for taste and style that never robbed the opera of its considerable emotional fire'.

We all went to see *Hello Dolly* and when it came to the finale of the musical Carol Channing advanced on the catwalk to be right in front of our seats in the theatre and sang 'Well, hello Joanie, and hello, Adam' and so on. Adam was amazed and couldn't understand how Carol knew we were there. He was further dumbfounded when we were escorted back to see her and she was so sweet to him. Of course, I deduced the whole surprise was because Barbara Matera had made Carol's costumes for the show and we had very likely been sitting in the house seats. It was a terrific thrill for Adam who went back to school in London shortly after. It was a thrill for us, too. What a wonderful Dolly she was.

We were off to Cincinnati, giving a concert there on January 9 with the Cincinnati Symphony Orchestra including a repeat of the Glière Concerto. This work was becoming extremely popular with both orchestras and audiences and scored a big hit when finally released on record by Decca in 1968 under the title of *Russian Rarities*. The same concert was again repeated in the New Orleans Municipal Auditorium with their Philharmonic Symphony Orchestra on January 19.

Before our trip to New Orleans we went to Boston where we taped an hour-long programme for NET in Channel 2's huge studio there. The show was called *An Hour With Joan Sutherland*, produced by Curtis Davis and Kirk Browning, with Terry McEwen as host-compère. Marilyn Horne and John Alexander were assisting in this TV show – Marilyn with me in the duet 'Serbami ognor' from *Semiramide* done in concert fashion and John in the staged duet 'Vieni fra queste braccia' from *I Puritani*. I also sang some favourite arias of Handel, Arne, Ricci and Meyerbeer, together with 'The Gipsy and the Bird'.

After the concert in New Orleans on January 19 we flew to New York – for more fittings with Barbara Matera – then on to Boston on the twenty-fifth to rehearse *Semiramide* with Sarah Caldwell for the Boston Opera, with performances on February 5 and 7. Marilyn Horne was my son Arsace, André Montal Idreno and Joseph Rouleau Assur.

I'm never sure who or what prompted Marilyn to wear a moustache and beard as Arsace. She made her entrance on a 'ship' which travelled straight down the centre of the raked stage and the sight of her very pregnant, rotund figure in a long draped kaftan with a stove-pipe helmet and jaunty Assyrian-style beard from ear to ear was too much for everyone at the Dress Rehearsal and the whole House dissolved into helpless laughter. This included Richard and the orchestra. Her opening line didn't improve matters – 'Eccomi, alfine in Babylonia!' ('Here I am, at last in Babylon!'). As well as Marilyn looking just like the cartoon character the Little King, there was trouble with the 'ship'. It tended to travel too fast and give the impression it would go off its rail and sail on into the orchestra pit.

The critic of the *Boston Traveller* (Alta Maloney) wrote:

> Miss Sutherland arrived at the altar in a chair carried by soldiers, white doves fluttering briefly. From that moment the audience was spellbound. Probably if it had not been snowing, they would like to have carried her away in it after the curtain calls.
>
> Miss Horne, who has a remarkable range – even with a beard – sailed downstage to the docks on a boat, her aria of arrival winning her own enthusiastic applause.
>
> But the moment when mother and son embraced and sang to each other words of longing and comfort was truly glorious. When it was over the roar from the audience forced them into an unusual mid-scene bow.

The doves mentioned were skilfully recaptured by members of the chorus and returned to their coop which was kept underneath the back of the highly raked stage. All very fine, but when we reached the last scene of the opera and I began to sing the beautiful prayer begging forgiveness they all joined in with very determined cooing, giving the long, legato line of the short aria a strange syncopation. Weenie was therefore stationed by their coop for both performances to say 'Shh' when the aria began – and they actually obeyed and kept quiet.

In the *Christian Science Monitor* of February 6, 1965 Harold Rogers wrote an excellent preamble to his review on the Golden Age of Opera, asking:

> ... What was this Golden Age? It was that period around the turn of the century when singers truly prepared for their careers. Voices were trained to sing with the accuracy of instruments. ... In our day, however, singers have aimed for the quick success. We have had the occasional coloratura ... But until Joan Sutherland and Marilyn Horne appeared on the scene the Golden Age of Opera was a thing of the past.

The above – and the rest of the review – was very gratifying, but also sad comment on the state of vocal tuition and preparation during the mid-twentieth century. Unfortunately, I fear the vocal training has deteriorated even further at the time of writing some thirty years later and so many promising young voices are all too quickly experiencing problems after making splendid début performances, disappearing from the scene in a very few years. They do not appear to have learned and really developed a basic vocal technique. Their musical ability is far ahead of their capacity to sustain long and difficult roles on the stage, being unable to cope with the support and projection of their voices over a large (and very often over-loud) orchestra in modern acoustically imperfect theatres.

Next stop Miami and four *Lucias* which were the first in which Luciano Pavarotti and I sang together and were his North American début. Originally Renato Cioni was engaged to do them but cancelled at the last moment. Richard had heard Luciano sing an audition in 1963 and suggested he be engaged. He was already contracted to come to Australia with us for the Williamson tour, and the rest is history.

We had a little free time to enjoy the comfort of our bungalow on Key Biscayne, also testing our skill on their 'Pitch and Putt' course. I'm afraid I swiped at the ball which hit a palm tree, bounced off it and caused a nearby female player to duck in alarm – but I made the first green. We also got to know Luciano a little and felt we had a charmer for the Australian public and a good trouper.

Back in New York briefly for a taping for the *Bell Telephone Hour* of the 'Jewel Song' from *Faust* and 'Ah, fors'è lui' from *La Traviata*.

At this time the *Norma* recording had been issued, together with

Richard's ballet collection, *Pas de Deux*. Both had a good reception by the critics. The *Gramophone* critic wrote of *Pas de Deux*:

... Mr Bonynge obviously likes the stuff, and one of the great virtues of the record is the sympathy with which he conducts it. The many touches of rubato are precisely gauged and the tunes, silly and otherwise, come alive in a surprising way, while overlaying the mediocrity there is tremendous and, as they say, infectious gaiety. The music is beautifully played and superbly recorded.

The critic in *Cue* magazine (whose name I do not have) wrote at the end of his review of *Norma*:

... Here is that well-known electricity of the Sutherland–Horne 'team': the famous duet and the long passages between them contain some of the most triumphant singing on discs. I have listened intently to this felicitous *Norma* four times; if it does not become a best-seller, I'll move meekly into the Victor dog's doghouse.

The rehearsal period for the *Faust* in Philadelphia on March 9 (my début as Marguerite) was minimal – but somehow the opera held together. It was probably the fact that several of the singers had been in the Vancouver performances with Richard, and I was just inserted into Irving Guttman's already existing production. Richard Verreau was Faust, Richard Cross Mephistopheles, Cornelis Opthof Valentin and Margreta Elkins Siebel.

Max de Schauensee, in the *Evening Bulletin* of 10 March, wrote:

... Miss Sutherland presented her new role with all the éclat and personal stamp of the star performer she assuredly is. It was carefully planned and sung with a brilliance that had been anticipated.

What had not been anticipated was the soprano's complete suitability for the role and the dramatic power that raised her acting high above the norm of what one generally sees in grand opera.

Another surprise was Miss Sutherland's excellent French diction. This was not the case with her great Australian predecessor of another generation – Mme Nellie Melba.

He went on to say:

... The diva's husband, Richard Bonynge, was on the conductor's stand and gave an excellently paced and shaded account of Gounod's best opera. He restored Siebel's aria 'Si le bonheur' (a charming melody) and several pages of duet between Faust and Marguerite in the final scene, which were heard only in the very earliest performances of the opera. Mr Bonynge always turns up with interesting musical excavations that are of value.

A further performance of *Faust* with the same cast was given at the Bushnell Auditorium in Hartford on March 16, then Richard flew to Bloomington, Indiana, to rehearse for our concert on March 21. We were very impressed with the standard of the Indiana University Philharmonic Orchestra and enjoyed our visit very much.

This was our last engagement in the United States for eighteen months and we were off to Jamaica two days later to spend two and half weeks at Noël Coward's seaside property Blue Harbour, enjoying the relaxed Caribbean atmosphere and Noël's hospitality. There was a main house in which was situated the dining-room, pleasant lounging terraces and the bedrooms of the permanent household, including Cole Lesley ('Coley') and Graham Payn. There were two guest bungalows, one of which Weenie had and the other Ric and myself. The whole property was on an incline covered with flowering tropical vegetation, descending to its own small beach and salt water swimming pool.

We had been met on arrival at Montego Bay by Coley and driven via Ocho Rios to the house near Port Maria. Coley had warned us there was a water shortage, due to lack of rain. Weenie vows the locals must have thought we were some kind of Rain Gods, as it rained heavily the first two nights we were there, with much drumming on the roof and the wind sighing and rustling through the palm trees and tightly closed storm shutters. The sea was a bit rough at first, but very soon the garden boys had the pump going, filling the sheltered swimming pool where we spent most of our days. During our stay we were interviewed by Betty Best, a journalist from Australia, and a lengthy article ultimately appeared in the *Australian Women's Weekly* as advance publicity for the Williamson tour. Accompanying the article were many colour photographs taken by (and with) Peter Sellers who also visited Blue Harbour briefly with his wife Britt Eklund. It was difficult to be vaguely serious when he was about as his particular sense of the ridiculous ruled most of the day.

Noël lived on a little plateau above Blue Harbour, reached by jeep up a very bumpy, unmade road. The house was called Firefly and the view from it spectacular. Here he worked every morning until lunch-time, when we usually went up to join him for the meal, with him coming down in the evening for dinner. He loved Firefly and was ultimately buried there at his favourite viewpoint. He wrote and painted there in semi-solitude, but loved company at certain times.

We met several of Noël's friends on the island, including Mrs Blanche Blackwell who lived nearby. She was a wonderful hostess, very vivacious and a splendid swimmer. She was able to take us on a couple of occasions to Golden Eye, the home of the late Ian Fleming, where the whole party went snorkelling in the beautiful bay below the cliff-top house, encountering some quite large and frightening sea creatures, including a very nasty looking eel and a barracuda or two.

During our stay the idea evolved of recording a disc of Coward songs with Noël participating and we worked on them with him. He suggested that Douglas Gamley might do the arrangements as he had done for the forthcoming disc of Christmas carols titled *Joy to the World*. Both of these discs were big hits, the Gamley arrangements being part of their attraction.

The author James Pope-Hennessy was another guest for a few days and May (the lovable cook-housekeeper) concocted wonderful dishes for all, using the plentiful seafood – notably black crab. There was also a rather lethal drink of coconut milk and gin known as the 'Clemence Dane Mixture', as that notable lady had thoroughly approved and imbibed it during her stay at 11 a.m. each day.

After a wonderfully relaxing holiday we boarded the small six-seater air bus to fly low along the coast to Montego Bay and take the plane to New York on April 11. I had final fittings with Barbara Matera for my new costumes for Australia then, on the fifteenth, we went back to London – just in time for Easter weekend.

During the stay of two months in London we rehearsed and performed six *Lucias* and six *Sonnambulas* at the Royal Opera House, Richard conducting them for the first time in the House. Luciano Pavarotti sang his first Elvinos. Several of the singers in both operas were members of the Australian tour, including Luciano, Joe Rouleau, Margreta Elkins and Joseph Ward, and these performances served as pre-rehearsal for us all, as had the *Faust* in Philadelphia.

After one of the *Lucia* performances Dame Nellie Melba's niece, Helen Lempriere, and her husband, Keith Wood, came backstage and presented me with a silver monogrammed pin box that Melba had kept on her dressing-table – a lovely token in view of our imminent return to Melbourne.

Also during this period in London we recorded *Joy to the World* with the NPO, which included Douglas Gamley's spirited and imaginative handling of the items, particularly 'The Twelve Days of Christmas'. Richard managed to record *Rosina* by the eighteenth-century William Shield and a collection of overtures as well.

At the end of May Weenie and Paul Garner went to Locarno to attend to the removal of the furniture and household goods to Les Avants. In spite of the still very cold weather everything was installed to Paul's satisfaction, later to be moved several times and taken out completely for storage while we extended the back section of the house, adding a large garage, laundry, music room, four bedrooms and several bathrooms, plus a tower on one corner to increase the length of the rooms on that angle. The original façade remains unaltered.

My earliest studio portrait, Sydney, c. 1931.

(right) My father at the Highland
gathering Sydney, 1930, two years
before his death.

(below) Mother and Richard at
Glyndebourne, 1956.

(opposite) A publicity photograph taken in London, 1952.

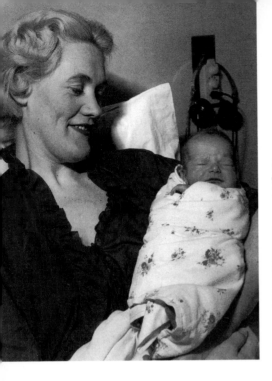

(left) Adam's first day –
Queen Charlotte's Hospital,
13 February 1956.

(right) Bidding goodnight to Adam
before going to the theatre, 1959.

(left) Outside the Teatro Massimo, Palermo,
January 1961 with Richard and Adam.

Richard, Lady Harrison, Princess Alexandra, myself and Sir Eric Harrison, the Australian High Commissioner, talking after a recital, London, 1959.

(Left to right) Regina Resnik, me, Birgit Nilsson, Danilova at a party in New York, 1962.

(above) Joking with Noël Coward at his home in Les Avants in the mid–Sixties.

(below left) With Placido Domingo – a surprise visit to my dressing-room, Sydney, 1990.

(below right) With Clifford Grant at the Sydney Opera House Trust Dinner, 1990.

Rocca Bella, Minusio, 1964.

Chalet Monet in winter.

Rocca Bella, Whale Beach, from the lower garden, 1993.

(above) In the garden of St John's Church. The wedding party, left to right: Jean-Paul Ingold, me, Richard, Ruthli, Adam, Helen, David and Jean Wahba, Josef Lang (best man) and Rachel in front.

(below) Richard was presented with the Order of Australia in February 1984. His mother is on the left, and Weenie next to me.

With one of her great costumes, Barbara and Arthur Matera at the Sotheby sale preview.

Some of the gowns displayed for the Sotheby's sale.

(above) A favourite family photo – a
winter walk on Whale Beach: Adam,
Vanya, Richard, Natasha, Helen.

(right) An outing to Taronga Zoo
in Sydney with 'Didi'.

(left) Richard's sixtieth birthday party,
with Natasha and Vanya.

Richard and me, October 1989, Newcastle-upon-Tyne.

The opening of the new section of the National Portrait Gallery by Her Majesty The Queen, taken in front of my portrait by Ulisse Sartini (left), with Mrs Peggy Haim and Prince Philip just behind her.

At Whale Beach during the Bicentenary. Back row left to right: Rachel, Ric, Adam, me, Ruthli. Front row: Vanya, Helen, Natasha, Jean–Paul, Chester.

PART THREE

The Return to Australia
and Further Tours in America and Japan
1965–1975

❖ 1 ❖

ON JUNE 11, THE day after the last *Sonnambula*, we left London, travelling to Australia via Hawaii, where the pleasant few days spent there broke the long journey and (we hoped) helped rid us of some of the jet-lag before arriving in Melbourne. Ruthli and Paul were with us, Weenie having gone to Sydney a few days earlier, then on to Melbourne to open up the house that Williamson's had rented for our stay. Gudrun remained in London to look after Adam until the end of his school year, then travelled with him out to Sydney to stay with his grandmother until we arrived for the six-week season there.

We had a change of planes in Sydney and various relatives and friends had come to the airport to welcome us back. But we were escorted past them all, barely able to give a wave of the hand, surrounded by eager press photographers all jostling for the best 'shooting' position. In a small, stuffy VIP room we were subjected to a barrage of questions, flash bulbs, microphones and TV cameras and became increasingly agitated and angry. The behaviour of the press was outrageous and undisciplined, eliciting the remark from Richard that they resembled a bunch of orang-utans. We could laugh over it afterwards but questions like 'How does it feel to be back in Sydney?' are impossible to answer when you've just stepped out of a plane from the other side of the world and not seen the city for fourteen years.

J. C. Williamson's had arranged the use of a very comfortable house for us in Toorak, an inner residential suburb of Melbourne. We barely had time to unpack before it was time to go to a welcoming reception in the then relatively new Southern Cross Hotel and dinner with Sir Frank and Lady Tait, John McCallum (Managing Director of 'The Firm', as Williamson's was affectionately called) and his wife Googie Withers. We doubtless talked about the forthcoming rehearsals but at least they did not begin until Monday, allowing us three more days to get our bearings.

We enjoyed a performance by Marcel Marceau in Her Majesty's Theatre where we would be performing ourselves in three weeks' time. It was a good omen that Marcel's tour was preceding ours and having such a huge success. We were happy to meet again after the show and laughed about the recurring coincidence of our being in the same place at the same time.

I began work on each of three operas – *Lucia*, *Traviata* and *Semiramide* – which were the first of five works in which I was appearing, the others being *La Sonnambula* and *Faust*. The remaining two operas on the schedule were *L'Elisir d'Amore* and *Eugene Onegin* – this last being on in the first week of the season with *Lucia* and *Traviata*. One opera a week was added to the repertoire so that, by the end of the Melbourne season, it was complete.

To set roughly each of these opening works was a good move, enabling the double cast to know what was happening on-stage. Most of the artists had already performed their roles elsewhere and it was a way of bringing the members of the Company together and finding out if extra musical coaching was required by some, as well as providing everyone with an overall idea of the staging.

Richard had assembled a quite formidable cast of young English, Australian and American singers, with just one Italian – Luciano Pavarotti. He was the first person to be contracted, agreeing to sing three performances a week from his repertoire of Edgardo in *Lucia di Lammermoor*, Alfredo in *La Traviata*, Elvino in *La Sonnambula* and Nemorino in *L'Elisir d'Amore*. John Alexander of the Metropolitan Opera sang Edgardo, Alfredo, Faust and, in *Eugene Onegin*, the role of Lenski. The third tenor was Alberto Remedios from Sadler's Wells Opera engaged for Edgardo, Faust, Lenski and Alfredo. Also in the tenor ranks were Joseph Ward from Covent Garden – to sing Idreno in *Semiramide*, Elvino, Nemorino, Gaston in *La Traviata* and Monsieur Triquet in *Eugene Onegin* – and André Montal, a young American, to perform the roles of Idreno, Elvino, Arturo, Gaston and Monsieur Triquet.

For the soprano team Richard had chosen people capable of singing the leading roles in the five operas in which I was appearing, as well as the remaining two – *L'Elisir* and *Onegin*. All the operas were to be performed in the original language except *Eugene Onegin*, which was sung in English.

The beautiful English soprano Elizabeth Harwood, then at the beginning of her career, joined the Company to sing Lucia, Amina, Adina in *L'Elisir d'Amore* and Lisa in *La Sonnambula* on the nights that I sang Amina. Doris Yarick (wife of Richard Cross) sang Marguerite in *Faust*, Tatiana in *Eugene Onegin*, Lisa in *La Sonnambula* and Giannetta in *L'Elisir d'Amore*, also appearing (in true Company style) as the Princess Azema (who has almost nothing to do) in *Semiramide*. Margreta Elkins had sung as a mezzo-soprano but was experimenting with a change to the soprano range. She sang Adina, Tatiana and Siebel in *Faust*. Another Australian, Joy Mammen, sang Violetta, Tatiana, Lisa and Giannetta.

For mezzo-sopranos we had Covent Garden's Monica Sinclair, the

Australian Lauris Elms who had also been singing at Covent Garden, the American Dorothy Cole and the Scot Morag Beaton. Monica and Lauris shared the difficult part of Arsace in *Semiramide*, also Olga in *Eugene Onegin* and Martha in *Faust*, with Monica singing Flora in *La Traviata* and Lauris the part of Annina. Morag Beaton sang Larina (*Onegin*), Teresa (*Sonnambula*), Annina, Alisa, Siebel and one performance of Tatiana. Dorothy Cole was Larina, Teresa, Flora, Alisa and Martha.

The baritones were the Dutch-Canadian Cornelis Opthof and Australians Robert Allman and Ronald Maconaghie. Opthof sang Enrico (*Lucia*), Germont (*Traviata*), Belcore (*L'Elisir*) and Valentin (*Faust*); Allman the same four roles, as well as Onegin, and Maconaghie sang Belcore, the Marquis in *La Traviata*, Oroe in *Semiramide* and Zaretsky in *Onegin*.

The four basses were the French-Canadian Joseph Rouleau, two Americans – Spiro Malas and Richard Cross – and the Australian Clifford Grant. Rouleau sang Raimondo in *Lucia*, Dulcamara in *L'Elisir*, Prince Gremin in *Onegin*, Assur in *Semiramide*, Mephistopheles in *Faust* and Count Rodolfo in *La Sonnambula*. Cross sang Raimondo, Assur, Gremin, Mephistopheles and the Baron in *Traviata*. Malas sang Dulcamara, Assur, Gremin, Rodolfo and the Baron, and Grant Raimondo, Gremin, the Doctor in *Traviata* and the Ghost in *Semiramide*.

All the members of the Company were prepared to sing smaller roles – and did, except those who had three major parts to perform every week. Many members of the chorus sang minor roles and had long careers as soloists either with the Australian Opera (now Opera Australia) or abroad (especially with the ENO) for more than twenty-five years. These included Donald Shanks (leading bass with the Australian Opera, who sometimes sang the Doctor in our *Traviata*), Tom McDonnell (who sang Alessio in *La Sonnambula*), Sergei Baigildin (who sang Normanno in *Lucia* and one Lenski) and Mary Hayman (who sang Giannetta in *L'Elisir d'Amore*). Judith Turner sang such roles as Santuzza and Brünnhilde with the ENO later and John Heffernan (John Aron) was in the London production of *Phantom of the Opera*. Many of the 1965 chorus only retired from the Australian Opera in 1988–9, including Elizabeth Allen, Josephine Bermingham, Pauline Garrick and John Durham.

As well as directing five of the operas, Norman Ayrton did a fine job of co-ordinating the rehearsal schedule. Martin Scheepers directed *L'Elisir d'Amore* and *La Sonnambula*, as well as choreographing the ballets and dancing in the *Faust* Wallpurgis Night scene.

Gerald Krug and Georg Tintner (both with the Elizabethan Theatre Trust Opera) and William Weibel of the Metropolitan Opera were Assistant Conductors. They also worked with the chorus and as *répétiteurs*. In this latter task they were joined by Caroline Lill who became a backbone of the Australian Opera music staff, and by Brian Stanborough and Gwen Halstead. Richard conducted four times a week as a rule and attended every one of the one hundred and twenty performances given on the tour.

As for myself, I sang a total of forty-two performances – twelve Violettas, eleven Lucias, eight Semiramides, six Aminas and six Marguerites. At the beginning of the tour Luciano Pavarotti recalls that I sang the Dress Rehearsal of *La Sonnambula* one morning in full voice and a performance of *La Traviata* the same night. Many of the other singers had as much to sing, but I felt responsible for the success of the season and tried to cope with endless interviews and receptions as well to boost the public's interest in this first-rate Company.

The opening night of the tour was a triumph, but the closing night of the Melbourne season was one neither Richard nor I will ever forget – nor, I think, will anyone who was there. After applause lasting for a full forty minutes, with the whole Company on stage in formal dress, as well as those who had taken part in the final performance of *La Sonnambula*, the audience began chanting 'Home, Sweet Home' repeatedly. A terrible old upright rehearsal piano was wheeled on from somewhere in the wings and Richard accompanied me in the old song, such a favourite of Melba. The theatre was full of great joy and love, and all of us were thrilled by the public response.

The Age reported:

Flowers and streamers blanketed the stage, women in evening gowns stood on seats and applause continued for forty minutes.

and the *Melbourne Herald*:

The effect was magical and I doubt whether anything like it has ever been seen in Australia before.

There were numerous hilarious incidents during the tour. One of our baritones who, for emotional reasons, had 'drowned his sorrows' overmuch, was brought to the theatre very drunk, incapable of making himself up, and was attended to by friends in the chorus. They somehow got him to the stage and pushed him on – where he swayed about and went straight off the other side. He got back on, was pushed around all night as Belcore in *L'Elisir* – and sang his most accurate performance of the season.

Another night a baritone singing Germont in *La Traviata* went blank as he made his entrance to Flora's party. He froze and there was what seemed like an enormous pause, with the prompt (Adelio Zagonara, famous old comprimario from La Scala) practically jumping out of the prompt box to attract his attention. Just as Luciano decided he might as well sing the phrase for him our Germont loudly uttered 'Cortigiani!' (practically the same notes from *Rigoletto*). The whole cast collapsed into ill-concealed giggles.

Moffatt Oxenbould was very young at the time and was one of our stage managers. He was frequently taken for our son, in spite of the total lack of resemblance. He is first to acknowledge that the experience gained on that tour was a very solid background for his years as Artistic Administrator and now Artistic Director of Opera Australia.

It was a very happy and excited group that left for Adelaide on August 15 – some thirty-eight of us on one plane and over a hundred more on the Overland Express from Melbourne or by private car. The season in Adelaide was to begin the next day with *Lucia*. There was not such an obvious reaction to the performances, it being a much more conservative and reserved city in those days. But the public enjoyed all the operas and the Company was fêted, with civic receptions, cocktail parties, visits to the vineyards of the Barossa Valley and the like. In the midst of all this we received the sad news that Sir Frank had died at Portsea (Victoria) on August 23 aged eighty-one. He had realised his dream of bringing home Australia's leading singer of the day (as he had Nellie Melba in the past) to great acclaim – not only for her, but for the whole Company. His work was done.

As the tour took place during the long summer school break for Northern Hemisphere dwellers many of the artists brought their young families with them from America and combined their work with sightseeing. Adam had come down to Melbourne for a week to see a number of performances and was delighted to find some young people who would be travelling on to Sydney, where they could all go on a few excursions. He was preoccupied over having enough flowers to throw on stage at the end of the opera as he did in Europe. Weenie collected some daffodils and some other flowers that had seen better days from our flower vases, while Paul Garner culled what he dared from our rented house's garden. Adam managed to land several well-aimed bunches near his mum and some of the other children joined his act.

It had been difficult convincing the public that not only the performances with myself as leading soprano were worthwhile. The nights and matinées when I was not on stage were very poorly attended at first, but gradually the audiences realised there was star quality in singers like Luciano, John Alexander, Joseph Rouleau, Elizabeth Harwood, Cornelis Opthof and other members of the Company. The Melbourne *Age* remarked that the Sutherland–Williamson season had 'proved that there is still a wide public for opera which will respond to the correct stimulus'. And the impression that the Company made, not only in Melbourne but in all the cities it visited, certainly provided a whole new generation of opera-goers – ready and waiting for the Australian National and State Companies to achieve the same high standards. This they have done, in their various new performing arts centres, including the then partly finished Sydney Opera House.

After the two-week season in Adelaide we flew to Sydney and managed to escape to our rented apartments in Altona, a lovely old house in Wunulla Road, Point Piper, not far from where I was born. It had a wonderful view and harbour frontage, complete with swimming pool and boat-shed. During our stay Vincent Price was also in residence and later gave me his marvellous cookbook.

Although the opening night in Sydney was considered somewhat anti-climactic after the extravagant audience behaviour in Melbourne, the exuberance grew and we actually played an extra week there (six instead of five) before going to Brisbane for just one week instead of the originally planned two. We, of course, had relatives and friends in Sydney who couldn't understand that we were unable to visit and meet them as freely as we would like. We had to continue to perform at our peak on all the publicised occasions and it left us precious little time to relax, especially with the added obligatory Company receptions, inspection of the Opera House site, presentations of awards, visits to various charitable organisations and hospitals, guest of honour at a well-known ladies' club or two – quite exhausting. All I wanted to do was spend some time with Adam in Altona's lovely garden looking at the beautiful harbour, remembered so well from my childhood, or do some of my needlepoint.

This I had started doing as a result of Richard asking me what I proposed to do between performances in Australia, as I would need to take as much rest as possible with such a heavy schedule. I said I would probably read and he suggested that I try and do the piece of tapestry needed to cover an antique fire-screen he had bought for number 36. I found the perfect design in Harrods just before we left London for the tour – and have continued needlepointing to this day, making wall hangings, rugs, chair covers, cushions, nursery pictures for our grandchildren and presents for friends. I also infected some of my friends and colleagues with the bug – Marilyn Horne, Gigi Capobianco, Barbara Matera, Huguette Tourangeau and many others. They all found it very relaxing and a great way to pass the time on planes, in airports, waiting in rehearsals or recording sessions and (if you had time) between scenes in the dressing-room.

There was the problem of having enough time to do things with Adam, but at least he was there. Ruthli and I took him to Taronga Zoo, also an excursion on the harbour with a picnic and games on Clark Island. He had to return to London with Gudrun and go back to school before the end of the tour but had enjoyed his time in Australia so much that the seed was sown for his desire to live there. I visited my old school, St Catherine's at Waverley, and New South Wales Conservatorium of Music to meet the students.

After the thirteenth week of the tour we went to Brisbane, had a splendid week there and, on the last night (October 16), celebrated Margreta Elkins's birthday and Ric's and my wedding anniversary, as well as the end of a highly successful artistic venture.

Weenie stayed on in Sydney for her holiday and Ric, Ruthli and I left for London via Tahiti, San Francisco and New York, along with Chester Carone who had been in the Sutherland–Williamson chorus and had joined the household staff as a general assistant, particularly with the driving and trying to organise Ric's packing, plus being an excellent 'do-it-yourselfer', photographer, movie-camera buff and tape-recorder addict.

We stayed on the Tahitian island of Moorea, arriving with most unnecessary clothing, including my fur coats which Udi and I carried over our arms. An American tourist asked me good-humouredly, 'Where on earth have you come from, Alaska?'

I have never really enjoyed a humid climate and, in spite of our lovely bungalow by the water, the abundance of tropical flowers and fruit and the sweet Tahitian people, I was most uncomfortable and couldn't wait to leave for San Francisco and New York, where I had my photograph taken on a visit to Roddy McDowall which he published in one of his great collections *Double Exposure – Take Three* in 1992.

We finally arrived back in London on November 9 where we saw the enchanting Zeffirelli production of *Romeo and Juliet* at the Old Vic theatre.

$\diamond$ 2 $\diamond$

ON DECEMBER 2 I flew to Geneva with Coley and stayed in Les Avants for a few days, then went to Vienna to record the Beethoven Ninth Symphony with Marilyn Horne, James King and Martti Talvela, Hans Schmidt-Isserstedt conducting. We all had a good time, there not being that much to sing, enjoying meals together (especially with 'Jackie' Horne) and doing some Christmas shopping. I returned to Les Avants on the eleventh and much preparation was made for our first Christmas in Chalet Monet. Adam and Gudrun arrived on the seventeenth and he was delighted that Gudrun was able to give him his first skiing lessons. His Christmas loot included a pair of skis, a sled and an Instamatic camera – this last a gift from Noël Coward. It was so foolproof that I had one myself for several years, not being too happy fiddling with 'dins' and 'ASAs'.

There was a huge old sled in the cellar of the chalet – probably used to haul luggage and supplies from the village to the house in the worst weather. Our drive is fairly steep and had a good covering of snow, so we thought we'd try a run down it. I was sitting on the sled waiting for the rest of the family to decide who would share the first run when Adam gave a playful push and I shot off down the hill, through the gateposts and across the road, only stopping in the piled-up snow left by the commune snow plough. Everyone thought that was a great joke, but there was a much funnier incident later when Ric, Adam and our two Italian doctor friends took the big sled down the steepest part of the main run, failed to make the curve and all flew off head first into the piled-up snow. We onlookers laughed hilariously, but the sledders were not amused.

Christmas Eve we spent in Chalet Monet, giving and receiving presents by our tree, but on Christmas morning, at about 11.30, we went over to Chalet Coward and added to their guests, giving and receiving more gifts. This ritual was carried on every year, with their household and guests coming to us after dinner on Christmas Eve to our tree and our contingent going to Chalet Coward for somewhat lethal champagne cocktails and their tree, returning home for our huge Christmas lunch.

After Christmas we began recording Rossini's *Semiramide* in London

192

with Marilyn Horne and Joseph Rouleau. When issued, the critics all lauded the singing of the Semiramide–Arsace duets, together with their respective arias, and the recording has stood up well.

We spent a pleasant New Year's Eve giving a little dinner party with friends at number 36 – Joseph Rouleau, Spiro Malas, Norman Ayrton, Marilyn Horne and Russell Braddon.

The *Semiramide* sessions were nicely spread, due to availability of the orchestra. This meant some free nights and one of them was spent at that great British Christmas treat 'The Panto'. We all went to see *Cinderella* with Danny la Rue and Alan Haynes as the Ugly Sisters, a riotous take-off of Fonteyn and Nureyev having us convulsed, with tears ruining my make-up. Danny la Rue passed a drink to Alan Haynes with the quip, 'Here, dear, if you take this you'll sound like Joan Sutherland.'

On January 16 the recording of Bellini's *Beatrice di Tenda* was commenced, with Richard again conducting the LSO. Josephine Veasey sang Agnese, Cornelis Opthof Filippo Visconti and Luciano Pavarotti Orombello. When issued, the set received criticism for the uneven balance of the supporting roles, but Richard's conducting was praised for securing 'a kind of orchestral and choral finish that we seldom hear in this music'.

During the recording of *Beatrice* Richard and I did a TV show for the BBC, with Nadia Nerina and Christopher Gable dancing scenes from *Cinderella*, Moura Lympany playing the third movement of Grieg's Piano Concerto and the Australian guitarist, John Williams, some Bach transcriptions. I performed yet another *Lucia* Mad Scene, together with 'The Gypsy and the Bird' and Noël Coward's 'This is a changing world'.

Adam struggled along with his piano practice, sometimes with me sitting by doing my needlepoint and trying to encourage his not very promising efforts. He had a happy knack of asking questions which gradually veered away from piano-playing to singing – or anything that took his fancy – so that his prescribed time was usually up before much progress had been made with his current pieces. He was much more interested in James Bond and *Our Man Flint* at the local cinema and all the sporting programmes on television, particularly soccer and skiing. It was great to spend time with him and actually be at home for his tenth birthday.

On Sunday, February 20, we had a concert in the Albert Hall, with Richard conducting the London Philharmonic Orchestra. For some reason, none of our regular drivers was available to take us to the hall, a car and driver from another firm being engaged for the trip by our usual company's boss. The two heavy bags of music went into the car first, with my big gown and theatre case on top, along with Ric's tails; and when the gown, tails and small case were unloaded off went the car, carrying all the orchestral parts with it – we knew not where. Fortunately, the driver returned to his own garage and was tracked down by telephone, returning to the Albert Hall with all speed, somewhat calming the panic and permitting the concert to begin only five minutes late.

This was our last public appearance in London for a few months, the next being the opening night of Sandro Sequi's delightful production of Donizetti's *La Fille du Régiment* on June 2. Half the audience from the Albert Hall Concert seemed to line up to say goodbye and the crush of people outside was enormous. One would have thought I was leaving for the moon, but it was all very heart-warming.

The Times wrote under the heading 'The tingling precision of Sutherland':

> Prima donna concerts are so often predictable and unsatisfying – 'everything by starts and nothing long' – that we should salute Joan Sutherland and Richard Bonynge most cordially for having contrived a programme which they gave with the London Philharmonic Orchestra in the Albert Hall last night.
>
> ... In this aria ('Bel raggio') she threw off chains of fleeting arpeggios very lightly on the breath and with a tingling precision that was physically exhilarating, and she brought out one high note which spun round the huge hall with such radiance that one expected the eyes as well as the ears to be dazzled by it.
>
> Because Miss Sutherland concentrates on so-called bel canto opera it is easy to forget how big her voice is, bigger now than in the days when she sang Evchen and Desdemona. Glière's Concerto for soprano and orchestra came as a salutary reminder. This is a 'two-movement work', beautiful in an old-fashioned vein for its date, 1942–43; in the first movement one might have been listening to Tchaikovsky's Tatiana...
>
> ... The concerto might have been made for her – and what a lovely Tatiana she would be!

The next morning we were off to Copenhagen, where we did two performances of *Lucia* in a very stark, modern setting at Falkoner Centret on February 25 and 28. There were also two performances of *L'Elisir d'Amore* and I could not forgo the opportunity of seeing and hearing Giuseppe di Stefano. But it was a sad occasion. Di Stefano left out passages, sang some down an octave and generally massacred the role of Nemorino. He left town very quickly.

It was here in Copenhagen that we first met John Winther who later became the General Manager of the Australian Opera and with whom we worked so closely some ten years later in Sydney. We also visited the British and Australian ambassadors, the Royal Danish Ballet – and I bought some splendid pieces of needlepoint to work.

Back in London, Adam had been trying his hand in the kitchen making 'cup cakes' that were more like bullets, but these were dutifully munched by us all under the ever-watchful eye of the cook until every crumb was consumed.

On March 10 we began recording *Love Live Forever – The Romance of Musical Comedy* with more splendid arrangements by Douglas Gamley and Ric conducting the National Philharmonic Orchestra. Although I tried to learn the pieces 'as writ' in advance, the actual arrangements were sometimes late in reaching me – like the morning of the recording sessions. Ric and Douglas had agreed on keys which sometimes gave me a rather high vocal range to cope with at the last minute, however we managed. It was fun singing numbers from *The Student Prince, The Boys from Syracuse, The Desert Song, Rose Marie, Balalaika, Show Boat, Maid of the Mountains* and *Tom Jones*, as well as some great Viennese and French operettas.

After the recording sessions we flew to Antwerp where we did a concert for the Belgian Radio in the Queen Elisabeth Hall.

Back in London again we began recording excerpts from Graun's *Montezuma* with Lauris Elms, Joseph Ward, Elizabeth Harwood, Rae Woodland and Monica Sinclair. This was followed immediately by excerpts from Bononcini's *Griselda*, again with Lauris Elms and Monica Sinclair, together with Margreta Elkins and Spiro Malas, both discs with the London Philharmonic Orchestra.

On April 3 I began rehearsals of *Don Giovanni* at La Scala with Lorin Maazel. Nicolai Ghiaurov was Don Giovanni; Wladimiro Ganzarolli Leporello; Pilar Lorengar Donna Elvira; Luigi Alva Don Ottavio and Mirella Freni Zerlina. Mr Maazel was very against our singing any appoggiature and as I had sung the opera at Glyndebourne, Vancouver, Vienna, Dublin and in London, where they were considered an essential of Mozartian style, I questioned his judgement and he remarked that I knew Mozart personally, of course. After he had further words with me, and then the management, we were able to sing our appoggiature. Pilar and I were also told by Mr Maazel that we would, of course, wear ballet slippers in the performance. 'Certainly not,' we chorused. 'They make us walk badly in those big costumes.' These, although very attractive, were mid-Victorian in period and most un-eighteenth century. We realised that even without shoes we were both taller than he and would dwarf him at the curtain calls anyway, so wore our usual footwear with a small heel.

On the opening night there was an error on the part of the Commendatore's ghost in the supper scene of the last act and the vocal trio fell apart, one half of the orchestra following one singer and the other another, gradually winding down like an old gramophone and stopping completely. Mr Maazel was conducting without a score and had to ask the leader for a rehearsal number to get everything going again.

We managed to come up to Les Avants for the Easter weekend and do some work in the garden, Chester and Weenie ridding us of some unwanted privet bushes and Richard complaining I was pulling out all the nice flowers – which were actually weeds. But time was short as we had to go back to Milan.

Between performances of *Don Giovanni* we flew to Paris for a concert in the Théâtre des Champs Elysées with the Orchestre National de l'ORTF on the twenty-eighth.

Back to Milan again for my last Scala performance and on to Stuttgart the next day, with a concert on May 3 there, repeated on May 6 in Hamburg in the Musikhalle. Saturday the seventh saw us back in London with rehearsals for *La Fille du Régiment* beginning on the Tuesday – three weeks of hard work and much laughter in the tomboyish production devised by Sandro Sequi and which remained my interpretation of Marie for the rest of my career. We had a splendid cast, with Luciano Pavarotti as Tonio, Spiro Malas as Sergeant Sulpice, Monica Sinclair as the Marquise of Birkenfeld and Edith Coates as the Duchesse de Krakenthorp. The costumes were by Marcel Escoffier and the scenery by Anna Anni.

The opening night (June 2) was a gala in aid of the Opera House Benevolent Fund in the presence of the Queen Mother, who said afterwards she enjoyed it so much she would like to come again. Among others there that night were Danny Kaye, Julie Christie, Rudolf Nureyev and Margot Fonteyn.

When the regular first performance (June 8) was assessed by the press, many of the critics were shocked at the levity and what they called 'vulgarity', but the public (and the cast) had a great time and some of the less inhibited critics obviously enjoyed themselves. Whatever they thought of Sandro's approach to the production they could not fault the singing and general musical style of the performance. Even the Duchesse of Edith Coates, who didn't sing a note, was a gem of a portrayal that has never been equalled.

For me it was a great discovery – the first comic part I played and such a change to remain alive and well at the end of the opera. Those involved in the production considered Sandro's handling of it pure genius and certainly the best way for me to cope with the part, making capital of my stature. At one point Luciano fell into my arms and I was actually able to catch and support him through all those early performances – but not by the time we reached the Met. He had already gained a great deal of weight.

There were six more *Filles* that season (between June 11 and July 2). In between them we recorded Gounod's *Faust* at Kingsway Hall in

London, with Franco Corelli as Faust, Nicolai Ghiaurov as Mephistopheles, Robert Massard as Valentin, Margreta Elkins as Siebel and Monica Sinclair as Dame Martha. With only one French singer in the cast it was amazing that only Corelli's pronunciation was criticised. *Music and Musicians* of April 1967 says:

> The revelation here is the conducting of Richard Bonynge who handles the score with tremendous verve and a superb grasp of the architecture of the big scenes – aspects of the performance which the vivid, spacious recording effectively underlines.

In the *New York Times* of February 19, 1967, Howard Klein concluded his long assessment of the *Faust* with

> In all, this recording is a major effort. Sutherland's Marguerite is a total creation of a role and is thoroughly personal. Although there may be better French singers, one cannot imagine another singer making the role such a triumph of dramatic singing. From the innocence of her Jewel Song to the ecstasy of her call to Faust from her garden window – 'Viens, viens' – and the big, long-held high C at the conclusion of the scene and then the final triumphant grandeur of the trio – hers is a Marguerite not to be encountered elsewhere.

When we had reached the session set aside for the recording of the final trio, Corelli was not feeling well so it was decided to record it with just Ghiaurov and myself. Both of us had other commitments and the orchestra (London Symphony Orchestra) couldn't extend their availability so this was my first experience of creating a master tape on to which the tenor was 'tracked' at some later date suitable to him. It was very tricky and I was never happy doing it, as I felt both the basic tape and then the 'voice-over' became too rigidly controlled, with no possibility of surge and flow if the result was to appear musically together. But the recording companies frequently resorted to the system when problems developed at the last minute.

Our young German girl Gudrun left us in June 1966 and we were very sorry to see her go. She still keeps in touch, phoning the Chalet from time to time.

With the *Faust* sessions and performances of *La Fille du Régiment*, I was fairly busy but still managed trips to Hardy Amies to fit a charming, light and cool, crisp white organza gown and long coat for my concert in Monte Carlo on June 21. The programme was again basically the same as in the previous orchestral concerts, with me substituting Donna Anna's 'Non mi dir' from Mozart's *Don Giovanni* for the Handel arias. The Glière Concerto was again an enormous success and it was delightful to meet their Most Serene Highnesses The Prince and Princess of Monaco for the first time. We were invited to a simple family lunch the following day out of doors and were completely under the spell of Princess Grace. The concert was part of the centenary celebrations of Monte Carlo.

Back to London for the remaining *Fille* performances, as well as rehearsals for a concert on June 30 with the English Chamber Orchestra for the Bach Festival in Oxford Town Hall. The programme consisted almost entirely of Handel works, with the exception of one of them – the Corelli Concerto Grosso, Op. 3 No. 2. We stayed with the former Ambassador to Italy, Sir Geoffrey and Lady Meade, who lived near Oxford.

On the last night of *La Fille du Régiment* Spiro and I played a joke on Luciano. He had remarked when I was presented with flowers after a performance that he'd much rather have spaghetti. So Spiro bought some and during the interval I dressed up the boxes with carnations, making a quite fetching bouquet of flowers and pasta. I presented it to Luciano at the curtain calls. He laughed a lot and took it with him when he flew back to Italy the next day to give to Adua his wife.

With these engagements we concluded our public appearances for the season, but there were still six *Faust* recording sessions, an odd Noël Coward one and four more *Love Live Forever* (the Musical Comedy–Operetta) sessions to complete.

We also managed to dine with Roddy McDowall, go with Blanche Blackwell to Noël Coward's *Double Bill*, enjoy luncheon with James Bailey and one with Hilary Watson in his charming garden, along with Dame Alicia Markova and other friends. A flurry of packing also took place – costumes had to be sent in advance to America and we were all leaving for our summer holidays, most of us to Les Avants, with Weenie going on to Australia.

✧ 3 ✧

ADAM HAD GONE with a friend to Majorca for the first part of his school holidays and we picked him up in Geneva on the twenty-fifth, very happy with his visit. We had a lovely long holiday this year even managing to spend a week with our friend Dr Gallacci in Arenzano, near Genoa, enjoying the Italian coast and his splendid hospitality. On August 30 we returned to London, travelling on to San Francisco on September 3 where we began rehearsals on the fifth for *I Puritani*. We were very happy to be staying with our friends in Sausalito who spoiled us with trips to various beauty spots on free days, as well as splendid meals.

At the opera we were at home with old friends. Arturo was sung by Alfredo Kraus, Giorgio by Nicola Ghiuselev, both making their San Francisco débuts, as were Clifford Grant and Dorothy Cole. I was most unhappy with the costumes so I wore those I'd had in Boston for which I was grateful.

On the opening night, Lady Bird Johnson presented me with a huge armful of wonderful red roses. She was most charming and both Richard and I were happy to see her again and know she had enjoyed the performance.

According to *Opera News*:

> Miss Sutherland has never appeared here to better advantage than in this overdue local première of Bellini's *I Puritani* ... the unending chain of Bellini's melodies were lovingly conducted by Richard Bonynge.

There were five performances in San Francisco (between September 20 and October 8, with a performance in Sacramento on October 5). It was at the matinée on October 2 that Marilyn Horne first introduced us to that charmer Rock Hudson – a Scorpio subject like myself.

Richard and I returned to New York via San Antonio and Atlanta, where we gave concerts on October 15 and 20. In San Antonio the programme consisted of works by Corelli, Mozart, Cherubini, Rossini, Verdi and Donizetti, with the San Antonio Symphony Orchestra. The programme with the Atlanta Symphony was comprised of some J. C. Bach, Mozart, an aria, 'Non han, calma', from Graun's *Montezuma*, Rossini, Maillart and Delibes. While in Atlanta, we were invited to lunch at Mimosa Hall by the President of the Women's Symphony Committee and felt we were walking back in time – it conjured up the beautiful mansions in *Gone with the Wind*.

Back to New York for a concert in White Plains, then to Philadelphia where minimal rehearsals were held by Irving Guttman for two performances of *Lucia*, on November 1 and 4.

The week of November 7 to 13 was spent rehearsing and recording another *Bell Telephone Hour* and an *Ed Sullivan Show*. The *Telephone Hour* must have been the one on which I sang the Bell Song from *Lakmé* and 'Io non sono più l'Annetta' – this last seated on a swing in a huge, fluffy white crinoline. It was my contribution to the show entitled *The First Ladies of Opera* and also on the programme were Renata Tebaldi, Leontyne Price and Birgit Nilsson, each delivering two of their favourite arias. The show was presented at the end of 1966 – on New Year's Eve.

We flew to Los Angeles for three performances of duets and arias with Marilyn Horne for the Music Center Opera Association in the Dorothy Chandler Pavilion on November 19, 21 and 26. I sang the Bell Song and a moving aria from Graun's *Montezuma*, and Marilyn and I sang Act 2 Scene I of *Norma*.

After the final duo concert we travelled to Houston and performed with members of the Houston Symphony in Jesse H. Jones Hall, a programme drawn from the works we had already done in Atlanta, San Antonio and Westchester County Center.

In New York once more we were rehearsing for the production of *Lucia* at the new Met at Lincoln Center. It all looked very glossy after the old theatre, more like a de-luxe cinema, but seemed very vast and open. The backstage facilities were certainly an improvement on the old House but it all felt strange and too modern at first. It was amazing, too, that with all the extra stage areas we *still* had trouble crossing it due to banked-up scenery.

Richard made his début as a Met conductor on the opening night with Anselmo Colzani as Enrico, John Alexander as Edgardo and Nicola Ghiuselev as Raimondo.

Harriet Johnson, in the *New York Post*, wrote of Richard:

> ... He obviously knew the score almost by heart and his instinctive sympathy with the voice extended to everyone. He showed how authoritative he could be during the long finale to Act II when he inspired the soloists to sing an excellent 'Sextet' and then go on with chorus and orchestra to a rousing conclusion. He has absorbed the traditions of the style and made them his own.

Richard Tucker sang the role of Edgardo later during this season.

After the first performance we went to Washington for a concert with Orchestra in Constitution Hall, again staying with the Australian Ambassador, now his Excellency Mr John Keith Waller and Mrs Waller, the latter also an avid needlepointer.

The usual round of dinners and parties took place over the Christmas and New Year period, together with minimal rehearsals with Karl Böhm for *Don Giovanni* in which I was to sing Donna Anna for the first time at the Met in early January. Adam stayed in Europe this Christmas as he wanted to perfect his skiing and we were very busy. Richard continued to do some performances of *Lucia* at the Met with Gianna d'Angelo, Roberta Peters and Renata Scotto in January and February. The *Don Giovanni* was in the wonderful sets devised by Eugene Berman and originally staged by Herbert Graf. Don Giovanni was Cesare Siepi, Donna Elvira Pilar Lorengar, Zerlina Laurel Hurley, Don Ottavio Alfredo Kraus, the Commendatore Justino Diaz and Leporello Ezio Flagello. Some of the critics expressed surprise at my complete control of Donna Anna's music, having heard me only in the later Donizetti and Bellini bel canto repertoire and forgetting (or not knowing) of the excellent training I had undergone at Covent Garden and Glyndebourne in the Mozart works. They were certainly complimentary, the *New York Times* commenting on the 'power and passion' also the 'energy and brilliance of attack that made tremendous impact' in the first act.

On January 20 I had travelled down to Philadelphia and rehearsed with the Orchestra and István Kertész for their Pension Fund Concert on the twenty-first. From this concert until February 16 Richard and I were both shuttling between New York and Boston for rehearsals and three performances of *Don Giovanni* with Sarah Caldwell's company whilst still continuing our Met dates and concerts. Without Weenie and Chester to help organise us we would have been unable to cope – I also had fittings with Barbara Matera.

On February 1 we flew to Toronto and rehearsed that afternoon and the next morning for a concert in Massey Hall with the Toronto Symphony – the Corelli Concerto Grosso in D Minor, Op. 6, No. 4, 'Non mi dir' (*Don Giovanni*), Divertimento in D Major, K 136 of Mozart, 'Non hàn calma' (*Montezuma*) by Karl Heinrich Graun, 'Ernani, involami!' from Verdi's *Ernani*, the overture to *Les Dragons de Villars* of Maillart and the Bell Song from Delibes' *Lakmé*. John Kraglund of the *Toronto Globe and Mail* wrote a somewhat sarcastic account of the concert, rounding it off with: 'Although the Bell Song from Delibes's *Lakmé* has been mercifully absent from concert repertoire of late, it was pleasant to discover that Miss Sutherland can almost make it worth listening to.'

Back to Boston from Toronto for final rehearsals and the *Don Giovanni* there opening on February 6. Oliver Smith's sets were interesting. I had my own costumes and was not asked by Sarah Caldwell to remove or change any part of them on stage – which the Don, Elvira and Zerlina seemed constantly to be doing. The Don was Justino Diaz, Donna Elvira was sung by Margreta Elkins, Zerlina by Huguette Tourangeau and Don Ottavio by Loren Driscoll. Leporello was sung by Donald Gramm, that versatile and highly talented baritone with whom it was a joy to work. Sadly, he died all too young in 1987.

Richard was supposed to travel to New York for rehearsal between the first and second performances but there was an overnight continuing blizzard and all planes were grounded. We both went to New York after the second Boston *Don Giovanni* as Ric had *Lucia* at the Met on the ninth and an evening concert rehearsal on the tenth in New Jersey. Fortunately we were able to stay with our friends the Kaufmans, who not only provided us with transport to and from rehearsal and the concert but also with their particularly relaxed and informal hospitality. The concert was on the eleventh in the Newark Symphony Hall and was a repeat of the Toronto programme.

Ric had another *Lucia* at the Met on Monday the thirteenth and we were back in Boston on the evening of the fourteenth for the last *Don Giovanni* on the fifteenth. To New York again on the sixteenth, Ric's final *Lucia* on the seventeenth, a party on the eighteenth given by Anya Dorfman, a business lunch with Ann Colbert in our apartment in the Village on the nineteenth and on the twentieth we were off to Bloomington, Indiana, and places north and west for the next two months.

We were greeted and fêted at Indiana University and on this visit we had dinner with Zinka Milanov who taught there at that time. Zinka and I had a long discussion about the standards of vocal technique and the ability of students to comprehend how much work should and *must* be done to perfect a solid technique no matter how good their young, natural voices are. Without a sound technical understanding of what they do and why, they run the risk of being unable to cope with heavy schedules of work, travel and the obligatory press interviews, especially if they are not feeling well and are tired. Their careers will be very short-lived. Zinka was very outspoken and said that far too many vocal students she was obliged to take were never going to be made into opera stars, certainly not by her. 'They sound like little cats!' she said.

Richard and Chester went to Vancouver for rehearsals of *Lucia di Lammermoor* and I went with Weenie to Montreal for a concert on February 28 in the Forum with the Montreal Symphony and Wilfrid Pelletier conducting. The huge audience of 12,000 loved 'Ah fors'è lui' and the *Hamlet* Mad Scene. Maestro Pelletier was a superb conductor and we got along very well.

A few more days in New York and Weenie and I were off to join Richard and Chester in Vancouver for six performances of *Lucia* with the Vancouver Opera spread over the last three weeks of March. We had rented a house for the period and felt very much at home, with plenty of time to meet with old friends and enjoy the beautiful surrounding countryside.

After the last *Lucia* we stayed in Vancouver for a couple of days, studying Delibes's *Lakmé*, which we were to perform for the first time in Seattle. On April 1 we all drove down there from Vancouver – not too long a distance and, with all our bits and pieces of luggage, very convenient, as well as a pleasant sightseeing trip of that north-western corner of the United States.

Some of our colleagues in *Lakmé* were old friends. The Brahman Priest Nilakantha was sung by Joshua Hecht, Mallika by Huguette Tourangeau, Gerald by Frank Porretta, Frédéric by Cornelis Opthof. The opera was produced by Glynn Ross with a group of local dancers choreographed by Mara – a leading authority in the United States of Cambodian and oriental dance. I heard that the sets were from a touring production of the *King and I* or *South Pacific*. Whether or not, they served admirably and the opera was a great success. It opened on April 10, with four further performances to the twenty-second. There was surprise expressed by members of the press that I should undertake the role of Lakmé which had been such a favourite of the diminutive Lily Pons, still very well remembered by North American opera-goers. Although they mostly belittled the opera as 'dull' or 'teary weary', it was also described as 'one of the finest creations of the nineteenth-century French lyric theatre'. Whatever the critics thought of the opera as a whole, they paid tribute to the fine singing of the cast, especially that of Huguette Tourangeau and myself in the lovely first-act duet and also a 'glitteringly accurate Bell Song'.

For myself, although always apprehensive with a new role, I very much enjoyed it and found the short entrance prayer thrilling to sing, also the duets with Frank Porretta very moving and vocally rewarding. My costumes were stunning, Barbara Matera having created a magnificent one for my entrance from the temple, sewn from head to foot across the front in green cabochon 'emeralds' the size of pigeon eggs with a fan-shaped head-dress of peacock feathers. The audience used to gasp each night when I came on stage.

Home to London, where Richard stayed for only a day before leaving for Vienna by car with Chester driving to commence rehearsals for Joseph Haydn's *Orfeo*. Weenie and I joined them there the following week for two and a half weeks' rehearsals for the first ever performances of the opera in Vienna, during its Festival in the Theater an der Wien. Although written to be performed in 1791 in London, it never reached the stage until 1951 at the Florence Maggio Musicale.

The cast was a very fine one, consisting of Nicolai Gedda as Orfeo, Spiro Malas as Creonte and New Zealander Mary O'Brien as Genio – whose aria was robbed by the directors for me to sing in the third act as I had nothing in that act otherwise, *not* because Mary couldn't sing it. The producer was Rudolf Hartmann and there was a great deal of chorus and ballet work involved. The set was terrifying, consisting of an ironing-board-shaped springboard on a turntable with very little else other than a cyclorama on to which scenery was projected. Because of the latter, entrances and exits could only be made at a certain point and then one had to walk around the perimeter of the solid stage within the 'cyc', usually while the 'springboard' revolved like a guillotine on an angle ready to knock you on the head or decapitate you if you misjudged the rate of revolve. This gave the audience a change of scenery and unnerved the cast. We were also expected to use the whole length of the springboard but found the tip of it very unstable and, as neither Nicolai nor I was a lightweight, it embarrassed us, as well as unsettling us to feel the board react as if our next move would be to dive off into the darkness. We were assured it couldn't break but the sensation of instability was too much for either of us and we avoided venturing further than just beyond half-way to the tip. The costumes were somewhat strange, with the chorus looking like some sort of monsters on wheels when they were supposed to be trees. During a rehearsal the two solo dancers had long, witch-like hair but after the male had become entangled in his during a lift and practically strangled, both wigs were torn off and thrown into the wings, never to reappear.

We had been able to rent a comfortable apartment and were delighted to find the services of a housekeeper went with it. Richard fell for her in a big way, especially when she presented a dish of stuffed peppers (which he loves) for a meal. Her name was Mara Trifunovic, a Yugoslavian from Belgrade, and she had worked for both Karajan and Wieland Wagner. She expressed a desire to revisit Britain some day. Richard pounced, and asked her would she like to come and work for us helping Ruthli and taking over most of the cooking. She was already in her late sixties, I imagine, but agreed in a flash – so we had another member of staff.

We did a great deal of sightseeing in and around Vienna, with Weenie and Chester photographing everything, and my Instamatic was kept busy too. While Chester was on one of his roving jaunts in the city with his camera he noticed a man extracting a package of what he thought was chewing-gum from an automatic vendor in the street. He investigated the machine and (with no real knowledge of the language) worked out that if he inserted so many coins he would receive a packet of three. 'Just what I need,' he thought and promptly did as bidden. With a loud till-like ring, out popped the packet – *not* of chewing-gum but three condoms.

With Spiro Malas in our cast together with Nicolai and his wife Stacey and John Alexander, also at the Vienna Festival, singing in Korngold's *Die tote Stadt* with Marilyn Zschau, Adèle Leigh the darling of the Volksoper, a blossoming friendship with Ronald Schneider and holidaying friends like the two Jacks from San Francisco, we had plenty of happy meals with one or more of them particularly out of doors in Grinzing. Irwin Gage was also involved in the musical production of the *Orfeo* with Ronald Schneider.

The opening night was on May 21, with further performances at intervals until June 6. The gloomy visual production was considered 'not acceptable' by the *Christian Science Monitor* but its critic, Rudolf Klein, also noted: 'The singers saved the evening and were stormily applauded.' Whether the Vienna public enjoyed the opera or not, the pile of fan mail and requests for photographs was huge and I had to make a special trip to Fayer to satisfy demands.

On June 7 Weenie, Mara and I flew to London, with Ric and Chester setting out on the return trip in the car with much extra luggage gained by Ric in the old books and music shops.

On June 13 Ric and I were invited to dine at 10 Downing Street and had a most enjoyable evening with the then Prime Minister Harold Wilson.

Next came a revival of *La Fille du Régiment* and a few critics even admitted enjoying the tomboy approach to Marie. The opening night was a Saturday so Adam was able to come and join in the fun. The *Fille* nights were always very relaxed and happy, and as the opera was performed with dialogue there were times when a few changes crept in. One classic night that none of us will forget was after I'd sung my off-stage trumpet-like cadenza prior to my first entrance. Sulpice (Spiro Malas) asked his question 'Mais qui vient?' ('Who's coming?') and before I appeared accompanied by a drum roll a young male voice from way up in the amphitheatre very audibly replied: 'IT'S JOAN!'

Another time, after the Tonio–Marie duet Luciano kissed me rather excessively during the applause, looked thoughtful, moved downstage looking at Richard in the orchestra pit, spread his arms and shrugged saying, 'Scusi, Maestro.' In the singing-lesson scene Monica Sinclair had a habit of substituting a topical name for that of the forgotten maestro who had composed our little number. They ranged from politicians to music critics and performers, always raising a laugh, particularly when the subject was present at the performance, such as Georg Solti (Musical Director of the House at that time) or Edward Heath.

We took Adam and his friend Peter Eastwood to Battersea Fun Fair, with Chester giving us an amazing display of sharp-shooting at one of the many galleries. I found I had lost the urge to be suspended upside down in the 'Rocket' or whatever it was called and opted for the Dodgems, only to be severely bumped by another car, badly bruising my elbow.

There was a gala performance in aid of the Royal Opera House Benevolent Fund on July 4 at which the Queen Mother was present. Scenes were presented from three different operas: the Presentation of the Rose from *Der Rosenkavalier* with Georg Solti conducting, the Study Scene from *Don Carlos* conducted by Edward Downes and Richard conducted the Mad Scene from *Lucia di Lammermoor* for me. Except for Grace Bumbry (Princess Eboli) and Boris Christoff (Philip II) in *Don Carlos* all the rest of the singers were British and, at one time or another, members of the Covent Garden Company.

We recorded *La Fille du Régiment* with the Covent Garden Orchestra and then went off to Les Avants. One evening we decided to attend the appearance of a local Yodel Club at Chatelard, the boarding-school for girls in the village. We called in to Noël Coward for coffee first and all trooped down the hill for the concert. Richard, Noël and I were ushered into specially reserved seats – the only ones in the hall. The Yodel group had been involved in an accident *en route* and when they *did* arrive were somewhat shaky. Noël amused himself making wicked asides during the alpenhorn excerpts, flag throwing (and dropping) to Ric and me and it was impossible not to laugh. We tried to hide the fact but Udi and the rest of the household were sitting behind us and could see our shoulders shaking. This, although embarrassing Udi, started them laughing too and we couldn't wait to go outside at half-time. Noël said he'd had enough and persuaded us to go back to Chalet Coward, where he and Ric sat at the two pianos and provided those of us who'd gone with something more to the 'Master's' liking. Udi was mortified and thought we had behaved *very* badly, especially in front of the children. She was probably right, but I don't think yodelling is heard to advantage indoors, not to mention the alpenhorn – rather like the bagpipes.

After our holidays we opened at the King's Theatre, Edinburgh with *Orfeo* on August 25. Luciano was also singing in the Edinburgh Festival – the role of Tybalt in Bellini's *I Capuleti*. We had rented a charming house with an Aga cooker and I was not sure how to handle it, considering myself very lucky to have Mara there, who seemed to manage famously.

✦ 4 ✦

AFTER THE LAST *Orfeo* we went briefly to London, then back to Switzerland for a week. Adam and Ruthli went to London for the resumption of the school term at the Lycée and Chester drove Ric and me to Arenzano for a week or so by the sea, before going on to stay at the Château de la Chèvre d'Or in Eze Village. From this charming hotel high on the Corniche Chester drove us to Monte Carlo each day where we recorded *Lakmé* with l'Orchestre National de l'Opéra de Monte Carlo between October 1 and 12 with Alain Vanzo, Gabriel Bacquier, Jane Berbié and Monica Sinclair.

We enjoyed another relaxed luncheon at the palace, our conversation touching on the problems of maintaining a normal family life for our children. We had decided to give up the London house, enlarge the chalet in Les Avants and live there permanently, so we were trying to find a school that would be within reasonable distance of the chalet to permit Adam to come home for weekends whenever possible. Prince Rainier was a great advocate of Le Rosey and suggested we arrange an entrance exam with the Headmaster, Dr Johannot. We knew of the school as Anya Dorfman's grandsons were pupils there and the information was stored for future action. It was at this time that the owner-director of the Chèvre d'Or raised the possibility of Adam pursuing a career in the hotel industry. He was a charming old man, a diligent host and he proposed our looking into the various good hotel schools in Switzerland, as Adam already seemed adept at languages and interested in regional foods. I laughed, saying we were jumping ahead and that Adam still had several years of schooling before we could think seriously of a career, but it was certainly an idea to be kept in mind. He even offered to take Adam on his staff for a trial run.

By October 16 I had gone briefly to London and on to Vienna to record the Verdi *Requiem* with Marilyn Horne, Luciano Pavarotti, Martti Talvela and the Vienna Philharmonic Orchestra with Georg Solti conducting. These combined forces made quite an impact, with sound and more sound reverberating around the Sofiensaal – it was hard to believe that one's voice could possibly be heard. But John Culshaw and the Decca crew performed their usual magic.

Back in London by the twenty-fourth and rehearsing for Handel's

Messiah to be given on Sunday, October 29 in the Festival Hall with the LPO. The other soloists were Monica Sinclair, Peter Baillie and Raymond Myers, with Richard conducting.

Bellini's *Norma* went into rehearsal at the Royal Opera House on November 6. Sandro Sequi was the producer and there were performances on November 30, with six more in December and January 1. Franco Tagliavini was Pollione, Joseph Rouleau Oroveso and Marilyn Horne Adalgisa on the first five nights, and Margreta Elkins sang the last three. The rather stark, rocky sets were very effective and resembled Stonehenge. They were designed by Pier Luigi Pizzi, as were the heavy-wool, nun-like costumes. These hung and 'moved' beautifully, but we were all grateful that we were wearing them in December–January as they were *very* warm. The loose weave of the over-garments also had a tendency to become hooked on jutting rocks. However, the most hilarious moment was when Marilyn, after our first duet together, walked up the ramp as I was singing 'Ma di, l'amato giovane'. I heard a loud thump and a not well stifled four-letter word, turned and saw Marilyn on the ground shaking with laughter and trying – successfully, I might add – to continue with her next phrase as I helped her to her feet again. She had not managed to catch all the folds of the costume in her hand as she went upstage and actually walked up the front of her gown which toppled her over. Again the Norma–Adalgisa duets were the high spots of the opera for the critics and they all remarked on a greater clarity and understanding of my delivery of the Italian text, with expectations of further growth in the role. David Webster, when he came backstage after the first night, said: 'Given a couple more performances to shake in this will be one of the greatest the world has ever seen.'

We had a lovely supper party at number 36 after the first night with the cast and friends, the last of whom left at about 3.30 a.m. when I went up to bed with a shoe in each hand – tired, but happy.

Before going off to Switzerland for the long Christmas weekend, we managed to visit a few theatres, including a ballet matinée at the Royal Opera House of *La Fille mal gardée* with Adam and Ruthli, all of us practically clog-dancing down Bow Street towards the Strand to find a taxi afterwards, we were so impressed and amused by its brilliant and humorous choreography.

With the remaining *Norma* performances immediately after Christmas, we could only stay for less than a week at Les Avants, during which time we were deciding what additions we wanted to the house and realising we would probably have to vacate it entirely until the work was done.

The New Year of 1968 slipped in very quickly before the final *Norma*. Then it was rehearsals immediately for the concert performance of

Meyerbeer's *Les Huguenots* to be presented in the Albert Hall on Sunday, January 7. This was a very ambitious venture by Michael Scott and Denny Dayviss to present great operas in a semi-staged fashion, operas that had not been heard live in London for many years. *Les Huguenots* was the first in the series and scored a huge success. Alan Sievewright had designed a special stage for the singers to use and a very informative programme with many illustrations. It was a lovely cast with Martina Arroyo, Huguette Tourangeau, Anastasios Vrenios, Dominic Cossa, Nicola Ghiuselev and Robert El Hage in the main roles. The venture had a big success with the public and the critics were impressed with the singing of Martina Arroyo and Huguette Tourangeau (both making their London débuts) as well as ourselves. The orchestra was the Philharmonia with the Ambrosian Singers providing the considerable chorus work.

The following week Richard was recording the ballet by Friedrich Burgmüller *La Péri* and I was supposed to record the Glière Concerto, but this had to be postponed as I succumbed to a throat infection and wanted to be in good voice for a recital Richard and I were giving on January 14 in the Theatre Royal, Drury Lane for the London Academy of Music and Dramatic Art to help raise funds to furnish their exciting new theatre. Fortunately all was well and the recital was accomplished, with Ric and Chester going to New York the next day aboard the *Bremen* with all the heavy luggage for our three and a half month stay in the United States, whilst Udi and I went to Les Avants for talks with the architects regarding the alterations to Chalet Monet. We went also to Gstaad to meet and talk with Dr Johannot, the head of Le Rosey.

It was a hectic week, with Douglas and Ailsa Gamley staying at the chalet, and many appointments in and out of Les Avants somewhat hindered by a phenomenal snowstorm which blocked the drive and necessitated 'all hands to the snow shovels'. We had no snow plough at that time and I thought Douglas would pass out as we tried to dig a path to the gate. Udi and I tried to organise for the removal of everything from the chalet which would take place in the spring during Adam's Easter holiday, with Udi in charge as we would be in America.

Somehow everything was accomplished and we flew back to London, where I only stayed for two nights before flying off with Weenie to New York on January 25. By the twenty-eighth I was rehearsing for the *Bell Telephone Hour* presentation *Opera – Two to Six*. This was a unique venture, presenting a well-known operatic duet, trio, quartet, quintet and sextet from *Tosca*, *Faust*, *Rigoletto*, *Die Meistersinger* and *Lucia di Lammermoor* respectively. The other artists in the programme were Tito Gobbi, Nicolai Gedda, Phyllis Curtin, Jerome Hines, Mildred Miller and Charles Anthony. I sang in the *Tosca*, *Rigoletto* and *Lucia* excerpts. The show was directed by Kirk Browning.

Following the TV, rehearsals began for a very different work: the Haydn *Orfeo* in Carnegie Hall on February 7 and 10 with a cast much the same as it had been in Vienna and Edinburgh.

I was still managing to fit in a few massage sessions with Jenny whenever I was in New York as I found her manipulation so beneficial and relaxing. The back was much stronger but the hectic pace, heavy costumes and long flights took their toll and I was always glad to see Jenny's beaming face.

We had two recitals – one in Symphony Hall, Newark, and the other in the Academy of Music, Philadelphia, on February 13 and 16.

Then on to Salt Lake City, where we performed with the Utah Symphony in the Salt Lake Tabernacle on the twenty-first. The acoustic of the Tabernacle is well known and we had a most enjoyable stay, as well as a warm reception to the following programme:

Overture to *Berenice* HANDEL
'Al tua seno fortunato' (*Orfeo*) HAYDN
Divertimento in D Major, K 136: Allegro, Andante, Presto MOZART
'Au beau pays' (*Les Huguenots*) MEYERBEER
Symphony No. 6 in C Major: Adagio-Allegro, Andante, Scherzo: Presto,
    Allegro Moderato SCHUBERT
Mad Scene (*Lucia di Lammermoor*) DONIZETTI

The next day was spent travelling back to New York via Denver, Colorado, and on the twenty-fourth we flew to New Orleans. We arrived when the city was bustling with preparations for the big Mardi Gras celebration on Shrove Tuesday and stayed at the Royal Orleans Hotel. Although Richard, Weenie and Chester went and mingled with the riotously dressed (or undressed) crowd, I had a fantastic view of Rex from my hotel window above the corner of Royal and St Louis. Chester and Weenie were both great camera fiends (movie and still), so we have a few outrageous reminders of the day, Kodak refusing to print some of the more risqué shots.

With all the continuing excitement we still managed to rehearse (minimally) and perform *Lucia* twice – on February 29 and March 2 in the Municipal Auditorium. We had a few friends in the cast – Dominic Cossa sang Enrico, Spiro Malas Raimondo and Michele Molese Edgardo. The performance was notable in the critics' eyes not only for the eight curtain calls for the Mad Scene, but for the restoration to the opera of the duet with Raimondo preceding the wedding scene, the 'tower scene' duet between Edgardo and Enrico, and the appearance of Enrico in the middle of the Mad Scene. All these items make more sense of the story line although they were at that time almost invariably cut.

Back in New York we spent a splendid evening with Zinka Milanov at her apartment, listening to her very droll reminiscences.

On Tuesday, March 5 we travelled to Boston for rehearsals for *La Traviata*. There was a mix-up over dates and Richard and I were horrified to find that there was a large audience at the only stage and orchestra rehearsal which acted as the Dress Rehearsal and, we heard afterwards, they had paid for their seats. I was fighting off a cold and hadn't intended to sing all of the opera full voice, certainly none of the high notes, but faced with a house full of people under the impression that this was a performance what could I do? It was all very upsetting. Anastasios Vrenios was my handsome Alfredo and the sets were those designed by Franco Zeffirelli for the Dallas production in which there was a flash-back during the first-act prelude (from the figure of Violetta in bed as in the last act) to the scene of her party – very effective if it works. Our performances took place on March 11 and 13 during violent snowstorms.

Back to New York and the first big gala in the new house of the Metropolitan Opera held on the sixteenth. It was a benefit for the Metropolitan Opera Guild and the Benevolent and Retirement Funds. All the artists – and there were twenty or more – sang items they had never sung at the Met previously. It was a grand concert and the *Daily News* of March 18 remarked:

> It is tragic that the all-star performance at the Metropolitan Opera, Saturday night, for the Opera Guild, was not recorded on film because, years from now, this would be a priceless recollection of the opera giants of the time. In dazzling succession we were thrilled by the magnificent voices of Joan Sutherland, Renata Tebaldi, Richard Tucker, Franco Corelli, Fernando Corena, Robert Merrill, Leontyne Price, Jan Peerce, Roberta Peters, Leonie Rysanek, Carlo Bergonzi, Giorgio Tozzi, Mario Sereni, Bonaldo Giaiotti, Sherrill Milnes, Sándor Kónya, George Shirley and John Macurdy. The conductors included Thomas Schippers, Richard Bonynge, Fausto Cleva and George Schick ... There has never been such a feast of great music and those of us who were there can consider ourselves rarely privileged.

There were also several other singers on the programme: Cornell MacNeil, Teresa Stratas, Nicolai Gedda, Ezio Flagello and James King, and Francesco Molinari-Pradelli also conducted some excerpts. So much for press accuracy. I sang 'Au beau pays' from *Les Huguenots* and also the Final Scene from *Faust* with George Shirley and John Macurdy.

On the twenty-first Richard, Weenie, Chester and I went to Philadelphia by train, arriving in time for a rehearsal of *Norma* at 8 p.m. We had two performances of the opera (on March 26 and 29) at the Academy of Music. The rehearsal period for the soloists was sketchy, nor was there much orchestral time, but there was some sort of 'dress' rehearsal minus costumes on the Sunday afternoon – without the chorus costumes either: we only saw these on the opening night. I was very thankful I had my own from Covent Garden as the men's garb looked like bits and pieces from a very old-fashioned Wagnerian production, with horned helmets and fur-fabric tunics, and I dreaded to think what might have been my fate! I could not resist a 'Ho-Yo-To-Ho!' when I saw them backstage and was glad they were mostly behind me in the big chorus scenes, otherwise my sense of humour would most certainly have got the better of me. Poor Richard had to watch them and had great difficulty concentrating. They were certainly the funniest idea of Druids we ever came across in 120 performances of *Norma*.

These performances remain in our memory for quite another reason. Montserrat Caballé (whose husband Bernabe Marti was singing Pollione) suddenly appeared backstage on the opening night, saying there was no way she would have missed the opportunity to hear us sing together. 'Besides,' she said, 'I am going to sing Norma myself soon and I thought I could learn from hearing you.' We all went to supper together and as she was 'not feeling very well' Montserrat ordered just a plate of spaghetti with cheese, enjoying it so much that she asked for a repeat order. While waiting for the second plate she danced with Bernabe, throwing herself into the movement and mood so much that her very built-up hair-do started to topple. How she laughed! We had a wonderful time together – but she was meant to be in Chicago where she was singing with the Lyric Opera and had flown down to Philadelphia for the night.

I was supposed to sing a concert in Columbus, Ohio, on April 2 and all the travel and rehearsal arrangements and social engagements are listed in my diary, but Weenie's says 'cancelled – bad cold'. I am afraid I have no recollection of either the concert or my staying in New York nursing a cold but, as I have no programme for the event, can only presume it *was* cancelled. However, by the sixth we did a concert entirely of Handel works at Hunter College, New York, which was repeated on the eighth and the two were special benefits during their twenty-fifth anniversary concert season.

On to Seattle for four *Don Giovanni* performances ending on the twenty-fourth. Allen Klein designed the set (which we all thought of as a 'moonscape') and Bliss Hebert produced. Gabriel Bacquier was a splendid Don, with Donald Gramm singing Leporello, Christine Murphy Elvira, Huguette Tourangeau Zerlina and Anastasios Vrenios Ottavio. Barbara Matera's beautiful gowns for me as Donna Anna stood out magnificently on the somewhat unrealistic set but had a tendency to catch on its rough surface (rather like the coarsest sandpaper) not only impeding progress but ripping the hems of the voluminous skirts.

Barbara had protective false hem turnings sewn on to each gown to prevent this.

From Seattle we flew to Toronto, where Ric and I performed a recital in the Macmillan Theatre for the CBC which was recorded for broadcasting twice at the end of May. It has lately been issued on video.

While in Toronto, Ric prepared a concert for the Canadian Broadcasting Corporation entitled *The Age of Bel Canto* with the CBC Opera Orchestra and four very fine young soloists. They were Patricia Brooks, Huguette Tourangeau, Pierre Duval and Cornelis Opthof, and they sang 'a programme of rarely performed operatic highlights'. These included works of Pacini, Balfe, Auber, Rossini, Ricci, Donizetti, Bellini, Meyerbeer and Verdi.

We returned to London and had a meeting with Mr John Corlette, headmaster of Aiglon College, who happened also to be visiting London. We were very impressed with his ideals and arranged to visit the school late in the summer, with a definite view to sending Adam there at the beginning of the next school year that September.

After two recording sessions for the Glière Concerto we went to Switzerland to meet again with the architects regarding the alterations to Chalet Monet and, as well as a most enjoyable lunch with Noël Coward, to pay a visit to Aiglon College. We had flown the car over to Geneva so after our various meetings we drove to Florence on May 14, where rehearsals for *Semiramide* began on the fifteenth. We again stayed at the Villa San Michele in Fiesole and had some pleasant excursions – to San Gemignano, Siena and the surrounding Tuscany countryside – with Sandro Sequi who was producing the opera.

The sets by Pier Luigi Samaritani were spacious and suggestive of Babylonian grandeur, while the costumes by Peter John Hall were very ornate in rainbow colours with massive head-dresses in keeping with the lofty backdrops.

In spite of the last-minute substitution by Renato Capecchi for Wladimiro Ganzarolli, the performances (opening on June 1) were very well received, with Richard gaining praise for his 'musicality throughout, his control of the score (many details were carefully and lovingly clarified) and his serious preparation'. This from William Weaver in the *Financial Times*, who also wrote glowingly of my own performance. However, he was not happy with most of the other members of the cast and grumbled that the spectators had a right to expect adequate singing when a seat in the stalls sold for almost ten pounds! There were three further presentations of the opera, the last on June 9.

On June 12, Richard and I did a song recital in the charming Teatro della Pergola, also for the thirty-first Maggio Musicale Fiorentino. At the end of the first group I sang 'With Plaintive Notes' from Handel's *Samson* which Ric was transposing into a slightly higher key. Unfortunately, as we moved into the middle section of the aria something went amiss with his method and I found the delightful air very difficult – Ric had managed to raise the pitch a whole fifth and I was endeavouring to execute limpid trills and turns a fifth higher than written. We battled on to the end of the aria and it brought the house down – the most successful piece in the whole recital with comments from the press about this amazing feat. We have a tape to prove it.

After Florence we drove to Rome to record *Semiramide* for the RAI. This has now appeared on CDs under the Nuova Era label. The major cast change was Mario Petri as Assur. During our stay I had time to order some gowns from Heinz Riva, with whom we managed to go to Porto Ercole for the weekend.

On June 29 Weenie and I flew to London, then to Aberdeen where I received my first Honorary Degree – that of Doctor of Laws (LLD) at the Graduation Ceremony of the University of Aberdeen. I was more nervous than before a performance. That evening we made our way to Leicester, where the next day I was conferred with the Honorary Degree of Doctor of Music by the Chancellor of the University of Leicester.

Back in London the weekend was spent brushing up Handel's *Messiah* for a performance the following Wednesday (July 10) in the Albert Hall, in the presence of HRH Princess Alexandra. This was the Handel Commemoration Concert in aid of the National Portrait Gallery's Handel Appeal, where we raised the funds to purchase the splendid Thomas Hudson portrait of the composer for the Nation. As a memento the Trustees and Staff of the National Portrait Gallery presented me with a beautifully framed lithograph of Handel's statue in Vauxhall Gardens.

Rehearsals began at home for *Don Giovanni*, as we were recording the opera in Kingsway Hall between July 15 and 30. As Don Giovanni in this set we had Gabriel Bacquier, with Werner Krenn as Ottavio, Pilar Lorengar as Elvira, Marilyn Horne as Zerlina, Donald Gramm as Leporello and Clifford Grant as the Commendatore. Richard conducted the English Chamber Orchestra.

This recording tried to recapture the qualities of the original performances in Prague – size and timbre of the orchestra, use of appoggiature and ornamentation of repeats by the singers, and a harpsichord continuo supporting the entire opera, not just the recits. All these contributed to a transparency and cleanness of texture, as opposed to the heavier orchestrations and unornamented vocal lines to which the twentieth-century listener had become accustomed. When reviews of the recording appeared two years later they were very mixed, each reviewer eager to air his knowledge of Mozart generally and *Don Giovanni* in particular. Perhaps Martin Bernheimer in the *Los Angeles Times* summed it up the best with 'If the new *Don Giovanni* does nothing else, it will make the old unadorned Mozartian manner seem a bit drab. Great singing, of course, can rise above any stylistic limitations. Mediocre singing cannot.'

There was general praise for the singers, although some quibbling about the casting, with my diction again receiving criticism. It sounded perfectly clear to me on rehearing the set at the time of writing, and I found it had a great deal of dramatic impact from *all* the cast.

✦ 5 ✦

TOWARDS THE END of the recording sessions the household prepared to go to Prcanj on Boka Kotorska, Yugoslavia, to spend a month in a charming (if somewhat primitive) old house that had once belonged to Mara. As the chalet was a total mess we needed somewhere to have a family holiday. At the beginning of that week Paul Garner had developed hepatitis, so to be on the safe side we had all been immunised against it *en masse* by Adam's charming doctor and thus had punctures on various parts of our anatomy. Better sure than sorry.

We flew to Dubrovnik and were then taken by car to Prcanj enjoying the sight of that huge sound going right to Kotor and completely navigable by large ocean liners and cruise ships. We found the little house had its own water frontage and a rambling old garden at the back with a vine-covered terrace where we ate all our meals – except when it rained. The main problem was dodging the wasps and bees.

Jan and Susan Rubes arrived on Sunday with their three boys, Jonathan, Chris and Tony. They were travelling down from Jan's first visit to his homeland (Czechoslovakia) after many years in Canada and he was in quite a high-emotional state. They had a campervan and were going to cross from Yugoslavia to Italy, continuing their holiday there. We had happy times together visiting Kotor, Ulcing, Budva and Sveti Stefan for swimming and picnics. The swimming was perfect right in front of the house and we set up tables and chairs and beach umbrellas where we played cards and mah-jong and the sun worshippers took advantage of the splendid weather. One of the great delights was to hear one of the local fishermen calling early in the morning something that sounded like 'Ree ... bay ...', which we knew meant there'd be fresh sardines grilled on the barbecue for lunch. No matter how many Mara bought we could always have eaten more, they were so delicious.

Norman Ayrton and Heinz Riva both came to stay and we made excursions to Dubrovnik, Petrovac and Perast. The whole area was dotted with beautiful old and crumbling stone houses from the great Venetian period and we were upset to learn of the damage done to the area by the earthquake they later suffered. What it must be like now after months of terrible civil war one cannot begin to imagine – all that destruction and imposed hardship for what? Serbs, Croats, Bosnians, Herzegovinians, Montenegrins all lived happily together in 1968 – or so it appeared when one travelled around, visiting local markets and bargaining for goods. How could those smiling, graceful people wilfully destroy not only the beautiful old towns but the lives of so many old and young alike?

Returning home, Adam went off cheerfully enough with us to Aiglon College where he shared a somewhat spartan room with two other boys – and a magnificent view of the Dents du Midi as did most of the school. I think we all felt lumps in the throat more than he, and Ruthli was very hard put not to cry – until we got into the car and drove off. We were requested by his Housemaster (Mr O'Hara) not to be in touch by phone too much and, although Adam could have the weekend away from school any time, work and sports fixtures permitting, he also advised us not to take advantage of this before half-term as it was better for the pupil to settle into the school routine over the first six weeks or so. He was a very charming man whose position was later taken by Mr and Mrs Elliot also living at Belvedere (Adam's house) with their family and always approachable over any problems, which seldom arose.

Adam was fortunate (he always says) to join the school at the same time it became co-ed – with a dozen or so girls (sisters of current pupils) on a trial run. This project was a huge success and a great atmosphere developed with the addition of the girls' dormitory and many more of the fair sex. The Lycée had, of course, been co-ed and I think Adam might have found Aiglon more difficult had it remained solely for boys. As it happened, after his first term there, and Christmas divided between New York and London, he couldn't wait to get back to the school and all its activities, particularly the skiing, ice-hockey and soccer.

Back in London, at the Festival Hall on Friday, October 4. Richard was very elated to be conducting *Lucrezia Borgia*, which was his first performance of the work and the London début of Montserrat Caballé. She had appeared three years previously at Glyndebourne but had not at that time been heard by the London public. Her performance of *Lucrezia* was exemplary, particularly the wonderful entrance aria and scena 'Come bello'. Richard had decided the part would be a great one for me and I demurred, saying I could never sing that aria as magically as Caballé. He was not one to accept 'no' for an answer, certainly from me, so of course I *did* sing the opera on stage many times and hope I created my own brand of magic. In the Festival Hall production Ruggiero Raimondi sang the role of Alfonso (Lucrezia's husband) and Eduardo Giminez was Gennaro, Huguette Tourangeau Orsini.

Frank Granville Barker wrote in the December edition of *Music and Musicians* after a most favourable assessment: 'Richard Bonynge controlled his soloists, chorus and orchestra with the combination of expertise and affection that makes him probably the finest Donizetti conductor of the day.'

It was at this time that I was sitting for June Mendoza for what is Richard's favourite portrait of me. It was painted in my dressing-room at number 36 below the short stairway leading to my bathroom and is all in shades of blue and brown. I think I look rather haughty, with what was then my long auburn hair hanging to my shoulders. June also painted me as Lucia and it is a wonderfully pathetic portrayal of me in the Mad Scene that is well known as a record cover and has been used frequently for publicity. There is a portrait of Ric also by her which I claimed for my bedroom and it is, along with her other works, an incredible likeness.

At the end of the second week in October Ric and Chester went to New York, where Ric began rehearsals for *Il Barbiere di Siviglia* for the Met on the fourteenth. I remained in London for a further three weeks, enjoying a lull in performing, although completing my sittings for June Mendoza, doing a big photo call in my *Traviata* costumes at number 36 for Bill Houston Rogers, various interviews with journalists, keeping in touch with friends and making trips to the theatre.

On October 25 Ruthli and I flew to Basel to attend the sixtieth birthday party of both her parents and, after it, must have been up at the crack of dawn to take the train to Montreux, pick up the car from Millasson's garage and drive to Chesières-Villars to meet Adam when he was free at 12.30. We had a happy lunch and shopping excursion in Montreux, buying food for him to take back to school and more sports equipment. It was great to be with Adam again and hear him talk about the school and its routine. He had never been one to gossip about his school life but the prospect of 'expeditions' with the boys and skiing beginning in the latter part of the term and continuing after Christmas when the real snow fell had him very excited. After a quiet Sunday and a huge lunch we returned him to Aiglon in the early evening in time for Chapel. I think it was harder for us all to say goodbye than when he had entered the school in September.

On Tuesday, November 5 I flew to New York and on the seventh (my forty-second birthday) *Il Barbiere di Siviglia* opened at the Met and I enjoyed the sparkling performance immensely with Teresa Berganza singing Rosina, Mario Sereni Figaro, Luigi Alva Count Almaviva, Giorgio Tozzi Don Basilio and Fernando Corena Dr Bartolo. Richard received excellent reviews, with one critic saying: 'Mr Bonynge's appearance in the pit is the best news the Met has given us in years. His musicality is impeccable and the vitality of his leadership was reflected in the outstanding results he obtained.'

The performances were videotaped for television by the Japanese Broadcasting Company (NHK) using their newly developed 'image-orthicon' tube which, being four times as sensitive as those in common use, made it possible to film without extra lighting. The cameras were very much smaller than hitherto and four were discreetly positioned about the House, causing very little disturbance or inconvenience to the audience. It was the beginning of a whole new approach to the televising of live performances and certainly made a huge difference to the performers. Whereas previously there had to be special moves by the singers, favouring certain cameras to facilitate the filming, now the cameras and their crews were able to tape the production as conceived by the stage director with little or no changes. This performance also launched the possibility of producing live opera on video as a commercial proposition.

After the performance Ann Colbert and Terry McEwen had planned a wonderful supper party at the Four Seasons Restaurant to celebrate both *The Barber* and my birthday, and it was a great pleasure to relax with so many colleagues and friends.

There were ten *Barbers*, which Ric conducted through the Christmas Season until January 11, 1969, with some cast changes, George Shirley singing Count Almaviva, Sherrill Milnes Figaro and Roberta Peters Rosina.

Ric and I began rehearsing both *Sonnambula* for the Met and *Lakmé* for Philadelphia, with Ric to-ing and fro-ing for his *Barber* performances. It was small wonder he was stricken with the particularly virulent influenza that was prevalent that fall. He managed to cope with one of the two *Lakmé* performances in Philadelphia on the nineteenth, but missed one on November 22. Ric spent the following six days in bed. He thus missed the début of Luciano at the Met – a matinée of *La Bohème* with Mirella Freni on November 23. I went, however, escorted by Terry McEwen, and witnessed the beginning of 'Big P's' hold on the New York public as he charmed and delighted them with his honest and somewhat naïve performance.

The *Lakmé* in the Academy of Music was the usual 'hit or miss' production of the Philadelphia Lyric Opera, with precious little rehearsal and a non-(or semi-) professional chorus. Dear Ray Fabiani relied very much on his leading singers holding everything together on stage, and frequently not only vocally. On this occasion (as usual) the costumes were only allotted to the chorus on the opening night. Some of the men were dressed as British soldiers and the rest as beggars, street vendors and Indian supporters of the Brahman Priest Nilakantha, father of Lakmé. In the second act, after my singing of the Bell Song during which Gerald inadvertently reveals his presence to Nilakantha, I had left the scene and was waiting in the wings. On-stage, Nilakantha was plotting with his followers to trap and kill Gerald who had intruded on to sacred ground near the temple and must die. Gabriel Bacquier was Nilakantha and as he began his denunciation to his men he realised that two were dressed in British army uniforms. In a very loud stage whisper he told the startled 'Brits' to 'get ze 'ell out of 'ere' or words to that effect, then continued unfolding his plan as though nothing had happened. The two choristers looked at each other in a stunned way, hesitated and ambled off, wondering why they shouldn't be there as the producer and chorus master had told them to be. None of them, I fear, knew the story line too well but I had a good laugh in the wings and Gaby was puce in the face with a mixture of exasperation and laughter.

The rest of the cast consisted of Huguette Tourangeau again singing Mallika, Alicia Maraslian Mistress Benson, Maxine Makas Ellen, Jacqueline Pierce Rose, Anastasios Vrenios Gerald and Cornelis Opthof Frederic. It was a very strong cast and, in spite of the odd production mishaps, was warmly appreciated by the public and critics.

Several friends visited from New York including Gladys Swarthout. There was a cute comment in the *Philadelphia Evening Bulletin* referring to the fact that the 'Amazonian Aussie-born soprano' had high notes that 'could have cracked the Liberty Bell all over again'. I wasn't sure it was a compliment.

Due to high fever from the flu attack, Ric was forced to miss most of the later rehearsals for *La Sonnambula* at the Met, although he managed to conduct the final Dress Rehearsal, finding the production in good shape. Fortunately he had another two days before the opening night on Monday, December 2. Already our desire to separate the rehearsal period from the first night by two days if possible proved to be an asset – in Richard's case this time as it meant he was almost recovered from the influenza virus and was able to conduct a more than satisfactory performance.

Unfortunately, John Alexander, who was singing the role of Elvino, succumbed to the flu (which had felled a number of Company members) half-way through the opera and George Shirley, who had been standing by, sang the last act. John had apparently warned the Met he was not feeling well that morning but had agreed to do his best. He was a great colleague and what I call a no-nonsense singer. The opera was broadcast from the matinée at the Met on Saturday, December 21.

The month was very busy, not only with Ric's performances of *The Barber*, as well as nine more of *La Sonnambula*, but some concerts, an *Ed Sullivan Show* (on the eighth), Adam and Ruthli arriving on the tenth and all the usual excitement leading up to Christmas and the New Year. Of course, Adam had a great deal to tell us about his sporting feats at Aiglon – not too much about the study side, but it was obvious that he was enjoying the life there. He came to the Met several times and went skiing with Jan Rubes and his family who were staying near Silver Mine ski run in New York. Christmas and New Year were hardly holidays for us – *La Sonnambula* on the twenty-fourth, *The Barber of Seville* on the twenty-fifth (to which we all went), with *The Barber* on New Year's Eve and *Sonnambula* on New Year's Day. The rehearsals for the *Ed Sullivan Show* were on December 4 and 7, with a full day's work on the day of the telecast, the eighth.

On the thirteenth Ric and I flew to Boston in the early evening to rehearsals next day with members of the Boston Symphony Orchestra and Anastasios Vrenios for a concert in aid of the Orchestra Pension Fund.

With the heavy performing load over the Christmas and New Year period it seemed no time at all before Adam and Udi had gone back to Europe.

$$\diamond\ 6\ \diamond$$

NEW YEAR'S DAY 1969 was another *La Sonnambula* with further performances on January 4 and 9, then off to Columbia, South Carolina, for January 13 – a recital with piano. The programme consisted of an early group of Handel and Dalayrac, followed by songs of Bellini and Rossini with the Sleep-walking Scene from *La Sonnambula* to end the first half. The second half opened with songs by Richard Strauss, Reger and Abt, followed by two groups of French songs by Gounod, Bizet, Massenet, Fauré and Delibes.

We returned to New York briefly, enjoying an evening with Jennie Tourel before travelling on to Indianapolis for a concert with the Indianapolis Symphony Orchestra on January 19 which was repeated in Wabash on January 21, and another recital in Minneapolis, Minnesota, on January 29.

This was our final concert of the winter season in the United States and we were happy to go back to London – via Switzerland to clarify a few details regarding the chalet reconstruction. Easter was made the deadline and packing and removal of the contents of number 36 were to begin immediately after Easter Monday.

We arrived in London on February 2 to rehearse for *Semiramide* which we were giving for the London Opera Society in the Theatre Royal, Drury Lane on Sunday, February 9. Marilyn Horne sang Arsace, Raymond Myers Assur, Clifford Grant Oroe and the ghost of Nino, and Anastasios Vrenios Idreno, with the New Philharmonic Orchestra.

The critics welcomed the opportunity to hear Rossini's work, if only in concert, and several implied that the Royal Opera House should have mounted a production of it for the Rossini centenary.

Much organising had to be done to ensure that we could vacate number 36 after Easter, but it didn't mean we could just concentrate on the move. We were rehearsing for a concert performance of *Alcina* with the London Philharmonic Orchestra in the Royal Festival Hall on February 19. Margreta Elkins sang Ruggiero, Monica Sinclair Bradamante, Mary O'Brien Morgana, Ryland Davies Oronte, John Gibbs Melisso and Kiri Te Kanawa Oberto. At the same time we were recording *Messiah* with the English Chamber Orchestra. The other soloists were Huguette Tourangeau, Werner Krenn and Tom Krause.

This was a controversial recording, the vocal line being quite heavily ornamented by Richard, and was ahead of its time. Not content with those projects Richard was also making a disc with Renata Tebaldi of arias and songs.

I was originally to record the album of French arias in this period but it was fortunately postponed to September in Geneva. There had also been an advance booking for Bologna for performances of *I Puritani* which were cancelled. I was quite exhausted and took the advice of Ivor Griffiths and went and stayed with Ruthli in the little Hotel Sonloup, just above the chalet, from where we watched the seemingly very slow progress of the transformation. The views from the hotel are superb and it has been refurbished and upgraded since then, but my bill for seven nights for two of us was only 434 Swiss francs with an extra 97 francs for phone calls, etc.

We spent another week at the Hotel Victoria in Glion where Richard joined us and we picked up Adam from school for a jolly weekend together. The chalet still looked only half ready, but the move was planned and must go ahead.

On April 1 we began recording Meyerbeer's *Les Huguenots* at Kingsway Hall with a splendid cast – Anastasios Vrenios as Raoul, Nicolai Ghiuselev as Marcel, Gabriel Bacquier St Bris, Martina Arroyo Valentine, Dominic Cossa de Nevers and Huguette Tourangeau Urbain. We also had Kiri Te Kanawa in the cast doubling as Maid of Honour and one of the young girls. Richard conducted the New Philharmonic Orchestra and the Ambrosian Singers in what evolved as a veritable best-seller.

Fortunately, my role as Queen Marguerite de Valois was not very long and was concentrated in two sections of the lengthy opera. This meant that I was able to be at number 36 to keep an eye on the removal operation. Four huge trailers were despatched to Les Avants. The chalet was not at all ready for the move, the main floor including kitchen, laundry entrance halls, salon and dining-room being unpaved and uncarpeted. Chandeliers had to remain in crates, along with busts and innumerable porcelain figures. The washing machine and drier were connected and the laundry was where everyone took their meals, jokingly watching clothes revolving in the machine and calling it our television set.

Once the second trailer arrived in Les Avants, Richard and I moved into the Waldorf Hotel, it being in walking distance of the recording studio at Kingsway Hall. Mara, Weenie, Adam and Chester went by car to join Ruthli and Paul at Chalet Monet, where the workmen were threatening to walk off the job if any more furniture came to impede their progress. Some of the bedrooms were ready, mostly those on the top floor, but amid all the chaos Adam's bed couldn't be found so he was sleeping in his sleeping bag on the floor of Ruthli's room. I think he was rather glad to go back to the sane environment of Aiglon College on April 28.

We completed the *Huguenots* recording on April 25, after many farewell dinners with friends. On the following day we flew to Switzerland and added to the chaos in the chalet – but not for long. By May 5 Richard, Weenie, Chester and myself were in Buenos Aires, leaving Paul and Udi to cope with working out the remaining decorating details, of which there were plenty, and the placing of the furniture in the house, which they managed admirably.

In Buenos Aires we were to do five performances each in new productions of *La Traviata* and *Norma* at the fabled Teatro Colón and orchestral rehearsals began the day after we arrived. We loved the city and were very impressed by the beautiful villas, not far from our apartment hotel. We made many friends and went shopping and sightseeing. We felt very much at home in Buenos Aires and were often out walking in the city. Although there were many graffiti and slogans telling the Americans to 'go home', we had no fear of being attacked in the streets and only witnessed a few minor demonstrations during our stay of two months.

Sandro Sequi was the producer of both the operas and there were a few old friends scattered through the cast with whom we enjoyed very late suppers of huge Argentinian steaks at two or three in the morning – the performances only commencing at 9.30 p.m. In *La Traviata*, Renato Cioni sang Alfredo and Piero Cappucilli Giorgio Germont. There were five performances between May 17 and June 1, and they all went very well, with Richard gaining praise for 'a lighter' reading of the score than was customary, especially in the preludes to Acts 1 and 4.

There was a ten-day break between the final *Traviata* and the beginning of rehearsals for *Norma*. We took a trip to La Paz, Cuzco, Machupicchu and Lima. We had a wonderful time, although the altitude in La Paz affected all of us, Richard rather more than Chester and myself. The trip to the market in La Paz was fascinating and Chester had great difficulty in getting any film of the colourful vendors, who persisted in throwing either one of their many skirts or a corner of a poncho over their heads to protect themselves from 'the evil eye'. We took the train along the high plateau to Guaqui, on the shore of Lake Titicaca, where we boarded an ancient steamship called the *Inca Queen* or S.S. *Inca*, which made the overnight crossing of the lake to Puno, arriving at about seven on the following morning. I swear it hadn't been decorated since 1895. We were very intrigued by the reed boats used by the fishermen, resembling those of the early Egyptians.

We travelled by train to Cuzco and discovered the local tipple – Pisco Sours. Refreshing they were, but also quite lethal. We wandered about the charming city and saw many remains of Inca civilisation. We took a train to Machupicchu and were amazed by the grandeur of the place and how, with such simple methods, this ancient people had been able to irrigate their land and establish a foolproof system of reckoning the seasons with their 'hitching post of the Sun'. How the hill-top community had been built without sophisticated equipment is a great quandary. We flew to Lima, then back to Buenos Aires. The trip was something we will never forget and we have remained very grateful that it was possible to fit it in then as we have never revisited South America.

Rehearsals for *Norma* began almost immediately and also a round of dinner parties, where we heard for the first time the enchanting Paraguayan harp.

We discovered from our friends that there was a great feeling of unease as to the deteriorating political situation. There were also a series of explosions in a chain of supermarkets, something like twelve of a total of fourteen being blown up while we were in Buenos Aires. Indeed, Chester went to his usual market early one morning only to find it a smouldering wreck. Fortunately, the bomb had gone off before the workers got there and there were no casualties but Chester returned to us very perturbed – he had been in the place the night before, right by the shelves housing the cereals where the bomb had been hidden.

Norma was designed by Pier Luigi Pizzi and produced by Sandro Sequi with Fiorenza Cossotto as Adalgisa, Charles Craig as Pollione and Ivo Vinco as Oroveso. The Chorus Master was Romano Gandolfi and Armando Krieger was one of the resident *répétiteurs*, with both of whom we worked again in the late 1980s and early 1990s. The performances were extremely successful although there was the inevitable comparison of the Sutherland *Norma* as opposed to Callas. The public was vociferous.

Norma was given five performances between June 21 and July 2. On July 3 we flew to Los Angeles, where we stayed at the crazy old Chateau Marmont on Sunset Boulevard (home of many film stars in the past) to rehearse and perform a concert at the Hollywood Bowl on July 8. The audience of some 14,000 enjoyed their evening 'under the stars' and we moved on the following day to Portland, Oregon, where we gave a recital with piano on the tenth, followed by another in San Francisco on July 12. We stayed on there for a few days, travelling to Chicago on the fifteenth for a concert at Ravinia with the Chicago Symphony. This was a repeat of the Hollywood Bowl concert, this time for an audience of about 5000, and Richard and I were busy performing encores with piano for a good half-hour after the orchestra had packed up and gone home.

Our final recital was in Ottawa on July 20 and we were very happy to fly home to Les Avants on the following day to commence our summer holiday in the refurbished Chalet Monet. Adam was home from school and several friends stayed for a few nights. We also did some recording in Geneva for Decca with the Orchestre Suisse-Romande, including the *Romantic French Arias* and *Coppelia*.

The collection of French arias is one of my favourite recordings as there are so many varied items, some of which had either never been recorded or not for many years. It was an exciting repertoire to work on and some of that excitement seems to remain on the disc.

OFFENBACH   *Robinson Crusoe*   'Conduisez-moi vers celui que j'adore'

MEYERBEER   *Dinorah*   'Bellah! ma chèvre chérie! ... Dors, petite'

CHARPENTIER   *Louise*   'Depuis le jour'

OFFENBACH   *La Grande Duchesse de Gérolstein*   'Dites-lui qu'on l'a remarqué'

AUBER   *Fra Diavolo*   'Non temete milord ... Or son sola'

BIZET   *Les Pêcheurs de perles*   'Me voilà seule ... Comme autrefois'

OFFENBACH   *Les Contes d'Hoffmann*   'Les oiseaux dans la charmille'

MASSENET   *Cendrillon*   'Ah! que mes soeurs sont heureuses'

GOUNOD   *Mireille*   'O légère hirondelle'

OFFENBACH   *La Grande Duchesse de Gérolstein*   'Vous aimez le danger ... Ah! que j'aime les militaires'

MEYERBEER   *L'Etoile du nord*   'C'est bien lui que chaque matin ... La, la, la air chéri'

GOUNOD   *La Tribut de Zamora*   'Ce Sarrasin disait'

MEYERBEER   *Robert le Diable*   'En vain j'espére ... Idole de ma vie'

LECOCQ   *Le Coeur et la main*   'Un soir Pérez le capitaine'

MASSE   *Les Noces de Jeannette*   'Au bord du chemin qui passe à ma porte'

GOUNOD   *Faust*   'Si le bonheur'

BIZET   *Carmen*   'La marguerite a fermé ... Ouvre ton coeur'

MEYERBEER   *L'Etoile du nord*   'Vielle sur eux ... Vaisseau que le flot balance'

Richard's recording of *Coppelia* was also a favourite and has remained very popular.

It was during this late summer break that Mara decided she was going back to Vienna and then to Yugoslavia. She had been a great help and we were very sorry to see her go but she was beginning to feel her considerable age and wanted to return to her homeland where she could be near her son. She kept in touch with Udi for some time and we later heard of her death.

Paul Garner also left, finding the constant living at a distance from the city and its musical activities difficult. As he did not drive he had to rely on our local train to get him home from a performance in Lausanne or Geneva and the last connection from the main line was so early that he always had to miss the last act of an opera or the second half of a concert. So he wanted to work back in London, which we quite understood. He rejoined us for a time later on.

Weenie had decided in Buenos Aires that it was time for her to move on too. She had come for a six-month trial after a severe illness had halted her nursing career – and had stayed for over eight years. She continued to live in Europe – in the Spa country near Heidelberg – and visited nearly every year to keep our press-cuttings books up to date, but has now returned to Australia. Without her this screed could not have been attempted. She stayed until the end of 1969, leaving us on January 4, 1970.

After his birthday on September 29 Ric went to London where he recorded both the *Homage to Pavlova* set and two discs of Handel overtures. I followed in early October and on the sixth we gave a recital in St John's, Smith Square in aid of their Restoration Fund.

The Church of St John the Evangelist was built at the behest of Queen Anne and was considered the most purely baroque church in London. The twice reconstructed interior survived until May 1941, when the church was completely gutted by an air attack on London. Her Royal Highness The Princess Margaret became Patron of the 'Friends of St John's' and through the organisation's work the church was restored as closely as possible to Thomas Archer's original design. The ceiling was given an acoustic treatment and the church (known as Queen Anne's Footstool) has become a valued additional venue in the heart of London's Westminster for concerts and recordings. Our recital was the initial public event in the presence of Princess Margaret and we have since returned to St John's both to record and give a further concert.

On October 8 we took the car on the Air Ferry to The Hague where we performed with the Residentie Orkest in the Congresgebouw on the eleventh. From The Hague we travelled by car to Hamburg, where we had rented an apartment as our stay was from October 12 until December 21.

In Hamburg we performed Handel's *Giulio Cesare* in a very glamorous production, the sets designed by Ming Cho Lee with costumes by José Varona, produced by Tito Capobianco, and his wife, Elena Denda ('Gigi'), choreographed the many balletic scenes. The cast was splendid, with Huguette Tourangeau as Caesar, Tom Krause Achillas, Ursula Böse Cornelia, Lucia Popp Sextus and myself as Cleopatra.

With the luxury of a complete month's rehearsal the production was very integrated and there was ample time to incorporate all the carefully studied movements devised by Gigi. The costumes were extraordinarily beautiful and great trouble was taken by the members of the Hamburg Opera wardrobe to meet the demands of José Varona. The set was a series of stairs and galleries rising to the back of the stage, with large movable central 'screens' to complement the finely executed fluted columns at stage level. Altogether the production appeared as a breathtaking baroque 'masque' glittering with gold, bronze and silver.

But not only the appearance of the work was perfection. The singers all appreciated the precision and beauty of the overall production and, in spite of some difficulties negotiating the rather narrow stairs in large costumes (fortunately, not too heavy) with musically measured steps, sang and performed at the height of their ability.

The Caesar of Huguette Tourangeau was exceptional, with an insight into the Handelian style, together with a dramatic intensity, that was something I had not encountered before in these operas. I was astonished at how masculine this ultra-feminine woman became on stage and it helped my own reactions and performance during our scenes together.

There had been a lot of laughs during the rehearsal period, especially with Tom, Huguette and Lucia, as we enjoyed each other's company and dined together a good deal. We all had difficulties with wrong-footing in some of our Gigi-inspired movements, getting very tangled up at times and laughing at our own efforts. But when it came to the performances they ran perfectly smoothly and caused quite a sensation with the Hamburg audiences and critics alike.

The opera was presented ten times between November 9 and December 21. During a break at the end of November Richard flew to London to complete the *Homage to Pavlova* recording and Chester, Huguette and I drove home to Les Avants for a few days.

We had all done shopping for Christmas and the car was loaded with all sorts of presents for family and friends about which Chester was worrying all the way to Basel and the Swiss customs. When we arrived they noted how low the back of the Skylark was and asked us to open the huge trunk. We thought they would ask the price of all our presents, but their query was over a very large stack of cardboard folders that Richard had bought through the Hamburg Opera Library to store and properly catalogue some of his unbound music. For me to explain this to a German-speaking customs officer and assure him that the large stacks of folders were for personal use and not going to be sold was quite difficult. Not one of us spoke the language and I was grateful for Huguette's French as mine was very rusty, also for her charm and personality. Finally, after much waving of arms and explanations in three languages, we were allowed to leave.

We spent five days at the chalet and flew back to Hamburg on December 5. We agreed to return early in 1971 and do further performances of *Julius Caesar*, also a new production of *Lucia*. Rolf Liebermann (the Intendant at that time) had been very persuasive over luncheon and had assured me it would be as interesting and beautiful a *Lucia* as the original Zeffirelli. This I doubted, but agreed to come to Hamburg and find out – I was not disappointed.

We spent a very happy Christmas and New Year (1970) with me studying and polishing *L'Elisir d'Amore* which we were to commence recording at the end of the second week of January together with a couple of *Messiah* sessions. We managed a fair amount of sledding with members of the Coward household. Our road is a splendid run from just beyond Sonloup above us down to the railway station in the village and we enjoyed going up with our sleds on the funicular ('the funi'), partaking of fondue together at the hotel there and sledding down the hill for a further Schnapps in the village. Sometimes we had dinner in our own homes and did several runs during the late evening. It was great fun always and the shrieks of laughter still occur today with a whole new generation – dependent, of course, on the amount of snow we have.

Adam returned to school on Friday, January 9 and we flew to London the next day, leaving Udi in charge of the chalet until our return the following July.

❖ 7 ❖

OUR RECORDING SESSIONS began almost immediately and after three sessions for *L'Elisir d'Amore* and two for *Messiah* we left for New York on January 19. It was straight to work with rehearsals and a concert in Philadelphia for the Hundred and thirteenth Anniversary Concert and Ball of the Academy of Music – a Gala which was conducted by Eugene Ormandy who was celebrating his thirty-fourth year on the podium of the Philadelphia Orchestra as music director and his seventieth birthday. I was a co-soloist with Placido Domingo and the pianist John Browning played the Rachmaninoff *Rhapsody on a Theme of Paganini*. It was a pleasure (as always) to sing in that lovely theatre and the Concert and Ball were a great success. I was delighted to work with Ormandy who was very charming and friendly. The then President Nixon and Mrs Nixon joined in the applause, demanding several encores. Variations on the theme of 'Happy Birthday' were played for Eugene Ormandy's seventieth, having been kept as a surprise for him. He remarked, 'I knew something was cooking, but I did not know what.'

On January 27 we gave a recital for the CBC in Ottawa which was recorded by them to be transmitted nationally at later dates. We repeated the same recital at Ann Arbor for the University of Michigan on January 30 and Constitution Hall, Washington on February 8.

For the rest of February we remained in New York, rehearsing for the new production of *Norma* being staged by Paul-Emile Deiber with sets and costumes by Desmond Heeley at the Met. The repaired revolving stage was being used for the first time since its unfortunate breakdown during rehearsals for the opening of the new House. We luckily had no problems. The idea of the set was rather like the Zeffirelli *Alcina* with a sculptured unit set presented from different angles for each of the acts. It worked very well and our costumes, too, were very effective.

Marilyn Horne was making her Metropolitan début singing Adalgisa and, as always, we enjoyed working and spending time together. Carlo Bergonzi was the Pollione and Cesare Siepi the Oroveso.

The opening night was a Guild Benefit on March 3, with ten further performances in New York. We then went on tour with the Met, doing

Norma in Boston, Philadelphia, Cleveland, Atlanta, Memphis, Dallas, Minneapolis and Detroit. The performance of *Norma* in Philadelphia on April 27 was for the Philadelphia Lyric Opera with Ezio Flagello as Oroveso, Pedro Lavirgen Pollione and Huguette Tourangeau Adalgisa. Richard conducted the Lyric Opera Orchestra. He also had a couple of *Lucia* dates during the tour with Gail Robinson and we then did two performances of *Lucia* back in New York at the Met. The Met had good use of our *Norma* production in its initial season and the long run of performances – twenty between March 3 and May 28 – certainly removed any hazards that greatest of roles may have held for me.

The opening night in New York was 'magnificent', 'memorable', 'A triumph' and Marilyn had a resounding success. Our voices had a special blend and we always felt a great rapport when singing together. Neither of us forgot that it was Bellini's genius that presented us with the wherewithal to cast the spell.

Irving Kolodin of the *Saturday Review* regretted that I had been singing too little in the new theatre:

> Such a career as hers, however long, is always too short, and to have a year or two of it spent entirely elsewhere is a deprivation New Yorkers can ill afford. She returns with vocal splendor undiminished, with her all but inhuman accuracy wholly at her bidding, and the fastidious kind of musicianship, that is almost as much a 'trade-mark' as her extravagant coiffure, more subtly employed than before.

I was thrilled by some of my telegrams on the opening night, particularly one from that great Norma of the late Twenties, Rosa Ponselle, reading:

> Norma has always been close to my heart and I know you will bring her close to the hearts of the thousands who will hear you tonight. A great role needs the talent of a great artist. The Met is fortunate to be able to present you both to its public. *In bocca al lupo* and God bless you.
>
> Rosa Ponselle

Although there were so many performances of *Norma* we found time for other engagements. I did yet another *Ed Sullivan Show* on March 8 – with Marilyn Horne, singing the much-loved duet from *Norma*. During rehearsal Ed Sullivan gave us one of his notorious mis-pronunciations, calling Marilyn's character in *Norma* 'Aggledisa'. We were rather sorry that he was corrected and during the actual telecast introduced her very distinctly as singing the role of Ad-al-gi-sa.

We also repeated our recital in London, Ontario, on March 30 and in Chicago on May 4, as well as performing in the Gala Benefit for Richard Tucker at the Met on April 11, celebrating his twenty-fifth anniversary at the House. I sang in the first act of *La Traviata*. This was followed by the second act of *La Gioconda* with Renata Tebaldi as Gioconda, then the third act of *Aida* with Leontyne Price as Aida. Richard Tucker sang all three heroes. He was fifty-five at the time and had sung more than four hundred performances for the Metropolitan Opera alone, attracting an enormous following. He sang the three large excerpts extraordinarily well that night and was besieged in his dressing-room by a horde of admirers, finally managing to escape to a nearby French restaurant to host a delightful supper party for the entire cast of the evening and many of his friends.

The two *Lucia* performances in New York in the first week of June featured Placido Domingo in his first Edgardos at the Met – his arm in a black sling, having injured it in a bicycle accident the weekend before. These *Lucias* with Placido were the first of many exciting performances of the opera together.

Ric and I returned to Switzerland by the 12.35 'Midnight' flight to Geneva immediately after the last performance. It made it possible for us to leave some of our heavier clothing at home before going on to England for a month.

The first of our engagements there was a recital for the Bath Festival in Bristol on June 11. Prince Charles was on a tour of the Duchy of Cornwall and attended it.

The following week we revised our *Norma* production at the Royal Opera House and caught up on London friends – Nadia Nerina and her husband Charles Gordon, the Gamleys, Hardy Amies – and Ruthli arrived from Switzerland for two weeks. Marilyn and I sang *Norma* on June 25, with a further four performances.

On June 30 a 'Gala Performance in Tribute to Sir David Webster' was given in the Royal Opera House. He had announced his retirement after twenty-six years as General Administrator of the Company. Some sixty soloists, the Covent Garden Orchestra and the chorus all participated, together with seven different conductors. The majority of the artists were British and were or had been members of the Company, with foreign visitors James McCracken, Martina Arroyo, Regina Resnik, Tito Gobbi and Ermanno Mauro, all of whom had worked at the Garden from time to time, also taking part. Her Majesty Queen Elizabeth The Queen Mother was present, accompanied by Prince Charles, and the gala was given in aid of the Royal Opera House Benevolent Fund and the Snape Maltings Foundation (Aldeburgh).

Although I was listed in the large Souvenir Programme to sing 'Casta diva' from Act 1 of *Norma*, I actually sang the Mad Scene from *Lucia di Lammermoor*. It was a splendid night, culminating in a Company line-up on the bare stage and a presentation to Sir David. When responding to Lord Drogheda's speech Sir David thanked the Queen Mother for her twenty-five years of patronage of the Opera House, going on to say: 'We've been at it twenty-five years and we haven't done badly, in fact we've done jolly well ... I believe that now we have the best opera company in the world.'

All the artists respected him and were sorry to see him retire from office. They certainly agreed with his comment, especially those who had experienced the inadequacies of some companies abroad. Richard and I had always appreciated his frankness and advice. He had fostered my career in no uncertain fashion and had given Richard the opportunity to conduct in that great House at a very early stage of his career. We will never forget his faith in our abilities. Unfortunately, Sir David did not enjoy his retirement for very long as he died within a year.

During the first two weeks of July we recorded *L'Elisir d'Amore*. Luciano Pavarotti and Spiro Malas were both in the recording and Richard conducted the English Chamber Orchestra. We also had an 'Aussie Reunion' party at Joseph Rouleau's home as so many members of the Sutherland–Williamson Company were in London at that time. It was a very jolly gathering and an opportunity for all to catch up on our family events since the 1965 tour.

On July 12 we returned to Les Avants, Adam having started his summer holiday that weekend. At the end of the following week we all went and stayed with our friends in Arenzano near Genoa for ten days, enjoying the seaside. The month of August was spent at Chalet Monet entertaining a succession of house guests.

The fourth of September saw us back in New York with a very heavy schedule for Richard at the Met. He was rehearsing revivals of *Norma* and *La Traviata* and also Gluck's *Orfeo* in a new production, all of which went into performance between September 17 and 25.

Norma opened on September 17, with five further performances, the last on October 17. The cast was much the same as earlier in the year with Fiorenza Cossotto singing two Adalgisas and Ruggero Raimondi and Ivo Vinco the role of Oroveso at times. Franco Tagliavini was Pollione on opening night. The Met loved changing casts.

La Traviata was next – on the following night, with Teresa Zylis-Gara, Giacomo Aragall and Robert Merrill in the leading roles. This was repeated on the twenty-second. One New York critic remarked on how beautifully the soloists sang, especially the more intimate scenes of the opera. He went on to say: 'What was best of all was the mellow blending of the orchestra and voices, something for which conductor Richard Bonynge deserves much credit. On that count we have rarely heard better.'

The new production of *Orfeo ed Euridice* opened on September 25 with Grace Bumbry as Orfeo, Gabriella Tucci as Euridice and Gail Robinson as Amore. The sets and costumes were by Rolf Gérard. This was a benefit evening for the Metropolitan Opera production Friends, and there were a further eight performances with Ruza Baldani taking over as Orfeo.

On October 12, after fairly minimal rehearsal, I sang the first of four *La Traviatas*. The last was on the evening of the 1970 'Ball in the Opera House', held after the performance. It also celebrated the twenty-fifth anniversary at the Met of Robert Merrill who was singing the role of Papa Germont in that night's *La Traviata* and was guest of honour at the Ball. This was the third twenty-fifth anniversary performance in which I had participated during the year and congratulations were certainly due to Bob Merrill for his long and varied career with the Met and elsewhere. He was always a most courteous and friendly colleague with a great sense of humour and we worked together frequently and well.

My opening *Traviata* cast (according to the programme) from October 12 consisted of:

Giorgio Germont	Sherrill Milnes
Flora Bervoix	Frederica von Stade
Gastone	Charles Anthony
Baron Douphol	Robert Goodloe
Marquis d'Obigny	Gene Boucher
Doctor Grenvil	Louis Sgarro
Annina	Loretta di Franco
Giuseppe	Luigi Marcella
A gardener	John Trehy

One newspaper report (the *New York Times* of October 14) mentions the

SUPERB *TRAVIATA* PRESENTED AT THE MET

Joan Sutherland sang Violetta and Sherill Milnes the elder Germont both for the first time this season in *La Traviata* at the Metropolitan Opera Monday night, and it was just as if the company had taken off into the stratosphere, compared with some other recent *Traviatas*.

It wasn't a matter of super-high notes, but of super-high quality. This kind of singing is what the Met is made for: warm, full, luscious, glorious, close to the ultimate in satisfaction.

The role of Violetta fits Miss Sutherland like a glove, and every moment sparkled with beauty and meaning. Mr Milnes was in top form, with deep, seamless tones and extraordinary musicianship.

Everyone rose to the occasion. Richard Bonynge's conducting was crisp and flexible, Giacomo Aragall was a lilting Alfredo, and all others in smaller roles, including Raymond Gibbs in his first Douphol with the company, responded accordingly.

As neither Giacomo Aragall's nor Raymond Gibbs's name appeared on the printed programme for the evening, could there have been an announcement preceding the Act 1 curtain that these substitutions would be made? Or was there a printed slip inserted in the programme that has fallen out and been lost? The *Annals of the Metropolitan Opera* lists Aragall and Gibbs for that performance. I expect it is correct. Neither Richard nor I can remember who sang – not surprising in Richard's case, with such a heavy schedule at the time. In spite of this we still managed to enjoy dining with friends – Terry McEwen, the Toller Bonds, Gabriel Bacquier, Geri Souvaine, Spiro and Marlene Malas and the Materas, with a record signing session at Korvettes and several photo sessions and interviews. There was also one *Traviata* with Luciano singing Alfredo.

We left for Seattle on November 1 where we were presenting a new production of *The Tales of Hoffmann*. The sets were designed by Allen Charles Klein and my splendid gowns were by José Varona and executed once again by Barbara Matera who made the trip to Seattle to ensure they were workable and able to be changed readily enough. As I was singing all four 'loves' of Hoffmann and there were big make-up changes as well, this was very important. Gigi Capobianco had been kind enough to evolve and do a 'trial run' while I was in New York of a superb make-up for Olympia (the doll). This made a relatively easy change to that of Giulietta, but it was still rather hectic to get everything in place including myself on the stage in a dazzling gown looking languid and bored, before the curtain went up on the second act.

I was happy to be singing this opera again after about fifteen years, when I'd sung in it at Covent Garden and on tour with that Company, but only two of the roles together, never all the female roles on the same night. It was my singing of Olympia, I believe, that had finally convinced the Royal Opera House administration that I was definitely a coloratura, in spite of the richer quality of my voice than was customary for that type of soprano. At the Garden the opera had been in English and now we were performing it in the original French. This created a problem with the dialogue for most of the cast, and many were the sessions we had, just repeating and perfecting it together in our apartment. It was also a big challenge to make each character we played different vocally as well as visually.

We had an excellent cast, with John Alexander singing the title role. I sang the roles of Olympia, Giulietta, Antonia and Stella. The Muse, Nicklausse and the Mother's Voice were sung by Huguette Tourangeau. Counsellor Lindorf, Coppelius, Dapertutto and Dr Miracle by Joshua Hecht. Spalanzani, Schlemil and Crespel by Jan Rubes. Andrès, Cochenille, Pittichinaccio and Frantz by Gerald Thorsen. Bliss Hebert was the perfect producer. Joshua Hecht was a fairly last-minute replacement for the bass Norman Treigle who refused to participate in the version arranged by Richard. This parallels as closely as possible Offenbach's original intentions and clarifies many points in the work. Treigle claimed the Seattle Opera had not forwarded the version in time for him to learn it.

The production had a big success, both musically and visually. My José Varona-designed costumes helped me enormously to assume the various personalities I portrayed and the Olympia and Antonia scenes had their customary knock-out effect on the audience.

In the *Seattle Post Intelligence*, Rolf Stromberg wrote, after a glowing account of the opening night:

> This is the opera version that stirred some contention over what is rightly the accepted edition. Bonynge did his work with balance and good taste. It seemed fitting, and was highly effective. Inasmuch as Offenbach didn't finish this, Bonynge's editing of it – as he contends, more in the spirit of Offenbach's original intent – is certainly acceptable. It is above all artistically valid.

It was a very successful venture for me and, although a very busy night in the theatre, I enjoyed it immensely. So much so, in fact, that I continued to sing all the roles in *Hoffmann* from time to time up until January 1985.

After three further performances in Seattle we returned to New York with Richard rehearsing at the Met the following day for further performances of *La Traviata*. He conducted one on November 28 with Anna Moffo and Alfredo Kraus and I returned to that opera on December 2, also with Alfredo. I sang a further performance with Placido Domingo as Alfredo and we attended a celebration of Placido's seven hundredth operatic performance. There was a huge cake which seemed in danger of setting the restaurant on fire with its 700 flaming candles.

The following week it was back into the role of Norma with three performances at the Met including the matinée broadcast on Saturday, December 19 with Marilyn, John Alexander and Paul Plishka.

Back in Switzerland for Christmas with Adam, I revised *Julius Caesar* for the Hamburg Opera and we performed this and *Lucia di Lammermoor* between January 18 and April 18, 1971.

Between the *Julius Caesar* dates we rehearsed *Lucia di Lammermoor* with a very interesting and demanding stage director, Peter Beauvais. He was the only person since I had worked with Zeffirelli on *Lucia* who was able to broaden my interpretation of the character and add further depth to her personality. Beauvais was primarily a television producer at that stage of his career and he kept making little TV screens by holding his hands up in front of him and 'dollying' in on his subjects.

It was rather disconcerting, and he was adamant about our holding certain poses and positions. This was all very difficult when we were working in a concrete-floored semi-basement rehearsal room with no scenery, and his assurance that the lighting and his use of spotlights would be a great feature of most of the scenes didn't help at all. One day, after we had spent a day and half on the mechanics of the Mad Scene for me alone, holding the prescribed positions, I found I couldn't remember any of them – or the words and music. I had to be excused from rehearsing the scene any further that day and was a nervous wreck.

When we finally got on stage it became more obvious what his intentions were and we could see why we had to be so meticulous about moving only an inch or so at times, as he had engineered various pools of light and the results were extremely effective. He also actually showed Lucia gibbering on the floor by her blood-soaked husband at the beginning of her Mad Scene – again in a pool of light. The scene was a huge success, being a Zeffirelli–Beauvais combination.

The sets and costumes were by Jürgen Rose and the cast was splendid, both Placido Domingo and Gianni Raimondi as Edgardo, Tom Krause as Enrico and Kurt Moll as Raimondo.

After five weeks' rehearsal the opera opened on March 7 to acclaim from the public for the singers and their well-nigh flawless work. However, they made it obvious that they did not like the designs of Jürgen Rose and the production as a whole. This was a great shame as not only had we all grown to accept and admire Beauvais's conception, but also we had a further twelve performances of *Lucia* in the House. The audiences in Hamburg had been used to a more 'up-dated' approach to such works and apparently disliked the realistic, traditionally authentic costumes and staging. The Wedding Scene and Mad Scene were quite wonderful, as Peter Beauvais had used retired actors and circus performers as extras. Some of these were very old and were splendid as relatives of the two clans involved, instead of young choristers having to make up and act as grandmothers and great-aunts. Another great feature was the inclusion of the tower scene, most often cut. It is very dramatic and makes a deal more sense of the plot when performed. We have always included it when possible.

My brother Jim arrived in Hamburg in time for the opening night and also attended the reception afterwards given by the Hamburg-Süd Shipping Company and Howaldts-Werke–Deutsche Werft. My brother had been Secretary of the P & O shipping company in Sydney and it was a coincidence that he should be in Europe prior to my launching a new ship for the German companies – *Columbus Australia* – early the following week, on Tuesday, March 9. This was a 21,250-ton turbine container ship which was to ply on the Columbus Line container service between the US East Coast and Australia–New Zealand. There was a very happy dinner-dance given at the Hotel Vier Jahreszeiten after the launching and I was presented with a splendid Donizetti autograph.

It was not the last time I saw the *Columbus Australia* by any means. It frequently appeared at the container terminal on Manhattan and I have often seen it steaming in and out of Sydney Harbour. Indeed, it became quite a good-luck symbol, arriving at times on the same day as an important concert or performance at the opera.

The *Lucia* on April 14 was attended by the ill-fated Göran Gentele who was to be Rudolf Bing's successor at the Met. We had dinner together after the performance and spent a pleasant hour or so with him. He seemed a charming man with very definite ideas for the future. On July 18, 1972 he and his family were involved in a motor accident while on holiday in Sardinia and he was killed.

Several friends visited Hamburg and we had enjoyable meals with them, also with some of our colleagues there including Placido and Marta Domingo, André Montal, Richard Cassilly, Tito Capobianco, Tatiana Troyanos, Richard and Doris Cross and the Australian soprano, Marie Collier.

On April 30 Richard and I did a recital for Aiglon College Development Fund in the Victoria Hall, Geneva, which was an amazing success with the boys and helped their school building fund a little.

The next day, Marta Domingo came to Les Avants and after a jolly lunch went house-hunting with Paul Garner and Ric. The Domingos were very keen to buy a residence in our area at that time, but found nothing they liked. Paul's help to Marta on this occasion was, I am sure, what prompted the Domingos to consider him as a secretary-organiser for Placido. This Paul actually became on leaving us and he has remained in that position for more than twenty years. We see him from time to time and laugh over some of our recollections.

On May 2 Ric and I flew to Madrid where we had a concert with the Orquesta Sinfonica de la RTV Espanola in the Teatro Real on the fifth at 11 p.m. Between rehearsals we managed to enjoy the Prado Museum – a small section of it.

The day after the concert we flew to Liverpool and gave a recital for the Royal Liverpool Philharmonic Society. It was back to London the next day and a visit to Ivor Griffiths late in the afternoon for a check-up. I had a heavy schedule for the next two weeks and was feeling a bit tired and croaky of voice. All must have been well as I was rehearsing Handel's *Rodelinda* for the rest of the week, giving two concert performances of the work on May 14 and 16. These were with Richard conducting the English Chamber Orchestra in Brighton as part of the Brighton Festival. Huguette Tourangeau sang Bertarido, Robert

Tear Grimoaldo, Norma Procter Edwige, Maureen Lehane Unulfo and Christian du Plessis Garibaldo.

We took part in an operatic concert on May 23 in the Royal Albert Hall in the presence of the Duke and Duchess of Kent in aid of the Self-Help Foundation, established in 1967 by Father Denis Madigan to 'help people of Papua and New Guinea help themselves'. Many Australian diplomats and politicians were present and were surprised and rather alarmed when a young gentleman leaped from his seat on to the platform and presented me with a crumpled posy of yellow flowers after having knelt at my feet and embraced me. It caused quite a gale of laughter.

Alberto Remedios, Thomas McDonnell and Josephte Clement assisted in the concert, with Richard conducting the London Philharmonic Orchestra. We were very embarrassed by the lack of attention given to the assisting artists, all of whom gave their services. Richard and I were presented with a set of silver teaspoons depicting native Australian fauna and a very handsome painting by Dermot Hellier of a Murray River landscape.

✦ **8** ✦

WE SPENT THREE weeks in Les Avants for a rest and study period. Richard's mother and father had arrived in Europe towards the end of our engagement with the Hamburg Opera and had been doing various tours, returning to Chalet Monet as their base. It was good to spend some time together, as well as restudying the role of Gilda in *Rigoletto* which we were to re-record in London in mid-June. Richard and Chester took Betty and Carl Bonynge on a trip to Paris and back, visiting the Loire valley. José and Mary Varona also spent a few days with us.

By June 12 we were in London again and, as well as recording sessions every day, I sat each morning for June Mendoza who was painting the well-known portrait of me as Lucia. It was very convenient as Decca never planned morning sessions and June was happy with the light between 10.15 a.m. and 12.30 p.m. She captured a great sense of Lucia's hopeless and helpless state. It was quite relaxing chatting with her about the doings of her large family and ours in her Chelsea studio and the portrait was done in nine sittings instead of the ten blocked in the diary. It was used as the cover for the *Lucia di Lammermoor* recording made that July.

Both the *Rigoletto* and *Lucia* recordings featured Sherrill Milnes and Luciano Pavarotti with Martti Talvela, Clifford Grant and Huguette Tourangeau in *Rigoletto*, not forgetting the young Kiri Te Kanawa as the Countess Ceprano. Nicolai Ghiaurov (Raimondo) and Huguette Tourangeau (Alisa) sang with us in *Lucia*. The LSO was conducted by Richard for the Verdi opera and the Royal Opera House Covent Garden Orchestra and chorus for the Donizetti.

I remember with such pleasure a visit with adorable Dame Edith Evans. 'What can we do with our Joanie?' she said. 'When she sings she has the voice of an angel and when she speaks, the voice of a schoolgirl!'

A very sad occasion was the Memorial Service held for Sir David Webster on Friday, July 2. I was asked to sing but declined as I felt too emotionally involved. Ric and I attended and thought the service rather overcrowded with artists *without* me.

Adam's summer holidays began on July 8 and he and Ruthli came

240

over to London for a week, with Adam going on to Majorca with one of his friends. Home in Les Avants we spent time with Sir Noël Coward, and his household, together with Cathleen Nesbitt who was visiting at the time, came to watch our annual fireworks display on 1 August – the Swiss National Day.

Ric's parents were still with us in between their various tours through the British Isles and Scandinavia. We were very glad to have bought the Chalet Amina across the road which helped to accommodate everyone, easing the household congestion a trifle. We made a few local trips – to Gstaad to have lunch with Anya Dorfman, to the Folkoric Market in Vevey each Saturday, to Lausanne and Gruyères, and I even had time for some dental work including a nasty extraction.

On August 19 we commenced recording *Les Contes d'Hoffmann* in Geneva at the Victoria Hall. (Richard also did a disc of three Romantic cello concerti with Jascha Silberstein during the same period, both with the Orchestre de la Suisse-Romande.) The cast for the opera was as follows: Placido Domingo was a wonderful Hoffmann, Huguette Tourangeau an adorable Nicklausse/Muse, with Gabriel Bacquier at the top of his form as the villains. Jacques Charon from the Comédie Française replaced Peter Ustinov as Spalanzani at the last minute and showed real genius.

At this time, with the Orchestre de la Suisse-Romande Richard also recorded a disc, *Arias from Forgotten Operas*, with Huguette Tourangeau. He dug up a few surprises including an aria from Balfe's *Ildegonda nel Carcere* and an amusing bravura rondo from Auber's *Le Cheval de bronze*.

We left for the United States on September 5 and stayed three or four nights in New York, seeing a performance of that breath-taking show *Follies*. Barbara Matera had made the costumes which were sumptuous and beautiful beyond belief. After a wonderful night in the theatre we had supper with her and Arthur at Elaine's.

Then off to Chicago for *Semiramide* in the production from Florence which the Lyric Opera had borrowed from the Teatro Communale. The cast was again made up of friends and former colleagues, Sandro Sequi producing. Marilyn Horne, Spiro Malas and Pietro Bottazzo sang with me. *Semiramide* continued to be a huge success with the public. As the opera had not been presented in the United States within living memory, opera-goers from all over the country wanted to see and hear it, quite apart from the regular Sutherland–Horne worshippers. Even with all its peculiarities of plot, it remains a great night's entertainment in the old tradition.

Our next opera was Donizetti's *Maria Stuarda* which was a new work for both Richard and me. We had a good three and a half weeks' rehearsal and time to enjoy the comfort of the Sausalito home of Jack

Shelton and Jack Juhasz, where we were again staying. The production was originally designed by Pier Luigi Pizzi and borrowed by the San Francisco Opera from the Teatro Communale, Florence. As new costumes had to be made for me I requested they be designed by José Varona and executed by Barbara Matera. The result was spectacular. Barbara flew out for the final stage rehearsals to be sure that everything was 'hanging' correctly and to make any last-minute adjustments. Due to what I called the 'raked stage craze' hemlines were always a problem. Tito Capobianco and Gigi (Elena Denda) were again producing and we had some good times together.

I had read as much as I could about Mary Stuart and felt a great deal of sympathy for her. Somehow either she or her supporters always seemed to go about things the wrong way and her desperation was increased by the numerous failures of their planning and plotting. Her prolonged pleading to Elizabeth the First for recognition prompted Schiller (on whose play the libretto of the opera was based) to bring about a very dramatic meeting between the two which never, in fact, took place historically. Huguette Tourangeau was a most convincing Queen Elizabeth and we enjoyed rehearsing and performing that scene immensely. Both of us had large, rewarding roles and found they were well written to attain the contrast between the two queens' personalities, quite apart from the very different natural qualities of our voices.

It was Huguette's début with the San Francisco Opera as well as in the role – and there were a few extravagant headlines for the opera and both of us. Cornelis Opthof also received praise for his début with the Company. He was a most sympathetic Talbot and his participation in Mary's Confession Scene helped make it my favourite in the opera.

I had never worked with Stuart Burrows, who sang Leicester, and found him very charming and considerate. We enjoyed our big scene together in Act 2, in spite of the quite severely raked stage. It was unfortunate that I made a fast entrance down the 'rake' and had a horror of not being able to stop from toppling into the orchestra pit. Quite apart from my own body weight, the costume was very heavy and there was a great deal of added impetus. It created a lot of problems with hems and trains and I had difficulty remaining erect, always having consciously to lean backwards. It did not help my chronic weakness in the lower back.

Following five *Stuardas* we flew to Salt Lake City, where we performed again with the Utah Symphony in the Salt Lake Tabernacle. The programme consisted of:

SCARLATTI-TOMMASINI   *The Good Humored Ladies*
DONIZETTI   'Regnava nel silenzio' (*Lucia di Lammermoor*)

MOZART   Symphony No. 40 in G Minor K 550

VERDI   Overture to *La Forza del Destino*
LEO FALL   Operetta Medley
VERDI   'Ah, fors'è lui' (*La Traviata*)

As always, we enjoyed our stay in the city, brief as it was, and were off to New York the day after the concert.

Richard's parents had taken a cruise through the Mediterranean to the Middle East from Genoa and back to Venice during our time in San Francisco. Unfortunately, Carl Bonynge became unwell whilst on the trip, the first sign of a type of leukaemia which led to his death in 1976. Both Mother and Dad made light of the problem, extolling the trip and not wanting to worry us, but Udi confirmed that Carl was not well at all and we were glad that the United States tour would soon be over and we could go home and see for ourselves the state of his health.

We remained in New York, although rehearsing for two performances of *Lucia di Lammermoor* for the Philadelphia Lyric on December 7 and 10. Veriano Luchetti was my Edgardo on this occasion and our old friend Cornelis Opthof Enrico. The *Philadelphia Bulletin* printed an advance article about the production which stated:

> Cornelis Opthof plays Lucia's *sister*, who deceives her into thinking her lover has chosen another woman. Opthof is a Canadian *baritone* who has sung with the Lyric before.

And some people believe everything they read!

We had two more dates: a concert in New Orleans with the Symphony and Huguette Tourangeau and a recital in the Kennedy Center in Washington. The second half of the New Orleans concert consisted of the whole of Act 2 Scene I of *Norma* with Huguette and myself, a 'house-bringer-downer' if ever there was one. The Kennedy Center Recital on December 17 was the one remembered not so much for my singing as the fact that prior to the last item before the interval a woman in the audience politely asked, 'May I ask a question?'

I smiled, nodded and said 'of course'.

'May I ask, why do you always use your music?'

(I always sang my latter recitals with my music on a stand in front of me.) I laughed and said, 'Because I have a rotten memory, and if I don't use my music I don't sing!'

(Applause, cheers, cries of 'Brava') – and the recital continued with the Donizetti song 'Il Sospiro'.

I had tried using a 'palm card' also the 'little book' with just my words (which were the chief and very real problem) but as my sight deteriorated the print was too small and close. I then started using the music stand which permitted me to read ahead much better. As most of the music I sang was of a period nature and doubtless had been performed at eighteenth- and nineteenth-century musical evenings in such a way with a music stand it became part of the regular presentation and gave me more confidence, especially once I started wearing contact lenses and could see the music so much better. The recital platform never appealed to me as much as the opera stage – I think I preferred to hide myself in another character and let *her* sing instead of me. Anyway, we reached the end of the evening without further interruption, leaving for Geneva and home the following night.

As usual we had our Christmas tree with presents on the twenty-fourth and went over to the Chalet Coward on Christmas morning for their present opening – and the customary champagne cocktails. Greta, Ike and Emma Elkins were staying with us, also Adam's friend Vanya Gant and Betty and Carl Bonynge, so we had quite a jolly crowd, together with Noël, Graham, Coley and their guests.

Richard flew to London on December 26, as he had some recording sessions, and returned in time for the New Year. I had succumbed to a mixture of exhaustion and a very bad cold so took to my bed for the first three days of 1972. I have never seen anything joyous in the beginning of another year and seldom stay up to welcome it in. My infectious state was a great excuse to stay away from the revellers.

After a few recording sessions in London at Kingsway Hall we went to Rome, where we gave a recital at the Accademia Nazionale di Santa Cecilia, collected some concert gowns from Heinz Riva and arrived in New York on February 2. On the sixth we were both presented with Honorary Doctorates of Art from Rider College in Trenton, New Jersey. This was during the rehearsal period at the Met for *La Fille du Régiment* which was to open on February 17 in the sets and costumes bought from Covent Garden, with Sandro Sequi again producing. Marcel Escoffier had designed a vivandière costume with baggy pants tucked into boots, but I felt more comfortable wearing the military jacket with the very full skirt over several petticoats that Barbara Matera had made for the *Who's Afraid of Opera* TV series and fitted very well into the scene. The whole cast was completely involved and sang superbly. My old friend Luciano Pavarotti (with his nine high Cs), Fernando Corena, Regina Resnik and Andrea Velis were with me.

For the spoken role of the Duchesse de Krakenthorp the Met had engaged that great old diva of the Forties and Fifties Ljuba Welitsch. There had been several prolonged bursts of applause during the opening night performance (February 17) after various well-delivered items, but Welitsch had barely appeared at the top of her entrance stairs when the House exploded into wild applause, stopping the show dead before she opened her mouth to say her few lines. She was remembered for her sensational Salome, among other roles, and it was a very touching tribute from the audience.

The critics actually agreed that the opera was great entertainment and fun, without any of the singers sacrificing vocal quality. Harold Schonberg (in the *New York Times* on February 19) wrote of my performance:

> She was often genuinely funny, and seemed to be having a good time, but there was none of the self-parody that one had feared. She showed that she was a good mimic, she moved with more grace than she had done in any role at the Metropolitan (she even did a few elegant dance steps in the second act) and she had a few deadpan routines that brought down the house.
>
> And she sang beautifully. Her voice was under fine control. As always, she threw out many notes in alt, but those Ds and E flats, impressive as they may be, are not the real glory of the Sutherland voice. The rich sound, coupled to extraordinary flexibility, is the real glory. Miss Sutherland spun out arch after arch of pure tone. What is more, it was expressive tone. There has not been more beautiful or expressive singing in any opera house than in Miss Sutherland's second-act* romance, 'Il faut partir'. This was bel canto at its best – secure in technique, melting in tone delicately shaded, long-breathed.

The opera was given twelve times and there were some cast changes during the run, with Donald Gramm singing Sulpice, Monica Sinclair the Marquise and both John Alexander and Enrico di Giuseppe the role of Tonio.

Richard and I had taken a much-needed break of a week in Jamaica between the end of March and April 6. We again stayed at Noël Coward's Blue Harbour and enjoyed a lovely evening at Bolt House, the home of Mrs Blanche Blackwell who had a charming group of Jamaican folk singers to entertain us.

We returned to New York refreshed and in time to see the showing of the first of the *Who's Afraid of Opera* series (*The Barber of Seville*) on April 9, with the second opera (*La Fille du Régiment*) being shown on April 16. There was enormous coverage of the two shows in the press, both before and after. Although the critics were not entirely impressed, the public response was tremendous and the whole series of operas was shown several times, ultimately being issued for sale on video. Aimed at a junior audience, we had a phenomenal response from

---

* Either he meant 'first-act' or, if second-act, the aria is 'Par le rang et par l'opulence'.

parents and teachers as well. We recorded eight shows: *Traviata, Faust, Rigoletto, Lucia, La Périchole* and *Mignon* as well as the two above.

On March 17 and 18 we had given recitals at Raleigh College, North Carolina, and on April 11 at the Academy of Music, Philadelphia. These were received as well as any we had given as recitalists in the US, especially in Philadelphia where no superlatives seemed to be sufficient praise for us by the critic of the *Evening Bulletin* – from his headline, 'Joan Sutherland Wows Audience', to his final line: 'Sutherland is still incomparable, and, with the help of her husband last night, unbeatable.'

On April 22 the Metropolitan Opera Guild sponsored a benefit to honour Sir Rudolf Bing, aged seventy-one, who was to retire at the end of the season after twenty-two years as General Manager. There had been a great number of changes during his regime, not the least of which was the move into the new house at Lincoln Center. He had not been the most approachable person; however, if agreement was reached over repertoire in talks with him you could be sure that his word would be honoured. Luciano and I sang the duet from *Lucia di Lammermoor* quite early in the programme and I was able to go and sit in 'the Golden Horseshoe' for the rest of the night. Of all the remaining items the one that amazed me most was the singing of the duet from *La Forza del Destino* by Richard Tucker and Robert Merrill. Here were two stalwarts of the Met scene, both having performed there for over twenty-five years, raising the roof with their vigorous and brilliant tone. It's not given to many to maintain that vibrant quality after years of constant use of their voice. They certainly had managed.

There was a long list of eminent singers including Martina Arroyo, Birgit Nilsson, Leonie Rysanek, Leontyne Price, Gabriella Tucci, Anna Moffo, Fernando Corena, Placido Domingo, Montserrat Caballé, Jon Vickers, Jerome Hines, Grace Bumbry, Pilar Lorengar, Lucine Amara, James McCracken, Irene Dalis, Cornell MacNeil, Ezio Flagello, Mario Sereni, Rosalind Elias, Roberta Peters, Sherrill Milnes, Teresa Stratas, Paul Plishka, Teresa Zylis-Gara, Gail Robinson, John Macurdy, Dorothy Kirsten, Enrico di Giuseppe, Cesare Siepi, Franco Corelli and Regina Resnik. I trust I have omitted no one. Regina sang a parody of Orlovsky's aria from *Die Fledermaus* – 'Chacun à Bing's Gout' – after the Presentation and Response from Sir Rudolf. He had written a cute letter to all of us in the Gala, a copy of which appears below.

TO ALL THOSE ARTISTS WHO ARE SO GENEROUSLY
PARTICIPATING IN MY FAREWELL GALA

This is a request to help speed up the happy proceedings during the Gala.

Will all artists please accept their applause after finishing their number and, indeed, allow that applause to develop to certainly deserved proportions, but once they leave the stage as directed by the Stage Director, please do not return. For obvious reasons, we cannot have duplicating bows and if for no other reason, because we all wish to get home before breakfast!

Thank you very much!

The day after the Gala we flew to Boston – the first city on the Met's spring tour. Here we opened the season on April 24 with *La Fille du Régiment*. (Ric had a *La Traviata* performance the following night with Anna Moffo, Franco Bonisolli and Robert Merrill.) This cast remained fairly constant for the whole tour which, as well as Boston, included Cleveland, Atlanta, Memphis, New Orleans, Minneapolis and Detroit. The main changes were the roles of Alfredo (sung by both Placido Domingo and Enrico di Giuseppe), and Flora which was sung by Frederica von Stade from Atlanta on.

We usually had the *Fille* and *Traviata* performances on successive days but in New Orleans Ric had a matinée *Traviata* with *La Fille du Régiment* in the evening. Tiring as it was for him it meant we could take the short flight back to New York after each double commitment instead of staying the full six weeks out of town.

Between the opera dates we also gave recitals at Michigan State University and Ohio State University in Columbus. We flew on to Atlanta from Columbus for Ric's *Traviata* on the tenth and *Fille* on the eleventh, after which we had a delightful dinner with Blanche Thebom, recalling our Dallas performances of *Alcina* in which she had sung Ruggiero and other happy occasions.

We went north again on the twelfth and spent the weekend with Barbara and Arthur Matera in their gingerbread home at Athens, NY, and again had a hilarious dinner with Zinka Milanov together with Martin Waldron.

Martin was the owner of a beautiful four-storey house on Prospect Park West, Brooklyn, with a splendid view of the park and, from the roof, back to Manhattan and the Statue of Liberty. When we decided not to rent again the Greenwich Village apartment Martin suggested we might like to look at the two top floors of his house which were a self-contained flat. This we could use as a base on our visits to New York as he did not wish to have permanent tenants but would enjoy having us stay whenever we came to the United States. We had accepted his kind offer and the arrangement worked out exceptionally well right up until my retirement. Certain of our friends were against our being in Brooklyn but we loved it. Quite apart from the park itself, there were the Botanical Gardens, the Library and the splendid Museum and excellent food stores all within walking distance. As for the distance from Manhattan and the Met, it more often than not took as long to cross that island from east to west as it did to travel by car or taxi from Prospect Park West, via the tunnel and the West Side Highway to Lincoln Center. We were also a good deal closer to both La Guardia and Kennedy airports.

So the day after our dinner with Zinka we were off to Memphis where we performed *La Fille du Régiment* on May 17 and then on to New Orleans on the eighteenth. We were able to spend some time with Anni Frind, that sweet soprano who had sung with Berlin and Dresden Operas before the war and was living now with her husband Joseph Sperling in New Orleans. Not only did she present me with the fan she had used in *Die Fledermaus* but she sent Richard and me tea-chests full of her scores and sheet music, all much treasured.

After New Orleans we flew to Minneapolis for more *Traviatas* and *Filles*, going to Detroit on 1 June for our final tour performances.

Back in New York, Ric conducted *La Traviata* at the Met on June 7 after a *Rigoletto* Dress Rehearsal in the morning. Our first *Rigoletto* performance for the June Festival at the Met was the matinée on June 10. The cast was very strong, prompting Harold Schonberg to write a glowing review in the *New York Times* of Monday, June 12. He said:

OPERA: RICH *RIGOLETTO*
ALL-STAR MET CAST LED BY JOAN SUTHERLAND

A strong blow in favour of all-star casts was delivered Saturday afternoon by the Metropolitan Opera. The opera was *Rigoletto*, and it had Joan Sutherland as Gilda, Luciano Pavarotti as the Duke, Sherrill Milnes as Rigoletto and Ruggero Raimondi as Sparafucile (all, incidentally, singing their respective roles for the first time in New York). The heavens above the equator on a calm moonless night could not be starrier.

There are those who look with suspicion on all-star casts. Silly they. Certainly this *Rigoletto* was the greatest thing of its kind as long as one can remember. For there are stars and stars. There are singers – and one does not have to go far to mention names – who abuse great voices to gratify their nasty, illiterate little egos. Those are the ones who give the star system a bad name. But when you have a group of artists such as were heard on Saturday, all working together, all trying to get the most out of the music, all with championship-caliber voices – well, grand opera and great singing are still alive.

He went on to give individual praise, later writing:

The conductor also was new. Richard Bonynge directed his first *Rigoletto* at the Metropolitan, and it was by far the finest thing this listener has ever heard him do.

Matteo Manuguerra sang the title role for the third and fourth performances, while Ivo Vinco sang Sparafucile at the second and third.

Ruggero Raimondi had managed to carry me in the sack from the inn to Rigoletto and dump me at his feet without any apparent strain. However, Ivo complained that he had a 'very bad back'. He said he, 'of course, could manage to carry the Signora, but his back ...!' So Richard suggested the Met engage a muscular assistant to Sparafucile who could do the job – which they did, and it worked perfectly.

We spent another weekend with Barbara and Arthur Matera in Athens and had three more *Rigolettos* on June 14, 19 and 22, and Ric also conducted *La Traviata* on the seventeenth and the matinée on the twenty-fourth. With all of that we managed to perform with Marilyn Horne and her husband Henry Lewis (who was Music Director of the New Jersey Symphony Orchestra at the time) in a gala concert to celebrate the fiftieth anniversary of the Orchestra at the Garden State Arts Center, Holmdel, New Jersey. This Center was the most modern and well-planned outdoor venue in which I have performed and we enjoyed the experience very much.

On July 2 Ric flew off to London to record with Renata Tebaldi an album of Italian songs. The title of the disc was *Serenata Tebaldi* and Richard accompanied Renata at the piano in a charming collection of songs from the eighteenth and nineteenth centuries. These have now been reissued in a different form on CD.

In Les Avants we had a month's study-holiday with Udi in the last stages of pregnancy and not very comfortable or well. We made a few local excursions and had our usual celebration of August 1 with fireworks on the terrace and a visit from Coley and Graham. By this time Noël was not at all well and couldn't come.

The following week we went to London, Adam as well. He stayed with his friend Vanya Gant, going to Dublin for a few days while Ric and I recorded. Together we did a session or two of our recital disc *Songs My Mother Taught Me*, with Ric recording a ballet.

At the same time I recorded Puccini's *Turandot* with Zubin Mehta conducting the London Philharmonic Orchestra. With Pavarotti, Caballé, Ghiaurov, Krause and Pears to complete the cast it was quite a formidable line-up on stage. I even wondered if it would be prudent to reinforce it, as only Tom Krause and Peter Pears could be termed light-weight. I must say it was a thrilling experience and for a while I contemplated singing the role in the theatre. However, after due consideration, I decided to leave the public with the impression I gave on the recording of the icy princess.

Once again we visited with London friends and learned during our stay that Udi had given birth to a little girl on 18 August, to bear the name of that great actress of the early nineteenth century, Rachel. Richard was to be godfather so he chose her first name, with Udi adding her sister's name, Maya.

After the last *Turandot* session on August 23 I flew home to Les Avants and went to see Udi and the baby each afternoon. I was sorry to have to leave again for San Francisco so soon. But Udi's parents were down from Basel, as was Tana, her sister-in-law, so we packed our bags yet again and flew to New York on the twenty-eighth for three days so that I could attend fittings for costumes with Barbara Matera, travelling on to San Francisco on August 31.

We began rehearsals with Tito Capobianco for the *Norma* at the San Francisco Opera. As usual, we had a hard-working and pleasant cast of friends. Pollione was sung by John Alexander, Adalgisa by Huguette Tourangeau and Oroveso by Clifford Grant. One of my 'children' was little Nadia Webb, the daughter of one of the best prompters in the profession, Susan Webb. Many are the lives Susan has saved, including mine.

The San Francisco Opera was celebrating its fiftieth anniversary season and heralded the event with 'Opera Week'. This began with a lunch-time gathering in Union Square with Mayor Alioto presiding. I was presented with a State of California commemorative book on behalf of Governor Reagan and Mayor Alioto presented me with the key to the city. After a very short response from me I sang 'Ah! fors'è lui' and 'Sempre libera' from *La Traviata* and after what the press described as a 'thunderous ovation' I sang 'The Last Rose of Summer' accompanied by Richard at the piano. This had apparently last been sung to a Market Street gathering by Luisa Tetrazzini in 1900. The Sixth Army Band provided 'exit music' and we had enormous difficulty, in spite of heavy official aid, in negotiating our way through some 10,000 people crowding the exits to the square. It certainly was a great advertisement for the Opera!

The season opened on September 15 to rave reviews. The costumes (designed by José Varona, as were the sets) were much lighter and floating in texture than those I had worn previously, giving the appearance of Greek or Roman goddesses rather than tough, primitive Druids. They certainly moved beautifully, although, as they were made of chiffon and georgette, they tended to waft and catch on 'bushes' and trees. I wore these costumes again later in Toronto and decided they were definitely the most beautiful I ever used as the Druid Priestess.

Headlines appeared reading:

A TRIUMPHANT BELLINI OPENING

SUTHERLAND MAKES *NORMA* RIPE FOR REVIVAL IN SAN FRANCISCO

SUTHERLAND BRILLIANT NORMA

Alexander Fried, in the *San Francisco Examiner*, wrote:

> ... Her voice is amazingly full-sounding for a soprano who can flit through the heights and ornate vivacities of coloratura singing. Her coloratura accuracy and trills were immaculate. Her upper scale has a uniquely glorious, liquid purity.
>
> There was a rare inward poise and vision in her quiet singing of Norma's famous 'Casta diva' aria, in which she begs for peace because war between her Roman lover and her Druid land would be unendurable.

After the opening performance an Opera Ball was given with the cast of the opera and notable guests present. These included Governor and Mrs Ronald Reagan, the Italian Consul General, Prince Luigi de Giovanni, Mayor Alioto and a host of other Californian dignitaries. Richard and I, although quite tired, enjoyed the celebration and I even managed to dance with Tito Capobianco who had staged the opera so strongly. There is a press photo of us in which I seem to be telling him I'll be his partner but he could be minus a few toes before getting back to his place at the table.

There were four further performances of the opera and between the last two *Normas* Ric and I went to Vancouver to work with Irving Guttman on Donizetti's *Lucrezia Borgia* which we were to perform for the first time there at the end of October.

It was at this time that the press published a list of fees that the leading singers' agents quoted as 'opening prices' in negotiations for the said artists' services. This was the result of a survey carried out by Michael Scott and published originally in the July issue of *Opera*, the British monthly magazine. The report caused quite a stir among colleagues and managements, being considered privileged and private information and, in most cases, incorrect fees were published. If nothing else, it showed the public why, allied with the cost of lavish scenery and costumes for new productions, their subscription rates to the various opera companies were steadily increasing. Compared with the remuneration demanded by the then current pop stars for an appearance, the singers' fees were extremely reasonable and this the opera-going public recognised. They continued to support their particular favourites, frequently travelling great distances to do so.

On October 11, Ric accompanied Huguette Tourangeau in a recital in Santa Rosa, after which rehearsals began in earnest in Vancouver for *Lucrezia Borgia*. The producer was Irving Guttman, Artistic Director of the Vancouver Opera Association, together with those of Edmonton and Winnipeg at that time. The costumes and sets were by José Varona, with my gowns very lavishly executed by Barbara in velvets and silks with heavy appliqué and embroidery. It was a first performance on stage of the opera for all of us and we worked very hard together to make the production a success. Louis Quilico played my husband Don Alfonso, Duke of Ferrara, John Alexander was Gennaro and Huguette Tourangeau Maffio Orsini.

There were six performances in Vancouver and three in Edmonton. Richard had made judicious cuts in the score which tightened the action and the result was a very exciting operatic experience. I had enjoyed the concert performance which Ric conducted in London with Caballé as Lucrezia but to sing the part on stage myself I found enthralling – one of my favourites – from my opening aria to the closing scene with its great duet and aria.

The production was hailed as a triumph for the Vancouver Opera and we were all highly complimented. One critic spoke of Richard as having 'the combination of expertise and affection that makes him probably the finest Donizetti conductor of the day'.

A constant reminder of these performances and of Vancouver is the gold effigy of myself as Norma given to me by a staunch supporter of the VOA and a particular fan of mine. He had requested the figure to be copied by a local goldsmith from the splendid Barry Glass photograph taken during my début performances in *Norma* and presented it to me on the opening night of *Lucrezia Borgia*. I wear this beautifully crafted memento on a neck chain more than any other piece of jewellery.

It had been sixty-eight years since the opera had been performed in North America and interest in the *Lucrezia Borgia* production remained during its performance in Edmonton. It was already becoming excruciatingly cold in that prairie city and we were very happy to return to Les Avants on November 23.

We only stayed for a little over a week, then travelled to London to rehearse and record two more shows for the *Who's Afraid of Opera* series – *Lucia* and *La Périchole*. As the filming took place at Shepperton Studios we remained just a week in London for the sound recording and blocking rehearsals, then spent the five days of filming at a quaint country hotel in Surrey within easy distance of the studio.

Home to Les Avants on December 15 where there were the usual pre-Christmas preparations and guests, with much skiing for the young ones or sledding for the oldies. We also attended the christening ceremony of Rachel at the village church and, on Christmas Eve, Noël Coward paid his final visit to us. He was not at all well but was determined to join in the festivities. He nursed Rachel who gurgled and smiled, prompting Noël to remark that Ruthli should watch how she was 'playing to the audience and the cameras already'. She was living up to her namesake.

On December 26 we flew to New York for the Dress Rehearsal of *La Fille du Régiment* and a New Year's Eve performance of the opera, after which we had dinner with Barbara and Arthur Matera at Elaine's to celebrate the coming of 1973.

LA FILLE DU RÉGIMENT took up most of January.

Owing to the tragic death of Göran Gentele the previous summer, Schuyler Chapin (who had worked a great deal with Leonard Bernstein and served as Vice-President of Lincoln Center) had been appointed acting General Manager of the Met. In May 1973 he was to be awarded the full title of General Manager. Rafael Kubelik had been engaged by Gentele as Music Director, remaining in the position only until the spring of 1974 due to various personal and health reasons.

As Schuyler Chapin was endeavouring to organise the Met's future programming he was meeting with the 'regular' performers while they were in New York to get to know them and discuss their possible repertoire and availability. We had a pleasant lunch with him on January 8 and found him very knowledgeable and delightful company. We ultimately became friendly with him and his family, especially his wife Betty. She was a warm, amusing hostess and we always enjoyed a relaxed evening at their New York apartment. Sadly, Betty died on June 17, 1993 from bone cancer.

On January 14 we attended a gala performance at 9 p.m. of *Oh, Coward* at the New Theater. This was the same compilation of Noël Coward favourites that we had seen in London under the title of *Cowardy Custard*. Noël was there and tottered down the aisle just before the lights dimmed on the arm of Marlene Dietrich, both looking exceptionally frail. One wondered who was supporting whom. It was a riotous evening and the last time we saw either of those great personalities. Noël travelled on to Jamaica where he died on March 26 and was buried on his property of Firefly at the 'Master's' favourite vantage point. Dietrich, although living for many more years, gradually retreated from public view.

We had our usual round of dinner and late-supper parties with Terry McEwen, Geri Souvaine, Donald Gramm and his friend Don Dervin, the Materas and various other Met colleagues and friends. On January 26, Ric and I flew to Ottawa, where we did a recital on the twenty-seventh for the CBC which was broadcast at a later date. It also appeared on a pirate disc. The programme was quite long, one of our 'mixed bags', being the basis for further recitals in Atlanta, Long Island and New Rochelle.

'O quand je dors'	LISZT
'Die Lorelei'	LISZT
'L'esclave'	LALO
'Berceuse'	CHAMINADE
'Puisqu'elle a pris ma vie'	MASSENET
'Aimons-nous'	HAHN
'Guide au bord ta nacelle'	MEYERBEER
'Chanson de Zora'	ROSSINI
'A mezzanotte'	DONIZETTI
'Ernani, involami' (*Ernani*)	VERDI
'Lament of Isis'	GRANVILLE BARKER
'Love's Philosophy'	ROGER QUILTER
'The Unforeseen'	CYRIL SCOTT
'Oh, that it were so'	FRANK BRIDGE
'The Gypsy and the Bird'	BENEDICT
'Il Trovatore'	PONCHIELLI
'La tua stella'	MASCAGNI
'Stornello'	CIMARA
'Seranata'	TOSTI
'Ah, que les hommes sont bêtes' (*La Périchole*)	OFFENBACH
'Tu n'est pas beau, tu n'est pas riche' (*La Périchole*)	OFFENBACH

On 10 February there was a Guild Benefit Gala at the Metropolitan Opera. It opened with Act 3 of *Aida* with Leontyne Price, followed by Act 3 of *Un Ballo in Maschera* with Elinor Ross and Luciano Pavarotti and we closed it with the Mad Scene from *Lucia*.

The next day we flew home and were able to take Adam for a birthday dinner in Villars before flying to London. Chester took the car to facilitate our British travel and we drove to Cardiff on February 17, giving the same recital as above. London the following week was a whirlwind of activity with rehearsals, wig and costume fittings for the TV shows and a concert for the Stars Organisation for Spastics, this last at the Albert Hall on February 23. The Duchess of Kent was present and also attended the delightful supper party given jointly by Mrs James Ogilvy, Nadia Nerina and her husband Charles Gordon at the Berkeley Hotel in Knightsbridge. Many stars of the London stage and screen were present, including Roger Moore, who was Chairman of the organisation at that time. I sat next to him during the meal and was very struck, not only by his handsome appearance but by his great charm and easy manners. Richard was quite dazzled by the Duchess of Kent and Roger Moore's wife, Luisa.

The SOS has done wonderful work to help in the care and entertainment of spastics of all ages since 1955. This concert, in which I sang the Mad Scene from *I Puritani*, some Leo Fall and Offenbach, raised some £15,000 for their appeal. Richard conducted the Royal Philharmonic Orchestra in the Schubert Symphony No. 6 and a suite for Orchestra from Massenet's *Esclarmonde*, as well as my vocal numbers and it was a very sparkling evening.

A 'Welcome back' banner was held up by fans in the Albert Hall and Sydney Edwards was most complimentary in his short resumé. He said in the *Evening Standard* (which had been a sponsor of the concert):

> The Voice (no wonder the Italians at La Scala [*sic*] called her La Stupenda) was in fresh marvellous form.
>
> Not only was there a stream of pure, precise top notes that filled the hall in Bellini and Offenbach but in some rather, light-weight operetta there was also a smooth, poised floating line.
>
> This was the art of Sutherland at its most pleasurable.

I might remind that it was my appearance at La Fenice in Venice as Alcina that prompted the 'La Stupenda' title, not La Scala – but it stuck.

On March 25, 26 and 27 I have six hours blocked in my diary each day for 'BBC–TV' and have been unable to recall the programme. It must have been the show produced by Patricia Foy with myself and Margreta Elkins.

After recording the music in three long sessions and rehearsing for a couple of days, we drove to a hotel in Surrey to settle in for the forthcoming week's filming at Shepperton of two more in the *Who's Afraid of Opera* series. With make-up and wardrobe calls, final rehearsals and false starts this entailed a solid ten hours a day in the studio. But it had its relaxed and funny moments, as we now got to know the puppeteers and cameramen and shared a lot of jokes between 'takes', often brought about by a filmed mishap.

We had a week of doing nothing but a couple of dental appointments and household shopping and we got home in time to pick up Adam (now a 'gentle giant' of seventeen) from Aiglon for his Easter holiday.

The following week our calm was broken by the arrival of a BBC–TV crew, together with Patricia Foy. She inspected the layout of the house, lining up possible shots, and we worked through the next two days filming interviews and 'local colour'. Unfortunately there seldom is much colour at the end of March so high in the mountains and, although I warned that the light very often disappeared in the afternoon, interviews were filmed in the morning in the house and outdoor shots in the afternoon through fog and the remains of the snow. It was *not* a year with an early spring, which is a glorious sight, but the film crew said they were satisfied.

My happiest memory of that week was being invited by Adrienne (Allen) and Bill Whitney to their home in La Tour-de-Peilz and meeting that fascinating artist Kokoschka who also lived close by at Veytaux further along the lake near the castle of Chillon. Ric and I were taken with his elegance and humour and he had the most piercing, wonderful eyes. He wanted to paint me – but I didn't see the point of fourteen or more sittings to appear on canvas looking like a fried egg. His early work was very beautiful but I have never been able to understand 'contemporary art'. As it happens, Kokoschka was practically blind by then and didn't continue painting, or live much longer. He was already very old – but a charmer.

We had a pleasant three weeks at home with friends visiting, Ric taking a trip to Paris to hunt for old music and time spent with Adam, Udi and Rachel. One of our lunch parties was with Kurt and Nancy Adler and Lotfi Mansouri. Kurt and Nancy had ideas of purchasing a house in the area and Lotfi already lived just outside Geneva so the talk was about real estate rather than opera for a change.

After enjoying the arrival of spring at Les Avants we returned to London where we had rented a small house in Lennox Gardens Mews for our two-month stay. It was very quiet and convenient – especially to Harrods and all the Knightsbridge–Sloane Square shopping areas.

Rehearsals for *Mignon* and *Rigoletto* in the *Who's Afraid of Opera* series began and we moved to Surrey for the five days' filming. I found *Mignon* one of the best of the little videos but could never understand why the producers of the series saw fit to dub a decidedly dull bass-baritone voice on to Ian Caley's dialogue. As Ian's tenor voice was very light at the time the gruff, growly sound of his speech in this and the *Faust* is ludicrous – a great shame. I found it was a terrific joke to be dressed as Titania, with cute wings and a fantastic fairy costume by Barbara Matera, at my age – and stature. I finally got to play the fairy!

The *Rigoletto* was rather a hoot, too, my costume for the last scene being a cross between Dick Whittington and Puss in Boots. It was the source of much laughter on the set, especially with the cameramen. These last were very taken with Huguette Tourangeau who flirted somewhat mercilessly as Maddalena with André Turp in this same scene, as well as being a charming Mignon.

Returned to London, Richard was rehearsing for the Decca recording of Massenet's *Thérèse* with Huguette Tourangeau in the title role, Ryland Davies as Armand de Clerval and Louis Quilico as André Thorel. The short two-act work had been performed first in Monte Carlo in

1907 and was popular until about 1930. This was the first recording ever made of the opera and initiated the Massenet revival.

Ric was exceptionally busy during this period, recording not only *Thérèse* but *I Puritani* with myself, Pavarotti, Ghiaurov and Cappuccilli, the Delibes *Sylvia* ballet with the London Symphony Orchestra and a set of arie antiche with Renata Tebaldi and the New Philharmonia Orchestra, which also played for *Thérèse*. As well as all this he rehearsed and conducted eight performances of *Lucia di Lammermoor* at the Royal Opera House with myself, Luciano Pavarotti as Edgardo, Louis Quilico as Enrico and Gwynn Howell as Raimondo. Between the seventh and eighth *Lucias* he flew to Amsterdam for two days' rehearsal of *Rodelinda*.

In between all those activities we still found time for a Sunday lunch at Hardy Amies' old home in Eldon Road, a fiftieth birthday party at the Connaught and various after-performance meals with friends.

We stayed at the Hotel des Indes in The Hague as all rehearsals for *Rodelinda* were held in the nearby Circus Theatre at Scheveningen, together with the first performance. The production was another collaboration of Tito Capobianco with José Varona and some of the cast were again old friends, so it was a most enjoyable time both in and out of the theatre. The weather was mostly pleasant and we could walk along the sea front by the Kursaal in Scheveningen or explore The Hague and its museums in our free time.

Huguette Tourangeau was a most glamorous Bertarido, Cora Canne Meijer (with whom I had sung at Glyndebourne in 1956) sang the role of Unulfo, Margreta Elkins was Edwige, Eric Tappy was Grimoaldo and Pieter van den Berg sang Garibaldo. The production was one for the Holland Festival of 1973 and a great deal of work was entailed for only four performances. The first was at Scheveningen, the second in Rotterdam at the Schouwburg and the last two in the Stadsschouwburg in Amsterdam.

The press was mostly incomprehensible due to the language; however, various English, Italian and American journalists at the Holland Festival assured us in their estimations of the performance that it was, in William Mann's words, 'received with rapture'. He went on to say:

> A glorious opera it surely is, but the style is not mastered at once. Miss Sutherland has learnt that style, in part at least from her husband Richard Bonynge who conducts *Rodelinda* sprucely and with firm attention to characterization.

In *Opera News* of September 1973 Judith Mindszenthy wrote:

> On June 25th the Circus Theatre of Scheveningen offered fans of baroque opera a chance to see and hear the magnificent Holland Festival production

of *Alcina* [*sic*]. The Netherlands Chamber Orchestra, under Richard Bonynge's baton gave this stylized work a discreet but firm backbone in the lively dance tempos. Joan Sutherland brought to Rodelinda her matchless technique for long ornamental trills but was also impressive in the radiantly expressive music of passion and sorrow (as in 'Ho perduto') fury and jubilance (the final 'Mia caro bene'). Equally brilliant was the Canadian mezzo Huguette Tourangeau in the role of Bertarido, written for castrato. Her agile voice, both heroic and poetic, was matched by endearing stage presence: the duet 'Io t'abbraccio' with Miss Sutherland was a highlight.

One of the performances was recently released on compact disc.

After the last performance in Amsterdam we were on vacation for about six weeks, although Richard flew immediately to Bologna to record a solo disc with Luciano entitled *Pavarotti in Concert*. The disc comprised arie antiche of Bononcini, Handel and Scarlatti, followed by five of the beautiful Bellini songs, four Tosti songs, three by Respighi and concluded with the rousing 'La danza' of Rossini. Ric conducted the Orchestra del Teatro Communale di Bologna for the recital and we later recorded *Maria Stuarda* together with them, with Ric also recording *La Favorita* with Pavarotti and Cossotto.

There had been a fairly continuous release of our discs over the 1972–3 period. These included the *Tales of Hoffmann*, the second *Lucia di Lammermoor* with Pavarotti, Milnes, Ghiaurov, etc., and *Rigoletto* was also issued with Pavarotti, Milnes, Talvela, Grant and Tourangeau – all to great reviews and enormous public success. This created, together with the TV shows, a much wider supporting public and it was becoming increasingly difficult to go about unrecognised. It was therefore with great relief that we put away the luggage and spent time in our own home enjoying the garden and long summer evenings with occasional house guests and visits with a few local friends.

We went to dinner with James Mason and his wife Clarissa, together with Ric's (and, I think, James's) favourite antique dealers from Montreux, M. and Madame Annichini, and I remember a splendid terrace barbecue luncheon for about twenty-five at Chalet Monet.

We flew to San Francisco on August 18 for *Die Fledermaus* with Lotfi Mansouri as Stage Director. Unfortunately I had slipped and hurt my foot when trying to take down some decorative lanterns during a sudden thunderstorm at the chalet. It was still quite painful and I was unable to dance and flit about the stage according to Lotfi's direction so was packed off to the doctor. No bones had been broken and, after a couple of injections, I could have danced all night.

We had great fun during rehearsals and later in the performances. It was an excellent cast and all of us were happy to be preparing a comedy. The Alfred was Ragnar Ulfung who was hilariously funny and made great capital out of his lack of height beside me, nuzzling the low-cut bosom of my négligé as though it was on his eye level or jumping up one step if he wanted to impress. Judith Blegen sang Adele and was very pert and cute, playing her violin in the prison 'audition scene'. She, too, was quite petite and played to the height of the Eisenstein, Nolan van Way, who was a perfect height for me.

Bruce Yarnell was Dr Falke, all six foot seven of him, and very accomplished he was. It was a terrible shock to us all to learn later that he had been killed when the light plane he had been flying crashed. He had offered to take us up for a quick joy-ride earlier, which we had declined. Our old friend Spiro Malas was Frank and Huguette sang Orlofsky with Walter Slezak playing the part of Frosch. Walter was quite adorable – like a favourite teddy bear – but he could not stop embroidering his role and it became less funny, rather than more so. This seems to be a general Frosch failing.

We had some riotous meals together, notably at our favourite Mexican restaurant Ramonas, where the charming owner served us with her famous lemonade – Margueritas ad libitum.

The headlines were all full of praise after the opening:

FLEDERMAUS – A HIT!

MAD, MAD NIGHT AT THE SAN FRANCISCO OPERA

OPERA HOUSE IN AN UPROAR

DIE FLEDERMAUS – IT'S A LOVELY, FUNNY, ENTIRELY WINNING SUCCESS

DIE FLEDERMAUS LEAVES THEM HUMMING

SAN FRANCISCO OPERA'S FLEDERMAUS REAL WINNER

DIVA TURNS COMEDIENNE – FLEDERMAUS SPLASHILY PERFORMED ON COAST

Arthur Bloomfield wrote in the *San Francisco Examiner* of September 10 under the heading:

DIVA GREAT IN *FLEDERMAUS*

Removed from the vales of fragile bel canto maidens Joan Sutherland took on her first Rosalinda in Johann Strauss's flirtation-filled Die Fledermaus Saturday night at the Opera House and emerged a winner on all points.

Furthermore, with keen singing-acting talents all over the stage, zestfully piloted by director Lotfi Mansouri, and a very elegant Richard Bonynge in the pit, this was a *Fledermaus* to make numerous competitive versions look pale indeed.

What company, one's tempted to ask, is offering a *Fledermaus* with a Rosalinda who sings the Czardas in grandly-voiced Hungarian, an Adele who plays a good fiddle during her Audition aria, and an Alfred who not only kicks up a vocal storm but plays a pair of spoons like castanets?

And where on this side of the Atlantic is there an opera orchestra which responds to Bonynge's immensely stylish beat with such glow, snap and, most important, the right lightness.

He went on to praise Ragnar Ulfung's performance, calling him 'that pint-sized jack-in-the-box of an Alfred' and 'surely the most virtuosic performer you're likely to encounter in the role of Alfred, ham tenor extraordinaire and Rosalinda's hottest old flame'.

We had all worked hard rehearsing the dialogue to make it very clear but to move it along at a good pace and endeavour to get the laughs without appearing to force them. I had fun working on my Hungarian for the Czardas, not to mention my Zsa Zsa Gabor accent as the fake Hungarian Countess. When Adele appeared at Orlofsky's party during the Dress Rehearsal, instead of saying: 'It's Adele – and in *my* gown,' I took in Judy Blegen's petite figure and added, in horror, 'CUT DOWN!'. It brought the house down and remained a laugh-getter through all my future Rosalinda performances. Barbara Matera had produced three wonderful costumes for me and they were a delight to wear – so elegant.

Ragnar taught Spiro and me to play the spoons one night at a dinner with friends and we decided to surprise him at the last performance. Ragnar always picked up two spoons from the supper table at the end of Act 1 and played along with the orchestra, so Spiro and I each concealed a pair in our costume and brought them out together, playing reasonably well and shocking Ragnar. His face was a picture and for a fraction of time he even stopped his virtuoso performance. Then we all went on playing and singing, laughing with the audience.

We fitted in a couple of recitals in Cupertino and Claremont Colleges and I then returned to San Francisco for a signing session of the newly released *Turandot* recording while Ric stopped off in Vancouver to attend a news conference there at which it was officially announced that he had been appointed Artistic Director of the Vancouver Opera Association, having signed a three-year contract. He had appreciated the challenge of the 1965 season in Australia, for which he had done the casting, and was looking forward to injecting some new life into the Vancouver Company with which he had enjoyed performing so much.

His plans were greeted by the press with a mixture of interest, excitement and scepticism. He wanted to form a resident company of young Canadian singers who would not only provide supporting roles and understudies in the main season but have their own season of (hopefully) three chamber operas. He also envisaged expanding the existing performance system to two distinct seasons in the spring and fall instead of the then current three to four separate operas per year. He was eager to start auditioning the young Canadians who might form the nucleus of his proposed group to work permanently in Vancouver with either himself or his future assistant, Miss Bliss Johnston, and his main desire was to improve the quality and general status of the Company, plus to provide an interesting repertoire. Irving Guttman's contract expired in June of 1974 and Richard had heavy commitments for two years ahead; however, the VOA Board was happy with his agreement to spend what time he could in Vancouver over that transition period towards a more full-time situation in due course. What was needed was a managerial drive for funding, in conjunction with publicity for the forthcoming seasons – not the province of the Artistic Director.

✧ 10 ✧

WE HAD ONE more recital in Fresno, California, before leaving the West Coast for Chicago and *La Fille du Régiment* with the Lyric Opera. Sandro Sequi was again the Stage Director and we had other firm friends in the cast – Spiro Malas as Sulpice, Alfredo Kraus as Tonio, Regina Resnik as the Marquise and Jennie Tourel in her last stage appearance as the Duchess of Krakenthorp. We were in the city for a month high up in an apartment hotel not too far from the theatre. Regina had an apartment there as well and we spent a good deal of time together. We also frequently saw our old ex-Decca friend David Harvey who was then with the Chicago Symphony.

Rehearsals went very smoothly and we opened on October 20 to more rave reviews for all and surprise at my enjoyment of a comedy role. A string of photographs appeared in the *Chicago Sun-Times* of my 'malleable face – on a par with the great voice for range of expression'.

There were five more performances, then back to New York for *Les Contes d'Hoffmann* at the Met. Again we had fine friends in the cast – Huguette Tourangeau as Nicklausse and the Muse, Placido Domingo as Hoffmann, Thomas Stewart as all the villains and Andrea Velis as Andrès, Cochenille, Pitichinaccio and Frantz. At some later performances John Alexander sang the part of Hoffmann and the young James Morris the role of Crespel.

We were very comfortable in the big apartment in Martin Waldron's house in Brooklyn and enjoyed entertaining friends there for dinner. Prior to the opening at the Met of *Hoffmann* dear Jennie Tourel died and we were able to attend the service for her at Riverside Chapel. She had been a great interpreter of the French repertoire and a much-respected teacher at the Juilliard School of Music.

The first night of *Hoffmann* was on November 29, followed by a gala supper in the Grand Tier for the Metropolitan Opera Guild. There were six further performances in December, then home to Les Avants for Christmas with Adam and the rest of our household family. There were five more performances in January–February, the final a matinée broadcast. Twelve in all – with the tour and the 1974 June Festival performances bringing the grand total to something like twenty.

The critics all had to air their differing views about the various versions of the Offenbach opera but agreed that this production was extremely well sung and the version more than acceptable. Speight Jenkins wrote in the *New York Post*:

THOUGHTFUL, WELL SUNG *HOFFMAN* AT THE MET

The new production of *Les Contes d'Hoffmann*, introduced last night at the Metropolitan Opera, places the poet Hoffmann in the central focus of every eye and makes the often ambiguous plot into a coherent whole. A brilliant new edition of the score well-conducted by Richard Bonynge and an interesting and controversial production by Allen Charles Klein (Designer) and Bliss Hebert (Director) found an ideal Hoffmann in Placido Domingo.

The Spanish tenor has given many great performances in New York, but never has he reached the level of vocal, musical and dramatic skill that he achieved last night...

... In the extended epilogue Hebert made clear Hoffmann's rejection of women for poetry, and Bonynge's transfer there of the Act II septet, now a quartet as Offenbach intended, ended the show with a musical bang of cosmic proportions.

Joan Sutherland demonstrated the incredible musicianship, beauty and weight of voice that is hers to command. Her jerky movements and accurate, full-voiced coloratura as Olympia could not be bettered: she passed the mezzo sections of Act II satisfactorily and sang Antonia with rich and expressive tone, managing some of the other-wordly quality that makes the girl really interesting.

After the opening of *The Tales of Hoffmann* at the Met Ric and I were thrilled to receive the following telegram:

My dear Joan Sutherland,

I am very happy for you and with you that yesterday's *Hoffmann* was such a great triumph for you and Maestro Bonynge. Please let me thank you for this wonderful, unforgettable evening. I am looking forward to hearing you again on Monday December 3, Wednesday December 19 and, Gods willing, February 2. As always yours,

Maria Jeritza

Between the *Hoffmanns* we fitted in a Sunday matinée recital at Brooklyn College and I saw *A Little Night Music* with that much-missed character Jack Metz, vocal coach extraordinaire.

During that return trip to New York, I was laid low by a violent three-day gastric flu bug and, after eleven years with the Metropolitan Opera without one cancellation I finally had to relinquish my performance on January 29. Thank heavens there was a very able cover for the roles in Colette Boky who acquitted herself admirably at such short notice. Three days in bed and I was able to cope with the matinée broadcast, although by this time John Alexander who was to sing Hoffmann had succumbed to the bug and the role was taken over by Harry Theyard. The short, violent attack played havoc with the Company members for about a month.

The day after the broadcast we flew to Miami, where we had three performances of *Lucia di Lammermoor* and one in Fort Lauderdale.

The Philadelphia Lyric Opera gave two performances of *Maria Stuarda* in Tito Capobianco's San Francisco production, with a further performance in Hartford, Connecticut.

I was certainly relieved to be recovered from the flu attack, whilst John Sandor had to sing the difficult role of Leicester at short notice as John Alexander was still unwell. The critiques were all very favourable, the *New Yorker* devoting a good deal of space to the background of *Maria Stuarda*'s libretto and its parallel with the Schiller play. After some slight reference to Donizetti's musical handling of the work the critic continued:

... But the most affecting music in *Maria Stuarda* comes in the sequence of numbers that lead up to Mary's execution, her famous 'Confession Duet' with Talbot, the agonized comments of the chorus as they glimpse the dreadful preparations, the transfiguring 'Prayer', in which Mary's voice soars above theirs, and her noble concluding aria. All this is in Donizetti's best vein, and it brought out the best in Miss Sutherland's art. She was in fine voice, and acted with unusual force and authority, much helped by her rich costumes, which stood out against Pier Luigi Pizzi's austere settings.

There was the usual spate of luncheons and dinners – one very fondly remembered lunch with the marvellous old conductor Max Rudolf.

It was as well that there was a three-week period to the end of March when I could enjoy being at Chalet Monet without any travel or public appearances. My half-sister Ailsa Hargreaves paid us a visit, staying for a while, and I had the opportunity, too, to see how Rachel was growing and developing.

Adam came home from Aiglon for his Easter holidays, then flew off to Lisbon to stay with a school friend, soon followed by us for our performances of *La Traviata*. We had chosen to stay at Estoril and travel the few kilometres along the coast to rehearsals at the lovely Teatro Nacional de San Carlos.

I was very happy to have sent my own costumes from the Australian 1965 tour in advance as the production was extremely stark, the same chairs appearing in every scene, whether in Violetta's house or Flora's party. The chorus gowns were not too inspiring and I was also happy to have the new wigs made for the *Who's Afraid of Opera* series. Alfredo

Kraus was Alfredo Germont and it was, as always, a great pleasure to work with him and Giorgio Zancanaro as Papa Germont.

Rehearsal time was very short and we worked on Good Friday evening and Easter Monday. On Easter Saturday and Sunday we did some sightseeing to Sessimbra, Setubal, the Pink Palace, and Sintra and attended a bullfight, finding it very exciting and quite a spectacle. The bulls were not killed in Portugal we were assured.

Adam had joined us at our Estoril hotel and was very upset that he was not permitted to enter the Casino there, due to his being under age. He was further aggravated when told he could not enter the theatre without a dinner-jacket on the opening night of *La Traviata* – the only performance he could attend as he was flying back to Switzerland the next day for his final term at Aiglon. He ultimately sat in a stage box which still had a grill from the last century to screen those not wanting to be seen in the theatre. He thought that was very special. He had on a business suit and tie but rules were rules, even for the son of the prima donna and conductor.

We were entertained by Ambassador Kelly and his wife Margaret at the Australian Embassy and found them a delightful pair. I still see Mrs Kelly in Australia occasionally.

The final performance was held in the large nineteenth-century circus arena which had a greater audience capacity than the lovely theatre – and an odour of animal excrement and sweat. This was not so noticeable on stage but almost overpowering in the dressing-rooms. However, the audience was wildly appreciative and the curtain calls were very numerous, and we arrived back in Estoril in the early hours of the morning very tired and happy.

What was our surprise and alarm when our charming driver telephoned about 8 a.m. on the next day to tell us there had been a Revolution around 2 a.m. and no one could leave the country. All flights were cancelled and we would have to stay. We then heard from Ambassador Kelly who was very calm and practical, telling us that in his opinion it would all quieten down in three days and we'd be able to leave. The border was closed for three days and we sat in Estoril and enjoyed the fine food there and surrounding towns.

Regina Resnik was preparing a production at the San Carlos and was confined to her Lisbon hotel, with cannons pointing from the square at her windows and some firing guns. She was very anxious and was glad of our reassurance via our Ambassador that the crisis would be over in three days. He finally facilitated our exit from a chaotic airport.

Ruthli was relieved to see us back and it was a quick turn around, as we had a flight to New York two days later. We began the Met tour of *Hoffmann* in Detroit, then flew to Atlanta. After a recital in

Birmingham, Alabama we flew on to Memphis, then to Dallas and Minneapolis for further *Hoffmanns*. After that a trip to Kansas City for a recital there in the Capri Theater and back to New York for the weekend and a dinner date with Anya Dorfman and Peter Mennen of the Juilliard School of Music.

There were two more *Hoffmanns* at the Met in May, together with final fittings with Barbara Matera for my costumes for Australia, and then we, together with Chester, were on our way to Sydney via Mexico City, where we broke our journey and spent four days relaxing and sightseeing.

On June 6 we left for Tahiti where we spent ten days enjoying the not too tropical climate and flew on to Noumea where we were joined by Huguette Tourangeau who had flown from Canada to spend six days with us recovering from jet-lag. We all arrived in Sydney on June 22 completely rested and looking forward to our reunion with colleagues from the 1965 tour and performing in the much-documented Sydney Opera House for the first time.

Although I had been asked to return and participate in the opening of the house, I had not been available when, after all its construction and Union delays, a date was finally set for the big event. These performances of *The Tales of Hoffmann* were taking place at the first available time and, as usual, the press was agog to know our opinions of the complex before we'd had a chance to work there.

Tito Capobianco and José Varona had devised a glorious production for our return to our own country and we were supported by the best of the Australian Opera. Several of these artists had been to Europe, sung with opera companies in Britain and Germany, and had major roles with the Australian Opera upon their return. Anson Austin, for example, was singing the very small role of Nathaneal but had already appeared as Ferrando at Glyndebourne. John Pringle who sang the Count in *The Marriage of Figaro*, Papageno, Marcello in *La Bohème*, Figaro in *The Barber of Seville*, sang the other student, Hermann. They seemed happy to be part of the production and were studying the way Tito worked to help develop the characters. Anson and John both sang in many later productions with Richard and me, and were first class in their field.

The programme devised for these performances was beautifully illustrated with full-page colour reproductions of seven of José Varona's designs, together with photographs and biographies of all the cast, with special attention given to Richard and myself, along with the hope that we would return to Australia more often than hitherto.

It had been a great pleasure to renew acquaintance with Moffatt Oxenbould, who had been Stage Manager for the 1965 tour and was now Assistant to the General Manager, developing a lasting friendship. The spirit of the whole Company was one of always wanting to do better and with this, over the twenty years of our association, they have certainly succeeded. The general standard of the Australian Opera productions meets with and surpasses that of many of the world's leading houses. It is one of the very few repertory companies remaining – one where the operas are frequently cast completely from Company members. The number of guest artists from abroad is limited by the strong Unions as well as financial considerations and the Company is a wonderful training ground for young singers from the whole Southern Pacific area.

The opening night on July 13 was an enormous success with the audience and critics, the latter writing their reviews under headlines such as:

A SMASH HIT BY OUR JOAN – BUT IT'S SOLD OUT

TRIUMPH IN THE OPERA HOUSE

THE SONGBIRD AT HER PEAK

STUPENDOUS!

There were reports that up to $400 had been offered for a seat by fans from as far away as Western Australia and an announcement made to the public by the General Manager, John Winther, at the end of the opening night that we had been made 'Honorary life members of the Company' and that we would return for future seasons was greeted with cheers. One dissenting voice came from Felix Werder of *The Age*:

> This was another of those lowbrow rejects from vaudeville which the Australian Opera keeps on keeping on. The classic recipe of presenting superstars in Mardi Gras situations.
>
> There was no sense of vocal characterisation; it all sounded the same. There was no intellectual grasp of shapeliness of phrase, no subtle chiaroscuro in the voice production.
>
> ... And though she was better in Act III as Antonia, it was only because she abandoned the French style altogether and gave us *Lucia* instead.

You can't please everyone!

Adam had completed his schooling and left Aiglon on July 3, almost immediately travelling to Australia via the United States. This was the 'long way' but some of his friends were returning to their homes in the States and it would mean he had company on the trip, at least as far as California. He arrived in Sydney very upset as the flight had gone to Melbourne first, where he had to go through customs. An eighteen-year-old looking scruffy from the round-about and lengthy trip must have appeared a likely drug smuggler and he had been obliged to turn out the whole of his luggage and submit to a body search. When he asked who repacked everything the reply was, of course, 'You do, mate!' His anger quickly abated and he proceeded to enjoy the pleasures and hospitality of the city. It was great to have him with us.

We gave a recital in the Concert Hall of the Opera House on July 6, a selection of the items from the North American tour. Nadine Amadio later wrote in *Music and Musicians*:

> If anyone had doubted the artistry and intelligence behind the Sutherland voice or had considered *Hoffmann* a lightweight showpiece, her recital in the Opera House concert hall the previous Saturday would have dispelled any doubts. So much better than on record her voice really rang with exultant vitality. She invested every word and note with meaning. There was never a hint of indulgence or excess. Just a radiant polish on every note.
>
> Unlike many sopranos with big voices, Sutherland was able to scale herself down and handle for example a group of French songs with extreme delicacy. Her voice suits the large new concert hall to perfection, and carried with ease even at the softest level. In a crowd-pleasing gesture, unparalleled since the days of Melba, she closed her recital with a sentimental 'Home, sweet home'. The audience responded with the kind of enthusiasm reserved for pop stars.

Both of us had family to visit in Sydney and it was good for Adam to see his Bonynge grandparents again and his Sutherland cousins. We also spent a wonderful weekend at Jenolan Caves, the splendid and extensive system of limestone caverns just over the Blue Mountains west of Sydney. Adam was very impressed and has since taken his family there. We have also revisited them and loved the 'Twenties' atmosphere that still existed – doubtless now gone due to extensions and renovations. But the caves remain a breath-taking sight. We visited six of them on that first long weekend.

We were fêted – lunch at Government House with Sir Roden and Lady Cutler (an ex-St Catherine's girl), and a late supper after the opera performance at the Prime Minister's residence in Kirribilli with Gough and Margaret Whitlam who supported the arts in Australia during Gough's regime – and still do. This was a very cosy evening around the fire with much chatter and laughter. There were lunches and dinners with old friends from the Thirties and Forties and a great harbour picnic organised by Moffatt and his brother Christopher, now a very high-up Naval Commander – a Rear Admiral.

There were also many interviews and photo sessions, together with a further recital in Sydney on August 9 and one in Dallas Brooks Hall in Melbourne on August 13 and 17. Then it was back to Europe for all of us.

However, prior to our departure John Winther asked Richard to become Musical Director of the Australian Opera and he accepted. This decision meant a great deal of work and planning for him, especially with his concurrent post in Vancouver, but he never regretted it and thoroughly enjoyed both positions with all their 'fights and frustrations'.

✧ 11 ✧

ON ARRIVAL HOME Richard was off again almost immediately to Bologna where he was recording Donizetti's *La Favorita* with Luciano, Fiorenza Cossotto, Gabriel Bacquier, Nicolai Ghiaurov and Ileana Cotrubas. The heat in the Teatro Communale without air-conditioning was so intense that many of the orchestra were using battery-operated fans.

The *Favorita* recording was completed the day I arrived in Bologna supposedly to record Donizetti's *Maria Stuarda* with the same orchestra, Luciano, Huguette Tourangeau and James Morris. Whereas some ten days were reserved for the opera we only worked for the first three days. It was apparent that Luciano had not managed to learn his role and the rest of the sessions were cancelled, to be re-scheduled the following year. The Decca equipment had been specially shipped to Bologna and consequently had to be returned, then re-shipped whenever the recording could be continued to ensure the acoustic matched.

There were a few frayed tempers when the news broke – but it meant we had some extra free time so we piled into the car, along with Huguette and James Morris, and all returned to Les Avants where we had a very happy few days. Adam was at home and he, Chester, Richard and our guests decided to play cards one evening. Not being one to gamble, even for peanuts, I decided to go to bed and read my entertaining book. As a result I missed a hilarious game of strip poker in which Adam was endeavouring to protect Huguette from stripping and James was reduced to his birthday suit! We entertained Regina Resnik and Arbit Blatas for a few days, then we were off to San Francisco for Massenet's *Esclarmonde*.

We had a three-week rehearsal period and needed every minute of it as the work was completely unknown to all of us, not having been produced since the early 1930s and never recorded. There were a lot of magical effects and ballet which had to be timed to the second, and quick changes for me as the Enchantress-Princess Esclarmonde. Throughout the opera she remains veiled for all men except her father, Phorcas the Emperor. This created a further problem, especially as the costumes were not available for rehearsal and we weren't sure how the quick closing and opening of the veils would work. When the

271

costumes finally appeared I found they were impossible for me, being in the style of a kimono with a huge cummerbund around the waist to hold it together – an easy solution for a quick change but most unflattering to my figure. Beni Montresor had designed the spectacular scenery and the costumes, and I hated to make a fuss but I looked like a sack tied in the middle and I was supposed to be a seductress! An SOS was received by Barbara Matera and she evolved from the old Sybil Sanderson photo and poster quite magnificent regalia in about a week, bringing the costumes to San Francisco herself to put the finishing touches to them and find out, once again, 'how they worked'.

Sybil Sanderson was a young singer from Sacramento, California, who sang for Massenet at a party in 1887 and created the role of Esclarmonde for him when only twenty-four. Massenet fell in love with her voice (and probably her) and later wrote *Thaïs* for her as well. The score of *Esclarmonde* was actually completed in Vevey where Massenet, Sybil Sanderson and her mother were staying – just twenty minutes away from Les Avants.

The role was a big challenge, requiring security in the high and low extensions of the voice, and I found the invocations to the spirits, the duets with Roland (with whom I am enamoured) my solos – indeed, all of the music – the most erotic I ever sang. The wonderful Spanish tenor Jaime (Giacomo) Aragall sang with me, as well as my old friends Clifford Grant and Huguette Tourangeau.

We gave five performances and the audience was wildly enthusiastic, only ceasing their applause and leaving the theatre after the management raised the main house lights. Even most of the critics enthused with headlines like:

AN UNKNOWN MASSENET DRAWS CHEERS

ESCLARMONDE IS GOLDEN TRIUMPH

JOAN SUTHERLAND MARVELOUS IN *ESCLARMONDE*

MAGIC OPERA EPIC RISES TO THE HEIGHTS

SUTHERLAND MAGIC REVIVES THE DEAD

BONYNGES AWAKEN SLEEPING BEAUTY

Stephanie von Buchau wrote in *Opera News*:

An enraptured audience greeted the raising of the house lights after Massenet's *Esclarmonde* (October 26th) with a chorus of disappointed 'No!'s. If union regulations hadn't shortened the applause, we might still be standing there, cheering the lavish production in stunning colour-and-gold gauzes by Beni Montresor, beautifully lit by Robert Brand and directed by Lotfi Mansouri in a straightforward way that avoided the camp atmosphere this fairy tale might inspire.

We applauded Joan Sutherland, whose title role calls for an impossible combination of coloratura pyrotechnics and the weighty declamation of a Dido, both of which she gave in full, lustrous measure; and Giacomo Aragall, who unleashed a series of thrilling forte top notes while looking every inch the storybook hero...

Mostly we applauded conductor Richard Bonynge, first for his sensitive negotiation of the languorous eroticism in this score about romantic love, then for the courage to mastermind the project in the first place. (These were the first American performances in this century.) Grumbles were heard that the music is thin and the story silly, but they came from that grim minority who insist that the only worthy operas deal with today's social, economic or psychological problems.

Dale Harris wrote in *Music and Musicians*:

... Before the event one might have been dubious about the opera's chances, but at the triumphant conclusion of the first performance there was little doubt that Richard Bonynge's faith in it had been completely justified. *Esclarmonde* is indeed a thrilling piece of work ... By those who judge operas in accordance with the tenets of verismo the work has already been denounced as absurd, I on the contrary found it an eloquent, thrilling and imaginative discourse on themes of the greatest relevance like love, obligation and faithfulness.

Without Bonynge the resuscitation would never have taken place. Without Sutherland it could never have been thought of. The title role is long and fearsome. It calls for a big untiring voice, capable of handling a sustained lyric line, and at the same time it calls for great agility: Staccati in alt, trills, divisions and the like. At every point Sutherland was mistress of the situation. In voice and technique she has no rival today.

Martin Bernheimer, in the *Los Angeles Times*, said:

... Bonynge conducted with a sweep, drive and passionate commitment that should go far to discredit his lingering reputation as the diva's also-ran...

Miss Sutherland started out a bit tentatively in the first act but soon coped magnificently with the extraordinary demands – in turn lyric, dramatic and coloratura – of the titular empress-sorceress.

She brought melting lyricism, thunder, enchanting staccati and a few hair-raising high notes to the challenge, and thus made quibbles about dramatic aloofness and style clashes in costuming (she forswore Montresor's gowns) seem irrelevant.

The Bonynges would seem to have awakened a sleeping beauty.

I have never lost the surge of excitement generated by this music and it is one of the very few of my recordings to which I listen from time to time. It had a success at the Met and later at Covent Garden, this last somewhat dampened by several bomb scares which were unnerving and disrupting to both the cast and the audience. It was strange that the original score of the work which Massenet had given to Sybil Sanderson should be auctioned about this time and Richard was delighted to learn that his bid had procured it for him and it remains a very precious and important item in our collection.

In November we were in Phoenix, Arizona, for *Lucia di Lammermoor* where I had as my tenor the marvellously tall and handsome Franco Tagliavini. Phoenix was fascinating and we had time to visit some of the majestic beauty spots. The same production went to San Diego for three performances and we were very taken with the whole San Diego area. We were delighted to meet Emmy Sokolov, who lived in La Jolla. She was the widow of the co-founder and long-time Director of the Cleveland Orchestra, Nikolai Sokolov, and we developed a lasting acquaintance with her. We also fostered another long-standing friend-ship, that with Dr Peter Newbold in England.

I arrived home on 10 December, very anxious to visit my dentist as I had managed to loosen a large fixed bridge and Christmas was not far off with its many holidays. We had guests at the chalet for Christmas – our old friends Buddy and Geri Kaufman, along with Quaintance Eaton. Quaintance had decided to write a book about us and was staying for a while to add 'atmosphere' to her work. There was something of a clash of personalities between the two visiting ladies and a few biting comments flew around the dinner-table at times. But there was the usual excitement of the season and much laughter to dispel any tense moments. Quaintance also, one morning, wandered into the hallway outside Richard's bathroom 'trying to find her way out of the house' as he was passing, stark naked, from his shower to his dressing-room. He always does this, not expecting anyone to be about, and had quite a shock, although probably not as much as Quaintance. However, she was as blind as a bat.

With Christmas Day over, on December 26 we were off to London where rehearsals began immediately for *La Traviata* at the Royal Opera House. We stayed at the Savoy Hotel for the first hectic week, with the Dress Rehearsal as early as Saturday, January 4. The following day we moved into the apartment of Dr Peter Newbold in Stanhope Gardens in Kensington, which he permitted us to use in his absence. A very convenient arrangement, especially as it was possible to walk to Knightsbridge and all those tempting stores.

The *Traviata* production was by Luchino Visconti. There had been reservations when this 'black-and-white' updating to the turn of the century was first staged at the Garden and I was a little anxious as to the style of the costumes. However, I need not have worried as I found them very flattering (except perhaps the one for Act 2 Scene I) and believe that they suited me with my extra height rather more than they had Mirella Freni, the original Violetta of the production. The other members of the cast were excellent and mostly old friends. Alfredo Kraus was Alfredo with Louis Quilico as Giorgio, his father. Baron Douphol was sung by George Macpherson, Doctor Grenvil by Robert Lloyd, Marquis d'Obigny by Eric Garrett and Gaston by John Dobson. The statuesque Heather Begg sang Flora and Johanna Peters was Annina.

'Sutherland: Stunning', 'Flawless, exquisite, unique', 'A revival cast from strength', said the papers and although almost all praised the Sutherland vocal technique, many found my appearance much too healthy. Philip Hope-Wallace wrote in the *Guardian* of January 7:

I never thought to hear Joan Sutherland so good as Verdi's 'strayed one', the Traviata of the moving opera. Twelve years ago she used to vocalise the role with great brilliance but had not found her way into an effective interpretation.

Last night with the beautifully sympathetic and finely judged conducting of her husband Richard Bonynge – forget the nervous, tense, first act – who gave the soprano, and indeed all the characters, the really understanding support they need, the Australian Diva pulled off a most moving and memorable last act, with a gentle swell of pathos in 'Prendi, queste l'imagine' which went straight to the heart like the phrase 'Alfin son tua' in her *Lucia di Lammermoor* in which she conquered us years ago.

I don't honestly think Verdi's Traviata is a natural assignment for her: she is too big and healthy, too strong and vivid, not sad and delicate enough for some of the scenes, but her big second act duet with the splendid Quilico, a magnificent baritone too long absent and a grand stage presence, went most effectively.

There were five further performances and we gave a recital in Manchester on the nineteenth. I was again experiencing stiffness and pain in my back and neck and was paying regular visits to a kindly old specialist and to a masseur, without gaining much relief. Once more, travelling long distances was a bit of a problem and the ability to turn my head was minimal. In fact, I was persuaded by Dr Bach to postpone a two-and-a-half-week period in North America (between January 31 and February 19) to continue the treatment in London and then in Switzerland. This caused a small crisis with my American agents but most of the dates were reinstated in a later period. The only dates not immediately re-scheduled were the two concerts with Luciano planned for February 5 and 9 in Avery Fisher Hall. These had to wait longer to be honoured.

With massage sessions every weekday it was difficult to arrange my other appointments. There had been a disastrous cyclone (Tracy, by name) which struck Darwin (in North Australia) on Christmas Eve 1974. It had destroyed the city, killed about fifty people, injured hundreds and dispossessed thousands. We organised a Darwin Relief Concert to be held at the Royal Opera House on January 25 – a 'Midnight Matinée' – to be televised and recorded by Decca, the royalties received donated to boost the House takings. Everybody gave their services, including the Royal Philhar- monic Orchestra and all the singers. These were mostly antipodean but Graham Clark and Louis Quilico also kindly appeared with Heather Begg, Margreta Elkins, Clifford Grant and Tom McDonnell. HRH The Prince of Wales attended and was, as usual, very charm- ing. He had also been to the *Traviata* performance the previous Tuesday.

During our stay in London, Nicaragua issued a set of fifteen stamps featuring 'the greatest operatic singers of our time' in which I was depicted as Marie in Act 2 of *La Figlia del Reggimento*. The other singers in the collection were Caruso, Chaliapin, Callas, Gobbi, Björling, Flagstad, Pinza, Lehmann, Melba, de Luca, Ponselle, Martinelli, Nilsson and Melchior. It was an interesting set and I was flattered to be included with such 'greats'.

As Richard had to leave for Vancouver on January 28, Sylvia Holford very ably took over accompanying me for a recital at the Royal Shakespeare Theatre, Stratford-upon-Avon on the following day. This was the first of several recitals we presented together, the rest of them in the United States, all consisting of songs and arias by French and Italian operatic composers including also a few 'goodies' by Godard, Fauré, Cimara and Tosti.

I stayed on in London with Douglas and Ailsa Gamley for just over a week to continue my daily massage sessions, arriving home in Les Avants on February 12, just in time for Adam's birthday. He had to wait a year after leaving school before commencing his hotelier training at l'Institut International de Glion, just a short distance from our home. He had been spending his time learning to type, to speak a little Spanish and to drive a car, this last being something of a passion – no automatic power-steering for him.

I felt bad at having been forced to postpone the two big Lincoln Center Concerts with Luciano, but my neck and back were beginning to respond more to treatment and this I continued in Montreux Hospital's Physiotherapy Department, with Peter Kosmalla, a Finnish Chiropractor–Physiotherapist who practically took my head off – but gave me the most blessed relief. I continued to go to him for many months whenever I was at home.

Richard found his group of young singers in Vancouver (called the Canadian Artists Company) well prepared musically by Bliss Johnston and production rehearsals proceeded with Norman Ayrton for *The Good Girl* (*La Buona Figliuola*) by Niccolo Piccinni.

After the second performance Richard flew to Amsterdam where he was doing repeat performances of Handel's *Rodelinda* with Noëlle Rogers in the title role, the rest of the cast remaining much the same as that of June–July 1973. Richard and Huguette came to Les Avants for the weekend of March 8, returning to Amsterdam on the eleventh, and it was good to see them both, if briefly.

I left for New York on March 12 and flew with Sylvia Holford to Rochester where we stayed at the home of Dr and Mrs Aquavella and gave our recital on the sixteenth for the Rochester Civic Music Association. We repeated the programme at Cornell University, then I flew down to Philadelphia where stage rehearsals with Tito Capobianco were in progress for *La Traviata* with the Lyric Opera. Richard flew in from Amsterdam for two performances. Frank Little was the Alfredo and Cornelis Opthof the Giorgio Germont, with many in the cast young singers from the local music schools showing great promise and I enjoyed working with them.

This was followed by Donizetti's *Lucrezia Borgia* in the sets and costumes designed by José Varona for Vancouver and directed this time by Lotfi Mansouri. These three *Borgias* were my operatic début in Houston, having visited previously for an orchestral concert in November 1966 during the inaugural season at Jones Hall.

It was my tenor John Brecknock's US début and he made a most favourable impression, his nine years with the English National Opera serving him well. It was always a pleasure to work with him.

We had a 'free' week in Les Avants between the last *Borgia* and going to Las Palmas for *Maria Stuarda* at the Festival de Las Palmas in the Teatro Perez Galdos. The young orchestra and chorus were from the University of Michigan and were all very eager.

We had a wonderful time in Las Palmas and would have liked to stay on, but Richard had to leave for Vancouver to rehearse *Rodelinda* with what was now called the Resident Artists Group of the VOA. Unfortunately a strike situation curtailed the number of performances and Richard was having to cope with management problems as well. He has always been of the opinion that artistic decisions should be made by the musical and artistic directors and not by the Board and the general management. The functions of the latter were to raise funds, publicise the season and sell tickets, with which I wholeheartedly agree. These days there has been a great deal of trouble in the opera houses of Europe due to political appointments to artistic posts of non-musicians and people with no previous knowledge whatsoever of the day-to-day running of a theatre or of coping with its many problems – with disastrous results. Richard's outspoken attitude upset several Board members who wanted to continue to present the same 'safe' operas they believed ensured a good box-office return. He had to work hard to gain agreement to his proposed season of *Semiramide*, *Queen of Spades*, *Faust* (an old favourite with Canadian audiences) and *The Merry Widow*. He became more than ever convinced that too much time was spent by him at business meetings instead of getting on with the decisions regarding repertoire and artists, and working with the latter.

I joined him in Vancouver briefly and we flew together to Hawaii for a few days, travelling on to Tokyo for the Metropolitan Opera's tour of Japan. Neither of us had been keen to go but we were ultimately enchanted by the country's scenic beauty and culture, and amazed at the audience response. The theatres were large and very modern, as were the cities we visited, and the neat and often chic dress of the people, particularly the teenagers, was a delight.

We stayed at the Imperial Hotel in Tokyo and were greeted very warmly by John Butler, the Australian Trade Commissioner, and his wife Sally who were most hospitable and helpful. Richard and I were doing performances of *La Traviata* together and Richard also had one or two with Adriana Maliponte as Violetta. We did five *Traviatas* together – four in Tokyo and one in Osaka. There were several important dinners and luncheons, Japanese style, which we enjoyed immensely except for the problem of sitting cross-legged on a cushion on the floor for the lengthy meals. The Japanese had been accustomed to doing so and looking elegant since childhood, but we Westerners were twice their size and it was very awkward and embarrassing as one tried not to give the impression of being uncomfortable. My knees and back ache when I think of it.

We also had time to do some sightseeing in Tokyo and went to the little seaside resort of Atami – a favourite of the Japanese to escape the smoggy city – for an overnight stay. We travelled on one of the very rapid 'bullet' trains and were amazed at its speed and how quickly one had to get on and off. In Atami we felt extremely out of place among all the Japanese, most of whom donned their hotel room kimonos and walked the streets and beach promenade in them. We laughed at my efforts to wrap myself in one about ten sizes too small and even Richard was barely covered. We had giggled at our struggle to get in and out of the taxis in Tokyo and this was even funnier. We braved the town in our normal street clothes and were fascinated to see how each house, no matter how small, had its tiny bonsai tree or shrub in a lovely ceramic pot outside and although the resort was becoming westernised we saw more clearly than in Tokyo the Japanese way of life. We even went to a musical after dinner – a Broadway-type version of *Madame Butterfly* with an all Japanese cast and a very Japanese Pinkerton in an extremely blond wig. The costumes and effects were excellent but Pinkerton and the Consul had us struggling to control our laughter. We arrived back in Tokyo the following afternoon, having managed to catch a glimpse of the base of Mount Fuji, but there was so much low cloud neither of us is sure we were looking at the right hill.

That night we were invited to dinner by Akio Morita, the head of the Sony Corporation. He was a charming and brilliant gentleman. He showed us on a set in his study a video of the La Scala presentation of *La Traviata* and said that most of the world would have such sets within a very few years. Of course, this was hard to believe and we all thought the equipment would be far too expensive. How wrong we were.

We went to the Kabuki theatre and were entranced by the movement, the settings, costumes, make-up and the ability of some of the performers to appear so feminine. We were taken backstage and saw a few of the artists making up – sitting cross-legged on the floor.

Dorothy Kirsten was singing some of her final performances with the Met and we saw her lovely Mimi. We were slow to leave our seats and retire to the foyer at the end of Act 1, and were besieged by a group of very orderly young Japanese requesting autographs. We remained in our seats signing until the lights went down for Act 2 – and through the next interval as well. I never liked signing a programme for a performance in which I was not participating, feeling it was discourteous to those listed, but this time there was no escape. Most of the requests came from students who were very polite and didn't jostle or push but patiently waited their turn.

The company visited Nagoya and then Osaka. Richard and I were not in either of the operas in Nagoya so we went to beautiful Kyoto for a day and a half. We thoroughly enjoyed the whole tour and wondered if we would ever return for a more relaxed visit.

On May 28 I had been offered the appointment of Companion of the Order of Australia (AC) by the then Governor-General of the country, Sir John Kerr, and this was publicly announced on June 14. It is the highest civic award of the Order and is made for 'eminent achievement and merit of the highest degree in service to Australia or to humanity at large'.

Our next assignment was a recording of Franco Leoni's one-act opera *L'Oracolo*, a story of intrigue and murder in San Francisco's Chinatown, and then Massenet's *Esclarmonde*. *L'Oracolo* was produced for the first time at the Royal Opera, Covent Garden in 1905 and was a favourite with Antonio Scotti who sang the role of the opium dealer Cim-Fen at that première and chose to sing it as his farewell performance at the Met in 1933 with Vincenzo Bellezza conducting and Queena Mario as Ah-Joe. The opera had never been recorded and all of us involved in it found it highly dramatic and touching. Apart from myself as Ah-Joe, the young niece of the rich merchant Hu-Tsin (sung by Clifford Grant), we had Tito Gobbi as Cim-Fen, the proprietor of the opium den, Richard Van Allan as Uin-Sci, a learned doctor, and Ryland Davies as Uin-San-Lui, his son, who is in love with Ah-Joe, Huguette Tourangeau as Hua-Qui (the nurse of Hu-Tsin's son Hu-Cher) and Ian Caley a fortune-teller. When the *L'Oracolo* recording was released the reviews talked of the indebtedness of the work to Puccini, some with quotes like 'Poor man's Puccini?' and re-quoting Henry Krehbiel's assessment in 1915 of it as 'Puccini and water'. However, they had to admit it was 'a powerful and interesting work, starting where Puccini left off'.

Arthur Jacobs, in his review in *Hi-Fi News* of July 1977, says:

> ... The style is indeed kin to Puccini's in that work [*Il Tabarro*] but Leoni got there first: *L'Oracolo* was first given in 1905 (at Covent Garden); *Il Tabarro* dates from 1918. It is a powerful piece of its kind, well-deserving the prestige of a Bonynge/Sutherland recording. Not for the first time I am grateful to Richard Bonynge's lively initiative.

In fact Richard received praise from all the reviewers, being congratulated not only for being instrumental in reviving the work but for his handling of it and the 'wonderful atmosphere' evoked by him.

Most of the sessions finished at 6 p.m. so we had time to dine with friends, one of them being my former colleague Adèle Leigh, whose husband was attached to the Austrian Embassy in London. We had a great laugh over old times at the Garden, also some of her experiences at the Volksoper in Vienna. Peter Newbold organised a dinner party for that dearly loved British soprano Isobel Baillie whom we were delighted to see again, having heard her often in concert during our early years in London. She was a most charming lady with a quiet sense of humour.

On July 9 we commenced recording *Esclarmonde*. Three of the artists who had sung in the San Francisco performances, Aragall, Tourangeau and Grant, were with us and Louis Quilico, Ryland Davies, Robert Lloyd, Ian Caley and Graham Clark completed the cast.

In the sterile atmosphere of the recording studio one became struck again by the exotic and voluptuous orchestral sound supporting the sensuous and glittering vocal lines. Massenet's use of leitmotifs somehow became more obvious – or were we just waiting for them?

The basic seven themes – one each for Esclarmonde and Roland, two for feats of Magic, and a Tournament, a Nuptial and a Possession theme – varied and given to different instruments in the orchestra, seemed to gain further mysticism. It was a thrilling group of sessions enjoyed by all, I think, especially the orchestra.

When it was released it was named as 'Record of the Year' by the *Financial Review* (December 17, 1976).

> There has been nothing on record this year to approach the splendour and enchantment of the previously unknown opera *Esclarmonde* by Jules Massenet. One can only express the greatest admiration for Richard Bonynge who restored this magical opera to the repertoire and who gives such an exultant performance on this set. .... All other roles are excellent, particularly the Australian bass Clifford Grant.

After the sessions ended we were picked up at the Kensington apartment and taken to Biggin Hill airport where Richard, Huguette and myself were flown by Decca's private jet to Bologna to complete the *Maria Stuarda* recording with Pavarotti. We actually had two free days in that fair city while the engineers set up the equipment and re-created the same acoustic as previously. We completed the opera without further problems and Richard and I went to stay with our friends in Arenzano for a few days until the end of the month.

Towards the end of August we were in San Francisco again, preparing our first performances of Verdi's *Il Trovatore*. Luciano was also making his début in the role of Manrico, with Ingvar Wixell as Count di Luna and Elena Obratsova as Azucena. Rehearsals went smoothly in spite of a problem with the surface of the set – foam rubber 'cobblestones' which were covered in what seemed like black plastic garbage bags. This had a nasty habit of sinking under the weight of the singers (none of us light-weights) and ripping from the pressure of our heels, then tripping us when our toes caught in the resulting holes. At least it was comfortable to kneel and fall upon, and the whole opera was kept so dark that Richard complained he couldn't see any of us.

During the Dress Rehearsal, I began to experience pain in a tooth which became increasingly worse during the night. I had a very nasty abscess on the root of a front tooth, and surgery had to be performed and the abscess drained. Although the surgeon was very considerate he could not prevent the pain and swelling which resulted. The little operation was performed on September 10 and the opening night was on the twelfth! I doubted if I would be able to sing but in spite of great discomfort I got through the opera, very grateful that the next performance was five days ahead. This gave plenty of time for the pain and swelling to disappear, along with the stitches.

Elena Obratsova had complained of a sore throat on opening night and was replaced for the second performance on the seventeenth by Shirley Verrett, resulting in a second assessment of the presentation by the press in which I was noted as having 'healed'. Barbara Bladen, in the *San Mateo Times* of September 20, 1975, wrote:

> ... Her [Joan Sutherland's] recovered composure and eloquent interpretation of Leonora were received with near-hysteria by a sell-out audience.
> ... The House went wild at the perfection of all four principals as they threw themselves into the dark and tragic Verdi work. Obviously all tension was removed from the traditional 'circus' atmosphere of opening night, something the singers can't escape amid the heightened excitement of everyone involved on both sides of the stage.
> ... Conductor Richard Bonynge had the opera's ebb and flow cupped in his palm with flawless control.

Leonora in *Il Trovatore* was a role I enjoyed singing. It was a great challenge for me, having been sung by all the big Verdi sopranos of the past. With my background of so much Bellini and Donizetti, as well as 'lighter' Verdi roles, I wondered how I would fare in the long 'Miserere' scene – in fact, the whole last act. My faith in myself was given a boost by a mailgram to Richard and myself from Martin Waldron. In this, after a greeting, he continued:

> I recall being present at a rehearsal when Toscanini told Z.M. [Zinka Milanov] that the ideal voice Verdi had in mind for Leonora was the voice also for Violetta and Gilda – completely yours. Both of you will have a beautiful success.

Such messages received backstage amid the bustle of opening night always had a huge impact on me. It was heartening to know that friends were thinking of you although miles away and unable to be present, but taking the trouble to wish you well in some way.

I went on to sing Leonora in several different productions but never in one that felt right. The closest I came was at Covent Garden at the end of 1981. At least I had the wonderful costumes devised by Barbara Matera for this San Francisco début.

We had some interesting dinner dates – with Obratsova and with Dr Ancona, the son of the well-known baritone of the 1890s, Mario Ancona. Of course we asked the kindly old doctor his impressions of other singers he had heard in the Met seasons with his father – Melba, Jean and Edouard de Reszke, Pol Plançon, Calvé, Nordica, Arnoldson and the like.

Between *Trovatores* we did a recital with Huguette Tourangeau in San Diego for the Opera on September 23. The programme consisted of duets, half of which I never sang again but certainly enjoyed working on with Huguette, combining them with extracts from operas we performed together. I particularly remember singing the Letter duet from *Le Nozze di Figaro*, Act 3, Countess and Susanna; the duo for Lisa and Pauline from Tchaikovsky's *Queen of Spades*; a Sérénade from *Le Roi l'a dit* by Delibes; the Flower duet from *Madame Butterfly*, and the duet for Mimi and Musetta from Leoncavallo's *La Bohème*. We also sang duets from *Le Roi de Lahore*, *La Fille de Mme Angot* and *La Donna del Lago*.

After the last *Trovatore* performance we went to Pasadena, where we did our usual type of recital of songs and arias by French and Italian operatic composers. This engagement was my last for about a month, so I was happy to fly home to Les Avants, Richard going to Vancouver where he prepared and conducted four performances with the Vancouver Opera of Rossini's *Semiramide* with Norman Ayrton as Stage Director, Marvellee Cariaga as Semiramide, Huguette as Arsace and James Morris as Assur.

I spent a very pleasant few weeks in Les Avants with friends visiting on their way to or from other parts of Europe, managing to help tidy the garden before the winter and plant bulbs. By the end of October I was back in New York, where I appeared on the *Ed Sullivan Show* on November 1. The next day I flew to Chicago, meeting up with Richard coming from Vancouver, and rehearsals began for *Lucia* directed by John Copley.

After eight *Lucias* I flew home to Les Avants with Chester, and Richard went to Sydney, where he was to conduct performances of *The Magic Flute* with the Australian Opera, spending Christmas with his parents. Chester and Gertie Stelzel joined Richard in Sydney to help decorate the apartment in Potts Point that Richard had bought through our Company on his previous visit. As we were likely to spend some five months of each future year with the Australian Opera, especially Richard as its Musical Director, it had been decided to maintain a permanent abode.

PART FOUR

Happy Years with the Australian Opera
and Final Performances
1976–1997

✧ 1 ✧

THE PERFORMANCES OF *The Magic Flute* in January–February 1976 were Richard's début as Musical Director of the Australian Opera.

In the *Bulletin* Brian Hoad wrote: 'An auspicious sort of début for a musical director. Bonynge's light and lively approach ... restores to these guardians of enlightenment the warm glow of humanity which is rightfully theirs.'

Roger Covell in the *Sydney Morning Herald* wrote: 'A Mozartian conductor of authentic flair.' He also praised the début with the Company of Isobel Buchanan as Pamina. This pleased Richard immensely, as on hearing her sing for him in London he had been impressed by her charm and maturity of voice and been instrumental in her being engaged by the Australian Opera, where she became the darling of the Company with her amazing performances and ready wit. Roger Covell said of her:

> Miss Buchanan has a voice that registers with exceptional definition, even when she is using it as softly as possible. It has formidable reserves of power and fullness ... Mr Bonynge whose protégée she is, must have been heartened by her vindication of his faith, judgement and guidance!

Meanwhile, in Les Avants, we had a very quiet Christmas indeed with just Adam, Rachel, Ruthli and her family, with visits from and to Lotfi Mansouri. These were to establish a few ideas regarding the dialogue and general production of the forthcoming *Merry Widow* in Vancouver in April 1976, of which he was the Stage Director.

During January I had a marvellous time organising various household replenishments and improvements, including the ordering of an extra-long bed for Adam who was feeling cramped in any of the existing ones. I also arranged for the re-covering of our dining-room chairs. Richard had thought I might manage to needlepoint these, but as there are ten upright chairs and two large carvers, all with fair-sized seats and high backs, I decided we couldn't wait the necessary lifetime for these to appear.

Gertie Stelzel came back to Les Avants via London on January 30 and confirmed my fears that Carl Bonynge was seriously ill and would probably not live to see us again. I was very glad that Ric had been able to spend this last Christmas with his father and mother. Chester had gone on to Vancouver on January 19 with Richard, who had to finish preparation for *The Queen of Spades*. The Stage Director of these performances was our colleague and friend Regina Resnik (who also sang the role of the old Countess) with Arbit Blatas designing the sets and Suzanne Mess the costumes. The young Samuel Ramey sang Count Tomsky, probably for the only time in his career.

On February 1 I flew to New York to begin rehearsing for the new production of *I Puritani* at the Met with Sandro Sequi. Richard arrived from Vancouver on the eighth and rehearsals intensified over the next two weeks.

I Puritani had not been heard at the Met since the 1917–18 season when Elvira and Arturo were sung by Barrientos and Lazaro with De Luca singing Riccardo and José Mardones as Giorgio. For this new production, almost sixty years later, we had Luciano as Arturo, Sherrill Milnes as Riccardo and James Morris as Giorgio. The sets were designed by Ming Cho Lee, the costumes by Peter John Hall and the production by Sandro Sequi was hailed as a 'Stunning success', 'Electrifying', 'Memorable', with great praise for all concerned. There were ten performances during this first run at the Met with Cornelis Opthof and Ezio Flagello singing the roles of Riccardo and Giorgio for the last three.

Between performances I had fittings with Barbara Matera for costumes for the Sydney *Lakmé* later in the year. A short video for television was filmed at these sessions, along with wig fittings and a trip across New York by car, all to promote the new production of Delibes' work for the Australian Opera in July–August. We spent a weekend at the Materas' lovely gingerbread house in Athens, NY, by the Hudson River. Later we learned that Carl Bonynge had died on February 20 and were happy he had not lingered further.

On the last day of March we flew to Vancouver and rehearsals began for *The Merry Widow*. This was a very relaxing and happy time, staying with our friend Zena Wagstaff (first known by me in 1958 at that original Vancouver Festival) and working with so many old friends each day on Lehár's charming and evocative operetta. Many were the laughs at the antics of Phil Stark and Gordon Wilcock and when the timing of moves and dancing was off. There were also memory lapses in the dialogue, especially when further cuts were made, but everyone involved believed in and loved the work, and with Lotfi Mansouri's handling of the staging within José Varona's open art nouveau sets and stunning costumes everything came together with just the right amounts of comedy and nostalgia.

It was a splendid cast. Baron Mirko Zeta was sung by Jan Rubes, with Barbara Shuttleworth as Valencienne (his wife), Graham Clark as Camille de Rosillon, Graeme Ewer as Njegus and Gordon Wilcock and

Phil Stark as the unforgettable zany pair, Cascada and St Brioche. Margreta Elkins threw up her legs as Zo-Zo the can-can dancer. The version was based on that which Lehár did for London in 1907. Martin Scheepers choreographed the operetta with the added Act 3 Ballet Music arranged by Douglas Gamley, who also provided an overture of great sparkle and zest, and arrangements of my entrance aria and the closing item in the production *Love Live Forever* from Lehár's *Paganini* and sung by myself and the whole Company. This rounded off the finale, which otherwise is quite abrupt.

The costumes for all were very elegant and I loved mine, remarking that my mother had worn such gowns for real not *so* long ago. My big test came when I made my first entrance down a central staircase singing and acknowledging the 'gentlemen' vying for my attentions with a huge feathered hat on my head, in a long, fish-tailed gown, with a muff on one arm and a black feather fan and dance programme on the other. This was all choreographed and looked most impressive when everyone moved in the right direction at the right time. We had a few collisions during rehearsals. There were a lot of laughs with Pieter van der Stolk and myself trying to imitate Martin Scheepers dancing the 'Kolo' and much begging by us to make the steps simpler as we were so out of breath for our next dialogue, but we managed and the scene proceeded convincingly, our breathlessness rather adding a human quality.

The critics had a field day, stating it was *not* the work for 'La Stupenda' – there were no great high notes and coloratura flights, and that's what the audience expected from 'the greatest singer of the century'. They grudgingly admitted the production was beautifully presented – 'a visual delight' – with Richard appearing 'to have a sense of the light lilt and sweep needed to convey the Viennese qualities of Lehár's waltzes and melodies'. Whatever 'they' thought, the whole run of six performances was sold out (before the first night, I believe) and the audience reaction was great every time.

On May 5 Richard, Chester and I flew to Hawaii for three nights, before flying on to Sydney, where I finally saw the apartment about which I had heard so much. We arrived there at night, so the full magnificence of the view was only evident the next morning, when I marvelled once again at Richard's luck when house-hunting. The situation on the top floor of a grand old block of eight apartments commands an unbroken view straight up the harbour to the Heads, the natural entrance to Sydney Harbour from the Pacific Ocean. With its high ceilings, polished hardwood floors, enormous windows on the view and the attention already given it by Chester and Gertie under Ric's supervision it was already very much a home, and only seven minutes from the Opera House.

Ric and I left on May 15 for New Zealand, for a four-and-a-half-week tour for Radio New Zealand, and they organised everything incredibly well. During our stay we performed six orchestral concerts – two each in Wellington and Auckland, and one in Dunedin and Christchurch, with a recital in Hamilton, Napier, Wellington and Christchurch. There was an amusing gaffe in *Opera*: '. . . Joan Sutherland became the best of herself in the music which she had made most her own, the "Street Walking Scene" of Bellini's *La Sonnambula*.'

We became very friendly with Jeremy Commons and David Carson Parker who introduced us to some of their friends – and some good antique shops. On our free days we found all sorts of items for furnishing the Sydney apartment and interesting additions to the 'Sutherland–Bonynge Collection', also aided by Kenneth Dryland who was visiting his homeland.

Between the Hamilton recital on the twenty-fifth and the orchestral concert in Dunedin on the twenty-ninth we took the opportunity to go by a charter flight to Mount Cook for a night and on to Queenstown to spend the following night, arriving in Dunedin on the twenty-eighth. However, as we approached Mount Cook the pilot said the weather looked bad and he doubted if we would get away from there the following day. He therefore flew us on to Milford Sound where we were bowled over by the scenery, including the lovely Sutherland Falls. We stayed long enough to have a drink while the little plane was refuelled – and be attacked by hundreds of mosquitoes and midges – before flying on to Queenstown for the night.

Here, too, the scenery was spectacular, although quite different from the soaring walls of Milford Sound. We visited Arrowtown the next morning and in the afternoon took the Shotover River jet boat for a thrill.

After our Wellington recital and two orchestral concerts in Auckland, we visited Rotorua, the fantastic volcanic hot-spring area with bubbling mud and geysers and a wealth of Maori history. We were truly fascinated by the variety and range of natural beauty in the two lovely islands of New Zealand.

The tour ended with a recital in Christchurch Town Hall (a superb acoustic) and on June 7 we returned to Sydney.

The production rehearsals for *Lakmé* proceeded very smoothly, with Norman Ayrton his usual organised self and Richard and me trying to fit in the many requests for interviews and social engagements. There were eleven performances, the last done specially for television with the audience admitted for half price, as brighter lighting was used and there was some camera interference with sight lines. It was fortuitous that this video was made and survives, as the whole production (with the exception of my costumes which were on display in an exhibition) was one of those burned in a disastrous warehouse fire the following year.

The opera was almost entirely double-cast, the exceptions being myself as Lakmé, Clifford Grant as Nilakantha and Graeme Ewer as Hadji. The rest of the splendid performers were:

Mallika   Huguette Tourangeau and Margreta Elkins
Gerald   Henri Wilden and Anson Austin
Frederik   John Pringle and Pieter van der Stolk
Ellen   Isobel Buchanan and Beryl Furlan
Rose   Jennifer Bermingham and Cynthia Johnston
Miss Bentson   Rosina Raisbeck and Mary Hayman.

Of course, everybody had heard the Bell Song but the dramatic content of the rest of Delibes' work took the critics and audiences by surprise. The opera was performed in the original French, with both Marie-Claire and Renée Goossens coaching the language. The tenor Henri Wilden was from Mauritius and, of course, had no problem but the rest of the cast, including myself, were constantly being given corrections and reminders about our pronunciation.

The opening night was somewhat marred by a delay of about forty minutes to show the orchestra's displeasure over possible reduction of their numbers. However, we finally got on stage and managed to woo the somewhat angered audience back, with good reports in the press, particularly for Richard and the disgruntled orchestra – he 'got the best playing out of the Sydney Elizabethan Orchestra it has given this season' according to Roger Covell, who also remarked in the *Sydney Morning Herald*, 'Miss Sutherland's voice manifests itself in a state of flawless and remarkable steadiness of tone.'

The *National Times* thought Richard 'drew such luscious sounds from the orchestra that it was a crying shame they weren't playing something more worth the effort'. Felix Werder managed one of his barbed remarks with 'In this opera, the Australian Opera certainly shows its indulgence for vulgar taste and unlimited spending.' You cannot please everyone.

Between the second and third *Lakmé* performances I began a series of sittings for the portrait as Lakmé by Judy Cassab which now hangs in the foyer of the Sydney Opera House. These were always enjoyable two-hour periods between 11 a.m. and 1 p.m., when Judy found the light perfect in her studio, with conversation seldom lagging. She later painted more casual portraits of both Richard and me which we have in our Swiss home.

Richard had already begun rehearsals for the new production of *Carmen* before *Lakmé* opened and between the seventh and eighth nights of the latter, on July 31, the *Carmen* had its première. It was designed and produced by Tom Lingwood (then Resident Designer with the Australian Opera) and he managed to make the small stage of the opera theatre appear immense.

Huguette Tourangeau was an enchanting Carmen and there were three scheduled Don Josés. Donald Smith was taken ill prior to the opening night so Ronald Stevens stepped in, having a great success. Later in the season the role was sung by Nicola Filacuridi who had sung with me in 1960 in the Glyndebourne *I Puritani*. He had been living in Australia for some time and came out of retirement to sing a few performances. Isobel Buchanan had a further triumph as Micaela. Gregory Yurisich from Western Australia was just beginning his career and sang Morales. It has been a great delight for us to see and hear his progress internationally.

The press reports were, as usual, divided. Nadine Amadio wrote in the *Financial Review*:

> This was a glowingly beautiful performance with the honours going almost entirely to the conductor, Richard Bonynge. ... there was never a moment when the fascinating unfolding of the score did not hold the attention and move the emotion with its fine attention to detail. A delicate but very insistent tension held the work together magnificently. ... How extraordinary that an Australian conductor should so perfectly capture that silken evocation of the French dream of exotic romance. It is a subtle and elusive quality and Bonynge can communicate it better than any conductor performing today ... the orchestra played superbly under Bonynge and gave a memorable performance.

'Mr Bonynge's absurdly fast tempos right from the overture made most of the opera seem farcical, exaggerated and lollipop,' said David Ahern in the *Sunday Telegraph*. Maria Prerauer of *The Australian*, however, commented: 'I do not think Bonynge's speeds are too fast. Occasionally they are too slow.' Roger Covell wrote:

> Bonynge's understanding of the Frenchness of the opera is evident in every bar of his conducting. His relatively slow, controlled beginning to Act 2 is far more ominous and evocative than many a frenetic reading of this passage.

Richard only conducted the first six *Carmens* and then opened *The Marriage of Figaro* revival with the Countess sung by Isobel Buchanan. Our old friend from Covent Garden, Rosina Raisbeck, was Marcellina. The producer was John Copley, with the sets by Henry Bardon and costumes by Michael Stennett – an extremely elegant visual delight to complement the excellent singing.

During all this Huguette Tourangeau, Henri Wilden, John Pringle and myself gave a concert of duets, trios and quartets from opera and operetta in the ballroom of Government House in aid of the Royal Institute for Deaf and Blind Children, of which the Governor, Sir Roden Cutler (VC, KCMG, KCVO, CBE) was Patron. The evening was a huge success and I went to the Deaf and Blind Centre in North Rocks the following week to visit the children and see the work being done to help them. Ric and I were both made Life Governors of the Institute.

On Sunday, August 15, we attended a dinner party at Admiralty House, the residence in Sydney of the Queen's representative – the Governor-General of Australia. At this time Sir John Kerr was in office – and not at all popular, as he had been instrumental in removing the Prime Minister, Gough Whitlam. We enjoyed our evening with Their Excellencies and the other guests, being rather careful to avoid politics as a topic of conversation.

At the end of August we gave recitals in Adelaide and Canberra, after which it was home to Les Avants – for a week. Richard had not been home for almost a year, going straight to London for our recording for Decca of *Il Trovatore*.

We had a first-rate cast: Luciano, Ingvar Wixell, Marilyn Horne and Nicolai Ghiaurov, with Richard conducting the National Philharmonic Orchestra. In just over two weeks the opera was completed and Richard sped back to Les Avants briefly before returning to Sydney and accompanying the Australian Opera on a short tour to New Zealand, conducting four performances of *Rigoletto* in Wellington. Richard told me that the orchestra pit of the Victorian theatre was so small he had to 'perch on a bench in the front row of the stalls' with some of the orchestra overflowing into the boxes. There were also electrical problems, with a complete black-out just after Gilda's entrance which necessitated her (Joan Carden) remounting the stairs to make her entrance again when the lights were reinstated. There was another failure at the end of the opera and Gilda had to climb out of her sack in full view of the audience as the curtain did not descend.

Isobel Buchanan also sang her first Gildas on this tour, alternating with Joan Carden. The Duke was sung by Henri Wilden and Reginald Byers, with Raymond Myers and Robert Allman singing Rigoletto. Sparafucile was sung by Neil Warren-Smith and Maddalena by Margreta Elkins, whom Ric had encouraged to return from England to join the Company.

I, on the other hand, stayed a few extra days in London to have a polypus removed from my nostril. It was done very quickly and neatly after the last recording session in my trusted specialist's consulting room and I was told to revisit him four days later to get a clearance to fly home. I was delighted to have a few extra days to shop and see friends and paid a visit to Apsley House which I had never seen in all my years in London.

I spent three weeks in Les Avants and on October 24 Chester and I flew to New York, then Seattle on the twenty-eighth, meeting Richard there. Next evening we performed a recital for the Seattle Symphony Orchestra, Richard travelling by car to Vancouver after the concert whilst I spent the night in Seattle and travelled to Winnipeg where Richard joined me for a further recital on Sunday, October 31. I'm not sure how Ric managed that weekend, what with the jet-lag after the flight from the Antipodes and all the further travel, as well as having to concentrate on the two recital programmes, but by Monday afternoon we were in New York, where rehearsals for *Esclarmonde* at the Met began next day.

During that rehearsal period I notice we had very few other engagements, probably of necessity for Ric to spend some relaxed evenings in the apartment catching up on some sleep. One event we attended was the launching of Cole Lesley's book, meeting many old friends. We also spent a late afternoon in Korvette's store signing our recordings and I celebrated my fiftieth birthday at a splendid dinner party given by Buddy and Geri Kaufman at their home.

Esclarmonde opened on November 19 with several of the principals from the San Francisco season and the recording involved. Newcomers were John Carpenter as Enéas, John Macurdy as Cleomer and Louis Quilico as the Bishop. The production was borrowed from the San Francisco Opera and Lotfi Mansouri made his début at the Met with these performances. There were a few cast changes in the ten performances, with John Alexander singing Roland on the second and last nights, and Jerome Hines singing Phorcas. We were sold out and according to one press report scalpers were offering tickets at ridiculous prices.

Harold Schonberg wrote in the *New York Times* of November 20:

> ... No wonder Miss Sutherland was attracted to this opera. ... The big, soaring line was there, the golden sound remains unparalleled, and there was some radiant singing. Miss Sutherland's instrument is still unique.

Of Richard he said:

> ... This was one of his memorable performances. He led *Esclarmonde* with high style and spirit and with a firm rhythmic base not always encountered in his work in the past. Mr Bonynge was very careful to work with the singers, holding the orchestra to a level over which the voices could easily penetrate. Yet he did not neglect the scoring, and the orchestra sounded firm, sonorous and – most important – sensuous. It was a most satisfactory evening, and it well could spark a look at some other virtually forgotten Massenet operas.

For once the press reports were fairly unanimous in their praise of the production and those involved in it and the audiences were wild with enthusiasm every night.

On December 12 Richard and I took part in a concert held in the General Assembly Hall of the United Nations sponsored by the Australian Government for the benefit of UNICEF. It was a gala tribute on the thirtieth anniversary of the Fund and the concert bore the title 'The Rights of a Child'. There were many Australian performers from different fields participating including June Bronhill, Rolf Harris, the ballet dancers John Meehan and Marilyn Rowe, John MacNally, Barry Crocker and others including that courageous example to us all, Marjorie Lawrence, who sang 'Waltzing Matilda' from her wheelchair. The hosts were Zoe Caldwell and Cyril Richard and Sir Robert Helpmann was the Artistic Director. It was a wonderful evening which we both enjoyed, rounding off the programme with the final Sleep-walking Scene from *La Sonnambula* and 'Ah, fors'è lui' from *La Traviata*.

The day after the final *Esclarmonde* Richard flew to Australia and I, together with Chester, to Les Avants for Christmas 1976 and just over three weeks' repose at the chalet, entertaining the occasional guest and enjoying some sledding. By this time Adam had almost completed his hotel management course and, after a skiing trip to Mégève, he and his girl-friend visited and it was good to see him looking well and obviously enjoying his work.

$$✧ \; 2 \; ✧$$

IN AUSTRALIA RICHARD prepared the revivals of both *Lakmé* with Joan Carden in the title role and *Carmen* with Heather Begg. The hard-working versatility of the singers and répétiteurs in the Australian Opera is quite special, making it possible to double- and triple-cast the operas and providing well-prepared substitutes in an emergency. In this first season, for which Richard was entirely responsible for the repertoire, the Company gave 231 performances of twenty-one operas. He was only able to stay for the first two nights of *Carmen* and *Lakmé*, having commitments in Vancouver, where he was to prepare and perform Ambroise Thomas's *Mignon*. This production was directed by Norman Ayrton with Huguette Tourangeau as Mignon.

Sylvia Holford arrived at Les Avants on January 15 to run through our recital programmes and the following week we flew to New York and on to Iowa City for our first recital, then Buffalo for our second. Our next stop was Akron, Ohio, where our recital was for the 'Tuesday Musical Club' on January 27 – this being a Thursday. What was our horror during the night to hear the wind howling and battering the windows and, in the morning, a continuing blizzard, paralysing all traffic. We were due to leave for Danville, Kentucky, but were told it would be impossible. We spent a further night in our Akron hotel and were flown by a private jet to Louisville, then on to Danville by car. We arrived at our hotel at about 5 p.m., with the concert looming at 8 p.m. Somehow we refreshed our anxious and protesting bodies, collected our wits and presented ourselves on time. The reviews bore headings reading:

SUTHERLAND AT CENTER: A NATURAL WONDER

JOAN SUTHERLAND SPARKLES IN KENTUCKY DEBUT

and these were followed by such praise that Sylvia and I began to think we should have a blizzard after *every* concert. It was quite an experience.

We flew on to Sarasota, Florida – quite a change from the 'man-killing blizzard and cold wave that swept the Upper Middle West'. Here we had time to visit the fantastic Barnham and Bailey's Circus Museum having a free day before our recital in the Van Wezel Performing Arts Hall, with one of the strangest exteriors I have ever seen. It seemed like a great purple-and-white octopus crouching on the grass.

Then it was on to Miami Beach for the final recital at the Miami Beach Theater of the Performing Arts on February 3. Sylvia had been a perfect accompaniste and great travelling companion, and I was so happy she had been able to fit my tour into her schedule. We went off in different directions: Sylvia northwards and I to join Ric in San Juan, Puerto Rico. Here we did two performances of *Lucia di Lammermoor* with a Spanish cast: Giacomo Aragall, Pablo Elvira and Justino Diaz. We saw a little of San Juan and thought we might enjoy a vacation in Puerto Rico but, to date, haven't revisited.

We arrived back in Switzerland on the morning of February 13 – Adam's twenty-first birthday. No great celebration had been planned (according to his wishes) and it passed very quietly, giving his parents an unspoken reminder that they were 'getting on'.

After a week at home we were off to Amsterdam for rehearsals of *Maria Stuarda*, dodging about between Scheveningen and Hilversum with Chester driving us to whatever locale from Amsterdam every day. The stage director was Tito Capobianco and the cast was very strong with Huguette Tourangeau again singing her splendid Queen Elizabeth, Vittorio Terranova as Leicester and John Bröcheler as Talbot. There were eight performances spread between Scheveningen, Rotterdam, Utrecht, Amsterdam and Eindhoven. There was considerable coverage in the Dutch press and most of the critics were impressed by the work, whilst the audiences were unanimous in their enjoyment of the performances.

On March 13 Huguette and I attended a small gathering in aid of the Dutch Red Cross, of which the then Princess Margriet was honorary president. With her husband Prince Peter van Vollenhoven, she accepted a copy of the Decca recording of *Maria Stuarda* from us.

Richard made a couple of trips to London between performances where he was doing recording sessions of *Sleeping Beauty* for Decca and before the final performance of *Stuarda* we spent an afternoon at the wonderful tulip garden of Keukenhof. It was a trifle too early in the spring and we had the wildest weather possible with sunshine, sleet, rain, wind – everything in an hour or so. But Huguette who was with us made us all laugh and we did see some of the beautiful blooms in the conservatories at least.

We returned to Les Avants, Richard for only just over a week before going to Vancouver for performances of *Un Ballo in Maschera* (James Morris sang his first Renato) whilst I was able to stay for a whole month and enjoy Easter and the spring weather at the chalet, with the garden beginning to bud after its winter sleep. Sylvia Holford came for a few days to get the feeling of tempi from Richard for *Le Roi de Lahore* which she was going to work on with me for Vancouver in September, also *Suor Angelica* which I was to sing in Sydney in July.

Before the *Ballo in Maschera* performances began in Vancouver there were already rumours and counter-rumours that the VOA was having financial difficulties and that Richard's innovations were partly to blame. He was also accused of not using sufficient Canadian singers in the productions. This after he had tried to form a nucleus of young Canadians to participate in the various operas with roles suited to their voices, which plan had been abandoned as unworkable (i.e. requiring funding) after a couple of years. There were differing ideas about the worthiness of instituting a month's season in which three operas would have five performances each, as opposed to the old system of one opera every two months, and he also wanted the VOA to have its own group of orchestral players instead of using those from the Vancouver Symphony. Ultimately he formed this orchestra which was still in existence at the time of writing, but all these business discussions were burdensome when he was supposed to be concentrating on rehearsals. He answered the various comments well in the *Vancouver Sun*, interviewed by Susan Mertens. He rounded off the interview with:

> I understand full well that I'm never going to please everyone. So I must start by pleasing myself – only in that way can I do opera here with conviction.
>
> I will just continue to go along doing my best and let them judge me on that basis ... I don't mind that they disagree with me – it would take more than that to drive me away.

I joined Ric in Vancouver for the last *Ballo* on the thirtieth, then we flew on to Sydney, with a ten-day break on Bora Bora *en route*.

Before I left Europe I visited Adam in his studio apartment in Basel, where he was now working for Hilton International at the Basel Hilton, occasionally doing duty as Sous-Chef and even in charge when the Head Chef was on holiday. He mostly worked in Food and Beverage Control which he seemed to enjoy and, after twenty years' knowledge of Udi and her family, was fluent in the local dialect. Some of his co-workers were unaware of his British background.

Our stay on Bora Bora was delightful and a much-needed rest, as there was a heavy schedule to face in Sydney, where we arrived on May 14. We began rehearsals immediately for *Lucrezia Borgia* and *Suor Angelica*, Richard rehearsing *The Barber of Seville* and *Fra Diavolo*, with a few concerts for good measure.

There had been the disastrous warehouse fire just before Easter which destroyed sets and costumes of several regular repertory works like *Madame Butterfly*, *La Bohème*, *The Merry Widow*, *The Marriage of*

Figaro and others, all of which would have to be remade promptly. This further strained the Company's financial problems but there was no apparent cut-back of expenses for the lavish production of *Lucrezia Borgia* which Kristian Fredrikson had designed and which was produced by George Ogilvie. The opera had not been staged in Australia this century, inviting more public interest.

The large cast of male singers was a means of utilising many Company members and they did a great job. Although there was some carping among the critics, most of them admitted it was a splendid night in the theatre, with many compliments and much appreciation for Donizetti's magic. The opera was given ten performances at this time, and all were sold out, with many opera fans sleeping outside the Opera House to be sure of obtaining standing passes – or a possible return.

After the second *Borgia* Ric had his first night of *The Barber of Seville*, with five more performances to follow. He again had a delightful cast, with Paul Ferris as a charming Almaviva, John Pringle as Figaro, Huguette Tourangeau as Rosina, Alan Light as Doctor Bartolo and Clifford Grant as Basilio. This was a revival of the original production by John Cox, designed by Roger Butlin and looking a bit like a white pepper mill and mustard pot side by side, with a predominance of white costumes. I enjoyed the show immensely and Maria Prerauer remarked in *The Australian* that it was

> ... much more genuinely amusing than its late unlamented original some years back. This time round the pace was terrific, the humour spot on ...
>
> And it was mainly due to conductor Richard Bonynge, who once again demonstrated what a master touch he has with light-fingered comic opera. ... Under his baton the music was razor sharp, the coloraturas bubbling and sparkling.

I began having more coaching for *Suor Angelica* after the second *Borgia* as I had not completely memorised it – those words again! Richard was already into final rehearsals of Auber's *Fra Diavolo* – in fact he had a lovely week with the fourth *Lucrezia Borgia* performance on June 14, *Fra Diavolo* final Dress Rehearsal on the fifteenth, the second *Barber of Seville* on the sixteenth, the first *Fra Diavolo* on the seventeenth, a 1 p.m. *Barber of Seville* matinée and the fifth *Lucrezia Borgia* at 7.30 p.m. on the eighteenth. He must have been quite exhausted but seemed to thrive on performances Friday night followed by the matinée and then the evening performances on Saturday, juggling the Rossini, the Auber and the Donizetti. He was also attending rehearsals of *I Pagliacci* and *Suor Angelica* during some days. I had quite enough on my plate with just two operas to think about.

The *Fra Diavolo* was a riot of fun in Henry Bardon's 'penny plain –

tuppence coloured' sets, with glamorous costumes by Michael Stennett and a romp of a production by John Copley. Even the cover of the programme was printed as a Victorian cut-out toy theatre. The cast obviously loved the piece and the performances John Copley drew from all of them were a joy for the audience. Isobel Buchanan showed onstage the wicked sense of humour we all knew she possessed, as well as singing like an angel as Zerlina. Robert Gard was a suave, believable Diavolo and Anson Austin the sergeant Lorenzo in love with Zerlina – both tenors well able to manage the very high tessitura of their roles. Dennis Olson and Heather Begg were a hilarious comic duo as Lord and Lady Allcash. Giacomo and Beppo, the brigand confederates of Fra Diavolo, were played by Neil Warren-Smith and Graeme Ewer with Italo-Australian accents and modelled on the interpretation of the characters by Laurel and Hardy in the old film of the work.

Most of the press loved it all, pointing out that the patrons were leaving the theatre 'with a song or two in their hearts as well as a twinkle in the eye'. But there were also comments as to what it must have cost – with counter-comments that it was worth every penny. Nadine Amadio wrote in the *Financial Review*:

> ... Bonynge's glittering performance, stylishly French and full of the atmosphere of the period, was the most outstanding contribution to the work. It pointed the wit, whipped up the froth and constantly bubbled and sparkled under the vocal lines ... The involvement of a fine cast of principals led to some superb ensemble singing displaying the craft behind Auber's froth ...

During the season we were saddened by the resignation of John Winther for whom we had much admiration. He had enormous theatrical flair and tried to see both sides of any situation. There had been disagreements between the Board and Winther, who left to become head of the Conservatorium in Newcastle. Richard had learned a great deal from him and missed John.

The Board of Directors rather quickly appointed Peter Hemmings, who had recently left the Scottish Opera. There was little hope of Richard and him agreeing, as he immediately spoke of my singing Elizabeth I in Britten's *Gloriana*, Lady Billows in *Albert Herring* and Emilia in *The Makropoulos Case* for the Australian Opera. Apart from some unprintable remarks on my part regarding such repertoire I also stated firmly that I would prefer to stay at home and tend my garden.

The stage director for *Suor Angelica* was Moffatt Oxenbould who had produced the complete *Trittico* some years before and his feeling and understanding of the work were a great help to me. All of the ladies in the Company loved the opera and there was an excellent rapport between us all – something I was to notice again much later when we did *The Dialogues of the Carmelites*. Was the atmosphere created by the fact that we were all women together, or was it imposed by the surroundings and trappings of the convent life? Whatever it was, it gave the piece a deep-seated sincerity. We only did four performances and I was sorry there were so few as I enjoyed singing something of the verismo repertory and I believe the role suited me very well. The imposing figure of Rosina Raisbeck as the Princess made me feel very small and helpless, and all the smaller roles were splendidly cast with Isobel Buchanan as the Nursing Sister, Elizabeth Fretwell the Monitress, Heather Begg the Abbess and Cynthia Johnston as Suor Genovieffa.

There was general surprise from the press at my ability to handle the part of Angelica with such vocal security and conviction, never having heard me in a verismo work before. The reviews were in agreement for once and very flattering indeed. Brian Hoad rounded off a long article in *The Bulletin* by saying:

> With the strong musical support of Richard Bonynge in the pit and intelligent stage direction from Moffatt Oxenbould, Sutherland handles all the demands magnificently. As the ordinary nun of the opening scene tending her garden with much horticultural devotion, she is for once unrecognisable as Sutherland. The interplay with her sister-nuns is ensemble work at its most sensitive. The explosive meeting with her aunt is played out with all the new-found dramatic power of her lower registers. And in the closing scene, the more familiar Sutherland soars heavenwards as only she can.
>
> There is, with reason, a continuing argument surrounding Angelica. Nobody but a religious imbecile, it is claimed, could accept that final vision of the Virgin, glittering as Puccini commanded, like some kewpie-doll from Luna Park. Yet that depends on just how well your Angelica has realised her role. She should, by that stage, have brought her audience to the edge of tears, viewing the vision through misty eyes, as Angelica herself is seeing it. That seldom if ever happens, and the argument persists. But tears, at precisely the right moment, is what Sutherland finally achieves. In doing so, she has restored to this opera the greatness which Puccini until his dying day believed it possessed, despite the public mockery. And Puccini has given to Sutherland one of the most dramatically satisfying and moving roles of her long career.

I certainly found the physical representation of the glittering Madonna and Child essential to the finale, a visible miracle that absolved Angelica's sin. One critic suggested that in this day and age the vision could surely be achieved by lighting and or laser beams. I saw it done – at the Met – and it meant nothing. The impression was that something had gone wrong with the lighting and it could have been no help at all to the Angelica to attain that final fervour and climax before death.

One of the greatest aids to interpreting a role is to *believe* it – not always easy. There is a limit to the strength of one's belief, but the surrounding scenery and some stage magic combined with the reality help artists to convey their emotions and enthral their audience.

Little Gregory Howett as the Child was a charmer, at first seemingly shy, but after his opening-night taste of the applause he became quite miffed when he was only allowed one or, at most, two curtain calls.

Richard had been awarded the CBE in the Queen's Birthday Honours in June for his 'service to the performing arts'. He received the insignia from the Governor in Sydney the following February, being unable to attend the General Investiture. During this visit I was presented with my insignia as Companion of the Order of Australia by the Governor-General (Sir John Kerr) at Admiralty House.

Practically the whole Company of singers appeared in a concert on July 24 in the Opera House Concert Hall in aid of the Royal NSW Institute for Deaf and Blind Children. All the participants generously donated their services and various business organisations added their support to the venture. It was a very lengthy programme of ensembles, mostly from operas not in the repertoire, accompanied by Richard and Sharolyn Kimmorley playing two pianos. The items included excerpts from *Ernani*, *La Sonnambula*, *Saffo*, *Esclarmonde*, *Martha*, *L'Oracolo*, *La Rondine*, *L'Amico Fritz*, *L'Italiana in Algieri*, *Il Matrimonio Segreto*, *Poliuto*, *La Périchole*, *Der Tsarevich*, *Ruddigore*, *The Bohemian Girl*, *I Lombardi* and several other works, some in the repertoire. There was a 'Surprise Trio' listed and Rosina Raisbeck, Heather Begg and I sang 'Three Little Maids from School' from *The Mikado*. The adjective was hardly apt, as I was the shortest of the three. The concert was such a success that it was repeated on February 18, 1978.

I received a letter of apology from the then Prime Minister (Malcolm Fraser) for missing the original performance as he had meetings in Canberra considering the budget and confirming that his wife and daughter were able to attend. There was a fuss because his wife and daughter used the private Government jet to facilitate their trip. I'm sure much worse waste occurs that's never reported.

The day after the concert we again had the pleasure of luncheon with the Governor and Lady Cutler at Government House and two days later, on July 27, left for home, on an Alitalia flight via Bombay and Rome. Unfortunately, on leaving Bombay there was an explosion, one of the engines caught fire, the fuel was jettisoned and we returned to spend twenty-six hours in Bombay with only our hand luggage and the clothes we stood up in, having had to surrender our passports and tickets to facilitate alternative transport when available. It was monsoon time and every so often the heavens would open, the rain would pour down, stop, the sun would half appear and the earth steam like a boiling cauldron. We took a taxi ride for a couple of hours to see something of the city, visiting the Gandhi Museum and various other places of interest, but found it predominantly depressing and unbearably humid, so retreated back to our mouldering hotel near the airport to try and get some sleep before the next leg of the trip – whenever that might be.

✧ 3 ✧

WE REACHED LES AVANTS on July 29, a rather bedraggled threesome with no desire to revisit India. Chester had taken some cautious video films, worried that the rain would suddenly fall and ruin his camera, and I have a few misty snapshots as reminders. Our relief at being home was increased by the fact that we had seats for all the family to see the pageant of the Fête des Vignerons in Vevey on the night of August 3. From 1797 this Fête had been presented in the market place of Vevey and followed a similar pattern, with a spectacular cortège and pageant depicting the four seasons and their effect on the growth of the vines and the ultimate picking of the grapes, making and finally drinking the wine. The Fête was held roughly every twenty-five years but there had been some differing periods between each one, due to wars or other circumstances. In the nineteenth and twentieth centuries they were held in 1819, 1833, 1851, 1865, 1889, 1905, 1927, 1955 and now this one between July 30 and August 14, 1977.

Although there was great anticipation of the event it far exceeded our expectations. The costumes and décor were very beautiful, with the pageantry and dancing splendidly executed. There was an orchestra of eighty-six with combined choirs from within the canton of Vaud, bands of fifes and drums and an extraordinary number of some 4000 participants in the specially constructed arena facing towards the lake and the Savoy Alps. All the people involved in the pageant were amateurs – local residents who had rehearsed in their own area, only joining together during the final days before the opening of the Fête. Just one professional actor played and spoke the role of Le Roi de la Fête and it was amazing that everything locked into place so well. The participants paid for their costumes with a promise that, should the general costs of the Fête be covered, they would be reimbursed. Some of the costumes on the floats depicting Spring, Summer, Autumn and Winter were most elaborate and the various local cantonal costumes very colourful. All the children performed perfectly and obviously enjoyed themselves. Towards the end of the entertainment there was a regrouping of everybody involved and many other cantons were represented in their traditional costumes. This I thought was very important as too many of these beautiful folkloric costumes have been

304

considered old-fashioned or obsolete. It was a wonderful entertainment and we hope we may see the next Fête, planned for 1999 – perhaps with our grandchildren.

By August 7 we were in London with recording sessions starting the following day in Walthamstow of *Lucrezia Borgia* and *The Merry Widow*. It was a friendly cast for *Borgia* – Marilyn Horne as Maffio Orsini, Giacomo Aragall as Gennaro, Ingvar Wixell as Don Alfonso, Graeme Ewer as Rustighello, Nicola Zaccaria as Astolfo, Richard Van Allan as Gubetta, also Graham Clark, Lieuwe Visser, John Bröcheler and Piero de Palma as the friends of Gennaro. The orchestra was the National Philharmonic which also played for *The Merry Widow*.

We had Werner Krenn as Count Danilo, Valerie Masterson as Valencienne, John Brecknock as Camille de Rosillon, Regina Resnik as Zo-Zo, Graeme Ewer as Njegus, and two very comic characters from our *Who's Afraid of Opera* series, John Fryatt and Francis Egerton, as Vicomte Cascada and Raoul de St Brioche. We had fun at these sessions, all of which were in the afternoon, leaving us free in the evening to relax with friends or go to a theatre.

By September 2 (after a quick trip to Les Avants) we were in Vancouver for rehearsals of Massenet's *Le Roi de Lahore*, together with *Don Giovanni*, while Richard also had *La Fille du Régiment* to rehearse and perform in this trial season of three operas during the same period. During rehearsals we heard of the death in Paris of Maria Callas who was only in her early fifties. She had been instrumental in launching the revival of the bel canto works of Bellini and Donizetti at the bidding and encouragement of those great old operatic maestri Tullio Serafin and Vittorio Gui. Without the productions conducted by them, singers like Caballé, Gencer, Sills, myself and others might never have had the opportunity to explore that extensive and almost forgotten repertoire. We were all quite shocked by her death and to learn how isolated and lonely she had become.

The first of the operas to open was *Le Roi de Lahore* for which Fiorella Mariani had designed very colourful sets and costumes which were a huge success, giving a very exotic hint of eleventh-century India. Sandro Sequi was the producer, bringing the characters very much to life and making some exciting and extraordinarily beautiful tableaux. The role of Timour, the High Priest was sung by James Morris with Cornelis Opthof singing the part of Scindia, villainous minister of King Alim and uncle of Sita, a temple priestess with whom he is in love. Sita (my role) loves a mysterious stranger who appears every evening in the temple. She is condemned to death for supposedly not keeping her vows of celibacy. Suddenly King Alim appears and reveals that he is the mysterious admirer, revoking the death sentence and agree-ing to atone for his offence by leading his troops against the

Muslim besiegers, accompanied by Sita and her bodyguard Kaled, a young officer, sung by Huguette Tourangeau. Timour blesses Alim in Indra's name. During the battle King Alim is mortally wounded by Scindia and goes to Paradise. The God Indra, sung by Spiro Malas, grants his desire to return to earthly life but stipulates that he must die when Sita does. The lovers are briefly reunited and Sita kills herself rather than marry Scindia, taking Alim with her to Paradise – quite a story. The opera was first performed in Paris in April 1877.

The vocal line I found quite difficult and awkward to negotiate at times, but it was a very atmospheric work. Some critics had snide remarks to make like 'Operatic Turkey made more edible when it tastes of Joan Sutherland' (this in the *Toronto Star* on October 11 which happened to be Canadian Thanksgiving Day). Others seemed to evaluate and appreciate the opera. '*Le Roi de Lahore* has been too long neglected,' said Ray Chatelin in *The Province*, while Susan Mertens in the *Vancouver Sun* headed her review with 'VOA revives a sleeping pedigree'. There were five performances of the piece in Vancouver and four in Seattle.

The second opera in the Vancouver season was *La Fille du Régiment* in the old Covent Garden sets of Anna Anni – still looking quite good – loaned by the Metropolitan Opera. Sandro Sequi again produced the opera with Costanza Cuccaro as Marie, Graham Clark as Tonio, Fernande Chiocchio as a super-aristocratic Marquise of Birkenfeld and Pierre Charbonneau as Sulpice. *Fille* was a hit, 'a well-balanced and pleasant diversion', 'a delight to the eye and to the ear' according to the press and I whole-heartedly agreed. It was such fun to sit in the audience and see the opera for a change, so well performed by those singers – I loved it.

Next on the agenda came *Don Giovanni* which I had been rehearsing whenever possible since the second week in Vancouver. Norman Ayrton was the producer and the production was designed by Robert Prevost, courtesy of the National Arts Centre Ottawa. There were four performances between October 7 and 22. James Morris was our Don and, according to Susan Mertens in the *Vancouver Sun*, 'He is Errol Flynn, Tyrone Power and Douglas Fairbanks rolled into one. Raunchy in white satin breeches and silver earring – an arrogant, unrepenting, fatally fascinating cad.' Spiro Malas was Leporello, of whom the same lady said he displayed 'both considerable buffo talents and a voice that responds with the strength and flexibility of an acrobat'.

Pierre Charbonneau was both the Commendatore and Masetto with Cesar-Antonio Suarez singing Don Ottavio to my Donna Anna. Marvellee Cariaga was Donna Elvira and Huguette Tourangeau sang Zerlina. Richard and I both admired Cesar-Antonio's voice and, with his height and stature, he was a splendid foil for me. We all tried to help him to ignore his anxiety over the role but he remained a very nervous singer.

So, between September 4 and October 22, Vancouver Opera had mounted the mini-season of three very different operas with a 'Holiday Weekend Package' of three over the US Columbus Day and Canadian Thanksgiving weekend. It had been hectic for the Company, especially the singers involved in more than one opera. Bliss Johnston coached the operas and there really was a Company feeling among the artists who all enjoyed the experience.

The day after the last *Don Giovanni* we drove down the Coast to Seattle where we had the performances of *Le Roi de Lahore*, then Richard left for Australia where he did *Carmen* with the Australian Opera in Brisbane, the Company drawing 'its best crowds in that city [Brisbane] for nearly a decade'.

Richard arrived back from Australia and after two and a half weeks' rehearsal we opened at Covent Garden on December 15 with *Maria Stuarda*. The following day we did a quick weekend trip back to Les Avants, as we would not be home for Christmas and had only a couple of days there after the London dates before flying to Sydney for the summer season. We organised lighter clothing, music and Christmas presents and hastened back to London for the second *Maria Stuarda* on the twentieth.

The whole run of *Stuarda*, directed by John Copley, was exciting and celebrated my twenty-fifth anniversary performances at the Royal Opera House. A special programme had been devised with photographs of me in various roles and the fans were most generous with their tokens of flowers, cakes and other goodies, along with thunderous applause. The critics had a field day paying compliments and I was happy to share the success of the opera with my colleagues and friends in the cast, Huguette Tourangeau, David Ward, Stuart Burrows and Heather Begg.

We scrambled off to Les Avants to pick up our luggage and leave for Australia, arriving there on January 3, 1978. When previously in Sydney we had gone house-hunting north of the city and found a splendid property on Careel Head. It overlooked Whale Beach and the mouth of the Hawkesbury River, with an uninterrupted view north and east, and we were able to enjoy our spare time in that wonderful, relaxed seaside atmosphere.

But rehearsals had to be attended and, as well as *The Merry Widow*, Richard had to prepare Verdi's *Nabucco*. Lotfi Mansouri was again producing *The Widow* and the attractive costumes (and hats!) were by Kristian Fredrikson. The performances were taking place in the Concert Hall which was possible in this early part of the year, being high summer with no regular Symphony rehearsals and concerts. The

Company did some superb productions in this bigger hall with no proscenium or curtain, using artful black-outs and fade-outs, and a fixed basic set which covered the organ and choir stalls and usually incorporated a high gallery with a long staircase, providing a great entrance for the prima donna. I used to climb up behind the scenery fairly early in order to regain my breath before entering. Plenty of old friends were in the cast including Gordon Wilcock as Baron Zeta, Isobel Buchanan as his wife Valencienne and Anson Austin as Camille de Rosillon. Graeme Ewer again sang Njegus with Ron Stevens and Pieter van der Stolk sharing the role of Danilo. The grisette Zo-Zo was played by Heather Begg. There was, of course, no orchestra pit, the players sitting where the first few rows of seats would be normally. This made the orchestral sound a little harder to control but I loved the more open feeling of the stage and that the vocal sound was reaching much further than in the opera theatre, with more ring and gloss – without any extra effort, in fact with less. We gave thirteen performances.

Some of the critics thought it was wasting my voice to appear as the Widow, others that it was a great vehicle for me, some that the Concert Hall was the wrong venue for it, others that it was right. Whatever they thought, once again the audience loved it and the critics had to admit that it was a very beautiful production, with brilliant lighting changes for the various scenes. The whole cast had a great time during the run, glad of some light relief from the heavier repertoire.

Brian Hoad wrote of me in *The Bulletin*: '... Her sense of fun is irresistibly contagious, her warmth is palpable, her romantic affections naively touching and sincere and she sings like the legendary Pontevedrian nightingale.'

David Gyger, in *Opera Australia*, said:

Joan Sutherland makes a magnificent Widow ... she sang, acted, danced and talked ... her way through Lehár's classic operetta role ... with absolute aplomb ... It was something of a paradox that Sutherland herself, who has often been criticised for her incomprehensibility got the words across best of anyone – whether she was singing or speaking.

In the *Financial Revue* Nadine Amadio wrote:

... Her amused and tolerant sophistication was underlined by her occasional head-thrown-back laugh which had all the beauty and flair of a modern Garbo. It seems that once again one of the most musically productive partnerships in the world of opera, that of Sutherland and Bonynge, has notched another victory.

I was very touched to read in H. R. Forst's piece in the *Daily Telegraph* that he thought it was almost certain that Vilia had never been sung quite as beautifully, with other numbers sounding 'unique in radiance and splendour'. He went on to say that 'Lehár would have felt greatly honoured to include our phenomenal Joan Sutherland in the list of his interpreters.'

Robert Morley, who was appearing in Australia at the time, was so annoyed at certain critics carping about the cost of the production that he wrote to *The Australian*:

> It is the function of your theatre critic surely to appraise the performance he attends, not to pine wistfully for another fare. In disparaging the choice of *The Merry Widow* as a suitable vehicle for your great opera star he ignores the thousands who, like myself, loathe and detest grand opera and were stunned into delight by the knowledge that we were going to watch and hear the wonderful tunes sung by Miss Sutherland.
>
> In all the years I have been coming here I have never seen anything in this always unpredictable country that so warmed my heart or filled me with admiration as this production.
>
> Of course it must have cost a fortune, of course the money could have been spent on other projects – it always can – but to those who, like myself, were lucky enough to be there it was a one-in-a-lifetime experience, and they are almost always expensive.

In fact the production was revived six times at least, with many of the same cast members, including Rosina Raisbeck as Praskovia still going strong aged seventy-two. I don't know how she managed it.

We had many social engagements – another luncheon at Admiralty House with the 'new' Governor-General and Lady Cowen, also Richard's private investiture at Government House where he received the insignia of a Commander of the British Empire, followed by lunch. Richard opened with *Nabucco* on February 17 and after a few nights we left for New York. Rita Hunter later that year made her Australian début in Adelaide in the same production, which also went to Melbourne. She had a big success in both cities and was a distinguished addition to the Company.

No sooner had we arrived in New York than rehearsals began for us at the Met for *Don Giovanni*, which opened on March 10 with six performances to follow. The very fine cast was headed by James Morris as the Don, Gabriel Bacquier as Leporello, I sang Donna Anna, John Brecknock Don Ottavio, Julia Varady Donna Elvira (these last two making their Met débuts) and Huguette Tourangeau Zerlina. This was the last run of performances in the wonderful sets by Eugene Berman which had been refurbished through the generosity of Mrs Edgar Tobin and her son Robert. The performance was televised on March 16.

Harold Schonberg, in the *New York Times*, said:

... Miss Sutherland is in very good voice these days. The sound is as golden as ever, and firmer than it was several seasons back. It is hard to think of any living soprano who could have projected 'Or sai chi l'onore' with equal command and color. ... In a few held notes of 'Non mi dir' there was a slight beat; otherwise the singing was sheer magnificence, and the coloratura went with signal-generator accuracy.

He went on to say:

Mr Bonynge paced a fine performance. He has been growing artistically in recent years, and his rhythms had none of the misplaced accents of yore. He is still a little too polite, a little too anxious to accommodate his singers, but there is a thorough grasp of the music in his mind and at the tip of his baton. The Eugene Berman sets hold up magnificently.

This is a *Don Giovanni* on the highest of today's standards, and in some respects it ranks with the great ones of the past.

This period was not too arduous as we knew all our colleagues so well *and* the opera. Luciano was also in New York for *L'Elisir d'Amore* at the Met and we had a jolly luncheon with him. We visited that fun show *On the Twentieth Century* which had some great effects.

After the last Met performance, Richard and I had a few days before going to Kalamazoo, where we gave a recital on April 4 at the Western Michigan University. We then moved on to Salt Lake City, giving our recital in the Tabernacle. The *Salt Lake Tribune* reported:

SUTHERLAND BRILLIANT IN S. L. RECITAL

Joan Sutherland is living testimony to the proposition that no other musical instrument is capable of the myriad shadings, the subtle textures of a truly brilliant, impeccably trained voice.

She proved that Friday night in recital at the Salt Lake Tabernacle where she appeared with her husband and accompanist Richard Bonynge. ... His fluid, delicate accompaniments, particularly in the series of songs 'Le Serate Musicali' by Rossini were fully as interesting as Miss Sutherland's magnificent voice.

One loved to receive appreciation from the critics but always had to bear in mind that their evaluation of a performance was just for that particular evening and there were many more hurdles to jump before you could relax and rest on your laurels. One had, in a way, to ignore the good crits as much as the not so good to avoid the risk of becoming over-confident.

We had further recitals in Minneapolis and Memphis, where we were very touched to get the following telegram:

We had planned for nearly a year to have the great joy of attending your Memphis recital but a nasty cold prevents this. Know you and your great art will be immensely successful. Warmest regards to you both and congratulations to Richard Bonynge for CBE.

Marjorie Lawrence

We both had great admiration for her and were sorry she had been unable to make the trip so we could see her again.

On once more to Tulsa, Oklahoma, and New Orleans where we gave our final appearance in the US until January 1979.

After so many years of spending months in the United States we now would be in Australia for five months of every year, the rest of the time being taken up with recordings and performances in Europe and occasionally in America and Asia. We also hoped to have a little more time at home, although this happy state for me was delayed for about ten years – and Richard at the time of writing is still as busy as ever.

Back home we participated at the chalet in the television show *A Life on the Move*, written and directed by Brian Adams (the writer of *La Stupenda*) for the ABC. We also recorded a lengthy recital programme for Decca, Richard accompanying me at the piano.

On June 3 we travelled to Tokyo to give a recital there and in Nagoya. The television crew were with us most of the time, filming the concerts and our visits to the beauty spots in Kyoto and Nara *en route* to Nagoya. We had experienced the Japanese audience response to the opera performances of the Met tour, so were a little prepared for the tumultuous applause and adulation of the public. We felt more like pop or rock stars as the whole mass of people swarmed forward to the platform wanting to touch a hand or part of my gown or Richard's trousers. It was a bit frightening as well as flattering.

We visited South Korea and performed in Seoul on June 13. There was a fantastic Korean luncheon banquet in the palace – once again sitting on the floor. We had thought the clamour of the Japanese audience incredible but that of the Koreans was even more over-whelming. They were very orderly, but obviously adored the art of song and have produced many fine young singers in recent years. Richard was very thrilled with some large Korean paintings which he bought and, along with some Japanese prints, they help decorate the Sydney apartment.

We left for Australia on June 14 and began rehearsals immediately for *Norma*, designed by Fiorella Mariani and produced by Sandro Sequi, with Richard also doing final rehearsals of *The Marriage of Figaro* and a new production of *Don Giovanni*. At the end of our first week there we went to the house at Whale Beach for the day, taking the two Italians with us to show them our beautiful coastline. Fiorella had the brilliant idea of adding a bedroom and bathroom over the top of the existing sitting-room and kitchen with a stair going up from the main floor. This was accomplished, with a music room on the other side of the upper floor, in due course. What started out as a weekend retreat has grown into an extremely comfortable dwelling, complete with cliff-top swimming pool.

Norma had not been heard in Australia for over sixty years. This production was very beautiful with a silvery-blue moonlit glow in the big 'Casta diva' scene and interesting costumes and sets generally. It was later televised and issued on video. We gave thirteen performances of the opera between July 5 and August 26 and I happily sang all of them. H. R. Forst's headline in the *Daily Telegraph* read: 'Just the part to show her voice of the century in its most startling aspects ... If you want to hear La Stupenda and what really has made her stupendous, this is the opera to choose.'

Brian Hoad, in *The Bulletin*, wrote:

... Sutherland masters the dramatic and vocal complexities to perfection ... The vast humanity she radiates seems to fire the whole production. It is the sort of magical performance rarely found even in a lifetime of opera going. It is the sort of performance which left its audience for the most part dumbfounded, precipitating one of the wildest receptions the Sydney Opera House has ever witnessed or is likely to for a long time.

Roger Covell wrote in the *Sydney Morning Herald*:

Sutherland impersonates her always as a woman strong in passion but never a monster or a tigress. The womanliness is in her manner and above all, in a voice as beautiful as it is sure and agile. Don't miss *Norma* if you care about opera. It is a rare opportunity to see and hear the greatest living interpreter of the part in an inimitable performance.

Before Fiorella and Sandro went back to Italy we had a little dinner party for them at the apartment on Potts Point. Other guests were Leona Mitchell, Jack Metz, Moffatt Oxenbould, Graeme Ewer and Sharolyn Kimmorley. There was much laughter before and during the meal, after which someone suggested a few silly childish games, one of which was Stack. This required everyone to lie one on top of the other in a pile on the floor, which they did, laughing hilariously. Sharolyn and Leona would have been the smallest and Jack's roly-poly figure was quite a problem. As the stack fell apart in a sea of arms and legs Leona remarked in her wonderful Southern drawl, 'You are retarded!' She was undoubtedly right.

There were many social functions and interviews both for the press and television during this stay in Sydney, making each week very full, but I always kept completely free the night before my performances and the whole of the day leading up to them. This, I'm sure, made it possible for me to fulfil my obligation to the Company – and the public. I spent the quiet days making curtains for the sitting- and dining-rooms at Whale Beach.

The new *Don Giovanni* opened on July 19 and Ric conducted eight performances. James Morris made his Australian début as the Don, Joan Carden was Donna Anna, Lone Koppel-Winther Elvira, Isobel Buchanan Zerlina, Henri Wilden Ottavio, Neil Warren-Smith Leporello, Donald Shanks the Commendatore and Lyndon Terracini Masetto. George Ogilvie was the director, with sets by Hugh Coleman and costumes by Kristian Fredrikson.

In the *Sydney Morning Herald* Roger Covell wrote:

> ... Casting from strength, the Company has brought together musical director, voices, production and design in one of the major successes of its performing career. ... Richard Bonynge and the Elizabethan Sydney orchestra began the evening auspiciously on Wednesday with a well-shaped overture. Singing and playing from then on registered Bonynge's direction with a distinctive eloquence and care for detail. The plaintive orchestral phrases in the accompanied recitative for Elvira's 'Mi tradi' sang with languishing affection. Overripe? I do not think so.

Already Richard was rehearsing John Copley's new production of *La Traviata* designed by Henry Bardon with costumes by Michael Stennett in which I appeared the following year. This time, however, it was the vehicle for Kiri Te Kanawa's début as Violetta looking and sounding just right.

How Richard managed to fit in a concert at Chalwin Castle (alas no longer standing) with his principal string players (Ladislav Jasek, Pamela Munks, Irena Morozov and Hans Gyors) I don't know. The group rehearsed at the apartment a few times with Richard enjoying so much playing chamber music again. The programme included the Mozart G Minor Quartet, the Schubert B flat Trio and the Schumann Quintet in E flat. Earlier, on August 13, we had given a recital for the National Lieder Society of Australia in the Opera House, my opening number being the glorious Mozart Concert Aria 'Non temer amato bene'. I think Richard was probably preparing himself for the Chalwin Castle concert by including that aria, giving his fingers plenty of exercise.

We were very sorry to say farewell to Lone Koppel who had been a strong member of the Company for some years, singing unforgettable performances of Marie in *Wozzeck*, Jenůfa, and Jenny in *Mahagonny*. She went back to her home theatre in Copenhagen, returning to Sydney from time to time to give a few of her great dramatic interpretations.

As I only had performances of *Norma* and these were well spaced, I accepted many invitations to social functions which Ric could not attend due to all his commitments with the Company. Although I quite enjoyed the various parties that is not really the life for me. I couldn't abide the life of a social butterfly, flitting from one gathering to another day after day. I am much happier entertaining a few friends at home – or reading a good book.

In April of 1978 Hamilton McClymont succeeded Barry Thompson as General Manager of the Vancouver Opera. Richard had realised his lack of availability to that Company and accepted the title of 'Consulting' Artistic Director. He had completed casting for the 1978–9 season and his contract was due to expire in 1980. Whatever the problems that had arisen during his time with the Company, he had certainly managed to present some very interesting artists and performances and had the initiative to inaugurate the Vancouver Opera Orchestra. He was happy to have had the experience with the Company and appreciated the support he received from members of the community there.

During September we had several house guests and I was glad that Richard was home again after his last *Traviata* on 10 September. He needed to relax and catch his breath for the next round of events. He had recorded in Brisbane a Mozart disc with Isobel Buchanan, John Pringle and the Queensland Symphony Orchestra, as well as coping with his very heavy season in Sydney. Now he was able to enjoy the company of our friends and we even made a short excursion to Italy to stay with Douglas and Ailsa Gamley at their house in San Bartolomeo di Andora, after which there was a further steady flow of visitors to the chalet.

Richard was back in Australia by October 21 to conduct the performances of *Nabucco* in Adelaide and Melbourne with Rita Hunter which were such a success for her, also for Robert Allman as Nabucco.

I remained at the chalet studying my Wagner arias, due to be recorded in London at the end of November after *Suor Angelica*, and some Mozart arias. Ric and I arrived in London on November 16 – he from Australia and I from Switzerland, with recording beginning on the eighteenth. 'L'amero' and 'Ach, ich fühl's' were the first two pieces and we worked steadily at Kingsway Hall recording practically every day until we left on December 2 for Amsterdam.

We were fortunate in *Suor Angelica* to have Christa Ludwig giving a powerful performance as the Princess, Anne Collins was the Abbess, Elizabeth Connell the Monitress, Enid Hartle the Mistress of the Novices, Isobel Buchanan Sister Genovieffa and Marie McLaughlin Sister Osmina. Della Jones was Sister Dolcina and Janet Price the Nursing Sister. Although we did not have the benefit of a long rehearsal period, as for the theatre, the rapport between the group was evident when the recording was released. However, I never felt we reached the same pitch of atmospheric feeling as the staged performance – a common shortcoming of the sterile recording studio.

On November 26 we performed at the Royal Opera House in the inaugural gala concert of the Australian Musical Foundation in London in the presence of HRH The Prince of Wales. With us were John Williams, John Brecknock, Yvonne Kenny, Gregory Dempsey, Jonathan Summers and Malcolm King. Richard and Douglas Gamley conducted the orchestra of the Royal Opera House and the narrator was Dame Edna Everage. Prince Charles asked kindly after Norm (Dame Edna's husband), to be told he was in hospital in Sydney waiting for a donor for a prostate transplant. 'Don't look at me,' the Prince is reported to have replied quickly, adding with a big smile, 'Never on Sunday.'

On December 2 we took an evening flight to Amsterdam where we began rehearsals for *Norma* at the Circustheater in Scheveningen, opening on the fourteenth in Amsterdam, with further performances in Scheveningen, Rotterdam and Utrecht. It was during this series of performances that I experienced one of my most embarrassing vocal moments. Between my big entrance recitative and commencing 'Casta diva' I turned upstage to cut a mistletoe branch and took the opportunity to clear a little phlegm before beginning the aria. To my horror I croaked the opening words – I hadn't cleared my throat but had lodged the phlegm securely like a veil or web right across it. I really sounded like a broody hen. After the first two words I stopped singing, shrugged my shoulders, loudly *did* clear the obstruction and continued singing without further problems. There was more applause that night than ever for the aria.

Unfortunately, it is always possible for this to happen – one is only human. The thing to do in such a case normally is to 'sing through' the little unwelcome guest. For this reason singers warm up (hopefully only a little) in their dressing-rooms before their entrance on stage. However, the opening phrase of 'Casta diva' is quite low in the voice and sung very softly, and there was no way I could have regained the purity of tone without doing what I did. Some of my colleagues have had much harsher treatment – especially tenors – and have withdrawn from performances because of the cruel audience reaction to similar problems.

It was announced in the New Year Honours List that I had been made a Dame Commander of the British Empire – the third Australian singer so honoured. The first was Nellie Melba in 1919, then Joan Hammond in 1974. We had known beforehand but had kept quiet about it, as requested, so there were several celebrations held on both sides of the Atlantic – and the Equator in due course. I was thrilled by such recognition but also felt I had even more to live up to.

After the last *Norma* in Holland Richard left for New York to rehearse

Werther at the Met and I flew home to Les Avants – with Amsterdam airport in chaos due to a howling, icy blizzard. Sharolyn Kimmorley was with me and we kept hearing that Richard's plane was further delayed. Whereas he had been due to leave well before us, we boarded our flight not knowing if he would take off. The wind was so strong, with so much ice, that the walkways couldn't be used and we had to trudge from the terminal to the plane through the gate. One gentleman carrying a bulky 'baby bag' had to chase after bibs and jackets which flew from the partly open bag. Richard actually took off just in front of us and we were happy to get away finally.

I only stayed home for four days, long enough to make sure that all was well, see Adam briefly and fly to New York on January 7 – with clothing for the summer in Australia, as well as a couple of weeks in the US and Canada. Ric was well into rehearsal at the Met and we gave a recital in Philadelphia at the Academy of Music on the eleventh, followed by one in Toronto at Massey Hall.

Back again to New York for the long-awaited 'Great Performers at Lincoln Center' concert with Luciano, Ric and myself. There was a huge amount of publicity for this event, with joint and personal coverage in the newspapers about our early lives and future plans. Some of the New York press broached the subject of my cancellation (many months in advance) of the proposed performances by me at the Met of Constanze in *Il Seraglio*. Although I had wanted to sing the role much earlier in my career for Glyndebourne, I had been deemed 'too big' for the production on their stage! Some twenty years later I was asked to do a long run of the opera (about thirteen performances) at the Met, plus the tour. After studying the role carefully for some time I felt I was unable to sustain the tessitura for so many performances in a large house like the Met (and some of the tour venues) without problems and possible last-minute cancellations. So Ric and I thought it was better to withdraw, giving plenty of time to find a replacement. The Met then, seemingly out of pique, cancelled performances of *The Merry Widow* which had been agreed upon and the *Semiramide* production planned with Marilyn Horne – with the management saying the three productions had been a 'Package Deal'. There had been no mention of this to us but the result of the situation was that I did not perform an opera at the Met between the end of March 1978 and the beginning of November 1982.

Richard had his opening night of Massenet's *Werther* at the Met on January 18 with Alfredo Kraus as Werther, Régine Crespin as Charlotte and a demure Kathleen Battle as Sophie. The production was by Paul-Emile Deiber with sets and costumes by Rudolf Heinrich. It was the first time Richard had conducted the work and he received a great deal of praise. The *Christian Science Monitor*'s Thor Eckert Jr said:

Richard Bonynge, in one of his rare appearances without wife Joan Sutherland, brought the final touch of authenticity to this revival. He understands the smouldering style of the score, and the continuous fabric of near-eruptions. The effect, particularly with a cast so keen on intimacy, was steeped in the tradition Mr Bonynge so completely understands.

Ruthli and Rachel arrived on Saturday, January 20 and attended the 'Live from Lincoln Center' concert with Luciano on Monday the twenty-second. The audience for this event was bristling with excitement – and members of every opera, concert and symphony management, together with conductors who could get there. It was like giving a mammoth audition. There was so much light for the TV cameras that Luciano and I could pick out and name everyone to more than half-way down the body of the hall. After our first number we begged that the lighting be dimmed a little.

What a success that concert had, the initial one of several the two of us did together, as well as the wonderful one when Marilyn Horne joined us. The coverage in the American press was enormous, with the use of every superlative in the book. The headlines were ecstatic:

PERFECT MATING OF PURE SOUND

TWO VOICES IN ONE

JOAN, LUCIANO AT THEIR BEST

THEY COULD HAVE SUNG ALL NIGHT

OPERA FANS GO WILD

Harold Schonberg, in the *New York Times* of January 23, wrote the review of a lifetime for us all:

... Joan Sutherland and Luciano Pavarotti have appeared together on the operatic stage, but joint recitals of this calibre cannot be bought in every five-and-dime. They had an orchestra, expertly conducted by Richard Bonynge, to support them, and they went through a standard segment of the Italian and French literature, singing solos and duets.

They are stars; and stars cannot get to be stars unless they have something unique to offer. What both of these singers offer in abundant measure is voice, voice, voice...

... and there is not a pair of singers alive who could have matched this prodigal outpouring of voice. They enjoy singing with each other, and they were stimulated by the enthusiasm of the audience, which did everything but tear up the seats in its excitement. Neither singer did anything to upstage the other, they had confidence in their voices, and enough confidence in each other to blend together and take rhythmic liberties to maximum effect. It also should be said that Mr Bonynge was with them, as soloists and duettists, every inch of the way. And so it was a triumph for both. This is what Italian Opera is all about: a maximum of voice coupled to musical taste, and it is given to very few singers of any generation to have it. There have been reports that an official of the Metropolitan Opera has said that the house could do very well without stars of the Sutherland–Pavarotti type. If that is a true statement, the man who said it is out of his ever-loving mind.

Whether it was Mr Schonberg's last remark that prompted a feeler from the Met to re-establish our good relations or not I cannot say, but such an approach was made with a clearing of the air and relaxing of the tension between us.

There has always been for me a great sense of excitement to be on stage participating with great voices, each one somehow sparking the others into even more fabulous vocal feats, and with the audience reaction as well, such evenings were exhilarating beyond measure and what we all hoped might be the outcome of our efforts. Certainly this concert was a night to remember! The performance has been issued on LP, CDs and video.

Udi and Rachel had been sitting right in the front of the hall and joined in the throwing of flowers on to the stage, forming a carpet, and the TV presentation was such a success that it was re-broadcast a week later. By this time, however, Udi, Rachel and I had flown to San Francisco for a few days *en route* to Sydney, where we arrived on January 29. Rehearsals for a revival of *The Merry Widow* began next day and Adam and Richard arrived later that week. The *Widow* opened on February 9 with eight further performances.

Towards the end of February I paid a visit to my old school (St Catherine's, Waverley) to give my name to the new Junior Library. There had been many improvements since my previous return there and I received a great welcome from the headmistress, teachers and the girls.

I attended some rehearsals for *La Traviata* during the last weeks of February and also sat for a portrait by Michael Stennett. Although known for his splendid costume designs he has always been very versatile, painting landscapes, still-life and portraits. Indeed, his designs for the theatre often bore the shape and visage of the interpreter of the character. He ultimately painted several portraits of me – as Violetta, Anna Glawari (*The Merry Widow*), Adriana Lecouvreur, Amina in *La Sonnambula*, as well as the large painting which depicts the whole family and household, including our dog.

We travelled to Melbourne the first weekend of March, after the final *Merry Widow*, and opened in *Traviata* at the large old Palais Theatre in St Kilda on March 10. The Palais capacity was 3000 and had apparently been sold out for some weeks, with scalpers asking up to $300 for a seat. The theatre was in poor condition, although I found the acoustics excellent. It was on a block of land between the Luna Park fun fair and the sea, and at times the roof was violently shaken by the wind. It was also possible to hear the screams of riders on the roller-coaster and other fairground noises. This added immensely to the atmosphere of carnival in the last act of one of our *Traviatas* but was not always quite so appropriate.

On March 14 I was most surprised to find myself the subject of the television show *This Is Your Life*. Adam, Ruthli and Rachel came down to Melbourne and Terry McEwen, Russell Braddon, Norman Ayrton and Margreta Elkins were flown in for the show. Marilyn Horne, Franco Zeffirelli and Luciano Pavarotti all appeared briefly on film. It was wonderful to see them all.

By this time, Adam had transferred from the Basel Hilton to the Sydney Hilton, from where he was moved to the Sydney Airport Hilton upon its opening. Here he spent several happy years in Food and Beverage Management. So we had the pleasure of his company whenever we were in Australia.

We flew to Brisbane on March 27 for four performances of *Norma*. I remember my dressing-room in this old theatre (Her Majesty's) for the tantalising aroma which wafted up from the pizzeria underneath. By the time of the last interval I was certainly looking forward to my supper.

The memory of these *Normas* always reminds me of the evening one of my 'children' became bored with just sitting quietly at my feet and started blowing raspberries fairly continuously during 'Mira, o Norma'. By patting and stroking his arm and shoulder I tried to distract him and was relieved when the time came for Clotilde to take him and his brother off. To the dismay of us all he went off imitating a steam train, 'choo-chooing' at every step. Our self-control was really put to the test.

While in Brisbane we managed to make a few excursions further north along the coast to see the beautiful beaches and to the town of Toowoombah. I also presented some prizes at the Queensland Conservatorium of Music, one recipient being Lisa Gasteen.

Back in Sydney we spent a little time at Whale Beach and saw the preview of Brian Adams's TV film *A Life on the Move*. Then we were 'on the move' again, back to Les Avants by April 14, where I was able to do some necessary springtime gardening for a week before we went to Paris for a recital on April 26 at the Paris Opéra, then to Munich for another at the Staatsoper.

We spent May Day in Stockholm walking in the old town and taking a canal trip, both to see something of the city and to shelter from the biting wind. The Old Town we found charming and had dinner there practically every evening of our stay. We visited Drottningholm and saw all the wonderfully preserved stage machinery in the old theatre. On May 6 we did a concert performance of *Lucia di Lammermoor* in the Konserthuset with the Swedish Radio Symphony Orchestra and a cast of fine singers. Graham Clarke sang the role of Edgardo and the young Gösta Winbergh was Arturo. During the performance our watches and my lovely Jenny Lind medallion were stolen from our dressing-room, causing much consternation to members of the management of the Hall and the Swedish Radio. Fortunately, they were ultimately retrieved by the Swedish police and returned to us. The newspapers reported that the performance 'made the Stockholmers behave like a Southern football audience'. We enjoyed our visit and returned on future occasions.

Back to Les Avants for a week, then by car to Asolo, where we gave a recital on May 14 in the Teatro Duse, my first appearance in Italy since 1972. We laid flowers on the grave of Eleonora Duse as a sign of our respect for her great art. One understood the attraction this lovely hill town held for her and other artists and writers such as Freya Stark.

Another week or so in Les Avants, then back to Sydney for the winter season there, with my first and only performances of Elettra in *Idomeneo*. Richard also had *Die Entführung aus dem Serail* and a new production of *The Queen of Spades*, as well as *Traviata* with Joan Carden. We did *Don Giovanni* in Melbourne, again at the Palais in St Kilda.

Earlier in the year a group of regular opera-goers asked that they be able to form a Joan Sutherland Society. Their aim was to encourage interest in our young singers and help them by raising money to provide grants or scholarships. They organised various functions and asked that Richard and I attend a relaxed dinner with them each year which we always enjoy. At the time of writing the Society still carries on its good work and its assistance is much appreciated.

The *Idomeneo* production was bought from the Victorian State Opera, designed by John Truscott and produced by Robin Lovejoy. Leona Mitchell sang a most beautiful Ilia, Margreta Elkins was Idamante and Ronald Stevens and Sergei Baigildin both sang Idomeneo. I very much enjoyed singing Elettra and was sorry that due to the illness of both our tenors on July 10 we only did seven performances instead of the eight planned. There was no third person able to sing a role like Idomeneo at such short notice – so the Company asked me to sing in a performance of *La Traviata* instead. This I did, with nobody having any time for rehearsal, except that we had all been together in Melbourne earlier in the year. It has been hailed as the best *Traviata* we ever did in Sydney. Everyone was on top form with an audience reaction that really sizzled and spurred us all on to do better.

Roger Covell wrote:

... the Company's work came together with exceptional decisiveness and urgency. Sutherland sang with phenomenal accuracy and brilliance ... her partners responded memorably to the challenge of the occasion.

... Richard Bonynge's direction was full of character and strength. The evening was a personal triumph for him.

Maria Prerauer in *The Australian* headed her report:

JOAN IS SHEER JOY!

She sang like some angelic visitation from on high. She could scarcely have been more impressive or unleashed more ravishing tones if she had been preparing for a month.

... Honours should also go to tenor Anson Austin and baritone Robert Allman for likewise jumping in as her true love and his heavy Victorian papa.

Roger Covell wrote in the *Herald*: '... As always, such a dramatic challenge brings out the athletic best in Sutherland. Her rapid notes whizz past in perfect formation, yet with tone of a size and quality that are truly heroic.'

The following week Richard opened the run of seven performances of *The Queen of Spades* in Sydney. This was produced, as in Vancouver, by Regina Resnik in sets by Arbit Blatas. Rosina Raisbeck sang the role of the Countess for most of the season with Regina herself singing the last three before the Company moved on to Adelaide. Marilyn Richardson sang Lisa, with Gregory Dempsey as Ghermann. John Pringle sang Tomsky and Gregory Yurisich Yeletsky. Richard very much enjoyed the preparation of the work, appreciating Regina's great insight and ability to impart her enthusiasm and understanding of it to all the cast. I found it an extremely compelling performance with incredible dramatic peaks and overall tension not always experienced in the opera house.

On July 24 Richard, his mother and I flew to Canberra for a private investiture and luncheon at Government House there. The Governor-General, Sir Zelman Cowen, as the Queens' representative in Australia, 'invested' me with the insignia of Dame Commander of the Order of the British Empire, after which we had a very pleasant lunch with His Excellency and Lady Cowen, together with the Chairman of the Australian Opera, Charles Berg, and his wife, Robyn, all flying back to Sydney early in the afternoon as Richard had a performance of *The Queen of Spades* that night.

On July 29 we flew to Melbourne and opened at the Palais in *Don Giovanni* on August 4 with a further five performances. With so little rehearsal it was as well I had revised the role of Donna Anna the previous year for the Met.

I went to see a performance by Les Ballets Trokadero de Monte Carlo at the Princess Theatre. The troupe was an all-male company and I'd wanted to see them for some time, as Peter Anastos was a long-time fan of mine and I had heard so much about their clever adaptations. I had a great laugh, and was photographed with some of their 'ballerinas'.

By August 20 we were back at the chalet and off to London on the twenty-fifth to record in Kingsway Hall Massenet's *Le Roi de Lahore* with Luis Lima as Alim (the King of Lahore), Sherrill Milnes as Scindia, Nicolai Ghiaurov as Indra, James Morris as Timour (the High Priest) and Huguette Tourangeau as Kaled. Richard and I were very pleased that Decca decided to record this opera and with such a fine cast. We were both glad we had done the staged performances in Vancouver and Seattle which gave us a more dramatic conception of the work and helped to enliven the discs.

A quick trip to Les Avants, then to Glasgow, where we did one of our recitals at the Theatre Royal.

Back to New York on September 23 for another of the 'Live from Lincoln Center' concerts – this time with Marilyn Horne and myself. As well, Richard had rehearsals and performances of *Werther* at the Met and we did a recital at Ann Arbor, Michigan, and another in Cincinnati, Ohio. Richard was flying back and forth to New York for his rehearsals at the Met and his performances there which began on October 6. There were also press conferences and TV interviews with Jackie (Marilyn Horne) and orchestral rehearsals for the Avery Fisher Hall concert which took place on Monday, October 15. This was another resounding success with Jackie and me doing our 'party pieces'. The headlines read:

SUTHERLAND, HORNE DAZZLE THE AUDIENCE

BRAVO! BELLA! BRAVA!

A GLORIOUS REUNION

SUTHERLAND & HORNE: TOGETHER!

Not only were the fans in the audience impressed but the critics were full of praise for our 'togetherness', seemingly unimpaired since we were heard together nearly ten years previously singing *Norma* at the Met – and again the concert was televised. How fortunate we have been to have such visual as well as sound recordings of our performances.

The following day it was Richard's and my Silver Wedding anniversary and we could hardly believe that twenty-five years had gone by since that day in 1954, both of us wondering then what the future held in store. Now that we have experienced our Ruby anniversary the wonders of the past *forty* years flash by ... What thrills we have shared, what friends, what travels, what love and generosity – how fortunate we have been!

During 1979 our great Wagnerian soprano, Marjorie Lawrence, died aged seventy-one and we remembered her with great affection and admiration of her fortitude after being stricken by polio in 1941.

Time certainly never stood still and on October 18 we left for Switzerland, then for London to re-record *La Traviata*. This was the first digital *Traviata* to be issued and, I believe, became the first CD opera issued by Decca. The quality of the sound was very striking in its clarity and, of course, the lack of surface noise. I must say, at the ripe old age of fifty-three I felt some trepidation as to the reception my second Violetta might get. However, I was agreeably surprised and happy with the press reports (some of which were laced with superlatives) and even reasonably pleased with the overall performance myself.

After the final session we flew direct to Adelaide, South Australia, where Richard had the opening night of *The Queen of Spades* the following Saturday, with three more performances there. Chester came with us as usual and we rented a pleasant apartment in North Adelaide for our stay in the city on tour with the Australian Opera. On November 22 we opened in *The Merry Widow* and also performed one of our operatic concerts with the whole Company participating in aid of Children's Medical Research. We always enjoyed visiting Adelaide as there are some excellent antique shops and wonderful wine country not too distant from the city, which has many fine buildings of Adelaide Sandstone and well-kept parks and gardens.

We travelled to Melbourne and opened in the *Widow* on December 6, the first of five performances. Ric had three *Queen of Spades* performances, as well as readings for *The Magic Flute*. Tired, but very happy, we flew to Switzerland on December 16 giving us a very full week of shopping and organising for Christmas and our usual influx of guests for the holiday period. We had been very reliant on our charming secretary, Tessa Trench, during this busy year and appreciated her thoughtful attention to the many books and scores on the shelves. She has continued to mend, clean and polish them for us although she is now working full time in England. She had worked for Decca in London and we had known her there before she joined our gypsy life, back and forth with us to the United States and Australia, catching up with her family in England whenever possible.

ON THE FIRST day of 1980 we were off to London for our second recording of Bellini's *La Sonnambula* beginning in Kingsway Hall the next day. This version was with Luciano as Elvino, Ghiaurov as the Count, Della Jones as Teresa and Isobel Buchanan as Lisa. I was shocked to realise that the previous Decca discs of the opera had been made in Florence almost twenty years before.

We were back in Les Avants by the evening of January 10, having a brief five days there before flying to Sydney on the sixteenth. We spent a quiet weekend at Whale Beach and began rehearsing for the Australian Opera's new production of *Lucia di Lammermoor* on Monday, January 20. The Australian audiences had eagerly awaited performances of this opera and were not disappointed in the production by John Copley in sets designed by Henry Bardon and costumes by Michael Stennett. The original performances were in the Concert Hall of the Sydney Opera House with its superior acoustic and were a huge success.

There were some twenty-two performances of *Lucia* during that year – eight in this summer season in Sydney and six in the winter, with four in Adelaide and four in the Melbourne Palais during the Company tour. Not only were the sets and costumes very fine, but the whole cast's make-up had been devised and supervised by Charles Elson, a superb make-up and wig specialist from New York. He had worked for several of the companies in America where I had sung, and he came to Sydney, with his assistant Dennis Beaugevin, to provide the whole Company with a revitalised approach to their make-up. I had never looked more glamorous – even the critics noticed. Maria Prerauer, in *The Australian* of February 7, wrote:

> ... Her stunning performance of the Mad Scene stopped the show for five minutes as the audience shouted and applauded.
>
> Dame Joan sang as Sydney has never heard her. And she looked superb – like a young and radiant girl.

The following day, on the Arts page of the same newspaper, Maria Prerauer gave a further review of the opening night:

... As her luscious voice effortlessly soared, swooped, pounced and trilled like a lark on the wing she could have been at the triumphant beginning of a brand new career rather than just about to celebrate her 21st anniversary [in the role].

Her vocal riches could perhaps have been expected. The surprise was her physical transfiguration (there seems no other phrase for it) into a radiant young Scots girl ... She seems to have found the secret of turning back the clock.

During the run of these performances Richard conducted six *Magic Flutes*, with five more during the winter season in August–September.

One of my engagements during February was a luncheon on the nineteenth celebrating the seventy-fifth anniversary of Rotary International at which I was presented with the Sydney Club's 1980 Award for Vocational Service by the Governor of New South Wales, Sir Roden Cutler. This beautifully printed citation and the accompanying medallion remain an important part of my collection of awards and honours.

We spent as much time as possible between shows at Whale Beach and left Sydney on March 3, taking the Concorde on its short-lived service to London from Singapore. Neither Richard nor I enjoyed this flight and we can well understand that it was very soon scrapped. Although the speed of the plane took several hours off the flying time it was far too cramped for such a lengthy journey. One large passenger (an ex-wrestler) was unable to extricate himself from the lavatory, requiring verbal assistance from the cabin staff which finally released him – just prior to the removal of the door.

Rehearsals for the Covent Garden production of *Lucrezia Borgia* began almost immediately. The week before, Brian Adams's documentary *A Life on the Move* was shown – the product of being trailed half-way around the world for months by him and his camera crew. Intended to whet the viewers' appetite for the BBC opera transmission of *Borgia*, it also brought me an extra mound of fan mail. However, the miles of film had been cleverly cut by Brian into an entertaining video and Richard and I were quite pleased with it.

Lucrezia Borgia had not been seen at Covent Garden for over ninety years and there was consequently a great deal of anticipation. As always, I was happy to be at the Royal Opera House and also to be working again with Alfredo Kraus with whom I had done so many performances in Europe and the United States.

The opening night of the opera was a Gala in aid of the Royal Opera House Benevolent Fund and the Development Appeal Fund in the presence of Her Majesty Queen Elizabeth The Queen Mother, accompanied by the Prince of Wales. Her Majesty rather admired my last-act coronet – beautifully made theatrical paste – whilst hers glittered with real diamonds.

The public loved the whole production and were very welcoming to me at all seven performances. The critics were also warmed and stirred by the piece, with much talk of the 'melodic' and 'tuneful' music which is so difficult to equate with the historical 'viper' so many believed Lucrezia to have been. The revival of the opera was deemed a huge success and it remains the performance most favoured by the majority of Sutherland fans at the Garden. I was presented by Sir John Tooley with my silver Royal Opera House commemorative long-service medal at the conclusion of one of the performances.

After a pair of recitals in Stuttgart and Vienna we were off to Rome in the car for seven more performances of *Lucrezia Borgia* at the Rome Opera.

We rented a house in Velletri, a secluded villa with a beautiful garden in the countryside a good thirty or so kilometres south of Rome, beyond Castel Gandolfo where the Pope has his summer residence. I remember a lovely camellia tree laden with blossoms and, inside the house, china cats everywhere you looked. Between ourselves we called the house 'Pussy Palace' or 'Cat Castle' and laughed a lot at some of the more outrageous figures. Being used to all the Staffordshire figures in our own collection they didn't bother us overmuch – but it was difficult to find a space to set a coffee cup or drink.

There had been a strike at the Rome Opera by the corps de ballet earlier in the year during performances of *Giselle* with Rudolf Nureyev and Carla Fracci, and another of the chorus in May, forcing the theatre to cancel altogether a performance of *Simon Boccanegra*. The opening night of *Lucrezia Borgia* on May 15 was another opportunity for the disgruntled chorus to express its displeasure. All the soloists were dressed and ready, and a quarter of an hour before curtain-up it was probable that the opera would be performed *without* the chorus. About three minutes to go and an announcement was made to that effect. This prompted the chorus to change their minds and the performance went ahead with everybody somewhat distracted by the uncertainties of the evening. The audience was glad to be entertained after all and greeted the opera with vociferous applause and many flowers thrown from boxes and balconies. In spite of the problems it was declared a triumph.

We had friends in Rome like Sandro Sequi, Fiorella Mariani and Heinz Riva, also Michael Stennett who not only was adjusting costumes for the *Borgia* cast but was full of his forthcoming trip to Australia, having designed the costumes for the AO's *I Masnadieri* production in July of 1980. It was good to be able to spend time with them. Although I had just picked up some new clothes from Hardy Amies while in

London, I ordered some more outfits from Heinz and had great pleasure attending fittings at his atelier on the Piazza di Spagna and enjoying his company shopping or lunching together.

The Australian Ambassador and Mrs Robertson held a splendid reception at the Embassy on May 31 after that night's performance and on Monday, June 2 we went to a matinée performance given by Michael Aspinall in our honour which was great fun – a send-up of *all* 'Prima Donnas'.

Chester drove Richard and myself to Rome airport where we joined a flight to Hong Kong connecting with the Qantas flight to Sydney, arriving in time to spend a weekend at Whale Beach. Richard then flew to Melbourne to record and we settled into rehearsals for Verdi's *I Masnadieri*.

Chester was travelling back to Les Avants from Rome with the car, before joining us in Sydney together with Tessa Trench on June 9. Only Tessa arrived, as Chester was involved in an accident with a bus in Piacenza and was hospitalised for some days. Fortunately he had already checked in to a hotel and the owner was extremely helpful as the Volvo wagon was a write-off and Chester could speak little or no Italian. Dear Heinz Riva drove up from Rome to visit him and help, and some of his co-patients were apparently very friendly in spite of the language barrier. Chester actually rented a car and drove back to Les Avants when he was released from hospital as there was so much baggage he said he couldn't manage it on to a train. He had a nasty wound on his head, having hit and cut it on the rear-vision mirror. We felt he should have rested longer in Piacenza but he said he couldn't wait to get away. Ruthli had been relaying messages to and from us and was very worried until he reached the chalet – and continued to worry until we were able to telephone and assure her he had ultimately arrived safely in Sydney.

The accident had been caused by an overgrown tree blocking a STOP sign at the intersection. In a strange town at dusk the sign was completely invisible and the bus had hit the passenger side of the car, spinning it round and concussing Chester. He laughed over the Italian police telling him they *had* to fine him although they knew the sign was obscured – the princely sum of 2000 lire. Apparently a woman had been involved in an accident at the same spot during the previous week and nothing had been done about the tree. Good for his pocket but no salve to Chester's hurt pride at never having had a major accident all the years he'd been driving.

Rehearsals were going ahead for *I Masnadieri* and we took every possible opportunity of going to Whale Beach at the weekends. Adam was a frequent visitor, arriving late after his work at the Hilton Hotel. He had by this time acquired his first car, a natty second-hand Alfa

Romeo which he loved, hating eventually to part with it for something more accommodating for a wife and family.

The producer of *I Masnadieri* was Peter Beauvais who had made such an impression with his handling of the Hamburg *Lucia* and he created some of the same atmosphere with the awkward libretto of this Verdi piece. The cast was very well chosen and I was happy finally to sing with Australia's great tenor Donald Smith. In some thirty years of our careers in Europe and Australia we had never been in the same production at the same time. Donald Smith was cast as Carlo, Robert Allman as his scheming brother Francesco, Clifford Grant was their father Massimiliano and Bruce Martin sang the role of Moser the Pastor. With sets by Allen Lees and Michael Stennett's costumes it was the opera chosen to celebrate the tenth anniversary of the Australian Opera with a Gala performance on July 2, 1980.

Unfortunately there was a flu virus doing the rounds of the Company but although I had a brief attack during rehearsals I was recovered in time for the opening. Not so Robert Allman who was decidedly unwell, with Donald Smith also not feeling on top form. The first night went very well in spite of this, but by the third performance Donald Smith had to retire after the first act and Paul Ferris finished the opera that night. Paul was the official 'cover' for the role of Carlo and although he had studied the music he had never rehearsed on stage. He managed exceptionally well, sewn into Donald's costumes, the defects covered by a cloak. His main worry, he said, was the pistol he was supposed to fire at a given point. Be that as it may, the audience appreciated his saving the show, as did the rest of those on stage. The following Monday's *I Masnadieri* (July 14) was cancelled completely and reinstated on August 5 so as not to disappoint subscribers. With all the illnesses and replacements we managed to fulfil the remaining nine shows with Paul Ferris courageously singing Carlo's role – a part that was vocally too heavy for him but he coped very well.

Of my own performance, W. L. Hoffmann of the *Canberra Times*, after pointing out the fact that it was the first time I had made my début in a major role in Australia, wrote:

The special qualities which Verdi wrote into the role of Amalia for Jenny Lind particularly suit Joan Sutherland's voice, and she was right at the top of her form. Her first aria 'Lo sguardo avea degli angeli' was sung with such refinement, ease and beauty as to stir the audience into an enthusiastic response, a reaction which was repeated many times during the evening ... Richard Bonynge conducted, with excellent control of the musical disparity between the first two acts, which are typical early-Verdi, and the final acts which look forward to his later style. He obtained fine playing from the Elizabethan Trust Orchestra – the ovation that he received individually at the end showed that Sydney opera goers at least recognise the musical quality he has brought to the Australian Opera as its Musical Director over the past four years.

During the same period as *I Masnadieri* was on Richard was also conducting nine performances of *Rigoletto* with Joan Carden, Raymond Myers, Anson Austin, Bruce Martin, Donald Shanks and Heather Begg.

We had a hilarious dinner with Leona Mitchell and husband Elmer at their apartment – Leona was singing in *Manon Lescaut* with the Company. There were several charity functions to attend, the Joan Sutherland Society dinner and we managed to see that clever duo of Hinge and Brackett who had so amused us on television. We had a laugh-filled meeting backstage. I also visited a Benedictine convent where I was entertained at a delicious tea party by the kindly and scholarly sisters. There was a quick trip to Canberra too, to accept my Honorary Doctorate of Laws from the Australian National University on August 7.

We did six *Lucias* during this winter season between August 22 and September 6, and Richard rehearsed an almost complete cast change for the revival of the 1977 *Fra Diavolo* production – then conducted a couple of performances before flying to join me in San Diego.

As General Director of the San Diego Opera at that time, Tito Capobianco had asked Beverly Sills and myself to alternate the roles of Rosalinde and Adele in his production of *Die Fledermaus* in October of 1980 and we had both thought it a fun idea. Beverly planned these as her last appearances, her commitment as General Director of the New York City Opera leaving her no time to perform. She had sung both roles during her lengthy career, whilst I had only sung Rosalinde, although I vaguely knew Adele's arias having heard them so often.

We rented a house by the sea – a charming bungalow complete with swimming pool high on the rocks of La Jolla with a spectacular view. We loved it – and were able to use it again on a later visit.

There was consternation when Tito Capobianco learned that, due to Union problems at the New York City Opera, Beverly would have to do at least six round trips from New York to San Diego between September 26 and October 19 – right through the final rehearsals and the four listed performances plus the Gala Benefit matinée. The stress of the commutes and important meetings was enough, without having to rehearse not one but two major roles. Beverly was game enough but it was decided that we each stay with the one character throughout the run. 'Why couldn't I have known this before I worried and fretted to learn Adele!' was my first thought, but then I was greatly relieved to know that I only had to remember Rosalinde's words and music. It meant I could relax and enjoy the whole experience much more than if we'd chopped and changed – and I'm sure Beverly felt the same.

We had barely met previously and all enjoyed each other's company very much. Ric and Beverly are both crossword addicts and compared their timings completing the NY Times's daily puzzle, Ric coming in second – which he set about changing. Without several books of these puzzle reprints he never goes on a long trip, getting very cranky if they run out before he manages to replenish his stock. They are his answer to my needlepoint.

We had another friendly cast with Giuseppe Campora as Alfred, Alan Titus Eisenstein, Joseph Frank Dr Blind, Jake Gardner Dr Falke, Spiro Malas Frank, Regina Resnik Prince Orlofsky and Leonard Frey Frosch. Tito had worked with Beverly a great deal during his years at the New York City Opera and, of course, with Ric and me on several occasions. Regina Resnik was also a friend from Covent Garden days in the early 1950s and Spiro Malas always a happy-go-lucky, warm-hearted colleague and family friend. Together with Alan Titus we got along famously, with many laughs between and during rehearsals.

It was Richard's fiftieth birthday on September 29 and Tito organised rehearsals so that we could all meet for a celebration dinner on the evening of Sunday the twenty-eighth – Ric's actual birthday had rehearsals morning, afternoon and evening.

How Beverly managed to appear so calm and collected during that very taxing time I don't know. Doubtless her years of experience and disciplined approach to her work helped get her through.

The opening *Fledermaus* was a 2.30 p.m. Gala Benefit on October 5, followed by a Gala Dinner Party in the ballroom of the lovely old Hotel del Coronado

In honor of Beverly Sills and Joan Sutherland
(alphabetically speaking)

according to the invitation. It certainly was a sparkling evening with champagne flowing both on stage and at the dinner, where Beverly and I were each presented with a large and very heavy cut-crystal bowl.

The five performances of Strauss's bubbly operetta were a huge success. Of course the press and the fans had been eagerly awaiting the 'Duel of the Divas' as Martin Bernheimer of the *Los Angeles Times* headed his critique. In fact, one feels they were all amazed that the only sparks that flew were those generated by Beverly, myself and the rest of the cast, firing the whole show with the gaiety and fun which set the audience laughing until they cried. The expected 'rivalry' had always been in the minds of the opera-goers because both Beverly and myself had sung so much of the same repertoire over the years and each had our staunch followers. What the public saw at those rollicking shows was how we truly felt, and we – and they – loved it.

Whereas there is often a surprise number at Orlofsky's party (the *Don Quixote pas de deux* on these occasions) at the end of the gala who should walk on to the stage but Sherrill Milnes to give a tribute to Beverly and myself – and to sing the fabulous Drinking Song from Thomas's *Hamlet*, the role with which he would enchant Australian opera-goers in 1982.

The critics' headlines were mostly akin to those of Martin Bernheimer's:

BELOVED DIVAS TRIUMPHANT IN *FLEDERMAUS*

SOPRANOS MAKE A 'DREAM TEAM'

SUTHERLAND, SILLS REALLY HIT IT OFF

SILLS/SUTHERLAND: THE PAIR A DUO AT LAST

But some of them remarked:

... This production of *Fledermaus* was intended mainly as an opportunity to hear two great sopranos – Sills for the last time. *Fledermaus* is a fun creation. It is meant to allow the audience to have a good time and leave the theatre humming the melodies to those beautiful Strauss waltzes. The audience left the Civic Theatre having enjoyed itself, humming the Strauss melodies – and knowing it had witnessed something historic.

The whole run in San Diego was a delight and our admiration for Beverly as a person and artist grew with each performance. She was so happy, although nostalgic to be retiring from the stage, and I began to consider more seriously my own thoughts of doing likewise.

During the preceding two years, arrangements had been made by Eric Gustafson to exhibit some fifty of my personal costumes at the New York Public Library at Lincoln Center in their main gallery. Barbara Matera spent a great deal of time helping to show the beautiful gowns to advantage, together with their accessories and many of the original designs. The exhibition was called 'Designs for a Prima Donna: Dame Joan Sutherland' and ran from October 7 to December 12, but although the reports of it were very favourable, I will always regret I was unable to make the trip to New York to see it due to my commitments both in San Diego and immediately afterwards in Australia.

By this time Adam was already seeing a great deal of Helen Wahba, both at the Hilton where they were working and during their free time. They joined me at Whale Beach for the weekend and I flew to Melbourne on the Sunday where Richard was already taking rehearsals.

Our four *Lucias* and Ric's four *Rigolettos* were all well received in the old Palais Theatre, the *Lucia* cast remaining much the same, with Paul Ferris and Lamberto Furlan sharing the role of Edgardo. The opening *Lucia* on November 5 elicited superlatives from the critics regarding the state of my voice 'after 21 years in the artistic limelight' as John Sinclair wrote in the *Herald*:

... there was this marvellous voice, spinning a line with dream-like delicacy and a heart-breaking gentleness of tone and phrase.

... In the past I have heard her sing the role differently; more brilliantly at La Scala in 1961 and more impeccably in Melbourne in 1965. But never has she sung it so beautifully.

Last night her involvement in, and mastery of the role was so consummate that, for the first time, I felt that I had witnessed the performance of a very great artist.

Ian Hunt, in *The Australian*, wrote:

THE LEGEND CONTINUES

The Palais Theatre was packed for the long-awaited return to Melbourne of Joan Sutherland in the role which established her as a legend in her own time. Sutherland and Lucia have become synonymous in the world of opera...

With performances of *Lucia* on November 5, 8, 11 and 14 my birthday on the seventh was a reasonably quiet affair, but Adam and Helen came down to Melbourne for the weekend and we spent a little time together. I was made aware that Helen, too, was a Scorpio subject with her birthday ten days or so after mine. Ric and I liked her very much and were unsurprised and extremely happy when they later announced their intention to marry. We spent some pleasant hours with Lorraine and Peter Walker and their family during our stay and attended the launching of Brian Adams's biography *La Stupenda*, leaving for Adelaide on the sixteenth for a further four *Lucia* performances.

Boris Godunov was in the repertoire of the Australian Opera tour and Richard and I decided to go to see it again in Adelaide as we had enjoyed it so much in Sydney. During the Inn Scene the fowls, which had behaved well in Sydney when released through the window on to the set, were not so 'theatrical'. To quote from a passage in Richard's book *Joan Sutherland and Richard Bonynge with the Australian Opera*:

In fact, they kicked up an almighty ruckus during rehearsals so it was decided to sedate them. The sedative obviously had too strong an effect and when they were thrown through the window upstage they landed with a clunk like bags of cement. Halfway into the scene they began to show signs of life. Whenever tenor Gordon Wilcock sang, they squawked along. As the drug wore off they became more unruly and were all over the stage. Gordon, singing Missail, gave one of them a kick out of his way and all hell broke loose – there were fowls everywhere creating a fearful racket! Two of them flew off stage into the pit – one landed on the head of the first horn, who didn't miss a note, and the other at the foot of the conductor, Peter Seymour where it lay rather dazed. At the end of the act Peter left the pit carrying off his prize. I doubt the scene was ever applauded so vociferously.

We arrived back in Les Avants looking forward to Christmas and entertaining a series of house guests including Moffatt Oxenbould, Graeme Ewer, Peter Bloor – all friends from the Australian Opera. Dr Peter Newbold paid his customary Christmas visit and Sylvia Holford was another good-humoured guest, with Richard Toeman of the music publishing house of Josef Weinberger Limited in London paying a brief visit regarding the firm's forthcoming publication of the version of John Gay's *The Beggar's Opera* jointly devised by Richard and Douglas Gamley. This would be given its first airing by the Australian Opera in February 1981. Adam spent Christmas with us and it was at this time that Michael Stennett somehow managed to paint his large picture of the whole family and household including our dog, Asta. Not only were we all faithfully reproduced but a corner of our music room as well, with portraits on the walls of me in several roles, together with odd bits and pieces of memorabilia.

We flew to Sydney on January 3 with immediate rehearsals of *Otello*, a work I'd not done since the late Fifties at Covent Garden, and I had enjoyed re-studying it with Richard and Sylvia over Christmas. Angelo Marenzi sang the role of Otello, John Shaw and Robert Allman were Iago and I was happy to sing Desdemona again. George Ogilvie was the producer and the costumes were by Kristian Fredrikson. Carlo Felice Cillario conducted the ten Sydney performances in the Concert Hall of the Opera House.

Cillario has a great sense of humour and loves spending a portion of each year in Australia, having done an enormous amount for the Australian Opera musically. He continues to encourage the singers and orchestra and I've seldom seen him without a smile on his face – only when something (or someone) is incorrect during rehearsal or performance. I remember being on the receiving end of his smile during a performance of the big third-act ensemble in *Otello* whilst, with a turn of his head to the left, the smile changed to a glare at a couple of other singers who were meandering along, apparently oblivious of his beat and dragging the tempo. In a flash one of Carlo's hands pinched his nose, the other made the motion of pulling a lavatory chain, then his head quickly turned towards me again, his face wreathed in that seraphic smile. At such a dramatic point of the opera it was, perhaps, naughty but the miscreants got the message and paid attention hence-forth.

On another occasion during the run I had forgotten to wear flesh-coloured underwear and was sporting a pair of black, lace-trimmed panties. During the singing of the Willow Song in the last act the fastening on the cotton underskirt of the see-through nightie came undone and the underskirt fell to the ground. I stepped out of it and Heather Begg as Emilia scooped it up and carried it off on her exit. Left to sing the Ave Maria still wearing my voluminous cloak-like dressing-gown (which *should* have gone off with Emilia) I wondered what to do – take it off and run the risk of the black panties showing or go to bed with the heavy mantle still on? I did the latter and only one person (who'd been to a previous performance) made any comment.

Without our trusty Tessa Trench with us on that Sydney trip I fear there would have been many problems with forgetting appointments, rehearsal times, dinner engagements, etc. Richard not only had the rehearsals and performances of *The Beggar's Opera* to cope with but was travelling back and forth to Melbourne.

We managed to escape to the house at Whale Beach for most weekends even if there was a Saturday evening performance. Adam and Helen came whenever they could, as well as Ric's mother and aunts and various friends for lunch on Sundays. I also paid visits to the garden centres and plant nurseries near the house to help replenish the garden.

The Beggar's Opera opened on February 7, with ten performances in Sydney. The production was presented as the making of a film of the work in Hollywood during the Thirties, with some very clever sets and costumes by John Stoddart and directed by Anthony Besch. Half the Company appeared in this frolic and they and the audience enjoyed themselves immensely. The accompaniments had a decided flavour of a movie musical.

The critics were divided in their opinions but mostly in favour, particularly of the orchestrations of Douglas Gamley and the whole atmosphere achieved by Ric with the singers and orchestra. In the *Sydney Telegraph* Nadine Amadio wrote:

> *The Beggar's Opera* in Hollywood has come to the Opera House and the audience loves it. So they should. It's great entertainment and as a showpiece for the Australian Opera cast it underlines their extreme professionalism ... This time it has been 'Hollywoodised' and why not send up Tinsel City? It's as good a way of mocking man's vanity as satirising politicians or art trends.

Our last two performances for the summer season were on February 28 – mine of *Otello* and Ric's final *Beggar's Opera* – and we were off to

Europe next day. The only problem was a strike by the Qantas cabin crews; and we ended up going to Geneva via Fiji, Honolulu, San Francisco and Amsterdam, arriving on the evening of March 2. I had lengthy visits to my dentist over the next three days and we were in London by Friday evening, March 6, commencing recording *The Beggar's Opera* for Decca next day.

If the Australian Opera production was 'Hollywoodised', this recording came pretty close with the cast involved. Angela Lansbury was Mrs Peachum, with Alfred Marks as Mr Peachum and the gaoler, and Kiri Te Kanawa as Polly. James Morris sang Macheath, with Regina Resnik as Mrs Trapes, Stafford Dean as Lockit and myself as Lucy Lockit. Graham Clark was Matt, Anthony Rolfe Johnson Filch, Ann Murray sang Jenny Diver and Ann Wilkens was Dolly Trull, with John Gibbs as Jemmy Twitcher, Michael Hordern as the Player and Warren Mitchell as the Beggar and the Drawer. The orchestra was the National Philharmonic.

I flew straight to New York on March 12 when I had finished recording my pieces, having had a great time working with everyone, especially Angela Lansbury who was so worried about her singing. We singers all assured her *we* were worried about our dialogue, making us all square.

In New York we had our third 'Live from Lincoln Center' concert with both Marilyn Horne and Luciano Pavarotti scheduled for March 23. There was such a response at the box-office that a second concert was organised at 3 p.m. on the twentieth – the only time we could all be available together. Both concerts in Avery Fisher Hall were a riot, with prolonged applause for all of us. Apart from our usual repertoire we sang the trio finale from Act 4 of Verdi's *Ernani* with Marilyn Horne singing the baritone part of Don Carlo as had Marietta Alboni during the last century, and the trio 'La barca s'avvicina' from Act 4 of *La Gioconda* (Ponchielli). As an encore, the trio 'Angiol di pace' from Bellini's *Beatrice di Tenda* was sung after the allotted time for the broadcast – doubtless caused by the very prolonged applause during the evening. It was an interesting flash-back to include this piece from the opera in which Marilyn and I had both made our débuts in New York twenty years previously.

The event was thrilling for us all as participants, not just for the audience – there was that wonderful feeling of each voice acting as a charge to the others and generating great brilliance to the overall vocal sound. It was always a pleasure to sing with either Marilyn or Luciano, but to appear together in that way was something very special to us all, Richard as well. The resulting video and CD are there to remind us of a most spectacular night during our careers. Peter G. Davis in the *New York Times* wrote:

In its essentials, the concert could be heard as an old-fashioned glorification of the human voice, not as much as an instrument to achieve penetrating expressive ends but as a phenomenon to be wondered at for itself alone. Viewed in that light, perhaps these three singers did, after all, give us the concert of the century.

The whole venture had generated a great deal of excitement which was somewhat dulled by a ghastly 'gala party' – overcrowded and unbearably noisy – which Richard, myself and some of our friends left as quickly as possible. We were flying to Pittsburgh the next evening (March 24) with a rehearsal the following morning of a concert Luciano and I were giving with the Pittsburgh Symphony. The strain on the voice trying to talk above the disco noise level plus the jostling fans was too much for me with the Saturday concert in view and my own form of discretion was 'the better part of valour'.

The Pittsburgh concert was the usual mixture of duets and arias and, as always, I was struck by how much longer than the tenor arias mine were. But the audience and critics enjoyed the concert immensely with headlines reading:

PAVAROTTI AND SUTHERLAND: NOTHING SHORT OF SPECTACULAR

OPERATIC SUPERSTARS IN STUNNING TRIUMPH

We moved on the next day to Memphis, Tennessee, for a single performance of *La Traviata*. The day after on to Rock Hill, South Carolina – the scene of our American recital début twenty years previously – where I was given an honorary degree of Doctor of Music by the President of Winthrop College.

Next off to Toronto for six *Normas* with the Canadian Opera. Richard spent the first three days of rehearsal in bed with a heavy bout of flu aggravated by exhaustion, but Lotfi Mansouri kept the production rehearsals up to schedule until Ric was back on deck and the performances took place as planned. Adalgisa was sung by Tatiana Troyanos, Pollione by Francisco Ortiz and Oroveso by Justino Diaz. Although I had known Tatiana for ten years or so I had never actually sung with her. She had worked with Richard in *Werther* at the Met and we had met socially in Hamburg when we were there at the same time. She was a fascinating person with great senses of drama and fun, and I enjoyed working with her. It is hard to realise that this lovely artist is no longer with us, having succumbed to a pernicious cancer in 1993.

We spent a very pleasant month in Toronto, leaving immediately after the last performance for Los Angeles where we spent the night, travelling on to Melbourne via Auckland and Sydney. I had six performances of *Otello* with Cillario conducting again and Richard was conducting eight of *The Beggar's Opera*.

We had a small apartment and frequently visited friends in the Company and some of our old Melbourne friends including Lorraine and Peter Walker, Lady Tait, also John and Patricia Davies where I met Geoffrey Dutton and enjoyed his engaging conversation.

Then it was back to Sydney for some brush-up rehearsals of *La Traviata*. Richard was working very hard during the same period with seven *Traviatas*, nine performances of *Les Huguenots*, two of *Rigoletto* and three of *La Buona Figliuola*, as well as rehearsing the new production of Handel's *Alcina*.

La Traviata opened on June 17 and Maria Prerauer headed her review in *The Australian* with:

TRAVIATA IS DAME JOAN'S

All Sutherland has to do to enchant an audience is to stand there and open her mouth and let those radiant tones stream out – rich, creamy, velvety and wholly unique in quality. So compelling is the legendary magic of her magnificent soprano that she can still bring down the house by the sheer impact of her singing alone.

Roger Covell's headline read 'Violetta Compelling but hardly Consumptive', referring to my stature and physique, although I was still not quite recovered from my persistent nasal infection and felt decidedly ready for the sanatorium.

The opening night of Handel's *Alcina* was on June 26 between the third and fourth *Traviatas*. Sir Robert Helpmann produced the opera in sets and costumes of great beauty by John Pascoe, with Richard conducting. Complaints were voiced at the cost incurred (some three hundred thousand dollars) but it was worth every cent for the pleasure of looking at such dazzling elegance and hearing this astounding masterwork performed so faithfully and well by the totally Australian cast which included Joan Carden, Margreta Elkins, Heather Begg, Angela Denning, Anne-Maree McDonald, Paul Ferris and Donald Shanks. Richard received unstinted praise for his conducting of the work, as did John Pascoe for his settings and costumes, and Sir Robert for his knowledgeable production, eliciting from John Cargher in *The Age*: 'The Australian Ballet should not have allowed Sir Robert Helpmann to leave. Any producer capable of making a high-grade popular entertainment out of a Handel opera is nothing short of a genius.' Very true, in a way – but our previous experiences with Handel's masterworks had taught us that the composer's genius could carry an audience into ecstasies of delight, even without the visual trappings astounding the eyes.

I was particularly interested in the *Alcina* production as I was to perform in one of its revivals in 1983. Meanwhile, between the *Traviatas* and rehearsals for *Les Huguenots* I went house-hunting with Helen as she and Adam had announced their marriage plans, fixing on January 23, 1982 for that all-important event, and Richard and I wanted to give them their first home as our wedding present. We found a charming Federation house in Kensington which was ready to walk into and easy to maintain for a busy working couple.

June and July 1981 brought with them three and four performances a week for Richard plus rehearsals, and those for *Les Huguenots* were very concentrated. With such an immense work and a huge cast, it was a great credit to the Company that it could mount the opera at all, let alone in such a very busy season – with only one guest artist in Marilyn Zschau as the heroine Valentine. It was a grand performance designed by John Stoddart (sets) and Michael Stennett (costumes), directed by Lotfi Mansouri, which celebrated the twenty-fifth anniversary of the Company. Prior to the Dress Rehearsal the whole company assembled on stage for a slice of a huge cake and to drink a toast to the Company's past and future. The cake, a replica of the opera house with its 'sails' and long flights of steps, measured one and a half metres square. I plunged in the knife and watched the cake consumed rapidly by the 220 Australian Opera Company members – 200 more than initiated the then unnamed group twenty-five years previously in Adelaide. The Company had only borne the title of the Australian Opera for ten years.

The large cast, in order of appearance, consisted of:

Le Comte de Nevers	John Pringle
Tavannes	Paul Ferris
Thoré	Donald Lister
De Retz	Gregory Yurisich
Cossé	Ron Stevens
	Robin Donald (Aug. 18, 22)
Méru	John Fulford
Raoul de Nangis	Anson Austin
	Richard Greager (July 31, Aug. 5, 8, 11)
Marcel (Raoul's Huguenot servant)	Clifford Grant
Leonard (de Nevers's valet)	Melinda Sharman
Urbain (Marguerite's page)	Anne-Maree McDonald
	Judith Saliba (Aug. 11, 15, 18, 22)
Marguerite de Valois	Joan Sutherland
First maid of honour	Beryl Furlan

Second maid of honour	Rosemary Gunn
Valentine (daughter of de St Bris)	Marilyn Zschau
Le comte de St Bris	Bruce Martin
Bois-Rosé	John Murray
First young girl	Angela Denning
Second young girl	Judith Saliba
	Helen Borthwick (Aug. 11, 15, 18, 22)
First gypsy girl	Elizabeth Fretwell
	Nicola Waite (Aug. 18, 22)
Second gypsy girl	Lesley Stender
	Kathleen Moore (Aug. 11, 22)
Nightwatchman	Erik Badcock
First monk	John Antoniou
Second monk	Robert Eddie
Third monk	John Durham

Most of the critics appreciated the overall strength of the Company's effort in mounting so successfully this mammoth work. Brian Hoad wrote in *The Bulletin*:

... The singing, often excruciatingly difficult, is uniformly a delight. Sutherland is vocally immaculate and splendidly imperious ... *Les Huguenots* is an apt gesture on the part of the Company, on the occasion of its 25th Anniversary, to show just how far it has progressed musically.

There were, however, a few negative remarks in the press, Maria Prerauer complaining in *The Australian*:

For the money squandered on this superseded Victorian monstrosity the Australian Opera could have staged at least one Wagner *Ring* cycle music drama or *Tristan and Isolde* or *Parsifal*, or Strauss's *Elektra*.

Perhaps Maria was not feeling well at that time, as she gave another very caustic crit in the same newspaper to the performances later in the season of Piccinni's *La Buona Figliuola*, stating:

It is less an opera than an early (1760) ancestor of those empty musical comedies by Lortzing now blessedly exposed to public view only on German-speaking stages. Musically, the hurdy-gurdy score has about as much inspiration as a barrel-organ.

Les Huguenots was given nine times. There had been so much work for the wardrobe staff with all the anniversary productions that costumes were not always ready in time for dress rehearsals (a problem in *most* Companies) and I treasure a note from Bill Paterson, that very special cutter and fitter, addressed to 'Marguerite de Valois' and saying:

Herewith – one velvet gown. Am afraid collar isn't finished and train will have to be pinned.

Sorry it's not complete but I thought I had better throw a stitch or two into Marilyn [Zschau as Valentine].

Love Bill

At the end of the first week of August we were shocked and saddened by the horrible accident suffered by my half-brother Jim and his wife Fran. They were hit by a car which mounted the pavement at a pedestrian crossing, Fran being killed instantly and Jim sustaining terrible injuries to his limbs. I had spoken with Fran on the telephone only two evenings previously and found it hard to accept their daughter Ruth's frightful call with the news of the accident. My brother's recovery was very slow but he is possessed of an unshakeable faith and spirit and is still coping with the vagaries of his six very lofty offspring, their feats and follies. They have all done very well, especially in the fields of science and agriculture.

After the last *Huguenots* performance we were off the next day – Richard and Chester to San Francisco and Tessa Trench and myself to Les Avants. Richard was performing *Semiramide* in the much discussed Pier Luigi Pizzi 'all white' production and I had a month's break at home with friends visiting and some gardening and advance preparations for Christmas.

Richard's performances of *Semiramide* opened on September with Montserrat Caballé in the title role, Marilyn Horne as Arsace and James Morris in his San Francisco Opera début as Assur. I arrived in San Francisco on 19 September, in time for the matinée next day, and was very amused by Montserrat's outrageously lofty wig and the male soloists' costumes which appeared to consist of a mantelpiece on the shoulders with a pepper pot for a hat. The vocal prowess of those three was never in doubt. It was a delight for me to sit in the audience and listen to that grand music after having sung it so often myself.

The rehearsals for *The Merry Widow* began on September 21 with Lotfi Mansouri directing his production from the Canadian Opera Company. The cast was a very jolly one, with several old friends involved, notably Phil Stark as Baron Zeta, Judith Forst as Valencienne, Anson Austin as Camille de Rosillon and Håkan Hagegård as Danilo. A polished performance brought glowing reviews from most of the critics. There were one or two who raised the question as to whether *The Widow* was really opera house fare – somewhat ridiculous in view of the nine sold-out houses. Of course, the plot is 'frivolous', the situations nostalgic and nothing to do with today's world – thanks be! – but the music transports us to that more gracious way of living and weaves its magic spell long before we hear of the nymph Vilia.

Of my own performance Richard Pontgious of the *San Francisco Examiner* wrote:

> No finer romantic and playful diva could he [Lotfi Mansouri as Director] have than Joan Sutherland, whose regal Anna Glawari may be without peer. Sutherland's vocal and theatrical expressiveness are enchanting. She carries herself lightly, plays seemingly spontaneously with the dialogue, and wins reactions from her audience with a simple turn of the head, the lift of an eyebrow, a knowing smile.

Alongside this and other reviews of similar vein in my press book was a rather vitriolic one delivered by Donna Perlmutter of the *Los Angeles Herald Examiner*, saying (among another nine or ten paragraphs of personal slaughter):

> Everyone knows that La Sutherland has old-fashioned prima donna proportions, is about as agile as a behemoth and no longer looks young enough to portray the luscious, young thing that Mae Murray, then Jeanette MacDonald and finally Lana Turner realized on the silver screen.

I wonder what this lady thinks of some of our current young singers of 'old-fashioned prima donna proportions' while still in their thirties? She was most careful to point out that I was fifty-five at the time. I'd had the opportunity of hearing several of those 'old-fashioned' ladies who sang like angels compared to the forced, un-focused, wobbly, out-of-tune voices of far too many singers today with Hollywood proportions – and otherwise.

Among the many notes of good wishes in my dressing-room that first night was one from the Lighting Director of the show, Joan Sullivan, saying:

> I had the privilege of working on another production in which you sang – a *Lucia* in Chicago in 1975. It was my second season in professional opera. I remember vividly an evening performance after a night crew and a daytime dress rehearsal of another production. During the scene change into the fountain scene, while I was checking your lights, you asked me to express your thanks to the crew for being there doing your show in spite of our extreme fatigue. Now, six years and many productions later, it is my turn to thank you for enriching this production of *The Merry Widow* with your talent and grace. It has made my job a joy.
>
> My sincere best wishes for a successful opening.
>
> (signed) Joan Sullivan
Lighting Designer

On October 17 Richard and I flew to San Diego to participate in a Gala Benefit Concert for the San Diego Symphony sponsored by the San Diego Opera. The concert raised some $41,275 from ticket sales and helped to sustain the orchestra through a bad financial period. Sadly, as I write, they are again in trouble, in fact disbanded – temporarily we hope.

We returned to San Francisco the next day to complete our *Merry Widow* dates – the last we would do during the regime of Kurt Herbert Adler. Retiring after thirty-eight years as General Director of the San Francisco Opera, he managed to arrange a final season featuring many of the artists he had supported in their early years in America, Richard and myself included. Leontyne Price, Nilsson, Pavarotti, Caballé, Horne, Domingo, Berganza and many others appeared, and the season was a fitting tribute to his years of holding a tight rein on the Company.

On November 15 Richard flew to Geneva and Tessa, Chester and myself to New York. Tessa's help had been invaluable during this trip and she continued to sort out affairs in New York for a few days while I took the shuttle to Washington on the evening of the third to appear in the 'Gala Tribute to George London' the next day at Kennedy Center. After he stopped singing in 1967, George became the first artistic administrator of the Center and later was head of the Washington Opera. While touring Germany in this capacity in 1977, he suffered severe brain damage as a result of cardiac arrest and required constant nursing and daily physiotherapy. This gala concert was to raise funds for the then newly formed Opera Singers' Disability Fund which would contribute to George's care and provide medical assistance to other handicapped singers. Nora London, George's lovely wife, had been totally responsible for his care and was greatly involved with the organisation of the concert. I sang Donna Anna with George in the first Vancouver Festival of 1958. He was already a great international star and I have never forgotten how helpful and encouraging he was to me, then virtually unknown outside Britain and Australia. At the end of the concert a TV excerpt from a 1964 *Bell Telephone Hour* was shown of George London singing the final scene from *Boris Godunov* – his 'mightiest' role. Sadly George was unable to be present, but I was assured in a charming letter from Nora that he would watch a film of the whole evening the very next day. Three hundred thousand dollars was raised.

A two-week break in Les Avants was a busy one, catching up on mail and preparing for performances of *Il Trovatore* at Covent Garden. Adam and Helen arrived for a stay of five weeks and made a few short trips to other parts of Europe. One of these was to Rome, where Helen had final fittings for her wedding gown with Heinz Riva, who had promised Adam he would make his chosen bride's gown as a wedding present several years previously. The gown – and that for her attendant and flower girl, Rachel – came back to Les Avants on the train with the 'lovebirds' and both were packed up for the trip to Sydney.

As Giorgetta in *Il Tabarro*, 1952 – the end of year performance which helped me gain a contract at the Royal Opera House.

As Clotilde, my first Bellini role, in *Norma*, Covent Garden, 1952, with Maria Callas and Ebe Stignani.

(left) As the Countess, in *The Marriage of Figaro*, Covent Garden, 1953.

(below) As Frasquita in *Carmen*, Covent Garden, 1953/4.

(left) Richard playing the
harpsichord continuo in the
Alcina performances at
La Fenice, 1960.

(below) With Dino Dondi
in Bellini's *Beatrice di Tenda*,
La Scala, Milan, 1961.

a Scala
gliani
irica 1960 61

in "BEATRICE DI TENDA"

(above) *La Fille du Régiment*, Covent Garden, 1966, with Spiro Malas and Luciano Pavarotti.

(below) Singing with Marilyn Horne in *Norma* at Covent Garden, 1967.

(above) *Rodelinda* in Amsterdam, 1973, with Huguette Tourangeau as Bertarido.

(below) Singing the Czardas at Orlofsky's Party, *Fledermaus*, San Francisco, 1973.

(above) Violetta in *La Traviata* at Covent Garden, 1975.

(below left) The Australian Opera *Lakmé*, 1976, with Huguette Tourangeau as Malika.

(below right) As Esclarmonde at the Met, 1976.

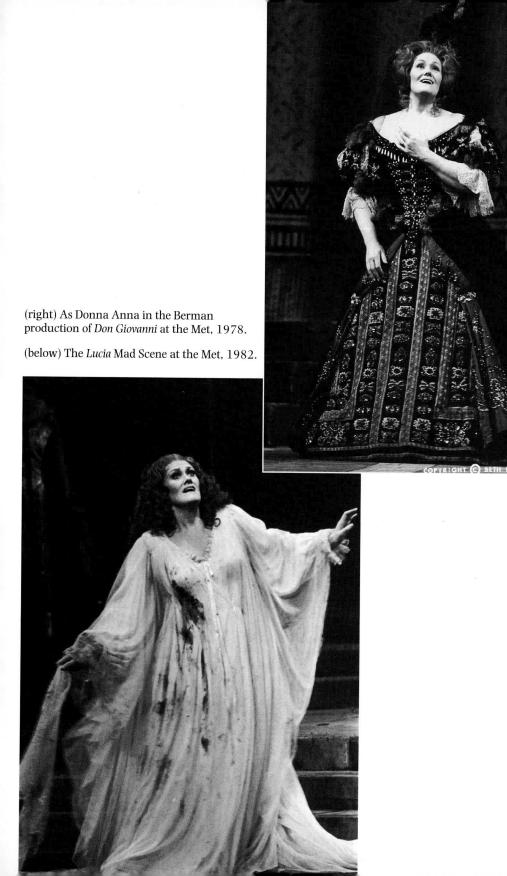

(right) As Donna Anna in the Berman production of *Don Giovanni* at the Met, 1978.

(below) The *Lucia* Mad Scene at the Met, 1982.

Australian Opera's *Alcina*, 1983, with Margreta Elkins and the bearers.

With Margreta Elkins after a performance of 'Mira, o Norma' in the concert hall of the Sydney Opera House, February 1983.

(left) *Semiramide*, the 1983 Australian Opera production, with Bruce Martin as Assur.

(right) The 1983 Met production of *La Fille du Régiment*, with Alfredo Kraus, left, and Ara Berberian.

(below) Adriana's denunciation in *Adriana Lecouvreur* for Australian Opera, 1984.

The 1984 Canadian Opera production of *Anna Bolena*, with Judith Forst as Jane Seymour.

As Olympia with Graeme Ewer as Cochenille in the Australian Opera 1984 production of *The Tales of Hoffman*.

Curtain calls with Ric after *The Merry Widow* in Sydney, 1988.

On Our Selection cast at Kate's wedding. Back row: Noah Taylor (Joe),
Geoffrey Rush (Dave), Murray Bartlett (Sandy), Essie Davis (Kate),
Celia Ireland (Sarah), Cathy Campbell (Lily), Pat Bishop (Maude White).
Front row: Robert Menzies (Cranky Jack), Leo McKern (Dad),
me (Mother), David Field (Dan).

(left) The magnificent
Australian Opera
farewell.

(right) The Covent
Garden farewell,
New Year's Eve 1990.
Left to right: Louis Otey,
Marilyn Horne, Ric, me,
Luciano Pavarotti and
Nancy Gustafson.

On November 24 we flew to London and rehearsals at Covent Garden began the next day. The day after I was conferred by Her Majesty Queen Elizabeth The Queen Mother with a Fellowship of the Royal College of Music. As President of the College, the Queen Mother also presented the diploma of the Honorary Degree of Doctor of Music to His Royal Highness The Prince of Wales. There was a phenomenal group of recipients of the FRCM with me that afternoon – Denis Arnold, Julian Bream, Sir Geraint Evans, Reginald Goodall, Alexander Goehr, Marie Goossens, Lorin Maazel. It was quite a jolly affair, with a fine concert featuring some of the students. I especially remember the playing of the young clarinettist Michael Collins. We had tea with the Queen Mother who was in great form.

During rehearsals for *Il Trovatore* in a concert to aid the Australian Musical Foundation at the Royal Opera House, I had the pleasure to appear with the Australian pianist Eileen Joyce and the violinist Stéphane Grappelli.

The sets for *Il Trovatore* were designed by Filippo Sanjust in a production originally by Luchino Visconti dating from seventeen years before. Michael Stennett had designed beautiful costumes for me and I found the sets the most believable and workable of any of the *Trovatore* productions in which I was involved. Yuri Masurok was Count di Luna, Franco Bonisolli Manrico with Elena Obratsova Azucena. Chris Renshaw restaged the opera. During rehearsal I begged Franco to be *sure* to help me to my feet after pleading with the Count in the Act 1 trio – otherwise I would have to stay there until the curtain fell. My knees were not giving me the necessary leverage to raise myself and the quite heavy costume without some support. He usually forgot.

In the *Guardian*, Edward Greenfield wrote:

With her husband guiding her from the orchestra pit Dame Joan rose to the occasion with the bigness which marks her out as a diva of the grandest possible tradition. Her critics can quibble about this or that detail, but Dame Joan still combines dramatic weight, sheer size as well as beauty of voice, with range and control plus dazzling flexibility of coloratura (with added decorations) to have one forgetting the years.

A rather funny photograph of Bonisolli and myself appeared in *The Times* on 4 December with the caption: 'Joan Sutherland and Placido Domingo at the London Opera Centre rehearsing *Il Trovatore*.'

We had many social engagements during our time in London, one very happy occasion being the West End Theatre Awards on December 6 at the Café Royal, at which Richard and I presented the Opera Awards. A reception was held by the High Commissioner for Australia and Mrs Garland at Australia House, followed by a dinner party at their residence in Hyde Park Gate, and we got to see a host of our friends very informally. There were the usual demands for interviews for press, radio and television and, very important to me, fittings with dear Lilian of Hardy Amies for my ensemble to be worn at Helen's and Adam's wedding.

We spent a very happy Christmas in Les Avants with Helen and Adam, who left for Sydney on the twenty-seventh, to prepare themselves for their wedding on January 23.

Ruthli, her husband Jean-Paul and Rachel were already in Sydney when we arrived and we began immediately to organise the house and garden for the wedding reception just a couple of weeks away. We had a short rehearsal period for *Lucrezia Borgia* and the Triple Bill that Ric was also doing of Shield's *Rosina* and Offenbach's *Ba-ta-clan*, together with William Walton's *The Bear*, this last conducted by David Kram – quite varied entertainment on one night.

At the end of that week the Australian Opera had planned a concert performance of *La Traviata* in the Sydney Domain as part of the Festival of Sydney. This was the first of many such free events each summer in the open air, but the original date of January 16 was rained out and the concert took place two days later with the weather still rather unstable and stormy. In fact, after Act 2 there was such a downpour that we thought the last act would be cancelled so changed into our street clothes, only to be told that the show would continue in spite of the wet grass and anxiety of the orchestra that their instruments might suffer damage – there was next to no overhead protection for the stage. This problem on-stage was rectified for succeeding years and many thousands attended each concert, bringing their picnic baskets and rugs to spread on the grass.

The day for the wedding, Saturday, January 23, arrived and great was the excitement. The ceremony was held at St John's, Darlinghurst, one of Sydney's oldest churches, which looked lovely decorated with white roses, lilies, carnations and tuberoses. Helen's bouquet was of the same flowers (without lilies) and the whole bridal group wore either white, pale grey or beige, with Rachel in a mini replica of Helen's gown in pale pink with a wreath of tiny pink roses on her head. There were not very many guests – about seventy, I think – and after several photographs outside St John's we all drove to Whale Beach where the caterers had everything under control. We had been told we were crazy to have an outdoor reception at the end of January as it always rained, but we were very lucky and just a few drops fell from a passing cloud late in the afternoon. It was the happiest occasion, after which the newly-weds left for their honeymoon on one of the islands off the Queensland coast and we stayed at the beach for the rest of the weekend to catch our breath.

The first *Lucrezia Borgia* was on February 3 and the 1977 production had been rebuilt for the Concert Hall, giving it an extra grandeur and a more opulent and exciting acoustic. There were ten performances and Roger Covell wrote: 'She could keep this role in her repertoire for another ten years.' In fact, I *did* sing Lucrezia seven years later in Barcelona and Paris.

There was an anti-Donizetti outburst from John Carmody of the *National Times* stating:

Donizetti writes like a student who has just discovered the diminished seventh chord. What other justification – other than the glorification of Joan Sutherland – can the Australian Opera possibly have for doing such an inferior, unimportant piece?

Richard also rehearsed and conducted four performances of *Norma* during this Sydney season with Rita Hunter as the Druid Priestess. I much admired the quality, size and agility of her voice. I went to Rita's dressing-room during the Dress Rehearsal and was amazed to find her demolishing a huge plate (it looked like a whole loaf) of white bread sandwiches. When I exclaimed 'How *can* you, and then sing?' her placid reply was something to the effect of 'It's a big role and I've got to keep my strength up – it's a long time before I get my dinner!'

We went to Whale Beach every possible weekend and Adam and Helen came most times, cooking for us on our last night there.

We gave a recital on March 9 for the Western Australian Opera Company in the Perth Concert Hall which was recorded for TV and later sold as a video. Richard had never been to Perth and I had not been to that fair city of the West for over thirty years. We both wished we'd had more time to enjoy it and its beautiful surrounding countryside but we were off to Europe the day after the recital.

After a week in Switzerland we flew to Stockholm to do a concert for the Swedish Radio of *Lucrezia Borgia*. Gennaro was sung by Gösta Winbergh, Maffio Orsini by Doris Soffel and Don Alfonso by Ulrik Cold. The visit was over all too soon and we flew to London the day after the concert to record *I Masnadieri* in Kingsway Hall. The male roles were sung by Franco Bonisolli as Carlo, Samuel Ramey as Massimiliano and Matteo Manuguerra as Francesco. I had found Bonisolli quite a funny character but during the recording sessions he was obsessed with the idea that 'his enemies' (presumably Pavarotti and Domingo) were endeavouring to undermine his abilities by sabotaging his sessions. This was by making the hall 'too hot', 'too draughty', 'too noisy' by turn, giving Decca's crew – and the orchestra – a few problems. At least he sang well.

Richard remained in London recording *Les Sylphides* and the *Hamlet* ballet music, travelling to Venice on the eighth, where I joined him the same day from Switzerland in time to freshen up and attend a civic reception in the Doge's Palace. The Associazione 'Omaggio a Venezia' had organised a concert dedicated to the great nineteenth-century prima donna Maria Malibran to be performed in the charming theatre named after her – because, by not accepting a fee for her performance of *La Sonnambula* in the House (then the Teatro Emeronittio), she saved the theatre manager from bankruptcy. In gratitude the theatre immediately became the Teatro Malibran.

A beautiful souvenir programme had been devised by Bruno Tosi with parallel biographies of Malibran and myself, noting the fact that our concert on April 9, 1982 was only one day later than Malibran's appearance in the same theatre (on April 8) 147 years previously. We both had phenomenal success with two Bellini roles – Amina in *La Sonnambula* and *Norma* – together with Donna Anna in *Don Giovanni* and the title roles in *Maria Stuarda* and *Semiramide*. Arias from most of these works were included in the programme, together with Susanna's 'Deh, vieni non tardar' (Malibran sang Susanna) from *Le Nozze di Figaro*, and a piece written by Malibran herself 'Le beau page'. Between the vocal pieces were three 'Souvenirs dramatiques' composed by Charles de Beriot (1802–70), a highly successful violinist of his day and husband of Maria Malibran.

The theatre was in chaos when Richard and I arrived for a camera–sound test (the whole evening was televised by RAI) with cables and lights tangled up in a mass of floral garlands and decorators – there seemed no possibility of the House being in order in time for the concert. But, in true Italian fashion, all was relatively calm by evening and the concert proceeded. It was followed by a dinner at the Hotel Cipriani – 'ore 23.15 circa' to quote the invitation, but it was *much* later due to the Easter holiday canal traffic no doubt. Some old friends were present and we were happy to be greeted by Renata Tebaldi looking as beautiful as ever, also our friends Regina Resnik and her husband Arbit Blatas.

The following day we were driven to Genoa, where we gave a recital in the Teatro Margherita on Easter Monday, April 12, of arias from works of Mozart, Rossini, Donizetti, Bellini, Verdi, Meyerbeer, Gounod and Massenet. Simone Alaimo assisted, singing four bass-baritone arias.

Then it was off to Amsterdam for rehearsals for *Lucia di Lammermoor* beginning the next day at 10.30 a.m. Once again we spent a good deal of time criss-crossing Holland for rehearsals and performances, as well as quite a lot of sightseeing. On this visit the opera opened in Amsterdam at the Stadsschouwburg on April 29 for three performances, then played in the Circustheater, Scheveningen for two more, followed by Utrecht, Eindhoven, Rotterdam and back to Amsterdam for a final two. Richard had to be in Australia for rehearsals of

Thomas's *Hamlet*, so the last three *Lucia* performances were conducted by Stuart Challender.

We had some pleasant outings with Chester driving us to Keukenhof where the bulbs were in full bloom. I ordered an enormous number for the garden in Les Avants, forgetting that I had very little time to plant them in October.

I joined Richard in Sydney on June 3, where Sherrill Milnes came from New York to sing the title role in *Hamlet*. A fine cast of Australian singers had been prepared by the Company's music staff and their hard-working French language coach Marie-Claire. Unfortunately, Joan Carden who was to have sung Ophélie was involved in a serious car accident, and this gave a great opportunity to young Jennifer McGregor, who thoroughly enchanted the public and press, giving her best performances in the Company to that date. Lotfi Mansouri produced the opera in sets by Alan Lees, costumes by Desmond Digby and choreography by Robert Ray. The cast was very strong, with Heather Begg as the Queen, Bruce Martin as Claudius, Richard Greager as Laërte, Robin Donald sang Marcellus, John Fulford Horatio, Clifford Grant the Ghost, John Wegner Polonius, with Gordon Wilcock and John Germain as the grave-diggers.

There had been severe criticism of the Australian Opera for mounting this opera based on old reports of performances, but the critics – or most of them – admitted their surprise at finding the work really good theatre. Roger Covell summed up his critique with 'Thomas's Hamlet is worth reviving and well worth attending.' I more than agreed with him, experiencing a wonderful night at the opera with all the characters, from Sherrill and Jennifer right through to the grave-diggers, giving sterling performances.

I had been rehearsing for the new production of Johann Strauss's *Die Fledermaus* since my arrival in Sydney and, as always, enjoying it immensely. Anthony Besch was the producer, with designs by John Stoddart. I was not very happy with the period of his costume – the 'apron and bustle' look with, for me, a much-too-short bodice giving a high, hard waistline and a far too long appearance to the skirt. A few changes were made and I ultimately wore some of my own comfortable gowns from America.

There were twelve performances and partly a double cast, with Robert Gard and Ronald Stevens playing Eisenstein, Anson Austin and Paul Ferris as Alfred, Monique Brynnel and Jennifer McGregor as Adele, Orlofsky was sung by Heather Begg, Blind by Gordon Wilcock, Falke by Michael Lewis, Frank by Gregory Yurisich and Frosch by Graeme Ewer. The ABC television-FM radio simulcast on July 10 was viewed by an estimated 2.5 million and a mound of 45,000 letters were sent to the Australian Opera requesting souvenir programmes and expressing the viewers' appreciation of the opportunity to watch 'Live from the Opera House'. This response from all over Australia resulted in the continuing practice of opera simulcasts, and the subsequent issuing of video cassettes of the performances.

After the last *Fledermaus* on August 4 I flew back to Switzerland, while Richard remained in Sydney for a few more days to complete his eight performances of Massenet's *Manon* which had opened on July 17 with Glenys Fowles in the title role.

We had a pleasant three weeks in Les Avants studying *Adriana Lecouvreur* and revising *Alcina*, before departing at the end of August for San Francisco and seven performances of *Norma*. The production was that from 1972, re-staged by Lotfi Mansouri with Marilyn Horne singing Adalgisa – the last time we performed together in those roles. It was also the Company's first season under the General Directorship of Terence McEwen. Ezio Flagello sang Oroveso and Ermanno Mauro Pollione.

The newspaper headlines proclaimed:

A *NORMA* TO JOIN WITH THE LEGENDS

SUTHERLAND, HORNE SET STANDARD IN *NORMA*

BONYNGE CONDUCTS ORCHESTRA TO GLORIFY VOICES, EMPHASIZE THE DRAMA

A TRIUMPHANT NIGHT AT THE OPERA

NORMA SHIMMERS WITH VOCAL EXCITEMENT

The *San Francisco Examiner* critic (Richard Pontgious) wrote:

... Sutherland's 'Casta diva' so excited the jammed Opera House crowd that the ensuing cheers and applause interrupted the performance for several minutes. Her duet with Horne 'Mira, o Norma' brought down the house.

I received a lovely letter from Kate Regan of the *San Francisco Chronicle*:

Dear Miss Sutherland,

Your performance in yesterday's *Norma* was one of the superb experiences of my life. It was more than marvelous in itself: it illuminated for me, not an opera aficionado, all the possible magic of the art. *Now* I understand! Of course, the friend who accompanied me warned, 'It'll be a long time before you hear anything like that again.'

Your performance in the third act had, for me, the sweep and nobility and inevitable tragedy of Greek theater. I began by thinking how intelligent your singing and acting, then simply was lost in the drama, suspense and beauty of your presentation. And, of course, your voice and Miss Horne's blend so exquisitely, that the first and second acts, especially the duets were thrilling.

Thank you so much.

Sincerely,

(signed) Kate Regan
Critics Department

There was a four-day break between shows in September which enabled us to enjoy a trip to Lake Tahoe and various places *en route* with our friends the Jacks. One stop was the huge and outrageously decorated MGM Casino where we gained and lost a few dollars on the one-armed bandits. But the Californian and Nevada countryside was breath-taking – always a joy for us when visiting the West Coast.

On October 3 we returned to Les Avants, where Richard held some pre-rehearsals for the cast of *La Sonnambula* which he was to conduct at the San Carlo in Naples in December–January. The rehearsal time was so short then that the leading singers agreed to come and work with him at home. I met Cecilia Gasdia (Amina) for the first time and had the pleasure of seeing my old friend Sandro Sequi who was to produce the opera. I enjoyed listening to the young people work, while endeavouring to plant most of the bulbs I had ordered from Keukenhof. I was particularly impressed by Gasdia's fresh, pure sound, her musicality and quality of voice.

On October 12 we flew to London where we performed in a gala concert at the Royal Opera House, celebrating the thirtieth anniversary of my first appearance there. I had excellent support from Doris Soffel and Jonathan Summers in a programme which delighted the audience. Edward Greenfield wrote in the *Guardian*:

Magic and professionalism...

Joan Sutherland's whole career has been a supreme demonstration of the two together...

After the dazzling display earlier with coloratura of such agility and precision still there to amaze in so big and warm a voice – the spun lines of legato [in 'Io son l'umile ancella'] were heartachingly beautiful. Adriana may modestly finish with the thought that, 'my voice is no more than a breath that with every new day must die' but few breaths could be more memorable than this!

Next day it was an early start (an 8.45 a.m. pick-up by Charlie) for the airport and a flight to New York. However, instead of leaving at 11 a.m. the plane was delayed until about 2.45 p.m. which made the trip seem very long and tiring. At least we had a day to recover before beginning rehearsals on October 20 for the Met and a gala concert for the Richard Tucker Foundation in Carnegie Hall on Sunday the twenty-fourth. The Foundation to perpetuate the memory of America's great tenor provides financial support to young singers, the chief grant being the Richard Tucker Award which is given annually to promising young Americans who already have had a certain amount of performing experience. The winners up to the time of this 1982 concert had been Rockwell Blake, Diana Soviero, Barry McCauley and J. Patrick Raftery, all of whom profited greatly from the award.

Thomas Fulton shared with Richard the conducting of arias and duets given by Giuseppe Giacomini, Alfredo Kraus, Sherrill Milnes, Roberta Peters, Paul Plishka, Olivia Stapp, Shirley Verrett and myself, with Grace Bumbry as the Mistress of Ceremonies. The concert was simultaneously broadcast live. It was a happy night and a fitting tribute to Richard Tucker's memory.

Rehearsing the revival of *Lucia di Lammermoor* continued in earnest the following day for my return to the Met after an absence of five years or so. Once again Alfredo Kraus was singing with me as Edgardo, with Pablo Elvira as Enrico, Paul Plishka as Raimondo and Ariel Bybee (who had sung with me in *Maria Stuarda* in San Francisco in 1971) as Alisa. There were some changes of cast during the run of eleven performances with Brian Schexnayder replacing Pablo Elvira, James Morris singing Raimondo and Dano Raffanti the last two Edgardos.

The press was loud in its praise and the audiences even more so with very prolonged applause. As Harriet Johnson wrote in the *New York Post*:

> Miss Sutherland received so many and such prolonged ovations – one irrepressible fan yelled 'Welcome back!' shortly after she appeared – that the opera hadn't even begun the final scene at the time it was all supposed to be over.

From Thor Eckert Jr:

> Miss Sutherland sings with all the agility and style one remembers, with the timbre and the range virtually intact, only a certain caution reminding us that it was more than 20 years ago that she exploded on to the New York opera scene with her electrifying Met début in the same role. She maintains, in her way, the high standards set then, and to this day there has been no one who can sing this music in so large-scale, so glorious and virtuoso a fashion.

Other headlines read:

SUTHERLAND KNOCKS 'EM DEAD AT THE MET

DAME JOAN DAZZLES

SUTHERLAND MAGNIFICENT

and many more in like vein.

With a stay of nearly two months in New York we had time to visit many friends including Spiro Malas and family on Shelter Island, the Chapins, the Materas for my birthday weekend at Athens (NY) and many other colleagues who were resident or passing through the city. There was the Metropolitan Opera Guild Annual Luncheon on November 3 at the Waldorf Astoria at which I was Guest of Honor and received a charming gift – an eight-inch-high Steuben glass koala bear – from the Chairman, Lawrence (Larry) Lovett.

Michael Stennett was a visitor to new York and we went together to the Museum of the City of New York for the Worth Exhibition, the Met Museum where the magnificent Belle Epoque gowns were on display and also to the Charles James exhibit at the Brooklyn Museum, all of great beauty and interest to both of us.

On December 14 I flew back to Switzerland, with Richard going to Naples for *La Sonnambula*. Ruthli and I prepared for the customary festivities and Richard flew in late-afternoon on Christmas Eve, going back to Naples on the twenty-seventh to complete his five *Sonnambulas* at the San Carlo. Chester and I flew to Australia on the thirtieth, being met at the airport by my daughter-in-law Helen who was already pregnant, the baby being expected at the end of April or early May 1983. Richard flew in from Naples on January 5 and the round of rehearsals began again for a very busy eight weeks in Sydney.

The 'Opera in the Park' *Fledermaus* was a huge success, with the audience being spared the downpour of the previous year until after the concert. As the guest at Orlofsky's party in Act 2 Leonie Rysanek sang 'Meine Lippen Sie küssen so heiss' from Lehár's *Giuditta*. Leonie was appearing with the Australian Opera as Tosca at the time and we happily reminisced over our days in the Fifties and Sixties.

Luciano had said often he'd love to return to Australia, having such happy memories of the 1965 season, and he finally came to sing three *Bohèmes*, as well as appearing in a grand gala with Richard and myself at the Sydney Opera House. This took place on January 23 and netted a box-office sum of nearly $300,000 – the largest ever for an indoor event in Australia. As well as being simulcast, it was later marketed on video and it was one of the highest-rating single performances in Australian television history, according to a survey which estimated an audience of six million viewers.

The cartoonists had a field day when Pavarotti professed to have an allergy to stage dust. He spent some time in a house very near us at Whale Beach and we had the pleasure of his company at Rocca Bella, where he insisted on making a spaghetti lunch and enjoyed a swim and many laughs over our almost twenty years' association.

During our stay the Art Gallery of New South Wales had an exhibition of twenty paintings chosen by Richard and me in their series Celebrity Choice; I also received the Charles Heidsieck Champagne Award for Excellence.

During rehearsals for the new production of Gounod's *Romeo et Juliette* Richard had been telling me how beautiful it appeared to be. Even so, I was quite unprepared for the breath-taking realisation on the concert hall stage and returned to see it as often as I could manage. Kenneth Rowell had designed and Sir Robert Helpmann directed this spectacular production, with the casting perfect from a visual and vocal point of view. Juliette was sung by Glenys Fowles with Anson Austin as Roméo, John Pringle as Mercutio, Clifford Grant as Friar Lawrence together with Heather Begg, Anne-Maree McDonald, Paul Ferris, Anthony Warlow, Donald Shanks/Bruce Martin, Robin Donald, John Antoniou, John Wegner and Constantine Mavridis – a completely Australian cast and with the exception of Glenys all members of the Company.

The press was justly favourable, with Richard receiving great praise for his musical interpretation of this and the several other operas from the French repertoire he had introduced to Australian audiences with such success during his reign as Musical Director of the Australian Opera.

Alcina was revived in February with myself in the title role, that with which I'd made my Italian début in Venice in 1960. Barbara Matera had designed and made magnificent new costumes for my appearances in this magical Handelian piece, which was directed and choreographed by Sir Robert Helpmann. The sets and costumes (other than my own) were designed by John Pascoe and the production incorporated many wonderful effects based on the old stage machinery of the Drottningholm Theatre. It was challenging to work with Sir Robert after having known him from my early days at Covent Garden. He was a director who talked little in rehearsal and spent the time repeating scenes until he was completely satisfied – tiring, but very good for memorising and having the show run smoothly.

My entrance as the enchantress Alcina was made reclining in a shell-shaped litter carried by four hefty body-builders who wore the briefest of briefs, feathered turbans and a lot of jewellery. A fifth walked in front carrying a huge feathered fan. It was most effective, but I am no light-weight and wondered every night if the muscle men might collapse, especially with the added weight of the heavily embroidered and decorated costume. But all went well and the only problem was on the final night when I was supposed to disappear at the end of the opera in a flash and a puff of smoke. Unfortunately the flash failed so

I moved as planned – and the flash went off under my enormous gown. There was a frightful smell and a warm feeling at the back of my legs, inspection by Sandy, my dresser revealing a huge hole in the back of the fortunately fire-proofed skirt. I had wondered why the smell had followed me on-stage for the curtain calls.

The opera was given seven times, with Ruggiero sung by Margreta Elkins, Bradamante by Lauris Elms, Morgana by Jennifer McGregor, Melisso by John Wegner, Oronte by Richard Greager and Oberto by Anne-Maree McDonald. George Kennedy, in the *Sun*, wrote that *Alcina*

has become the most important repertory piece of the Australian Opera at its revival last week. The sheer beauty of John Pascoe's dazzling settings and Sir Robert Helpmann's sensitive production perfectly mirrored Handel's music-theatre which was a never-ending struggle for recognition in the hotbed of opera seria.

The performance was crowned by Dame Joan Sutherland's playing of the name part. The ravishing beauty of her voice, the easiness of how she executed the most difficult passages in Alcina's six arias and how she tormented herself in between love, hate, jealousy, bitterness and despair kept one sitting at the edge of the seat. The capacity audience certainly were rewarded by a tremendous account of 'Ah, mio cor' in Act 2 when she learns that Ruggiero plans to leave her – one of the greatest that even Sutherland could have given.

It had been an enormous pleasure to work with Margreta again in *Alcina* and to share together the excitement of the audience reaction as we had in London twenty years before.

There were fierce, catastrophic bushfires in Victoria and South Australia at the end of February and on the twenty-seventh, the day after the last *Alcina*, over thirty soloists from the Company with conductors Geoffrey Arnold, Stuart Challender, Peter Seymour, David Kram, William Reid, Carlo Felice Cillario and Richard, together with the chorus and orchestra, joined in a benefit concert for victims' relief at 4 p.m. – so that Richard and I could appear in the first half of the programme and still manage to catch our plane back to Europe that evening.

✧ 5 ✧

A WEEK IN Les Avants to catch our breaths and we were off to Genoa for performances of *La Traviata* at the Teatro Margherita there. We stayed with our friend Tito Gallacci in Arenzano and were looking forward to working again with Lamberto Furlan who had returned to Italy from Australia. The director of the theatre suggested to me that he sing the role of Alfredo and I, of course, agreed. After a very slight 'crack' in the tenor solo of Act 1 'Un di felice', the audience voiced its disapproval momentarily. The opera proceeded without further interruption until the last act duet 'Parigi o cara' when catcalls and booing erupted from a portion of the house, the rest calling for silence and wanting the opera to continue. Lamberto had done nothing to warrant such an outburst – I had sung that duet many times with better-known tenors having far more pitch problems – and I said quietly to him 'We don't have to try and sing against that – come on', nodded to Richard and the three of us returned to our dressing-rooms. All hell broke loose, the theatre in an uproar, but I refused to return, changed into my street clothes and left, together with Richard. We saw Lamberto being propelled back on-stage by the Director of the theatre to complete the last few minutes of the piece with the soprano who was to take over the role of Violetta after my contracted three appearances.

For too long the Italian opera houses have all had their claques, with the artists paying for applause at the 'right' moments during the evening or taking the unpleasant consequences. I think it has been an iniquitous state of affairs and found the booing and hissing delivered ill mannered. No-one sings badly on purpose, and if they have been engaged to sing a role that is unsuitable for them then it is the management's fault. It had been stated in the press that I insisted on Lamberto singing, but this was untrue. Perhaps the opera-goers had some favourite who they thought should be singing or, as was confided to me, the public wanted to be rid of the current Opera Director. Whatever the reason, there had been a spate of like incidents all over Italy that season and the unruly audience behaviour was deserving of our action. Such occurrences have broken the nerve of many a colleague and Lamberto was not immune. I was told by some young fans: 'The boos were not for you, signora,' to which I replied, 'I don't care *who* they were for. It is just unacceptable behaviour and I will never sing in Italy again.' They were to have been my last performances there, anyway.

We returned to Les Avants the next day and I was able to get on with studying *Hamlet*, which we began recording in London early in April. Sherrill Milnes repeated his fine performance of the name role, with James Morris as Claudius, Barbara Conrad as Gertrude, Gösta Winbergh as Laërte and John Tomlinson as the Ghost. The Orchestra and Chorus of the Welsh National Opera were again used by Decca, resulting in an atmospheric performance.

I had completed my singing of Ophélie's music by April 13 and returned to Les Avants that day to continue memorising Cilea's *Adriana Lecouvreur*, but I was finding it increasingly difficult to remember the words.

On May 1 we flew to San Diego and commenced rehearsals with Tito Capobianco for *Adriana*. On May 4 Natasha, our first grandchild, was born and we were over the moon. It was like old times, having a whole three weeks to rehearse and settle into a new work, and I enjoyed the role of Adriana immensely, both musically and dramatically. With John Bröcheler as Michonnet, Arnold Voketaitis as the Prince de Bouillon, Stella Silva as the Princesse and the handsome Vasile Moldoveanu as Maurizio, it was a very strong cast and my costumes designed by Michael Stennett were perfection. It was Tito's final presentation as General Director for the San Diego Company and it was exceptionally well received. Headlines after the opening night read:

ADRIANA: FITTING EXIT FOR TITO

TITO'S LAST GIFT: SUTHERLAND'S ADRIANA AN UNSURPASSED NIGHT AT THE OPERA

LA STUPENDA'S SILVER LARYNX STILL SHINES BRIGHTLY

From *The Tribune*, San Diego, May 23:

... Sutherland's performance, indeed, was unsurpassed. It's hard for this observer to believe she could sing better than she did last night. Her voice, at 56, is incredible: admirably powerful at the top, grand in its phrasing, rich in its tone, never small in scale. Cilea's lush lyrical score suits her fullest beauty. And – if all this isn't enough – there's an unexpected acting skill that emerged last night, a facet of Sutherland that's always paled next to her voice prowess.

The spoken dialogue over the orchestra in Act III where she recites a speech from *Phedre* using it to denounce her hostess, the princess, was handled with the subtlety and finesse of the most sensitive interpreter.

Placing herself in front of her adversary, Sutherland poignantly upbraided her. She held her threatening pose for some moments, turned, and made a stunning exit. It was done with such intuitiveness that Sarah Bernhardt (if alive and present) would have grown green with envy.

We left for Sydney on June 2 and were met by Adam, Helen and our granddaughter Natasha. After a weekend at Whale Beach we plunged into rehearsals for *Trovatore* and a concert we did on June 12, with the Elizabethan Sydney Orchestra for the Australian Opera Auditions Committee of New South Wales. This organisation raises funds to aid young singers, presenting a Joan Sutherland scholarship each year. I sang arias by Mozart, Handel, Shield and Bellini, and Richard unearthed a concerto by the very young Rossini.

The designer of the opera was Australia's Sir Sidney Nolan who, with fellow Australian producer Elijah Moshinsky, had staged *Samson et Dalila* at Covent Garden with considerable critical success. Their collaboration now brought a very stark *Trovatore* to the Sydney Opera House, softened by Luciana Arrighi's mid-nineteenth century Risorgimento costumes. I'm sure the result of the all-glossy-black rectangular set with some movable sections, lit to highlight the singers, was much more effective for the audience than helpful to the performers whose imagination really had to work overtime. The programme was even printed in white on black paper. We teased Sid Nolan a great deal about his 'fried-egg' moon, his mountains which resembled the Olgas in Central Australia and his Ned Kelly-like figures of a mother and child as a backdrop to Azucena's revelation.

The Spanish tenor Francisco Ortiz had been engaged to sing the great role of Manrico but after rehearsing well he fell ill close to the first night and Welsh Kenneth Collins, who was to do some later performances, made the trip from Britain to save the day. Not only did he do so admirably but he liked Australia so much that he became a resident and has filled the dramatic tenor roles for the Australian Opera with gusto and his ringing high C ever since. Ken's very late arrival didn't allow for much rehearsal together so everyone was more or less giving him a gentle push or inclining the head and eyes in the right direction for him to move on the opening night. With Lauris Elms as Azucena and Jonathan Summers as Count di Luna, we did nine performances, one of which was televised and issued on video.

The opening night was a gala, with the then Prime Minister (Bob Hawke) and other politicians present. I have a humorous reminder of the occasion in a newspaper photograph of Bob on his knees in front of me, head bowed and clasping my right hand in his. It was taken outside my dressing-room.

Maria Prerauer praised the production as 'visually, dramatically and vocally stunning'.

'Dazzling night at the opera', was Nadine Amadio's headline in the *Sunday Telegraph*, continuing:

> ... With all the leading singers in top form, the opening had a sense of great occasion ... Dame Joan Sutherland's handling of the demanding role of Leonora was an example of professional opera stagecraft and stunning vocal beauty...
>
> When one added to this great singing, the powerful imagery of Sidney Nolan, the surprisingly calm authority of Richard Bonynge and the strong chessboard direction of Elijah Moshinsky, it resulted in a memorable night of opera.

It was an extremely busy season for Richard who conducted nine performances of *Lucia* with Jennifer McGregor, after her success in *Hamlet*, bringing her youthful charm to the leading role. He also performed *The Barber of Seville* six times with Håkan Hagegård as Figaro, Gregory Yurisich as Bartolo and Jennifer singing Rosina.

During August, five performances of Rossini's *Semiramide* were given. Originally these were to be a 'semi-staged concert version'. However, some stock sets and costumes were put together and a more than acceptable production devised. The administration was pleased with the inexpensive result and thought, as there was always criticism of their huge expenses for lavish staging, their move would be appreciated. There were only complaints about the lack of grandeur, in spite of the opera being well directed by Moffatt Oxenbould, having a splendid cast and above all giving the public the opportunity to see and hear a work they had been requesting since the 1965 Williamson tour.

Lauris Elms sang Arsace, Bruce Martin Assur and Anson Austin Idreno, Constantine Mavridis the High Priest (Oroe) and Clifford Grant the Ghost of Nino. The critics had a field day tossing compliments or derogatory remarks about the 'low budget' production, but had to concede that the opportunity to hear Rossini's electrifying opera so well sung was a plus for the Company.

On August 21 we flew back to Switzerland for two weeks to catch up on household needs, dental appointments, the mail and some revising of *La Fille du Régiment* and *Esclarmonde*.

On September 6 we flew to New York where we had two and half weeks to rehearse *Fille*, opening on the twenty-seventh at the Met. It was a pleasant time of year to be in the 'Big Apple' and we were quite relaxed doing an opera we knew so well.

On the afternoon of Friday the sixteenth we went straight from a morning rehearsal to spend the weekend with the Materas in their lovely old house at Athens in upstate New York. On Saturday the menfolk went 'antiquing', leaving Barbie and me to potter in the house and huge garden and meet them in Catskill for lunch. Unfortunately, I tripped when coming down their steep and narrow back stairs (much closer to our room than the main staircase) pitching forward and framing my head in the small window at the bottom, broken glass seemingly everywhere. Barbie had a frightful shock and after sponging off the blood bundled me into her car and took me to Catskill Memorial Hospital. There I was vacuum-cleaned in case of further glass splinters and stitched on the left side of my neck where there was a nasty curved cut. I moaned to the charming doctor that it would show when I wore my second-act costume, whereupon he provided me with the finest of flesh-coloured sticking plaster and the wound is barely visible in some of the photographs taken two days later at the Met stage and orchestra rehearsal. The close-ups were not usable, but by the opening night a week later a dab of make-up did wonders. Now the small scar is just one more age wrinkle in my neck.

Alfredo Kraus sang Tonio, Ara Berberian was Sulpice and the Marquise was sung at the first performance by Gwynn Cornell due to Regina Resnik's indisposition. She joined the cast at later performances, along with Spiro Malas as Sulpice. Andrea Velis was Hortensius, much to our delight, and we gave eight performances. The critics were quite impressed by the ability of Alfredo and myself to sustain our roles at our ripe old age of nearly fifty-seven.

OLD PROS AT THE MET — KRAUS AND SUTHERLAND BRING DOWN THE HOUSE

A LESSON IN MUSIC'S POWERS

were a couple of headlines, with Donal Henahan stating in the *New York Times*: '... Although reference books insist she is a few weeks short of 57, the ear refuses to believe it. She is a genuine phenomenon, a bit of operatic history walking among us.'

This was the 100th anniversary season of the Metropolitan Opera and it was heralded on TV on September 28 by the presentation of *Lucia di Lammermoor* taped the previous November 13 with Kraus, Pablo Elvira and Paul Plishka.

As extra publicity for their Centennial the Met staged a televised gala on October 22. About 100 artists appeared during the eleven-hour marathon, with an afternoon and evening section and a dinner break between them. Backstage was organised chaos, with singers arriving while those who had performed already had not vacated their allotted dressing-rooms, make-up artists and dressers milling about trying to capture their next charge and stage management lining up the next-but-one performer in the wings so there'd be no hitches in the flow of the programme.

Of course, the gala was a very mixed bag and the ladies were all out to impress with their gowns. I think I might have beaten the lot in Barbara Matera's wonderful shaded green chiffon with its cobweb-like cape glittering with crystal drops and bugle beads. I was happy to be in the afternoon section and enjoyed seeing so many friends backstage – Kiri Te Kanawa, Placido Domingo, Nicolai Gedda, Tatiana Troyanos, Eva Marton, Sherrill Milnes, Jess Thomas, Mirella Freni, Régine Crispin, Alfredo Kraus, Leona Mitchell to name just a few.

Donal Henahan wrote in his lengthy review in the *New York Times*:

> ... The afternoon session, like the evening one, was a disconcertingly mixed bag...
>
> But it provided euphoric moments, chief among them Joan Sutherland's glittering 'Bel raggio lusinghier' from *Semiramide*. The Australian prima donna's appearance touched off the loudest and most sustained ovation of the program.

After the last intermission in the evening the curtain went up on twenty-five of the Met's former stars seated at the rear of the stage. These wonderful artists had, in their heyday, been the glamorous idols of the opera-going public. We had heard many of them, known them and even worked with some. Cesare Valletti, Risë Stevens, Ramon Vinay, Dorothy Kirsten, Eleanor Steber, Zinka Milanov, Bidu Sayão, Ferruccio Tagliavini and Jarmila Novotná were greeted with a storm of applause from those who remembered their many triumphs. A very special touch during all the anniversary celebrations was an invitation from Edward Koch, then mayor of the City of New York, to attend a reception in the Met's honour at Gracie Mansion.

One wonders if the Met gala prompted Thor Eckert Jr to write his article later in the month of October entitled 'All of opera's big voices seem to be fading away'. After an introduction speaking of Wagnerian (and other) disasters at the Met in recent years, he continued:

> Where are the big voices today? Will we ever get back to a time when a Kirsten Flagstad could – as anyone who ever heard her will confirm – flood a house with sound? Will there ever be another Birgit Nilsson, to mention someone from the immediate past? Incidentally, *Variety* reported that she has finally sung her last concert, thus bringing to an end the resplendent career of one of the supreme mistresses of the art of singing.
>
> When Leonie Rysanek and Joan Sutherland finally decide to exit – one hopes that will be years away – there is danger that the really large voices ideal for certain slices of repertoire will no longer exist.
>
> Rysanek refers to her breed as a dinosaur. She has spent her entire career as jugendlich (youthful) dramatic soprano and has never dared

assault the heavier roles such as Elektra (except on recordings), Isolde or Brünnhilde, roles that managements have been hounding her for years to take on.

Sutherland, who started out being a Wagnerian soprano and then switched to the bel canto coloratura literature with startling success, also possesses a large sound. Last season at the Met in *Lucia di Lammermoor* she sat on stage near the end of the first act, singing at half volume, and one was aware of her voice effortlessly expanding into the theater. And when she chose to let go at full tilt, the sound shot through the hall.

Why is it that this type of voice is virtually nonexistent today?

His article went on to give what is definitely, for me, the answer.

... Nowadays young singers are expected to be fully matured, finished professionals by the time they reach 30. Yet big voices rarely come into complete focus for another 10 years, and by then those young singers who *might* have progressed are at the ends of their careers – victims of the too-much-too-soon syndrome that seems to have polluted so many of our lively arts today.

How right he was – and still is, unfortunately. Since retiring from performing I have accepted requests to adjudicate at some of the many important vocal contests held annually world-wide and the overall decisions I and most of my colleagues on these juries reach are unanimous. The majority of the contestants are lacking a solid basic vocal technique. Many of them are splendid musicians, capable of learning and interpreting the most difficult works. But all too often they sing with a complete lack of understanding of how to breathe and then support the voice on that breath, and project a properly prepared and well-focused, beautiful sound.

I have been asked very complicated questions by established singers which imply their use of all sorts of incredible gimmicks which strain their vocal equipment and do nothing to preserve and improve their young, natural voices. They will doubtless get by on their looks, youthfulness and musical ability for a limited time, but when problems arise due to the constant studying, rehearsing, performing, travelling, coping with their personal and family affairs, they will have no hope of sustaining their careers. Too little time has been spent perfecting their technique before they are singing publicly – and roles that are, nine times out of ten, far too heavy for them at their stage of vocal development, if ever. Most of the great bel canto singers of the past studied for something like eight years before being permitted by their teachers to sing publicly. Now, it seems, two or three years is a maximum, with no period of seven years in a company like Covent Garden steadily 'learning the ropes' and progressing from role to role.

They are off and running from one Company to another within their own country, then abroad, with TV and recordings thrown in. No wonder they don't survive, but I cannot understand how the public can accept and acclaim their breathy, wobbly, shrill, off-pitch 'singing'. Yes, Mr Eckert, they *are* unwitting victims of the too-much-too-soon syndrome.

On October 25 we arrived back in Les Avants for a few days (during which I managed to make the Christmas pudding!) before leaving for London on the thirtieth. Rehearsals began the next day for Massenet's *Esclarmonde* which the Royal Opera House had brought from San Francisco via the Met. It was, as always, great to be spending time in London at the Garden, especially as the opera house now had its great rehearsal room in which production calls were held instead of at some hall away from the theatre. Lotfi Mansouri again supervised his original production of the opera with Ernesto Veronelli making his début at Covent Garden as Roland. Diana Montague sang Parséis, Ryland Davies Enéas, Gwynne Howell the Emperor Phorcas and Jonathan Summers was the Bishop of Blois. Although rehearsals went well the production seemed somehow doomed. I was forced to cancel the second performance (December 2) due to a throat infection and on two other occasions the opera was interrupted by bomb scares. These were very unsettling as we had to vacate the theatre in costume and wait about in the music library across the street until the security officers gave permission for the performance to proceed.

The production was not greeted with the success it had achieved in San Francisco and the Met, possibly due to the much smaller stage and lack of depth to the set. It was classed as 'old-fashioned', 'excruciatingly banal', 'good viewing for the pre-panto season' by some critics, others talked of 'the colourful and beautifully lit stage designs' and 'lavish settings'. The musical attributes of the work were not always to the critics' taste either, although *The Stage* headed its report with 'British première triumph for Joan'.

It was indeed the first time *Esclarmonde* had been produced in Britain, although given its original première by the Opéra Comique on May 14, 1889. Despite other Massenet works being presented frequently in the United Kingdom his magic-filled *Esclarmonde* waited almost a hundred years for its appearance. The audience greeted the opera warmly, but there was somehow not the exhilaration experienced in the American performances.

Adam and Helen came from Sydney to London for five days in early December, bringing Natasha to spend Christmas with us, and we managed some shopping excursions together before they continued to Les Avants. On December 17 we returned home ourselves, in good time to prepare for the family Christmas celebrations prior to leaving for Australia again in early January, 1984.

Richard was already rehearsing *The Magic Flute* with Yvonne Kenny as a charming Pamina, Richard Greagor as Tamino and Christa Leahmann as the Queen of the Night, also Anthony Warlow making his very promising début as Papageno. Shortly after the opening of the *Flute* the annual 'Opera in the Park' concert was given on January 14, this time with a performance of *Lucia di Lammermoor*. It was just a few days short of the twenty-fifth anniversary of my first *Lucia* at Covent Garden in 1959. There was a large crowd of about 100,000 and just as the opera ended down came the rain, drenching the majority of the audience. It was a typical Sydney summer storm, passing quickly, having cooled the air – and the crowd.

As soon as I had arrived I'd begun rehearsing for the Australian Opera's first new production of the year, Cilea's *Adriana Lecouvreur*, which we gave nine times. John Copley directed the opera, with beautiful sets and costumes designed by Alan Lees and Michael Stennett, evoking the era of Sarah Bernhardt and the Comédie Française of her day. I loved this role very much and there was a strong cast, with Anson Austin as Maurizio, Heather Begg as the Princess, John Shaw as Michonnet, John Wegner as the Prince and Graeme Ewer as the Abbé. Jeffrey Black, of whom much has since been heard in Europe and America, made his début as the Major Domo but in the television performance sang the role of Quinault extraordinarily well at very short notice due to the indisposition of Robert Eddie.

There was a great deal said in the press about the opera being merely a vehicle for the star, with only one decent tune. However, some praised it as the lyrical drama it is. W. L. Hoffmann in the *Canberra Times* said:

> This is an excellently sung, played and staged production of this lovely, lyrical opera; that it has taken eighty years to achieve a performance in Australia is quite surprising. It makes a welcome addition to the repertoire and is a change from the seemingly endless repetition of the round dozen popular Puccini and Verdi operas we have been getting in recent years.

Peter Robinson in *Australian Financial Review*: '*Adriana* is a gross waste of a national treasure ... ludicrous, banal, extravagant.' However, the *Daily Mirror* thought:

> Dame Joan Sutherland enchanted a sell-out audience as the star of a new production of Cilea's romantic drama *Adriana Lecouvreur* ... Dame Joan richly dressed in Michael Stennett's gorgeous costumes not only looked and acted like a theatre star but sang magnificently.

Whatever was written at the time, the opera was released on video after the simulcast and can be viewed at will by all.

This was the first time surtitles were used in Australia and there were some complaints. As they appear above the proscenium arch and can only be seen by consciously looking up at them I cannot understand the objections. Not many of the opera-going public are fluent in foreign languages and the titles are extremely well devised and projected.

The Australian Broadcasting Commission presented a feature to celebrate the tenth year of my association with the Australian Opera in February – *Sutherland, A Celebration*. In it I was rehearsing *Adriana*, also talking about and introducing excerpts from various roles which I had sung with the Company such as *Don Giovanni*, *The Merry Widow*, *La Traviata*, *Lucia* and *Die Fledermaus*.

Richard conducted several performances of *The Merry Widow* that season which meant he stayed on in Sydney for a few days after Tessa and I left for Switzerland, where we were based for an unbelievable two months with the occasional trip within the country or to a nearby French town. I spent two weeks studying Donizetti's *Anna Bolena* with Richard and Sylvia Holford and a good deal of time in the garden.

On May 4 Richard, Chester and I flew to New York, where I had a lengthy fitting with Barbara Matera for the *Anna Bolena* costumes designed by Michael Stennett for the Toronto production of the opera. On May 6 we continued to Toronto, where we had leased a charming house in 'Cabbage Town' within easy distance of the theatre. Rehearsals for *Bolena* began immediately and, with Lotfi Mansouri directing, they moved along with considerable ease. I had been having some difficulty memorising the role of Anna, finding similarities in many musical and verbal phrases to other Donizetti and Bellini works I had already performed. This concentrated two-week rehearsal period with all the cast members was quite arduous but certainly helped to stabilise my interpretation of the character within the bounds of the very haunting music.

When the costumes arrived for the stage rehearsals I was amazed at the length and beauty of the train to be worn in the opening scene. Before donning it I remarked with a laugh that I would be 'nailed to the floor' by it, unable to move due to its weight. I was proven correct and at least a metre of the rich material had to be removed, still leaving a goodly length with the heavily embroidered and befurred fantail to be controlled by me crossing and recrossing the large stage. The opening aria for Anna is quite difficult, so I had to look as though I wore that train every day and appear to toss off the scene as part of the usual court gossip. It was not easy, but the effect was quite stunning and I worked out a way of manipulating the train by clutching it discreetly from either side and giving a firm pull in the direction I wished it to go. Fortunately for me it usually responded.

With James Morris as Henry VIII, Judith Forst as Jane Seymour,

Michael Myers as Percy, Janet Stubbs as Smeton and Ben Heppner (then a member of the Toronto Opera Ensemble) as Hervey, it was a very strong cast and the towering sets by John Pascoe with Michael Stennett's exquisite costumes for all created a splendid atmosphere for us, aiding the dramatic content and giving the public a visual and vocal treat.

The critics, too, were impressed. John Kraglund, in the *Globe and Mail*, wrote: 'It was unquestionably Sutherland's night, as the 57-year-old singer demonstrated remarkable control in lyrical and coloratura passages, as well as surprisingly effective interpretive powers musically …' All the critics remarked on the production's visual splendour with 'tremendous respect' for Richard and his 'clearly inspirational effect on chorus and orchestra' and the stage direction of Lotfi Mansouri, involving not only the singers but a couple of horses and several hunting dogs. After five performances we repeated the opera twice in Detroit. The Toronto *Bolena* production was shared by Detroit, Houston, San Francisco and Chicago, and not all the stages were able to cope with the massive scenery, causing unfortunate delays between scenes.

The weather in Detroit was very hot and humid and the costumes were predominantly made of velvet, heavy brocades and wool – all of us were drenched in perspiration as there was no air-conditioning. While one scene change was negotiated, I remember standing in the wings for eighteen minutes fortunately adjacent to an outside door which, left open, created a slight draught of cooler air. Unfortunately, the long wait was too much for one of the horses who, once the stage was ready, entered and promptly relieved itself – right on top of one of the small attendant page-boys. He went off to be cleaned up but was still wailing in the interval that the horse had 'shat' on him. He was not the only casualty as some chorus members fainted due to the heat.

In all of these early performances I valued very much the presence of Judith Forst as Jane Seymour. Her disciplined professionalism on stage, her infallible musicianship, together with her lovely voice and off-stage charm and friendliness endeared her to me and helped enormously to create the necessary rapport between Anna and Jane.

Next on our agenda were three performances of Verdi's *I Masnadieri* in San Diego. We again stayed in the comfortable bungalow on top of the cliff on the edge of La Jolla and enjoyed relaxing there after the day's work, watching the surfers and sea birds.

Although Tito Capobianco was no longer Director of the San Diego Opera he returned to produce *I Masnadieri*, which opened the Company's 1984 Verdi Festival. Unfortunately, the Company appeared to have economised on the set, a series of ugly ramps and platforms having little or nothing to do with the confusing plot of the opera.

There was also a hasty substitution for the role of Francisco, due to the illness of William Justus. The two-weeks rehearsal period was barely enough. The ultimate cast consisted of Alfredo Zanazzo as Massimiliano, Gordon Greer as Carlo, Antonio Salvadori as Francisco and Kenneth Cox as Moser.

The critics were not impressed by the work as a whole, dubbing it too old-fashioned a libretto for a modern audience. They wrote about the Company claiming it was a West Coast première of the opera, although it was possibly the first complete performance on the American stage. They also spoke of the association of the work with Jenny Lind, Albert Goldberg writing in the *Los Angeles Times*:

> ... How Lind sang the music can only be conjectured, but one can think of no contemporary soprano who could dispose of this long and taxing chore with the ease and musicality of Sutherland. The years have imposed no obvious penalties on her. Her tone is as pure as ever, her facility as smooth and unerring, her top notes as uninhibited. She is a diva – the real, genuine article.

During the run we saw a performance of *Sugar Babies* with Ann Miller and Mickey Rooney, both of whom were incredibly agile and funny. One remembered their early films and knew how long and hard they had worked, and here they were still giving such pleasure to a huge audience.

Tessa went back to Switzerland on June 29. As usual for us, it was 'up and away' on July 1, driving to Los Angeles to take the Qantas flight to Sydney, where we arrived on the third.

Without any previous word from the Company during his four-month absence, Richard was met with the news that Mr Veitch and the Board had decided there was no need for a Music Director and that Moffatt Oxenbould would now be called Artistic Director as opposed to Artistic Administrator. He and Richard had always worked well together (and still do) with Moffatt attending to Ric's share of administration due to his (Richard's) dislike of any office work, his heavy workload rehearsing and performing and his absences abroad for half of the year. He continued as Musical Director until the end of 1986 and still is very interested in the Company. I quote a passage from Richard's book on our years with the Australian Opera:

> Although the Board behaved in an ungentlemanly manner, they did me a favour – it was the same decision I would have had to make sooner or later. My tastes in music are my own but they correspond exactly to what, before my time with the Company, was missing from the Australian Opera repertory. There was little understanding of bel canto, there was almost no French repertoire and no exploration of the eighteenth century.

I believe I opened these doors and that Joan and I left a legacy which is continuing and will continue. I don't believe the time and energy were wasted. I now look back on my eleven years with the Company as Musical Director with great satisfaction and very happy memories. I dare say some of my decisions were better than others but I regret none of them.

So, after the situation was digested by us, it was on with the winter season, Ric opening on July 14 with a triple bill of *Trial by Jury*, a *pas de deux* from Offenbach's *Le Papillon* and finally the same composer's farce *Ba-ta-clan*. It was a hilarious night in the theatre, with splendid casting and, as one critic wrote, there was 'hardly a straight face left in the Opera House'. The sight of Gordon Wilcock as the Learned Judge looking just like Humpty-Dumpty and the antics of the Defendant (Anthony Warlow) and the Plaintiff (Anne-Maree McDonald) had me laughing throughout. Added to these we had John Fulford as Counsel for the Plaintiff, John Germain as the Usher and Donald Solomon as a Clerk of the Court, all giving rollicking interpretations and singing well in spite of the swift-moving humour. The *Ba-ta-clan* cast remained the same as before.

Rehearsals had been going on for a revival of *Les Contes d'Hoffmann* with a predominantly new cast. We still had Donald Solomon's Luther, Robert Eddie's Schlemil and Graeme Ewer's telling and droll performances of Andrés Cochenille, Pitichinaccio and Frantz. The four baritone roles were now sung by Jonathan Summers, with Horst Hoffmann making his début with the Company as his namesake. Horst, with his very wide-ranging repertoire, stayed with the Company as resident tenor and has given some incredibly fine performances. The Muse and Nicklausse were sung by Bernadette Cullen, with Anthony Warlow as Spalanzani, Pieter van der Stolk as Crespel, and Jeffrey Black and Christopher Dawes as the Students. *Hoffmann* was given at this time to mark our ten years' association with the Australian Opera, having appeared together in the same production on our first visit in 1974.

W. L. Hoffmann in the *Canberra Times* wrote:

SUTHERLAND AND BONYNGE IN A CELEBRATION

continuing:

The sheer brilliance and magic of the sound in Olympia's aria of the first act was spellbinding. This performance aroused a sustained ovation from the audience, an ovation only surpassed at the end of the wonderful trio which concluded with Antonia's death ... Richard Bonynge directed the performance with all the care and style that he brings to the French operatic repertoire ... The ovation that Richard Bonynge received when he made his first appearance in the pit, and the warm enthusiasm for Sutherland's singing, demonstrated a personal warmth and affection, and gratitude for the pleasure and many memorable moments that they have brought to opera audiences over the past ten years.

I remember particularly the Dress Rehearsal to which Helen brought Natasha to see the Olympia scene, although only fifteen months old. She was very well behaved, and apparently wanted to 'sing along'. A photograph was taken with Horst, Ric, Natasha and myself. She had also been briefly to the Dress Rehearsal of *Adriana Lecouvreur* at the beginning of the year. Until they were at school full time both Natasha and Vanya were able to visit the Opera House this way.

The acknowledgement on-stage at the end of the first night by the Company and opera-goers of our work in Australia was heart-warming and much appreciated by both of us. We were also very touched by Moffatt's introduction in the programme which paid tribute to our ten-year association with the Company, including the Artists' Benevolent Fund, Young Artists Programme, the park and charity concerts, simul-casts, etc. Our interest in all of the Company's activities has never waned and we continue to be impressed by the talent displayed by many of the young singers who ultimately make their mark in Europe and the United States. Richard is still, at the time of writing, performing regularly in the Company's winter season.

On August 19 Stuart Challender and Richard shared the conducting for a concert entitled 'Musicians for World Peace' supported by the United Nations Association of Australia. I sang the *Lucia* Mad Scene and 'Casta diva' and of the other artists remember vividly the playing by Paul and Maud Tortellier of the *Paganini Variations on a Theme of Rossini* – they were incredibly stylish, yet gave the impression of a hilarious music-hall turn.

With the *Hoffmanns* out of the way I started rehearsing the role of Madame Lidoine (the New Prioress) in Poulenc's *Dialogues of the Carmelites* which the Australian Opera was mounting for the first time. I had resisted re-learning this role (sung at Covent Garden in 1958) but was ultimately glad I had – it was a wonderful cast and the production by Elijah Moshinsky, designed by John Bury, was extremely moving. Isobel Buchanan was Blanche, Lone Koppel the Old Prioress, Heather Begg Mère Marie, Anne-Maree McDonald and Fiona Macon-aghie Sister Constance. Geoffrey Chard sang the Marquis, Paul Ferris the Chevalier, Richard Greager the Priest with John Fulford, Pieter van der Stolk, Gordon Wilcock, John Wegner, Anthony Warlow and John Germain all taking part. Patricia Price, Cynthia Johnston, Beryl Furland, Marie-Thérèse Driscoll, Luise Napier, Hellen O'Rourke and Deborah Riedel were among the remaining sisters, all of whom added to the emotional climax of the work – a real Company opera.

There were nine performances, with the press giving ecstatic reviews, particularly for Richard. As he remarked, 'This great Catholic masterpiece survived being conducted by a Protestant and directed by a Jew.' I, too, fared well with the crits, apparently having given 'a rare and vintage performance'. The opera was simulcast and issued on video.

Richard also conducted four performances of *The Marriage of Figaro* at this time with another splendid cast – Joan Carden as the Countess, Glenys Fowles as Susanna, Bernadette Cullen as Cherubino, Michael Lewis as the Count, John Pringle as Figaro, Graeme Ewer Basilio, Rosina Raisbeck Marcellina and Pieter van der Stolk Bartolo.

I accepted an honorary degree of Doctor of Music from Sir Hermann Black, Chancellor of the University of Sydney, in a beautiful ceremony there on September 12 and Richard was in the same year made an Officer of the Order of Australia for his services to music. I also attended an evening at St Catherine's school, renewing acquaintance with old friends and meeting members of the School Foundation.

Darlene Newman had been a constant visitor to Sydney during the Company's winter seasons which coincided with her long summer break as a professor at Fresno, California. Tessa had the desire to be less of a gypsy and return to a fixed abode in London and it was decided that Darlene would take Tessa's place for a time.

After the last *Carmelites* we returned to Switzerland for a week and arrived in San Francisco on October 7 to rehearse *Anna Bolena* with the Toronto sets and costumes and, except for myself, a complete change of cast. Once again we stayed in Sausalito, missing the presence of Jack Shelton who had died after a long illness since our previous visit. Rehearsals went well over a two-and-a-half-week period, the opening being on October 25 with a further six performances scheduled. I was forced to cancel on October 31 due to a nasal and throat infection. Olivia Stapp was able to replace me, so the show went on.

Livia Budai had been miscast by the management as Jane Seymour and, after struggling through the rehearsals and the opening night, was then replaced, fortunately by Judi Forst. Livia was a lovely colleague with a splendid and huge voice and should never have been placed in this position. She had just finished a successful run of Azucenas and the roles were not compatible. Kevin Langan sang Henry VIII and Rockwell Blake as Percy sang a series of somewhat outrageous variants as only he can. During the run both Judith Forst and I celebrated our birthdays (although our ages differ greatly) and were given a rousing reminder by the chorus and Company when the curtain dropped at the end of the performance on the sixth. I also was pleased and flattered to be presented with the San Francisco Opera Medal after the final night by Terry McEwen, the General Director of the Company at the time.

We flew back to Switzerland on November 14 and went to London on the eighteenth to do our second recording of *Norma* with Montserrat Caballé, Luciano Pavarotti and Samuel Ramey. Fortunately I was not required to sing anything until the twenty-fifth, for which I was very grateful as the heavy schedule of the performances and travel had finally caught up with me and I was feeling tired. Richard had plenty to do with the orchestra and other cast members meanwhile. The recording in Walthamstow Town Hall proceeded with the Welsh National Opera Orchestra and Chorus without any hitches. Montserrat was a great source of fun and never wanted to repeat sections of her role as Adalgisa. During one session Richard and the Decca producer suggested that a further take might be useful. Definitely not, she decided, making an excuse of tiredness or strain – and practically skipped off the stage making a smiling aside to me that now she would go shopping in Knightsbridge.

Ric's mother arrived in London on November 28 and travelled back to Les Avants with me on December 5, Richard staying a further few days in London to complete the recording. My niece, Ruth Sutherland, and Dr Peter Newbold joined us a few days before Christmas and we had a happy time together. Betty Bonynge was a great walker, unfazed by the snowy and slippery road, and we had the fun of trips with her to Les Diablerets and to Gstaad on our local train in the picturesque winter weather.

✧ **6** ✧

AFTER A LOVELY break at home we were off again on January 3, 1985, arriving in Sydney on the fifth to begin rehearsing for a new production of *Norma* and 'Opera in the Park'. It was a performance of *The Tales of Hoffmann* that year, held on January 12, finally under a canopy for the performers. A grand crowd spread themselves on the grass of the Sydney Domain and enjoyed the evening in spite of problems with the sound. Unfortunately the prevailing evening wind invariably interferes with all the meticulous preparations by the technicians and those members of the audience of some 100,000 beyond a certain distance from the stage had difficulty hearing. But it was a rousing success with several MPs and Government officials present, including Prime Minister Bob Hawke and that great character and ex-Prime Minister Gough Whitlam with wife Margaret – and no rain to mar the proceedings. The public even cleared their picnic rubbish to the vicinity of the overflowing bins – 'The only litter left on the grass was the mounds of ice from emptied "Eskies",' quoted the *Sydney Morning Herald*.

Although I sang in the Domain concert I had made two trips to Sir George Halliday the previous week as I again had an uneasy throat and slight deafness, doubtless a legacy of the long flights and changes of atmosphere. The good doctor assured me on the first visit there was nothing serious amiss, advised a prescription, caution when rehearsing (if I must) and a second visit to check all was in a good state to sing in the park. He was a wonderful, down-to-earth person and much admired by his colleagues and patients.

We escaped to Whale Beach whenever possible at the weekends and rehearsals went on despite a certain amount of dissatisfaction within the Company over its policy at the time which had created a very heavy work-load for the singers. Far too many performances were given of Australian works that would probably never be seen again but required a great amount of work from all involved in their preparation. A letter was sent by the performers to the newspapers stating their lack of confidence in the Board and the Management, which they considered were spending far too much money on extra administration staff and over-luxurious offices.

But 'the show must go on' and we busied ourselves with *Norma*.

This was in fact a substitution for a previously projected then cancelled run of *Esclarmonde* presented in the Concert Hall, for which Kenneth Rowell had designed fabulous sets and costumes. He was then asked to create this new *Norma* for the same venue 'on a shoestring', owing to lack of funds, presumably due to the redecoration of offices for the ever-growing Administration. Whatever the reasons he did manage to give us a workable set and very apt and flattering costumes. Horst Hoffmann was a striking figure in his 'bronze' breastplate and sang Pollione extremely well. The Adalgisa was well sung by Sandra Hahn, a young Australian soprano who had been studying in Italy for some years.

There had been reports in the local press that I was proposing to retire from the stage and singing generally, and these influenced some of the reviews of *Norma*, which opened on January 22, with a further eight performances. Werner Baer's review in the *Manly Daily* read:

SINGING IS STUPENDOUS

La Stupenda is still the greatest. All the recently published suggestions concerning her pending retirement from international singing appear totally unfounded considering her magnificent showing in the present very effective production of *Norma*.

... Sutherland dominates the stage and story ... Norma was one of the early roles and successes of Dame Joan, and there is still nobody to match her in fiery and most convincing singing.

Maria Prerauer of *The Australian* wrote:

... As Norma, Dame Joan Sutherland, looking glamorous and impressive in a series of flowing all-white, all-black and all-red gowns returns to one of her most renowned roles, adding great dignity and even a new dash of temperament to the part. And she sings the smooth bel canto phrases, even the famed 'Casta diva' with admirable poise and restraint, resisting any temptation simply to let fly.

The audience loved every bar of it, breaking again and again into sustained applause.

Unfortunately, I suffered a recurrence of the earlier throat infection and had to relinquish the last two *Normas*. I was relieved that there was an extremely able understudy, Christa Leahmann, whose singing of the difficult role earned her great appreciation from the audience.

Richard was also conducting a new production of *Don Pasquale* with Gregory Yurisich in the title role, Rosamund Illing as Norina, Richard Greager as Ernesto and Michael Lewis as Dr Malatesta. It was another low-budget production but through the ingenuity of designer Roger Kirk and producer Stuart Maunder it worked beautifully and the singers were delightful. I enjoyed several performances and again bemoaned with Richard the fact that this was a Donizetti role I had never sung.

We were to participate in a televised gala of *Les Contes d'Hoffmann* from the new Victorian Arts Centre on March 7 with the whole Sydney Company. There had been a dispute with the Unions over the travel allowance to be paid on tour and nothing had been resolved prior to the Company's arrival in Melbourne – or by the evening of the seventh. The result was that what was to have been the opening of the Australian Opera's Melbourne season and my final performance of *Hoffmann* was called off – forty minutes after the curtain had been due to rise. Although this strike was a great disappointment to the cast (who had been hopefully waiting, made-up, in their dressing-rooms) it was more so for members of the audience, some of whom had flown from New Zealand and even the United States to witness this, my last interpretation of Offenbach's diverse heroines. It resulted in the refunding by the Australian Opera to its patrons of a considerable sum of money (which it could ill afford) and the large television audience missing out on seeing that beautiful production. It could not be rescheduled as we were obliged to leave for Europe the following day.

Arrived in Les Avants for a brief period we experienced a great fall of snow over several days during which Richard and I revised the pieces I was to sing with Luciano in the first two mammoth concerts we had been persuaded to do by Herbert Breslin and Tibor Rudas. The idea never appealed to me as the venues were to be so huge and I recalled the college stadiums of our early days in the US with the sound problems we had experienced. After being assured (never convinced) that all this would be taken care of by expert technicians we had agreed and the publicity exploded for these ventures in Phoenix, Arizona, on March 27 and Atlantic City, New Jersey on the thirtieth.

Rehearsal for Luciano and me was fairly minimal, with Richard taking the Phoenix Symphony through the arias and duets thoroughly without us. We had sung the pieces together elsewhere many times.

Some 11,000 people attended the event, 2000 school children having seats at the rear of the orchestra. The sound engineering was controlled by Jimmy Lock who had done so many of our recordings with Decca and we were confident we had the best result possible under the circumstances. I was still in two minds about the whole project, feeling there was far too little contact with the audience and little – if any – artistic worth, with all the amplification and TV screens. But off we trooped via New York to Atlantic City where the concert was in the Convention Center, sponsored by Caesars Atlantic City Casino with the New Jersey Symphony Orchestra. This necessitated Richard's rehearsing with the orchestra in Newark *en route* to Atlantic City from New York, with a further rehearsal on the afternoon of the concert in the Convention Center.

On the bottom of the 'Gold' concert tickets (price $250 per person) was a detachable strip for a 'Cocktail Reception' at 10.30 p.m. on the Friday evening in the Emperor's Ballroom which we were expected to attend. I *must* have said if the promoters wanted a concert the next night they'd better forget it – 6.30 p.m. would be bad enough, but 10.30? They must be joking – or mad! Was I talked into 'putting in an appearance'? I don't remember. Granted, Ric and I had a huge (and very glitzy) suite courtesy of the Casino for our brief stay, but we were both uneasy with all the overblown publicity as it seemed more like a circus than 'popularising opera by bringing it to the people'. We fled to London the next day, taking the Concorde from New York around midday to arrive at 10.30 p.m. and stagger to bed.

In London it was back to business as usual with another round of *Lucias*. Carlo Bergonzi was singing Edgardo for the first time at Covent Garden and it was a great pleasure to work with him again. We joked about our ages but the years certainly didn't show in his voice, least of all in his final scene.

Henry Pleasants of the *International Herald Tribune* wrote:

LUCIA LONDON TRIUMPH

Lucia di Lammermoor with a 58-year-old grandmother as Lucia and a 60-year-old Edgardo who is certainly a father and quite possibly a grandfather, appearing in a Royal Opera Zeffirelli production dating from 1959? It would have seemed a geriatrically daunting prospect had not the Lucia been Joan Sutherland and the Edgardo the extraordinarily durable Carlo Bergonzi. Not entirely surprisingly, the première proved a tumultuous triumph for all concerned, especially for Dame Joan, returning to Covent Garden in the production that launched her to stardom almost exactly 26 years ago (and she was no beginner even then).

The performance was interrupted twice in the middle and at the close of the 'mad scene' for prolonged and noisy acclamations, and at Sutherland's final curtain call the audience rose in a standing ovation.

What a singer she has been – and still is. And what a performer ... Bergonzi, nearing the end of a career that he began as a baritone 37 years ago, husbanded his resources for the taxing final scene and offered a lesson in vocal art and vocal resourcefulness.

All the dailies and weekend newspapers used superlatives in their headlines and texts, and some also reported the rain of spring flowers from the audience.

Before Lucia's entrance in Act 1 there is a long harp introduction and in the Zeffirelli production she was seated by the fountain, the curtain going up a few bars before her opening phrase. One night the curtain remained down longer than usual and I thought Richard would be panicked but he hadn't noticed, enjoying the excellent playing of the harpist. Just as the final notes were played the curtain creaked up about a half metre and jammed. The offending curtain was lowered, apologies made to the audience and the scene commenced again with the curtain being taken up manually. While we were again hidden from view I remarked that it was not only the tenor and I who were 'geriatrics'.

It was a great joy to feel the generosity of the audiences and critics and a wonderful farewell in that House to the role that had sky-rocketed me on to the international circuit. I was also very touched to receive a hand-written letter from David Sigall, one of the young directors of our long-time agents in London. It read:

Dear Joan,

We Hartog trainees do not tend to write other than business-like letters – and short at that!

There are however occasions when our training has to be stretched.

To say that it was a privilege to have been present at your *Lucia* on Friday goes just a little way in expressing my reaction to your over-whelmingly glorious performance. I thought I had heard everything after *Daughter* in New York but *Lucia* on Friday was something I shall remember and talk about for very many years to come...

Before the run of *Lucias* was over I began recording Handel's *Rodelinda*, with Alicia Nafé, Isobel Buchanan, Huguette Tourangeau and Samuel Ramey. Richard was also completing his recording of the ballet *Manon*.

On May 5 we returned to Les Avants where my brother Jim and his new wife Nancy spent a few days with us, and on the nineteenth Richard and I flew to Stockholm via Copenhagen, taking a private jet from there because of some airline strike. We were able to view the Northern Lights from the pilot's seat – a magnificent spectacle, showing not only the 'top of the world' but all the glittering lakes and streams of Sweden glistening below us. In Stockholm we gave a concert performance of *Norma* with Doris Soffel as Adalgisa and Horst Hoffmann as Pollione – a 'tall trio'.

The next day we took an early flight to London where I recorded Handel's *Athalia* with Christopher Hogwood, his Academy of Ancient Music players and Emma Kirkby, James Bowman, the charming and sweet-voiced boy Aled Jones and Anthony Rolfe Johnson. The old (or reconstructed to ancient specifications) instruments used were frankly a bore, wasting enormous amounts of time being tuned and constantly losing pitch again. The piece was interesting but the recording came at a time when I was somewhat musically saturated and would rather already have been in Sydney at the beach with the family.

On June 1 that wish was granted, although our flight from London was delayed by engine trouble in Singapore and we were diverted to Melbourne, arriving in Sydney after lunch instead of before breakfast. Then we went into rehearsal for two gala concerts with Marilyn Horne – in Melbourne on June 9 and Sydney on the twelfth, with a programme similar to that we had sung at Lincoln Center in New York. Glowing reports by all the Melbourne papers of the concert preceded us to Sydney where we had to repeat 'the miracle'. And this, apparently, we did, prompting Maria Prerauer to write after a four-paragraph introduction to set the scene:

> ... And when the divas finally opened their mouths and began their vocal incantations, what they conjured up was nothing less than magic in its most potent form. Suddenly something akin to mass hysteria, in its best sense, went sweeping around the hall. This critic at least has never felt anything quite like it.
>
> ... The two phenomenal voices went on flooding the hall with golden tone, looping the vocal loop, scattering trills and turns and pyrotechnics as they went.
>
> ... I doubt whether the TV cameras could have picked up the kind of alchemy that was going on in the hall. But in years to come people will be telling their grandchildren about this night. Naturally, they will not believe a bar of it.
>
> Who could? That is, not unless they were there.

It had been wonderful to work again with Marilyn and we were all sorry not to have had more free time together.

Richard had already been rehearsing *The Mikado* and conducted the first six performances of the Company's thirty-six during the season. 'G & S' is very popular in Australia and most of the Australian Opera singers are dab hands at it. The cast was indeed splendid and enjoyed the very funny production as much as the audience.

I was immediately rehearsing for seven performances of *I Puritani* with romantic sets by Henry Bardon, beautiful costumes by Michael Stennett and produced by Sir Robert Helpmann. Anson Austin sang the role of Arturo and was quite happy with its stratospheric range. Michael Lewis sang a splendid Riccardo, Donald Shanks a sympathetic Giorgio. W. L. Hoffmann wrote in the *Canberra Times* of 'a night of magnificent singing'.

> ... Sutherland in a cast, and singing at her best, seems to elicit a high response from every member of the cast and this is the case here. The chorus too, sings with character and spirit and Richard Bonynge, conducting the performance with his innate feeling for the spirit of these 'bel canto' operas, also obtains beautifully expressive playing from the orchestra.

... This is a notable presentation of *I Puritani*, with singing which very few opera houses in the world could match. Those who see it are fortunate indeed in hearing Sutherland in one of her most distinguished and exciting coloratura roles.

On July 8 a lavish book compiled by Richard entitled *Designs for a Prima Donna* was launched at the Opera House. Produced by Craftsman Press, it contained sixty-three beautiful colour plates of many of the costume designs by such artists as José Varona, Michael Stennett, Franco Zeffirelli, Kenneth Rowell, John Piper, Kristian Fredrikson, Wakhevitch and Anna Anni, together with explanatory notes on each costume and the role for which I had worn it. There were only 500 copies printed and they are treasured by as many opera lovers as could afford it. The mystery is where did Richard find the time to do all the preparation necessary before presentation to the publishers?

He was supposed to conduct the first four of a run of *Così fan tutte* performances but spent the opening night in bed with a heavy bout of flu. However, he did the next three and on July 18 Darlene and I left for Les Avants, with Chester and Richard going to New York where Ric had rehearsals and performances of a production of *Norma* with the New York City Opera.

I was delighted to have a six-week period at home with no performing at all and splendid summer weather. Much time was spent in the garden and Sylvia came to work with me on the role of Ophélie in Thomas's *Hamlet* which I had agreed to sing in Toronto in October. Lotfi Mansouri was impressed by my singing in the Decca recording and had managed to break down my resistance to doing the part on-stage – aged almost fifty-nine. His argument had been (when I said I was worried about studying anything new at my age) that I already must know it very well, having recorded it so recently and he dismissed my strong reservations regarding my age and appearance. In an evident fit of madness suited to Ophélie I agreed, mostly because I *had* enjoyed singing the role and now I had to memorise those words. At least I knew the Mad Scene very well, having sung it in so many concerts.

On August 14 our grandson Vanya was born and there was much rejoicing at the news. Richard was especially pleased to know there was to be a further generation of Bonynges. He and Adam had been the last of an old Huguenot family.

Richard and Chester arrived back from New York on August 31 after his 'strange production' of *Norma* and we were off to London on September 4 to record at Walthamstow Assembly Hall the *Bel Canto Arias* disc for Decca. This comprised eight arias by Donizetti, Verdi, Bellini, Meyerbeer and Rossini, more than half of which I had never sung in public. New to me were arias from Donizetti's *Il Castello di*

Kenilworth, Verdi's *Attila*, Donizetti's *Betly*, Meyerbeer's *L'Africaine* and Rossini's *Guillaume Tell*.

Rehearsals for *Hamlet* began in Toronto on the sixteenth and we were pleased to work again with John Bröcheler who sang Hamlet. Leslie Richards was Gertrude, Donald Shanks Claudius and Mark Dubois was Laërte. Michael Stennett had designed delightful costumes for me, especially that for the Mad Scene. But even wearing them I had quite a problem, being very conscious of my age and knowing that everyone in the cast was younger by far. Lotfi worked hard to persuade me I had been right to agree to sing Ophélie and Richard, too, made several attempts to convince and encourage me. Ultimately I had to accept that the opening night was on October 4 so I would have to do the best I could with that haunting music.

The press spoke a good deal abut the opera being 'a period piece' and, having been absent from the general repertoire for many years, being a 'historical curiosity'. The overall production and fine cast received due praise. Of my own contribution to the work William Littler of the *Toronto Star* wrote: '... Make no mistake about it, the lady from Sydney remains a phenomenon. She proceeded through the various stages of the Mad Scene, tossing off trills and caressing melodies with a combination of clarity and tonal beauty that remain the envy of her colleagues.'

Harold Schonberg in the *New York Times*:

... Is there a more experienced soprano than Miss Sutherland on the operatic stage today? She knows so well how to pace herself and how to overcome her physical liabilities. And she still has, after over 30 years on stage, a dependable technique. Through most of the opera she was in total control, only a few pinched and flurried high notes betraying her age. Her sound was often still ravishing. The Sutherland scoop, of course, was there, it always has been part of her style. Her admirers ignore it. Such gallant singing by so gallant a veteran brought down the house, as well it should have.

Hermann Trotter's report in the *Buffalo News* stated:

Sutherland's voice is still a marvel and can bring audiences to their feet, as it did at the conclusion of Ophélie's extraordinary mad scene. This is not of the frenetic, wailing variety, but a calm and calculated recounting by the unfortunate young girl of all the reasons why 'her husband' Hamlet never would desert her, a soliloquy couched firmly and totally in unreality.

Her voice retains both its ring and its range, as well as fine agility. About the only musical concession to time is a slight tendency for the vibrato, which warms and colors the voice, to veer in the direction of wobble on occasion.

And to be perfectly candid, it is a dramatic impediment when the youthful Ophélie looks many years the senior of Hamlet's mother, Gertrude ... in their touching duet of advice-giving.

So *someone* noticed!

There were five further performances in October and we had time to spend with visiting friends from New York and San Francisco. We had fun with Susan and Jan Rubes and viewed his recently made film *Witness*, in which he played the grandfather exquisitely. He has always exuded such honest sympathy and charm and was featured in several more films with great success.

With Darlene in tow we all moved on to Chicago. Here we had seven *Anna Bolena* performances, again in the Toronto sets and costumes. We had asked the Chicago Lyric Opera to find us an apartment or house to rent for the month and arrived to find we were housed in a glorious pseudo-French château in Highland Park with a splendid garden, a huge kitchen and minimal cooking utensils of a modest size. Stefania Toczyska sang Jane Seymour very dramatically, Paul Plishka looked every inch Henry VIII and Riccardo Percy was sung by Chris Merritt. The young and gifted soprano Nova Thomas was my 'cover' there and we enjoyed her wonderful Southern accent and stories, as well as her vocal ability. The opera opened on October 30, with a further six performances in November. Richard had two more *Normas* with the New York City Opera and in spite of his to-ing and fro-ing we still saw a lot of the countryside (and junk shops) of Illinois and Wisconsin.

On November 20 we were back in New York for the first of three concerts of *Anna Bolena* – in Avery Fisher Hall on the twenty-fifth, the Wang Center in Boston on December 1 and the Kennedy Center in Washington on December 6. The New York concert was with the New York City Opera Orchestra and televised for the 'Live from Lincoln Center' series. The singers for all three performances remained the same and we were a very compatible group. Judith Forst again sang the role of Jane Seymour, Jerry Hadley that of Percy, Henry VIII was sung by Gregory Yurisich and Smeton by Cynthia Clarey. All the artists were well received and I had many compliments, along with the current talk of my proposed retirement and ripe old age. Bill Zakariasen, in the *Daily News*, said: 'Despite the fact that she's just this side of 60, Dame Joan Sutherland is arguably the greatest singer currently practising her art.' The critics and audiences in Boston and Washington also appeared to enjoy the concerts and we were certainly glad to have completed what had been a mammoth year for this soprano of 'almost 60'. Home we went on December 7 for our Christmas celebrations.

Nineteen eighty-six saw us all on our way to Australia, arriving there on January 4 – in Perth at 3.40 a.m. Chetty and Darlene went on to Sydney, but we had a concert with the Western Australia Opera Company and WA Arts Orchestra, together with Bernadette Cullen in Perth. We found time to enjoy a Garden Party and dinner at Government House with His Excellency the Governor and Mrs Reid, also a luncheon trip on the river and a visit with Greg Yurisich to his parents' home, Olive Farm Vineyard just outside the city. The concert was a great success, very similar in content to the ones with Marilyn Horne, Bernadette's young mezzo-soprano voice blending beautifully in our duets.

Richard and I arrived in Sydney on January 11 – the same day that Adam went to New York on a course for Hilton International. But Helen, Natasha and Vanya joined us all at Whale Beach for the rest of the weekend, then we went into rehearsal for a revival of *Lucia di Lammermoor* and what was to be our last 'Opera in the Park' – a performance of Verdi's *Rigoletto*. I'd not sung the role of Gilda since the June Festival at the Met in 1972 and although scheduled for January 18, it had to be postponed due to torrential rain. The concert then took place on Monday the twentieth, with the title role excellently sung by Michael Lewis. Richard Greager was the Duke, Donald Shanks was both Monterone and Sparafucile and Rosemary Gunn was Maddalena. The *Sun* on January 21 remarked:

Saint Joan of Sydney made her annual pilgrimage to the people last night and, once again, the people loved it.

... Someone recently remarked that she sounds like a young soprano – except that there isn't a young soprano who sounds half as good!

David Gyger wrote:

Age plus physique alone would of course all but preclude Joan Sutherland from playing Gilda on stage these days; but she can sing the role as stupendously as ever – and proved so beyond doubt on Monday, January 20th.

... The particular personal triumph of the night as I saw it was the conducting of Richard Bonynge, which displayed at every turn precisely the right mix of musical passion and dramatic fire required to do full justice to the work in performance.

There were five *Lucias* in the Concert Hall – in January–February – and the performance was simulcast and released on video. I felt they photographed me really well. Although I was featured in many of the critical headlines:

LA STUPENDA OFFERS THE STUFF OF LEGENDS

DAME JOAN'S LUCIA A TRUE MASTERPIECE

MIRACLE VOICE JOAN STILL SOARS

LA STUPENDA SUPERB IN THE TITLE ROLE

ANOTHER TRIUMPH FOR LUCIA

the whole cast was warmly acclaimed and each performance seemed to grow musically and dramatically.

Richard also conducted five performances of a new *Magic Flute* at this time in the rather stark production by Carl Friedrich Oberle (designer) and Göran Järvefelt. I missed John Copley's romantic production. With further performances in July–August there was double and sometimes triple casting with Gran Wilson singing all the Taminos, Amanda Thane and Yvonne Kenny sang Pamina, Håkan Hagegård, Jeffrey Black and John Fulford Papageno, Christa Leahmann Queen of the Night with Donald Shanks as Sarastro. The Three Ladies were very well sung by various combinations of Rosamund Illing, Nicola Waite, Bernadette Cullen, Patricia Price and Rosemary Gunn, and Graeme Ewer was Monastatos.

During our last week in Sydney we were guests at Randwick racecourse where the Australian Jockey Club commemorated our visit by naming all the races on the day's programme after well-known Australian Opera figures, including Race No. 5 – the Dame Joan Sutherland Handicap – and Race No. 9 – the Richard Bonynge Welter Handicap. We each had to 'sash' the winner of 'our' race. It was a wonderfully relaxed day and whetted our appetite for more. I had amazing luck with my selections – so much so that Arthur Fitzgerald who had organised the outing was asking what I intended to back. Adam and Helen, both interested in the sport, were able to join us – their house was less than five minutes' walk from the trainers' entrance to the course.

We also visited a wonderful exhibition of paintings at the Art Gallery of New South Wales from the Heidelberg School, featuring works of Australians Tom Roberts, McCubbin, Conder, Bunny, Nerli, Ashton, etc.

On March 1 we flew to Wellington, New Zealand, where we opened their Festival of the Arts with the New Zealand Symphony Orchestra, giving two concerts with them and a recital with piano, arriving back in Switzerland on March 14.

The next two weeks were spent in Les Avants polishing the songs from the movies, arranged by Douglas Gamley for the recording *Talking Pictures* to be made in London the first week of April. We'd had fun deciding which pieces to include on the CD – I'd been a great Grace Moore, Deanna Durbin, Jeanette MacDonald fan and, of course, Miliza Korjus, so had certain priorities.

We went to London on March 30 for our film songs and Richard began his second recording of *Giselle*. By April 8 we were in Barcelona, together with Chester who had driven me down in the car. As always in Spain we made some day trips in the beautiful countryside surrounding Barcelona and visited several museums including the Picasso and Costume (Textile) collections.

Our rehearsals for *Norma* at the Liceo went well and we opened on April 21. The role of Adalgisa was ably sung by Doris Soffel with Jesus Pinto as Pollione and Giorgio Surjan as Oroveso. The singing was of a high standard but the sets left much to be desired. Norma's dwelling was furnished with Empire couches, one decked with a frilly lace baldachin. I couldn't look at it without wanting to laugh so kept my eyes very much on Richard in the pit. However, the public enjoyed it. At one stage rehearsal the gong in the last act was held by two virtually naked ballet boys who, we were told, would be painted gold for the performances. As I had to strike the gong forcibly to call the populace together I was worried that I might miss my target. Fortunately the idea was scrapped.

After our four *Norma*s we travelled back to Les Avants in the car to find Adam, Helen and the children had arrived at the weekend. It was fun to have them with us and on Natasha's birthday we went to the circus and took her to see the bears in Bern.

At the beginning of June we were to perform *La Fille du Régiment* with the Pittsburgh Opera, produced by Tito Capobianco who was also General Director of the Company. Rockwell Blake was Tonio with Claude Corbeil as Sulpice, and I made my first entrance from the back of the audience, beating my drum, although the climb on to the stage was a bit breath-taking. Richard Schulz, the music critic for the FM station had this to say:

> Dame Joan Sutherland was the lively, sparkling Marie in Donizetti's *Daughter of the Regiment* at Heinz Hall in the last production of the season for Pittsburgh Opera. If you had a tape measure I guess you could prove that her figure is not girlish, and if you looked in the Almanac you could prove that she is not a teenager, but you couldn't prove either of those statistics by how she looked and sounded on stage in the Thursday night performance. She looked enchanting ... And vocally, Dame Joan sounded like heaven's own special angel. The voice was clear as a bell: floating high notes, coloratura, incredible control, and climactic interpolated high notes made this a Sutherland that is even better than the legend – for recordings don't completely capture the clarity of the voice that has thrilled audiences for more than 30 years.

On June 11 we travelled to Houston for the final four *Anna Bolena* performances that had been scheduled for us in the Toronto production.

There were cast changes, with the delightful Susanne Mentzer singing Jane Seymour, Jane Bunnell the role of Smeton and Jerry Hadley was a most musical Riccardo Percy. Nicola Ghiuselev was our Henry VIII here and it was pleasing to work with him again after so long. We had a lovely apartment for our stay there and a charming hostess, Eileen Hricik, who ferried us everywhere, including a trip to the old opera house in Galveston. There was also a hurricane scare.

On June 29 we flew to Honolulu and on to Kauai, where we stayed at the Coco Palms Hotel for a few days, a charming old place alas no longer there, having been practically demolished by the violent hurricane which hit the island a few years ago.

In Sydney on July 5 we were greeted by Adam, Helen and the children, then went to Rocca Bella for the rest of the weekend. Back to the city for rehearsals for the Australian Opera's *La Fille du Régiment* – produced by Sandro Sequi along the lines of that first production of his in 1966. As always, it was fun to work with him and the cast of friends – Anson Austin, Heather Begg, Gregory Yurisich, Gordon Wilcock and Marie-Claire as the Duchess of Krakenthorp. The sets were by Henry Bardon with costumes again by Michael Stennett. Rehearsals for *Fille* had begun while we were in Kauai, so it was no time at all before the show was on, opening on the twenty-second, with six further performances.

'Sutherland: icing on the Regiment', said Fred Blanks in the *Sydney Morning Herald*. He continued:

> ... We know how old she is, and we imagine Marie ... being at most one third of that age, but it matters not a scrap. Indeed, the wonder of it is how convincingly Joan Sutherland still carries off her role, with that knack of tomboy foolery and face-pulling that suggests the young girl at heart ... the magic of those coloratura runs and particularly of those characteristic trills, continues. To say that she has found her second wind would be quite misleading, for she has never lost her first.

Roger Covell wrote in the *Sydney Morning Herald* at the end of December:

> DAME JOAN, SINGER AND COMEDIENNE, SHOWS THE OTHERS HOW IT'S DONE
> *No* experience in 1986 has been quite like attending a performance of the Australian Opera's *Daughter of the Regiment* with Dame Joan in the title role.
>
> Being away for the opening and catching up with the production only at a matinée late in the season I expected mild pleasure but no revelation.
>
> Yet the feeling in the theatre as the opera proceeded was too striking to let pass unchronicled. I can only describe it as a process of complete communication and sympathy between performers and audience.
>
> Yurisich, Austin and the others put their best into the afternoon; but

the truly memorable part of the occasion was the audience's relationship with Sutherland. It was an expression of absolute trust in and total commitment to the personality and gifts of the performer.

Some opera-goers have sniffed at the traditional (old-fashioned, if you like) nature of the production. One or two people may assume that the audience's unquenchable love for the leading lady was no more than a case of habitual heroine-worship. I do not think so.

Sutherland held the audience with her usually good comedienne's craft and the unaffected charm of her stage presence. I was put in mind of the legends of Nellie Stewart and Gladys Moncrieff at their best.

She has managed to establish a relationship with the Australian public which bears comparison with the musical comedy queens of a former age as well as, of course, earning an international operatic reputation at the highest level. That is a rare, probably an unrepeatable combination. It deserves notice.

It also deserves emulation by as many singers in the Australian Opera as possible, indeed by all operatic singers. It is not enough to deliver the notes or even to go through plausible dramatic motions; the potent appeal of musical theatre at its best depends on presence and communication.

'Last curtain call for Sutherland?' asked Jeremy Vincent in the *Melbourne Herald* on August 27. He went on to describe the scene at the Sydney Opera House after the final *Fille*, when I was showered with balloons, daffodils and streamers – 'her last scheduled performance with the Australian Opera Company'.

During our stay we took part in Vanya's christening and his first birthday – how time flies! We flew to Honolulu on the twenty-fourth where we were supposed to give a concert on August 29. However, there was an orchestral strike and picketing of the hall, so the event was cancelled. We spent further days at the Coco Palms on Kauai where I began to feel discomfort in the sinus area and ears. Was I carrying the infection that had attacked many members of the opera company over the past few weeks?

Hoping I would feel better on arrival, we left for San Francisco on August 28 for four more Sutherland–Pavarotti extravaganzas. It was quite obvious that I had contracted something, but by Sunday (three days later) equally obvious that I couldn't rehearse and might not be able to do the concert planned for Tuesday, September 2. It was Labour Day weekend in the States and all the doctors were unavailable. Fortunately our friend Jack Juhasz was able to contact Dr Saviano who kindly saw me at Children's Hospital on the holiday Monday and, diagnosing a perforated ear-drum, forbade my participation in either the next night's concert or the one planned for Saturday, September 6 in the Hollywood Bowl. Both ears were badly abscessed and I was very deaf. I felt dreadful and was in a lot of pain – agony might be a better word. Although some treatment and painkillers were prescribed I was assured that nothing much could be done until the inflammation subsided. Meanwhile I should see him the next day and again at the end of the week to determine whether I could at least fly to New York, if not to Chicago for the third projected gala. He did not want me to fly at all but I felt if I was in New York, even if the Chicago concert on the twelfth had to be cancelled by me, I might be recovered enough to sing the final one at Madison Square Garden on the sixteenth. Dr Saviano reluctantly permitted me to travel, on condition that I saw another specialist as soon as possible in New York.

I was able to get in touch with Dr Wilbur (Jim) Gould on Sunday, September 7 who saw me several times, starting Monday morning that week. He was appalled at the state of the ears and eustachian tube and did many tests of my hearing – all rather negative. He said after two visits there was no possibility of my doing either concert and that I had better accept the fact. I had fitted with Barbara a huge, glamorous black concert gown for the New York appearance after my first visit to the doctor. Herbert Breslin had come to this (along with a photographer and writer) against my wishes, not wanting to believe that the 'big draw' event in Chicago was an impossibility and probably that at Madison Square Garden would have to be cancelled by me too. In discussions after the journalists' departure, probably to alleviate his own panic, he laughed and said that of course I'd manage it – that I *never* cancelled. But this time I was forced to. Although the pain had diminished I was terribly deaf and once the final decision was made, the day before that of the Chicago concert, I asked Dr Gould if I could go home. He didn't like the idea at all but I pointed out that I was better out of New York when the news broke or I'd be worried to death by phone calls – which I couldn't hear, anyway. Finally he gave me his permission to take the direct flight to Geneva on Saturday, September 13 and I was relieved to collapse in my own home. I remained deaf for a further three weeks, more so in one ear than the other, giving me a lopsided feeling and making it difficult for me to know where any sound I *could* hear was coming from. My family seemed to materialise suddenly because I couldn't hear them walking into the room.

Of course, the cancellation made the New York headlines:

SUTHERLAND DROPS OUT OF CONCERT

DAME JOAN OUT OF 4 CONCERTS

JOAN SUTHERLAND CANCELS CONCERT AT THE GARDEN

This last headline was in the *New York Times* on Wednesday, September 10 and the article which followed also bore a statement from Dr Gould.

Dame Joan Sutherland is under therapy for a continuing ear infection which has temporarily affected the acuity of her hearing, thereby prohibiting her from the fulfilment of her engagement at Madison Square Garden.

The concert went ahead with Madelyn Renée assisting Luciano in a similar programme to his usual solo arena appearances. Although I hadn't enjoyed the concerts from an artistic angle there *was* a certain excitement about them and this series had been organised as a tribute to both of us – Luciano for the twenty-fifth anniversary of his operatic début and myself for having sung twenty-five years at the Met. I felt very embarrassed and upset that, after all the hard work and publicity, I had to withdraw. Fortunately there was (for me) a fairly long free period before having to record in London and slowly the hearing improved, although it has never become as acute as it was.

✧ 7 ✧

THERE HAD BEEN continuous criticism of the Australian Opera management in the press for months and the singers had joined those requesting the resignation of Patrick Veitch and Charles Berg who was Chairman of the Board. Charles had been involved with the Company for several years, giving both his time and money and attracting business associates to support and sponsor the opera. He retired and died quite soon after. On October 16 the *Sydney Morning Herald* reported:

> Meetings of staff from the Australian Opera have been called for today in order to announce the departure of the Company's General Manager, Mr Patrick Veitch.
>
> The announcement will bring to an end a long period of controversy within the Company, whose singers called for Mr Veitch's resignation in February this year.

Mr Veitch's contract had been due to expire two years later, at the end of 1988.

Towards the end of September Tessa Trench paid a welcome visit to Les Avants and again busied herself tidying up books and trying to sort out letters. Darlene had left things in very good order before returning to her university work in Fresno. We had discussed the possibility of her staying as a full-time secretary, but her father had been very unwell in Ohio and there was her long-service pension to be taken into consideration. She had enjoyed the constant trips and was a great organiser, getting along well with everyone. Now she visits from time to time in Sydney and we are always delighted to see her. She helps keep our diaries up to date and reminds us of the mail waiting to be answered.

My period of rest at home was very beneficial and I refrained from singing as long as possible, only 'feeling my way' during the last week or two, knowing I had to revise *Anna Bolena* to record it in London in mid-October. Recording sessions began on the fifteenth – with the middle of the long and varied final Mad Scene at 'Oh! chi si duole?' and continuing with the short but very exposed arietta 'Al dolce guidami'. It was not the most sensible 'opener' after my problem, however it had to be done some time so why not straight away?

Since retiring I have frequently heard this whole Mad Scene sung by competitors in vocal contests, most of whom had no idea of its difficulties and pitfalls, just ploughing through it. 'Al dolce guidami' appears to be a straightforward, simple piece but its range, sustained fragility and dreamlike quality are quite taxing, requiring great restraint after previous dramatic outbursts in a staged presentation – with more of them to come. It is a gem and should sound like it.

Enrico VIII was sung by Samuel Ramey, Lord Riccardo Percy by Jerry Hadley and Jane Seymour by Susanne Mentzer. We were delighted to make the acquaintance of Bernadette Manca di Nissa and her lovely voice singing the role of Smeton.

By October 25 we were in New York, rehearsals having begun at the Met for a revival of *I Puritani*, to celebrate the twenty-fifth anniversary of my association with the Metropolitan Opera, on November 14, with a total of nine performances. Before these began I had celebrated my sixtieth birthday, dining with Barbara and Arthur Matera and some friends, including that clever Broadway designer Florence Klotz, at the Materas' apartment.

The cast of *I Puritani* had an excellent Riccardo and Giorgio in Sherill Milnes and Sam Ramey, with Salvatore Fisichella as Arturo for half of the run, Rockwell Blake then taking over. There was the usual participation in interviews, record and book signings (*The Joan Sutherland Album*, a chronological picture book), various dinner parties, and Richard also had a concert for the Richard Tucker Foundation in Avery Fisher Hall. A luncheon was given for me by the Met to celebrate my twenty-five years with them and a large cake, iced and decorated with a replica of the huge arched windows of the Metropolitan Opera house, was served.

The programme for *I Puritani* contained photographs from several of the roles I had sung at the Met – as my first Lucia in the old house, Norma, Marie in *La Fille du Régiment*, Olympia in *Les Contes d'Hoffmann* and Elvira in *I Puritani*. In itself this was a delightful tribute.

Donal Henahan of the *New York Times* had this to say of the opening night:

This is the kind of night it was: when Joan Sutherland made her first entrance in *I Puritani*, the Metropolitan Opera House resounded with such a prolonged stomping, screaming ovation that the performance came to a dead halt. La Stupenda, as opera history will know her, finally gave up, left the stage and returned to start over, allowed at last by her happy fans to take on the persona of Bellini's famously unstable heroine, the on-again, off-again madwoman Elvira.

Any appearance by the Australian diva these days is likely to put an audience into delirium, but last evening's could not help being special, coming as it did just 12 days short of the 25th anniversary of her Metropolitan début in *Lucia di Lammermoor*. At every opportunity, the audience paid tribute to the evening's heroine by howling and ululating in fearsome unison, as if ordinary applause could not satisfy the demands of this historic event. Miss Sutherland, surely the youngest-sounding 60-year-old soprano in modern operatic history, responded with an astounding display of bel canto craft and staying power. The voice, though used more cautiously than it once was, retains remarkable freshness and technical security, evident in the lively brilliance of her 'Son vergin vezzosa' as well as the alternating pathos and febrility of 'Qui la voce'.

After the matinée performance on the thirteenth I was presented with a silver tray during the final curtain calls by Bruce Crawford, the Met's General Manager, and honoured later at a supper party given by him for the cast at the Opera Club.

Christmas was fast approaching so we wasted no time after the last *I Puritani*, flying to Geneva the next evening to spend a relaxed ten days in Les Avants with the family and friends from England and Australia.

On New Year's Eve we were off to New York again, staying just two nights before travelling on to Washington where we had a concert at Kennedy Center on January 4, 1987. In the *Washington Post* the next day Joseph McLellan wrote:

Two months after her 60th birthday and 25 years after her Metropolitan Opera début, Joan Sutherland is still 'La Stupenda'. If anyone doubted this fact in last night's standing-room audience at the Kennedy Center, a few minutes of listening would have been enough to prove the point.

... The Australian soprano's richness of tone is remarkable throughout her wide range. Her agility in the stratospheric regions above the treble staff remains amazing, not merely for a voice as big as hers but for any human voice at all. Under the always considerate baton of her husband, mentor and accompanist Richard Bonynge, her powerful voice soared through and above the sound of a well-chosen 60-piece freelance orchestra.

We were back in New York the next day, where rehearsals began on the sixth for a Met gala on the eleventh in aid of their Pension Fund and celebrating again my twenty-five years at the Met, together with Luciano's twenty-five years as a professional singer. We performed Act 1, Scene II of *Lucia di Lammermoor*, Act 3 of *Rigoletto*, and Act 3 of *La Traviata*, complete with sets and costumes, and the evening was taped for transmission in the TV series 'Live from the Met' that March. Leo Nucci, Ariel Bybee, Julian Robbins and Isola Jones sang with us.

It was something of a hassle to get the scenes sorted out in the time available.

The *Lucia* and *Traviata* were not too much of a problem but I'd not done Gilda on stage since the Met's June Festival in 1972, although I had sung the 'Opera in the Park' concert in Sydney the previous January. At my age and somewhat increased weight, I was worried about being carried on in a sack and dumped at Rigoletto's feet. The problem was solved, also my garb as a boy. I asked for extra dim lighting although it is a gloomy night scene anyway and the Lighting Designer (Gil Wechsler) obliged, making it almost impossible for me to negotiate the scenery. Apart from a few minor hitches the evening went well and the audience went wild. Thor Eckert Jr of the *Christian Science Monitor* wrote:

> It was a sentimental evening, with longtime fans and recent converts to both singers' art gathered for an SRO [standing room only] performance. Miss Sutherland has remained true to her voice, which makes her still capable of tossing off clean, clear runs and singing high notes, as well as displaying other facets of that wonderful Sutherland gift that have long made her performances sellouts.
>
> Mr Pavarotti, somewhat her junior, succumbed early in his career to some of the glamour and pressures of being a superstar, which meant stepping into a repertoire for which his light tenor was not built. He has found ways to make much of the new repertoire work for him. But when faced with a role that used to be one of his glories – Edgardo in *Lucia* – the vocal price he has paid was obvious.

Mr Eckert had again shown his perceptiveness regarding the human voice as he did with his 'too-much-too-soon' article and was, in a way, reaffirming and confirming that opinion.

Dale Harris in the *New York Post* summed up his assessment of my performance with: 'At the age of 60, she remains one of the vocal phenomena of the century. Twenty-five years after her sensational Met début as Lucia, she can still give the world a few lessons in the art of singing.'

Many of my colleagues wrote warm letters of congratulations and I was especially touched by one from dear John Alexander with whom I had sung so much and who had been such a stalwart member of the 1965 Australian Tour.

After the Met gala Richard and I continued with the tour started in Washington, visiting Boston, Pasadena, San Diego, Tulsa, Dallas and Miami. We repeated the Washington concert in all these cities, Richard of course having to rehearse a different orchestra each time. Some of the groups were from the local opera companies (who also sponsored some concerts) so were possibly familiar with the repertoire, whilst other players were from chamber orchestras with no (or very little) experience of the operatic repertoire. How grateful I was that Ric was mostly able to rehearse without my having to sing, or even *be* there. I would come to the second rehearsal and sing just as much as was necessary for judging pauses, etc., although he had anticipated them all. The tour was for five weeks, including Washington and the Met gala with Pavarotti, and Richard and I enjoyed very much not only the appearances but the opportunity to see old friends in many of the cities and to meet some new ones.

We flew back to Les Avants on February 6 and on the fifteenth returned to London to complete the *Anna Bolena* recording begun the previous October. By the twenty-first we were back home again in Les Avants, where I embarked on learning *Ernani* for the recording to be made in May and revising *Adriana Lecouvreur* for performances with the Canadian Opera in Toronto. This last work I knew well and loved to perform but of the *Ernani* I knew only the big aria 'Ernani involami' and needed quite a bit of work to 'sing the role into my voice' so that there would hopefully be no problems at the recording sessions.

By March 15, Chester, Richard and I were in Toronto and rehearsals progressed well, with John Copley producing the opera as he had in Sydney. Cornelis Opthof was a sympathetic Michonnet and it was good to see him again after quite a long time. The Prince de Bouillon was sung by Gary Relyea, the Princesse by Lorna Myers and the hero Maurizio by Alberto Cupido. The chorus was superbly rehearsed by that wizard chorus master Donald Palumbo. The opera opened on April 3, with five further performances. There were violets everywhere – on the programme cover, the invitations to dinner and after per- formance suppers – but the flowers were not poisoned as in the opera.

There seemed to be disappointment that the role did not require great flights of coloratura singing which the critics encouraged the audience to notice. The opera had apparently not been staged in Canada before and there was the customary criticism of Cilea's work. For myself, I was delighted to dispense with all the agility and enjoyed the opera's dramatic high spots for Adriana together with, for my taste, emotional and effective music.

On April 19 we went to New York for a few days, flying on to Houston on the twenty-third and giving another concert with Luciano. It was given the title of 'The Sutherland–Pavarotti Extravaganza' and sponsored by the Houston Grand Opera, with many parties and dinners in our honour. About 12,000 attended the event in the Summit and a good time appeared to be had by all.

Back we went to Geneva the day after, managing to spend two weeks there before going to London to record *Ernani* with Luciano, Leo Nucci, and Paata Burchuladze. As I remember there were not too many problems during the taping – the usual false starts, creaking boards, coughs, vagaries of pitch, external noise and just plain wrong entries and errors. But at the time of writing the disc had not been issued. Whatever the reason, between sessions we managed to enjoy meeting with friends and Richard went to some of his favourite antique shops and auctions. We had a very happy weekend with our friend Peter Newbold at Lord and Lady Aberconway's home in North Wales, Bodnant, with its spectacular rhododendron garden in full flower.

Home in Les Avants I spent a busy week planting geraniums – and anything else that took my fancy. We had a luncheon at the Hotel Victoria in Glion to celebrate Udi's thirty years as part of our family and Weenie and Marion arrived at the end of the week to keep the press books up to date. Without their regular visits this book could never have been written – not by me anyway!

The biography that Norma Major had been writing over a period of five years was published and on sale from May 31 in London. Norma had never intruded while writing, although checking with us from time to time, appreciating our need for privacy and relaxation between engagements. However, she managed to pen a very faithful and precise account of our lives, with a fairly accurate discography and list of performances to the date of publication. The book was revised, updated and republished in 1994. Putting together my own recollections with the material all to hand in our series of press books and personal agendas, I can appreciate just how much Norma had to glean from opera house archives and libraries.

The Joan Sutherland Album, the collection of photographs arranged chronologically as a pictorial biography of our lives by Richard and myself, was also mentioned in some of the book reviews during this summer, although published the previous year.

On June 5 Richard and I took the TGV Express to Paris in the evening, spending a pleasant weekend there. On the Sunday we were taken by Jean-Marie Poilvé, our French agent, to visit Pierre Jourdan, who in turn took us to Compiègne to view a portion of the Palais Royal and its attached unfinished theatre. Pierre was endeavouring to have it cleaned (the pigeons had nested in it for years) and completed to provide a venue for festival performances. This he ultimately accomplished and the Théâtre Français de la Musique has been functioning for several seasons of opera and operetta. Although the whole project intrigued both of us very much and we were made patrons (Membres Bienfaiteurs), we have unfortunately not managed to attend a performance there yet. An interesting point about the situation of the theatre is that it stands on the site of a destroyed Carmelite convent – that of the Sisters of Compiègne featured in *The Dialogues of the Carmelites*.

On June 8 we gave a recital in l'Opéra de Paris – the Palais Garnier, of course. '*Joan Sutherland triomphe à l'Opéra,*' wrote Claude Samuel and the audience did, indeed, go wild, showering the stage with flowers, as noted in *Le Monde*: '*Avalanches d'iris, d'oeillets et de roses pour saluer l'entrée de la célèbre diva australienne. Et ovations délirantes pour la remercier de son récital.*' It was a wonderful night, with many compliments on my black-and-silver bouffant concert gown designed by Barbara Matera, as well as the singing.

Next day we returned on the TGV to Les Avants and on June 12 arrived in Warsaw, where we performed the same recital on the fifteenth – moved from the fourteenth due to the visit of the Pope, as demonstrations were expected. Also due to the visit of His Holiness, we were lodged in a picturesque, if somewhat dilapidated country château about forty kilometres outside the city which must have been a gem in its heyday. It was being lovingly restored and was at that time a type of retreat or holiday hostel for Polish writers and artists with a well-built and decorated wooden annexe for extra guests across the road at the edge of a forest. Richard and I were lodged in the suite of (I think) the Minister of Culture, which was a remaining part of the original small castle on the property and separate from the main villa.

When we had unpacked our toilet articles in the bathroom I had noticed a bucket and watering can filled with water under the hand basin and wondered why. It was not long before we found out. There were frequent electrical black-outs which meant that the pump for distributing the water was not working, so the filled cans were for such an emergency. They had their own generator there but I fear that was pre-war and tended to break down. One night, Richard and I sat in the study outside our huge bedroom in our dressing-gowns with only candles to provide light for Richard to do his crossword puzzle and me some needlepoint. We felt like characters from *A Month in the Country* or some such piece. It was very romantic but taxing on the eyesight.

The concert was a great success with the public and we were entertained to dinner by the Australian representative, Mr Seccombe, and his wife. Happily we had the time to visit the Chopin house at Zelazowa Wola and the palace of Wilanow with its garden. Unfortunately, the trees had been burned, presumably by the air currents from Chernobyl after the disaster. We managed to see the refurbished 'Old Town' and had the desire to revisit Poland at our leisure. So far it has not been possible, although Richard later made a recording in Krakow.

At the end of June Pierre Jourdan and Jean-Marie Poilvé visited, Pierre wishing to make a television documentary about us, having had success with previous ones, particularly that with Teresa Berganza.

We talked a great deal about the possibility but I felt I had enough to do and that it was too late for such a project so it never happened.

On July 12, Adam, Helen and the children arrived for a six-week stay, also Helen's mother, Jean, and a procession of friends right through July and August into September. We had not been at home for a lengthy period like this since we started going to Sydney for the Australian Opera's winter season and it was rather like the years we spent in Ticino, with house guests all the time. We were delighted to keep them amused by taking day trips to some of the not too distant beauty spots and even did a three-day trip up to Lake Constance, Arenenberg, St Gallen, Einsiedeln and back through the mountains and the Valais. Everyone enjoyed themselves and we were able to have full benefit of our garden. We went to a matinée at Circus Knie on tour in Bern for the children – and the rest of the family – before they all returned to Australia.

I had not had to perform for four months – a foretaste of retirement and I *loved* it! But on September 20 we flew to Stockholm, where we did *Puritani* for the Swedish Radio, with César-Antonio Suarez as Arturo, Knut Skram as Riccardo, Ulrik Cold as Giorgio and Raymond Björling (another member of that great singing family) in the small role of Bruno. We were handsomely entertained and one morning were able to visit the outstanding collection of antique Royal costumes and regalia displayed in the palace.

We decided to return to Les Avants before going on to Edinburgh – to pick up some winter clothes to go with the summer ones so we could continue on to America after our UK commitments. We had four busy days at home organising our luggage for the next five and a half months, as after the American dates we would go to Australia, not returning to Les Avants until the second week of March 1988.

We gave concerts with the Scottish Chamber Orchestra in the Theatre Royal, Glasgow on the fourth and in Usher Hall, Edinburgh, on the seventeenth. We had another look at Holyrood House and the museum during our stay and were given a fantastic dinner party by the sponsors, the Royal Bank of Scotland, in their beautiful Georgian bank after the Edinburgh concert. The day after, we had a leisurely drive via Sir Walter Scott's home, Abbotsford, to visit our old friends Brian Sack and Francis Coulson. We spent the night at their famed hotel Sharrow Bay on Lake Ullswater near Penrith. What wonderful hosts they are and such a delectable menu. We were sorry to have to leave so promptly but had to get to London in good time for recording the next day.

This was a collection of *Romantic Trios for Soprano, Horn and Piano*, with the horn played by Barry Tuckwell and Richard at the piano. It was recorded in Henry Wood Hall and most of the songs were in

German or French, with one Donizetti piece in Italian. We had a little trouble gauging pauses and tempi suitable for both Barry and myself but the disc was completed without too much fuss.

A frightening memory of that London visit was the hurricane that swept through during the night of October 15. We had an evening session until 9.30 p.m. and by the time we had eaten and gone to bed we were quite tired. Richard slept like the dead but I was awakened by the sound of a constant rushing wind and the rattling of doors in the apartment. The next morning when I opened the curtain in the sitting-room which faced the garden square I couldn't believe the destruction there – branches broken and blown into the street and all sorts of rubbish, as well as damaged cars. The television news was very explicit about the damage and we wondered if we would manage to get across the river to the recording hall with all the huge trees broken down along the Embankment. However, it was amazing how the police and fire departments coped with the emergency and moved the debris with very little inconvenience. If we had been working with an orchestra I imagine the session would have been cancelled, as so many transport services were disrupted. It was truly sad to see the damage to Kensington Gardens and Kew.

One bizarre occurrence was the fact that we had a free day on the previous Tuesday and visited Michael and Robin Onslow with Ann and Charles Aberconway. Michael was worried about the avenue of elm trees at Clandon that had been attacked by Dutch Elm Disease and many of them completely ruined, leaving ugly remains and gaps. He asked Charles what he thought would be the best way to tidy up the surviving trees to replant. There were several suggestions, but they were all needless three days later – the storm had felled the lot.

Rehearsals for the new production of *Il Trovatore* began at the Met on October 20 on what was probably my least favourite set in almost forty years on the stage. It was a series of rostrums connected by steps with high risers and very narrow treads – not at all large enough for my size 42 shoes. To add to the hazards the set had an ultra-shiny black surface and, apart from showing every footprint, was rather slippery. The stage was polished after every scene. Then when Count di Luna's attendants came on stage fully dressed for the first time in their expensive metal armour, not only did they clank and clash during their own entrance but through the off-stage muted singing of the chorus of nuns. The hollow rostrums banged and thumped like bass drums at every step too. The armour was scrapped but the rostrums still resounded, so one had to creep about not to ruin the musical phrases. I hated that set and refused to walk from stage level up. Down was bad enough but, with the heavy costumes and no support at all, to climb up was impossible so once I had entered from two levels above there was nowhere to go but down. The castle was a series of huge columns (meant to represent towers) on wheels which were placed at different angles further on- or off-stage, rather like the Australian Opera set which at least had a solid floor. At every performance I had the impression I was working in a rehearsal room with no scenery at all and I don't think Luciano liked the production any more than I did. Maybe the lighting was fantastic but I will never know.

However, before we reached the stage rehearsals, Richard and I performed in the twelfth annual gala concert in Carnegie Hall for the Richard Tucker Music Foundation, together with Livia Budai, Justino Diaz, Giuseppe Giacomini, Alfredo Kraus, Richard Leech, Pilar Lorengar, Eva Marton, Sherill Milnes and Harry Dworchak – the winner of that year's Richard Tucker Award. The conducting was shared between Richard and Anton Guadagno and I sang the duet from Act 1 of *La Fille du Régiment* with Alfredo Kraus, although the printed programme says otherwise. The concert was on October 25.

Once again, for the weekend prior to the Dress Rehearsal at the Met we went to Barbara and Arthur Matera's house in Athens, New York – but there was no accident on the stairs this time, just my very happy sixty-first birthday.

We opened at the Met on November 12, with nine further performances including the matinée broadcast on the nineteenth. Luciano was Manrico, Leo Nucci was di Luna and Azucena was shared by Livia Budai, Elena Obratsova, Shirley Verrett and Mignon Dunne. The reviews were *not* complimentary, speaking of the

> Met's cold-blooded *Trovatore* and Ezio Frigerio's cold and utilitarian set – a stageful of highly polished stairs and six monumental blank columns that motored about, changing places for different scenes – evoked no atmosphere except Opera House Cheap

as Heide Waleson wrote.

Tim Page said:

> This is an ugly and ill-conceived *Trovatore*, built, incomprehensibly, upon an omnipresent staircase that suddenly burst into flames at the conclusion of the opera.
>
> The staircase is flanked by what resemble greased Victorian table legs that move back and forth toward the middle of the stage like the sinister trees in *Babes in Toyland*. Backgrounds include a skyscraper that seems part William Blake, part Niagara Falls and a flaming red mountain that resembles Mt Kilauea erupting that suddenly appears behind Pavarotti during 'Di quella pira'.

At least the critics and the audience showed their disapproval, dismay and anger at the non-production but that did not help the artists, all of whom were inhibited by this bare and wasteful monstrosity.

We had time to see some American friends and also some shows – *Anything Goes* was our favourite and although *Les Misérables* was the rage we thought it boring. We also saw *Cabaret* and were delighted by Regina Resnik's performance. She was splendid, but I don't know how she managed to sustain all those appearances. We also attended Ira Siff's ('Madame Vera Galupe-Borszkh) Second Annual Farewell Recital specially performed for me. He did wonderful send-ups of my *Lucia* and *Hamlet* Mad Scenes and we appreciated his great knowledge of style in some of his less flamboyant offerings such as Dido's Lament, a Tchaikovsky song and Poulenc's 'Chemins de l'amour'. He frequently sang better than the divas he was lampooning.

During the year I had been honoured to receive the Arturo Toscanini Critics' Award for my work 'representing lifetime achievement as a performing artist'.

Richard, Chester and I flew to Sydney arriving on the twenty-second and going to Whale Beach, where Ruthli and her family joined us on the twenty-fourth and we all spent a happy Christmas and New Year together there with Adam, Helen and the children, with their other grandma, Jean, their great-grandma Bonynge and great-grandfather George (Jean's father).

This was Australia's bicentennial anniversary year of the founding of the original British colony in Sydney on January 26, 1788. The preparations for the celebrations had been considerable, along with the public anticipation, and we all looked forward to watching the harbour events from our splendid vantage point, the windows and roof of our apartment at Potts Point. The 'great day' was some weeks away so on January 4 rehearsals began for the revival of *The Merry Widow* of which I was to do six 'gala' performances and Glenys Fowles was singing a further nine, so Richard would be busy. Rehearsals of this favourite Company frolic were fun and at the end of the first week we had a birthday lunch at Whale Beach for Grandma Bonynge, with Weenie and Marion and friends Pat and Ann from Leura (in the Blue Mountains). It was a lovely family gathering. The following week was full of Dress Rehearsals, especially for Ric, who had two of everything because of the double casting, treble, in fact, as Christine Douglas did a couple of performances due to the indisposition of Glenys Fowles.

The arrival of the Tall Ships in the harbour on January 18–19 was eagerly awaited and what a sight that was! Hundreds of the local small craft gathered to salute and escort the magnificent sailing vessels up the harbour to their berths at Darling Harbour and we were able to watch the scene from our windows.

Sadly, Christmas Day was the last time we saw great-grandfather George, who had refused all treatment for his advanced cancer. His funeral was on January 20 and I felt such sympathy and great admiration for Jean and Helen, who had coped with three terminal illnesses and deaths in their family within a very short time: David Wahba, Jean's happy and lovable husband whom she had helped nurse through the final stages of cancer, Mollie her mother who had been incapacitated by several strokes and in a nursing home for a long period and now talented, cheerful George. We understood when Jean soon after decided to sell their house complete with granny flat and move to a much smaller, cosy bungalow of her own styling, with a manageable garden, just around the corner from Rocca Bella at Whale Beach. That trip was also the last for us to see Ric's mother, whose health rapidly deteriorated that year. She died peacefully in hospital where she had gone for tests. Vanya and Helen were two of her last visitors, having spent a very happy time with her.

The Widow opened on the twenty-first with practically all the critics latching on to the 'merry' of the operetta's title:

LA STUPENDA THE MERRIEST OF WIDOWS

FANS MERRY ON JOAN'S CHAMPAGNE

JOAN IN A MERRY MOOD FOR SYDNEY

STUPENDA BACK FOR MERRY BICENTENARY

A special gala programme had been printed with many photographs and the Company's new General Manager, Donald McDonald, wrote a small preface to the elegant programme saying:

> It would be unimaginable for the Australian Opera to celebrate the bicentennial without the participation of Joan Sutherland and Richard Bonynge.
>
> These Gala performances of *The Merry Widow* provide us with the opportunity to honour and celebrate the unparalleled contributions to the world of opera, and Australia's place in it, which have been made by these two great artists.

The cast was mostly made up of members of the Company well-versed in their roles, with Ron Stevens again giving us his suave Danilo. Alan Jones commented next day:

> ... What a performer! It was a night as spectacular as the tall ships, the First Fleet Re-enactment, and Darling Harbour rolled into one, packed Opera House. A 61 year old soprano, perhaps the world's greatest ever, totally dominated, entertained, and then hypnotised an audience which couldn't get enough and when it ended and the Merry Widow found her lover the scenes were almost mayhem.

Everyone in the theatre rose to their feet, balloons and streamers cascaded from every part of the Opera House and Joan Sutherland and her husband, Richard Bonynge, had crafted yet another triumph.

Why don't we make this woman Governor-General? If we're talking about giving women a go let her tell her story to all Australia. How do you preserve such artistry at 61?? How do you continue to make the sacrifices necessary for success at 61 years of age? Isn't that a lesson we could all learn?

We made a quick trip to our extraordinary Jenolan Caves with Ruthli, Jean-Paul and Rachel before they returned to Switzerland on the thirtieth after having seen the celebrations in the presence of the Prince and Princess of Wales, the Parade of Sail on the harbour, then the magnificent firework display on January 26.

There were luncheons and dinners, both Richard and I sat for portraits by Judy Cassab, there were many interviews and my unveiling of a tribute to me commissioned by the Sydney City Council. It was a bas-relief in marble, beautifully sculpted by Peter Schipperheyn, the subject a human ear. The sculptor said the piece symbolically represented the enjoyment given by my singing. I was very flattered by the tribute which is on one of the walls of the Sydney Town Hall directly opposite the one to Dame Nellie Melba.

We also gave a short recital on February 19 in the ballroom of the Queen Victoria building for the Children's Hospital Fund. After the end of the concert, the General Superintendent of the hospital, Dr John Yu, reeled into our 'dressing-room' and I thought he was feeling faint. He said he was, waving a piece of paper. He had just been given a cheque for a million dollars towards the Fund for the new Children's Hospital being built on the outskirts of the city. Helen and I paid a visit to the old hospital a week or so later and saw the magnificent plans for the new one which opened in November 1995 and is a huge success. John Yu was named 'Australian of the Year' for his untiring efforts to establish this great modern facility for the children not only of Sydney, but those in outlying districts anywhere in the country who can be flown by helicopter directly to receive the best available treatment.

We spent a great amount of time at Whale Beach and I saw Helen and the children frequently. But on March 3 we were on the move again, flying to Adelaide, where we gave on the sixth a similar concert to those performed in America, this time for the Adelaide Festival with the Adelaide Symphony Orchestra. We returned to Sydney on the seventh, managed next morning to visit the exhibition of treasures from the Hermitage in St Petersburg showing at the Art Gallery of New South Wales and left the same evening for Europe.

While in Sydney there had been discussions between Edmund Capon, the Director of the Art Gallery of NSW, Diana (Di) Heath, Moffatt Oxenbould and ourselves about the possibility of holding an exhibition of my costumes in the gallery as a tribute. It was a wonderful idea and Richard and I were excited by it, but I pointed out that most of my costumes were in Les Avants, the rest in New York and it was a long way to Australia. Edmund had assured me that the gallery was used to that – had I not been to many of its visiting exhibitions? 'All very well,' was my response, 'but surely this would be different – and such a weighty and bulky consignment.' When and how this would all be brought about was somewhat vague, but the date was set for 1989–90. On arrival in Les Avants one of the top priorities was to inspect the gowns and accessories in the loft of Chalet Amina (our 'overflow' guest house). Trying to decide what to include was difficult as there were so many.

On April 3 we gave a concert in New York with the Orchestra of St Luke's which we thoroughly enjoyed. The reviewers' headlines waxed lyrical with:

DAME JOAN DELIVERS

GREAT DAME TRIUMPHS IN LINCOLN CENTER CONCERT

DAME JOAN STILL IN FINE FORM AT LINCOLN CENTER

THERE'S NOTHING LIKE THIS DAME

On April 4 we flew to Rochester, New York, and stayed in the home of Dr and Mrs Aquavella from where we travelled to Syracuse to rehearse and sing a benefit concert for the Syracuse Opera on April 7. Andrea Griminelli, the Italian flautist, appeared with us playing the Rondo Russo from Mercadante's Concerto in E Minor for flute and strings and the brilliant *Fantasy* on Bizet's *Carmen* arranged by Francis Borne.

We visited Rochester's Art Museum and also the fascinating Kodak photographic museum, before returning to New York on the afternoon of the eighth, managing to see that spectacular show *Phantom of the Opera* (with Michael Crawford) before going to Baltimore on the thirteenth for a concert with the Baltimore Symphony. We spent time in the wonderful Museum of Fine Art bequeathed to the city by a wealthy collector-benefactor and on April 17 were back in Les Avants for a two-and-a-half-week stay.

Rehearsals for *Anna Bolena* began on May 5 at Covent Garden and I was very at ease with the other members of the cast. Susanne Mentzer was again Jane Seymour, with Dimitri Kavrakos as Henry VIII, John Aler as Percy and Eirian James as Smeton. The opera was beautifully designed and produced by John Pascoe.

On May 15 we appeared in a gala for the Australian Musical Foundation in London – a 'Bicentennial Celebration' at the Theatre Royal, Drury Lane attended by Her Royal Highness Princess Alexandra. The artists were predominantly Australian, including Barry Tuckwell, Sir Charles Mackerras, Douglas Gamley, Susanne Kessler, Malcolm Donnelly and others with Dame Edna Everage compèring *Peter and the Wolf*. The young American singer Nova Thomas sang the part of Adalgisa in the Act 2 Scene I of *Norma* duet with us.

The opera opened on May 30 for six performances. 'Joan Sutherland Scores Another Triumph at 61,' said the *International Herald Tribune*. 'High Note that may be Dame Joan's Swan Song,' headed the report in the London *Daily Mail*, concluding with '... So if this is indeed farewell, Dame Joan is going out on a musical high. Vocally, it is a miraculous climax to an illustrious career.'

We saw many old friends during our seven weeks' stay in London and visited some of the city's museums, including the Queen's Gallery. We also appeared in the gala for Sir John Tooley who was retiring, having been General Director of the Royal Opera House between 1970 and 1988 and worked in the house for a total of thirty-three years. It was a grand night, with so many artists both from the opera company and the ballet paying homage. My contribution was the *Lucia* Mad Scene as requested, with Richard conducting.

Back to Les Avants on the twenty-third, with Tessa making a brief visit, also friends, the McNutts, from Tunbridge Wells. On July 3 Richard and I flew to Munich, where we gave a recital in the Philharmonic Hall. On the sixth we flew on to Catania where we received the 'Bellini d'Oro' award and gave a recital in the large Teatro Metropolitan, followed by a delicious dinner on the eighth. As it was extremely hot in Sicily and the theatre was without air-conditioning, Richard and I were perspiring freely – so much so that in my final item the perspiration trickled into my left eye, washing out my contact lens which I was fortunately able to retrieve from my cheek with a not too obvious raising of my hand. Our clothing was more soaked than after doing a complete opera.

Back at the Chalet Monet on July 9 I was free for about seven weeks and able to enjoy the summer again, with friends visiting from time to time. Richard and Chester left for Sydney on July 23, as Richard had performances there of *Fra Diavolo* with the Australian Opera.

On September 4 I flew to London and was taken by car to Fairy Hill, a charming old seventeenth-century country-house hotel outside Swansea in South Wales. Richard had flown direct from Australia and recording for *Adriana Lecouvreur* began in Brangwyn Hall in the city on the sixth. These sessions had been difficult to arrange, due to everybody's other engagements, and Luciano had said he could only do two sessions before he left for America, leaving the bulk of his role to be recorded during the time set aside for us in December. With the whole orchestra and chorus of the Welsh National Opera gathered, and the rest of the cast waiting, Luciano, when he arrived, elected to do Maurizio's aria and it was quite obvious to us that he did not know it as well as he should. During the recent summer he'd had the benefit of two coaches, the second of whom, Maestro Tonini, highly respected for his many years at La Scala, was much embarrassed at the sessions. I suspected Luciano had refused to work on the role, preferring to swim and relax. I could not understand why, if he didn't know the piece, he had bothered to come to Swansea at all. He left for America while those of us still in Swansea continued recording until the ninth. Decca secured a promise from Carlo Bergonzi to sing the role of Maurizio in the December period, dropping Luciano completely from this opera.

I went back to Switzerland very upset that the recording had been disrupted and by Luciano, of all people. Richard flew to Toronto where he was preparing Tchaikovsky's *Queen of Spades* for the Canadian Opera.

I again had a long break of five weeks at the chalet, relishing the lack of pressure and the realisation that soon I would be spending much more time in my home.

On October 16 I flew to New York and on to Washington on the eighteenth, where Richard joined me, between his Toronto performances, for a concert in Kennedy Center on the twenty-first, with the Sydney Symphony Orchestra on its very successful Bicentennial tour. The programme was repeated on October 24 for the United Nations Day concert at the UN and televised by the ABC.

A further concert with the orchestra in Carnegie Hall on the thirtieth featured a different programme, with me singing the big aria from *I Masnadieri* and that of Zerlina from *Fra Diavolo*, and Richard also conducting the ballet music from *Esclarmonde*.

On the thirty-first we returned briefly to Les Avants, leaving again by car on November 6 for Barcelona, where we were to do four performances of *Lucia*. Alfredo Kraus sang the role of Edgardo. Once again there was a good deal of gossip about our both being in our early sixties and still singing these roles well after thirty years. Alfredo and I had some interesting talks abut vocal production, weighing the different method of approaching the upper register of the voice practised by each of us. Neither of us felt we could succeed using the other's technique. It was an indication of the difficulties that can exist between teacher and pupil – how to overcome conflicting ideas of obtaining the same result. Our rehearsals were not arduous and we managed several trips in the car between them. *Lucia* opened on November 21 to great acclaim, with the fans raining printed cards down during the curtain calls stating 'Joan–Alfredo – Gods of the Opera'.

On December 1 we left in the car for San Sebastian where we stayed the night at the Hotel Maria Cristina, travelling on the following day to the Château de Pray-Amboise. The next night we spent at Château Montreuil, driving to Calais and on to Swansea the next day for another stay at Fairy Hill to complete the *Adriana Lecouvreur* recording – with Carlo Bergonzi replacing Luciano. The opera was one that Carlo had apparently always wanted to record and he was delighted when Decca asked him to take over. We all had a wonderful time, enjoying the great garden and even greater cuisine at the hotel. The remainder of the cast were all very friendly and we got to know the Bergonzis better than ever before. The other singers were Francesco Ellero D'Artegna (Il Principe di Bouillon), Cleopatra Ciurca (La Principessa), Leo Nucci (Michonnet), Michel Sénéchal (L'Abate di Chazeuil), with Bryn Terfel as Quinault. Our sessions were very calmly accomplished and we had a wonderful 'Christmas party' on the last night.

The next day (December 11) we drove to London and on the thirteenth Richard and I went by train to Manchester where we were both made Honorary Members of the Royal Northern College of Music, the President of the College, Her Royal Highness The Duchess of Kent conferring the Fellowship awards. Richard's Presentation was made by the late Sir Charles Groves and mine by my ex-colleague from Covent Garden days and respected teacher at the College, Joseph Ward. It was a lovely ceremony and during the course of the afternoon I met and was photographed with that lean giant Paul Whelan who was studying at the College, never dreaming I would be judging his fine performances in the Cardiff Singer of the World Competition a few years later.

We spent another jolly Christmas at home, with my nieces Ruth and Helen as well as Dr Newbold joining our festivities. After the holidays were over I turned my attention to completing the sorting of my costumes and accessories to be sent to Australia for the proposed exhibition at the end of the year and they were expertly packed and transported from the house for shipping in mid-January 1989.

By January 22 we were on our way again, this time to California for *Norma* with Opera Pacific at the stunning new Orange County Performing Arts Center at Costa Mesa. We had rented a charming house on Balboa, one of the several islands off the coast. David di Chiera of Detroit was also General Director of Opera Pacific so we were immediately among friends, with John Pascoe designing and directing the opera. César-Antonio Suarez was Pollione, Nova Thomas sang Adalgisa and Georgi Seleznew was Oroveso. John Pascoe had designed a production with costumes that might have resembled those worn in first performances of the opera in the early 1830s – crinolines rather than the more classical Roman lines usually favoured. The gowns were very beautiful, but I felt a bit strange after having worn the 'slimmer Druid look' for so many years. We had a wonderful month in Costa Mesa, with four nicely spread performances, and went to Disneyland with Nova (who told us all the 'best rides') and John Pascoe.

On February 25 we flew back to New York where I prepared those costumes required for the Australian exhibition ready for shipping.

Then, on March 12 I sang, with Richard at the piano, my last performance at the Metropolitan Opera after over twenty-five years' association with that Company and its grand history of the greatest operatic performers. It was not easy to control my emotions during the programme, with memories of all my 'triumphs' there and in the old House flooding in. But the outburst of applause at the conclusion of the concert was a wonderful send-off and I felt great joy to know that such appreciation and warmth still existed for me in the hearts of those who had listened. The next day we left again for Switzerland and I was able to organise numerous large tubs of bulbs and other early spring flowers on the chalet's terraces.

During the second week of March Sian Griffiths, who had worked for some years as manager of Artists and Repertoire for Decca, London, arrived for a stay of a couple of months to sort out our 'office', in rather a muddle since Darlene's departure. She had left Decca and was happy to go back and forth between the chalet and her home in London and we all enjoyed the four years or so she spent more or less with us before taking up a post with the BBC. Her musical knowledge was invaluable, plus the fact that she was an avid and very able gardener.

April 3 found us in Detroit again to perform *Norma* in John Pascoe's production for the Michigan Opera. David di Chiera and his wife Karen were splendid hosts during our stay, Karen or their good friend Hans Rogind acting as chauffeur. I had a slight recurrence of nasal infection – those long air trips the cause again perhaps? – so did not attend all the rehearsals. It was fortunate that I had been in the production with the same cast in February and knew what the director wanted.

I had received a lovely letter from the Governor of the State of Michigan, James J. Blanchard, thanking me for the artistic contributions I had made not only to the citizens of Michigan but to the whole musical world and wishing me success in these, my final performances of *Norma*. This letter, more than anything hitherto, made me realise that soon I would sing not only the last performance of a specific work, or in a specific city, but really remove myself from the stage altogether. With a minimum of regret I felt, on looking back, how lucky I had been and what a wonderful life we had both had because of our combined talents. They were to be my last *Normas* so they'd better be good, I thought. Apparently I succeeded, with glowing headlines again:

A BREATHTAKING SWAN SONG

JOAN SUTHERLAND'S THE REASON TO CHEER *NORMA*

Richard and I arrived back in Switzerland on April 24 and next day, together with Chester, flew to Athens for a holiday, driving through southern and eastern Greece with our Greek-Australian friends in a very comfortable minibus which they had already picked up at the airport. The weather was perfect for the whole of our trip – just a few rainstorms, particularly on the Greek Easter Sunday. Having Dr Dervos and his sister Maria as part of our group of six was wonderful as they knew the country so well and of course spoke the language. Chester and Shahab Ispahani did most of the driving. We not only visited the Peloponnese, with their fine historical theatres, temples and museums, but Delphi, Meteora, and north to Volos and Pelion – a wonderful, relaxing holiday which whetted our appetite for more similar trips. We also spent a week visiting ancient sites along the west coast of Turkey.

We returned home on May 13 and Chester drove us to Barcelona on the sixteenth. We opened with *Lucrezia Borgia* at the Liceo on the thirty-first with four following performances. Alfredo Kraus sang the role of Gennaro, Martine Dupuy Maffio Orsini, Michele Pertusi Don Alfonso and Piero di Palma was Rustighello, with a group of good young Spanish singers. The Australian Opera lent me the costumes designed for me there by Kristian Fredrikson for which I was grateful as it meant I was at ease wearing them and needed no fittings or alterations. They blended very well with those the theatre hired from Tirelli of Rome. I especially liked my silver-and-black costume for the last scenes. The critics extolled the ability of Alfredo and me to sustain such operatic roles at our age, coupling our performances with those in the earlier *Lucia*, saying we had both provided a great lesson in vocal ability and control.

With such splendid weather we made several trips to nearby beauty spots – Sitges, Villanova, Tarragona – and one day went with Francisco Ortiz (with whom I had sung) to some very interesting old towns previously unknown to us.

On June 15 we flew to Paris, where the whole company from Barcelona gave a concert performance of *Lucrezia Borgia* at the Théâtre des Champs Elysées on the seventeenth as part of the Festival of Paris. The theatre was packed, in spite of the city's celebrations. The critic of the *International Herald Tribune* wrote: 'The performance here offered enough fireworks to match those going off simultaneously nearby at the Eiffel Tower.'

Next day we flew to London to attend the Annual Decca Conference as Guests of Honour and on the twentieth were back in Les Avants, where we stayed for just over a week, leaving for Sydney via Bangkok, where we spent five days sightseeing from the lovely old Oriental Hotel.

On July 8 we arrived in Sydney, leaving most of our luggage and flying on to Melbourne on the eleventh. Here I sang with Douglas Gamley and his Australian Pops Orchestra in the Melbourne Concert Hall items predominantly from favourite operetta works featured on our recordings. It was a very happy night for my farewell performance in Melbourne. The stage was banked with flowers, with more thrown by the capacity audience, along with a bombardment of balloons and streamers – quite a send-off, with more to come.

The next day we went back to Sydney where Richard began rehearsals for *The Pearl Fishers* and I a round of social engagements. I visited the site for the Joan Sutherland Performing Arts Centre at Penrith, to the west of Sydney at the foot of the Blue Mountains. That whole western area had developed rapidly over the last twenty years and there was no suitable facility for touring musical groups or the presentation of local talent. This centre was to provide not only an excellent 650-seat auditorium with a stage capable of carrying seventy orchestral musicians comfortably, but a group of ten or so rehearsal or teaching studios available for hire. The main hall was to be named in Richard's honour. Both of us were very impressed by what we saw on the site and looked forward to the opening of the Centre in due course.

It was marvellous to find the Opera Company in such a relaxed state after all the bickering between management, Board and company members over a number of seasons. Under the new General Manager, Donald McDonald, things were calm and happy and Donald has restored and maintained the old family feeling that had existed before the storms. He and his wife Janet have been exactly what the Company needed.

After the second *Pearl Fishers* I returned home, arriving on August 17. This meant I could enjoy the rest of the summer in the garden and around the house, before going with Ruthli to Egypt in mid-September on a British Museum tour. Ruthli had been fascinated by Egypt since she was about fourteen and I likewise, although Richard preferred European culture and dreaded possible stomach problems in the Middle East. He was unable to make the trip anyway, as he had engagements with the opera in Catania to perform *Nina Pazza per Amore* by Paisiello and Bellini's *I Puritani*.

The Egyptian tour bore the title of 'Pharaohs and Christians' and combined the pharaonic sites with some of the still practising early monasteries and Coptic museums. There were also two excellent lecturers in George Hart and David Buckton. Sir Steven Runciman, that charming, much-travelled expert on Byzantium, was also a member of our party. In spite of the constant early starts (to beat the heat of the day and crowds of tourists) we had a wonderful tour, taking in all the important sights of Cairo, Memphis, Sakkara, Giza and Alexandria, a trip to Mount Sinai and the Monastery of St Catherine and its collection of priceless icons and manuscripts and the monasteries of St Paul the Theban and St Anthony. On to Luxor, Karnak, the Valley of the Kings with its great tombs, including Tutankhamun, the Temple of Queen Hatshepsut, Deir el Medina, the Colossi of Memnon, Esna, Edfu, Kom-Ombo, Aswan, Philae's transported Temple of Isis, the High Dam and a trip to Abu-Simbel. It was hectic, but the few days on board our Nile cruiser were relaxed, despite the early starts and the tummy problems. Almost everybody on the tour had succumbed at one time or another to 'Tutankhamun's Revenge', but our friend Dr Dervos had come equipped with a variety of medicaments for every ailment and was much in demand.

Richard and I went to London on October 4 where we gave a recital at St John's, Smith Square in aid of their organ appeal. This was a gala affair in the presence of Her Royal Highness The Princess Margaret, Countess of Snowdon and it was twenty years since Richard and I had inaugurated St John's as a concert hall on October 6, 1969. In the interim the hall had enjoyed great success and continues to do so, being an ideal venue for more intimate performances. The evening was yet another in the round of farewells and actually my last full solo appearance in London.

On October 8 we travelled to Newcastle where we gave a gala concert on the eleventh in the newly restored Tyne Theatre and Opera House in aid of the Prince's Trust. This was with the Northern Sinfonia and I sang the four big arias from *Norma*, *I Masnadieri*, *Fra Diavolo* and *Lucia* (the Mad Scene). This concert was unfortunately interrupted due to a bomb scare, which turned out to be a harmless unidentified parcel.

We flew to Dallas on the eighteenth where we were to do four *Merry Widows* between November 1 and 11 – my farewell performances in the United States. I had made my American début with the Dallas Civic Opera on November 16, 1960 and almost thirty years later, on November 11, that wonderful American career was over. The whole period in Dallas was a joy, with Louis Otey as a very dashing Danilo, and a fine supporting cast. We renewed acquaintances with old friends both in and out of the Company and it was a wonderful gesture of Nicola Rescigno and Plato Karayanis to present me with a com-memorative book of letters from colleagues and friends in and out of the operatic world, including a charming one from George and Barbara Bush. Nicola had conducted for so many of my early international appearances, among them the Dallas début, and it was a pleasure to see him again at this very memorable event in my life. The compliments were innumerable, with dinner and supper parties, luncheons and just homey visits with some of the original 1960 Dallas hostesses, still supporting the Opera and helping to entertain the artists.

One rather hilarious problem arose when the Rolling Stones staged a 'comeback' appearance at the Fairground on the same night as *The Merry Widow* and all sorts of detours and police escorts were organised. Our main worry was would the noise of the Stones' concert penetrate the walls of the Music Hall. But all was well and both entertainments went off without a hitch.

After all the excitement of the Dallas farewell it was hard to collect our wits and baggage and fly off to Hong Kong the next day. Here we stayed at the Peninsula Hotel and had only to cross the road to rehearse at the new Hong Kong Cultural Centre. We did a concert with the Hong Kong Philharmonic Orchestra on November 19 as part of the opening festival of the Centre. We were escorted to various beauty spots and restaurants by a group of very sweet young Hong Kong Chinese working for the festival and found time to shop. I met that delightful fashion designer Diane Frés who arranged for me to view a large range of her latest models, for which I fell heavily. One wonders what will happen to such enterprising businesses as hers after July 1997. 'Sutherland shows she's still in sensational form' quoted the *South China Morning Post*.

As in most of the cities visited during this final tour an assessment of our whole career together appeared in the press and it was again brought home to me that in another year I would already have done my last performances with the Australian Opera. Meanwhile we flew to Sydney for the splendid exhibition of my costumes and memorabilia, which was to open on December 7 at the Art Gallery of New South Wales. Moffatt Oxenbould had written a splendid book – *Joan Sutherland – A Tribute* – which not only singled out my favourite roles with accompanying photographs and artists' designs but gave a complete list of performances and dates at the back. This little book is a concise and graphic account of my forty-three years as a singer, beautifully presented by the publishers.

Many of my friends belonging to the backstage staff had helped with the preparation of the display, particularly Shirley Germain of the wig department with Bill Paterson and my dresser, Sandy Windon, who all made sure that the mannequins looked as realistic as possible. It was Sandy who remarked when quizzed by one of the many interviewers: 'There is Joan Sutherland, the Queen and God. It's that simple!' What a headline *that* made!

The memorabilia – letters, programmes, designs, photographs – were beautifully displayed and the overall effect of the exhibition was breath-taking. It remained on view in Sydney until February 11 during the Annual Festival of Sydney, then toured to Adelaide and Melbourne. The opening was a huge success with a superb dinner party the following night at the gallery and I was happy to be named 'Australian of the Year'.

We returned to Les Avants on December 10 and enjoyed a visit from Adam, Helen, Natasha and Vanya, also Grandma Jean. We had a great time together, although Richard was off to Paris on New Year's Day for performances of *Maria Stuarda* with Lella Cuberli, and Adam and Helen spent a few days there, too.

Chester and Richard left for San Diego mid-January for performances of *The Dialogues of the Carmelites* and *La Fille du Régiment*, travelling to Melbourne on March 12 where he did twenty-six performances of Emmerich Kálmán's *The Gypsy Princess* with the Australian Opera in Melbourne and Sydney.

When Richard arrived in Australia the company and opera-goers all over Australia were shocked and grieving over the untimely death of John Fulford at forty-three. Not only did he have a baritone voice of quality, great versatility and sense of the stage but he was a charming and humorous colleague. I admired his performing of Enrico in *Lucia di Lammermoor* with Jennifer McGregor in the theatre and he sang the role with me in the outdoor concert of the opera in 1984. His Papageno and Guglielmo suited his personality as well as his voice. His death was a great loss to the Company and to the musical scene generally.

Meanwhile I enjoyed my freedom in Switzerland, along with a few interviews for European magazines and radio. Tessa paid one of her welcome visits and Ruthli and I had a quick trip to Paris for four days in March, courtesy of Decca who organised all manner of entertainment and interviews. We were even given a tour of the Bastille Opera House which I thought more suitable for an aquatic centre. They were in final rehearsals for the opening of *Les Troyens* and already having large problems.

Our house is on four floors and to climb from the lowest to the top level was becoming more arduous for all of us. We had decided to install an elevator and, after much deliberation with architect, builder and the elevator company, the work was commenced in early May. Ruthli and I had protected the surrounding area of the projected well as best we could and began to dread the upheaval. But although there was considerable demolition and reconstruction it was amazing how smoothly the work was accomplished with a minimum of dust – considering. It was as well Richard and Chester were away and we had no guests, so we could use the vacant rooms and Richard's library to store books, music, paintings, breakables – which all had to be put back on completion of the work. Richard and Chester arrived back from Australia on May 17 – shocked at the chaos but satisfied with the progress made.

On the twenty-third we picked up a Volkswagen minibus, hired for our trip to Hungary and Czechoslovakia, again with Erik Dervos, Shahab Ispahani and their Hungarian friend Marti Clare (who had been on the Egyptian tour), setting off the following day for Innsbruck. We stayed one night there, then spent another at Schloss Wimsbach with the Weisweillers (also on the Egyptian tour) and on to Vienna, via a visit to Bad Ischl and the Lehár Museum, then over the border into Hungary and south to Pecs, viewing everything we could on the way. From Pecs (the original university town) we crossed east via Hortobagy as far as the Russian border, mostly on back roads, then north and west again to Budapest. We had a wonderful time, with Marti explaining and cajoling curators to let us see wooden painted churches, museums, gardens – all manner of places we couldn't have been without using the Hungarian language. We visited Tokaj, Eger, Debrecen and, for Richard, Miskolc which is mentioned in *The Gypsy Princess*.

We spent some days in Budapest and saw another Kálmán operetta, *The Circus Princess*, also, on the way to Czechoslovakia, visiting Kálmán's home on Lake Balaton. The trip from Bratislava via Brno and visits to several of the old castles *en route* to Prague were a real eye-opener. How was it possible to restore perfectly so many – Lednice, Valtice, Mikulov, Trebic, Telc and the magical pink castle of Cervena Lhota?

Prague was a city we had longed to see and we were not disappointed. That trip whetted our appetite but so far we've not been back. However, we saw a great deal in our few days there, including an enjoyable performance of *Russalka* – no Mozart unfortunately. On another musical level we had loved the 'gypsy' ensembles in the Hungarian restaurants, complete with cymbalum players – some better than others – but giving us a wealth of Lehár and Kálmán.

We had read an article in one of London's Sunday papers about how dreary the food was throughout both countries – nothing but dumplings and never any salad or fresh vegetables to be had. This we found completely untrue, and I fear that writer had not been sufficiently brave to try some of the local specialities.

On the way back to Les Avants we spent a night by the Alpen See near Füssen, visiting King Ludwig's Neuschwanstein and Hohenschwangau next morning, before hitting the road home.

Having visited in a short space of time the surviving antiquities of Greece, Turkey and Egypt and now making this amazing journey through a portion of Europe so steeped in history – political and musical – I wondered just what our generation was leaving for posterity. The atom bomb and Internet, perhaps?

At the end of July I went to Sydney to begin rehearsals on the thirtieth for *Les Huguenots* – my very last operatic performances. Richard had already done nine performances of *The Gypsy Princess* with five more to go, several of which I attended and thoroughly enjoyed. Deborah Riedel as Sylva Varescu was charming and I couldn't recognise in her the timid sister from *Dialogues of the Carmelites* at all. It was such a polished performance and we all thought Deborah was on the way to an international career.

We had visits from Darlene, Tessa, David di Chiera, Yvonne Kálmán and Helmut Klumpp, various dinners, including the large Opera Auditions one which Adam organised at the Airport Hilton Hotel where he was Food and Beverage Manager at the time. There were many TV and newspaper interviews all asking what I would do when I retired, with book and record signing sessions as well as the rehearsals. I was glad that my role in *Huguenots*, although important, was not particularly long. There was an abundance of laudatory articles in the national press, with photographs old and new and a collection of funny – sometimes hideous – caricatures of the Sutherland mien. Had mother been alive I could hear her saying: 'There you are! Didn't I tell you not to pull so many faces?'

Richard and I gave a short recital at St Joseph's school where a portrait of me by Pamela Griffith was unveiled and the Joan Sutherland Centre at Penrith was officially opened on August 14 with a concert and the usual speeches. I only sang a very short programme of about twenty minutes' duration as the Centre is a good distance from the city of Sydney and we had early rehearsals for the opera next morning, but it was obvious that the complex had succeeded in providing a very necessary music venue for that western area.

With so many social commitments it was hard to squeeze in visits with Adam, Helen and the children, but at least we were within easy distance – not the other side of the world.

The opening night of *Les Huguenots* was on September 3, with six further ones in September and the final one on October 2. Already the front of the *Sydney Morning Herald* special supplement bore a full-page colour photograph of me acknowledging applause in the Domain after the *Lucia* there in 1984 and inside there was a two-page spread by Michael Shmith on 'The Final Season' with more black-and-white photos. This old Sydney newspaper – the oldest – never used colour on weekdays. I still had a month of performances (nicely spread) to get through before the one on October 2 which would really 'bring down the curtain'. Meanwhile every newspaper in the world seemed to take up the cry, especially those in Italy:

OPERA'S LEADING DAME RETIRES

STUPENDA BOWS OUT QUIETLY

SUTHERLAND UN ADDIO

LA SUTHERLAND SI RITIRA — 'RICORDATEMI COME ERO'

LA STUPENDA NON CANTERÀ PIU

JOAN, LA 'STUPENDA' ABBANDONA LA LIRICA

JOAN SUTHERLAND WILL NICHT MEHR SINGEN

JOAN, ADDIO AL BELCANTO

and many more.

The cast was made up of some of the original singers in the production – Anson Austin as Raoul, Clifford Grant as Marcel, John Pringle as de Nevers, Sergei Baigildin as Bois-Rosé and Neville Wilkie as Night Watchman, Amanda Thane sang Valentine, John Wegner Le Comte de St Bris, Suzanne Johnston Urbain and the rest of the cast was a group of younger artists than those in 1981. We got along famously and I think they were quite excited to be part of these nights of a near-pandemonium response from each audience.

Many had come from New Zealand, Britain, Spain and the US – even Placido Domingo turned up. I think it had been about ten years since our paths had crossed and he, as usual, was flying off to another engagement immediately with no time for us to catch up on family and friends. But it was good at least to say hello in my last-act costume.

A superb programme had been printed for the run of *Les Huguenots* with many coloured photographs of the roles I had sung with the Australian Opera, as well as some of my earlier Covent Garden roles. There was a letter from the Prime Minister, Bob Hawke, and a note from the General Manager of the Banque Nationale de Paris for Australia who, with the Regent Hotel, sponsored these performances. There was also a note from Donald McDonald in which he pointed out that I had sung 265 performances of twenty-three different roles for the Company, as well as conveying the Company's affectionate greetings.

The book that Richard had written on our years with the Australian Opera, including the 1965 Williamson season, was launched on September 7 and it is an excellent record of our performances with the Company, with a large collection of photographs from the productions. It is a great souvenir.

On September 18 I was honoured to receive the Dame Joan Hammond Award from Dame Joan herself at a gala dinner. Nick

Enright had written a very funny 'Ballad for two Dames' which he delivered. It was a happy evening, especially for us two 'Dame Joans'. The award is made for the greatest contribution to opera in Australia during the previous year – or an outstanding contribution over a number of years. We managed to escape most weekends to Whale Beach, sometimes for a little longer, and I saw Helen and the children as often as possible.

Suddenly it was October 2 and my last full stage appearance. What excitement there was backstage, everyone 'popping in' to my dressing-room before the show, something I had never enjoyed, but this night *was* special, so I forced myself to control the butterflies and not talk too much – superhuman effort. I don't think for one minute it was my best performance of my big aria and duet in Act 2, sung in rather a dream, but the applause was fairly tumultuous and I breathed a sigh of relief, as my only other appearance would be very brief and so the ordeal of that final fling on-stage was nearly over. Donald and Moffatt had given a great deal of thought to the celebration to occur at the end of the opera that night, aided and abetted by Stage Management and, indeed, the whole Company. It was a triumph of organisation and the result spectacular.

After my final scene I had returned to my dressing-room and changed into a big, black, sparkling gown. The whole *Huguenots* cast took their picture call at the end of the opera, with the major Principals entering one by one from prompt and OP side, lining up and, after several bows, the stage was cleared behind the tabs which were then taken up again to reveal me standing alone mid-stage in a battery of follow spots. I walked slowly down-stage to be joined by the *Les Huguenots* company, followed by the whole of the Australian Opera Company. With much applause and shouts of 'Brava', 'Stupenda', 'Diva', 'Joan', showers of flowers, streamers, a balloon drop (I'm not sure in what order) I finally somehow managed to sing 'Home, Sweet Home' in the Melba tradition, accompanied by Richard and the orchestra. More tumultuous applause and foot stamping – and a great 'Farewell' sign lit up above the breadth of the stage. Then, after Richard returned to the stage, Moffatt and Donald gave brief speeches, Donald making the presentation of a huge crystal urn on a heavy base, quite spectacular empty, magnificent when filled with flowers, as it later was. Of course, I had to respond and haven't a clue what I said – and then I got the shock of my life. Fireworks pouring and spouting from the Gallery, boxes and proscenium. It was like the Bicentennial all over again.

And, if that was not enough, there was a splendid reception and dinner at the Regent of Sydney. Thank goodness the performance had begun at 6 p.m., otherwise the dinner would have been much later than it was. What an incredible gathering of friends and colleagues, including the Prime Minister and the then Treasurer, Mr Paul Keating and Mrs Annita Keating, Mrs Hazel Hawke, also the Premier of New South Wales – the Honourable Nick and Mrs Cathryn Greiner. There were welcomes and toasts and the introduction by Ted Wright, General Manager of the Regent (whose guests we were) of the specially devised dessert 'La Stupenda'. This was masterminded by the Regent's Executive Chef, Serge Dansereau, and, although disastrously delicious, was too complicated to figure on many future menus around the world.

Clifford Grant also 'retired' that evening, although he has made several forays back into some roles, especially in Britain.

We finally staggered home to our apartment at some early hour of the next day and, fortunately, were *not* leaving for Europe immediately. We had thought it better to wait until the fourth to return home – there was quite a bit of cleaning up to do.

Judging by the number of press cuttings which poured in, I think every country in the world printed one report at least of that unforgettable night. The London *Observer* gave a better account than I could of that farewell. The writer (Peter Conrad) was after all in the audience, seeing it from a different angle.

The curtain calls were a masterpiece of festive *mise-en-scène*. Ushers distributed streamers and daffodils (it is spring in the antipodes) for us to throw; clouds of netting discharged showers of coloured balloons from the ceiling.

After a long pause, the curtain rose again on a stage grandly occupied by Sutherland alone. She had changed from Marguerite's red velvet court dress into a spangly black-and-silver gown, and she advanced intrepidly into the bombardment of blooms and balloons, and grateful cheers, which crashed against her like surf. Wreathed in streamers, she looked a little like one of those departing liners which used to glide out from the piers opposite the Opera House and take young pilgrims like her off to conquer the northern hemisphere...

... Anticipating her release into private life, she told the audience, 'I hope I'll be back before too long to become one of you out there.' At that a neon galaxy flared into life behind her and spelt out 'Farewell', while enough explosions for Armageddon detonated at the back of the theatre.

Fireworks whirled and spun inside the building, and advanced in successive shell burst towards the proscenium which suddenly gushed fire and blazed round her.

I truly expected Sutherland to lift off and drift skyward – like some miraculous figure in a baroque painting, like Dame Edna on her crane – to be installed within the Southern Cross. But she walked slowly into the wings through the parting sea of her colleagues, and despite all our baying and stamping and screaming she didn't reappear. We won't look upon her like again.'

It was, indeed a 'Stupendous' farewell.

October 5 saw us back in Les Avants with Richard going off to Barcelona to perform *Roberto Devereux* at the Liceo with Edita Gruberova as Elizabeth and Doris Soffel as Sara. I took the splendid train from Geneva to Barcelona on the thirtieth to a performance. I did not like the production at all but the singers were in good form and I often just listened rather than be aggravated by looking at the sets.

Two friends from the Joan Sutherland Society in Sydney were on a European holiday and, after attending the opera in Barcelona, were going on a five-day tour of southern Spain. As I had only ever been to Madrid in the south, I decided to go with them, visiting Cordoba, Seville, Ronda, Granada and back to Madrid before flying home to Switzerland, where Richard and Chester travelled by car the same day.

They were off again – to London for the Covent Garden rehearsals of *Die Fledermaus*. Originally I was to have sung the role of Rosalinde as my farewell to the Royal Opera. However, after having seen a model of the set and the stairs I would have to negotiate, I had told the management reasonably early on that I couldn't possibly cope with them and I must reluctantly withdraw. I also doubted my ability to sing the role well enough by then. The Garden management was very understanding and Nancy Gustafson sang Rosalinde with great charm, with Louis Otey as Gabriel von Eisenstein. I was very sorry to disappoint the Company and public, as well as to lose the opportunity to perform again with Louis. It had been such a delightful collaboration in the Dallas *Widows*.

The Royal Opera House persuaded me to appear one last time in the party scene of *Die Fledermaus* on New Year's Eve. My old friends Marilyn Horne and Luciano Pavarotti made the trip from New York especially to be with me for my final public appearance. It was a touching gesture and it made me very happy. This brief appearance meant I was only required in London after Christmas so I could remain in Les Avants until then.

Richard came home for a very quiet Christmas and on December 28 we all flew to London for the Gala Farewell. Ric had ordered a great green gown from Barbara, which she brought to London herself as a surprise. I had trundled the huge black 'Farewell' gown there, not knowing of the conspiracy. Jackie and Luciano were in great form and the Farewell to end the farewells was emotional and nostalgic but nevertheless a triumph. We performed our duets and arias – 'Serbami ognor' from Rossini's *Semiramide*, 'Parigi, o cara' from *La Traviata*,

'Mon coeur s'ouvre à ta voix' from *Samson et Dalila*, Federico's lament from Cilea's *L'Arlesiana* – with 'Home, Sweet Home' again being my final offering. More streamers, glittering confetti, fireworks and a parting gift from the Company, presented by Jeremy Isaacs – the drum I had used in *La Fille du Régiment* dedicated to me in gold lettering. This now bears a plate-glass top and serves as a lovely occasional table for a glass or cup in the music room at Chalet Monet – it is even the right colour.

There was a crowded buffet supper party in the Crush Bar afterwards and I was happy to have such friends around me including so many of the Company, also Prime Minister John Major and his wife Norma, both fans from my very early days at the Garden. Ruthli and Jean-Paul came to that gala and it was like a fast-motion replay of the previous forty years.

Now I was really retired – no more studying and performing or worry about catching a cold and having to cancel – I could do as I pleased. That is, I could travel if I felt like it or stay home and potter about my house or garden. Before returning home, however, I spent a couple of weeks in London visiting friends, including tea at 10 Downing Street with Norma and doing some more interviews – they still happen to this day.

Richard was travelling back and forth between London (*Die Fledermaus*) and rehearsals for Balfe's *Bohemian Girl* in Dublin which was to be given a concert performance and recorded with Nova Thomas and Patrick Power in the leading roles. I decided to go to the concert and enjoyed it very much, also seeing Dublin again after over thirty years. I didn't stay for the recording sessions and was glad to relax at home after all the excitement of the preceding weeks. A few guests stayed at the chalet and I recorded a big television interview. Richard came home for only a few days before he and Chester went off with our Greek-Australian friends on a tour of Tuscany and some of the very interesting towns in northern and central Italy. It was rather early in the year for such a trip and I couldn't go as I had agreed to travel to Sydney and accept my 'Mo' Awards. These were given me as Performer of the Year and Australian Show Business Ambassador of the Year, both highly coveted awards. They are named for Roy 'Mo' Rene, the much-loved Australian music hall and radio comedian of fifty years ago.

I also had the pleasure of presenting the Australian Operatic Performance Award to the Australian Opera for their much-lauded production of *La Bohème*. It was a star-studded event in Sydney's beautiful old State Theatre on February 17, and Helen and Adam accompanied me. I managed to spend an extra week with them, attending Natasha's school swimming event, where she was a proud winner. We had the weekend at Whale Beach, then I travelled home at the end of February.

It was a sad time for Ruthli as her lovable father died early in March – he seemed to lose the will to live after the death of his wife a year or so previously. We miss them both as they used to visit us frequently and although they spoke no English and our Schweizer Deutsch is elementary, we had some jolly times together, especially playing cards.

Richard went to New York on March 8 to do performances of *I Puritani* at the Met. Edita Gruberova was Elvira and Arturo was sung by Chris Merritt who was replaced at very short notice by Stanford Olsen at one performance. Paul Plishka was Giorgio and Paolo Gavenelli Riccardo. Richard went straight from New York to Catania, where he had rehearsals for his performances there of *Semiramide* with Anna Caterina Antonacci as Semiramide.

I went to Cannes for the première there of RM Associates' TV Special *La Stupenda: A Portrait of Joan Sutherland*. There was a wonderful dinner party at Le Moulin de Mougins on the Saturday night and the screening late on Sunday morning. I travelled on to Catania to join Ric for a week and had a lovely time there exploring the city with him and enjoying very much three *Semiramide* performances with an interesting production. I particularly liked Anna Caterina Antonacci – a lovely singer. We also managed to visit Syracuse on the Saturday and, of course, the Bellini Museum in Catania.

In April I took a lovely garden tour in the south of Switzerland and north of Italy, then in May visited Schwetzingen, near Heidelberg, to participate in my first of many vocal competitions as a member of the jury. There were thirteen of us adjudicating, among them some old acquaintances and colleagues – Leyla Gencer that extraordinary Turkish soprano, John Mordler who had been with Decca and now is Intendant of the Monte Carlo Opera, Pier Luigi Pizzi whom I was happy to get to know much better than on our previous meetings, Gerhard Reutter, the Director of the Festival of which the contest was a part, with Maestri Gianluigi Gelmetti and Alberto Zedda. The contest was primarily to find young singers who wished 'to apply themselves to the work of Rossini'. The winners were to take part in the 1992 Schwetzingen Festival, in the interim gaining experience from work with both the Süddeutscher Rundfunk (Stuttgart) and the Rossini Opera Festival (Pesaro). My chief memories of those busy two weeks, apart from hearing some very promising voices, are of the exquisite Schwetzingen Castle gardens, visits to Speyer and its Cathedral, Heidelberg, a boat trip with the contestants on the Neckar and the Rhine on a free day and the delicious asparagus that was available at every meal, the area around Schwetzingen being the heart of asparagus farming. We were even offered asparagus ice-cream.

After a short visit to Antibes to attend a concert performance of *Maria Stuarda*, Rachel and I flew to Sydney, in time for Natasha's and Vanya's school holidays.

✧ **8** ✧

THERE WERE PLENTY of functions to attend including the official opening of the Joan Sutherland Studio at the Australian Opera Centre and that of the Sydney Opera Supperclub at the Intercontinental Hotel. The idea for the club was Wolfgang Grimm's, General Manager of the hotel, and Adam very much enjoyed setting it up and running it for some years.

While Ric was conducting thirteen *Carmens* and twelve *Magic Flutes* I was able to fulfil a score of engagements. These included a visit to Brisbane to unveil the foundation stone of the projected music centre–assembly hall–gymnasium for John Paul College at Daisy Hill, Logan City. I was most impressed by the whole atmosphere of the college and happy to visit again in 1996 to see the finished centre with all its facilities in use, particularly those providing teaching and rehearsal rooms for all instruments and the several singing groups. I spent a relaxed weekend and paid a visit to Greta Elkins, receiving on Monday, August 12 an Honorary Doctorate of Music at the University of Queensland's graduation ceremony.

We returned to Europe and enjoyed a month at home, Richard then recording *Lucia* with Edita Gruberova and travelling on to Adelaide to conduct *Madame Butterfly* with Yoko Watanabe.

I adjudicated at the forty-second Concorso Internazionale di Musica Giovan Battista Viotti in Vercelli and during my stay was presented with the 'Viotto d'Oro', given since 1958 for excellence in every field of the performing arts. Giuseppe Pugliese and Edward Greenfield wrote delightful tributes in the programme and the award is another of my treasures.

Shortly afterwards I was off to Caltanissetta in Sicily for their twenty-third Concorso Internazionale Vincenzo Bellini and delighted to find Gianni Raimondi among my colleagues on the jury. Maestro Giuseppe Pastorello and his family were most thoughtful organisers and we all enjoyed a trip to Agrigento on a free day.

I attended the 1991 Gramophone Awards at the Dorchester in London and presented Luciano with his award for 'Artist of the Year', receiving the award for 'Lifetime Achievement' myself.

After a few weeks at home, Richard and I went as guests of honour to Enna in Sicily for the city's Christmas Concert, then flew to Venice, having been invited to attend the gala opening of the opera season at La Fenice – a performance of *Don Carlos*. Little did we know it would be the last time we visited that beautiful and historic opera house, gutted by fire in January 1996, just two years after Barcelona's Liceo shared the same fate. At least I had the privilege and pleasure of singing in both of those perfect theatres, and at La Fenice I was dubbed 'La Stupenda'.

We had a quiet Christmas with our usual visitors and I flew to Sydney in time for Adam's and Helen's tenth wedding anniversary (January 23, 1992) spending a week with them before flying to Cairns with Jean Wahba to join the South Pacific voyage of the spectacular *Crystal Harmony*. Jean and I enjoyed the few days aboard, floating back to Sydney via the Whitsunday Passage, the Barrier Reef and Brisbane, but cruising was not really for either of us indefinitely.

By February 10 I was in Hobart to present the Moët & Chandon Fellowship of $50,000 to thirty-three-year-old Rosie Weiss of Melbourne. Rosie was very excited and told me she had listened to my old 1960 recording of *The Art of the Prima Donna* while she painted.

Back in Sydney for Adam's birthday I was in a quandary over my appointments. Shortly after my birthday the previous November, I had been advised that Her Majesty The Queen had chosen to award me the Order of Merit. This was the greatest honour, the Order being restricted to only twenty-four members at any one time and it is the Sovereign's personal gift. The Queen was to visit Sydney in February 1992 and I was asked to accept the beautiful insignia from her there, on the morning of the twentieth. I had already agreed to unveil the plans for the new Performing Arts and Communications Centre to bear my name at St Catherine's school that same evening so thought it would be a busy day for me. Then I was invited to attend a dinner with Her Majesty and HRH The Duke of Edinburgh at Government House, also on the same night. I could not disappoint St Catherine's, nor did I want to decline the dinner invitation. I confessed my dilemma to the Governor's aide and a police escort was arranged to speed me from St Catherine's to the dinner, where I arrived somewhat breathless, just ahead of the Royal party, wearing my decorations, including the new one, as requested.

The Order of Merit had been presented by the Queen very informally at Admiralty House, with only Adam and Helen present. We adjourned to the garden, giving the battery of cameras and journalists a field day, retreated indoors from them and, during a little chat, Her Majesty confessed that the Queen Mother pitied her – because she had to 'wear specs'. Her mother did *not*.

I was again besieged by journalists on my departure, asking my views on Australia becoming a Republic. To this I replied it was hardly likely I was in agreement if I accepted such Honours from the Queen herself. Really!

Back in Les Avants by February 24, I then went to Florence where I was fêted and presented with 'L'Aria di Baule' in the Palazzo Vecchio on March 6. I was given a green zippered Ferragamo portfolio to symbolise the case in which singers of the past carried the music of their favourite party pieces. Mine did not contain 'Home, Sweet Home' and has been exceptionally useful to carry my papers at all the vocal competitions since.

I was sorry that Richard was unable to be with me for any of these events but he had recording dates and later performances of *Maria Stuarda* in Barcelona with Daniela Dessi. I was glad to have some time at home but was soon on my way again to join the very large adjudication panel of the 1992 Queen Elisabeth International Music Competition in Brussels. It is a very exacting and prestigious vocal contest and my co-jurors were all splendid colleagues, most of whom I knew and had worked with. We had a very relaxed lunch at the Palace of Laeken as guests of Queen Fabiola, and the Chairman of the contest, Count Jean-Pierre de Launoit, arranged for me to visit the fabulous conservatories of Laeken, brilliant with azaleas, fuchsias, geraniums, hortensias, and the spectacular palm house. These are only open for about ten days per year and I have been fortunate to see them on both my adjudication trips to Brussels.

On a free weekend I went to Amsterdam to accept an Edison Award for my complete recorded works and was taken to the 1992 Floriade. Although I had gone to Keukenhof many times, also the Chelsea Flower Show, I had not seen anything as vast as that display of flowers and shrubs anywhere.

After the Brussels contest I had a few days at home, then went to Schwetzingen again to see the performance of Rossini's *Tancredi* with some of the young singers from the previous year's competition there. The leading role was sung by Bernadette Manca di Nissa and it was good to see the youngsters do so well, also to enjoy the beautiful gardens again. But I was happy to return to Les Avants where my own rhododendrons were in full flower and to pay a visit to the Château de Vullierens near Lausanne to see – and order – the magnificent irises on display there.

At the end of June I travelled to Oxford where I was the guest of Sir Claus and Lady Moser at the Warden's Lodgings, Wadham College. On the twenty-fourth I received the degree of Doctor of Music at the Ceremony of Encaenia. This took place in the Sheldonian Theatre and was very impressive, with its colourful processions and ritual. The Queen of Denmark was one of the six other honorands and a splendid lunch and garden party followed, the weather being perfect. I wandered in the beautiful college garden with Lady Moser and she and Sir Claus hosted a dinner party in the evening. I have very fond memories of that trip – and the almost non-stop meals. During my stay, I saw my niece, Ruth, and paid a visit to Sir Geoffrey and Lady Meade who had been so hospitable during our Milan trips in the Sixties. I was amazed at Geoffrey's unimpaired mind, in spite of crippling paralysis, and doubly happy to have reminisced with them as they both died not long after.

By July 7 I was back in London where I attended Her Majesty's luncheon for members of the Order of Merit at Buckingham Palace on the ninth. Once again the Queen was very informal and it was quite a jolly gathering including old friends like Sir Sidney and Lady Nolan, Sir Michael Tippett and Lord and Lady Menuhin. A group photograph was signed and sent by the Queen and Prince Philip – it sits on my spinet and is a constant reminder of the day. I rounded off that afternoon with a visit to Norma Major and was off to Sydney the following day to catch up with Ric who opened a production of *Maria Stuarda* with the Australian Opera on the thirteenth. We spent every possible weekend at Whale Beach or with Helen and the children.

I was co-adjudicator of the McDonald's Operatic Aria Contest and the Sydney Symphony Orchestra presented 'A Tribute to Dame Joan Sutherland and Richard Bonynge' on August 19, conducted by Carlo Felice Cillario. Sixteen singers took part in the items mostly from works we both had done with the Australian Opera, whilst we happily sat in the audience and enjoyed the evening.

Back in Europe again Ric went to Rovigo to prepare and perform Rossini's *Sigismondo* with a cast of very talented young Italian singers including Sonia Ganassi and Rossella Ragatzu, with that capable tenor Bruno Lazzaretti as Ladislav. His very rapid, accurate coloratura and wide range were outstanding. I enjoyed the work immensely. I travelled to Vercelli from Rovigo to participate in the Viotti Concorso again and was very impressed by the singing of Maria Costanza Nocentini in the competition.

A surprise visit was made by Tommy Byrne, Gilles Dupont and several of their colleagues to the chalet in honour of my birthday. They came from Geneva, bearing a huge birthday cake, champagne and beautiful personal gifts. Tommy has been a big fan for years and he and Gilles now have a superb restaurant, Le Lion d'Or, at Cologny near Geneva where they organised another even *more* splendid surprise in honour of my seventieth birthday in 1996. Ruthli was a party to both celebrations and managed to keep me completely unaware.

I joined Richard in Barcelona in time for his opening night of *Anna Bolena* with Edita Gruberova and to adjudicate at the thirtieth Francesco

Viñas Vocal Contest. There were 225 competitors from forty-two different countries in the contest, with Maria Costanza Nocentini and Akemi Sakamoto among the finalists, together with a very young and promising Spanish soprano, Yolanda Auyanet. The jury was a large one with Magda Olivero as President.

Albin Hänseroth, General Director of the Liceo, hosted a 'Homage' to me on November 21 in the magnificent first-floor foyer of the theatre. It is a fondly remembered gesture, especially in view of the disastrous fire in January 1994 which gutted the beautiful theatre.

At the end of the month I went to London for several commitments and attended the Memorial Service for Sir Geraint Evans in Westminster Abbey. I sat a few times for a portrait by Alessandra Alderson and was invited by Norma Major to attend a luncheon at Chequers honouring Mencap. During a tour of the lovely house Norma told me she was writing a history of it, which has since been published with great success. I thoroughly enjoyed the book, especially having seen the house.

Christmas was somewhat hectic, with Richard dashing home from recording sessions in Krakow, working with Sumi Jo preparing for a recording in London the following March, then leaving for Montpellier for performances of *Les Contes d'Hoffmann*.

I stayed at the chalet and sat for Ulisse Sartini, the Italian portrait painter. Ulisse had been commissioned through Mrs Peggy Haim to paint my portrait to be hung in the new contemporary wing of the National Portrait Gallery. I also sat for the sculptor James Butler, whose work I admired, and found it easy to relax with both artists. The finished Sartini portrait is very beautiful, if a trifle youthful and, when viewed by the Queen at the Gallery opening, elicited the question to me, 'Did you have many sittings?' I replied I had a longish one of about two hours, for Ulisse to take rolls and rolls of film, then a single 'check-up' session prior to the unveiling of the finished portrait. The Queen smiled and said, 'Oh, that's what *I* like!'

Richard was off to San Diego and then Australia, so I had time at home to catch up on the mail with our new secretary, Mrs Janine MacKenzie. She has been of the greatest assistance to us both, especially in deciphering our scribbles. Without her I don't know how this book would have been completed.

On April 28 Udi and I attended the long-awaited opening of the Auditorium Stravinsky in Montreux. It has a most remarkable acoustic and excellent adaptable seating, with the added asset of great views of the lake. Georg Solti conducted the London Symphony Orchestra and said the hall had the best acoustic in Switzerland and probably of any modern hall in Europe.

I later flew to London and reminisced with Georg and Valerie Solti over lunch at their home. That night I attended the Memorial Concert in the Festival Hall for Howard Hartog who had died the previous November. He had written us in November 1990, telling us he was terminally ill and thanking us for our collaboration over the years. I kept the letter, not only for its contents, but also because it was the longest we ever received from him – far removed from his characteristic one-liners or one-worders.

A pleasant few weeks at home enjoying the garden and gleaning information for these memoirs from our press scrap-books, then off to Cardiff for the BBC's 1993 Cardiff Singer of the World contest. *En route* I opened the newly developed Jackdaws, which provided further space for the varied activities of the Great Elm Music Festival held annually in the home and grounds of Bridge House, near Frome, by Maureen Lehane Wishart. Among the jurors in Cardiff were Marilyn Horne and Gérard Souzay, both of whom gave interesting master classes. Due to the high standard of the contestants it was difficult to arrive at a final decision but the exposure in the press and on television benefits all of them. The winner that year was Inger Dam-Jensen, with Paul Whelan winning the Lieder prize, but all the other finalists have been doing well.

I flew direct to Sydney after the final, where Richard was conducting a production of *La Périchole* which he'd told me was 'over the top'. This did not prepare me for the liberties taken with the plot, period and presentation. It was aimed to shock, was far too harsh and brittle and had lost every vestige of charm. Poor Offenbach!

From June 28 to July 23 I worked, together with Marlena Malas and Luigi Alva, with twenty young Australian singers in the First National Vocal Symposium. Their ages ranged from twenty-two to about thirty and we endeavoured to steer each of them on the right track for their particular vocal and interpretative abilities. The course was repeated in 1996.

We had a nasty scare when Richard developed stomach pains which he brushed aside until I called a doctor against his will. Fortunately the doctor came very swiftly to our apartment and, within an hour of examining the patient, he had Richard in the nearby hospital prepared for an immediate appendectomy. The attention he received during his brief stay removed his dread of hospitals and their treatment, and his room was seldom without visitors bearing gifts of flowers, fruit, chocolates and wine – 'for after'. The orchestra sent a card sympathising for his having 'pericholitis'. We spent an extra couple of weeks at Whale Beach before the doctor gave him permission to return home at the end of August.

Then we were off to London for the unveiling of Ulisse Sartini's portrait at the National Portrait Gallery. This was a memorable evening with, after the personal presentation of the portrait, a short concert given by Australian artists Yvonne Kenny, Peter Coleman-Wright and Geoffrey Parsons. An excellent dinner followed and we enjoyed the company of Prime Minister John Major and Norma, several other dignitaries and the then Director of the Portrait Gallery, Dr John Hayes, also Mrs Haim.

Returned to Les Avants, Richard went off to Savona for performances of Pacini's *Medea* and on September 19 Ruthli and I went to Monte Carlo where I had been invited to participate as a member of the Sydney Olympic 2000 Bid delegation. It was all very exciting mingling with the groups from the other 'bidders' – Manchester, Beijing and Turkey. Roderick (Rod) McGeoch and his assistant Margaret McLennan had organised a non-stop group of street performers; the press, radio and TV personalities were there in full force, along with top sports aces such as Evonne Goolagong Cawley and Kieran Perkins, not forgetting a selection of the current politicians and the much-loved Gough and Margaret Whitlam. Receptions, lunches at the Hotel de Paris and aboard Kerry Packer's yacht *Galu*, many interviews showing plans and proposed scheduling for the Games throughout the Sydney area were held, culminating in the Official Presentation to the International Olympic Committee of Australia's beautiful video film and lively speeches, which ultimately won for Sydney the Games in the year 2000.

I made a quick trip to Vienna as the guest of the Friends of the Staatsoper the weekend of October 2, then flew on to Italy to see the opening of Pacini's *Medea* in Savona, returning briefly to Les Avants. Richard went off to Dallas where he had performances of *The Barber of Seville*, with Cecilia Bartoli and a strong cast with whom he enjoyed working.

For me there were further European commitments: a weekend in Reggio Emilia as guest of the Circolo Lirico Giuseppe Verdi, receiving the eleventh Memorial Giacomo Volpi Award, then on to Caltanissetta where I was again adjudicating. One of the contestants was Anja Kampe, a pupil of Elio Battaglia, who reached the final of that twenty-fifth Concorso Internazionale V. Bellini. She was also in the 1995 Cardiff Singer of the World competition and I was pleased to hear how she had progressed.

Richard had performances of *La Fille du Régiment* with Edita Gruberova in Barcelona, with Heather Begg singing the Marquise de Berkenfeld. Before he returned to the chalet for Christmas Adam, Helen and the children arrived in Les Avants. To be sure of Natasha and Vanya learning to ski I organised a week with them in Zermatt and they were able to continue progressing at Les Avants as we had good snow that year for the local ski and sled runs. The young Bonynges returned to Sydney on January 6, 1994. Although we had all been disturbed by the news of the fierce bushfires around Sydney, Adam and Helen said they were not prepared for the widespread devastation they could see when coming in to land there.

I flew to Sydney in February for the opening and dedication of the Dame Joan Sutherland Centre at St Catherine's, which was a huge success. The multi-purpose structure has proved its worth, having provided space for all manner of artistic and musical pursuits, along with the technology opportunities of the computer room and learning centres. The new chapel is also a beautiful and versatile area which can be used for concerts and lectures. Two happy weeks were spent with Adam, Helen and the children and some time with Grandma Jean at Whale Beach, then it was back to Les Avants for me and on to Paris where I was escorted through the wonderful new areas of the Louvre by the Director and, on the evening of March 17, interviewed for their series 'Grandes Voix du XXe Siècle'.

I returned to the chalet and caught a glimpse of Richard who had been recording in London with Jerry Hadley and came home for a couple of days before flying off again – to San Diego, this time, for performances of *La Sonnambula* and *Les Contes d'Hoffmann*. After visiting friends in San Francisco I joined him there and saw both operas. We also had a day at the wild animal park and made a trip to the Anza Borego Desert with its wealth of cactus flowers.

Back home by mid-May I did a long interview with Eve Ruggieri for French television, then we relaxed for a month. During this time representatives from Sotheby's in London came to inspect certain items of memorabilia for possible sale, including my costumes and accessories. I loved all my 'disguises' but it seemed pointless to keep them in the attic to gather dust and rot, now that I no longer wore them. It was decided to organise a specific sale for them all in London on February 9, 1995, with everything being removed from Les Avants before I left for Australia in September.

I made a quick trip to Calais via Paris on the TGV in early July, naming and 'launching' one of the Eurotunnel shuttle locomotives and touring the whole French terminal area.

Between July 11 and 20 I was a member of the jury for the XXe Concours International de Chant de Paris, where there was great emphasis on the French recital repertoire.

Richard had performances of *Adriana Lecouvreur* with Yoko Watanabe and Patrick Power in Adelaide during August and a big Opera Gala concert with the Canberra Symphony Orchestra, before returning to Sydney for his rehearsals for *Les Pêcheurs de perles*. I joined him there in time for his opening night on September 16 and was again entranced by the work.

Rehearsals began on October 10 for the film *Dad and Dave On Our Selection*, a collection of stories by Steele Rudd of life on a most unproductive farm. Although I had finally agreed to appear in the film as Mother Rudd, opposite Leo McKern as Dad, I went to the first reading with the other members of the cast feeling very nervous and inadequate. I knew the Director (George Whaley), the Producer (Anthony Buckley) and the Designer (Roger Kirk) and had met Leo, but the rest of the cast I knew only by repute and from having seen them in Australian television films. I was happy to find them all amenable and very friendly – as curious about me as I was about them. My 'children' Geoffrey Rush (Dave), David Field (Dan), Essie Davis (Kate), Celia Ireland (Sarah) and Noah Taylor (Joe) were very circumspect at first, obviously on their best behaviour, but they soon relaxed into a real family atmosphere with Essie especially calling me 'Mum' off the set and the others following suit. By the end of the shooting of the film, I was 'Mum' to the whole group – and really felt like it.

I was delighted that Noah and Geoffrey had such a huge success in Scott Hicks's splendid film *Shine*. Their performances were certainly outstanding.

The readings and mini-rehearsals went on for two weeks, and during that time Ric and I celebrated our fortieth (Ruby) wedding anniversary quietly at the Opera Supperclub with just the family. Ric gave me a beautiful ruby ring which he'd had made in Sydney and I gave him ruby cuff-links that I'd bought in Burlington Arcade in London eight years previously while cutting through to Piccadilly. Adam, Helen and the children gave us a lovely commemorative Bilston enamel box.

I was transported to the Braidwood area on October 25 and housed for the whole seven weeks of filming at Settlers' Flat Lodge near Mongarlowe, a delightful property converted to receive about ten guests in beautifully decorated bedrooms with bath. Each room opened on to the surrounding veranda and views of the garden, paddocks and dams. Several other films had been made in that same part of New South Wales, not far from Canberra. The main street of the town still retains its Victorian appearance and there are some very grand and beautiful properties such as Mona and Bedervale – an earlier house designed by John Verge in 1836 and used in our film as the home of the despised squatter (J. P. Riley) played by Barry Otto.

Working with Leo McKern was a great joy and he was a fine example to all of us. All the production assistants, wig- and make-up artists were fun to be with and it was a very happy experience altogether. It was great to see wombats and kangaroos at dusk and I heard that Mongarlowe River is a sanctuary for platypus, too, although I didn't see any.

As the filming ended on December 16 I stayed in Sydney for Christmas. Adam, Helen, Natasha and Vanya came to Whale Beach and we had a great time, together with Grandma Jean.

I arrived back in Les Avants on December 30, happy to see Ric and the rest of the household again. He had been in Munich, Dallas and Verona since leaving Sydney, only returning in time for Christmas. On January 2 he went back to Verona, to complete rehearsals and perform *Les Contes d'Hoffmann*, so we at least spent the turn of the year together.

And so another year (1995) brought further 'jury duty' – in Dublin where the Veronica Dunne Bursary was to be awarded to a young Irish singer or one of Irish parentage born abroad. Veronica Dunne had been at the Royal Opera House with me in the Fifties and it was wonderful to see her again. She had been teaching for some thirty years in Ireland and this bursary celebrated her years of service to the vocal art.

Back in Les Avants on January 20 I went by train to Verona to see the *Hoffman* production – very lavish scenery but with a tendency to overwhelm the performers who were good in spite of it.

While in Verona we made a quick trip to Modena to hear some young singers auditioning for parts in *L'Elisir d'Amore* to be performed later in the year.

We returned home briefly, flying to London on February 3 to check on the display of my costumes, mounted by Kerry Taylor for Sotheby's, prior to the press viewing and sale. On February 8 a grand reception and viewing was held by Sotheby's in their gallery, followed by a special dinner given for certain of the guests including Barbara and Arthur Matera, Hardy Amies, John and Norma Major and others associated either with our careers or with Sotheby's. The sale was next day and it was a wrench in one way to see those superb costumes pass into other hands by the knock of a hammer. But I knew many of the recipients and that they would treasure them. The most ardent and successful bidder, Aaron Kleinlehrer from Australia, was determined to make his purchases the basis of a Dame Joan Sutherland collection in the proposed Theatre Museum in Sydney and I thank him most sincerely for his thought.

After a week in Les Avants I flew to Athens for the Maria Callas contest. On the jury with me were Victoria de Los Angeles, Elisabeth Söderström, Graziella Sciutti, Magda Olivero, Irina Arkhipova, Luigi Alva and others. We were disappointed in the overall standard of the competitors and did not award the actual Maria Callas prize.

From Athens I flew to Spoleto to help choose a group of young artists for inclusion in the forthcoming study group and possibly for the following season's Spoleto Festival.

The spring weather enticed me into the garden when I went back to the chalet, and Udi went walking with her sister, brother-in-law and Dolly, our Bernese shepherd dog. Unfortunately Dolly slipped on the wet leaves and cannoned into Udi whose leg was severely broken, putting her out of action for many months.

She insisted I go to Deutschlandsberg in Austria for the Ferruccio Tagliavini competition and there was some very good vocal material in the contest. A concert by the successful contestants was held in Graz on April 26.

After another short stay at home encouraging the garden, I was off to London to announce to the press that year's Cardiff Singer of the World competition as I had agreed to take Marilyn Horne's place on the jury. I seem to have become a regular juror for this contest as I am again participating in 1997.

So the days, months and years fly by, with no sense of my being 'retired'. We had a short period at the Britten–Pears school at Aldeburgh, then I paid a visit to Vercelli to attend Marilyn Horne's recital there and her receipt of the Viotti d'Oro, went to the Cardiff Singer of the World competition, to Budapest (again to choose young singers for *L'Elisir d'Amore*,) then off on holiday with Ric and friends to northern and western Greece, including Corfu.

There were more days in the garden at Les Avants, then I travelled to Sydney for Ric's performances of *Medea* and *Carmen*, and my participation in a second symposium for the Opera Foundation with Marlena Malas again involved. The requests continue to arrive for my services on adjudication panels and I *do* enjoy returning to some of the contests – notably the Cardiff, the Queen Elisabeth in Brussels, the Viotti, Deutschlandsberg and so on. I have also been grandly fêted upon reaching my seventieth birthday, both in Switzerland and London – nights I shall never forget.

EPILOGUE

Now my function in life appears to be that of judging how others sing, as opposed to being judged myself. The competitions are very numerous and provide a goal for the many contestants to work towards. Not all of them can be successful and some should never even be studying singing. However, a few show excellent and sometimes exceptional talent, going on to take their places as respected professionals. I wonder if they have any idea of the standards they must sustain despite the hazards and pitfalls, or the sacrifices they are forced to make to prevent exhaustion and illness when launched on a busy career? Success is one thing, sustaining it is something else. Perhaps this book may help them to cope – I hope so.

I have been so fortunate in having Richard to guide me, work with me and help me to enjoy not only our performing life, but also that very special family life so important to everyone. Our household has always been a happy one, based on great affection and love. We have also been on excellent terms with our agents, managements and performing colleagues, along with all those in the Decca recording group, our several secretaries and Udi – our companion-housekeeper for forty years; and my thanks and appreciation for the help of my editress Elsbeth Lindner. Her advice and assistance in reducing my ramblings to a reasonable size were of great importance. God bless them all.

LIST OF PERFORMANCES

Symbols
* debut performance; † also broadcast on radio; ‡ also broadcast on television.
p. producer; c. conductor; P. Pianist.
d. designer (*Where two designers are noted the first indicates the set designer and the second the costume designer*).

EARLY PERFORMANCES

Operatic Concert with Singers of Australia. Senta's Ballad (*Der Fliegende Holländer*), Bridal Chamber Scene (*Lohengrin*), Quintet (*Meistersinger*): 22 March 1947

Acis & Galatea (HANDEL) Galatea*; Eastwood Masonic Hall and King's School Sydney: with Ronald Dowd, Frank Lisle, 20 June, 19 July 1947

Dido & Aeneas (PURCELL) Dido*; C. Henry Krips; Town Hall Sydney: Shirley Wallwork (Belinda), Noel Melvin (Aeneas), Dowd (Messenger), 30 Aug. 1947

Tour with Riverina Music Clubs (N.S.W.) to Leeton, Griffith, Narrandera, Wagga Wagga, Cootamundra; repertoire included 'Voi lo sapete' (*Cavalleria Rusticana*), 'Porgi amor' (*Le Nozze di Figaro*) Sep. 1947

1948 *Concert* ABC Military Band; Sydney Town Hall: 4 Apr.
      Music Club Ryde-Eastwood, Sydney: 9 Aug.
      Music Club Manly, Sydney: 8 Sep.
      Music Club Rosebay, Sydney: 17 Sep.
      Music Club Killara, Sydney: 21 Sep.
      Music Festival Dich Teure Halle (*Tannhäuser*), *Softly sighs* (*Freischütz*) *Il est doux, il est bon* (*Herodiade*), songs by Richard Strauss, ballads; Wollahra All Saints: 7 Nov.

1949 *Olivet to Calvary* (MAUNDER); Sydney Town Hall: with Dowd and Melvin, 11 Apr.
      Concert Arts Council, Tamworth, N.S.W.: 8 June
      Tour with Riverina Music Club (N.S.W.) to Leeton, Narrandera, Wagga Wagga, Cootamundra: 13, 14, 15, 16 June

Tour Stars of Mobil Quest; Melbourne Town Hall, 15 Sept.; Hobart Town Hall: 10 Nov.; Adelaide Town Hall: 19 Nov.; Brisbane Town Hall: 27 Oct.; Newcastle Town Hall, N.S.W.: 1 Nov.; Sydney Town Hall: 3 Nov.

Music Club Nowra: 4 Nov.

Music Club Roseville: 9 Nov.

Music Club Ryde/Eastwood: 14 Nov.

Music Club Rose Bay; first shared platform with Bonynge as soloist: 26 Nov.

Celebrity Concert Lithgow Music Society, also with Bonynge; Union Theatre, Lithgow: 28 Nov.

Elijah* (MENDELSSOHN) also *Suicidio* (*La Gioconda*), *Il est doux, il est bon*, *Ritorna Vincitor* (*Aida*), *Pleurez mes yeux* (*Le Cid*); Queen Victoria Club, Eastwood Masonic Hall: 5 Dec.

1950 *Concert* Scottish New Year, Sydney Town Hall: 2 Jan.

Music Club Hurstville, N.S.W.: 20 Feb.

Stars of Mobil Quest: 19 Mar.

Concert Rockhampton, Queensland: 21 Mar.

Elijah; Parramatta City Hall, N.S.W.: 28 Mar.

Concert Cremorne Orpheum, Sydney: 2 Apr.

Music Club Killara, Sydney: 11 Apr. with Bonynge.

Recital Lismore, N.S.W.: 18 Apr.

Concert Broken Hill, N.S.W.: 27 Apr.

Stars of Mobil Quest Savoy Theatre, Woolongong, N.S.W.: 29 May

Concert Maryborough Town Hall, Queensland: 15 June

Concert Farewell to R. Bonynge; Rockdale Methodist Church: 17 June

Recital Cronulla, Sydney: 22 June

Recital Sydney Lyceum Club: 13 July with Bonynge

Samson (HANDEL) Dalila* & Israelite Woman*; Royal Philharmonic Society; c. Toy; Sydney Town Hall: 15 July

Concert Benefit for Rachel Foster Hospital; with Bonynge: 21 July

Tour Stars of Mobil Quest, Melbourne Town Hall: 6 Sept.; Brisbane Town Hall: 13 Sept.; Canberra Albert Theatre: 15 Sept.; Sydney Assembly Hall: 20 Sept.; Newcastle Century Theatre: 26 Sept.; Kalgoorlie Town Hall: 3 Oct.; Perth Capital Theatre: 6 Oct.; Adelaide Town Hall: 10 Oct.; Launceston Capital Theatre, Tasmania: 17 Oct.; Hobart Town Hall: 19 Oct.

Gala Concert Sydney Town Hall: 12 Nov.

Messiah* (HANDEL); Sydney Symphony Orchestra; c. Peterson: 25 Nov.

Concert Albury Choral Society; Plaza Theatre, Albury, N.S.W.: 7 Dec.

Carols by Candlelight South Australian Symphony Orchestra; c. Krips; Adelaide: 17 Dec.

431

1951 *Annual Scottish Concert* Sydney Town Hall: 1 Jan.
ABC Orchestral Concert Sydney Symphony Orchestra; c. Post; Sydney Domain: 11 Feb.
Music Club Returned Soldiers' Legion, Sydney: 13 Feb.
Music Club Wahroonga, Sydney: 16 Feb.
Music Club Orange, N.S.W.: 22 Feb.
Music Club Mosman: 3 Mar.
Music Club Longueville/Northwood: 9 Mar.
ABC Broadcast: 4 Apr. incl. *Suicidio* (*La Gioconda*)
Orchestral Concert Mildura Symphony Orchestra, N.S.W.; 16 Apr.
Farewell Recital Sydney Town Hall: 20 Apr.
Music Club Tuggerah Lakes: 30 Apr.
Broadcast 2GB: 4 May incl. *Dich Teure Halle* (*Tannhäuser*)
Concert Broken Hill: 10 May
Broadcast 2BL: 22 May
Concert Royal Empire Society: 24 May
Music Club Hunters' Hill/Drummoyne: 25 May
ABC Broadcast: 28 May
Grand Masonic Concert Parramatta Town Hall: 30 May
Judith (GOOSSENS) Judith*; James Wilson (Holofernes), Ronald Dowd (Bagoas); c. Goossens; Sydney Conservatorium: 9, 12, 18, 22 June
ABC Broadcast Brisbane: 27 June
Music Club Murwillumbah, N.S.W.; 28 June
Recital Kretscharan Club: 2 July
ABC Broadcast: 25 June

1952 *All at Sea* (GEOFFREY SHAW) Mrs Empson* (Act II only); Parry Theatre, Royal College of Music, London: 12 May
Il Tabarro (PUCCINI) Giorgetta*; Gordon Farrell/Kenneth Fawcett (Michele), Edward Byles (Luigi), Kenneth McKellar (Ballad Singer); c. Richard Austin, p. Carey, d. Peter Rice/Pauline Elliot; Parry Theatre, Royal College of Music, London: 16, 18 July
BBC Broadcast recital: 1 May
Broadcast from ABC London: 21 May
BBC Broadcast: 8 Aug.
BBC Broadcast: 19 Sep.
The Magic Flute (MOZART) First Lady*; Matters/Walters (Papageno), Lanigan (Tamino), Leigh (Pamina), te Wiata (Sarastro), Bak/Hollweg (Queen of Night), Howe, Watson (Ladies); c. Pritchard, p. West, d. Messel; Covent Garden: 28 Oct., 1 Nov., 6, 11, Dec.
Aida (VERDI) High Priestess*; Brouwenstijn (Aida), Shacklock (Amneris), Johnston (Radames), Williams/Walters (Amonasro); c. Barbirolli, p. West, d. Cruddas; Covent Garden: 3, 6, 14 Nov.
Recital (appendix 1); P. Gerald Moore; Wigmore Hall, London: 7 Nov.

Norma (BELLINI) Clotilde*; Callas (Norma), Picchi (Pollione), Stignani (Adalgisa), Vaghi (Oroveso); c. Gui, p. Enriquez, d. Barlow; Covent Garden: 8, 10, 13, 18†, 20 Nov.

A Masked Ball (VERDI) Amelia*; Edgar Evans (Riccardo), Walters (Renato), Watson (Ulrica); c. Pritchard, p. Rennert, d. Barlow/Stone; Covent Garden: 29 Dec.

1953　*The Magic Flute* First Lady; Geraint Evans/Matters (Papageno), Lanigan/Pears (Tamino), Leigh (Pamina), Nowakowsky/te Wiata (Sarastro), Hollweg/Bak (Queen of Night), Howe, Watson (Ladies); c. Pritchard, p. West, d. Messel; Covent Garden: 16, 19 Jan.

Aida High Priestess; Brouwenstijn/Hammond (Aida), Shacklock (Amneris), Johnston (Radames), Walters/Edwards (Amonasro); c. Barbirolli, p. West, d. Cruddas; Covent Garden: 28 Jan., 5, 11 Feb.

Aida Aida; concert performance; Central Hall, Plymouth: 4 Feb.

Aida High Priestess; Zadek/Lafayette/Kinasiewicz (Aida), Shacklock (Amneris), Johnston/Marlowe (Radames), Edwards/Walters/Williams (Amonasro); c. Barbirolli/E. Young, p. West, d. Cruddas; Royal Opera House tour: Cardiff: 16 Feb.; Edinburgh: 23 Feb.; Glasgow: 2, 14 Mar.; Liverpool: 18 Mar.; Manchester: 28 Mar., 1 Apr.; Birmingham: 11, 15 Apr.

A Masked Ball Amelia; Edgar Evans/Johnston (Riccardo), Walters/Edwards (Renato), Coates (Ulrica); c. Tausky, p. Rennert, d. Barlow/Stone; Royal Opera House tour: Cardiff: 18, 27 Feb.; Glasgow: 11, 13 Mar.; Manchester: 30 Mar., 2 Apr.; Birmingham: 13 Apr.

The Marriage of Figaro (MOZART) Countess Almaviva*; Geraint Evans (Figaro), Walters (Count Almaviva) Leigh/Dunne (Susanna), Mills/Zareska/Pollak (Cherubino); c. J. Gibson, p. Latham, d. Gerard; Royal Opera House tour: Edinburgh: 24 Feb.; Manchester: 4 Apr.; Birmingham: 18 Apr.

Wagnerian Concert Brangäne*; *Tristan und Isolde*: Act II; c. Barbirolli; Manchester: 9 Apr.

Elektra (STRAUSS) Overseer*; Schlüter (Elektra), Kupper/Kinasiewicz (Chrysothemis), Coates (Clytemnestra), Braun (Orestes); c. Kleiber, p. Hartmann, d. Lambert; Covent Garden: 13, 15, 23, 27 May

Aida High Priestess; Callas (Aida), Simionato (Amneris), Baum (Radames), Walters (Amonasro); c. Barbirolli, p. West, d. Cruddas; Covent Garden: 4, 6, 10† June

Norma Clotilde; Callas (Norma), Simionato (Adalgisa), Picchi Pollione), Neri (Oroveso); c. Pritchard, p. Enriquez, d. Barlow; Covent Garden: 15, 17, 20, 23 June

Aida High Priestess; Zadek (Aida), Shacklock (Amneris), Johnston (Radames), Walters (Amonasro); c. Barbirolli/E. Young, p. West, d.

Cruddas; Royal Opera House tour: Bulawayo, Rhodesia: 30 July, 1, 5, 10, 14, 19, 25, 29 Aug.
Gloriana (BRITTEN) Lady Rich*; Lanigan (Essex), Cross/Shacklock (Elizabeth I), Dalberg (Raleigh), Matters (Cecil); Royal Opera House tour, Bulawayo: 11, 15, 20, 22, 24 Aug.
Die Walküre (WAGNER) Helmwige*; Fisher (Sieglinde), Harshaw (Brünnhilde), Hotter (Wotan), Hook, Turner, Coates, Watson, M. Sinclair, Shacklock, Howitt (Valkyries); c. Stiedry, p. Schramm, d. Pemberton; Covent Garden: 19, 24, 26, 30 Oct.
Carmen (BIZET) Frasquita*; Rankin/Shacklock (Carmen), Johnston/ Edgar Evans (Don José), Rothmüller (Escamillo), Yeend/Leigh/Morison (Micaela); c. Pritchard/Downes, p. Asquith, d. Wakhevitch; Covent Garden: 2, 7, 10, 18, 26 Nov., 12, 28, 31 Dec.
Concert with Johnstone, Clitheroe; Odeon Theatre, Guildford: 5 Dec.
Aida High Priestess; Brouwenstijn/Hammond (Aida), Shacklock/Rankin/Watson (Amneris), Johnston (Radames), Rothmüller (Amonasro); c. Barbirolli/E. Young, p. West, d. Cruddas; Covent Garden: 2, 7, 11, 18, 26 Dec.

1954 *Aida* High Priestess/Aida*; Hammond/Sutherland (Aida), Shacklock (Amneris), Johnston/van der Zaalm (Radames), Rothmüller (Amonasro); c. E. Young, p. West, d. Cruddas; Covent Garden: 2, 22 Jan. (High Priestess), 4 Feb. (Aida)
Carmen Frasquita; Shacklock (Carmen), Edgar Evans/Johnston (Don José), Rothmüller (Escamillo), Morison/Stuart/Turner/Leigh (Michaela); c. Downes/Pritchard, p. Asquith, d. Wakhevitch; Covent Garden: 5, 12, 27 Jan., 9, 12 Feb.
Gloriana Lady Rich; Pears/Lanigan (Essex), Cross/Shacklock (Elizabeth I), Dalberg (Raleigh), Otakar Kraus (Cecil); c. Goodall, p. Coleman, d. Piper; Covent Garden: 29 Jan., 2, 16 Feb.; Royal Opera House tour: Cardiff: 11 Mar.; Manchester: 30 Mar.; Birmingham: 13 Apr.
Aida High Priestess; Hammond (Aida), Shacklock/Watson/Coates (Amneris), Johnston (Radames), Rothmüller (Amonasro); c. E. Young, p. West, d. Cruddas; Royal Opera House tour: Croydon: 24, 26 Feb.; Manchester: 3 Apr.; Birmingham: 17 Apr.
Die Walküre Helmwige; Fisher/H. Konetzni (Sieglinde), A. Konetzni (Brünnhilde), L. Hoffmann/Kamann (Wotan), Raisbeck, Toros, Coates, Watson, M. Sinclair, Shacklock, Denise (Valkyries); c. Goodall, p. West, d. Pemberton; Royal Opera House tour: Croydon: 5, 9 Mar.; Manchester: 2 Apr.; Birmingham: 6 Apr.
Carmen Frasquita; Shacklock (Carmen), Edgar Evans/Rowland Jones/Johnston (Don José), Rothmüller (Escamillo), Leigh (Michaela); c. Pritchard/Downes, p. Asquith, d. Wakhevitch; Royal Opera House

tour: Cardiff: 8, 12 Mar.; Manchester: 1 Apr.; Birmingham: 5, 16 Apr.

Der Freischütz (WEBER) Agathe*; Edgar Evans/Johnston (Max), Otakar Kraus/Dalberg (Kaspar), Leigh (Ännchen); c. Downes, p. West, d. Furse; Royal Opera House tour: Manchester: 23, 26 Mar.; Covent Garden: 13 May, 12, 16 July

La Buona Figliuola (PICCINNI) (BBC broadcast) Lucinda*; Cuénod (Armindoro), A. Young (Conchiglia), Morison (Cecchina); c. Mackerras; 22, 25 Apr.

Elektra Overseer; Schlüter (Elektra), Rysanek (Chrysothemis), Coates (Clytemnestra), Otakar Kraus (Orestes); c. Kempe, p. Hartmann, d. Lambert; Covent Garden: 30 Apr., 4, 12 May

Welcome to Her Majesty the Queen; Cantata for soprano and orchestra (BLISS); BBC Concert Orchestra; c. Sargent: 15 May

Der Ring des Nibelungen (WAGNER) Woglinde*, Helmwige, Woodbird*; Otakar Kraus (Alberich), Frantz (Wotan), Raisbeck (Wellgunde), Thomas (Flosshilde), Fisher (Sieglinde), Harshaw (Brünnhilde), Raisbeck, Toros, Howe, Iacopi, Johnson, Shacklock, Denise (Valkyries), Svenholm (Siegfried), Kuen (Mime); c. Stiedry, p. Hartmann, d. Hurry; Covent Garden: First Cycle: 27 May, 2, 8, 17 June; Second Cycle: 21†, 23†, 25†, 29† June

Concert Exsultate Jubilate (MOZART); c. Woolf; St Martin-in-the-Fields, London: 26 June

Aida High Priestess; Hammond/Shuard (Aida), Shacklock/Rankin (Amneris), Johnston (Radames), Walters/Geraint Evans (Amonasro); c. E. Young, p. West, d. Cruddas; Covent Garden: 3, 7, 19, 23 July, 14, 20, 28 Dec.

Carmen Frasquita; Rankin/Shacklock/Howe (Carmen), Edgar Evans/ Johnston (Don José), Geraint Evans (Escamillo), Hale/Leigh/ Morison (Micaela); c. Pritchard/Downes, p. Asquith, d. Wakhevitch; Covent Garden: 9, 21 July, 28, 30 Oct., 24, 30 Nov., 4, 7 Dec.

Promenade Concert Lisa's aria, Act I, *The Queen of Spades* (TCHAIKOVSKY); c. B. Cameron; Royal Albert Hall, London: 2† Aug.

The Tales of Hoffmann (OFFENBACH) Antonia*; Glynne (Crespel), Patzak/Edgar Evans (Hoffmann), Uhde/Otakar Kraus (Dr Miracle), M. Sinclair/Coates (Mother's voice); c. Downes, p. Rennert, d. Wakhevitch; Covent Garden: 17, 20, 23 Nov., 1, 13 Dec.

Der Freischütz Agathe; Edgar Evans/Johnston (Max), Dalberg (Kaspar), Leigh (Ännchen); c. Downes, p. West, d. Furse; Covent Garden: 22, 30† Dec., with Leigh, Evans, Johnston, Dahlberg; c. Downes; 15, 25 Jan. 1955.

1955 *The Midsummer Marriage* (TIPPETT) world première; Jenifer*; Richard Lewis (Mark), Otakar Kraus (King Fisher), Leigh (Bella), Lanigan

(Jack), Dominguez (Sosostris), Langdon, Coates (The Ancients); c. Pritchard, p. West, d. Hepworth; Covent Garden: 27†, 31 Jan., 8†, 11, 22 Feb.

The Tales of Hoffmann Antonia, Giulietta*; Edgar Evans (Hoffmann), Howitt (Nicklaus), Otakar Kraus (Dappertutto, Dr Mircale), Coates/M. Sinclair (Mother's voice), Glynne (Crespel), Sutherland/Hale (Giulietta), Morison/Sutherland (Antonia); c. Downes, p. Rennert, d. Wakhevitch; Royal Opera House tour: Glasgow: 28 Feb. (G), 5 Mar. (A/G), 7 Mar. (G); Edinburgh: 14 Mar. (G), 16 Mar. (A); Leeds: 21 Mar. (G); Manchester: 28 Mar. (G), 2 Apr. (A/G); Coventry: 11 Apr. (G), 13 Apr. (A)

Aida Aida; Shacklock/Coates (Amneris), Johnston (Radames), Geraint Evans/Walters (Amonasro); c. E. Young, p. West, d. Cruddas; Royal Opera House tour: Glasgow: 1 Mar.; Manchester: 5, 9 Apr.; Covent Garden: 23 Apr.

Missa Solemnis* (BEETHOVEN) BBC broadcast); other soloists: Cavelti, Pears, Standen; c. Schwarz; 15, 16, 20 Apr.

Concert with John Heddle Nash *Qual Farfalletta* (*Partenope*: HANDEL), *Ernani, involami* (*Ernani*), Duet *Bei Männern* (*Die Zauberflöte*), *Leise, leise* (*Der Freischütz*: WEBER), Duet *Ah! veglia, o donna, questo fior* (*Rigoletto*), 'Brindisi' (*La traviata*); p. G. W. Hodgetts; Brierley Hill, West Midlands: 27 Apr.

Der Ring des Nibelungen Woglinde, Helmwige; Otakar Kraus (Alberich), Hotter/Schoeffler (Wotan), Hale (Wellgunde), Halliday (Flosshilde), Rysanek/Hilde Konetzni (Sieglinde), Harshaw (Brünnhilde), Shuard, Hale, Coates, Iacopi, Berry, Shacklock, Howe (Valkyries), Svanholm (Siegfried); c. Kempe, p. Hartmann, d. Hurry; Covent Garden: First Cycle: 10, 14†, 27 May; Second Cycle: 8, 10, 17 June. NB: Sutherland did not appear in *Siegfried*.

The Tales of Hoffmann Olympia*; Edgar Evans (Hoffmann), Veasey (Nicklaus), Otakar Kraus (Coppelius), Nilsson/Tree (Cochenille), Geraint Evans (Spalanzani); c. Downes, p. Rennert, d. Wakhevitch; Covent Garden: 16, 18, 22 June, 20, 22 July

Aida High Priestess; Stella (Aida), Stignani (Amneris), Penno (Radames), Gobbi (Amonasro); c. Molinari-Pradelli/E. Young, p. West, d. Cruddas; Covent Garden: 11, 13, 16† 18 July

Promenade Concert Te Deum* (DVOŘÁK); c. Sargent; Royal Albert Hall, London: 8† Aug.

Euryanthe (WEBER) (BBC broadcast) Euryanthe*; Vroons (Adolar), Böhme (Ludwig), Otakar Kraus (Lysiart), Schech (Eglantine); c. Stiedry; 30 Sep., 1 Oct.

Recital P. Bonynge; Wigmore Hall, London: 7 Oct.

Celebrity Concert with other artists (further information unknown); P. Hardie; Manchester: 12 Oct.

Carmen Micaela*; Radev/Shacklock (Carmen), Johnston/Nilsson (Don José), Ronald Lewis (Escamillo); c. Downes, p. Asquith, d. Wakhevitch; Covent Garden: 20, 25, 31 Oct., 4, 14, 19, 24, 30 Nov., 27, 29 Dec.

BBC Broadcast London Symphony Orchestra; c. Goehr: 23 Oct.

Aida (concert performance) Aida; Nancy Thomas (Amneris), Byles (Radames); c. Walter B. Smith; Exeter: 30 Oct.

Golgotha* (MARTIN) British première (BBC broadcast); Marjorie Thomas, Midgley, Griffiths, Anthony; c. Sargent; Royal Festival Hall, London: 9 Nov.

BBC Welsh Broadcast 23 Nov.

1956 *Broadcast* 'The birth of an opera'; Royal Philharmonic Orchestra; c. Pritchard: 23 Jan.

La Clemenza di Tito (MOZART) (BBC broadcast) Vitellia*, Richard Lewis (Tito), M. Sinclair (Sextus), Vyvyan (Servilia), Pollak (Annius), Hemsley (Publius); c. Pritchard; Camden Theatre, London: 11, 12 Mar.

Verdi Requiem* c. Fleming; Coventry: 24 Mar.

Messiah c. Mansel Thomas; Cardiff: 30 Mar.

The Tales of Hoffmann Antonia; Robinson (Crespel), Richard Lewis (Hoffmann), Otakar Kraus (Dr Miracle), Shacklock (Mother's voice); c. Downes, p. Asquith, d. Wakhevitch; Covent Garden: 19, 21 Apr., 28 June, 9 July

The Magic Flute First Lady; Geraint Evans/Walters (Papageno), Lanigan (Tamino), Morison (Pamina), Kelly (Sarastro), Graham/Dobbs/Coertse (Queen of Night), Hale, Berry (Ladies); c. Kubelik/J. Gibson, p. West, d. Messel; Covent Garden: 24, 27 Apr., 3, 8, 12 May, 18, 20, 30 June

Concert Mahler's Fourth Symphony*; c. Kempe; Royal Festival Hall, London: 2 May

Concert of Sacred Music with Norma Proctor; Brecon, Wales: 6 May

Concert Magnificat* (MONTEVERDI); other soloists: J. Sinclair, Schneiderhan, Proctor, W. Brown, Pears; c. Walter Goehr; Royal Festival Hall, London: 13 May

Der Ring des Nibelungen Woglinde, Helmwige; Otakar Kraus (Alberich), Hotter/Pease (Wotan), Raisbeck (Wellgunde), M. Sinclair (Flosshilde), Fisher (Sieglinde), Harshaw (Brünnhilde), Shuard, Hale, Coates, Iacopi, Berry, Shacklock, Thomas (Valkyries), Windgassen (Siegfried); c. Kempe, p. Hartmann, d. Hurry; Covent Garden: First Cycle: 24, 28 May, 6 June; Second Cycle: 11, 12, 16 June. NB: Sutherland did not appear in *Siegfried*.

BBC Broadcast 24 July

Le Nozze di Figaro Countess Almaviva; Bruscantini (Figaro), Roux

(Count Almaviva), Rizzieri (Susanna), Canne-Meijer (Cherubino); c. Gui/Silem/Pritchard, p. Ebert, d. Messel; Glyndebourne: 6, 10, 14†, 18, 20, 27 July; Liverpool: 10, 12, 14, 22 Sep.

Die Zauberflöte First Lady; Geraint Evans (Papageno), Häfliger (Tamino), Lorengar (Pamina), Guthrie/Bernadic (Sarastro), Dobbs (Queen of Night), Canne-Meijer, M. Sinclair (Ladies); c. Gui, p. Ebert, d. Messel; Glyndebourne: 19†, 22, 25 July, 3, 7, 9, 11, 13 Aug.

BBC Broadcast c. Mackerras: 6 Aug.

Promenade Concert Martern aller Arten (Die Entführung aus dem Serail); c. Boult; Royal Albert Hall, London: 3† Sep.

Concert Jesu Joy of Man's Desiring (BACH), Mass in C Minor (MOZART); c. Wyn Morris; Llanelli, Wales: 7 Oct.

Mass in C Minor (MOZART) c. Victor Fleming; Coventry: 27 Oct.

The Magic Flute Pamina*; Geraint Evans/Walters (Papageno), Pears/Richard Lewis (Tamino), Dalberg/Kelly (Sarastro), Coertse/Graham (Queen of Night); c. J. Gibson/Kubelik, p. West, d. Messel; Covent Garden: 10, 13 Nov., 14, 18, 28 Dec.

BBC Broadcast c. Mackerras: 17 Dec.

1957 *Die Meistersinger von Nürnberg* (WAGNER) Eva*; Witte (Walther), Pease (Sachs), Dalberg (Pogner), Geraint Evans (Beckmesser), Pears (David), Marjorie Thomas (Magdalene); c. Kubelik/Goodall, p. Witte, d. Wakhevitch; Covent Garden: 28, 31 Jan., 8, 11, 13 Feb.

Carmen Micaela; Muriel Smith (Carmen), Johnston (Don José), Allman (Escamillo); c. Matheson, p. Asquith, d. Wakhevitch; Covent Garden: 5 Feb.

The Midsummer Marriage Jenifer; Richard Lewis (Mark), Glynne (King Fisher), J. Sinclair (Bella), Lanigan (Jack), N. Thomas (Sosostris), Langdon, Coates (The Ancients); c. Pritchard, p. West, d. Hepworth; Covent Garden: 21†, 28 Feb.

The Magic Flute Pamina; Geraint Evans/Walters (Papageno), Lanigan/R. Jones (Tamino), Dalberg/Kelly/Langdon/Rouleau (Sarastro), Graham (Queen of Night); c. J. Gibson/Kubelik, p. West, d. Messel; Royal Opera House tour: Cardiff: 8, 9, 12 Mar.; Manchester: 25, 29, 30 Mar.; Southampton: 8, 12, 13 Apr.

BBC Broadcast 'Mrs Billington', life of the eighteenth-century soprano with her favourite arias: 4 Mar.

Alcina (HANDEL) Alcina*; Carvalho (Ruggiero), Scheepers (Morgana), M. Sinclair (Bradamante), Kentish (Oronte); c. Farncombe, p. Besch; Handel Opera Society, St Pancras Town Hall, London: 19, 20 Mar.

Verdi Requiem c. George Weldon; Swansea: 4 May

Rigoletto (VERDI) Gilda*; Otakar Kraus (Rigoletto), Verreau/Midgley (Duke), Langdon/Rouleau (Sparafucile), Howitt (Maddalena); c.

Downes, p. Bailey, d. Gellner; Covent Garden: 8, 14, 17, 20, 28 May, 1 June.

The Magic Flute Pamina; Walters (Papageno), Lanigan (Tamino), Rouleau/Kelly/Langdon (Sarastro), Coertse/Graham (Queen of Night); c. James Gibson, p. West, d. Messel; Covent Garden: 25, 28 June, 6, 15, 17 July

Der Schauspieldirektor (MOZART) Mme Herz*; Lagger (Herr Frank), A. Young (Vogelsang), Labay (Mlle Silberklang), Griffiths (Herr Buff); c. Balkwill, p. Besch, d. Rice; Glyndebourne: 5, 7†, 9, 12, 14, 16, 18, 20, 23 July

Mitridate Eupatore (SCARLATTI) (BBC broadcast) Laodice*, Boyce (Farnace), M. Sinclair (Stratonica), Byles (Nicomede), J. Cameron (Mitridate); c. Appia; 16 Aug.

Emilia di Liverpool (DONIZETTI) (BBC broadcast) Emilia*; Cantelo (Bettina), McAlpine (Thomson), Alan (Asdrubale), Dowling (Claudio); c. Pritchard; 8 Sep.

Promenade Concert Quintet (*Die Meistersinger*) with Pease, Johnston, Nilsson, Howe; c. B. Cameron; Royal Albert Hall, London: 11† Sep.

Der Ring des Nibelungen Woglinde; Otakar Kraus (Alberich), Hotter (Wotan), Hale (Wellgunde), Marjorie Thomas (Flosshilde), Windgassen (Siegfried), Nilsson (Brünnhilde); c. Kempe, p. Potter, d. Hurry; Covent Garden: First Cycle: 25† Sep., 4 Oct.; Second Cycle: 7, 12 Oct. NB: Sutherland did not appear in *Die Walküre* or *Siegfried*.

Götterdämmerung (WAGNER) Woglinde; as above; Covent Garden: 14, 17 Oct.

The Tales of Hoffmann Antonia; Langdon/Robinson (Crespel), Johnston/Edgar Evans (Hoffmann), Otakar Kraus/Robinson (Dr Miracle), Elms (Mother's voice); c. Downes, p. Rennert, d. Wakhevitch; Covent Garden: 30 Oct., 5, 7, 13, 21 Nov., 2, 18 Dec.

Carmen Micaela; Resnik/Zareska (Carmen), Vickers/Johnston/Edgar Evans/Nilsson (Don José), Ronald Lewis/Dickie (Escamillo); c. Matheson/Kubelik, p. Asquith, d. Wakhevitch; Covent Garden: 31 Oct., 2, 8, 11, 15, 18, 20, 28 Nov., 10 Dec.

Otello (VERDI) Desdemona*; Vinay (Otello), Otakar Kraus (Iago), Lanigan (Cassio); c. Downes, p. Potter, d. Wakhevitch; Covent Garden: 21, 27, 30 Dec.

1958 *BBC Broadcast* Australia Sings: 22 Jan.

BBC Broadcast 'Sins of my old age' (ROSSINI): 16 Feb.

The Carmelites (POULENC) Mme Lidoine*; Walters (Marquis de la Force), Lanigan (Chevalier de la Force), Morison/Dunne (Blanche), Fisher (Mother Marie); c. Kubelik/Matheson, p. Wallmann, d. Wakhevitch; Covent Garden: 16, 18, 21†, 24, 27 Jan.; Oxford: 10 Mar.; Manchester: 24 Mar.

Rigoletto Gilda; Shaw (Rigoletto), Lance/R. Thomas/Kirkop (Duke), Langdon/Rouleau (Sparafucile), Berry (Maddalena); c. Downes, p. Gellner, d. Bailey; Covent Garden: 5, 8, 10, 13, 18, 21 Feb., 5 Apr., 27 May; Oxford: 12, 25 Mar.; Manchester: 26, 29 Mar.

Concert aria *Vorrei spiegarvi, O Dio* (ROSSINI), aria *Primo amore piacer del ciel* (BEETHOVEN); c. Blech; Royal Festival Hall, London: 19 Feb.

Carmen Micaela; Shacklock/Resnik (Carmen), Edgar Evans/Johnston (Don José), Ronald Lewis/Walters (Escamillo); c. Matheson, p. Asquith, d. Wakhevitch; Royal Opera House tour: Manchester: 20 Mar.; Covent Garden: 24 June, 7 July

*St Matthew Passion** (BACH) other soloists: Proctor, 'A. Young, J. Cameron, Cuénod, Hemsley, J. Ward; c. Pritchard; Liverpool: 4 Apr.

BBC Broadcast Beethoven's Ninth Symphony* with Baker, Jones, Evans, c. Schwarz: 6 Apr.

Concert Mahler's 'Resurrection' Symphony*; c. Barbirolli; Manchester: 14, 15 May

Applausus Musicus (HANDEL) (BBC broadcast) Temperentia*; M. Thomas (Prudentia), R. Lewis (Justilia), Cameron (Theologia); c. Newstone; 24 May

Centenary Gala I dreamt I dwelt in marble halls (*The Bohemian Girl*: BALFE) duet with Lanigan; c. Pritchard; Covent Garden: 10 June

Don Giovanni (MOZART) Donna Anna*; London (Don Giovanni), Rubes (Leporello), Andrew (Donna Elvira), Alarie (Zerlina), Simoneau (Don Ottavio); c. Goldschmidt, p. Rennert, d. Maximowna; Vancouver: 26, 29, 31 July, 5, 7, 9 Aug.

Recital CBC (no date) p. John Avison

Recital P. Bonynge; Sevenoaks, Kent: 4 Oct.

Der Ring des Nibelungen Woglinde, Woodbird; Otakar Kraus (Alberich), Hotter (Wotan), Hale (Wellgunde), Marjorie Thomas (Flosshilde), Varnay (Brünnhilde), Windgassen (Siegfried), Klein (Mime); c. Kempe, p. Potter (reh. only), d. Hurry; Covent Garden: First Cycle: 19, 29 Sep., 3 Oct.; Second Cycle: 6, 9, 11 Oct. NB: Sutherland did not sing in *Die Walküre*.

Samson Israelite Woman; Vickers/Lanigan (Samson), Lindermeier/ Caryle (Dalila); c. Leppard, p. Graf, d. Messel; Leeds: 14, 15, 16, 17, 18 Oct. (eve & mat.); Covent Garden: 15, 18 Nov., 12 Dec., 3† Jan. 1959

Recital P. Bonynge; *Tornami a vagheggiar* (ALCINA), *Bist du bei mir'* (BACH), *Let the bright seraphim* (*Samson*), *Parla* (ARDITI), *Mattinata* (LEONCAVALLO), *Regnava nel silenzio* (*Lucia di Lammermoor*); Horsham, Sussex: 25 Oct.

Te Deum* (BRUCKNER) & *King David** (HONEGGER); c. Sargent; Leeds: 19 Nov.

Don Giovanni Donna Anna; Geraint Evans (Don Giovanni), Lawrence (Leporello), Bartlett (Elvira), Clark (Zerlina), Troy (Ottavio); c. Balkwill, p. Besch; Dublin: 24, 26, 28 Nov., 1 Dec.

Grand Opera Concert with other artists, Radio Eirann Light Orchestra; c. O'Broin; Dublin: 29 Nov.

BBC Broadcast (ROSSINI): 4 Dec.

BBC Broadcast Cantata (BACH), *The Carmelites* (POULENC) British première, 'Te Deum' (BRUCKNER); Leeds Philharmonic Orchestra: 15 Dec.

Messiah other soloists: Proctor, Pears, Alan; c. Pritchard; Liverpool: 20, 27 Dec., 2 Jan. 1959

1959 *Lucia di Lammermoor* Lucia*; Neate/Gibin (Edgardo), Geraint Evans/Shaw (Enrico), Langdon/Rouleau (Raimondo); c. Serafin, p. Zeffirelli, d. Zeffirelli; Covent Garden: 17, 20, 23, 26†, 28 Feb.

Concert Beethoven's Ninth Symphony; c. Barbirolli; Manchester: 6, 7 May

Alcina (Radio Cologne broadcast) Alcina; Wunderlich (Ruggiero), Van Dyke (Morgana), Proctor (Bradamante), Monti (Oronte); c. Leitner; 15 May

Samson Israelite Woman; Vickers/Lanigan (Samson), Carlyle/Wells (Dalila); c. Leppard/J. Gibson, p. Graf, d. Messel; Covent Garden: 8, 12, 25 June

Recital P. Bonynge; Australia House, London: 18 June

Rodelinda Rodelinda*; Elkins (Bertarido), Herincx (Garibaldo), Baker (Eduige); c. Farncombe, p. Besch, d. Pidcock; Handel Opera Society, Sadler's Wells Theatre, London: 24, 26† June

Lucia di Lammermoor (DONIZETTI) Lucia; Alfredo Kraus (Edgardo), Shaw (Enrico), Langdon (Raimondo); c. Balkwill, p. Zeffirelli, d. Zeffirelli; Covent Garden: 10, 14, 16, 18 July

Don Giovanni Donna Anna; Waechter (Don Giovanni), Berry (Leporello), Scheyrer (Elvira), Gueden (Zerlina), Dermota (Don Ottavio); c. Hollreiser, p. Witt, d. Nehrer; Vienna Staatsoper: 14 Sep.

Don Giovanni (concert performance) Donna Anna: Waechter (Don Giovanni), Taddei (Leporello), Schwarzkopf (Donna Elvira), Sciutti (Zerlina), Alva (Don Ottavio); c. Davis; Royal Festival Hall; London: 18†, 20 Oct.

Concert Capitol Theatre, Horsham: 24 Oct.

BBC Broadcast ode to St Cecilia (HANDEL): 25 Oct.

Concert Qui la voce (*I Puritani*), *Care selve* (*Atlanta*), *Tornami a vagheggiar* (*Alcina*); c. Boult; Royal Festival Hall, London: 27 Oct.

Concert mad scene (*Lucia*); c. Harvey; Royal Festival Hall, London: 31 Oct.

Recital P. Bonynge; Manchester: 3 Nov.

Concert with other artists (further information unknown); New Theatre, London: 8 Nov.

Concert Beethoven's Ninth Symphony; other soloists: Boese, Vickers, Frick; c. Klemperer; Royal Festival Hall, London: 28, 30 Nov.

Don Giovanni Donna Anna; Waechter (Don Giovanni), Berry (Leporello), Lipp (Donna Elvira), Gueden (Zerlina), Dermota (Don Ottavio); c. Hollreiser, p. Witt, d. Neher; Vienna Staatsoper: 3, 5 Dec.

Otello Desdemona; Guichandut (Otello), Protti (Iago), Zampieri (Cassio); c. Wallberg, p. Karajan, d. Reinking/Wakhevitch; Vienna Staatsoper: 17, 19 Dec.

Messiah other soloists: Proctor, Pears, Alan; c. Pritchard; Liverpool: 30 Dec., 2 Jan. 1960

1960 *La Traviata* (VERDI) Violetta*; McAlpine/Lanigan (Alfredo), Walters/Quilico (Germont); c. Santi, d. Fedorovitch; Covent Garden: 8, 22, 27, 30 Jan., 4, 14 May

Concert Mahler's Fourth Symphony; c. Boult; Birmingham: 28 Jan.

Lucia di Lammermoor Lucia; Turp (Edgardo), Shaw/Geraint Evans (Enrico), Langdon/Rouleau (Raimondo); c. Balkwill, p. Zeffirelli, d. Zeffirelli; Covent Garden: 5, 8, 10, 13 Feb., 9, 13, 16, 22 Dec.

Alcina Alcina; M. Sinclair (Ruggiero), Cecilia Fusco (Morgana), Dominguez (Bradamante), Clabassi (Melisso), Monti (Oronte); c. Rescigno, p. Zeffirelli, d. Zeffirelli; Venice: 19, 21, 23 Feb.

Lucia di Lammermoor Lucia; Gianni Raimondi (Edgardo), Panerai (Enrico), Maionica (Raimondo); c. Serafin, p. Zeffirelli, d. Zeffirelli; Palermo: 11, 13, 15, 20 Mar.

Lucia di Lammermoor Lucia; Gianni Raimondi (Edgardo), Dondi (Enrico), Zaccaria (Raimondo); c. Rescigno, p. Zeffirelli, d. Zeffirelli; Genoa: 31 Mar., 3, 5 Apr.

Lucia di Lammermoor Lucia; Vanzo (Edgardo), Massard (Enrico), Rouleau/Mars (Raimondo); c. Derveaux, p. Zeffirelli; Opéra, Paris: 25, 30 Apr., 7 May

I Puritani (BELLINI) Elvira*; Filacuridi (Arturo), Blanc (Riccardo), Modesti (Giorgio); c. Gui/Balkwill, p. Enriquez, d. Heeley; Glyndebourne: 24, 26, 28 May, 1, 3, 5, 9, 14, 18†, 24, 26 June; Edinburgh: 24, 26, 31 Aug., 3, 8†, 10 Sep.

Verdi Requiem other soloists: Cossotto, Ottolini, Vinco; c. Giulini; Royal Festival Hall, London: 12 June; Edinburgh: 21† Aug.

Samson (concert performance) Israelite Woman; Lanigan (Samson);

c. James Gibson; All Souls, Langham Place, London: 19 June

Don Giovanni Donna Anna; Blanc (Don Giovanni), Geraint Evans/Bruscantini (Leporello), Ligabue (Donna Elvira), Freni (Zerlina), Richard Lewis (Don Ottavio); c. Pritchard/Gellhorn, p. Rennert, d. Maximowna; Glyndebourne: 1, 3, 5, 7, 9, 11, 16, 20, 22, 24†, 29 Jul., 3, 5 Aug.

Recital P. Bonynge; *Son vergin vezzosa (I Puritani), A, fors'è lui (La Traviata)*, mad scene *(Lucia)*; Worthing: 7 Aug.

Promenade Concert Di cor mio, Tornami a vagheggiar (Alcina), Regnava nel silenzio ... Quando rapita (Lucia); c. Sargent; Royal Albert Hall, London: 13† Aug.

Concert Di cor mio, Tornami a vagheggiar (Alcina), mad scene *(Lucia)*; c. Pritchard; Liverpool: 4 Oct.

La Sonnambula (BELLINI) Amina*; Lazzari (Elvino), Rouleau/ Ward/Robinson (Rodolfo), J. Sinclair/Eddy (Lisa), Berry (Teresa); c. Serafin/Balkwill, p. Medioli, d. Sanjust; Covent Garden: 19, 21, 25†, 28, 31 Oct., 3, 7 Nov., 1, 3, 5 Dec.

Recital P. Bonynge; St James's Palace, London: 27 Oct.

Alcina Alcina; Thebom (Ruggiero), Moynagh (Morgana), M. Sinclair (Bradamante), Zaccaria (Melisso), Alva (Oronte); c. Rescigno, p. Zeffirelli, d. Zeffirelli; Dallas: 16, 18 Nov.

Don Giovanni, Donna Anna; Waechter (Don Giovanni), Taddei (Leporello), Schwarzkopf (Donna Elvira), Ratti (Zerlina), Alva (Don Ottavio); c. Rescigno, p. Zeffirelli, d. Zeffirelli; Dallas: 20, 23 Nov.

Recital (appendix 4); P. Bonynge; Keele, Staffs: 29 Nov.

Concert Regnava nel silenzio ... Quando rapita (Lucia), Ah, fors'è lui ... sempre libera (La Traviata), O luce di quest'anima (Linda di Chamounix), mad scene *(Hamlet)*; c. Balkwill; Royal Albert Hall, London: 11 Dec.

Recital four Rossini songs, three Delibes songs; p. Bonynge; BBC: 24 Dec.

I Puritani Elvira; Iaia (Arturo), Ausensi (Riccardo), Gaetani (Giorgio); c. Rosada, p. Cardi; Barcelona: 30 Dec., 3, 6 Jan. 1961

1961 *I Puritani* Elvira; Gianni Raimondi (Arturo), Zanasi (Riccardo), Mazzoli (Giorgio); c. Serafin, p. Zeffirelli, d. Zeffirelli; Palermo: 12, 15, 17 Jan.

Lucia di Lammermoor Lucia; Cioni (Edgardo), Savarese (Enrico), Antonini (Raimondo); c. La Rosa Parodi, p. Zeffirelli, d. Zeffirelli; Venice: 24, 26, 29 Jan.

Recital (appendix 4); P. Bonynge; Rock Hill, S. Carolina: 2 Feb.; Danbury, Connecticut: 5 Feb.; Washington DC: 7 Feb.; Mount Lebanon, Pittsburgh: 11 Feb.; Oklahoma: 13 Feb.; Dallas: 15 Feb.; Englewood, NJ: 23 Feb.; Richmond, Virginia: 25 Feb.; Vancouver:

27 Feb.; Aurora, NY: 6 Mar.; Montreal: 9 Mar.; Toronto: 13†
Mar.

Concert Care selve (Atalanta), Nel cor più non mi sento (La Molinara:
PAISIELLO), *Gran dio che regoli (Ines di Castro:* BIANCHI), *Di cor mio,
tornami a vagheggiar (Alcina), Ritorna o cara (Rodelinda),* Let the
bright seraphim *(Samson);* c. Callaway/Stanger; Dunbarton Oaks,
Washington DC: 7 Feb.; Chicago: 3 Mar.

Concert sleepwalking scene *(La Sonnambula),* mad scene *(Lucia);* c.
Paul Kletzki; Dallas: 15 Feb.

Beatrice di Tenda* (BELLINI) (concert performance) Beatrice; Cassilly
(Orombello), Horne (Agnese), Sordello (Filippo); c. Rescigno; American
Opera Society: NY Town Hall: 21 Feb.; Carnegie Hall, NYC: 1, 11
Mar.

Bell Telephone Hour television, 'Willow Song' *(Otello),* mad scene
(Hamlet); New York; 17 Mar.

I Puritani Elvira; Filacuridi (Arturo), Taddei (Riccardo), Modesti
(Giorgio); c. Rescigno, p. Zeffirelli, d. Zeffirelli/Hall; Genoa: 22, 26,
29 Mar.

Lucia di Lammermoor Lucia; Gianni Raimondi (Edgardo),
Bastianini/Meliciani (Enrico), Modesti (Raimondi); c. Votto, p. Fri-
gerio, d. Nicola Benois; La Scala, Milan: 14, 17, 20, 27 Apr., 3 May
Beatrice di Tenda Beatrice; Campora (Orombello), Kabaivanska/
Varcelli (Agnese), Dondi (Filippo); c. Votto, p. Enriquez, d. Colonello;
La Scala, Milan: 10†, 13, 17, 19, 21 May

Lucia di Lammermoor Lucia; Vanzo/Turp (Edgardo), Shaw/Dinoff/
Quilico (Enrico), Rouleau/Godfrey (Raimondo); c. Pritchard, p. And-
erson (rehearsed only), d. Zeffirelli; Covent Garden: 6, 9, 12 June;
Edinburgh: 25, 28† Aug., 1 Sep.

Recital eighteenth-century arias; harpsichord Bonynge; BBC Edinburgh: 29 Aug.

Lucia di Lammermoor Lucia; Vanzo (Edgardo), Massard (Enrico), Ser-
koyan (Raimondo); c. Dervaux; Opéra, Paris: 16, 19, 24 June

Concert Di cor mio, Tornami a vagheggiar (Alcina); arias *(Beatrice);* c.
Pritchard; Edinburgh: 4 Sep.

Lucia di Lammermoor Lucia; Cioni (Edgardo), Ruzdak/Heater (Enrico),
Tozzi (Raimondo); c. Molinari-Pradelli, p. Yannopoulos; d. Ming Cho
Lee/Bauer-Ecsy; San Francisco: 23 Sep., 25 Oct.

Recital P. Bonynge; Lawrence, Kansas: 25 Sep.; Omaha, Nebraska:
28 Sep.; Atlanta: 30 Sep.; Syracuse, NY: 2 Oct.; Hartford, Connecticut:
4 Oct.; Montclair, New Jersey: 20 Oct.; San Francisco: 7 Nov.; Dallas:
11 Nov; New Brunswick, NJ: 20 Nov.; Princeton, NJ: 28 Nov.;
Washington: 11 Dec.; Great Neck, NY: 13 Dec.

*Concert Ombre pallide, Mi restano le lagrime, Tornami a vagheggiar
(Alcina);* c. Waldman; Grace Raney Rogers Auditorium, NYC: 9 Oct.

Lucia di Lammermoor Lucia; Tucker/Bergonzi (Edgardo), Zanasi (Enrico), Wildermann (Raimondo); c. Votto, p. Zeffirelli, d. Zeffirelli; Chicago: 14, 16, 18 Oct.

Concert sleepwalking scene (*La Sonnambula*), mad scene (*Lucia*), *Ah, fors'è lui (La Traviata)*; c. Paray; Worcester, Massachusetts: 23 Oct.

Lucia di Lammermoor Lucia; Cioni (Edgardo), Ruzdak (Enrico), Clabassi/Engen (Raimondo); c. Molinari-Pradelli, p. Yannopoulos, d. Cho Lee/Bauer-Ecsy; San Francisco: 25 Oct.; Los Angeles: 29 Oct., 4 Nov.; San Diego: 2 Nov.

Lucia di Lammermoor Lucia; Cioni (Edgardo), Bastianini (Enrico), Zaccaria (Raimondo), Domingo (Arturo); c. Rescigno, p. Maestrini, d. Zeffirelli; Dallas, 16, 18 Nov.

Ed Sullivan Show television, mad scene (*Lucia*); New York: 3 Dec.

Bell Telephone Hour television, 'Ernani involami' (*Ernani*); New York; 8 Dec.

Lucia di Lammermoor Lucia; Tucker/Peerce (Edgardo), Testi/Guarrera (Enrico), Moscona/Giaiotti (Raimondo); c. Varviso, p. Defrère, d. Rychtaric (1942); Metropolitan, NYC: 26 Nov., 2, 9†, 15, 21 Dec.

La Sonnambula (concert performance) Amina; Cioni (Elvino), Flagello (Rodolfo), B. Allen (Teresa), di Tullio (Lisa); c. Rescigno; American Opera Society, Carnegie Hall, NYC: 5 Dec.; Philadelphia: 17 Dec.

1962 *Die Zauberflöte* Queen of Night*; Geraint Evans (Papageno), Richard Lewis (Tamino), Carlyle (Pamina), David Kelly (Sarastro); c. Klemperer, p. Klemperer, d. Eisler; Covent Garden: 4†, 6, 8, Jan.

Lucia di Lammermoor Lucia; Gianni Raimondi (Edgardo), MacNeil (Enrico), Vinco (Raimondo); c. Sanzogno, p. Zeffirelli, d. Zeffirelli; Palermo: 21 Jan.

Concert Ah Ruggiero crudel ... Ombre pallide (Alcina), Qui la voce (I Puritani), mad scene (*Hamlet*); c. Bonynge; Rome: 25 Jan.

Lucia di Lammermoor Lucia; Turp (Edgardo), Lamachia (Enrico), Cohen (Raimondo); c. Rivoli, p. Pablo Civil; Barcelona: 28 Jan., 1, 3 Feb.

Bell Telephone Hour mad scene (*Lucia*): 2 Feb.

La Sonnambula Amina; Alfredo Kraus (Elvino), Vinco (Rodolfo); c. Votto, p. Visconti, d. Tosi; La Scala, Milan: 10, 13, 15, 18, 20 Feb., 12, 15, 18, 23 Apr.

Concert mad scene (*Lucia*), mad scene (*Hamlet*), *E strano ... sempre libera (La traviata)*; c. Erede; Antwerp: 23† Feb.

Concert Ombre pallide (Alcina), mad scene (*Lucia*), *Son vergin vezzosa (I Puritani)*, *Sempre libera (La Traviata)*; c. Erede; Amsterdam: 25 Feb.

Alcina Alcina; Elkins (Ruggiero), Vaughan (Morgana), M. Sinclair (Bradamante), Robinson (Melisso), Macdonald (Oronte); c. Balkwill, p. Zeffirelli, d. Zeffirelli; Covent Garden: 8, 10, 14, 17 Mar.

La Traviata Violetta; Turp (Alfredo), Quilico (Germont); c. Erede/Balkwill, p. Ayrton (reh. only), d. Fedorovitch; Covent Garden: 21, 24, 26, 29 Mar., 4, 7 Apr.

Concert Cavatina (Beatrice), O beau pays (Les Huguenots), mad scene (*Lucia*), *Addio del passato, Sempre libera (La Traviata)*, c. Balkwill; Royal Albert Hall, London: 1 Apr.

Beatrice di Tenda Beatrice: Cioni (Orombello), Elkins (Agnese), Zanasi (Filippo); c. Rescigno; Naples: 4, 6 May

Gli Ugonotti (MEYERBEER) Marguerite de Valois*; Simionato (Valentine), Corelli (Raoul), Ganzarolli (de Nevers), Cossotto (Urbain), Ghiaurov/Vinco (Marcel), Tozzi (St Bris), c. Gavazzeni, p. Enriquez, d. Nicola Benois; La Scala, Milan: 28, 31 May, 2, 7†, 12 June

Concert Ah, fors'è lui ... sempre libera (La Traviata), mad scene (*Lucia*); c. Rosenstock; Lewishohn Stadium, NYC: 24 July

Concert mad scene (*Lucia*); c. Cluytens; Chicago: 26 July

Concert Ah, fors'è lui ... sempre libera (La Traviata), Qui la voce (I Puritani), O beau pays (Les Huguenots), mad scene (*Hamlet*); c. Bonynge; Hollywood: 2 Aug.

Recital (appendix 4); P. Bonynge; Rosehill, Cumberland: 5, 7 Oct.

Television Show with Elkins; London Symphony Orchestra; c. Bonynge; Bristol: 13–14 Oct.

Semiramide (ROSSINI) Semiramide*; Simionato (Arsace),. Ganzarolli (Assur), Raimondi (Idreno); c. Santini, p. Wallmann; La Scala, Milan: 17, 19, 22, 26, 29 Dec., 1, 5 Jan. 1963

1963 *President Kennedy Inaugural Anniversary Concert* (see enclosed list); c. Bonynge; Washington DC: 18 Jan.

Concert mad scene (*Lucia*); c. Stowkowsky; Philadelphia: 26 Jan.

Bell Telephone Hour television, *La Sonnambula* final scene: 4 Feb.

Concert V'adoro pupille (Giulio Cesare), Regnava nel silenzio (Lucia), Bel raggio (Semiramide), Qui la voce (I Puritani); c. Bonynge/Varviso; White Plains, NY: 6 Feb.; Newark, NJ: 10 Mar.

Concert Piangero la sorte mio, V'adoro pupille (Giulio Cesare) Let the bright seraphim (Samson), Preghiera (Ines di Castro: BIANCHI), *Nel cor più non mi sento (La Molinara:* PAISIELLO), *The soldier tir'd (Artaxerxes:* ARNE); c. Bonynge; Englewood, NJ: 9 Feb.; Brooklyn College, NYC: 16 Mar.

La Sonnambula Amina; Gedda/Formichini/Alexander (Elvino), Tozzi/Hines/Flagello (Rodolfo), Chookasian (Teresa), Scovotti (Lisa); c. Varviso, p. Visconti/Butler, d. Gerard; Metropolitan, NYC: 21, 27 Feb., 4, 7, 14, 19, 23, 30† Mar., 2, 12 Apr.

Concert V'adoro pupille (Giulio Cesare), Nel cor più non mi sento (La Molinara: PAISIELLO), Let the bright seraphim (*Samson*), The soldier tir'd (*Artaxerxes*), mad scene (*Hamlet*); c. Bonynge; Boston: 23 Feb.

Dinah Shore Show television with Dinah Shore and Ella Fitzgerald: 17 Mar.

Concert recit & aria *Ernani involami (Ernani), Bel raggio (Semiramide), Und ob die Wolke (Der Freischütz),* mad scene *(Hamlet)*; c. Bernstein, Philharmonic Hall, Lincoln Centre, NYC: 26 Mar.

Concert Let the bright seraphim (Samson), The soldier tir'd (Artaxerxes), Io non sono più l'Annetta (Crispino e la comare: RICCI), *Bel raggio (Semiramide),* mad scene *(Hamlet)*; c. Bonynge; Los Angeles: 5 Apr., San Francisco: 7 Apr.; Washington: 27 Apr.

I Puritani (concert performance) Elvira; Gedda (Arturo), Blanc (Riccardo), Diaz (Giorgio); c. Bonynge; American Opera Society: Carnegie Hall, NYC: 16, 24 Apr.; Philadelphia: 18 Apr.

Recital (appendix 4) with Elkins; duet *Serbami ognor (Semiramide)*; P. Bonynge; Croydon, Surrey: 10 June

Giulio Cesare (HANDEL) Cleopatra*; Elkins (Giulio Cesare), Lawrenson (Ptolemy), Guy (Cornelia), Stahlman (Sextus); c. Farncombe, p. Ayrton, d. Warre; Sadler's Wells Theatre, London: 20, 22, 26† June

La Sonnambula Amina; Cioni (Elvino), Cross (Rodolfo), Cole (Teresa), Meneguzzer (Lisa); c. Bonynge, p. Mansouri, d. Nagy; San Francisco: 14, 17, 22 Sep.; Los Angeles: 2, 4 Nov.

Norma Norma*; Horne (Adalgisa), Alexander (Pollione), Cross (Oroveso); c. Bonynge, p. Guttman, d. McCance/Mess; Vancouver: 17, 19, 22, 24, 26 Oct.

Concert with Cole, Cross, Alexander; duet *Serbami ognor (Semiramide)* with Cole, *Bel raggio (Semiramide),* quartet *(Rigoletto),* duet *Sulla tomba (Lucia)* with Alexander, mad scene *(Hamlet)*; c. Bonynge; Vancouver: 29 Oct.

La Traviata Violetta; Alexander (Alfredo), Bacquier (Germont); c. Bonynge, p. Guttman; Philadelphia: 12 Nov.

Concert Let the bright seraphim (Samson), The soldier tir'd (Artaxerxes), Io non sono più l'Annetta (Crispino e la comare: RICCI), *Bel raggio (Semiramide),* mad scene *(Lucia)*; c. Bonynge; Toronto: 22 Nov.

La Sonnambula Amina; Alexander (Elvino), Tozzi/Macurdy/Giaiotti (Rodolfo), Martin/Chookasian (Teresa), Scovotti (Lisa); c. Varviso, p. Butler (rehearsed only), d. Gerard; Metropolitan, NYC: 5, 10, 23 Dec., 8 Jan. 1964

1964 *La Traviata* Violetta; Kónya/Labò/Gedda/Tucker/Morell (Alfredo), Sereni/Ruzdak (Germont); c. Schick, p. Guthrie, d. Smith/Gerard; Metropolitan, NYC: 14, 28 Dec. 1963, 2, 11†, 17, 21, 24 Jan.

Opera Gala La Traviata Act I: Violetta, Kónya (Alfredo); *Lucia* mad scene, in concert; *La Sonnambula* Act III: Amina, Gedda (Elvino), Tozzi (Rodolfo), Scovotti (Lisa); c. Schick/Varviso/Varviso; Metropolitan, NYC: 5 Jan.

Concert Let the bright seraphim (*Samson*), The soldier tir'd (*Artaxerxes*), Io non sono più l'Annetta (*Crispino e la comare:* RICCI), Bel raggio (*Semiramide*), mad scene (*Hamlet*); Cleveland, Ohio: 14 Jan.

Semiramide Semiramide; Horne (Arsace), Cross (Assur), Ruhl (Idreno); c. Bonynge; Los Angeles: 29, 31 Jan.

I puritani Elvira; Craig (Arturo), Cross (Riccardo), Malas (Giorgio); c. Bonynge, p. Caldwell, d. Burlinghame/Voelpel; Boston: 12 Feb.

Semiramide (concert performance) Semiramide; Horne (Arsace), Cross (Assur); c. Bonynge; American Opera Society, Carnegie Hall, NYC: 18, 20 Feb.

Concert Let the bright seraphim (*Samson*), The soldier tir'd (*Artaxerxes*), Bel raggio (*Semiramide*), Ah, non giunge (*La Sonnambula*); c. Bonynge; Hartford, Connecticut: 22 Feb.

I Puritani Elvira; Craig/Macdonald (Arturo), Bacquier (Riccardo), Rouleau (Giorgio); c. Bonynge, p. Zeffirelli, d. Zeffirelli; Covent Garden: 20, 23, 26, 30 Mar., 1, 4, 7, 10 Apr.

Lucia di Lammermoor Lucia; Morell/Tucker/Bergonzi (Edgardo), Colzani/Bardelli (Enrico), Wildermann/Ferrin (Raimondo); c. Varviso, p. Wallmann, d. Colonello; Metropolitan Opera House tour: Boston: 19 Apr.; Cleveland, Ohio: 23 Apr.; Atlanta: 16 May; Minneapolis: 23 May; Detroit: 26 May

Concert Ah, fors'è lui ... sempre libera (*La Traviata*), mad scene (*Lucia*); c. Ormandy; Michigan: 30 Apr.

La Sonnambula Amina; Alexander/Gedda (Elvino), Hines/Tozzi (Rodolfo), Chookasian/Kriese (Teresa), Scovotti (Lisa); c. Varviso, p. Visconti/Butler, d. Gerard; Metropolitan NYC: 3, 9 May

Concert: Pestalozzi Village Let the bright seraphim (*Samson*), Regnava nel silenzio (*Lucia*), sleepwalking scene (*La sonnambula*), mad scene (*Hamlet*); c. Bonynge; Berne, Switzerland: 4 June

Lucia di Lammermoor Lucia; Gianni Raimondi (Edgardo) Cappucilli (Enrico), Ferrin (Raimondo); c. Sanzogno, p. Wallmann; La Scala, Milan: 12, 15, 18, 20, 23 June

Lucia di Lammermoor Lucia; Kónya/Labò/Alexander (Edgardo), Merrill/Sereni/Harlea/Colzani (Enrico), Giaiotti (Raimondo); c. Varviso, p. Wallmann, d. Colonello; Metropolitan, NYC: 12, 16, 24, 27 Oct., 14, 20 Nov., 5†, 14, 24 Dec.

La Traviata Violetta; Ilosfalvy (Alfredo), Waechter (Germont); c. Bonynge, p. Mansouri; San Francisco: 1, 3, 5 Nov.; Los Angeles: 8, 10 Nov.

Opera Gala La Traviata Act I: Violetta, Alexander (Alfredo); c. Schick; Metropolitan, NYC: 29 Nov.

Concert Voi che sapete, Deh vieni, non tardar, Dove sono (*Figaro*), Bel raggio (*Semiramide*), Concerto for Coloratura (Glière), mad scene (*Lucia*) 19 Dec. only; c. Bonynge; Montreal: 8 Dec.; Houston: 17, 19 Dec.

1965 *Alcina* (concert performance) Alcina; Elkins (Ruggiero), Hurley (Morgana), M. Sinclair (Bradamante), Malas (Melisso), Montal (Oronte); c. Bonynge; American Opera Society, Carnegie Hall, NYC: 3, 5 Jan.

Concert Voi che sapete, Deh vieni non tardar, Dove sono (Figaro), Bel raggio (Semiramide); Concerto for Coloratura (GLIÈRE), mad scene (*Lucia*); c. Bonynge; Cincinnati, Ohio: 9 Jan.; New Orleans: 19 Jan.; Bloomington, Indiana: 21 Mar.

Semiramide Semiramide; Horne (Arsace), Rouleau (Assur), Montal (Idreno), Hoekman (Oroe and the Ghost); c. Bonynge, p. Caldwell, d. Senn/Pond/Voelpel; Boston: 5, 7 Feb.

Lucia di Lammermoor Lucia; Pavarotti (Edgardo), Sordello (Enrico), Cross (Raimondo); c. Bonynge, p. Stivanello, d. Wolf; Miami: 15, 20 Feb.; Miami Beach: 17 Feb.; Fort Lauderdale, Florida: 23 Feb.

Faust (GOUNOD) Marguerite*; Verreau (Faust), Cross (Mephistopheles), Opthof (Valentine), Elkins (Siebel); c. Bonynge, p. Guttman, d. Rome/Brooks van Horne; Philadelphia: 9 Mar.; Hartford, Connecticut: 16 Mar.

Lucia di Lammermoor Lucia; Turp/Macdonald (Edgardo), Bryn Jones (Enrico), Rouleau (Raimondo); c. Bonynge, p. Anderson (rehearsed only), d. Zeffirelli; Covent Garden: 3, 6, 8, 11, 17 May

La Sonnambula Amina; Pavarotti (Elvino), Rouleau (Rodolfo), Elkins (Teresa), Woodland (Lisa); c. Bonynge, p. John Copley (rehearsed only), d. Sanjust; Covent Garden: 26, 29 May, 1, 4, 7, 10 June

SUTHERLAND–WILLIAMSON TOUR

Lucia di Lammermoor Lucia; Alexander/Pavarotti/Remedios (Edgardo), Opthof/Allman (Enrico), Grant/Rouleau/Cross (Raimondo); c. Bonynge, p. Ayrton, d. Dorati; Melbourne: 10, 12, 14, 17 July; Adelaide: 16, 18 Aug.; Sydney: 31 Aug., 2 Sep., 2 Oct.; Brisbane: 11, 16 Oct.

La Traviata Violetta; Pavarotti/Alexander/Remedios/Montal (Alfredo), Opthof/Allman (Germont); c. Bonynge/Krug, p. Ayrton, d. Dorati; Melbourne: 20, 22, 24, 26 July; Adelaide: 25, 27 Aug.; Sydney: 16, 18, 20, 27 Sep., 6 Oct.; Brisbane: 13 Oct.

Semiramide Semiramide; M. Sinclair/Elms (Arsace), Rouleau/ Malas/Cross (Assur), Ward/Montal (Idreno), Maconaghie (Oroe); c. Bonynge, p. Ayrton, d. Dorati; Melbourne: 29, 31 July, 7 Aug.; Sydney: 4, 6, 22, 29 Sep., 4 Oct.

La Sonnambula Amina; Pavarotti/Ward (Elvino), Rouleau/Malas/Cross (Rodolfo), Cole/Elms (Teresa), Harwood/Yarick (Lisa); c. Bonynge, p. Scheepers, d. Dorati; Melbourne: 3, 5, 14 Aug.; Sydney: 11, 24 Sep., 9 Oct.

Faust Marguerite; Alexander (Faust), Cross/Rouleau (Mephistopheles), Opthof (Valentine), Elkins/Beaton (Siebel); c. Weibel, p. Ayrton, d. Dorati; Melbourne: 10, 12 Aug.; Adelaide: 21, 23 Aug.; c. Bonynge; Sydney: 9, 13 Sep.

1966 *Concert Di cor mio, Tornami a vagheggiar (Alcina)*, Concerto for Coloratura (GLIÈRE), *Bel raggio (Semiramide)*, sleepwalking scene (*La Sonnambula*); c. Bonynge; Royal Albert Hall, London: 20 Feb.; Antwerp: 18 Mar.

Lucia di Lammermoor Lucia; Antonioli (Edgardo), Colmagro (Enrico), Marchica (Raimondo); c. Bonynge, p. Colonello, d. Colonello/Casa d'Arte Fiori; Copenhagen: 25, 28 Feb., 3 Mar.

Don Giovanni Donna Anna; Ghiaurov (Don Giovanni), Ganzarolli (Leporello), Lorengar/Ligabue (Donna Elvira), Freni (Zerlina), Alva (Don Ottavio); c. Maazel, p. Squarzini, d. Allio; La Scala, Milan: 19, 21, 25, 30 Apr.

Concert Di cor mio, Tornami a vagheggiar (Alcina), Concerto for Coloratura (Glière), *Bel raggio (Semiramide)*, sleepwalking scene (*La Sonnambula*); c. Bonynge; Champs-Elysées Theatre, Paris: 28 Apr.

Concert Di cor mio, tornami a vagheggiar (Alcina), *Ah, fors'è lui (La Traviata)*, mad scene (*Lucia*); Stuttgart: 3 May; Hamburg: 6 May

La Fille du Régiment (DONIZETTI) Marie*; Pavarotti/Ward (Tonio), Malas (Sulpice), M. Sinclair (Marquise); c. Bonynge, p. Sequi, d. Anni/Escoffier; Covent Garden: 2, 8, 11, 14, 17, 23, 17 June, 2 Jul.

Concert with Orchestre Nationale de Monte Carlo; c. Bonynge, Opéra de Monte Carlo: 21 June for the Centenary of Monte Carlo

Concert Ombre pallide, Di cor mio (Alcina), *Care selve (Atlanta)*, Soft complaining flute (Ode to St Cecilia's Day: HANDEL); c. Bonynge; Oxford: 30 June

I Puritani Elvira; Alfredo Kraus (Arturo), Wolansky (Riccardo), Grant (Giorgio); c. Bonynge, p. Frusca, d. Sormani/Marcello d'Ellena; San Francisco: 20, 23, 29 Sep., 2, 8 Oct.; Sacramento, California: 5 Oct.

Concert Non mi dir (Don Giovanni), *Bel raggio (Semiramide)*, *Ernani, involami (Ernani)*, *Ah, fors'è lui (La Traviata)*; c. Bonynge; San Antonio, Texas: 15 Oct.

Concert Non mi dir (Don Giovanni), *Non 'àn calma (Montezuma:* GRAUN), *Bel raggio (Semiramide)*, Bell Song (*Lakmé*); c. Bonynge; Atlanta: 20 Oct.

Concert Non mi dir (Don Giovanni), *Non 'àn calma (Montezuma:* Graun), *Ernani, involami (Ernani)*, Bell Song (*Lakmé*); c. Bonynge; White Plains, NY: 26 Oct.; Washington: 17 Dec.

Lucia di Lammermoor Lucia; Molese (Edgardo), Colzani/Ausensi (Enrico), Sgarro (Raimondo); c. Bonynge, p. Guttmann, d. Brooks van Horne; Philadelphia: 1, 4, Nov.

Ed Sullivan Show television; 'Sempre libera' (*La Traviata*); New York: 13 Nov.

Concert with Horne; Selection from: *Non 'àn calma (Montezuma:* GRAUN), Bell Song (*Lakmé*), *Surta è la notte (Ernani)*, duet *Sous le dôme épais (Lakmé)*, duet *O rimembranza, Mira o Norma (Norma)*; c. Bonynge; Los Angeles: 19, 21, 26 Nov.

Concert Non mi dir (Don Giovanni), Non 'àn calma (Montezuma: GRAUN), mad scene (*Hamlet*), Bell Song (*Lakmé*); c. Bonynge; Houston: 30 Nov.

Lucia di Lammermoor Lucia; Alexander/Tucker (Edgardo), Colzani (Enrico), Ghiuselev (Raimondo); c. Bonynge, p. Wallmann, d. Colonello; Metropolitan, NYC: 12, 21, 24, 28, 31† Dec.

1967 *Don Giovanni* Donna Anna; Siepi (Don Giovanni), Flagello (Leporello), Lorengar (Donna Elvira), Hurley (Zerlina), Alfredo Kraus/Gedda (Don Ottavio); c. Böhm, p. Graf, d. Berman; Metropolitan, NYC: 4, 9, 12, 17, 28† Jan.

Concert Bel raggio (Semiramide), Son vergin vezzosa (I Puritani), Io non sono più l'Annetta (Crispino e la comare: RICCI); c. Kertesz; Philadelphia: 21 Jan.

Concert Non mi dir (Don Giovanni), Non 'àn calma (Montezuma: GRAUN), *Ernani, involami (Ernani)*, Bell Song (*Lakmé*); c. Bonynge; Toronto: 2 Feb.; Newark, NJ: 11 Feb.

Don Giovanni Donna Anna; Diaz (Don Giovanni), Gramm (Leporello), Elkins (Donna Elvira), Tourangeau (Zerlina), Driscoll (Don Ottavio); c. Bonynge, p. Caldwell, d. Smith/Simmons; Boston: 6, 8, 15 Feb.

Concert Non mi dir (Don Giovanni), Non 'àn calma (Montezuma: GRAUN), mad scene (*Hamlet*), Bell Song (*Lakmé*); c. Bonynge; Bloomington, Indiana: 23 Feb.

Concert Ah, fors'è lui (La Traviata), mad scene (*Hamlet*); c. Peletier; Montreal: 28 Feb.

Lucia di Lammermoor Lucia; Alexander (Edgardo), Cossa (Enrico), West (Raimondo); c. Bonynge, p. Guttman, d. Rinfret/Mess; Vancouver: 11, 15, 22, 25, 29 Mar.

Lakmé (DELIBES) Lakmé*; Porretta (Gerald), Tourangeau (Mallika), Hecht (Nilakantha); c. Bonynge, p. Ross; Seattle: 10, 13, 15, 19, 22 Apr.

Orfeo ed Euridice (HAYDN) First performance in Austria; Euridice* and Genio*; Gedda (Orfeo), Malas (Creonte); c. Bonynge, p. Hartmann, d. Ludwig; Theater an der Wien, Vienna: 21, 25, 29 May, 2, 6 June; Edinburgh: 25, 29 Aug., 1, 4, 6, 9 Sep.

La Fille du Régiment Marie; Pavarotti (Tonio), Malas (Sulpice), M. Sinclair (Marquise); c. Bonynge, p. Sequi, d. Anni/Escoffier; Covent Garden: 24, 27 June, 7, 11, 15 July

Opera Gala mad scene (*Lucia*); c. Bonynge; Covent Garden: 4 July
Messiah other soloists: M. Sinclair, Baillie, R. Myers; c. Bonynge;
Royal Festival Hall, London: 29 Oct.
Norma Norma; Tagliavini (Pollione), Horne/Elkins (Adalgisa), Rouleau
(Oroveso); c. Bonynge, p. Sequi, d. Pizzi; Covent Garden: 30 Nov., 4,
8†, 12, 16, 21, 28 Dec., 1 Jan. 1968

1968 *Les Huguenots* (concert performance) Marguerite de Valois; Raoul
(Vrenios), Cossa (de Nevers), Tourangeau (Urbain), Arroyo
(Valentine), Ghiuselev (Marcel), El Hage (St Bris); c. Bonynge; London
Opera Society, Royal Albert Hall, London: 7 Jan.
Recital (appendix 5); P. Bonynge; Theatre Royal, Drury Lane, London:
14 Jan.; Newark, NJ: 13 Feb.; Philadelphia: 16 Feb.; Toronto: 28†
Apr.; Florence: 12 June
Orfeo ed Euridice (HAYDN) First performance in America; (concert
performance) Euridice and Genio; Gedda (Orfeo), Malas (Creonte);
c. Bonynge; American Opera Society, Carnegie Hall, NYC: 7, 10
Feb.
*Concert Al tua seno fortunato (Orfeo ed Euridice), O beau pays (Les
Huguenots)*, mad scene (*Lucia*); c. Bonynge; Salt Lake City: 21 Feb.
Lucio di Lammermoor Lucia; Molese (Edgardo), Cossa (Enrico), Malas
(Raimondo); c. Bonynge; New Orleans: 29 Feb., 2 Mar.
La Traviata Violetta; Vrenios (Alfredo), Hedlund (Germont); c.
Bonynge, p. Zeffirelli, d. Hall; Boston: 9, 11, 13 Mar.
Opera Gala O beau pays (Les Huguenots), final scene (*Faust*): Marguerite,
Shirley (Faust), Macurdy (Mephistopheles); c. Bonynge; Metropolitan,
NYC: 16 Mar.
Norma Norma; Marti (Pollione), Elkins (Adalgisa), Malas (Oroveso);
c. Bonynge, p. Frusca, d. Brooks van Horn; Philadelphia: 26, 29 Mar.
*Concert Care selve (Atalanta), Da tempeste (Giulio Cesare), Ombre pallide,
Di cor mio, Tornami a vagheggiar (Alcina), Soft complaining flute* (Ode
to St Cecilia's Day: HANDEL), *With plaintive note (Samson)*; Hunter
College, University of NY: 6, 8 Apr.
Don Giovanni Donna Anna; Bacquier (Don Giovanni), Gramm
(Leporello), Murphy (Donna Elvira), Tourangeau (Zerlina), Vrenios
(Don Ottavio); c. Bonynge; Seattle: 16, 18, 20, 24 Apr.
Recital CBC; P. Bonynge; Macmillan Theatre, Toronto: 28 Apr.
Semiramide Semiramide; M. Sinclair (Arsace), Capecchi (Assur), Gara-
venta (Idreno), Ferrin (Oroe); c. Bonynge, p. Sequi, d. Samaritani/Hall;
Florence: 1, 4, 6, 9 June
Semiramide (Italian Radio broadcast) Semiramide; Sinclair (Arsace),
Petri (Assur), Mazzoli (Oroe); c. Bonynge; 28 June
Messiah other soloists: M. Sinclair, Baillie, Noble, Woolf; c. Bonynge;
Royal Albert Hall, London: 10 July

Lakmé Lakmé; Tourangeau (Mallika), Vrenios (Gerald), Bacquier (Nilakantha); c. Bonynge/Suppa, p. Frusca, d. Brooks van Horn; Philadelphia: 19, 22 Nov.

La Sonnambula Amina; Alexander/Shirley (Elvino), Giaiotti (Rodolfo), Pearl/Forst (Teresa), Boky/Clements (Lisa); c. Bonynge, p. Butler, d. Gerard; Metropolitan, NYC: 2, 6, 12, 18, 21†, 24, 27 Dec., 1, 4, 9 Jan. 1969

Concert with Vrenios; *With plaintive note (Samson), Da tempesta (Giulio Cesare)*, duet *E il sol dell'anima (Rigoletto)*, duet *Tornami a dir che m'ami (Don Pasquale), Ah, non credea (La Sonnambula)*; c. Bonynge; Boston: 15 Dec.

1969 *Recital* P. Bonynge; Columbia, S. Carolina: 13 Jan.; Minneapolis: 29 Jan.; Portland, Oregon: 10 July; San Francisco: 12 July; Ottawa: 20 July; St Johns, Smith Square, London: 6 Oct.

Concert Non mi dir (Don Giovanni), Al tua seno fortunato (Orfeo ed Euridice), O beau pays (Les Huguenots), Ah, non credea (La Sonnambula); c. Bonynge; Indianapolis: 19 Jan.; Wabash, Indiana: 21 Jan.

Semiramide (concert performance) Semiramide; Horne (Arsace), R. Myers (Assur), Vrenios (Idreno), Grant (Oroe and the Ghost); c. Bonynge; London Opera Society, Theatre Royal, London: 9 Feb.

Alcina (concert performance) Alcina; Elkins (Ruggiero), O'Brien (Morgana), M. Sinclair (Bradamante), Gibbs (Melisso), Davies (Oronte), Te Kanawa (Oberto); c. Bonynge; Royal Festival Hall, London: 19 Feb.

La Traviata Violetta; Cioni (Alfredo), Cappucilli (Germont); c. Bonynge, p. Sequi, d. Lumaldo/Lerchundi; Teatro Colon, Buenos Aires: 17, 21, 24, 29 May, 1 June

Norma Norma; Craig (Pollione), Cossotto (Adalgisa), Vinco (Oroveso); c. Bonynge, p. Sequi, d. Pizzi; Teatro Colon, Buenos Aires: 21, 24, 26, 29 June, 2 July

Concert Al tua seno fortunato (Orfeo ed Euridice), O beau pays (Les Huguenots), Casta diva (Norma); c. Bonynge; Hollywood Bowl: 8 July

Concert Al tua seno fortunato (Orfeo ed Euridice), O beau pays (Les Huguenots), Casta diva (Norma), Ah, fors'è lui (La traviata); c. Bonynge; Ravinia Festival, Chicago: 17 July

Concert Piangerò la sorte mia, Da Tempeste (Giulio Cesare), Al tua seno fortunato (Orfeo ed Euridice), O beau pays (Les Huguenots), sleepwalking scene *(La sonnambula)*; c. Bonynge; The Hague, Holland: 11† Oct.

Giulio Cesare Cleopatra; Tourangeau (Giulio Cesare), Ahlin (Ptolemy), Boese (Cornelia), Popp (Sextus), Kranse (Achilla); c. Bonynge, p. Capobianco, d. Ming Cho Lee/Varona; Staatsoper, Hamburg: 9, 12, 15, 19, 23, 27 Nov., 6, 10, 16, 21 Dec.

1970 *Gala* with Domingo; *O beau pays* (*Huguenots*), *Aria* (*Crispino*), duo Act
I (*Lucia*); c. Ormandy; Academy of Music, Philadelphia: 24 Jan.
Recital P. Bonynge; Ottawa: 27 Jan.; Ann Arbor, Michigan: 30 Jan.;
Washington: 8 Feb.; London, Ontario: 30 Mar.; Pauley Pavilion, Uni.
of Ca: 23 May; Winnipeg, Ontario: 25 May; Bristol, UK: 11 June
Ed Sullivan Show television with Horne 'Mira o Norma' (*Norma*); c.
Bonynge; New York: 8 Mar.
Norma Norma; Horne (Adalgisa), Bergonzi/Alexander/
Tagliavini/Cioni (Pollione), Siepi/Vinco/Giaiotti/Macurdy (Oroveso);
c. Bonynge, p. Deiber, d. Heeley; Metropolitan, NYC: 3, 6, 10, 14,
19, 23, 27 Mar., 4†, 9, 14, 18 Apr.; Metropolitan Opera House tour:
Boston: 22 Apr.; Cleveland, Ohio: 1 May; Atlanta: 7 May; Memphis:
12 May; Dallas: 16 May; Minneapolis: 20 May; Detroit: 28 May
Richard Tucker's 25th Anniversary at the Met Opera Gala La Traviata
Act I: Violetta; Tucker (Alfredo); c. Bonynge; Metropolitan, NYC: 11
Apr.
Norma Norma; Tourangeau (Adalgisa), Lavirgen (Pollione), Flagello
(Oroveso); c. Bonynge, p. Frusca, d. Brooks van Horn; Philadelphia:
27 Apr.
Lucia di Lammermoor Lucia; Domingo (Edgardo), Sereni (Enrico),
Macurdy (Raimondo); c. Bonynge, p. Wallmann, d. Colonello; Metro-
politan, NYC: 1, 5 June
Norma Norma; Alexander (Pollione), Horne (Adalgisa), Rouleau
(Oroveso); c. Bonynge, p. Sequi, d. Pizzi; Covent Garden: 25, 29 June,
3, 7, 11 July
Sir David Webster Opera Gala mad scene (*Lucia*): Lucia; Bryn Jones
(Enrico), Rouleau (Raimondo); c. Bonynge; Covent Garden: 30† June
Norma Norma; Horne/Cossotto (Adalgisa), Bergonzi/Tagliavini/
Alexander (Pollione), Vinco/Ruggiero Raimondi/Flagello (Oroveso);
Metropolitan, NYC: 7, 23, 28 Sep., 3, 7, 17 Oct., 10, 14, 19† Dec.
La Traviata Violetta; Aragall/Pavarotti/Bergonzi/Kraus/Domingo
(Alfredo), Milnes/Merrill/Sereni (Germont); c. Bonynge, p. Lunt, d.
Beaton; Metropolitan, NYC: 12, 22, 27, 31 Oct., 2, 5, Dec.
Les Contes d'Hoffmann 4 soprano roles*; Alexander (Hoffmann), Tou-
rangeau (Nicklaus, The Muse, Mother's voice), Hecht (Lindorf, Coppe-
lius, Dappertutto, Dr Miracle), Thorsen (Andres, Frantz, Pitichinaccio,
Cochenille), Rubes (Crespel, Schlemiel, Spalanzani); c. Bonynge, p.
Hebert, d. Klein/Mess; Seattle: 12, 14, 18, 21 Nov.

1971 *Giulio Cesare* Cleopatra; Tourangeau (Giulio Cesare), Ahlin (Ptolemy),
Boese (Cornelia), Popp (Sextus), Kranse (Achilla); c. Bonynge, p.
Capobianco, d. Ming Cho Lee/Varona; Hamburg: 28, 31 Jan., 9, 12,
17 Feb.

Lucia di Lammermoor Lucia; Domingo/Gianni Raimondi (Edgardo), Tom Krause (Enrico), Moll (Raimondo); c. Bonynge, p. Beauvais, d. Rose; Hamburg: 7, 11, 14, 18, 21, 24, 27, 30 Mar., 3, 6, 12, 15, 18 Apr.

Recital A benefit for Aiglon College; P. Bonynge; Geneva: 30 Apr.

Concert Da tempeste (Giulio Cesare), Ah, fors'è lui (La Traviata), O beau pays (Les Huguenots), mad scene *(Lucia)*; c. Bonynge; Teatro Real, Madrid: 5 May

*Recital*P. Bonynge; Liverpool: 9 May

Rodelinda (HANDEL) (concert performance) Rodelinda; Tourangeau (Bertarido), du Plessis (Garibaldo), Proctor (Eduige); c. Bonynge; Brighton: 14, 16 May

Concert Benefit for New Guinea with Remedios, Clément, Macdonnell; *Regnava nel silenzio (Lucia)*, duet *E il sol dell'anima (Rigoletto)*, trio *Tu ne chanteras plus (Hoffmann); Ah, fors'è lui (La Traviata)*; c. Bonynge; Royal Albert Hall, London: 23 May

Concert with Bacquier, Domingo, Tourangeau; excerpts *Les contes d'Hoffmann*; Orchestra de la Suisse Romande; c. Bonynge; Geneva: 25 Aug.

Semiramide Semiramide; Horne (Arsace), Malas (Assur), Botazzo (Idreno), Estes (Ghost), Ferrin (Oroe); c. Bonynge, p. Sequi, d. Samaritani/Hall; Chicago: 24†, 27, 29 Sep., 2, 8, 11 Oct.

Maria Stuarda (DONIZETTI) Maria Stuarda*; Tourangeau (Elizabeth I), Burrows (Leicester), Berberian (Cecil), Opthof (Talbot); c. Bonynge, p. Capobianco, d. Pizzi; San Francisco 12, 16, 21, 24, 27 Nov.

Concert Regnava nel silenzio (Lucia), Operetta Airs (Leo Fall), *Ah, fors'è lui (La Traviata)*; c. Bonynge; Salt Lake City: 30 Nov.

Concert with Tourangeau; *Casta diva (Norma)*, Act III *Norma*; c. Bonynge; New Orleans: 14 Dec.

Lucia di Lammermoor Lucia; Luchetti (Edgardo), Opthof (Enrico), del Bosco (Raimondo); c. Bonynge, p. Guttman, d. Peter Wolf, ass. Brooks van Horn; Philadelphia: 7, 10 Dec.

Recital; P. Bonynge; Washington: 17 Dec.

1972 *Recital* P. Bonynge; Rome: 22 Jan.; Raleigh, N. Carolina: 17, 18 Mar.; Philadelphia: 11 Apr.; Michigan: 5 May; Columbus, Ohio: 8 May

La Fille du Régiment Marie; Pavarotti/Alexander/ di Giuseppe (Tonio), Corena/Gramm (Sulpice), Resnik/Sinclair (Marquise); c. Bonynge, p. Sequi, d. Anni/Escoffier; Metropolitan, NYC: 17, 23, 28 Feb.; 4, 9, 14, 22, 25†, 30 Mar., 7, 15, 18 Apr.; Metropolitan Opera House tour: Boston: 24 Apr.; Cleveland, Ohio: 2 May; Atlanta: 11 May; Memphis: 17 May; New Orleans: 20 May; Minneapolis: 23 May; Detroit: 3 June

Sir Rudolf Bing Opera Gala duet *Sulla tomba (Lucia)*, Pavarotti
(Edgardo); c. Bonynge; Metropolitan, NYC: 22† Apr.

Rigoletto Gilda; Milnes/Manuguerra (Rigoletto), Pavarotti (Duke),
Ruggero Raimondi/Vinco (Sparafucile), Grillo/Godfrey (Maddalena);
c. Bonynge, p. Graf, d. Berman; Verdi Festival, Metropolitan, NYC:
10, 14, 19, 22 June

Concert with Horne; duets *Serbami ognor (Semiramide)*, *Mira o Norma
(Norma)*; c. Bonynge; NJ: 16 June

Concert P. Bonynge; *Sempre libera (La Traviata)*, *The last rose of summer
(Martha*: FLOTOW), Union Square, San Francisco: 11 Sep.

Norma Norma; Tourangeau (Adalgisa), Alexander (Pollione), Grant
(Oroveso); c. Bonynge, p. Capobianco, d. Varona; San Franciso: 15,
20, 24, 30 Sep., 6 Oct.

Lucrezia Borgia (DONIZETTI) Lucrezia*; Alexander (Gennaro), Quilico
(Don Alfonso), Tourangeau (Orsini); c. Bonynge, p. Guttman, d.
Varona; Vancouver: 26, 28 Oct., 1, 4, 8, 11 Nov.; Edmonton, Alberta:
17, 20, 22 Nov.

1973 *La Fille du Régiment* Marie; Pavarotti (Tonio), Corena/Gramm
(Sulpice), Sinclair/Resnik (Marquise); c. Bonynge, p. Sequi, d.
Anni/Escoffier; Metropolitan, NYC: 31 Dec. 1972, 6†, 11, 15, 19,
22 Jan.

Recital P. Bonynge; Ottawa: 27† Jan.; Atlanta: 31 Jan.; Long Island,
NY: 3 Feb.; New Rochelle, NY: 6 Feb.; Cardiff, Wales: 18 Feb.

Opera Gala mad scene (*Lucia*): Manuguerra (Enrico), Macurdy
(Raimondo); c. Bonynge; Metropolitan, NYC: 10 Feb.

Concert Qui la voce (I Puritani), Operetta Airs (Leo Fall), *Mon cher amant
(La Périchole*: OFFENBACH), *Waltz (Robinson Crusoe*: OFFENBACH); c.
Bonynge; Royal Albert Hall, London: 23 Feb.

Lucia di Lammermoor Lucia; Pavarotti (Edgardo), Quilico (Enrico),
Howell (Raimondo); c. Bonynge, p. Anderson (rehearsed only), d.
Zeffirelli; Covent Garden: 16, 19, 22, 25, 28, 31 May; 5, 9 June

Rodelinda Rodelinda; Tourangeau (Bertarido), van Bruggen
(Garibaldo); c. Bonynge, p. Capobianco, d. Varona; Holland Festival:
Scheveningen: 24 June; Rotterdam: 27 June; Amsterdam: 30 June,
3 July

Die Fledermaus (STRAUSS) Rosalinde*; van Way (Eisenstein), Blegen
(Adele), Ulfung (Alfred), Yarnell (Dr Falke), Tourangeau (Orlofsky);
c. Bonynge, p. Mansouri, d. Smith/Roth; San Francisco: 8†, 11, 14,
19, 30 Sep., 2 Oct.

Recital P. Bonynge; Cupertino, San Francisco: 22 Sep.; Claremont,
California: 26 Sep.; Fresno, California: 5 Oct.; Brooklyn College, NYC:
16 Dec.

La Fille du Régiment Marie; Alfredo Kraus (Tonio), Malas (Sulpice),

Resnik (Marquise); c. Bonynge, p. Sequi, d. Anni/Escoffier; Chicago: 20, 24, 26 Oct., 2, 5, 7 Nov.

Les Contes d'Hoffmann 4 soprano roles; Domingo/Alexander/Theyard (Hoffmann), Tourangeau (Nicklaus, The Muse), Stewart (Lindorf, Coppelius, Dappertutto, Dr Miracle), Velis (Frantz, Cochenille, Pitichinaccio, Andres), Morris (Crespel), Castel/Franke (Spalanzani), Harvuot/Holloway (Schlemiel), Munzer/Kraft (Mother's voice); c. Bonynge, p. Hebert, d. Klein; Metropolitan, NYC: 29 Nov., 3, 8, 11, 14, 19, 22 Dec., 17, 21, 25 Jan., 2† Feb. 1974

1974 *Lucia di Lammermoor* Lucia; Theyard (Edgardo), Opthof (Enrico), Morris (Raimondo); c. Bonynge, p. Stivanello, d. Bardon/Hall; Miami: 9, 16 Feb.; Miami Beach: 13 Feb.; Fort Lauderdale, Florida: 19 Feb.

Maria Stuarda Maria Stuarda; Alexander/Sandor (Leicester), Tourangeau (Elizabeth I), Corbeil (Cecil), Opthof (Talbot); c. Bonynge, p. Capobianco, d. Pizzi/Capobianco; Philadelphia: 26 Feb., 1 Mar., Hartford, Connecticut: 4 Mar.

La Traviata Violetta; Alfredo Kraus (Alfredo), Zancanaro (Germont); c. Bonynge; Lisbon, Portugal: 18, 21, 24 Apr.

Les Contes d'Hoffmann 4 soprano roles; Alexander (Hoffmann), Tourangeau (Nicklaus, The Muse), Stewart (Lindorf, Coppelius, Dappertutto, Dr Miracle), Velis (Franz, Cochenille, Andres, Pitichinaccio), Franke (Spalanzani), Morris (Crespel), Holloway (Schlemiel), Kraft/Munzer (Mother's voice); c. Bonynge, p. Hebert, d. Klein; Metropolitan Opera House tour: Detroit: 4 May; Atlanta: 7 May; Memphis: 13 May; Dallas: 16 May; Minneapolis: 20 May; Metropolitan, NYC: 27, 30 May

Recital P. Bonynge; Birmingham, Alabama: 10 May; Kansas City: 23 May; Concert Hall, Sydney Opera House: 6 July; Melbourne: 13 Aug.; Sacramento, California: 4 Nov.; Vancouver: 13 Nov.

Les Contes d'Hoffmann 4 soprano roles: Wilden (Hoffmann), Tourangeau (Nicklaus, The Muse), R. Myers (Lindorf, Coppelius, Dappertutto, Dr Miracle), Ewer (Frantz, Cochenille, Pitichinaccio, Andres), Maconaghie (Spalanzani), Eddie (Schlemiel), Dickson (Crespel), Connell (Mother's voice); c. Bonynge, p. Capobianco, d. Varona; Sydney Opera House: 13†, 16, 19, 24, 27, 30 July, 2, 6, Aug.

Recital P. Bonynge; Concert Hall, Sydney Opera House: 9 Aug.; Melbourne: 17 Aug.

Esclarmonde (MASSENET) Esclarmonde*; Aragall (Roland), Grant (Phorcas), Tourangeau (Parséïs), Kerns (Bishop); c. Bonynge, p. Mansouri, d. Montresor; San Francisco: 23, 26, 29 Oct., 2, 8† Nov.

Lucia di Lammermoor Lucia; Tagliavini (Edgardo), Darrenkamp (Enrico), Hale (Raimondo); c. Bonynge, p. Hebert, d. Bardon/Hall; Pheonix: 23, 26 Nov.; San Diego: 4, 6, 8 Dec.

1975 *La Traviata* Violetta; Alfredo Kraus (Alfredo), Quilico (Germont); c. Bonynge, p. Visconti (reh. Rennison), d. Faria/Marzot; Covent Garden: 6, 11, 16, 21, 24, 27 Jan.

Recital P. Bonynge/Holford; Free Trade Hall, Manchester: 19 Jan.; Royal Shakespeare Theatre, Stratford-upon-Avon: 29 Jan.; Rochester, NY: 18 Feb.; Ithaca, NY: 18 Mar.; Pasadena, California: 5 Oct.

Darwin Gala: Midnight Matinée. Aria & cabaletta *Oh nube! Che lieve (Maria Stuarda),* duet *Mira o Norma (Norma)* with Heather Begg; Covent Garden: 25‡ Jan.

La Traviata Violetta; Little (Alfredo), Opthof (Germont); c. Bonynge, p. Capobianco, d. Wolf Ass./Mess; Philadelphia: 25, 27 Mar.

Lucrezia Borgia Lucrezia; Brecknock (Gennaro), Devlin (Don Alfonso), Tourangeau (Orsini); c. Bonynge, p. Mansouri, d. Varona; Houston: 8, 11, 13 Apr.

Maria Stuarda Maria Stuarda; Tourangeau (Elizabeth I), Little (Leicester), Rae Smith (Cecil), Opthof (Talbot); c. Bonynge, p. Capobianco, d. Varona; Las Palmas: 29 Apr., 2 May

La Traviata Violetta; Alexander (Alfredo), Merrill (Germont); c. Bonynge, p. Lunt, d. Beaton; Metropolitan Opera House tour: Japan: 29 May, 3, 6, 9, 12 June

Il Trovatore (VERDI) Leonora*; Pavarotti (Manrico), Wixell (di Luna), Obratsova/Verrett (Azucena); c. Bonynge, p. Libby, d. Hager/Skalicki; San Francisco: 12, 17, 21, 27, 30 Sep., 3 Oct.

Recital with Tourangeau; P. Bonynge; duets *Sull'aria (Le nozze di Figaro), Regarde! (Pique Dame:* TCHAIKOVSKY), *Barcarolle (Les Contes d'Hoffmann), Viens Mallika (Lakmé), Mira o Norma (Norma), Tutti i fior (Madame Butterfly), Suvvia fuggiam perché (La Bohème:* LEONCAVALLO), *C'est le soir (Le roi de Lahore), Vivere io non potro (La Donna del lago:* ROSSINI), *Serbami ognor (Semiramide),* San Diego: 23 Sep.

Ed Sullivan Show television; New York: 1 Nov.

Lucia di Lammermoor Lucia; Pavarotti/Theyard (Edgardo), Saccomani (Enrico), Ferrin (Raimondo); c. Bonynge, p. Copley, d. Bardon/Hall; Chicago: 12, 15, 18, 21, 24, 28 Nov., 1, 4 Dec.

1976 *I Puritani* Elvira; Pavarotti (Arturo), Milnes/Opthof (Riccardo), Morris/Flagello (Giorgio); c. Bonynge, p. Sequi, d. Cho Lee/Hall; Metropolitan, NYC: 25, 28 Feb., 2, 5, 9, 13†, 17, 20, 25, 29 Mar.

The Merry Widow Anna Glavari*; van der Stolk (Danilo), Clark (de Rosillon), Shuttleworth (Valencienne), Rubes (Baron Zeta); c. Bonynge, p. Mansouri, d. Varona; Vancouver: 22, 24, 27, 29 Apr., 1, 4, May

Concert Non mi dir (Don Giovanni), Casta diva (Norma), mad scene

(*Lucia*); c. Bonynge; New Zealand: Wellington: 19† May; Dunedin: 29 May; Christchurch: 4† June; Auckland: 13 June

Concert Regnava nel silenzio (Lucia) Bell Song (*Lakmé*), *Qui la voce* (*I Puritani*); c. Bonynge; Wellington, NZ: 22† May; Auckland, NZ: 10 June

Recital P. Bonynge; Hamilton, NZ: 25 May; Wellington, NZ: 7 June

Recital P. Bonynge; Napier, NZ: 1† June; Christchurch, NZ: 16 June

Lakmé Lakmé; Wilden/Austin (Gerald), Tourangeau/Elkins (Mallika), Grant (Nilakantha); c. Bonynge, p. Ayrton, d. Digby; Sydney Opera House: 10, 14, 17†, 21, 24, 26, 30 July, 2, 6, 13, 18† Aug.

Recital with Tourangeau, Wilden, Pringle; P. Bonynge; duet *Serbami ognor (Semiramide)*, trio *Tous les trois (La Fille du Régiment)*, quartet & exerpts (*Rigoletto*), duet *Parigi o cara (La Traviata)* duet *Quanto amore* (*L'elisir d'amore*), duet *Mira o Norma (Norma)*; Government House, Sydney: 8 Aug.

Recital P. Bonynge; Adelaide: 21, 24 Aug.; Canberra: 27 Aug.; Seattle: 29 Oct.; Winnipeg: 31 Oct.

Esclarmonde Esclarmonde; Aragall/Alexander (Roland), Grant/Hines (Phorcas), Tourangeau (Parséïs), Quilico (Bishop); c. Bonynge, p. Mansouri, d. Montresor; Metropolitan, NYC: 19, 24, 27 Nov., 1, 4, 7, 11†, 17, 20 Dec.

United Nations Concert sleepwalking scene La Sonnambula), *Ah, fors'è lui (La Traviata)*; c. Bonynge; General Assembly Hall, United Nations, NYC: 12 Dec.

1977   *Recital* P. Holford; Ames, Iowa: 22 Jan.; Buffalo, NY: 25 Jan.; Akron, Ohio: 27 Jan.; Danville, Kentucky: 29 Jan.; Sarasota, Florida: 1 Feb.; Miami: 3 Feb.

Lucia di Lammermoor Lucia; Aragall (Edgardo), Elvira (Enrico), Diaz (Raimondo); c. Bonynge, p. Ayrton; Puerto Rico: 9, 11 Feb.

Maria Stuarda Maria Stuarda; Tourangeau (Elizabeth I), Terranova (Leicester), Cunningham (Cecil), Bröcheler (Talbot); c. Bonynge, p. Capobianco, d. Heeley/Vanarelli; Holland: Scheveningen: 10, 15 Mar.; Rotterdam: 12 Mar.; Utrecht: 18 Mar.; Amsterdam: 22, 27, 30 Mar.; Eindhoven: 25 Mar.

Recital with Tourangeau; P. Bonynge *Ah, non credea (La Sonnambula)*, duet *Barcarolle (Les Contes d'Hoffmann)*, *Io non sono più l'Annetta* (*Crispino e la comare*: RICCI), duet *Viens Mallika (Lakmé)*, duet *Serbami ognor (Semiramide)*; Amsterdam: 13 Mar.

Lucrezia Borgia Lucrezia; Stevens/Ferris (Gennaro), Allman (Alfonso), Elkins (Orsini); c. Bonynge, p. Ogilvie, d. Fredrikson; Sydney Opera House: 7, 11†, 14, 18, 22, 25 28 June, 5, 8‡ July

Suor Angelica (PUCCINI) Suor Angelica*; Raisbeck (Princess); c.

Bonynge, p. Ogilvie, d. Digby; Sydney Opera House: 16, 19, 22, 26 July

Opera in Concert Benefit for NSW Society for Crippled Children and NSW Society for Deaf and Blind Children; *Don Giovanni* quartet, Act I with Buchanan, Wilden, Yurisich; *Les contes d'Hoffmann* quartet, Epilogue with Bermingham, Wilden, R. Myers; *Esclarmonde* quartet, Act IV with Begg, Ferris, Grant; *Il trovatore* trio, Act I with Dowd, Shaw; *Bitter Sweet* (COWARD) duet *I'll see you again* with Pringle; *Three Little Maids* (GILBERT & SULLIVAN) with Raisbeck, Begg; *Lucia* sextet with Raisbeck, Byers, Ewer, Allman, Light; P. Bonynge/ Kimmorley; Concert Hall, Sydney Opera House: 24 July

Le Roi de Lahore (MASSENET) Sita*; Stevens (Alim), Tourangeau (Khaled), Opthof (Scindia), Morris (Timur); c. Bonynge, p. Sequi, d. Mariani; Vancouver: 23†, 25, 28 Sep., 1, 9 Oct.; Seattle: 27, 29 Oct., 2, 5, Nov.

Don Giovanni Donna Anna; Morris (Don Giovanni), Malas (Leporello), Cariaga (Donna Elvira), Tourangeau (Zerlina), Suarez (Don Ottavio); c. Bonynge, p. Ayrton, d. Prévost; Vancouver: 7, 12, 14, 16, 22 Oct.

An Evening with Joan Sutherland and Richard Bonynge Albery Theatre, London: 4 Dec.

Maria Stuarda Maria Stuarda; Tourangeau (Elizabeth I), Burrows (Leicester), van Allan (Cecil), Ward (Talbot); c. Bonynge, p. Copley, d. Heeley; Covent Garden: 15, 20, 23, 26, 29 Dec.

1978 *The Merry Widow* (STRAUSS) Anna Glavari; Stevens/van der Stolk (Danilo), Austin (Rosillon), Buchanan (Valencienne), Wilcock (Baron Zeta); c. Bonynge, p. Mansouri, d. Fredrikson; Concert Hall, Sydney Opera House: 19, 21, 23, 25, 26, 28†, 31 Jan., 2, 4, 6, 8, 9, 11 Feb.

Opera in Concert Benefit for deaf and blind children; *Don Giovanni* quartet, Act I with Buchanan, Wilden, Germain; *Les contes d'Hoffmann* quartet, Epilogue with Bermingham, Wilden, R. Myers; *Esclarmonde* quartet, Act IV with Begg, Ferris, Grant; *Il trovatore* trio, Act I with Stevens, Shaw; *Bitter Sweet* duet 'I'll see you again' with Pringle; *Lucia* sextet with Raisbeck, Ferris, Ewer, Allman, Grant; P. Bonynge/Kimmorley; Concert Hall, Sydney Opera House: 18 Feb.

Don Giovanni Donna Anna; Morris (Don Giovanni), Bacquier (Leporello), Varady (Donna Elvira), Tourangeau (Zerlina), Brecknock (Don Ottavio); c. Bonynge, p. Graf, d. Berman; Metropolitan, NYC: 10, 16, 18, 21, 25†, 27, 30 Mar.

Recital P. Bonynge; Kalamazoo, Michigan: 4 Apr.; Salt Lake City: 7 Apr.; Minneapolis: 9 Apr.; Memphis: 12 Apr.; Tulsa, Oklahoma: 14 Apr.; New Orleans: 16 Apr.; Tokyo, Japan: 7 June; Nagoya, Japan: 10 June: Seoul, S. Korea: 13 June; Concert Hall, Sydney Opera House: 13 Aug.

Norma Norma; Elkins/Begg (Adalgisa), Stevens (Pollione), Grant/Shanks (Oroveso); c. Bonynge, p. Sequi, d. Mariani; Sydney Opera House: 5, 8, 11, 14, 17, 20, 26, 29 July; 1‡, 4, 10, 23, 26† Aug.

Concert Casta diva (Norma), duet *Sulla tomba (Lucia)* with John Brecknock, Vilja (*Merry Widow*), mad scene (*Hamlet*), sextet (*Lucia*) with Brecknock, Kenny, Dempsey, Summers, King; c. Bonynge; Covent Garden: 26 Nov.

Norma Norma; Tourangeau (Adalgisa), van Limpt (Pollione), White (Oroveso); c. Bonynge, p. Capobianco, d. Hall; Holland: Amsterdam: 14, 17, 20 Dec.; Scheveningen: 23, 26 Dec.; Rotterdam: 29 Dec.; Utrecht: 1 Jan. 1979

1979 *Recital* P. Bonynge; Academy of Music, Philadelphia: 11 Jan.; Toronto: 14 Jan.; Opéra, Paris: 26 Apr.; Staatsoper, Munich: 29 Apr.; Teatro Eleanora Duse, Asolo, Italy: 14 May; Theatre Royal, Glasgow, Scotland: 16 Sep.; Ann Arbor, Michigan: 4 Oct.; Cincinatti: 7 Oct.

Concert with Pavarotti; duets *Libiamo, Un di felice, Parigi o cara (La Traviata), Ernani, involami (Ernani)*, mad scene (*Hamlet*) *I dreamt I dwelt in marble halls (Bohemian Girl)*, sleepwalking scene (*La Sonnambula*), duet *Sulla tomba (Lucia)*; c. Bonynge; Avery Fisher Hall, Lincoln Center, NYC: 22‡ Jan.

The Merry Widow Anna Glavari; Stevens/van der Stolk (Danilo), Austin (Rossillon), Furlan/Johnston (Valencienne), Wilcock (Baron Zeta); c. Bonynge, p. Mansouri, d. Fredrikson; Concert Hall, Sydney Opera House: 9, 12, 14, 16, 19, 22, 24, 28 Feb.; 2 Mar.; Adelaide: 22, 26, 28, 30 Nov.; Melbourne: 6, 8, 10, 12, 13, 15 Dec.

La Traviata Violetta; Austin (Alfredo), Allman (Germont); c. Bonynge, p. Copley (reh. Bremner), d. Bardon/Stennett; Melbourne: 10, 13, 16, 19, 24 Mar.

Norma Norma; Elkins (Adalgisa), Stevens (Pollione), Grant (Oroveso); c. Bonynge, p. Sequi, d. Mariani; Brisbane; 31 Mar., 3, 6, 9 Apr.

Lucia di Lammermoor (concert performance) Lucia; Clark (Edgardo), Cold (Enrico), Probst (Raimondo); c. Bonynge; Stockholm: 6 May

Idomeneo (MOZART) Electra*; Mitchell (Ilia), Elkins (Idamante), Stevens/Baigildin (Idomeneo), Wilden (Arbace); c. Bonynge, p. Lovejoy, d. Truscott: Sydney Opera House: 4, 7 (performance unfinished), 14, 17, 20, 25†, 28 July

La Traviata Violetta; Austin (Alfredo), Allman (Germont); c. Bonynge, p. Bremner (rehearsed only), d. Bardon/Stennett; Sydney Opera House: 10 July

Don Giovanni Donna Anna; Morris (Don Giovanni), Warren Smith (Leporello), Elkins (Donna Elvira), Moore (Zerlina), Wilden (Don

Ottavio); c. Bonynge, p. Ogilvie, d. Colman/Fredrikson; Melbourne: 4, 7, 10, 13, 16, 18 Aug.

Concert with Horne; duet *Barcarolle (Hoffmann), Tornami a vagheggiar (Alcina), Ah, fors'è lui* ... *Sempre libera (La Traviata),* duet *Serbami ognor (Semiramide),* duet *Viens, Mallika (Lakmé),* Vilja *(Merry Widow), Regnava nel silenzio* ... *quando rapita (Lucia),* duet *Mira o Norma (Norma);* c. Bonynge; Avery Fisher Hall, Lincoln Center, NYC: 15† Oct.

Opera in Concert Australian Opera in aid of Children's Medical Research; Adelaide Festival Theatre: 2 Dec.

1980 *Opera in Concert I Puritani:* quartet, Act I with Austin, Germain, Grant; *Son vergin vezzosa (I Puritani)* with Johnston, Austin, Pringle; *Maria Stuarda* duet, Act II with Donald Smith; *Pacific 1860* (COWARD) duet with Ewer, *Bitter Sweet* duet with Germain; *Rigoletto* duet, Act I with Austin; duet *Serbami ognor (Semiramide)* with Begg; *Rigoletto* quartet with Moore, Donald Smith, Pringle; P. Bonynge/Kimmorley; Concert Hall, Sydney Opera House: 26 Jan.

Lucia di Lammermoor Lucia; Greager (Edgardo), Allman (Enrico), Grant (Raimondo); c. Bonynge, p. Copley, d. Bardon/Stennett; Concert Hall, Sydney Opera House: 6, 9, 12, 15, 20, 23, 26, 29 Feb.

Lucrezia Borgia Lucrezia; Alfredo Kraus (Gennaro), Dean (Don Alfonso), Howells (Orsini); c. Bonynge, p. Copley, d. Stennett/Pascoe; Covent Garden: 26 29‡ Mar., 1, 5, 9, 12, 16 Apr.

Recital (appendix 12); P. Bonynge; Stuttgart: 21 Apr.; Wiener Konzerthaus, Vienna: 24 Apr.

Lucrezia Borgia Lucrezia; Piero Visconti/Taund (Gennaro), Roni/Luccardi (Don Alfonso), Zilio (Orsini); c. Bonynge, p. Copley (reh. Renshaw), d. Pascoe/Stennett; Rome: 15, 18, 21, 24, 28, 31 May, 3 June

I Masnadieri (VERDI) Amalia*; Donald Smith/Ferris (Carlo), Allman/Badcock (Francesco), Grant (Massimiliano); c. Bonynge, p. Beauvais, d. Lees/Stennett; Sydney Opera House: 2, 5, 8, 11, 17, 23, 26, 29 July, 2, 5, 9 Aug.

Lucia di Lammermoor Lucia; Greager/Ferris/Furlan (Edgardo), Allman/Badcock (Enrico), Grant/Shanks (Raimondo); c. Bonynge, p. Copley, d. Bardon/Stennett; Concert Hall, Sydney Opera House: 22, 25, 28, 31 Aug., 3, 6, Sep.; Melbourne: 5, 8†, 11, 14 Nov.; Adelaide: 19, 22, 26, 29 Nov.

Die Fledermaus Rosalinde; Titus (Eisenstein), Sills (Adele), Campora (Alfred), Gardner (Falke), Resnik (Orlofsky); c. Bonynge, p. Capobianco, d. Zack Brown/Oliver Smith; San Diego: 5, 8, 11, 16, 19 Oct.

1981 *Otello* Desdemona; Marenzi (Otello), Shaw/Allman (Iago), Ferris (Cassio); c. Cillario, p. Ogilvie, d. Girton/Fredrikson; Concert Hall, Sydney Opera House: 28, 31† Jan., 3, 6, 9, 12, 17, 20, 23, 28 Feb.; Melbourne: 20, 23, 26, 29 May, 1, 4 June

Concert with Pavarotti & Horne; trio Act IV (*Ernani*); duet *O remembranza (Norma)*; trio, Act I (*Norma*); duet, Act II, trio, Act IV (*La gioconda*); *Tu del mio Carlo (I Masnadieri)*; duet, Act I (*Otello*); final scene (*Il Trovatore*); c. Bonynge; Avery Fisher Hall, Lincoln Center, NYC: 20, 23‡ Mar.

Concert with Pavarotti; duets *Libiamo, Un di felice, Parigi, o cara (La Traviata), Tu del mio Carlo (I Masnadieri), Tornami a vagheggiar (Alcina)*, scena & duet *Signor ne principe (Rigoletto), I dreamt I dwelt in marble halls (Bohemian Girl), O beau pays (Les Huguenots)*, duet *Sulla tomba (Lucia)*; c. Bonynge; Pittsburg: 27 Mar.

La Traviata Violetta; Raffanti (Alfredo), Ryan Edwards (Germont); c. Bonynge, d. Karp; Memphis: 4 Apr.

Concert Tornami a vagheggiar (Alcina), Tu del mio Carlo (I Masnadieri), mad scene (*Lucia*), c. Bonynge; Rock Hill, S. Carolina: 7 Apr.

Recital P. Bonynge; Whitman Hall, Brooklyn College, NYC: 11 Apr.

Norma Norma; Troyanos (Adalgisa), Ortiz (Pollione), Diaz (Oroveso); c. Bonynge, p. Mansouri, d. Varona; Toronto: 28 Apr., 1, 4‡, 7, 10 May

La traviata Violetta; Austin/Greager (Alfredo), Summers (Germont); c. Bonynge, p. Copley (reh. Bremner), d. Bardon/Stennett; Sydney Opera House: 17, 20, 24, 27, 30 June, 4, 9 July

Les Huguenots Marguerite de Valois; Zschau (Valentine), Austin/ Greager (Raoul), Pringle (de Nevers), Macdonald/Saliba (Urbain), Grant (Marcel), Martin (St Bris); c. Bonynge, p. Mansouri, d. Stoddart/ Stennett; Sydney Opera House: 24, 27, 31 July, 5, 8, 11, 15, 18, 22 Aug.

The Merry Widow Anna Glavari; Hagegard (Danilo), Austin (de Rosillon), Forst (Valencienne), Stark (Baron Zeta); c. Bonynge, p. Mansouri, d. Laufer/Mess/Fredrikson; San Francisco: 3, 6, 9, 13, 16, 21, 25, 28, 31 Oct.

Concert Ah, fors'è lui ... Sempre libera, Addio del passato (La Traviata); c. Bonynge; San Diego: 18 Oct.

George London Tribute Concert O beau pays (Les Huguenots), p. Kohn; Washington: 4 Nov.

Concert with Bonisolli & van Allan; *Tirana gelosia ... Tornami a vagheggiar (Alcina), O beau pays (Les Huguenots)*, duets *Libiamo, Parigi o cara (La Traviata), Io non sono più l'Annetta (Crispino e la comare*: RICCI), final trio (*Faust*); c. Bonynge, Covent Garden: 29 Nov.

Il trovatore Leonora; Bonisolli (Manrico), Masurok (di Luna), Obratsova (Azucena); c. Bonynge, p. Renshaw, d. Sanjust/Stennett; Covent Garden: 10, 14, 18, 22† Dec., 1, 4 Jan. 1982

1982 *La Traviata* (concert performance) Violetta; Austin (Alfredo), Shaw (Germont); c. Bonynge; The Domain, Sydney: 18 Jan.

Lucrezia Borgia Lucrezia; Furlan (Gennaro), Martin/Allman (Alfonso), Cullen (Orsini); c. Bonynge, p. Ogilvie, d. Fredrikson; Concert Hall, Sydney Opera House: 3, 6, 10, 17, 20, 23, 26 Feb., 1, 4 Mar.

Recital P. Bonynge; Perth: 9 Mar.; Teatro Malibran, Venice: 9 Apr.; Genoa: 12 Apr.

Lucrezia Borgia (concert performance) Lucrezia; Winbergh (Gennaro), Cold (Alfonso), Soffel (Orsini); c. Bonynge; Stockholm: 26 Mar.

Lucia di Lammermoor Lucia; Derksen (Enrico), van Limpt (Edgardo), ven den Berg (Raimondo); c. Bonynge/Challender, p. Copley, d. Bardon/Stone; Holland: Amsterdam: 29 Apr., 2, 5, 24, 27 May; Scheveningen: 8, 11 May; Utrecht: 14 May; Eindhoven: 17 May; Rotterdam: 20 May

Die Fledermaus Rosalinde; Gard/Stevens (Eisenstein), Brynnel/ McGregor (Adele), Austin/Ferris (Alfred), M. Lewis (Falke), Begg (Orlofsky); c. Bonynge, p. Besch, d. Stoddart; Sydney Opera House: 25, 28 June, 3, 6, 10‡, 13, 16, 19, 22, 28, 31 July, 4 Aug.

Concert Act II, Sc. 1 (*Lucia*) with Allman (Enrico), Grant (Raimondo); c. Challender; Sydney Opera House: 25 July

Norma Norma; Mauro (Pollione), Horne (Adalgisa), Flagello (Oroveso); c. Bonynge, p. Mansouri, d. Varona; San Francisco: 11, 14, 17†, 21, 26, 29 Sep., 2 Oct.

Thirtieth Anniversary Concert with Summers, Soffel; *Com e bello (Lucrezia Borgia)*, duet '*Figlia!*' – '*Mio padre*' (*Rigoletto*), duet *Mira o Norma (Norma)*, duet *Dite alla giovine (La Traviata)* duet *Serbami ognor (Semiramide)*, *Czardas (Fledermaus)*, trio *Tu ne chanteras plus (Hoffmann)*, *Io son l'umile ancella (Adriana)*; c. Bonynge; Covent Garden: 17 Oct.

Richard Tucker Foundation Gala Concert Casta diva (Norma), duet (*Hamlet*) with Milnes; c. Bonynge; Carnegie Hall, NYC: 24 Oct.

Lucia di Lammermoor Lucia; Alfredo Kraus/Raffanti (Edgardo), Elvira/Schexnayder (Enrico), Plishka/Morris (Raimondo); c. Bonynge, p. Donnell, d. Colonello; Metropolitan, NYC: 1, 5, 10, 13, 20, 24, 27†, 30 Nov., 4, 9, 13‡ Dec.

1983 *Die Fledermaus* Rosalinde; Stevens (Eisenstein), McGregor (Adele), Ferris (Alfred), Pringle (Falke), Begg, (Orlofsky); c. Bonynge, p. Besch, d. Stoddart; Sydney Opera House: 10, 18 Jan.; Concert Performance: The Domain, Sydney: 15 Jan.

Concert with Pavarotti; duet *Libiamo, Addio del passato (La Traviata)*, *Qui la voce (I Puritani)*, duet *Prendi l'anel ti dono (La Sonnambula)*, *Io son l'umile ancella (Adriana)*, mad scene (*Hamlet*), duet *Sulla*

tomba (Lucia); c. Bonynge; Concert Hall, Sydney Opera House: 23‡ Jan.

Alcina Alcina; Elkins (Ruggiero), McGregor (Morgana), Elms (Bradamante), Wegner (Melisso), Greager (Oronte); c. Bonynge, p. Helpmann, d. Pascoe; Sydney Opera House: 5, 9, 12†, 16, 19, 22, 26 Feb.

Concert in aid of the bushfire in Victoria and S. Australia, with the participation of the entire Australian Opera; duet *Mira o Norma (Norma)* with Elkins (Adalgisa), *Lucia* sextet with Raisbeck, Ferris, Ewer, Fulford, Shanks; c. Bonynge; Sydney Opera House: 27 Feb.

La Traviata Violetta; Furlan (Alfredo), Montefusco (Germont); c. Bonynge, p. De Tomasi, d. Del Savio/D'Alessandro; Genoa: 17 Mar. (performance unfinished)

Adriana Lecouvreur (CILEA) Adriana*; Bröcheler (Michonnet), Moldoveanu (Maurizio), Silva (Princess de Bouillon); c. Bonynge, p. Capobianco, d. O'Hearn/Mess; San Diego: 22, 26, 29 May, 1 June

Concert Deh vieni non tardar (Figaro), With plaintive notes *(Samson)*, When William at eve, Light as thistledown *(Rosina)*, *Sediziose voce ... Casta diva (Norma)*, sleepwalking scene *(La sonnambula)*; c. Bonynge; Sydney Opera House: 12 June

Il Trovatore Leonora; Collins (Manrico), Summers (di Luna), Elms (Azucena); c. Bonynge, p. Moshinsky, d. Nolan/Arrighi; Sydney Opera House: 25, 28 June, 2‡, 5, 8, 13, 16, 19, 22 July

Semiramide Semiramide; Elms (Arsace), Martin (Assur), Austin (Idreno), Mavridis (Oroe); c. Bonynge, p. Oxenbould, d. Clark; Sydney Opera House: 5, 8, 13†, 17, 20 Aug.

La fille du régiment Marie; Alfredo Kraus (Tonio), Berberian/Malas (Sulpice), Resnik (Marquise); c. Bonynge, p. Sequi, d. Anni/Escoffier; Metropolitan, NYC; 27 Sep., 1, 5, 8, 11, 14, 19, 24 Oct.

Met Centenary Concert Bel raggio (Semiramide); c. Bonynge; Metropolitan, NYC: 22 Oct.

Esclarmonde Esclarmonde; Veronelli (Roland), Howell/Rea (Phorcas), Montague (Parséïs), Summers (Bishop of Blois); c. Bonynge, p. Mansouri, d. Montressor; Covent Garden: 28 Nov., 6, 10, 13, 16 Dec.

1984 *Lucia di Lammermoor* (concert performance) Lucia; Greager (Edgardo), Fulford (Enrico), Grant (Raimondo); c. Bonynge; The Domain, Sydney: 14 Jan.

Adriana Lecouvreur Adriana; Shaw (Michonnet), Austin (Maurizio), Begg (Princess de Bouillon); c. Bonynge, p. Copley, d. Lees/Stennett; Sydney Opera House: 27, 30 Jan., 2, 7, 11, 14, 18‡, 22, 25, 29 Feb.

Anna Bolena (DONIZETTI) Anna Bolena*; Morris (Enrico), Forst (Seymour), Stubbs/Segar (Smeton), Michael Myers (Percy); c.

Bonynge, p. Mansouri, d. Pascoe/Stennett; Toronto: 22, 25, 28‡, 31 May, 3 June; Detroit: 6, 9 June

I Masnadieri Amalia; Zanazzo (Massimiliano), Greer (Carlo), Salvadori (Francesco); c. Bonynge, p. Capobianco; San Diego: 21, 24, 30 June

Les Contes d'Hoffmann 4 soprano roles: Hoffmann (Hoffmann), Cullen (Nicklaus, The Muse), Summers (Lindorf, Coppelius, Dappertutto, Dr Miracle), Ewer (Andres, Cochenille, Pitichinaccio, Frantz), Warlow (Spalanzani), Eddie (Schlemiel), van der Stolk/Grant (Crespel), Price (Mother's voice); c. Bonynge, p. Capobianco, d. Varona; Sydney Opera House: 20, 23, 26, 30 Jul., 4, 7†, 11, 15 Aug.

Musicians for World Peace Concert Casta diva (Norma), mad scene (*Lucia*); c. Bonynge; Sydney Opera House: 19 Aug.

The Carmelites Mme Lidoine; Chard (Marquis de la Force), Ferris (Chev. de la Force), Buchanan (Blanche), Begg (Mother Marie), Koppel (Old Prioress), A-M McDonald (Constance); c. Bonynge, p. Moshinsky, d. Bury; Sydney Opera House: 1, 4, 8, 11, 15‡, 19, 22, 24, 26 Sep.

Anna Bolena Anna Bolena; Langan (Enrico), Budai/Forst (Seymour), Gettler (Smeton), Blake (Percy); c. Bonynge, p. Mansouri, d. Pascoe/Stennett; San Francisco: 25, 28 Oct., 3, 6, 9, 13 Nov.

1985   *Les Contes d'Hoffmann* (concert performance) 4 soprano roles; Austin (Hoffmann), Cullen (Nicklaus, The Muse), Yurisich (Coppelius), Lewis (Dappertutto), Swan (Dr Miracle), Ewer (Andres, Cochenille, Pitichinaccio, Franz), Warlow (Spalanzani), van der Stolk (Crespel), Price (Mother's voice); c. Bonynge; The Domain, Sydney: 12 Jan.

Norma Norma; Hoffmann (Pollione), Hahn (Adalgisa), Shanks (Oroveso); c. Bonynge, p. Renshaw, d. Rowell; Concert Hall, Sydney Opera House: 22, 26, 29 Jan., 2, 9, 12†, 16 Feb.

Concert with Pavarotti; duet *Libiamo*, *Parigi o cara* (*La Traviata*), *Io son l'umile ancella* (*Adriana*), *Son vergin vezzosa* (*I Puritani*), duet Act II (*Rigoletto*), *The Doll Song* (*Hoffmann*), *Vilja* (*Merry Widow*), *Regnava nel silenzio*, duet *Sulla tomba* (*Lucia*); c. Bonynge; Phoenix: 27 Mar.; Atlantic City, NJ; 30 Mar.

Lucia di Lammermoor Lucia; Bergonzi (Edgardo), Rawnsley (Enrico), Howell (Raimondo); c. Bonynge, p. Sutcliffe, d. Zeffirelli: Covent Garden: 13, 16, 19, 23, 26 Apr.

Norma (concert performance) Norma; Hoffmann (Pollione), Soffel (Adalgisa), Appelgren (Oroveso); c. Bonynge; Stockholm: 24 May

Concert with Horne; *Tornami a vagheggiar* (*Alcina*), *Vorrei spiegarvi* (*La cambiale di matrimonio*: ROSSINI), duet *Serbami ognor* (*Semiramide*), duet *Viens Mallika* (*Lakmé*), *The Doll Song* (*Hoffmann*), *Ne craignez rien* (*Fra Diavolo*: AUBER), duet *Mira o Norma* (*Norma*); c. Bonynge; Melbourne: 9 June; Concert Hall, Sydney Opera House: 12‡ June

I Puritani Elvira; Austin (Arturo), Shanks (Giorgio), M. Lewis

(Riccardo); c. Bonynge, p. Helpmann, d. Bardon/Stennett; Sydney
Opera House: 24, 28 June, 1†, 6, 10, 13, 16 July
Hamlet (THOMAS) Ophélie*; Bröcheler (Hamlet), Shanks (Claudius),
Richards (Gertrude); c. Bonynge, p. Mansouri, d. Skalicki/Digby/
Stennett; Toronto: 4, 7, 10, 13, 16, 19 Oct.
Anna Bolena Anna Bolena; Plishka (Enrico), Toczyska (Seymour), Zilio
(Smeton), Merritt (Percy); c. Bonynge, p. Mansouri, d. Pascoe/
Stennett; Chicago: 30 Oct., 2, 5, 8, 11, 14, 19 Nov.
Anna Bolena (concert performance) Anna Bolena; Yurisich (Enrico),
Forst (Seymour), Clarey (Smeton), Hadley (Percy); c. Bonynge; Avery
Fisher Hall, Lincoln Center, NYC: 25‡ Nov., Boston: 1 Dec.; Wash-
ington: 6 Dec.

1986 *Concert* with Bernadette Cullen; *Casta diva ... bello a me ritorna
(Norma)*, mad scene *(Hamlet)*, duet *Alle piu care imagini (Semiramide)*,
duet *Mira o Norma (Norma)*, *Io son l'umile ancella (Adriana)*, mad
scene *(Lucia)*; c. Bonynge; Perth: 10 Jan.
Rigoletto (concert performance) Gilda; M. Lewis (Rigoletto), Greager
(Duke), Shanks (Sparafucile), Gunn (Maddalena); c. Bonynge; The
Domain, Sydney: 20 Jan.
Lucia di Lammermoor Lucia; Greager (Edgardo), Donnelly (Enrico),
Grant (Raimondo); c. Bonynge, p. Wregg (rehearsed only), d.
Bardon/Stennett: Concert Hall, Sydney Opera House: 28 Jan., 1, 8‡,
14, 19 Feb.
*Concert Io son l'umile ancella (Adriana), Sediziose voce ... Casta diva ...
Bello a me ritorna (Norma), Qui la voce (I puritani)*, mad scene *(Lucia)*;
c. Bonynge; Wellington, NZ: 5‡ Mar.
*Concert Vorrei spiegarvi (La Cambiale de Matrimonio), Non temete,
Milord, Or son sola (Fra Diavolo: AUBER), Regnava nel silenzio (Lucia)*,
mad scene *(Hamlet)*; c. Bonynge; Wellington, NZ: 8‡ Mar.
Recital P. Bonynge; Wellington Town Hall: 11 Mar.
Norma Norma; Soffel (Adalgisa), Pinto (Pollione), Surjan (Oroveso);
c. Bonynge, p. Calusso, d. Villagrossi; Barcelona: 21, 24, 27 30
Apr.
La Fille du Régiment Marie; Blake (Tonio), Corbeil (Sulpice), Griffin
(Marquise); c. Bonynge, p. Capobianco, d. Malabar Ltd; Pittsburgh:
5, 7, 10 June
Anna Bolena Anna; Ghiuselev (Enrico), Mentzer (Seymour), Hadley
(Percy), Bunnell (Smeton); c. Bonynge, p. Mansouri, d. Pascoe/
Stennett; Houston: 19, 22, 25, 28 June
La Fille du Régiment Marie; Austin (Tonio), Yurisich (Sulpice), Begg
(Marquise); c. Bonynge, p. Sequi, d. Bardon/Stennett; Sydney Opera
House: 22, 26, 30 July, 2, 9‡, 16, 23 Aug.
I puritani Elvira; Fisichella/Blake (Arturo), Milnes (Riccardo), Ramey

(Giorgio); c. Bonynge, p. Sequi, d. Cho Lee/Hall; Metropolitan, NYC: 14, 18†, 22, 25, 29, Nov., 3, 6, 9, 13, 18 Dec.

1987 *Concert Sediziose voce ... Casta diva ... bello a me ritorna (Norma)*, mad scene (*Hamlet*), *Qui la voce (I Puritani)*, mad scene (*Lucia*); c. Bonynge; Washington: 4 Jan.; Boston: 15 Jan.; Pasadena, Ca.: 19 Jan.; San Diego: 23 Jan.; Tulsa: 27 Jan.; Dallas: 1 Feb.; Miami: 5 Feb.
Opera Gala Act I sc. 2 (*Lucia*), Lucia, Pavarotti (Edgardo); Act 3 (*Rigoletto*), Gilda, Pavarotti (the Duke), Nucci (Rigoletto), Furlanetto (Sparafucile), Isolo Jones (Maddalena); Act 3 (*La Traviata*), Violetta, Pavarotti (Alfredo), Nucci (Germont); c. Bonynge; Metropolitan NYC: 11† Jan.
Adriana Lecouvreur Adriana; Opthof (Michonnet), Cupido (Maurizio), Myers (Princess de Bouillon); c. Bonynge, p. Copley, d. C. M. Christini/Stennett; Toronto: 3, 6, 9, 12, 15, 18 Apr.
Concert with Pavarotti; *Addio del passato, Sempre libera (La Traviata)*, duet *Teco io sto (Ballo in maschera)*, duet *Depuis l'instant (La Fille du Régiment)*, *Com'e bello (Lucrezia Borgia)*, *Qui la voce (I Puritani)*, duet *Sulla tomba (Lucia)*; c. Bonynge; Summit Stadium, Houston, Texas: 25 Apr.
Recital P. Bonynge; Theatre de Athenee, Paris: 8 June; Warsaw: 14 June
I Puritani (concert performance) Elvira; Suarez (Arturo), Skram (Riccardo), Cold (Giorgio); c. Bonynge; Stockholm: 25 Sep.
Concert mad scene (*I Puritani*), *Com'e bello (Lucrezia Borgia)*, *Addio del passato (La Traviata)*, mad scene (*Lucia*); c. Bonynge; Theatre Royal, Glasgow: 4 Oct.; Usher Hall, Edinburgh: 7 Oct.
Richard Tucker Foundation Gala Concert duet *Depuis l'instant (La Fille du Régiment)*, with Alfredo Kraus; c. Bonynge; Carnegie Hall NYC: 25 Oct.
Il Trovatore Leonora; Pavarotti (Manrico), Nucci (di Luna), Budai/Mignon Dunne/Obratsova/Verrett (Azucena); c. Bonynge, p. Melano, d. Ezio Frigerio/Squarcipino; Metropolitan NYC: 12, 16, 21, 24, 27 Nov., 1, 5, 10, 16, 19 Dec.

1988 *The Merry Widow* Anna Glavari; Stevens (Danilo), Austin (de Rosillon), Anne Maree McDonald (Valencienne), Wilcock (Baron Zeta); c. Bonynge, p. Reh. Maunder, d. Fredrikson; Sydney Opera House: 21, 28 Jan., 3, 12, 17, 23‡, Feb.
Recital P. Bonynge; Queen Victoria Building, Sydney: 19 Feb. in aid of Sydney Children's Hospital.
Concert Tornami a vagheggiar (Alcina), *Qui la voce (I puritani)*, mad scene (*Hamlet*), mad scene (*Lucia*); c. Bonynge; Adelaide Festival

Theatre: 6 Mar.

Concert Sediziose voce ... Casta diva ... Bello a me ritorna (Norma) mad scene *(Hamlet)*, *Qui la voce (I Puritani)*, mad scene *(Lucia)*; c. Bonynge; Avery Fisher Hall NYC: 3 Apr.; Syracuse: 7 Apr.; Baltimore: 15 Apr.

Gala Concert duet *Mira o Norma (Norma)*, Nova Thomas (Adalgisa), sextet *(Lucia)*, Roden, Malcolm Donnelly, Patrick Donnelly, Ryan, Kessler; c. Bonynge; Theatre Royal, Drury Lane; 15 May

Anna Bolena Anna Bolena; Kavrakos (Enrico), Menzter (Seymour), James (Smeton), Aler (Percy); c. Bonynge, p. John Pascoe, d. John Pascoe; Covent Garden: 30 May, 3, 8, 13, 18†, 22 June

Sir John Tooley Opera Gala mad scene *(Lucia)*; c. Bonynge; Covent Garden: 19 June

Recital P. Bonynge: Munich: 5 July, Catania: 8 July

Concert Ah, fors'è lui ... sempre libera (La Traviata), Vilja (The Merry Widow), Ah non credea ... Ah non giunge (La Sonnambula); c. Bonynge; Kennedy Center, Washington: 21 Oct., United Nations NYC: 24 Oct.

Concert Dall'infame banchetto m'involai ... Tu del mio Carlo (I Masnadieri), Non temete Milord ... Or son sola (Fra Diavolo); c. Bonynge; Carnegie Hall NYC: 30 Oct.

Lucia di Lammermoor Lucia; Kraus (Edgardo), Vicenc Sardinero (Enrico), Harry Dworchak (Raimondo); c. Bonynge, p. Patane, d. Piantanida/Cavalotti; Barcelona: 21, 24, 27, 30 Nov.

1989   *Norma* Norma; Suarez (Pollione), Nova Thomas (Adalgisa), Selezneev (Oroveso); c. Bonynge, p. John Pascoe, d. John Pascoe; Orange County Performing Arts Complex Costa Mesa Ca: 11, 15, 18, 24 Feb.; Masonic Temple Auditorium, Detroit: 15, 19, 22 Apr.

Recital P. Bonynge; Metropolitan NYC: 12 Mar.

Lucrezia Borgia Lucrezia; Kraus (Gennaro), Pertusi (Don Alfonso), Dupuy (Orsini); c. Bonynge, p. Ionesco d. Ionesco/Tirelli; Barcelona: 3, 7, 11, 14 June

Lucrezia Borgia (concert performance) Lucrezia; Kraus (Gennaro), Pertusi (Don Alfonso), Dupuy (Orsini); c. Bonynge; Théâtre des Champs-Elysées, Paris: 17 June

Concert Music from opera and operetta including: *At the Balalaika (Balalaika*: POSFORD), *Falling in love with love (The Boys from Syracuse*: ROGERS), *Love live forever (Paganini*: LEHÁR), *My Hero (The Chocolate Soldier*: STRAUS), *I'll follow my secret heart* (COWARD), *The Nun's Chorus (Casanova*: J. STRAUSS), *Zigeuner* (COWARD), *Deep in my heart (The Student Prince*: ROMBERG), *O mon cher amant (La Perichole*: OFFENBACH), *Ah, fors'è lui ... sempre libera (La Traviata), Io non sono più l'Annetta (Crispino e la comare*: RICCI); c. Gamley; Melbourne: 15 July

Recital benefit for the Organ Appeal; P. Bonynge; St Johns, Smith Square, London: 5 Oct.

Concert Sediziose voce ... Casta diva ... (Norma), Dall'infame banchetto m'involai ... Tu del mio Carlo ... Carlo vive? (I Masnadieri), Non temete milord ... Or son sola (Fra Diavolo), mad scene *(Lucia);* c. Bonynge; Tyne Theatre & Opera House, Newcastle: 11 Oct., Hong Kong: 19 Oct.

The Merry Widow Anna Glavari; Louis Otey (Danilo), Douglas Ahlstedt (Rosillon), Joan Gibbons (Valencienne), Peter Strummer (Baron Zeta); c. Bonynge, p. Anne Ewers, d. Fredrikson/Laufer; Dallas: 2, 5, 8, 11 Nov.

1990 *Recital* P. Bonynge; St Joseph's College for Boys, Sydney: 9 Aug.

Concert opening Joan Sutherland Performing Arts Centre; c. Bonynge; Pennant Hills, N.S.W.: 14 Aug.

Les Huguenots Marguerite de Valois; Thane (Valentine), Austin (Raoul), Pringle (de Nevers), Suzanne Johnston (Urbain), Grant (Marcel), Wegner (St Bris); c. Bonynge, p. Mansouri, d. Stoddart/Stennett; Sydney Opera House: 3, 6, 10, 14, 20, 26, 29 Sep., 2‡ Oct.

Die Fledermaus Gala duet with Pavarotti *Parigi o cara (La traviata),* duet with Horne *Serbami ognor ... Alle piu calde immagini (Semiramide), Home Sweet Home,* c. Bonynge; Royal Opera House, Covent Garden: 31‡ Dec.

INDEX

471

INDEX

INDEX

INDEX